CITY OF HUMAN MEMORIES

Moubray Coat of Arms

CITY OF HUMAN MEMORIES

by

GUY DE MOUBRAY

Guy de Moubray

12 Sep 2007

The Memoir Club

© Guy de Moubray 2005

First published in 2005 by
The Memoir Club
Stanhope Old Hall
Stanhope
Weardale
County Durham

British Library Cataloguing in
Publication Data.
A catalogue record for this book
is available from the
British Library

ISBN: 1 84104 128 9

Typeset by TW Typesetting, Plymouth, Devon
Printed and bound by Antony Rowe Ltd, Eastbourne

To Daphne, beautiful, loving and brave

Contents

List of Illustrations

Preface

I have some doubts about writing my memoirs. There cannot be any more self-centred occupation. Should one indulge it? Is it just vanity? If one has had a distinguished life, having made an important impact on the affairs of one's country, it may almost be a duty to do so. But that is not my case. So why have I for two years now been writing my memoirs? In the first place – very mundanely – I find that when talking to family or friends and telling stories about my life, they frequently say, 'Have you written that down; it really should be recorded.'

I have had an unusually varied life. Some will be interested to read about a distant world in which children of colonial parents hardly ever saw their parents. Life in English private boarding schools in the 1930s will be of interest to others. I did not have what is sometimes called 'a splendid war', but my wartime experiences in the Army in Burma were quite unusual. At Oxford I was friends with Sandy Wilson and acted in his revues. Ken Tynan was also a friend and I acted in *Samson Agonistes* directed by him. Tony Crosland was my tutor and also a friend. My years in the Treasury, the Bank of England and the International Monetary Fund all have their interest. Two years working in Morocco was another unforgettable experience. Later still, I worked for some years in an unusual management consultancy. But this is just the skeleton of my life. I also have a lot to say about politics, and monetary and economic policy. My religion is very important to me; and it is an unusual one – many people have not even heard of Emanuel Swedenborg – and I devote a chapter to this.

But there is another reason for writing one's memoirs. It is in some sense a judgement on one's life. We are all going to be judged in the next world, and one can start the process by judging oneself. I have been quite severe on myself. I have become much more aware of just how unimaginative and selfish I was for many years in my marriage – and I speak quite frankly about this. A passage I came across recently in a sermon by an American New Church minister makes the point of how important our memories are to us:

> So much of the human mind is like the pattern of a city. There are houses in the mind, sheltering our memories. Chamber after chamber is occupied since earliest childhood to retain what we have thought, seen, heard, smelled, tasted, touched, willed, wanted, suffered, enjoyed. All this makes a huge city of ideas never to be forgotten – retained to eternity to be used if necessary. In this huge city of human memories live the wishes, the urges, the demands, the desires, the wants of man. These inhabit the houses and either use them properly or ruin them for habitation.

These memoirs are in some sense a diary, which it has taken two years to write, covering nearly eighty years. The style is therefore more spoken than written. It is as if I have been dictating them. I am deliberately retaining this very personal style, which I think reveals my character more truthfully.

CHAPTER 1

Family History

WHEN ALEC DOUGLAS-HOME RENOUNCED his peerage to become
Prime Minister in 1963, Harold Wilson, then Leader of the
Opposition, made some sneering reference to the 14th Earl of Home.
Douglas-Home rather neatly retorted that Mr Wilson was no doubt the
14th Mr Wilson. There is no great merit in being the 14th Mr or the 14th
Earl. All mankind has a long lineage. We are all influenced by heredity,
however little we may know about our forebears. And yet curiosity about
one's ancestors seems to be very general. American Negroes look back to
their African roots, American Presidents seek out their origins in obscure
Irish villages (Kennedy, Nixon and Reagan) and even among the poorest
peasants of Africa and Asia there seem to linger some vestiges of ancestor
worship.

The satisfaction of this curiosity is denied to most of us. We hear gossip
from parents, grandparents (if we even remember them), uncles and aunts.
By the time we are old enough to remember what we were told, they are
too old to be reliable. It is only illustrious families that have the
documentary evidence. In our patriarchal society the evidence is confined
to the male line, but since most sons of illustrious families marry women
from other illustrious families, detailed records can be traced back for many
generations. However since the number of forebears grows so rapidly with
each generation – only 6 generations back, we all have 64 forebears – even
the most illustrious families have gaps in the records. When the Lady Diana
Spencer married the Prince of Wales, one of the colour supplements of the
Sunday papers produced a chart showing their forebears for about six
generations and, if I have remembered it rightly, there were some twenty
gaps in her ancestry and even a few in that of her royal consort (no doubt
on the Mountbatten side!).

I was brought up to believe that the de Moubrays were an illustrious
family. I think I was only in my teens when I began to discover that this
was not really so. The de Moubrays are certainly an old family (by my
calculation there are 30 generations between the eleventh century Roger
de Moubray and young Ajax and Arthur de Moubray; thirty-one
generations from William the Conqueror himself, since one of our ancestors
married William's granddaughter). Strict documentation, however, does
not go back beyond the late fifteenth century with Sir David de Moubray
of Barnbougle in Scotland. And on at least two occasions the succession
came through the female line. The Moubrays are of Norman ancestry. The
name comes from the little town of Montbray in the Cotentin. The very

1

2   CITY OF HUMAN MEMORIES

early years of the family history are rather obscure. Roger de Moubray, brother of Geoffroy, the Bishop of Coutance, crossed with William the Conqueror in 1066 and fought at the Battle of Hastings. He had two sons, and almost certainly a daughter, Amicia de Moubray. The elder son, Robert, became Earl of Northumberland. In the *History of Inverkeithing and Rosyth* by the Revd. William Stephen we read:

> In 1088 he [Robert] joined in a rebellion against William II, and devastated Somerset; and at Alnwick Castle he defeated the Scots and slew King Malcolm III on Nov 13th 1093. In the following year he entered into a conspiracy to dethrone William II in favour of Stephen of Aumale [Albermale], a near cousin of the Royal House [in fact William I's nephew] . . . but he was captured by the King, and blinded, and imprisoned at Windsor [other accounts suggest the Tower of London], his estates being also forfeited. Though originally sentenced to imprisonment for life, after a period of incarceration amounting to 34 years, he was released in order to become a monk at the Abbey of St. Alban's, where he died.

He married Mathilda de l'Aigle and had no issue. The marriage was dissolved by Pope Paschal II under a principle of jurisprudence prevailing in France, whereby perpetual imprisonment was regarded as equivalent to civil death. Amicia de Moubray, almost certainly Robert's sister, married Roger d'Albini, son of William D'Aubigny, and had three sons, William, Nigel and Samson. William d'Albini, the elder son, became Earl of Arundel (the male line became extinct in 1243). He and his son, also William d'Albini, were both very active in Norfolk and Suffolk in the twelfth century. The second William married Matilda, daughter of Roger Bigod (associated with the castles of Orford and Framlingham).

Nigel d'Albini, the second son, was our ancestor. His first wife was Mathilda de l'Aigle, the former wife of his uncle Robert. That marriage seems to have been dissolved too. He married, second, in 1118, Gundreda de Gourney (granddaughter of William the Conqueror) by whom he had three children, Roger, Hamo and Henry. Roger, born 1120, assumed the name de Moubray and the title (Earl of Northumberland) of his great-uncle Robert by command of King Henry II. A detailed family history which I have only recently come across, says of him: 'In 1148 he accompanied Lewis, King of France, to the Holy Land, and there acquired great renown by vanquishing a stout and hearty Pagan in single combat!' He married Alice de Gant and had three children, Nigel, Robert and a daughter who became a nun at the Abbaye des Dames at Caen. Nigel, who died in 1192, married Mabel, daughter of the Earl of Clare, and had four sons: William, who was the ancestor of the Dukes of Norfolk, Sir Philip de Moubray (our ancestor, who died 'after 1233 and before 1240'), Robert and Roger. Sir Philip married Galiena of Waldeve and through her acquired the baronies of Inverkeithing and Dalmeny, thus establishing the Scottish branch of the family. I have shown this part of my memoirs to John Martin Robinson, archivist to the Duke of Norfolk, who says that this account is accurate. All this is shown in greater detail in the family tree (Appendix II).

The Scottish branch of the family were of no great distinction. They always seemed to back the wrong side – John Baliol, for example, rather than the Stewarts. So they became landed gentry in the County of Fife. The last member of the family to call himself de Moubray was Sir David, who died in the early sixteenthth century. No accounts of what my ancestors did and thought become available until my great-great-great grandfather George Moubray, the fourth son of Robert Moubray (1700–79). George, born 1740, was a Lieutenant in the Royal Navy and was killed in action. I have an account of all the ships he served on and an account of a battle he had in the Channel in 1778 with a French privateer, when in command of the cutter *Ferret*.

Whilst he was at sea, his wife Elizabeth Toby lived at Cockairnie, the estate in Fife, with his brothers, Robert and James. So their son George, my great-great-grandfather, was born at Cockairnie in 1773. As a boy he was brought up with his first cousins (whose portraits hang in the dining room here at Buxlow), Robert, later Colonel Sir Robert, and his younger brother Richard, later Admiral Sir Richard Hussey-Moubray and later still just Sir Richard Hussey, having inherited his mother's estates in Huntingdonshire.

George was the last member of our family to have been born in Scotland. He joined the Navy as a midshipman at the age of sixteen in 1789 and was stationed at Halifax, Nova Scotia. George wrote an account of his naval service. Perhaps the most interesting thing that happened to him in his early years was when he was a midshipman on HMS *Juno*. They had been active in the siege of Bastia in Corsica and were ordered to Toulon. During a brief period in 1793/4 Toulon was not held by the French revolutionary forces but by the Royalists and the English. *Juno* was delayed by bad weather, and arrived at Toulon somewhat later than expected, and sailed in – a difficult passage through a narrow strait – and found to their dismay that the French Republicans had retaken Toulon and had to beat a hasty retreat under fire from the shore. George did not know it, but Toulon was recaptured primarily because of the initiative of a young Lieutenant of artillery, Napoleon Bonaparte; it was no doubt Napoleon himself who was firing on *Juno*. A few days later George was transferred, still as a midshipman, to HMS *Victory*. Three months later he obtained his first command as Lieutenant of *Morelle*.

Regrettably his account ends in 1795. Perhaps he wrote some more which has since been lost. From internal evidence it is clear the account was written after 1820 because he refers to his 'late' Majesty King George III. So we know nothing of what happened to him during the next seven years when he was on the East Indies, Moluccas and China stations as Lieutenant of La Fujimi. And we have no account of his part in the Battle of Trafalgar, when he was First Lieutenant on HMS *Polyphemus*. He took command of the ship during the battle, when his captain was wounded. A cousin of

Capt. George Moubray RN 1773–1856, my great-great-grandfather

mine, Isabel's brother, Douglas, has recorded the following: '. . . he had the good fortune, during the gale that followed, to regain possession of the *Argonauta*, *Spanish 80*, and delivered her over to Admiral Collingwood off Cadiz. He afterwards took in tow the *Victory*, with the body of Lord Nelson on board, and conducted her to the mouth of the Straits of Gibraltar. Another account, however, says that the tow rope snapped in the gale and that some other ship had the honour of towing Nelson's body to Gibraltar.

He was promoted Commander on Christmas Eve of 1805. He then spent three and a half years in the West Indies, commanding the *Rhodian* and the *Morelle* (on which he had served in 1794/5). He married Eliza Yates in Jamaica and in the same year was promoted Post Captain. But with the end of the Napoleonic War he went on half pay for 32 years! Finally, at the age of 71, he was appointed Captain of HMS *Victory* in Portsmouth Harbour. The official history of HMS *Victory* contains the following paragraph:

> On the anniversary of the Battle of Trafalgar in 1844 Queen Victoria, on her visit to Portsmouth, passed near to *Victory*. *Victory* was at the time commanded by Captain George Moubray, who had served as First Lieutenant on the

Polyphemus at Trafalgar. The Queen noticed that *Victory* was decorated with flags, and her mastheads adorned with laurel and she inquired the cause. On being informed she immediately expressed her intention of going on board. Her Majesty, accompanied by Prince Albert, accordingly went over the ship. On being shown the spot where Nelson received his death wound Her Majesty read aloud the inscription 'Here Nelson fell'. She plucked two leaves from the laurel wreath in which the plaque was enshrined and carefully treasured them as a memento of the Hero. Her Majesty then went over to the poop rail where, over the steering wheel, is inscribed in gold letters the words of the memorable signal 'England expects that every man will do his duty'. This inscription was also adorned with laurel and flowers. With marked emphasis, Her Majesty repeated the words. Her Majesty and Prince Albert looked around from the Poop for a few minutes, and then the Queen asked to be shown where Nelson had died. The Queen proceeded to the cabin, in which the very spot is marked by a funeral urn (in paint), surmounted by Nelson's Flag, and on its top encircled in a wreath, are the words, 'Here Nelson died'. There was a pause here for several minutes, and it was remarked that Her Majesty was again much affected by the reflections that such a scene awakened.

George retired to the Royal Hospital Greenwich in 1846 where he died in 1856 as Senior Captain. Amongst his relics we have, believe it or not, a lock of his hair and, in the library, his commission as Lieutenant of the *Polyphemus* signed by Nelson just sixteen days before the Battle of Trafalgar. A despatch by Nelson to the Admiralty on 5 October 1805, which I have only just discovered, thanks to the Internet, explains why Nelson personally signed the commission:

Victory, off Cadiz, 5th October, 1805.
Sir,
Captain Morris of His Majesty's Ship *Colossus* having communicated to me the particular loss he would sustain in his present First Lieutenant becoming junior, in consequence of their Lordships having appointed Lieutenant George Moubray, who from his rank is senior to him; you will please to acquaint the Lords Commissioners of the Admiralty that, from a most thorough knowledge of the justness of Captain Morris' statement, and the very great good derived to His Majesty's Service from Captains being allowed confidential Officers as their First Lieutenants, and their Lordships having removed several Lieutenants of the *Colossus* that the present might continue First, I have, conceiving it to be their Lordships' wish, suffered the said First Lieutenant to remain in that situation, and appointed Lieutenant George Moubray to the *Polyphemus*, in consequence of Lieutenant Alexander Gordon of that Ship having been yesterday invalided, and found unfit for His Majesty's Service in this Country, as appears by a copy of the Report of Survey herewith transmitted, which I trust, for the reasons before mentioned, their Lordships will be pleased to approve. Lieutenant Gordon was First of the *Polyphemus*, and therefore Lieutenant Moubray will still be Senior.
I am, &c.,

His son, another George, was born in Jamaica in 1810. There is something wrong with the dates, because his parents are recorded as having married in 1812! He too had a naval career, but a much quieter one. He had essentially a desk job – a paymaster. However he did accompany Sir James Clark Ross on his expedition to the Antarctic with HM ships *Terror* and *Erebus* in 1841 – Moubray Bay is named after him. He received the Crimean and Turkish medals with Sebastopol clasp for service as resident Naval and Victualling Agent at Constantinople from 1854 to 1856. For six years (1856/62) he was paymaster of the Royal Yacht, the *Victoria and Albert*. He retired with the rank of Paymaster-in-Chief and died in 1887. He married Eliza Moore, daughter of George Moore (with an American mother), who, although British, was US Consul in Trieste. He came from an Isle of Man family; he had been born there in 1779, the son of James Moore, a partner in the firm of Moore, Carrick & Co, bankers in Glasgow, and grandson of Sir George Moore, Speaker of the House of Keys. Eliza's mother was American, Sara Nicholson, daughter of Judge Nicholson of Baltimore, Maryland, USA. Judge Nicholson's grandfather, Sir Francis Nicholson, born in 1660, was at one time Governor of Virginia and in 1688/9 Governor of New York (he sounds rather young for the position, so the report, 'Moore Family and Nicholson Family', may be unreliable). George Moore, one of my great-great grandfathers, seems to have been a remarkable man. I hope I have inherited some of his characteristics. His grandson, a Dutchman by the name of von Hemert, wrote this of him in 1926:

> I wish my children to remember and honour the family of my grandfather George Moore, the kindest, jolliest and most honourable gentleman, I have ever known.

George Moubray had six sons, the eldest of whom, George, never married; the second son, Charles, born in Trieste, was my grandfather; two died in infancy; Arthur, the fifth son, emigrated to the United States and then to Canada (two of his sons turned up in London during the Second World War but I know nothing more about them); and, finally, Herbert married Margarita Antinori from Perugia. I never met Herbert, but I did know Great-Aunt Rita. She was the mother of Isabel Moubray, who stayed here at Buxlow and who died in 1995.

Charles became a banker. Early in his career he was stationed in Mauritius where, in 1886, he married my dear grandmother, Berthe Laurence de Chazal. Laurence, as you well know, is in French a girl's name, but in honour of my grandmother that is my second name. My father, George, was born in Mauritius in 1888. Charles and Laurence lived and worked first in Mauritius and then in Madras for many years, where he was Manager of the Oriental Bank Corporation, also I believe in Cochin in Southern India – now known as Kerala. They retired to Lausanne in Switzerland sometime before 1910, Switzerland being then a very cheap place to live. Charles lost most of his money by investing everything in

French Government bonds which, when the French franc devalued after the First World War, lost much of their value. After Charles died in 1929 Granny left Switzerland and moved to Brussels. But more of that when we come to that time of my life.

Berthe Laurence, not quite 20 when she married, was one of thirteen children of Pierre Edmond de Chazal, who owned sugar plantations in Mauritius. The history of the de Chazals is set out in another book and does not need to be repeated here. Granny – 'Tante Laurence' to her many Mauritian relatives and 'Maman' to her children – was a great character. She spoke French in preference to English all her life, and her English had an unmistakable French accent and intonation. She seems to have been beautiful, impetuous and extravagant. Poor Charles; he certainly did not have the means, and probably not the character to cope with her. She told us years later how infuriating he would be at dinner parties, loudly correcting from the far end of the table any factual error she made – 'No, my dear, it was Friday, not Thursday!' Their children were always talking about Mauritius, the de Chazals and 'Maman', but poor Father was hardly ever mentioned. One of the few stories I remember is how he apparently infuriated his fellow bank officers, understandably, by insisting upon returning to his employers that part of his expense allowance which he had not actually needed.

Charles and Laurence had six children: Margaret, who died of diphtheria at the age of five; George, my father; Eileen, who also died of diphtheria aged three; Claire; Madeleine; and Kathleen. George was born on 18 August 1888 at Vacoes (Grandpère and Grandmère de Chazal's home) in Mauritius. He and the three remaining sisters spent the early years of their life in India. In those days sons were usually sent home at a very early age to be educated. I had always assumed that he had been sent home between the ages of 5 and 8. But I know that the Loretto School register shows him as having started in 1899 (aged 11) and as having left in 1905 (if he left at the end of the summer term he would have been just short of his 17th birthday). Viola has confirmed to me that he was indeed sent home at the age of 11, from Mauritius, not Madras as I had thought. He was apparently shipped home in the care of his uncle, l'Oncle Docteur. L'Oncle Docteur is reported to have accompanied him only as far as London and then just shipped him off to Edinburgh on the train alone! To be sent to Loretto was a bit of an aberration. The Cockairnie Moubrays had been sent to Loretto, at Musselburgh, a few miles outside Edinburgh; quite appropriately since they were lairds of Cockairnie, an estate in Fife only just across the Firth of Forth. But it was sheer romanticism to send young George there more than a hundred years since his great-grandfather had left Scotland to join the Navy. At the age of 11 he started in the prep school known then, and in my time, as the Nippers.

I presume that he must have spent some of his holidays with his grandmother in Upper Norwood (but she died in 1902). I know that he also stayed with the Welches, soap manufacturers in Manchester. Somewhat surprisingly, Buxton Welch had been a contemporary of George's at Loretto. He had been falsely accused of theft and George stood by him until he was exonerated; the Welch family then took the Moubrays to heart; not just George, but later on Madie and Kathleen. On my way to school some forty years later I spent a night with the two Welch bachelors. They remembered particularly his great appetite for macaroni cheese, the very dish with which they regaled me; they were delighted to see how good an appetite I had; in other words, I was just as greedy as my father had been!

After Loretto my father went to Switzerland where his parents had settled on retirement. He always told me that he had studied chemistry at Zurich University – but he never claimed to have a degree. He certainly could not have got one in only two years as the school register suggests. Granny told me that he had wanted to be a chemist, which she had frowned upon (almost certainly because she thought he meant to serve behind a counter making up prescriptions, a calling she would have thought 'beneath' her son). He had also shown an inclination to be a clergyman in the New Church (Swedenborgian) to which she (and all the de Chazals) belonged. But her devotion to the Church was not great enough to reconcile her to that as a calling for her son. Viola tells me that she understood that he was studying engineering and that it was his father who insisted on him leaving Zurich in order to enter for the Indian Civil Service. He went to a crammer's in London but did not do well enough in the exams to make the ICS and had to be content with the Malayan Civil Service. It must have been about now that George changed his name to 'de Moubray'. I wonder why. I think perhaps it gave him the confidence he seemed to lack – he had caved in to his mother very easily over careers. It may have been a defence mechanism against the endless talk of the 'de Chazals'; the French set great store on the *particule* as a sign of aristocratic birth. No Moubray had been called 'de' since about the beginning of the sixteenth century (Sir David de Moubray). Viola tells me that she had heard that when he was at Loretto he came across one of the Cockairnie Moubray's name carved into a desk and he had called himself 'de' and George thought that looked rather good!

He started in Malaya just before the First World War. He spent some time in India. New recruits were required to learn two languages. Malay obviously had to be one and for some rather obscure reason he chose as his second language Pushtu, for which he had to go to India. In Malaya Tamil would have been a great deal more useful. The photographs of him at this age show him to have been something of a dandy, large bow ties, a monocle and spats! (Another attempt at boosting his confidence?)

Meantime his two younger sisters, Madeleine and Kathleen, had been at school at Hamilton House in Tunbridge Wells – the parents, I think, remained in Switzerland. One of their close friends at H.H. was Katherine Layard, born in 1898 in Ceylon, daughter of Arthur Layard, a tea planter,

My parents' wedding reception at the Gallands' house in Lausanne – 1921

who seems to have retired in his 40s – somewhere around 1905 – to live
in a villa in Molyneux Park Road in Tunbridge Wells. He called the house
'Lanka' (the old name for Ceylon – now readopted by independent
Ceylon). The Layards were originally a Huguenot family, the most famous
of whom was Sir Henry Austen Layard, the excavator of Nineveh – he must
have been a great-uncle of Arthur's.

On George's first home leave – to Switzerland, where his parents were
– Madie and Kathleen invited Katherine Layard to come and stay; a
deliberate piece of matchmaking, which succeeded. George (this was 1921)
was already 33 and this was almost his last chance to find a wife; there were
virtually no unmarried English girls in Malaya, and his next home leave was
not to be until 1926. Katherine was one of three children (together with
my Uncle Frank and Auntie Peggy). She had driven an ambulance in the
later years of the war; mostly at Aldershot, where she had been very busy
in the frightful flu epidemic of 1918. She was known to her friends in the
service as 'Leyland', the brand name of her ambulance – no windscreen, just
a tarpaulin sheet to put across her lap when it rained. Her mother, Margaret
Carnegie-Arbuthnot (originally Capel), had died in 1918 – said to have
worn herself out with war work. Katherine was desperately afraid of being
kept at home to look after her dreary father. So she too had a very good
reason for marrying. I don't know whether they were really in love – I am
not sure that being in love was thought to be quite so important in those
days. Uncle Frank, years later, confided to Daphne how shocked his family

had been at the engagement; they found it very hard to take this dandified, very un-English colonial. The engagement was short; George's leave was coming to an end. They were married in Lausanne, where Charles and Laurence were living in a tiny villa, Villa Clary; the reception was held at the Gallands' much larger house (I stayed there in 1937). They spent their honeymoon motoring in Italy and on the French Riviera. Driving in Italy at that time must have been disconcerting; in some provinces, so my father told me, you drove on the right and in others on the left; the changeover would be indicated by a sign saying simply *Tenere la Sinistra*!

My elder sister, Daphne, was born in 1922. My mother had puerperal fever during the pregnancy and Daphne was born with very poor eyesight and subject to fits. She later became virtually blind and somewhat mentally retarded and spent all her life after about 1933 in a home. At the age of 81 she is still in a home in Jersey.

CHAPTER 2

The Early Years

MY FATHER WAS CHIEF MAGISTRATE at Kuala Lumpur, then capital of Negri Sembilan, one of the Federated Malay States, when I was born there on 15 March 1925. I used to think that it was almost unique to have been born there, but I was sitting next to Dulcie Gray, the actress, at Sandy Wilson's 70th birthday party in 1994 and said to her at one point, 'You won't believe this, but I was born in Kuala Lumpur.'

'Well,' she replied, 'so was I'!

The colonial tradition was still going strong and many of my contemporaries were born in colonies. As I have already noted, so were both my father and my mother.

I have virtually no recollections of the first five years of my life. I know that I came on home leave with my parents in 1926; I don't know whether we visited England, but I suppose I must have been shown off to my Layard grandad in Tunbridge Wells. My parents told me that they were turned out of a hotel in Switzerland because I disturbed the guests with my crying; even on the boat coming home my father appears to have had to spend a long time walking the decks to keep me quiet. I haven't been very easy to keep quiet ever since!

After their leave my parents returned to Trengannu on the north-east coast of Malaya, where my father was presumably a District Officer. Until my sister Viola was born, in 1928, I was the only white child in Trengannu – probably on the whole east coast. I grew up under the care of an amah (a Chinese nanny) and played with the local Malay children. I spoke a mixture of Malay and English and must have been as fluent in Malay as any child of four or five can be. I have been told that amah found me difficult – on one occasion she asked if my parents would leave their dirty bathwater in the tub; apparently to wash me in it afterwards was considered an infallible method of washing the devil out of me. I have a vague recollection of my mother playing a game with me when I had to wash my hands – each hand was a ship – the 'something' and the '*Borobat*'. Many years later she told me that these were Danish tramp ships plying up the east coast from Singapore – the captain of the *Borobat* was drunk most of the time and his ship often grounded on sand banks, being floated off at high tide when he had sobered up.

I discovered in 1945 that I had another recollection from this period. I was driving a jeep in K.L. when I recognised a distinctive smell. I followed it to a street stall, where durians were being sold. The durian is a large fruit in a case rather like a giant horse chestnut. I bought one and returned to

11

Me in Malaya aged about 3

the Officers' mess; none of my fellow officers could stand the smell and I was banished to the far end of the compound to eat it!

Before starting on the life that I do remember, a word or two about my parents. My father never really fitted in; he was always a bit foreign. I have no personal knowledge of what he was like in Malaya, but I don't think he was a typical colonial civil servant. He drank very little; not for him a burra peg at sundown. He was contemptuous of those in Government House; my mother told me that she often had to get him to tone down letters he wrote. I remember, after the war, that he once called some New Church clergymen with whom he disagreed 'silly buggers'; he may well have liked to say the same of the Governor and his staff.

However lacking in self-confidence he may have been when younger, he accomplished a great deal in Malaya. He loved the Malays; perhaps too much for Government House, for, apart from his time as Magistrate in K.L and a brief period as the occupant of Government House in Penang, he spent most of his time upcountry, mostly on the east coast, where everyone was Malay. His brother-in-law, John Dalley (husband of Auntie Peggy) on the other hand, in the police service, was an expert on the Chinese triads. Government House had to remember that in the west, in the tin mines and on the rubber plantations, there were mostly Indians, and in the cities and particularly in Singapore there were more Chinese than others.

In his country posts George became an accomplished horseman, and a very good polo player. He won lots of cups. The polo teams were made up for the most part of Malays – mostly Sultans of the Federated Malay States: Negri Sembilan, Perak, Kelantan, Trengannu, Pahang and Johore. He wrote a book, *Matriarchy in the Malay Peninsula* which became a standard textbook for students entering the exams for the Colonial Service. He was also a very good shot; particularly, I am told, of snipe, which are a great test of skill because of their rapid zigzagging flight. He also shot big game, tigers – there are no lions in Malaya. On one occasion he shot and killed a rogue elephant which was terrorising the neighbourhood. Another thing that set my father apart – in his mind, and probably not even known to those around him – was his religion. I don't think he was a particularly religious person during his time in Malaya – that came later after 1942. But anyone brought up in the New Church, as he was, and as I was to be later, sees everything through rather different eyes; the complete conviction that one is in this world in order to prepare for eternal life as an angel gives one a quite different perspective of everything that goes on in the world around one.

My mother, although she too loved the Malays, was a much more typical colonial; she loved parties, cocktails, tennis and golf. She rode a great deal and did a lot of work encouraging local handicrafts.

To return now to my life. I was five when we returned to Europe on home leave. I know from reading the Preface to my father's book that when he finished it in April 1930 we were living at Steep Farm near Petersfield in Sussex. I believe however that most of the summer was spent in Switzerland; the name Kandersteg has been familiar to me ever since, though I have no real memories of it. But there is a small sepia photograph in the dining room of a small boy squatting in a stream – that's me in Kandersteg. Why my parents left me in Europe at the age of five, I don't know. Eight might have been just as good an age. Perhaps it was just that I was 'difficult', that I was by then too old for an amah, and that there were no kindergartens in Malaya in 1930.

Even odder is that I was not left in England but in Belgium. The ostensible reason was to make me bilingual; but if so why not in France? Perhaps Belgium was cheaper; or perhaps it was that there were no progressive Montessori schools in France. Auntie Claire, who had been widowed after only a dozen years or so of marriage – she had lived in Cochin where her husband Hal Harrison Jones was a businessman – set up an extraordinary menage in the Avenue de l'Echevinage, in Uccles, a suburb of Brussels. I think Granny and Madie were with us initially, but later moved out to an apartment on their own; Claire never found it easy being in close contact with her mother, yet Granny was totally dependent on Claire, the only member of the family with any money. The household consisted of my sister Daphne and me and my two first cousins Claire and

Me at Kandersteg in Switzerland – 1930

Jack, the children of my Aunt Kathleen – with us presumably since with the farm doing so badly in what was by then the Great Depression, they couldn't afford to keep them. There were also two Belgian children, whose names I cannot remember – a boy and a girl – whose parents were separated; presumably providing additional income for the household. So we were really a kind of foster home, but for two-thirds of us with a foster mother who was a loving close relation.

This was the setting for my earliest very vivid recollection. In truth the memory is no longer vivid, but it must have been traumatic at the time. On 5 November 1930 my mother and I and Auntie Claire were invited to a Guy Fawkes party in the large house and garden of some English people. I hated it. I remember the host father lifting me up near the bonfire and saying, 'Shall we burn the Guy?' and all the children screamed, 'Yes! – Guy, Guy, stick him in the eye.' I was terrified. But worse was to come. I suddenly realised that my mother wasn't around. I found her in the porte cochère getting into a car to be driven away. She was leaving for Malaya (for three years!) to join my father who had already left. I clung to her skirts sobbing wildly. It must have been as awful for her as it was for me. I don't blame her for trying to get away without my knowing; she knew well enough that it was the only possible way of avoiding a 'scene'; miserably for us both, the scene nevertheless took place.

The next three years, though, were happy enough. The house seemed spacious – although when I made a point of visiting it when on a business trip to Brussels in 1989 it seemed very small. The new owner allowed me to look around; it had all been modernised and the telephone booth in the hall had been removed; the booth was memorable in that it was there that the flexible leather clothes brush was kept – useful for punishing small boys.

Just before the painful evening on Guy Fawkes' Day I had started school at the École d'Ecroly in Uccles. It was a progressive Montessori school attended by many of the diplomatic children in Brussels and also by many Belgians. My first class was run by Mademoiselle Poulet. She knew not one word of English, nor I think did any of the class, and I knew not one word of French. And yet very soon I learned to read and write and speak French. Mlle Poulet's face is blurred in my memory, but I can still vividly recall her bold simple handwriting in chalk on the blackboard – '*la poire*', '*la pomme*' – with little pictures beside them. Strange to say I don't remember ever having another teacher; perhaps she remained our teacher as each year we moved up. Nor do I remember any classes other than reading, writing and arithmetic – no Latin, no religious instruction, no geography. Or is it just my memory which is at fault? We used to collect frogspawn from a stream near our house; it went into the aquarium in the classroom and we watched the tadpoles progress.

Splashing around in water is always fun for small children, but it sometimes got us into trouble. One Sunday, dressed in our Sunday 'best' we were out in the yard with buckets. I am sure we thought we were doing something useful, but to the grownups we were just being 'naughty', making a thorough mess of our clothes. I think it was then that I was for the first time put across someone's knees and spanked. I don't believe I took it calmly; I seem to remember resisting, struggling and kicking; but my only reward was to be sent to bed to calm down. I also have a vague memory of being aware for the first time of the concept of injustice (and yet Piaget, I think it is, says that the human mind is not capable of assimilating abstract concepts before the age of 10 – perhaps 'abstract' is the clue – maybe I just had a concrete feeling that my punishment was not fair to me).

I have few memories of the school. I think I had a girl friend, and that her name was Andrée, that she was dark haired and that I once brought her a posy of flowers. I remember, quite early on, when I was about six years old, that whoever it was who fetched me from school didn't turn up. My sense of abandonment grew and grew as the crowd of waiting boys and girls slowly dwindled until only I was left, crying in despair and refusing to be comforted by a teacher. There was no doubt a simple explanation, but despair at that age is absolute.

The memory is strangely selective. For the three years from 1930 to 1933 only six or seven memories remain. Why these, one wonders? Why were they particularly vivid? For most of them it must have been the element of drama. One took place at lunchtime. We ate our meals at refectory tables, with a teacher at the head of each table with the older children near the teacher and the young ones like me at the foot of the table. We ate in complete silence (not what one would expect at a progressive school today). On this occasion I suddenly sneezed and coughed simultaneously (I don't do this often, but when I do it is very noisy). The Headmistress, Mademoiselle Amède, banged on the table and asked which child had screamed! There was complete silence. Being a literal child I was not going to own up; after all I had not screamed, only sneezed. After a long and embarrassed pause, the teacher at my table spoke up to say that '*le petit Guy*' had been the unwitting culprit. Everybody laughed and then quickly fell silent again. I don't think Mlle Amède believed her, but I was not punished.

The school covered the whole age range from five to eighteen. As far as I can remember the senior ones were all girls. I remember the embarrassment of having to dance around naked under a sprinkler, only just a few yards away from senior girls doing their needlework under the trees.

We seemed to travel everywhere in Brussels by tram, which ran like little trains on special routes between the carriageways of the roads; as they still did when I was there in 1989. My efforts to learn to read must have been very tiresome for Auntie Claire – and all the other passengers. I used to read out aloud laboriously in phonic style the advertisements. I can still remember *La – vache – qui – rit*. Now there's a product which has lasted! We used to visit the Bon Marché. On the top floor was a café where, if we were lucky, we could have banana splits or knickerbocker glories.

Our landlords, the Duponts, owned the casino at La Panne (the last town in Belgium before Dunkirk) and other properties on the coast. We spent one holiday in one of their houses in Nieuport. This was memorable for only one thing. Quite uncharacteristically, I think, I spent one evening in the basement painting a bicycle that didn't belong to me a most lurid yellow; and not only the bicycle but most of my clothes and a lot of me. I got into very hot water for that!

A few other random memories of Brussels. I remember going to see my first film (in sepia): the opera of *Don Quixote*, starring in the title role the famous Russian bass Chaliapin; in the world of music, he was as famous as Nijinsky in the world of ballet. For supper we usually had prunes and yoghurt which was always pronounced 'yaourt'. It was very much the new in thing; natural bacteria seeing off harmful bacteria. Auntie Claire was a sucker for all kinds of alternative medicine, the more outrageous the better. A few years later, when we were in England she got hooked on chews; whenever there was anything wrong with us we had to moisten and chew a piece of blotting paper, which was then posted to the homeopathic doctor. She would diagnose what was wrong by passing an ivory ball on a thread over it – the pattern of the swinging of the ball revealed what was wrong!

I remember one other holiday during those three years besides Nieuport. One summer we took a house in Hunstanton in Norfolk, on the Wash. I remember being told that it should be pronounced 'Hunston'. The north Norfolk beaches with pine trees coming right down to the shore (which I have never visited since) made a vivid impression on me. Could one, I wonder, today be on one of those beaches in the summer with nobody else in sight for miles?

Staying with us were the Spiers brothers, American sons of a New Church man who had I think recently become a widower, and whom Auntie Madie was making a play for. Years later, in Washington DC, Ronnie admitted that he and his brother had been terribly worried that their father might marry her. Even I have to admit that she would have made a very difficult stepmother. Ronnie, of whom more later, was last heard of as US Ambassador to the Bahamas!

There is only one event from that holiday that I remember. On a very hot night we dragged our mattresses into the garden (a walled garden) and all the children slept out. In the middle of the night there was a thunderstorm and we got soaked banging on the door to gain admission. It still seems odd that the grown-ups should have locked us out! One contrast between Belgium and what was to come later – school food. I remember, in particular, pork with prunes. Imagine that at an English prep school! Food enthusiasm must already have started. Auntie Claire was a competent but not imaginative cook, but both Granny and Madie cooked some memorable dishes, amongst which I particularly remember cauliflower salad and pattypan gourd salads with a dressing of hard-boiled eggs, olive oil, lemon juice and cream. Perhaps I am mistaken and this may have been a later memory in England. When I was writing one of these attempts at memoirs in 1996, Daphne had been reading some memoirs by Dirk Bogarde. He describes a train journey he made in India in 1945. She asked me how it compared with the journey I made in India in 1944. I read a few pages; my picture of India was quite different, but I will come to that at the right time.

The point of this interjection is to note that Bogarde leaps about by subject, rather than time. By contrast my memory is very chronological. I can tell you what I did in every year since 1930. Why should I be so chronological? I wonder if it is something to do with being the child of colonial parents? Life for them was dominated by the regular pattern of Home Leave. Every three years a long leave, starting and ending with a 21-day sea voyage. So every third year was very special from the family point of view. Imagine my mother disentangling herself from a sobbing child of five, knowing that they wouldn't meet again until the boy was eight. Most colonial wives just put up with it. Some, like Betty Rawlings, a friend of my mother's who lived in Aldeburgh, put children before husband and stayed in England. An alternative would have been to say to hell with colonial tradition and keep the children out East until they were older. This in fact was what my parents did later; Viola stayed with them in Malaya until 1939, when she was eleven. She and Audrey went to school in Cameron Highlands, a hill station near Kuala Lumpur. Mark you, they might not have done that with a boy! I have just been thinking: from the age of 5 to the age of 20 I must have been with my father for not much more than six or seven months in total (home leaves in 1933, 1936 and 1939); my mother just a little bit longer, because she didn't always go back to Malaya at the same time as my father.

Anyway, back to the chronology. 1933 – a home leave year. We must still have been in Brussels when they got home. I have a vivid memory of going round an abandoned garden with them there. It had clearly been abandoned for some years; all the borders and shrubberies were rank with weeds. I had not yet heard of *The Secret Garden*, but it made a great impression on me – perhaps because we were trespassing, which added an element of fear. We picked young nettles (so it must have been in the spring) and cooked them like spinach.

So it was good-bye to Belgium, until a brief holiday in 1935 and short visits in 1949 and later, as a management consultant in the 1980s. The whole family (without my sister Daphne who from about this time on, spent her life in institutions) moved to England. For the holidays we took a house in Wales, somewhere south of Harlech castle, on the wrong side of the main road which had to be crossed to reach the splendid beaches. Not that there can have been very much traffic in those days. I still couldn't swim and was learning. In the sea I wore a lifebelt which was a miniature version of those then used on ships for boat drill – a canvas waistcoat with cork sewed in to it. I have two other memories of that holiday. First, sailing with my father in some estuary; he tried to frighten me – and succeeded – by going out briefly into the open sea, which seemed to me to be particularly rough. The second was Granny and the Prune Stone! It was a great drama; the children were already in bed and the grown-ups were having dinner. Granny, who was then 66, was already treated as very elderly (she lived to be 90). In the course of dinner she began to choke – a prune stone caught in her throat. All local remedies failed. An air of panic pervaded the house. Granny was bundled into the back of the car – probably an old-fashioned Sunbeam with running boards – and my father set off for the nearest hospital at Aberystwyth,. Half an hour later a rather sheepish party returned; the jolt from crossing a humpbacked bridge had dislodged the stone. I don't suppose there are any humpbacked bridges on the main road to Aberystwyth today!

CHAPTER 3

Prep School in England

So to school in England. My father was returning to Malaya ahead of my mother, and as a novel way of going to boarding school for the first time, my mother and I accompanied him on the first twenty-four hours of the voyage. We boarded the SS *Comorin,* a P&O liner, at Tilbury Docks. The departure of an ocean liner is always dramatic. I remember standing on deck and seeing the shoreline recede, friends and family waving; many would not see those sailing again for many years. I remember next morning, a fine and sunny September day, watching the shoreline as we rounded Dungeness. Early in the afternoon we docked at Southampton and my mother and I disembarked. My father would reach Singapore in three weeks' time. My mother would join him later.

We bundled all the paraphernalia of prep school – trunk and tuck box – into a hired car (chauffeur driven, of course; there were no self-drive hired cars in those days) and set off along the coast for Seaford in Sussex, where my prep school, Normansal, stood high on Blatchington Down overlooking the town below. I remember a tearful parting and crying myself to sleep. I also remember another small boy of only six who was starting and was even more tearful than I.

The Headmaster, W.R. Seagrove, had been a Cambridge Athletics Blue and ran the school with his sister, Miss Rowena. He did not make the passing of exams the be-all and end-all of education. Common Entrance results were consequently not particularly brilliant, but most of the boys learned to enjoy their work The rest of the 1930s for me were made up of several strands which only rarely overlapped: school (Normansal from 1933 to 1938), which I will come on to later, holidays at 'home' (not as simple as it sounds since I didn't really have a 'home'; not only did I have no 'roots' as one would say today, but I cannot answer simply the question where did you spend your childhood?) and holidays abroad (1935, 1937,1938) and two more Home Leave holidays – 1936 and 1939.

Home – what did it mean? One centred around Granny and Madie with whom I frequently stayed, although I don't remember ever having 'my room' with my things in it. There was just a bedroom allocated to me when I was there. Initially Auntie Claire was with them too. She bought a house at No. 6 North Square in Hampstead Garden Suburb, facing the Free Church in the centre of the square. We can't have been there very long; I remember so little about it. The ménage broke up quite soon because, I think, Claire could not get on with her mother and sister. After all in India, for quite a few years, she had been undisputed mistress of the house. Claire

Auntie Claire, my father, my mother and Granny at 50 Northway 1936

was in loco parentis to me. She was my substitute mother from 1930 to 1943, when I joined the Army. Claire had all the money; Granny and Madie had very little of their own. Claire now bought for them 50 Northway, still in Hampstead Garden Suburb and not very far from North Square; just down the hill towards the bus stop. They were to be there until 1948. Claire must then have started looking after Grandad Layard in Tunbridge Wells.

But Grandad Layard's house in Molyneux Park Road was, I suppose, another 'home' of sorts. Grandad didn't really like children (he must already have been in his 70s), so I was never there for very long, but stayed mainly at Northway, but never for the whole of any holiday. Auntie Claire had plenty of help. Even though Lanka was a suburban villa (on 3 floors) built around 1900, there was a cook, Mrs Farrant (cooks were always 'Mrs' whether married or not), who commanded the kitchen; there were also a kitchen maid and a parlour maid (dressed in conventional black and white maid's uniform). They lived on the attic floor. For breakfast there was a sideboard in the dining room with an assortment of cold bacon (we would call it gammon today), sausages, bacon, eggs, kidneys, sometimes kedgeree

Granny in 1936

(real kedgeree with smoked haddock, not salmon), porridge, cereal and toast.

At lunch – I don't think I ever had dinner with my grandfather – Grandad used to sit at the head of the table, a large expanding table with drop leaves, with a decanter of whisky always at his right. Another servant was the faithful Gibbs, chauffeur, gardener, handyman. He had started as a coachman with the Chamberlain household in Birmingham. He made the whistling noise that grooms make when currycombing a horse when he was polishing the car.

We did not use the word car in those days; it was always 'the motor'. It was a large Austin with a glass dividing screen between the passenger seats and the chauffeur; a speaking tube for giving instructions; and a silver flower holder. Grandad was always wrapped in a rug when going for a drive around Ashdown Forest. Grandad had a bristly grey moustache which tickled when he kissed you – on arrival, at bedtime and on departure. When leaving there was always the ceremony of being handed a half crown to add to the pocket money.

What else do I remember of Grandad? He smoked – Gold Flake cigarettes. The Wellington chest in his drawing room held lots of miniature playing cards collected from packets of Gold Flake. I used them for playing patience. There were also lots of ivory mah-jong pieces. I also remember him in white ducks with a Panama hat on his way to play croquet with corseted ladies on the croquet lawn just off Molyneux Park Road. I gathered later that Claire found him murder to look after and would have left him but for the War; he died in 1941. Until then I spent very little time in Tunbridge Wells; but from 1941 until I joined the Army it suddenly became home, presided over by Auntie Claire. Viola and Audrey had joined us in 1939 when my parents went back to Malaya. But now we had no cook, no kitchen maid, no parlour maid. Gibbs was still around; the motor was probably still around in the garage, but since there was no petrol, Gibbs' main function was to grow vegetables in the garden. But more of Tunbridge Wells in its proper place, chronologically speaking.

The other 'home' and the nearest to a real home was with Auntie Kathleen (known as T.K.). She had married an Army officer just after the War, Leslie Moore, from a Worcestershire family. My first holiday with them must have been quite early in the 1930s when Uncle Leslie was still trying to run a small farm at Wisbech in Cambridgeshire. I remember very little of it. Whether it was there or later, I don't know, but I remember taking part in the old-fashioned farming activities – stooking corn, standing on the hay wagon tamping down the hay, watching the corn go into the thresher; I was even taught to milk a cow. I don't remember the house; I think it was a bungalow at the end of a dusty lane in a very flat landscape. I have a very clear memory of digging for horseradish in the banks of the lane. Uncle Leslie always liked very hot food – provided it was English; none of that foreign stuff. (Poor T.K. – she had been brought up on French cooking and had lived in India with her parents and knew nothing of English cooking.)

For the rest of the time that I spent with the Moores the background was a house in a field, at least half a mile from any other house, outside a village called Crowle in Worcestershire. A map would soon reveal where it was; but it was not very far from the City of Worcester, because I remember bicycling into Worcester to see my first Fred Astaire and Ginger Rogers film. I discovered in 1998 that it was the Manor House, Crowle. It had just appeared in *Country Life* for sale at £300,000. The particulars said in need of modernisation – see below!

It must be hard for anybody today to believe how primitive life in that house was in the mid 1930s. No mains water; no electricity; no bathroom; no indoor lavatory. The only water came from an outside pump; we learned to prime the pump (you always had to keep some water for that purpose in a bucket; if you forgot, you had to take the bucket all the way to the brook). T.K. cooked on a paraffin stove – two burners and an oven. The food at T.K.'s was always delicious; but always English at the insistence of Uncle Leslie.

I should have said that by this time his farm at Wisbech had failed, as did so many others in the Slump. He now acted as a peripatetic bailiff for a

Worcestershire land owner, visiting all the farms in his 'Baby Austin' – an Austin Seven. I had primitive driving lessons in the Baby Austin and once crashed into an apple tree, but no harm was done.

The loo was an outside affair, not a water closet, and for bumph we usually used scraps of newspaper. T.K. did all the laundry in a weekly wash in the copper – a large copper cauldron set over a wood fire. Saturday night was bath night; a galvanised iron bath tub was placed on the stone kitchen floor in front of the fire under the copper and was filled partly by cold water carried from the pump in a bucket and partly by hot water from the copper, ladled out with a scoop, a circular pot at the end of a long wooden handle. I remember bath nights as a special treat.

We used candles for going to bed and oil lamps for all other purposes. The main source of light in the drawing room was an Aladdin Lamp – an oil lamp with a gauze mantle which glowed with a bright white light, the lamp being fired by paraffin under pressure. You had to pump the pressure up before lighting it. If the mantle blackened it had to be corrected by sprinkling a pinch of salt over the chimney. Quite a performance, but so satisfying to see the black disappearing with a sparkle.

All this was to change. One of the first things was to install a large water tank in the attic and a Raeburn solid fuel boiler in the kitchen. That made a bath and a WC possible. But there was still no electricity and no mains water, so the water to the tank still had to be pumped from the well by hand; no longer by the old-fashioned long handled outdoor pump, but now an indoor pump fixed to the wall with a short lever which had to be pushed backwards and forwards. Everybody – at least every child – had to do so many pumps a day: was it 50? or more? Finally came electricity; the only real benefit it brought was an electric pump. I was really quite sad to see the end of oil lamps, Aladdins and bedtime candles.

I suppose it must have rained in the 1930s, but in my memory it seems to have been eternal sunshine. School was fun. No serious punishments and an enlightened headmaster in Mr Seagrove. We tended to study what we wanted to study. My form got rather stuck on Charles I and the Civil War. In 1936 I remember we acted in a play about Charles, in which I played the part of Sir Henry Vane, Private Secretary to the King. I know it was 1936 because we were still in make-up after the performance when we listened to Edward VIII's abdication broadcast on the 'wireless'. Earlier that year I remember also listening to the Home Service as it announced: 'The King's [George V] life is drawing peacefully to a close.' Little did we know that the King's physician had given him a lethal dose to speed him on his way to meet the deadline for the morning *Times*; it surely wouldn't have been proper to have the news broken by those vulgar little evening papers – *News, Star, Standard*.

In the dormitories it was the custom for one boy to tell a story after 'lights out' – not permitted but always done. The stories were usually about

Sexton Blake and always included smugglers in tunnels under the Downs and were often meant to be frightening. I was quite an impressionable boy; I remember taking a book out of the library by Jeffrey Farnol; I never got beyond the first sentence which was: 'The Frenchman beside me had been dead since dawn!' They were slaves in a galley!

The Downs were an important feature of our lives. We roamed for miles over them in organised paper chases. There were no hedges, no cultivated fields, just grass cropped by sheep and rabbits, with vetch, clover and thyme which released its subtle fragrance as it was trampled under foot. We went as far afield as the Cuckmere Valley –where there was Drusilla's (only visited with parents or friends' parents), which had a miniature steam railway and lovely high teas.

So far as I can remember school food was not at all bad. I bet the meat was overdone, though, and there was a fairly constant smell of cabbage. After breakfast every morning most boys were required to queue up at Sister's cubby-hole to be given whatever tonic our parents (or guardians) had prescribed. I think I had a tablespoon of Radio Malt (sounds odd doesn't it? – perhaps 'radio' was meant to show how modern it was). Others had Parish's Iron Food which they had to take through a straw so as not to blacken their teeth. I always wanted to see a boy with blackened teeth; but they all seemed to negotiate the straws successfully.

We had two services every Sunday – taken, I think, by the headmaster; I don't remember a priest. I particularly liked Evensong and the Nunc Dimittis – 'Lord, now lettest Thou Thy servant depart in peace.' On 11 November in every year we all stood to attention for two minutes at eleven o'clock to commemorate the Armistice.

Events abroad made little impact on me until 1939. I suppose I must have heard of Herr Hitler and Signor Mussolini. Come to think of it, I think I do remember the Italian invasion of Abyssinia and the tragic figure of Haille Selassie. I am sure, in fact, that we read *The Times* every day, because we had a relief map of the world in plasticine mounted on a pingpong table on which we placed little ships (with their names) and moved them every day in accordance with the Shipping News, which gave arrivals and departures of most major ships from all the ports in the world.

Insulated though we were from the world outside and barely aware of the massive unemployment in the country, one echo of it reached us at school. All the maids at Normansal were from the valleys of South Wales; they were probably the only earners in their families and sent most of their wages back to their parents. It occurs to me now that I have absolutely no idea where they lived. In the main part of the school the dormitories were in the attic and we never saw the maids except at mealtimes.

I had a very quick temper. I don't think I controlled it until I was grown up. I can still hear myself saying, 'If you don't stop [whatever it was I didn't like] I shall lose my temper,' and then becoming involved in fierce fights. I remember throwing a chair across a classroom at a boy called Wallace-

Cox, with red hair and a freckled face, whom I met years later in a London Underground. There was one refugee from Germany in the school. I regret to say that I hated Metzger, why I don't know. We even had a vicious fight, and had to be parted. I am sure he was very unhappy and he suffered very badly from hay fever.

I also remember the pop songs of the era: 'Jeepers, creepers, where'd you get those peepers, where did you get those eyes?'; 'I want to be happy and to make you happy too' and 'Tea for Two'. But the music was not all pop. One master introduced us to classical music. He had a gramophone and played the records with special fibre needles which had to be sharpened with a special cutter, rather like a cigar cutter. It was said to produce much better sound than the regular steel needles. He took us right through Tchaikovsky's Fifth Symphony. Whenever I hear that romantic soaring melody with which it opens, I am taken back to my school days. The melody later featured as one of the songs by the name of 'Moonlight and Roses' in a Deanna Durbin film which came along in the 1940s. Thinking of Germany; we saw their airships passing overhead on their way to the USA. I think we saw the *Hindenburg* on its final ill-fated voyage.

There is another memory from the mid 30s of climbing on to the school roof and sitting astride the ridge one summer's evening (permitted by the staff) to watch a most spectacular display of the Northern Lights – the Aurora Borealis. I don't think there has been as fine a display in the last sixty years.

We played a lot of sports. I was not at all bad at rugger and hockey, but no good at cricket – I didn't have an eye for the ball. In my final year I was the scorer for the 1st XI and travelled with them to Away matches. It was always fascinating to see other prep schools and to pass comment on the quality of their team teas. Amongst the schools we visited was Beaumont, where I was particularly impressed by their workshops in which boys were making stained glass windows. I also remember Ardingly with its lovely archetypal English cricket ground with beautiful trees. I also enjoyed swimming. We had an indoor unheated swimming pool, covered over in the winter with floorboards, where the school plays were performed. One summer I determined to swim a mile without stopping. I made it, but had to be helped from the pool, blue with cold. I was taken to the bathrooms and thawed out in a tepid bath to which hot water was added very slowly. All this was supervised by the Headmaster. He liked the sight of naked boys, but never, so far as I know, behaved improperly.

The school was divided into four 'houses': Oaks, Pines, Willows and Yews. There was no Head Boy, but there were four heads of house. In my final year I was head of Yews. That year we won the summer sports and Auntie Claire presented me with the Silver Cup; somewhere there is a photograph of the occasion. I seem to remember that I won the high jump. There were no mattresses in those days, just a sand pit, and I used what was then the latest technique called the 'Western Roll' – now superseded by the 'Fosbury Flop'! I also did pretty well at the pole vault – old-fashioned bamboo poles and a sand pit; no fibreglass and no mattresses either.

I had no particular friends but got on pretty well with most of the boys. There were two boys with what seemed to us rich parents who visited the school frequently during term. They were worth cultivating; I seem to remember quite a party being allowed out with them to have high teas with sausages and chips. One of the boys was called Sleigh; he had the distinction of having his own elaborate Hornby train set mounted on a pingpong table which he would allow others to play with.

Apart from that one visit on Sports Day I don't remember any relation visiting me at school in the five years that I was there. But wait: I must be wrong; I remember Granny being there when I was quite junior and embarrassing me greatly by saying to one of the senior boys, 'So you are one of Guy's friends.' I have since come across my very first photograph album and there are pictures in it of my father and mother outside the school with their yellow Triumph Gloria sports car and of them with Granny on the miniature railway at Drusilla's. So that must have been in the summer term of 1936 – a home leave year. It is rather extraordinary, I think, to know that Drusilla's still exists and that people still ride on the miniature railway. I remember sitting in the back of the Triumph Gloria – very cramped – and urging my father to go faster and being thrilled when the speedometer showed 72 m.p.h. This was on the road near Peacehaven in Sussex.

From the mid 1930s to about 1941 I spent nearly all my summer and winter holidays at the Manor House, Crowle with the Moores: Uncle Leslie, T.K., and my cousins Claire and Jack. Jack was about two years younger than me, but he was my constant companion. We spent months making an elaborate map of the area, which involved a lot of bicycle riding. We went enormous distances; probably nearer the end of the 30s we went as far as 25 miles away – 50 miles in one day!

We did a lot of fruit picking, for which we were paid. We picked mainly apples and plums. One of the earliest apples, which I particularly liked, was the Worcester Pearmain – not so popular these days because it doesn't keep. The brook was another great attraction. Jack and I used to boat on it in the bathtub, which we called the *Queen Mary* (that dates it, because I think she was launched in 1936). Another of my favourite occupations was making elaborate water courses, where little tributaries wended their way through the mud. I would spend hours making dams and new channels. We also made a secret tree house in an old lime tree. Food forms an important part in my memories. T.K. was a very good cook: an old-fashioned cook. Every year we used to have a pig killed and shared it with the butcher. T.K. would then use the whole half pig, curing and hanging the ham, curing the bacon and making brawn with the head; years later I discovered that in America brawn was called 'head cheese'.

Christmas and the New Year were always rather special. We used to have an enormous turkey; once we picked up the the turkey legs and began chewing them at the table and Granny who was there told us sharply that if we wanted to do that we should go to the kitchen; somebody then went back to the dining room to find Granny herself chewing a bone! After Christmas there was always a lot of turkey left over; Uncle Leslie made a habit of eating devilled turkey legs, dripping with mustard, really far too hot for him, but he persevered, going red in the face! At Christmas too, there were always the carol singers, who were invited in for cake and wine (certainly not grape wine, but elderberry or parsnip wine). At the New Year we always stayed up until midnight, and Uncle Leslie insisted on an ancient custom; it was good luck if the first person to enter the house in the New Year had dark hair, so Claire was pushed out of the back door and had to come round to the front to be admitted. I don't suppose anybody now knows that there were New Year carols. The boys from the village would always appear outside the front of the house at dawn on New Year's Day and sing their carols.

I was very fond of T.K. and I think she was of me. When I was still small enough I often used to sit on her lap to be cuddled – 'Spoony Guy' they called me.

In the summer we usually all went to Stratford-upon-Avon to see a Shakespeare play. Uncle Leslie would have us read the play through, each taking a part. I remember doing that round a table in the garden. I was not always culturally sound; one Christmas I was given as a present a copy of Dickens' *Oliver Twist* but handed it back saying I didn't really want to read it! Although my parents were abroad I always received presents from them – chosen and bought, of course, by Auntie Claire.

I don't think I ever spent the Easter holidays at Crowle. I must have spent some of the time at my grandfather's in Tunbridge Wells and also at Northway with Granny and Madie. In London we went to church every Sunday at the New Church in Pembridge Villas; it was a very long journey by bus (the number 2, I think) from Hampstead Garden Suburb. I used to go to Sunday School whilst the grownups listened to the sermon – and sermons used to be pretty long in those days. I was baptised into the New Church there in 1936; there being no New Church in Malaya, I had been baptised as an infant into a non-denominational Christian church. My father would not countenance an Anglican christening.

I remember being taken to the cinema by Auntie Madie to see a Jack Hulbert film; but when we arrived the previous film was still showing (there was always a double bill in those days) – some gangster film – and I remember hiding behind the seat in front so as not to see the shooting! In those days Hampstead Garden Suburb was very near the country; we used to catch the bus on the road at the bottom of Northway and on the way to Golders Green there were farms on the right with sheep and cattle.

But there were some quite different holidays. Our landlord in Brussels, M. Dupont, owned the casino at La Panne (the last town on the Belgian coast before the French border and Dunkirk). For some extraordinary reason, I was sent there on my own for several weeks in the summer of 1935; I say 'extraordinary', but presumably Auntie Claire felt that I ought to keep up my French and she felt she trusted the Duponts. The Casino was a complex with, besides the Casino proper, a cinema, a restaurant/café and tennis courts. My bedroom was just behind the projection booth of the cinema, so I heard the soundtrack as I went to sleep. I ate in the restaurant – a corner table – with Poupette, the Duponts' nine year old daughter, who was my main companion. I don't remember much about her except for one evening when she and I were invited to dinner by some friends of the Duponts. Even though aged nine and ten we were given wine to drink and Poupette became quite drunk and began to abuse our hostess – 'salle vache', etc. Poupette was taken up to bed and I was sent back to the Casino to tell M. Dupont that Poupette would not be back until the morning. I remember finding her father behind the bar; he was none too pleased.

I used to consort with teen-age boys behind the tennis courts. One of them, a Vietnamese (from what we then called French Indochina), introduced me to cigarettes; we smoked an American cigarette called Kool with menthol tips. Very cool – because tipped cigarettes were then very rare. All the French – and Belgians – smoked Gauloises, Gitanes.

Another adventure was with the Duponts' son of about 18. He asked me to crew for him on his sand yacht – the beach at La Panne was fantastically wide at low tide, very much like Deauville in Normandy – and there were many land yacht races from La Panne to Dunkirk. I thought he had chosen me for my crewing skills. But it turned out that the real reason was that I was so light. Sand yachts in those days had real wooden hulls like a boat. When we raced to Dunkirk we would be timed into Dunkirk and sent off again back to La Panne an hour later. Young Dupont, I later discovered, spent the hour loading his boat with bottles of brandy! On our way back we crossed the border without stopping. In Belgium brandy was a great deal more expensive. So I had my first experience of smuggling at the age of ten. I remember feeling sorry for the little old ladies in black with wicker baskets covered with a cloth who could be seen dodging in and out of the dunes, trying to avoid the customs officers. My only other memory of La Panne was of watching with fascination a pair of lovers in the restaurant, where the man was nibbling the girl's ear lobe – I simply could not understand it! This, by the way, was in public.

The next big holiday was in 1936 – a Home Leave year. My parents took a house in Ireland, Knockferry, on the shores of Lough Corrib in Galway. The party consisted of my parents, me, Viola and Audrey, Auntie Claire and Mary and Peter Dalley (my first cousins, the children of my mother's sister Peggy and her husband, Uncle John). John and Peggy's home leave did not coincide with my parents'. Uncle John was a police officer in Malaya.

We did not travel to Ireland all together. My parents took me by car with them, whilst poor old Auntie Claire took all the other children across the

Guy in a pool in Ireland 1936

Irish Sea by boat and then by train from Dublin. My parents and I set off by car for Liverpool. As I remember it, we travelled in a very large Sunbeam saloon. We couldn't possibly have squeezed everything in to the Triumph Gloria, but the photographs I have of us in Ireland show the Triumph Gloria, and yet when driving around Galway and Connemara, which we did (I remember the sight of the Twelve Bens in Connemara and also seeing the salmon in the water in the river beneath the bridge in Galway) with that number of people we must have had a large car. An unsolved problem.

Knockferry was on the south shore of Lough Corrib at its narrowest point. Every morning Peter and I would row over to the other side to collect our milk and bread. A lot of time was spent on the Lough. I always enjoyed 'messing about in boats'. At that time I used to read the *Swallows and Amazons* books by Arthur Ransome. My father did some fly fishing, which I never mastered and we also used to 'troll' for perch – what beasts they were to kill with their spiny dorsal fins. My father must have caught some trout, because I remember eating some freshly fried.

Returning home we drove through the Mersey Tunnel, which had only just been opened. I also remember visiting Stokesay Castle in Shropshire. I also remember my embarrassment at my parents' attempts at sex education – this consisted of all three of us having a bath together, which required a very large bath, which there was in the hotel in Liverpool. I didn't know

The Residency, Penang, where my parents lived 1937/38

where to look and didn't learn anything of any importance! The final memory of the holiday was when our car broke down near Craven Arms (in Shropshire?). We were driving along in this large Sunbeam, with my mother and me in the back when with a bang the back of the car sank on to the road– the 'Big End' had gone, whatever that may mean. The car had to be abandoned and all our luggage transferred to the station and we finished the journey by train.

My only other memories of 1936 are from school; already mentioned above. I have no memory of any tearful farewell to my parents. I think I had really got accustomed to not having them around. Of course, on this occasion, they went back with Viola and Audrey.

In 1937 I went on a holiday to Switzerland during the Easter holidays to stay with the Gallands in Lausanne; he was the honorary British Consul in Lausanne and his wife was from Mauritius and must have been a relation of the de Chazals. As I have already mentioned, my parents' wedding reception had been held there in 1921. They lived in a large house with a big garden, high up overlooking the Lake of Geneva. I did not in fact travel there on my own, but in the care of my great-uncle, l'Oncle René (de Chazal), my grandmother's brother. Although he lived in England, he was really very French. I remember how boring he was on the journey to Dover, and how he came to life when we docked at Calais and took the train to Paris; he put on a beret which he had kept in his pocket and lit up a Gauloise! The atmosphere on the dockside at Calais was quite unique; porters wearing traditional uniform with leather patches on their shoulders and their individual number on a big metal badge ran up and down shouting, '*Porteur, Porteur.*' It still seems strange to me to arrive at Calais and drive off the ferry with hardly anybody to be seen – no atmosphere of 'being abroad' – except for driving on the right. Our journey to Lausanne continued. At the Gare du Nord our train took what was then known as 'la ceinture' which circled Paris round to the Gare de L'Est where we changed trains.

My companion in Lausanne was the Gallands' daughter, whose name I now forget, who was about my age. Her great fame to a young boy was that she had had tetanus (lockjaw as we called it) and in her convulsions had bitten off the tip of her tongue. Why should young boys be so interested in such a gruesome detail? We played a lot in their very large garden and took boat trips on the Lake, visiting the Château de Chinon, as all tourists do. There were also other relatives there; in particular I remember Maurice de Chazal, a cousin, who was a young New Church minister, whom I didn't take to at all. He had a rather vulgar sense of humour, and was also, I think, a hypochondriac. At the Manor House at Crowle I remember seeing him lying ashen-faced on a sofa tucked up with a rug; we were given the impression that he was dying but he lived for many more years.

The journey back had a strange feature. Oncle René had moved on and I was put in the care of two elderly ladies, who had I think been teachers at Hamilton House in Tunbridge Wells. They were as naive as I was. On the train to Paris we were befriended by a man with one leg in plaster, broken, he said, in a skiing accident. He seemed quite charming. When we got to Paris he offered to take me off the ladies' hands and settle me in the hotel at the Gare du Nord. We went by taxi and I was put into a bedroom adjoining his. At bedtime, imagine my surprise when he came in to my room – no plaster cast, incidentally – and told me how difficult it was to be without his wife and tried to get into bed with me! I managed to fend him off after he had tried some intimate advances; and he retreated to his bedroom. Next morning he handed me over to the old ladies and we continued our journey to England without him. None of us had ever heard of paedophiles! I suppose I must feel lucky that nothing worse happened. I never told anyone about it. But the ladies were fine chaperones!

1937 was also memorable for the Coronation which, judging from my photo album, I must have witnessed. But more important was the Review of the Fleet at Spithead. My uncle, Frank Layard, younger brother of my mother, was a career naval officer. He went to Dartmouth (when it was still in fact at Osborne in the Isle of Wight) and joined the Navy as a Midshipman at the age of 16, just in time to serve at the Battle of Jutland. In 1937 he was a Lieut. Commander in command of a destroyer and I was invited to see the Review with him. I remember being very impressed when he was 'piped aboard'. The Fleet was a magnificent sight – hundreds of ships, enormous battleships, cruisers, destroyers and many smaller ships; and not just British, there were representatives from the Navies of Germany, France, Japan and the USA. We reviewed the Fleet in a launch from Uncle Frank's destroyer. Never again will such a sight be seen!

In a school play as Don John of Austria – 1937

Uncle Frank was the best-mannered man I have ever met and so charming. He married quite late (sometime in the mid 1930s) a very jolly lady, Joan. They once took me to the theatre, in Shaftesbury Avenue, to see *Treasure Island*. There were some remarkable effects, with the ship, the *Hispaniola*, on a heaving sea. But just as exciting for me was being driven to the theatre in the dicky of the Layards' sports car; I remember going round Piccadilly Circus. It must have been around 1937 that Uncle Frank first took me to his club in Pall Mall, the Junior United Services Club. As a young boy I was very impressed when the steward in the dining room asked me if I would like a second helping – here we go again, food! When he asked me if I wanted to go to the loo, he always said, 'Do you want to splash your boots?' Another archaism he employed was to refer to girls as 'popsies'. Uncle Frank lived to a great age, dying just two days before his hundredth birthday.

1938 was my last year at Normansal; I was to go to Loretto (the oldest public school in Scotland) in September. The next section of these memoirs will cover Loretto and the beginning of the Second World War, but first I will finish with the final holidays of the 1930s.

In the summer of 1938 we spent a holiday in Brittany. When I say 'we' I can never be quite sure who was there. I know that it was all arranged by Auntie Claire and that Claire and Jack Moore were with us. Was Auntie Madie there also? I don't know. We stayed in a guest house at Port Blanc. I have a vague feeling that the owners may have been distantly related; I know from my photograph album that the owner of Les Pervanches was a Mme. Sanglé-Ferrière. Perhaps she had been introduced by Claire de Pitray (the Comtesse de Pitray — excellent wines, incidentally, from the Château de Pitray), a Mauritian cousin. We were right by the sea and had a lovely time. I remember the crooked spire of the church at Plougrescant, kicked over, they said, by the devil. This was also the first time I was ever attracted by a girl; she was at least four years older than me, but I would gaze at her in admiration. She was called Agnes de Longueville.

From my album, again, I discover that we went by ship to Jersey (which was to play a part in my life after the war); changed ships there and sailed to St. Malo. We also visited Mont St. Michel. I remember it well, but needed the album to date the visit. 1939 was again a Home Leave year. My parents were due back for the Easter holidays and my father for part of the summer holidays. I knew that it had been planned that my parents and I were to go to Norway for a skiing holiday. I became very worried in March when the news of the Italian invasion of Albania seemed to presage war — not that I was worried about the war; I was just afraid that the Norwegian holiday might be cancelled! But, of course, it wasn't. It was a memorable holiday. We sailed from Newcastle on a Norwegian ship, the SS *Venus*. I remember on the station platform when the boat train arrived meeting Ingeborg Harmsworth; her mother Lady Harmsworth was Norwegian. I was quite taken by her (Ingeborg, I mean). We were staying in the same hotel at Finse on the Hardanger Glacier and I danced with her most evenings. We dressed for dinner and I wore my Sunday best from Loretto — a Hunting Stewart kilt with a black jacket with silver buttons on the cuffs. But I am leaping ahead. The sea journey was lovely; I don't remember how long it took. But I remember my first experience of Smorgasbord — delicious! We sailed up the fjord to Bergen, which was no longer snow-covered and went by train up to Finse. On the glacier all was deep snow. The hotel was by a lake, which was completely covered with ice and snow. As we arrived at Finse some of the skiing instructors came down the slopes pulling up right by the train in a flurry of snow —very impressive!

My father, who was then 51, had never skied before. So we all spent the first few days on the nursery slopes. The ski instructors were very impressed with 'the old man'. It was all very different then; the skis were of wood and they had to be waxed every day; the instructors showed us that different waxes were required for different snow conditions. Perhaps the biggest difference was that there were no chair lifts; we had to climb with fur strips attached to the skis to help them to grip and went up with the skis in a herringbone pattern. I made quite good progress and was entered in a slalom race (for those in the know, I am afraid I had only mastered the 'stem turn'). I was desperately keen to win, or at least to beat the young Canadian boy who was, of course, very experienced. It was an unusual slalom by today's practice; we were not timed but all started at the same time! I was in the lead with only about 25 yards to go to the finishing line, when, horror of horrors, I fell and the Canadian boy passed me; even though I scrambled up to finish, I only managed second place!

On the last day we (my parents and I) went for a full day's excursion accompanied by instructors. It was a beautiful sunny day and when we reached the top we had a picnic, sitting on our skis. Up to this point not a single downhill run, but we were now poised high up on the glacier looking down a steep mountainside to the tiny hotel on the far side of the lake. Remember there was no 'piste'; this was virgin snow. With a swoop they all set off for the bottom; for a moment my nerve failed me and I was all alone hundreds of feet away from the warmth of the hotel, but I took courage and followed them down. I think I fell twice, but it was an exhilarating experience.

On my return to school I wrote to Ingeborg at her public school (I don't remember which one it was) and mysteriously signed my name backwards 'Yarboum ed Yug'. For some reason the letter was not delivered and was returned to Loretto. Imagine my embarrassment when the Headmaster called me to his study and asked me if I called myself 'Yarboum ed Yug'! Perhaps in those days girls were not allowed to receive letters from boys at another school. Nowadays I suppose you would just send a text-message!

My parents being still in the country, they took me out for the half term holiday in June 1939. There were to be no more half term holidays —the war put an end to that. We went and stayed with Carew Moubray, the Laird of Cockairnie, the head of the family. Cockairnie was and indeed still is in Fife — Amicia visited it a few years ago. We then did a tour of the Highlands; I remember Glencoe, Oban and Fort William. We didn't see any sun; it was mostly Scotch mist and light rain. When we had to put the hood up it was my job to get out of the car and clip on the side windows made of a yellowish early version of plastic.

The last holiday of the 1930s was in the summer of 1939. We stayed with Uncle John and Auntie Peggy at their house in Marston Magna. I am not in fact quite sure that Uncle John was there; he may have already gone back to Malaya. Also present were Peter and Mary Dalley, Viola and Audrey and Auntie Claire. My mother was there too, but I think my father had already returned to Malaya. It was a lovely summer. Marston Magna was in Somerset, near Yeovil and Cadbury Castle, on the borders with Dorset and Wiltshire.

We drove around quite a lot in the superb car my mother had bought; a Minerva. The Minerva was a Belgian car, as prestigious as a Lagonda or Hispano-Suiza. It was enormous with a hood and running boards on which, within the grounds, Peter and I would ride. The children usually sat on the folded down hood with their feet between the grown-ups in the back seat, so we could easily manage, on a fine day, to carry five children and four adults. When my mother returned to Malaya in September the poor old Minerva was sold for scrap for £10!

The villages around Marston Magna had lovely names, Queen Camel in particular. We used to go swimming in the River Yeo at Chilton Cantelo. As it happened, I didn't have much of a holiday because I developed a streptococcal throat, which in the days before antibiotics was rather serious; I suspect it was what they referred to in the eighteenth century when they said somebody had died 'of a putrid throat'. I had a very high temperature and spent several weeks in bed. But there was already a new drug, sulphanilamide which had to be taken orally, and they were still very unsure about the dosage. Anyway I recovered, and by 3 September was convalescent in my pyjamas on a chaise longue, and it was outside in a sunny corner that we all heard Mr Chamberlain on the wireless telling us that we were now at war with Germany.

CHAPTER 4

Public School and War

SCHOOL AND WAR WERE INEVITABLY INTERTWINED. But the next section of these memoirs will be about Loretto. It seems quite strange to send a boy who had been at prep school in Sussex, and whose only homes had been in Kent and Worcestershire, to school in Scotland. My parents believed that they had made their choice on rational grounds. When on home leave in 1936 they had visited a number of public schools and talked to the headmasters. The one who impressed them most was Greenlees of Loretto. He was certainly an unusual man; he had been a paediatrician in Glasgow in the 1920s, but he had also been a great rugger player, a Cambridge Blue, indeed captain of the Cambridge XV and had later played for Scotland. By the time I got to Loretto he was getting on, probably around 60. It was decided that he should retire at the end of the summer term of 1939, but the man appointed to replace him never came; with the start of the war he joined the Army, and Greenlees stayed on to the end of the war. Greenlees was very tall and looked like an Old Testament prophet, with unusually long, for those days, white hair. I rather liked him, but I think he had lost touch with what was going on in the school below him.

I have no doubt that sentiment played a very important part in my parents' decision. My father was very proud of his ancestry and the elder branch of the family, in the person of Carew Moubray, were still lairds of Cockairnie. My mother was also very inclined to see herself as a Scotswoman. Her mother had been a Carnegie-Arbuthnot; their home which my mother had often visited as a child was called Balnamoon – pronounced Bonnymoon. My mother played the piano; her favourite music book was *The Oxford Scottish Song Book*. At the slightest opportunity she would be on the Road to the Isles. Carew himself had been at Loretto, some time in the 1870s, I think; others of the family had been there even earlier. Loretto was I think founded in 1827.

But the die was cast, and Loretto it was to be, starting in September 1938. After the end of the summer term at Normansal, Auntie Claire and I went up to Edinburgh to buy my school clothes from the outfitters in Princes Street. Loretto was much influenced by Arnold of Rugby – *mens sana in corpore sano*. So we wore very healthy clothes. All year round we wore shorts and open necked shirts. On Sundays we dressed up for chapel, wearing either kilts or, if purely Sassenach, morning coat and trousers. We also wore stiff white collars, Eton collars for those under sixteen or under six foot and polo collars for the others (I switched to polo collars before I was sixteen, because of my height). I remember how difficult it was to fasten the collar stud, although it was slightly easier when I switched to polo collars. The Moubrays having married into the Stewarts were entitled to wear the Hunting Stewart tartan, so I was kitted out in a kilt. Auntie Claire and I stayed in a boarding house and I was pleased when a man asked me if I would like a ride to the Braid Hills by car. I should have known better; as I have already said cars were then known as motors, so the trip was not by motor, but by tram car!

Loretto was not a bad school, but I was very unhappy there. There was much too much corporal punishment. In the three and half years that I was there I don't remember Greenlees ever beating a boy, but masters and prefects were allowed pretty free rein. I think I was beaten in every one of the eleven terms I was there. Loretto was above all a rugby school; believe it or not there were exactly fifteen prefects – the members of the Rugby First XV! They indulged in beating for the most trivial reasons. Only prefects were allowed on the grass lawn coming down to School House; for any other boy a foot on the grass when being chased was a beating offence. I remember being beaten for leaving a library book on the pegs in the cloakroom overnight and for mislaying the mouthpiece of my bugle. There was some kind of assembly after lunch where the prefects made announcements and read out the punishment list – which didn't take place for some time afterwards, so you were left with an agonising wait. I found the whole thing degrading. I have to say that some of the prefects carried out the beating in a fairly restrained manner, but there were one or two who enjoyed it too much. Just as bad was that the masters were allowed to beat; looking back I think in fact that I can remember only one master who did beat; I even remember his name – Donny Reid. He was the Latin master and would regularly beat boys in front of the class for making too many mistakes in their Latin unseens. Now he really enjoyed it, and used to try and draw blood. It certainly never improved my Latin; I just tried in prep to sit next to a boy who was good at Latin, and shamelessly crib. Years later, in 1943 I think, I was on a Tube in London when Donny Reid had the nerve to come up to me to say hello!

The other classics master, Mr Pateman, who taught Greek was pretty severe, but he did not beat. He had a contraption which he called an 'incita mentis'; it consisted of a compass point mounted on a wooden handle. He would get you to stand beside him: 'The aorist paradigm of *luo* in ten seconds!' If you failed he would jab the contraption into your biceps! Did it do any good? *Luo, lueis, luei, luomen, lueitis, luein* – is that right? But Pateman had a softer side to him; he gathered a group of us in his rooms in the winter evenings to sing unaccompanied Elizabethan madrigals. Another master, who couldn't have killed a fly, was Cuthbert-Brown, who taught French and German. We called him 'Coudebou' – presumably a dog French version of Cuthbert. I feel sure he would have retired had it not been for the war. He was going deaf and some of the boys used to tease him. They would say, 'Tickle your arse with a feather, sir'; 'What's that, boy?' he would exclaim. 'Particularly nasty weather, sir,' they would reply.

When term started we were in the midst of the Munich crisis and there were fears that war was going to break out. So one of the first things we did was to go to the dunes on the shores of the Firth of Forth and fill sandbags; I think we did this for about a week, at the expense of classes. The weather was fine and I started on a happy note. Loretto is in Musselburgh to the east of Edinburgh on the shores of the Firth of Forth. Musselburgh had been a mining town, with the seams going out under the Forth, so the beaches at Musselburgh were black and old ladies were frequently seen gleaning for coal. The school was alongside the golf course. I believe that the Musselburgh golf course is the oldest in the world; older even than St. Andrews. Strange to say I don't remember ever being given a golf lesson; not that it would have been possible after the war started, since the golf course was covered with obstacles to the landing of enemy gliders. In 2002 I saw an article in a paper about Loretto becoming the first school in the British Isles to offer golf scholarships! Another feature of Musselburgh is the race course of which I have absolutely no memory.

In that first term Carew Moubray very kindly came to see me at school, even though he was already in his eighties and Cockairnie was quite a long way away. I suppose we had tea together somewhere in the school; we did not, I think, go to one of the high tea cafés in the town. He told me about his time at Loretto. The only two things I remember are that he said they were so hungry that they used to catch rats and roast them over the bedroom fires and that he was in the cricket XI because there were only eleven boys in the school then!

Dormitories at Loretto were fairly small, not more than about eight boys in each. I started off in the House across the way from School House (I cannot remember its name). Each dormitory had a head of dormitory, who would have been about eighteen and who had failed to become a prefect because he wasn't good enough at rugger! The main task of the junior boy was to light a fire in the dormitory fireplace on Sundays, when we spent a lot of time in the dormitories; and what a job that was – no fire lighters, damp coal and damp wood; a lot of time was spent with a newspaper stretched across the fireplace trying to get a draught going. All the rest of the week the dormitories were cold – very healthy!

First thing in the morning we had to have cold baths – and a strange ritual it was; the taps in the cast iron baths were left running the whole time and one after the other we would flop into the bath with the displaced water running on to the tile floors and away through the drain. In my first term I had another duty; just before lights out I had to wind up the gramophone and put on a record by Hildegarde, a well known London cabaret artist, and the head of dormitory would sigh and drift off to sleep; with a wind-up gramophone you could not just wait for it to turn off, so I had to keep awake. The head of dormitory would regale us with stories of his visits to night clubs in London during the holidays. I wish I could remember the name of the tune which I had to play every night (something like 'Good night Sweetheart').

We had to take exercise every afternoon, whatever the weather. In the autumn term we played rugger, in the next term hockey and in the summer cricket. But if the weather was too bad for organised games we had to go for runs, which I hated because it was always wet, usually cold and anyway I didn't like running. I even remember some of the names of the runs – the short Wally and the long Wally. If the long Wally was decreed, prefects would be around to ensure that you didn't cheat by doing the short Wally instead. I remember one winter's day, after heavy snow, doing a very long run, longer than the long Wally, right up to the top of a nearby hill. The path to the top was in a gully which was at least eight foot deep in snow, so we had to run up beside the path, constantly slipping and falling into the snow. In the summer, if it was too wet for cricket, Greenlees would have us out on the rugger pitch practising passing! On Sundays, after church, we went for crocodile walks, wearing our Sunday best; the local 'keelies' (Scottish word for urchins) used to taunt us as we walked by, trying to flip up our kilts – 'Kilty, kilty cold bum, canna keep his arse warm!'

I was quite good at rugger, a prop forward, and by the autumn term of 1941 was in the Second XV. Had I stayed on another year, I am sure I would have graduated to the First XV – and presumably, have been made a prefect. If that had happened I might have left Loretto with much fonder memories, who knows? Talking of rugger, the whole school was taken to Murrayfield to watch the Calcutta Cup match between Scotland and England, but we only went once, in March 1939; no more took place during the war. I haven't mentioned it before, but one other item of school clothing was a light blue tweed plus-four suit, worn going to school at the beginning of term and going home again, but also worn on occasions such as the visit to Murrayfield.

I joined the school in the fourth form, one above the normal entrance form because of my Common Entrance results. I remember the names of some of my contemporaries. One, I know, was Marr, who I think is or was the father of Andrew Marr the BBC political correspondent, who is I know a Lorettonian. Another was Guy Robertson-Durham, the only other Guy I ever met as a boy. Not that it mattered what your Christian name was since we always addressed each other by our surnames. I remember reading Robertson-Durham's obituary in an old boys' magazine I used to receive. His main claim to fame seemed to have been that in 1946 he played golf with King George VI! My best friend, Doney Foulis, was in fact in the form below me. We did a lot together, including long bike rides in the summer (when those were permitted I cannot remember – Saturdays, I think). I know we did one long ride as far as Gullane on the coast. The whole area was deserted and one was not allowed on the beach; I think it had been mined. Strange to say Gullane is where Muirfield Golf Club is, and some time in the 80s I watched the Open there on television and saw a much older Doney Foulis presenting the prizes; he was then Captain of Muirfield Club. He once came to stay with me in Tunbridge Wells, and I once went to stay with him at his Highland home; I remember his nanny cooking delicious griddle cakes – essentially the same thing as American pancakes.

In the form above was Hector Laing, later Chairman of United Biscuits (the Laings being one of the Scottish biscuit families). He was later Sir Hector, a favourite of Maggie Thatcher's, a Director of the Bank of England, where I later met him at lunch in the Governor's dining room. But at school he was a very sad figure; he could not pass his School Certificate and was therefore never in the VIth form, but in the Remove, nor a prefect. I remember seeing him leaning against a wall looking completely withdrawn. I suppose he knew that he would get into the family business, whether he had any School Certificates or not.

Another contemporary was Jock Macpherson, a slim red-haired young man; I say young man because for some reason my first memories of him are in the VIth form. We spent a lot of time together in the VIth form library, working for our subjects in the Higher Certificate – mine were French and German. But we also concocted some kind of smoking mixture from basket weaving cane, which we then smoked up the chimney, so as to leave no smoke in the library. I saw Jock again after the war, meeting him in Victoria Street. But we then lost touch again. Years later, in the 1960s, I saw his picture in the *Financial Times* and got in touch with him. He was now a rising business star, Chief Executive of Northern Securities, building up quite a powerful conglomerate. By this time his hair had lost its colour, and he had become pretty stout – too much good food and not enough exercise. We met for lunch quite often; he would take me to the Savoy Grill and send me back to the Bank in his Rolls! Amicia and I once went to Royal Ascot in his box. I am afraid that things eventually went wrong for him; he was kicked off the board of the company he had founded; amongst other things, the shareholders objected to paying him for four Rolls-Royces. He died some years ago. Everybody in the school was in the OTC, now known as the Corps. We were attached to a Scottish regiment (The Royal Scots, I think) and wore a uniform with a kilt. I rather enjoyed rifle practice and parade ground drill, which all came in handy a few years later in the Army. Right up to the summer of 1939 there was a Corps camp after the end of term. In 1939 we camped somewhere near Dalkeith. I remember that the platoon I was with had to go through a wood; we took a mighty long time, the undergrowth was nothing but wild raspberries!

I very much enjoyed being in the school choir. We had a lovely chapel, which must have been built after the First World War because the inscription on stone tablets behind the altar was 'Greater love hath no man than to lay down his life for his friends'. I was in the choir throughout my time at school, starting as a treble, graduating to alto, tenor and, finally, bass.

I had quite a good voice, but not good enough to be a soloist. When I was a treble there was no one good enough and I and another boy sang the solo parts as a duet. I loved the anthems; quite my favourite was Purcell's 'Rejoice in the Lord always, and again I say rejoice'.

There was an organ, which I learned to play. It always required the presence of two people, because the pump was still manually operated. Services – two on Sundays and prayers once a day – were in accordance with the Church of Scotland liturgy, so we sang the metric psalms. There was no chaplain; we had visiting ministers. I remember one in particular, with a strong Scottish accent, with rolling Rs and sibilant Ss; his text was 'Be ye wise as serpents and harmless as doves'; try and imagine that with all the Ss and rolling Rs. At one point he said, 'Ye are all miserable sinners'; I am afraid we all sniggered, because as he said it, he was pointing at the Headmaster!

The chapel was a blaze of colour; all but about 16 of the 182 boys wore kilts. Some of the tartans were spectacular. I remember particularly the Buchanan tartan (Buchanan incidentally pronounced with the 'ch' as in loch and the second A long). A very interesting tartan was that of McCosh of the Isles, not in fact very colourful, pale whitish-blue. But what a wonderful name to have! Urquhart was another interesting one. I learned, of course, the correct pronunciation – 'Uchart' with again the 'ch' as in loch. On Sundays, when formally dressed for chapel we always had to wear a buttonhole. The buttonholes, already prepared, were in baskets. I remember particularly that in the autumn term they were always chrysanthemums with that distinctive perfume, which always reminds me of school.

The war had a big impact on our lives. In September 1939 several of the prefects from the summer term, one of whom was to have been Head Boy, did not return, because they had joined up. This had the unexpected effect that the new Head Boy was not in the rugger XV; what's more he was a 'swot'! During the period of the 'phony war', September 1939 to the spring of 1940, life went on much as it would have done in times of peace. But I do remember one incident quite early in the autumn term. We were on the games pitch; presumably I was on the touch line, because I was off games for the whole of that term (because of having taken sulphanilamide for my strep throat). We saw some aeroplanes over the Firth of Forth, and behind each plane would appear a puff of black smoke. Was this some training exercise, we wondered? We then realised that they were in fact German planes, and that our anti-aircraft fire was not being very effective. But they dropped no bombs and soon flew off over the sea.

In spite of rationing the school food was very good, plenty of fresh vegetables and lots of milk. There was a kind of pantry where jugs of milk were available at any time along with a barrel of ship's biscuits – real ship's biscuits, such as sailors would have had in the Napoleonic war; very hard and you often had to knock the weevils out before biting!

We followed the war news in newspapers – the *Scotsman* – and the wireless; always the nine o'clock news on the Home Service. The nine o'clock news on Sundays was always preceded by the national anthems of the Allies. This must have started early in the war, because I remember well that one of the anthems was Sibelius' 'Finlandia' – I don't think Finland was technically an ally; but they were fighting a fierce war with the Russians. I remember seeing pictures of troops in white uniforms on the frozen Lake Lagoda. I also remember some of the news of the Norwegian campaign in March 1940.

I say that we used to listen to the wireless, always in the dormitories, because nine o'clock was after bedtime. But until now it has never occurred to me to ask who provided the wireless sets; I think now that the school did not. We must I think have been listening to my very own set, given to me, as I remember, by Auntie Peggy, presumably because she no longer needed it, as she was returning to Malaya. It was a very early portable set, and it didn't have dry batteries as it would today, but a smaller version of a car battery. I used to have to take it to a garage in Musselburgh High Street periodically to have it recharged.

Besides listening to the news we also heard Churchill's speeches. They made a great impression. Passages such as the following are still very moving (June 1940):

> Hitler knows that he will have to break us in this island or lose the war. If we can stand up to him, all Europe may be free and the life of the world may move forward into broad, sunlit uplands. But if we fail, the whole world, including the United States will sink into the abyss of a new Dark Age. Let us therefore brace ourselves to our duties and so bear ourselves that if the British Empire and its Commonwealth last for a thousand years men will still say 'This was their finest hour'.

and again later that month:

> We shall defend our island, whatever the cost may be. We shall fight on the beaches, we shall fight on the landing grounds, we shall fight in the fields and in the streets, we shall fight in the hills. We shall never surrender.

Inspiring stuff.

Throughout the war we had Summer Time during the winter and Double Summer Time in the summer. Being as far north as we were this had a big effect on our lives; during the summer it didn't get dark until midnight and was not in fact very dark all night long. And in the winter it was not light until after nine o'clock in the morning. So our early morning walk across the golf links, breakfast and our first classes were all in darkness. The invasion of Holland, and then Belgium and France, on 10 May made a dramatic impact. We could hardly believe what we were hearing. Everybody had always said that the Maginot Line was impregnable. But the fall of France had a more dramatic effect on my life. I was due to take my School Certificate in June 1940 but my parents decided that England was no longer safe and that I should be evacuated to the United States. The

Maynards of Stonegate near Tunbridge Wells were close friends of my mother's and had relations living in Virginia, who were willing to take their three children, Joe, Buffy and David and the three Moubrays, me, Viola and Audrey. It was decided that I should take my School Certificate before leaving, but that it would be more convenient for me take the exams in Kent. So I left Loretto (as I thought, for the last time) in June and took the exams with the boys of Tonbridge School. For some reason my main memory of the exams was of the boy sitting at the desk in front of me; he had no hair at all, just like Duncan Goodhew the Olympic swimmer. I never went to America. The Maynards changed their minds and Auntie Claire then decided that she had better take us to some people she knew in New York. I believe that it was at about this time that a passenger ship was sunk on its way to America. This persuaded my parents and Auntie Claire that we should stay.

By the end of August and into September we (Viola, Audrey and I, together with the Maynard children) were camping on the Maynards' fruit farm at Stonegate, on the border of Kent and Sussex. We kept very busy fruit picking, apples and plums. But the main interest was the Battle of Britain which was taking place overhead; this was where the British Spitfires and Hurricanes intercepted the German bombers. The bombers were themselves escorted by German fighters, mostly Messerschmitts. We watched enthralled as the dogfights took place overhead, cheering madly when a German fighter began to fall out of the sky, streaming black smoke behind it, and groaning with misery when one of ours was hit. All around us there was a tinkle of falling shell cases. Nobody ever told us to take cover. We secretly hoped that one of the German planes would come down near us, so that we could go and take the pilot prisoner! I am often asked when I started cooking. Viola told me recently that Buffy and I were the principal cooks in the camp. There was in fact one other girl in our party, called Allison, I think, who was a friend of the Maynards. She was another of my early 'crushes'. I actually attended her wedding at Oxford soon after the war. She was at LMH. The speech at the wedding reception was made by a Canon, whose opening remarks seemed to me to be inappropriate in a man of the cloth. He said, 'A speech at a wedding reception should be like a woman's skirt, short enough to attract interest and long enough to cover the subject'!

Back to 1940. To my great disappointment I now had to return to Loretto. I think it must have been at about this time that I told Auntie Claire that I couldn't stand Loretto. She arranged to talk to Mr Seagrove, the Headmaster of Normansal, who said that he could arrange for me to be transferred to Malvern School. I am not sure why I did not accept the offer. I rather suspect that it was an example of 'British grit'; I felt that having put my shoulder to the wheel I had to be a man and stick it out.

The main feature of school in that winter of 1940–41 was the air raids. I don't think Edinburgh was ever the target of serious bombing, but many bombers passed overhead. Whenever the air raid sirens went we all had to go immediately to the air raid shelters, which were rather like an underground Nissen hut. The air raids were almost all at night. So we put on dressing gowns and a warm coat over that and trooped down to the shelters – in my case, the one for School House – with our pillows and tried to sleep in rather primitive bunk beds. Most of the raids were relatively short and we could return to our dormitories without having lost much sleep. But there was one night when Glasgow sustained a fierce bombing raid which lasted almost all night. It was dramatic, but not particularly frightening because no bombs were falling anywhere near us. All we heard was the steady drone of the bombers overhead and the explosions of anti-aircraft fire. The explosions in Glasgow were too far away to hear.

Travelling to and from school was quite eventful during the war. The trains were always packed with servicemen and there was never a seat, since I usually joined the train at Birmingham, having travelled there from Worcester. I seem to remember sitting on my suitcase in the corridor, surrounded by servicemen, mostly sailors, I think, presumably heading for the Clyde or the naval base at Rosyth. They mostly sat on their kit bags drinking beer from bottles; every now and then the cry would go up 'another dead'un' and an empty bottle would be rolled down the corridor.

One journey home was memorable for the state of Birmingham Station (New Street, I think it was). There was glass all over the platforms, the roof having been blown in. It was cold and there looked like being a long wait for the next train to Worcester. And there was no shelter in the Waiting Room. At this point some businessman came and asked me if I would like a trip in his Rolls-Bentley. No; this was not an improper invitation! We drove to Worcester without incident. I remember the luxury of the leather seats and the polished wood. Another travel experience was when I was returning to school. The train from Birmingham went to Glasgow and passengers for Edinburgh had to change at Carstairs Junction, not very far from Glasgow. I asked a porter to direct me to the platform for the Edinburgh train. He showed me a platform and when the train came in I climbed on board – with a seat this time – and stowed my suitcase in the rack overhead. Some time later the ticket collector came along and looked at my ticket. 'Young man,' he said, 'you're on the train to London.' I don't know whether the next stop was a scheduled stop or whether they stopped on purpose to put me off. Anyway it was a tiny station at Beattock, just north of Lockerbie. When I had been at Carstairs it was still daylight, but by now it was after dark. I don't think they had any idea how long it would be before there was a train back to Carstairs. I spent a long evening with the only two members of the station staff, being given cups of tea and biscuits. After a time the signalman had what he thought was a brilliant idea. He would try and stop the Royal Mail (the prestige service on the LMS – London, Midland and Scottish Railway). He equipped himself with an oil lantern with red glass and stood on the platform waving it at the Royal Mail as it approached. It took no notice and thundered by! Eventually I did get on to a train for Carstairs, got to Edinburgh and took a taxi to Loretto. It must have been around midnight; everybody had gone to bed except for Greenlees, who was waiting for me; no histrionics, just mild amusement!

During 1941 life went on as it had before. We followed the war news in the papers and on the 9 o'clock news. It was universally bad throughout the year. I remember being stunned to hear in June that Germany had invaded Russia. My immediate reaction was to say, 'Good, they will destroy each other,' but I had soon to accept the idea of Russia as our 'gallant ally' and all the propaganda put out about 'dear old Uncle Joe Stalin'. A Russian song called 'Meadowlands' was constantly to be heard with dear Russian peasants singing in the field. I was reminded of my mother's love of the Don Cossack choir, of which she had records.

An important date in my life was December 1941. War with Japan was to shift my life in another direction. Not that I knew that on the day of Pearl Harbour and the Japanese invasion of Malaya. My first concern was, of course, my parents. My father at that time was Resident in the State of Trengannu; that meant that he was the Senior Adviser to the Sultan and was de facto ruler of Trengannu. My mother told me the story of the occasion when a certain denomination of the state postage stamp ran out. It took months to get new supplies from de la Rue's in England and it was accepted practice to take another denomination of stamp and overprint it with the required denomination. Somebody in the Sultan's entourage came up with the bright idea of overprinting one sheet of stamps upside down. This made them a collector's item which could be sold at an inflated price. When my father found out he ordered the 'collectors' item to be brought to a meeting of the cabinet and insisted that the sheet should be burnt there and then!

But to return to December 1941; the Japanese landed at Kuantan in Pahang, to the South of Trengannu. My parents decided to try and get to Kuala Lumpur, three hundred or so miles to the south-west. They abandoned the house with everything in it, collected the Sultan and all his family, made a dash to the north-west and just caught the last train from Kelantan going south. They had no time to bury their valuables, but the local Malays looked after everything. After the war they returned my parents' silver to them (including the Queen Anne style silver teapot which I still have and all my father's silver polo cups). I am told that they even offered to send back the stuffed head of a bison which my father had shot and had mounted!

My mother then became a nurse and my father joined the Army (an Australian unit I believe) to help with his local knowledge and the language. We at home knew that they had managed to evade the Japanese so far. I don't think any of us realised how easily Singapore was going to fall. But that was still two months away.

Towards the end of term a notice appeared on the school board. The Government had realised that they had a desperate shortage of people who could speak Japanese and other oriental languages. As I discovered later there were only two or three Japanese speakers in the whole country. Quite a few English people spoke Japanese, but they had all been interned in Japan. So the Foreign Office announced that they were offering 300 scholarships for boys of 17 or 18 to learn Japanese, Chinese, Turkish and Persian at the School of Oriental and African Studies in London. Applicants would be called to take tests, oral and written, to test their aptitude at various centres in the United Kingdom; tests and interviews in Edinburgh were to be held in January 1942.

I decided to apply, partly because of what was happening in Malaya, but also, and to me even more importantly, because it was a means of getting away from school much earlier than would otherwise have been the case. In the normal course of events, I would not have left school until the end of the summer term in the year in which I became 18 – that would have been July 1943. The Headmaster was happy for me to apply. I believe I was the only boy at Loretto to do so.

I am pretty sure that I spent the Christmas holidays with the Moores at Crowle. It was to be the last one. I am sure that I thoroughly enjoyed it. The Manor House by this time had every modern comfort, electricity, running water, a bathroom and a lavatory. But I still tend to remember it best with the pump, Aladdin lamps and candles. I am not sure that I ever really made clear to T.K. how much I loved her. She had a very difficult life; Uncle Leslie drank far too much and spent a great deal of his time in the pub. I guess it must have been that holiday (I was approaching 17) that he took me to the pub to show off his tall nephew. I must have had something to drink; probably a half pint. but I remember being rather embarrassed by the, to me, false bonhomie.

I think it must have been the same holiday that Uncle Leslie decided to have a sucking pig. It was quite illegal; meat rationing prohibited the private slaughtering of animals. Uncle Leslie and I set off in his Baby Austin to collect the pig from the other side of Worcester. We were very apprehensive driving through Worcester when, at a red traffic light, the pig began to squeal. But, of course we were not found out. When served for dinner the whole pig was brought in to the dining room on a platter.

At the beginning of January 1942 I started what was to be my last term at Loretto. For the first part of the term we heard with horror of the rapid advance of the Japanese through Malaya and finally of the fall of Singapore. My mother was about to take one of the last boats out, when she heard that my father had been wounded and was in hospital. She decided that her first priority was her husband and she went to see him in hospital; she didn't see him for long; they were soon captured. Because he was military my father went to the prisoner of war camp at Changi Prison; and my mother was taken to the civilian internment camp at Sime Road. If she had taken the boat I doubt whether she would have survived; all the last boats, I think, were sunk.

My parents were to be separated for three and a half years, never knowing whether they would ever be free again. Aunty Peggy had got out on a boat before the final debacle and spent the rest of the war in Australia. Uncle John had established what amounted to a private commando force, 'Dalforce', I think he called it, harrying the Japanese behind the lines; he had a lot of contacts through his work in the police. He got away in a small boat, but got no further than Sumatra before being captured; he spent the rest of the war in a prisoner of war camp in Hong Kong. During the next three years we (Auntie Claire, I should say) received altogether three postcards from my parents which told us no more than that they were still alive.

The next important event for me was the Scholarship exam, which took place in Edinburgh in January. It was not a test of existing knowledge; there were no questions on French or German, both of which I was studying for my Higher Schools' Certificate. The tests were for aptitude to learn to read and write a foreign language and for which of the four languages one had the greatest aptitude to speak. The written tests included a passage in some unknown language (possibly an African one – Swahili perhaps) in which the English equivalent was written under every foreign word. You then had to translate into the foreign language a passage in English; all the grammar and vocabulary you required had been included in the illustrative passage. A most ingenious test, I thought. I wonder if a similar test is ever used today. I think I did pretty well in the written test.

The oral tests took quite a long time. One of the tests, again, I think, based on African languages, was to see if you could pronounce a word starting with the sound 'ng'; nobody English has any difficulty in pronouncing 'ng' in the middle of a word as in 'singer', but they often find it almost impossible to start a word with 'ng' or 'nk'; remember the name from Zimbabwe, Nkomo; most English people pronounce it as if it were spelled Enkomo. I had no difficulty with that, which is similar to sounds in spoken Japanese. But I found it quite impossible to make the sounds necessary for speaking Mandarin Chinese. That is a tonal language; and I was asked endlessly, it seemed, to say 'you' with a rising inflection, a falling inflection, or neither rising nor falling. I was quite unable to do so. I am sure I was also asked which of the four languages I wanted to study. I had no particular desire to speak any Eastern language; I was much happier with European languages. But because of what was happening to my parents, I expressed a preference for Japanese. So it was just as well that my aptitude turned out to be for that language.

I am pretty sure that the results were not announced for some weeks, but I never had any doubt that I would win one of the scholarships. The results came through before the end of term, but only just before I think. Throughout that term I acted 'demob happy' a phrase which had not yet been invented (that only came with the end of the war). I frequently broke the rules. I remember some time early in March going in to Musselburgh and buying several bottles of ale (I was not yet quite 17) and carrying them back to the dormitory after dark, hoping that no one in authority would hear them clanking under my coat. I was then Head of my dormitory, and none of the juniors would 'shop' me. I am sure they all enjoyed the drama of drinking beer in the dorm – I don't suppose any of us actually liked the taste. Looking back, I now wonder how on earth we disposed of the 'empties'.

A couple of other memories from that dormitory: my bed was right under the window and the window had to be kept open, whatever the weather. One night I had to drape a mackintosh across the foot of my bed to stop the snow from melting through my blankets. Another memory: the youngest boy in the dormitory was Shanks; I used to think how awful it must have been for him to see his name on every lavatory. I suppose he went into the family firm when he left school. The firm is still around today, called Armitage-Shanks. He also taught me one of my then favourite pop songs – 'You must have been a beautiful baby, cos Baby look at you now'.

CHAPTER 5

Dulwich and the SOAS

I AM SURE THAT THE ORIGINAL ANNOUNCEMENT mentioned three hundred scholarships but I don't think that there were that number when we first gathered; I would say rather less than two hundred:perhaps about 45 for each of the four languages. We met early in May 1942, after the Easter holidays. We were all billeted at Dulwich College and were treated as a special VIth Form. We were subject to discipline from the Headmaster of Dulwich, Mr Gilkes. The Japanese and Chinese groups were established in the Headmaster's House and the others some way away in another Master's house. Dulwich College still went on around us, but presumably with a smaller number of boys. The hero of Dulwich was a Sixth Former already renowned for his prowess at cricket – Trevor Bailey, who played for England after the war. I remember seeing him striding imperiously across the school yard, noticeable for his hair which was fashionably slicked down with Brylcreem.

Our lot, the Japs and the Chinese, met on the first evening in the hall in the Headmaster's House. He told us that we would be subject to school discipline; not that that made very much difference, for unlike the Dulwich boys, we left school every morning and commuted to the School of Oriental and African Studies (SOAS) in London from West Dulwich Station. But we were expected to dress neatly. Gilkes announced one morning after breakfast in School Hall that the standard of dress was not up to scratch and that he expected us on the next day to appear dressed as we would have been at our own schools. Typically bloody-minded de Moubray turned up next day wearing shorts, no tie and full length red stockings, as he would have done at Loretto. Gilkes was not amused, but had to accept it. Of course, I didn't do it again; imagine walking along Victoria Street dressed like that. Another element of discipline was that we had a roll-call every evening; it must have been quite late, because I know we frequently had dinner at restaurants in London.

The most striking thing about that first evening was that we were somehow dragooned into electing Peter Parker as our Prefect (I don't think he had a formal title). I always found Peter thoroughly irritating, sanctimonious and self important. He let us know that he had been Head Boy at Bedford, which to be fair must have been quite an achievement for a boy only just seventeen. He was, and remained throughout his life, on the left politically, Labour, but not Old Labour; I am sure that at one point he was an admirer of Hugh Gaitskell and later, I think, a Social Democrat following his Oxford girlfriend Shirley Williams. His politics, in other

49

words, were as different from mine as they could possibly be. I saw him again after the war at Oxford and later in the 1970s I was on a CBI/British Institute of Management Committee with him; he, of course, was Chairman. We clashed as always, but more of that at the right time. He became Chairman of British Rail (in the 80s I think), was knighted, and died in 2002.

Our course started with a very formal ceremony in the Senate House in Malet Street with speeches by Anthony Eden, the Foreign Secretary, and Leo Amery, who must, I think, have been Colonial Secretary; they were both already famous figures. Anthony Eden looked like a matinee idol and had a distinctive languid voice. Leo Amery was equally distinctive; he couldn't have been much over 5 ft tall. One of his sons was to be a traitor and executed, the other, Julian, became a Conservative Minister. The Head of the SOAS was present and rather extraordinarily for 1942 was a woman, Professor Edwards. The ceremony was a late afternoon affair, with cocktails. From then on the Foreign and Colonial Offices showed no further interest in us. Surprisingly, I don't remember anybody from the military being there; the focus was more on what we would do for our country after the war than on helping to win the war.

Our classes took place in the SOAS. Initially we had only two teachers. The principal one was Mr Yoshitake, who revealed a characteristic Japanese trait that I was to see more of later in the war. Being in British hands, he behaved as if he had no loyalty whatever to Japan or the Emperor and treated us with utmost courtesy and helpfulness. The other was a Formosan (what today would be called Taiwanese), whose name I cannot now remember. He was quite different, young and jolly and he absolutely hated the Japanese, who had now occupied his country since the middle 1930s.

Our first textbook was a grey paperback book from Yale. I still remember an extraordinary comment from its introduction; Japanese ideograms, it said, give you no indication whatever of the way they should be pronounced like, it said, some English surnames – and here one expected them to come up with a name like Cholmondely (pronounced Chumley), but no, the example they gave was Enroughty (pronounced, would you believe it, Derby!). Where they got that from I can't think. More of the SOAS later.

But first some more about our group at Dulwich. We lived, as I have said, in the Headmaster's House. There may have been dormitories there in the past, but now each floor was divided into cubicles down both sides of a corridor and we each had our private cell. I had three principal friends, all entirely different from each other; two of whom did not last out the eighteen months that the course lasted. The one who stayed the course was my closest friend, Peter Hobson. He was quite short and dark and had been educated at Leeds Grammar School. He didn't look at all English and indeed later, after the war, was able to pass himself off as Japanese and to my certain knowledge as Indonesian. By that time he had the advantage of being able to speak both those languages fluently with an impeccable accent.

SOAS at Dulwich

He already spoke several European languages fluently. His grandmother was Danish. Peter loved music, both classical and jazz, and played the piano.

My lifelong love of jazz began that summer in Dulwich. We had a group, despised by some of the purely classical music enthusiasts, who endlessly listened to jazz records — mostly on the Parlaphone label. We were purists and would not accept what we disparagingly described as 'swing'; that is to say that the big bands of the time were not accepted as jazz, such bands as Glenn Miller, Tommy Dorsey and even the Benny Goodman band (his small group, the quintet, was accepted). We listened to Louis Armstrong (with songs like 'Sweet Patootie') and Duke Ellington (and we were particularly impressed with the modernity of 'Black and Tan Fantasy' and tried to persuade the Classicists that it was great music on a par with Mozart and Beethoven, though of course it isn't; but the young like to have extreme views). Quite my favourite piece of Ellington was 'Blue Goose' with alto saxophonist Johnny Hodges, which I still listen to now and then in my car. I also loved Bix Beiderbeck, Mugsy Spanier and others. But I can admit now that I was not a real purist; I enjoyed Glenn Miller's 'In the Mood' and 'Chattanooga Choochoo' and I enjoyed Tommy Dorsey's trombone playing. Neither of my other two friends was in the jazz group.

The first was Mike Jacot; believe it or not his real full name was Pierre Louis Blaise Jacot de Boinod et de la Ferrière; he was of Swiss origin. He was tall, good-looking and absolutely charming and an incorrigible womaniser. He had a torrid affair with the girl in the ticket office at Herne

Hill station. Our common interest was in films. We both were smitten with the bug and saw ourselves as incipient film stars. We both signed up at Central Casting in Leicester Square for work as extras in films. The pay was unbelievably good, a guinea a day. He got a lot more parts than I did. I am afraid that we had absolutely no right to be extras; it meant playing truant from our classes and involved subterfuge in the evening, when we had to arrange for somebody else to answer for us at the roll call. But in fact I don't think it happened very often. Indeed I can now only recall two occasions, one at Pinewood Studios and the other at Welwyn Garden City Studios. To get to the studios meant making an incredibly early start; I think one had to report to the studios as early as half past six in the morning.

My first experience was in a film called *Demi-Paradise*, starring Laurence Olivier (whom everyone called Larry) and Penelope Dudley-Ward, who was the daughter of a former mistress of the Prince of Wales. Margaret Rutherford was also in the film, just as funny in real life as in her film roles. The Director was Anthony Asquith. I played the part of a soldier, a non-speaking role; one tried to convince the director that to be more realistic one should say at least a couple of lines – that would increase the pay to astronomical heights: £5 a day. The film is still occasionally repeated on Channel 4 or on BBC 2. Olivier played the part of a Soviet sailor being seduced by the lovably eccentric English way of doing things, hence the title *Demi-Paradise*. Asquith had the irritating habit of taking endless takes; I remember one particular shot where he took fourteen. It was a scene in which Olivier was in an English country town street discovering the oddities of a charity flag day. Margaret Rutherford played her usual fussy, fluttering woman, carrying a charity box hanging from her neck, and when she leant forward to pin a paper flower to his lapel she was supposed to trip and had to be caught by Olivier with his charming smile. On one of the takes Margaret Rutherford really tripped, this time over lighting cables on the floor. When I finally saw the film in a cinema, it was clear that that was the take printed; no acting, real laughter from Olivier. My scene, walking down a street with a couple of other soldiers, was finally cut so I never appeared on screen. But it was an adventure; and I still felt that that was the life for me. I had trouble from Peter Parker the next day; he had discovered that I had not actually been present at the roll call. He gave me a stern moral lecture.

The other day spent as an extra, at Welwyn Garden City, was for a film starring Vera Lynn. It turned out that I was wrong for the part; Central Casting had been asked for a pilot and I looked like the typical young fighter pilot, but when I got to Welwyn it turned out that what they wanted was a ship's pilot, who would have been much older. But I was paid my guinea and stayed all day watching the filming; my only surprise was to discover that Vera Lynn's offstage accent was broad cockney.

I remember going to the the theatre in Shaftesbury Avenue with Mike Jacot to a matinée of *No Orchids For Miss Blandish*. Mike knew one of the cast, an older woman who played the leading villain. Her co-star was Robert Preston, who was already drunk for the matinée. At some point he had to brandish a knife at someone and managed to throw it into the front row of the stalls!

As I have said, two of my friends did not stay the course. Mike Jacot was one of them. I really don't know why he left; perhaps it was too much playing truant, or it may have been woman trouble; or it may, quite simply, have been that he decided that Japanese was not right for him, and that the sooner he got into the forces, the sooner he could get out and start a career in films. In any event he left before the end of 1942. I met him once in Oxford Street after the war; he was already married with more than one child. I think I heard later that he had as many as five children. I nearly met him again in the late 1980s; I was talking to a colleague at KIA (of which more later) in Camden Town and somehow his name came up. It turned out that she knew the family and that Mike was now a successful producer of documentary films in Canada and was expected to visit the UK quite soon; but in the event we never met up.

My third friend was Sandy Wilson. When Daphne and I had him here to stay about twelve years ago and were talking about how awful Peter Parker was, he surprised me by saying, 'Of course, you and I, Guy, were the only two from decent schools' – Loretto and Harrow! At Dulwich we soon found that we had a common interest in film and the theatre. He was always writing plays; I used to sit beside him watching with fascination as he churned out line after line of dialogue; one of the plays, I remember, was set in the Outer Hebrides. I told Sandy of this many years later; he remembered the play and said that it had never been produced. Sandy also played the piano, and we had lots of sheet music of popular songs, of the Cole Porter variety. We went to the cinema with great regularity, travelling quite long distances to see special films, the Tooting Classic, for example. I think we went there with Peter Hobson to see *Stormy Weather* with Lena Horne. Another Lena Horne film I remember seeing was *Cabin in the Sky*, a copy of which I still have recorded on a video. One of my favourite films was *The Magnificent Ambersons* by Orson Wells, starring Joseph Cotton and Ann Baxter. Ann Baxter was the only film star I ever wrote to and I had for a time a signed photograph of her.

Watching so many American films gave me a lasting affection for America and the Americans. In those days I was a Democrat; I thought the Tennessee Valley Authority was a shining example of State intervention and admired Franklin D. Roosevelt. Today I am much more of a Republican and think Franklin's older cousin Theodore outshines him. I also was attracted to the American way of life. When standing in a queue for the cinema, I always tried to get into conversation with GIs. I thought the way they smoked cigarettes was really 'cool'; I don't know whether you can see this on films, but American men always opened their pack of Camel or Lucky Strike cigarettes by tearing off half the top of the pack, and they would then tap the closed part of the pack, and up would pop a cigarette. That's how I did it when in later years I smoked American cigarettes.

Sandy Wilson had relations in Rhodesia and used to suggest that after the war we should both go to Bulawayo where there was a theatre in which he could produce plays and I act. We also went to the theatre quite often. I remember seeing Vivien Leigh in *Doctor's Dilemma* – the play dominated by references to 'phagocytes'. We also saw Noel Coward in *Present Laughter* and *This Happy Breed* at the Haymarket; his leading lady was the lovely Judy Campbell. As I have said, fifty-two years later she was to sit opposite me at Sandy's 70th birthday party.

Sandy and I were also very keen on revues; he knew Hermione Gingold and we went to see her and visited her backstage. The revues inspired Sandy. He wrote one for the group at Dulwich, which was a great success; the only song I remember was 'Halo round the Moon'. Sandy's revues were mainly songs and sketches, but he was not strong on humour, unlike the Footlights revues of the 50s. I cannot think why I was not in Sandy's Dulwich revue. Japanese was just not up Sandy's street; for some reason I can still hear him pronouncing '*anata*' (Japanese for 'you') and sounding more like Noel Coward than Mr Yoshitake. He left well before the end of the course and joined the Army, stationed initially in South Wales, from which he sent us a letter. Later he went to Egypt and Mesopotamia – Iraq, I suppose. I met Sandy again at Oxford after the war.

London in 1942 was so very different from today. The streets were teeming with uniforms, Army, Navy, Air Force, British, American, Free French, Polish; I heard that one day somebody walked along Piccadilly in full Nazi uniform and was not stopped; it did not seem any more outlandish than many of the others! My memory of the summer of 1942 is that it was very sunny. We used to make a jolly boisterous group of young men on our way from Victoria Station to Tottenham Court Road. We usually went by bus; the old fashioned double-decker buses – the kind where you could leap onto the platform as the bus was moving. But there were also trams; one of the routes took them along the Embankment and up through a tunnel to Kingsway. There were trolley buses too. In spite of the sun everything was very dirty; the Clean Air Act was still fourteen years away. If you leaned against a tree in Green Park your back would be marked with soot; and most buildings were black. On the train up from Dulwich you passed house after house with black smoke streaming from their chimneys.

The Government had decreed that no restaurant could charge more then five shillings for a meal; restaurants like Simpsons and the Savoy Grill were not exempt, and covered their costs with a charge for table money and, no doubt, on the drink. No restaurant meals were lavish, but if as a hungry young man you did want to feel well fed the answer was a Chinese restaurant; and the only one in the West End was Leyon's in Wardour Street. There was no China Town in the West End; that was in Limehouse, near Wapping. I remember once trying to impress a girl. I took her out to eat at Martinez in Swallow Street, that strange little road that joins Piccadilly and Regent Street. The restaurant was on the ground floor and aperitifs were served on a wrought iron balcony on the first floor; when your order was ready the Head Waiter would call you down: 'Señor de Moubray'. I was only seventeen, but felt very grown up!

The blitz was over. There was still some bombing but it never seemed very important. I cannot remember ever going to an air raid shelter when we were at Dulwich. And the V1s and V2s had not yet started. I never actually experienced them, because they started after I had gone abroad and I didn't return until the war was over.

War fever can have some strange results. I have been told that Vaughn-Williams was walking above the cliffs near Dover two days after the First World War had been declared and was taken into custody at a police station on suspicion of being a spy; he had been making entries in a notebook – musical notations as it happened! He was released after a caution. A similar strange event happened to me at Dulwich. My interest in films had made me keen on unusual camera angles. I was crouching by the fence outside Dulwich College with my camera trying to frame the school in an interesting diamond shape when an officious young Army officer accused me of being a spy. He said that I obviously knew that there was a Royal Engineers' truck parked in front of the school with secret material. I wasn't even aware that the truck was there. But he hailed a passing policeman and I was hauled off to the police station, where I was kept in custody whilst they sent the film from my camera to be developed. Of course there was nothing to suggest that I was a spy and I, too, was released with a caution.

Work continued at the SOAS. There were now more teachers as a result of a swap of British and Japanese internees. One of them was Professor Daniels, a strangely remote man with very short sight and enormous spectacles. He was completely out of touch with the ordinary world. At his very first class he called the roll and was completely mystified by Mason; he had never come across a cockney and kept saying, 'Who is this Myson'? He had a beautiful Japanese wife, Otome. She always wore a kimono and was exquisite. Peter Hobson became very keen on her and had, I am sure, an affair with her. They were together so much that it is hard to believe that the Professor didn't notice; perhaps he thought it a small price to pay for keeping her as his wife. The shortage of Japanese speakers and translators was now so acute that the services started a lot of six months' crash courses, either for speakers or for translators, so the SOAS became awash with men in uniform, virtually all Army or Air Force. Some of the translators were posted to Bletchley for decoding work. I am surprised that they didn't curtail our course, or call us up. Even more surprising in recollection is that we maintained the usual peacetime terms and during our eighteen months we had two Long Vacs, and a Christmas and Easter holiday.

My home life was centred on Tunbridge Wells. I remember Granny and Madie being there quite a lot; perhaps they had decided to leave Hampstead Garden Suburb whilst there was still a threat of bombing. I had many friends, all around seventeen or eighteen. They were still at school and were not called up until about the time when I joined the Army. We played tennis and spent a great deal of time on bicycles. We spent hours on Ashdown Forest. Our games were incredibly innocent for a group of healthy teen-aged boys and girls. There were absolutely no sexual liaisons. We played childlike games such as 'wave', where whoever is 'he' captures people he can see and they can be released if they see one of the free ones 'wave'. It was great fun. Bicycling in the country around Tunbridge Wells, we hardly ever saw a car; with petrol rationing, the only drivers seemed to be doctors and the District Nurse (perhaps I am wrong; District Nurses probably had to use bicycles themselves). There were also occasionally military vehicles.

I had a girl friend; not in the modern sense; I was keen on her and, I think, she on me. But we never so much as held hands, let alone kiss. She was Diana Fletcher (with the Diana pronounced with the stress on the first syllable; not on the second as with the Princess). She lived not very far from Molyneux Park Road with her mother and her younger sister, Priscilla. I was invited to dine with them occasionally. I remember being surprised that the vegetables they served for four were no more than I expected to eat alone! Diana joined the forces before I did, joining the Wrens. She played an active part in the hunt for the *Bismarck*. I saw her occasionally in London in 1943. She was at LMH at Oxford when I was up, but we had no special relationship. She eventually married a Cambridge don and I had dinner with them in Cambridge at some point in the early 1980s. There were no other close friends. I remember one family with three daughters who were called Faith, Hope and Charity! and also one girl who was called William.

Another activity in Tunbridge Wells was the Home Guard. I was a kind of Private Pike, as in *Dad's Army*. We had proper uniforms and did various exercises in the woods. I once nearly killed the whole of my section. We were being shown how to throw hand grenades. We all gathered behind a wall of sandbags and were taught to remove the pin and lob the grenade over the wall and duck down until it had exploded. When it came to my turn I lobbed the grenade so high that it came down on our side of the wall! The corporal instructor showed amazing courage, he dived at the grenade and popped it over the wall before it exploded. It was a very lucky escape.

By the autumn of 1943 some of the Dulwich crowd began to be called up. I know that Peter Parker went early; he must have pulled some strings, because he was given an immediate commission as a second lieutenant. We were not given any choice of service. Peter Hobson was posted to the Navy and spent the rest of the war in Australia. Our course ended for the Christmas holidays and I was instructed to report to the Army after Christmas. I had been called up as a private. My number was 14700927!

Chapter 6

The Army and Service in the Far East

I REPORTED TO WARLEY BARRACKS NEAR BRENTWOOD in Essex either late in December 1943 or early in January 1944. Warley was the Headquarters of the Royal Fusiliers, but we were not inducted into a regiment; we were, I think, called General Service Corps. All newly conscripted soldiers started in this way. We were to have basic training in drill and weapons and to be assessed for which branch of the Army we were most suitable. The latter purpose was otiose so far as we were concerned; with our Japanese we were obviously intended for the Intelligence Corps – but Warley did not know that.

This was the first time I had ever been in contact with members of the working class. The major impression was the language. Every other word was the 'f' word. I don't think I had ever heard it before; and I was soon to learn many more Anglo-Saxon four-letter words. There must have been about ten of us from Dulwich in our draft and we were all put in the same Nissen hut, with bunk beds. Once we had been kitted out we all gathered in the hut to hear from Corporal Essex who was to be in charge of us for the next six weeks. Mason, whom I have already mentioned, was no more familiar with the language than we were. Corporal Essex asked if there any questions and Mason piped up, 'Corporal what's a bollocking?' Even I could guess that.

We soon became familiar with the life of a private. Basic training included instruction on how to assemble and dismantle a Bren gun, and shooting practice on the range. I was quite good with the Lee Enfield .303 rifle, but always seemed to miss the target with a machine gun. We also did drill, which of course I had already done in the OTC. We were also put through various aptitude tests; it became clear very soon that I was not cut out to do anything mechanical. To the instructor's disgust I didn't even put together two pieces and two screws to make a door handle – I tried to make it more Art Deco than practical.

We had to get used to other elements of Army life. I got to meet soldiers other than our Dulwich group in the NAAFI canteen. I remember two in particular. One was the son of the owner of a shop in Tooting which sold caged birds and birdseed; we got on very well together, and both of us enjoyed the experience of meeting someone with an entirely different background. The other was a cockney from the East End who was memorable primarily for his name; when I asked him his name he said 'Darshibow', but when he spelled it out it turned out to be D'Archambaud! He had no idea how he had come by such an aristocratic name; I suppose it must have been Huguenot – there were a lot I think in the East End.

Another feature of Army life was 'spud-bashing', sitting round a tub of cold water with a pile of potatoes and a knife and peeling them. Since we were going to eat them ourselves later, I could never understand why so many of the young men left the potatoes full of black eyes. Eating was quite an experience; we took a tray each and moved down the counter with food being dumped on our plates by ATS girls, who were so busy flirting with men that we often had gravy poured over our porridge!

After six weeks, sometime in February, we were sent to Rhosneigr in Anglesey for a three months' course of infantry training and fitness training on an assault course. I really did become very fit; I was by this time about 6 ft 5 ins and must have weighed 12 or 13 stone. I had no difficulty with the assault course, and managed long route marches across Anglesey in full kit, rifle, tin helmet and a pack on my back. Rhosneigr was an attractive seaside town, perhaps more of a large village. I don't know how it came about but I made friends with a couple who ran a café on the sea front; they had a daughter of about 16 who served in the café. In the evenings, after they had closed, they would let me in and give me a very good supper with eggs, bacon and sausages. I really don't know why, but it was very kind of them.

In May we were finally posted to the Intelligence Corps and sent to their Headquarters, which were in Wentworth Woodhouse, outside Sheffield. The house may have been grand, but we were billeted in the stables. We were subjected to more drill, this time by Regimental Sergeant Majors from Guards regiments. It was amusing to see, and hear, them drilling young I Corps officers: 'Pick your bloody feet up, Sir.' Some of the young officers were very wet, and you could understand why people outside the Corps referred to our cap badge (a Tudor rose in a wreath of laurels) as 'a pansy resting on his laurels'! We were not at Wentworth Woodhouse very long. We were put on a two weeks' motor cycle course; one week learning to ride and one week on maintenance of the machine. It is a pity that I only completed the first week; I still have absolutely no idea how an internal combustion engine works. But I loved riding a motorbike. We did a lot of what I suppose would now be called motocross, up and down rough fields and tracks. But we also went out on the open road. We wore no helmets in those days and I found it exhilarating to rush over the moors with the wind in my hair. On one occasion we were in a group riding across the moors to Scunthorpe and I got carried away. All the bikes were supposed to have governors limiting their maximum speed to 60 m.p.h. but mine was capable of at least 70. I overtook the whole squad including the corporal. He was surprisingly lenient, and after a very mild 'bollocking' no more was said.

Instead of doing the second week of the course, I was sent on embarkation leave – a week, I think. In the first week of June we prepared to leave. Four days after D Day we marched down to Sheffield station in full kit, but no rifles. Many women by the roadside called out, 'Good luck boys'; they thought we were off to Normandy. But then they couldn't see the tropical uniforms in our kit bags. We went by train to Gourock on the Clyde and embarked on a P&O liner, the SS *Maloja*. It seemed absolutely crammed with troops, but in the course of the voyage we took on at least a thousand more. I am sure there were cabins occupied by officers, but we were below decks with large wooden mess tables and hooks above for slinging our hammocks. The voyage to Bombay would in peace time have taken just over two weeks, but our journey took all of a month.

We spent the first two weeks in the Atlantic, probably going as far south as the Azores to avoid enemy submarines. The first few days were awful; the weather was bad and the sea was rough; hundreds of soldiers were being sea-sick all over the place. I have never been seasick, but I had to endure the stench. We then spent a week sailing through the Med, skirting the North African shore, again to avoid submarines. At Port Said the East began. But first we took on a very Western one thousand American troops. They were better paid than us and better fed. They treated us as if we were animals in the zoo; they would stand on a high deck throwing packets of their K rations down to the British troops, who scrambled to get them. Here began the worst part of the journey for me; from Port Said to Bombay I was appointed mess orderly. I had to scrub the wooden mess tables twice a day and polish all the tea urns until the Corporal could see himself to shave in them. And the heat was unbelievable. The trip through the Suez Canal was pleasant enough and interesting, but in the Red Sea, the heat became insufferable. There wasn't the slightest breeze, and anyway, since I was mess orderly, all the places on the open deck had been taken by the time I came up for air. I remember that the heat, lying off the port of Aden, was 140 degrees Fahrenheit. By the time we reached Bombay, on 10 July, I had lost about two stone; it was to be some fifteen years before I recovered the lost weight.

So to India in the last days of the Raj. I had, of course, never been to India, but the idea of India was deeply engraved in my mind. Auntie Claire had lived there for many years, and my grandparents had lived there too. I also had Layard relatives in the Indian Civil Service (ICS). My father had worked there during the First World War. I had read most of Kipling. I believed then, and still do now, that the British Empire was one of the most benevolent empires that ever existed and that their role in India, despite some blemishes, had on the whole been good for the people of India. Members of the East India Company had certainly been primarily motivated by the desire to acquire wealth, but in that they had not differed from their predecessors, the Moghul Empire. After the Indian Mutiny, the ICS had been motivated by an altruistic desire to bring to India stable government under the rule of law and to prepare India for eventual self-government. They no doubt expected that to take the form of a self-governing Dominion, rather like Canada, but the remarkable thing is how peaceful, on the whole, it had been. For nearly a hundred years India, with a population of millions, was governed by only a handful of British.

We landed in the monsoon. It was pouring with rain as we disembarked and marched to our train. Although I could not remember the tropics, I felt quite at home. The first arrival in the tropics always delights me; I feel bathed in the enveloping warmth and breathe in with pleasure the mixture of perfumes and spices. Our train, with a steam engine, of course, was incredibly long. We were not made very comfortable; as privates we were in Third Class carriages furnished with wooden slats. My knowledge of the climate of India is so poor that I don't know whether we arrived at the very end of the monsoon with the rain drifting southward or whether it was the very beginning and the rain had not yet moved very far north. I think, probably the latter.

In any event the first morning out of Bombay dawned bright and sunny. We were in the Deccan, the high plateau occupying the centre of the peninsula. As I awoke I saw out of the window that we were crossing a small bridge with the jungle behind. I dozed off again, and when I next looked out of the window we were crossing a small bridge with the jungle behind. It looked remarkably like the one I had seen earlier. It turned out to be exactly so. Our train was too heavy to get up the hill! Every time it had succeeded in going some way it had to roll down again. So the order was given for all the troops to disembark and walk alongside the train. There must have been at least a thousand troops on board. With its lightened load the train successfully negotiated the hill. With monkeys gambolling around us we hastily climbed aboard again.

I don't think we had the faintest idea of what our destination was to be. We were a small group of Japanese 'experts' in charge of an Intelligence Corps corporal. As it turned out we were bound for Abbotabad on the North-West Frontier and the journey was to last six days. Our train was so heavily laden that we made very slow progress; it took all of three days to get to Delhi. We made frequent stops, very often in the open countryside. We would take our tin mugs up to the engine and get hot water for tea, and we were fed from a kitchen truck, food being ladled into our mess tins. We made some stops at stations and then the platform would be swarming with Indians trying to sell us all sorts of food, fruit and trinkets. We didn't have much money; I don't remember what the pay was, but earlier in England it had only been about £1 a week. I bought at least one mango and have to say that it wasn't very nice – stringy and with a strong hint of turpentine flavour, about half the size of the mangoes you can now buy in supermarkets. We slowly began to pick up a smattering of Hindustani, the numbers of rupees or annas (*ek, do, teen, char, panch*).

At Delhi we lost a good number of passengers and coaches, but we didn't disembark. The train moved on the next day into the Punjab. By the late afternoon we reached a railway junction at Raiwind from which one line kept on north to Lahore and Rawalpindi and the other to Karachi. The corporal spoke to the engine driver and discovered that he intended to take the whole train to Karachi, when we were supposed to be going to Pindi.

He persuaded the driver to uncouple our coach and park us in a siding. We were to spend that night and the whole of the next day in Raiwind before another engine came. There were no longer any facilities for food or drink on the train and we resorted to the restaurant on Raiwind station. It was intended for First Class passengers, but we persuaded them to let us in. The waiters all wore white uniforms and elaborate turbans and smiled a great deal; it was the first time they had ever served private soldiers.

We spent the next day wandering around Raiwind. I cannot find it on any map, but apart from the railway junction it didn't seem to qualify as a town, no more than a large village. The inhabitants I think found us as strange as we did them. I am sure that they had never before seen a dozen or so Englishmen all at the same time; and for us it was our first real contact with Indians. We had no means of communication, although I think one or two villagers spoke some English. It was a beautiful day and we smiled at everyone, patted little children on the head and thoroughly enjoyed ourselves. They must have been Muslims, because all the women wore baggy trousers with very colourful tops. Raiwind must, I think, now still be in India, some miles from the Pakistan border, which means that only three years later with partition they must have had a horrible time; some may have got away to the west, but many of them must have been massacred by Hindus. What a world we live in that such beastly things can happen.

The rest of our journey was uneventful. At Pindi we transferred to a truck and were driven up into the mountains to Abbotabad, which is not very far from the border of Kashmir. We joined the Wireless Experimental Station, a unit of the Intelligence Corps. I don't remember doing any work there; we just waited around whilst the authorities decided on our next postings. Abbotabad was a real mountain town with a steep main street crowded with people and with shops all along both sides. We had plenty of time to wander around. The shopkeepers were very friendly, and although we had very little to spend, asked us in to drink cups of sweet spiced tea, with cardamoms, I think. We began to add to our local vocabulary. For example in the barracks we slept on *charpoys*, wooden frame beds with webbing across and with a biscuit mattress on top. To me one of the strangest experiences came every morning when an Indian would come to my bed and, whilst I was still lying down, lather my chin and shave me with a cut-throat razor. This was at a time when there was an active 'Free India' movement, not I may say noticeable in Abbotabad, and I could not help thinking how easy it would have been to cut my throat!

Eventually, in early August I was promoted to the rank of Sergeant; you could have stripes sewn on, but it was considered much more the thing to buy two badges of brass stripes which fastened to your sleeves by a safety pin. I was posted to the Wireless Experimental Centre (WEC) at New Delhi. Actually it was a mile or two out on a barren rocky hillside at, I think, Rohtak. I was only there for two or three weeks, but I had ample opportunity to see Delhi, both Old and New. It didn't take very long to get into town by tonga – a tonga is a two wheeled horse-drawn carriage with the passengers (not more than two) sitting at the back facing the direction from which you are coming. I visited the Red Fort in Old Delhi and wandered around the crowded bazaars. I also saw all the sights of New Delhi, the Lutyens buildings – the Viceroy's Palace, the Parliament and the boulevards. I used to enjoy sitting in a café on Connaught Circle (a Lutyensesque version of Finsbury Circus in the City of London) drinking iced coffee and nibbling roast cashew nuts. On one occasion a friend of mine (Sergeant Coates) and I had a guided tour of All-India Radio. At one point they allowed us to make a recording of our voices and had it played back to us. I carried out a mock interview: 'How long have you been in India, Sergeant Coates?' The playback was hilarious, my plummy accent was exaggerated and Coates' broad Yorkshire equally overdone. We sounded like the hammiest Music Hall turn.

To return to the WEC. Life was a little more civilised as a sergeant. We belonged to the Sergeants' Mess, but feeding was still pretty primitive. We ate sitting at tables out of doors under awnings but had to carry our food from the kitchens on metal plates; this was a very hazardous occupation, for there were kite hawks, we called them 'shite hawks', hovering overhead and if you were not careful they would sweep down and take all your food, knocking the plate out of your hands. I had a peculiar experience at the WEC; somebody came up to me and said, 'Robert.' I looked very puzzled and he said, 'Aren't you Robert de Mowbray?' Apparently I looked a bit like him and he had been at the WEC a short time before. There were four de Mowbray brothers from Lymington in Hampshire, three of them doctors (Robert, Michael and John), the fourth one, Stephen, a spy with MI5. Throughout my life they have appeared from time to time. I don't think they are related, but in the early 1950s, John nearly married my cousin Françoise Pezzani (known to her family as 'Fafise').

But to more serious things. The purpose of being at the WEC was to set up a small unit to carry out an entirely new project (at least in the Far East – for all I know such units may have already been operational in Europe) to listen in to enemy regimental radio. Regimental radios have a very short range and are broadcast on UHF radio waves and the eavesdroppers have, therefore, to be right up in the front line as near to the enemy as possible. The unit was to consist of one officer, Captain Kenderdine, who had worked in Japan and also in India and four Sergeants, G de M, Frank Greenland and Terry Nelson, who had both been at Dulwich with me. The fourth sergeant was Jock Lindsay who had done one of the Japanese speaking short courses at the SOAS. We were to pick up our equipment in Calcutta. But we were first instructed in the use of a UHF radio receiver; they were quite large. I seem to remember a unit probably about six times the size of the Apple computer on which I am writing this.

So sometime in September 1944 we set off for Calcutta by train and stayed there for a couple of weeks. At Calcutta station we encountered a memorable sight – a very tall Indian walking in the opposite direction to all those disembarking, wearing a white uniform with an enormous turban, exuding bonhomie, with flashing white teeth under a black moustache and to each soldier as he passed he said, in a loud voice, 'Cheer up, Cheer up.' I didn't think the soldiers looked particularly glum; perhaps he was just showing off the only two English words he knew.

Calcutta then, and now I am sure, was swarming with people. Thousands of people lived on the streets, although not I think on the main thoroughfare, Chowringee. The climate was oppressive with such a high humidity that one's arms were always damp with sweat and it was impossible to avoid 'prickly heat'. We went to the cinema quite frequently, not to see the films, but to keep cool; the Lighthouse Cinema on Chowringee was one of the first buildings to have air-conditioning. Keeping cool in India had always relied on *punkahs*, fans suspended from the ceiling and activated by *punkah wallahs* who often pulled the ropes with their feet, whilst lying on the floor. There were also screens made of grass matting, *khas-khas tattis* which were dowsed with a bucket of water every now and then. My only other memory of Calcutta is of an officer staying in the same house as us whom I had to wake up one morning; the first thing he did on waking up was to take a slug of neat gin and light a cigarette; the East had certainly got to him!

In Calcutta we changed our khaki uniform for jungle green with Australian bush hats, the kind where the brim on one side is tipped up. The day before we set off for Burma, Kenderdine came to see us and said that we would have all our equipment in a Chevrolet 15 cwt. truck and that we would also have a jeep; he would drive the jeep and he asked which of us would drive the truck. He was taken aback when we told him that none of us could drive and none of us had a driving licence! He decided that he would have to drive the Chevrolet and that he would, that very afternoon, take two of us out and teach us to drive the jeep. I was not one of those chosen. Terry Nelson was the one chosen to drive when we started. Next day, this must have been either at the very end of September or in early October, we reported to the station and our vehicles had to be loaded onto the train. Kenderdine, quite rightly, didn't trust any of us to do this, so he loaded both the truck and the jeep. We spent the night steaming north to Siliguri in the foothills of the Himalayas, the railhead for Darjeeling. It was a clear starlit night. Kenderdine may have had a carriage to sleep in, but we bedded down on top of the canvas roof of the Chevrolet, which was fine except for the constant shower of smuts from the engine.

Next morning we set out from Siliguri going due east through Northern Assam with Kenderdine alone in the truck and we four sergeants in the jeep. Terry Nelson was driving and was absolutely petrified; whenever he saw a vehicle half a mile or more away coming in the opposite direction he stopped until it had passed. I couldn't stand any more and said that I would take over; I knew how to change gear on a motorcycle and had crashed Uncle Leslie's Baby Austin into an apple tree; what more qualifications did I need? I drove very well, I think, but I knew nothing about the four-wheel drive mechanism and we were in fact in two-wheel drive, which began to matter several days later, as I shall explain. For the time being we were driving along unmade roads, but with a good surface, with virtually nobody in sight, with the occasional jungle fowl flying over the road. It was a lovely day, the war could have been, and was, miles away. We must have stopped to have a meal in our vehicles, but we made very good progress.

Late in the afternoon Kenderdine decided that we should stop for the night. He had found a *dak*-bungalow (a government staging house) marked on the map and we drove down a remote track until we found it. As an old India hand Kenderdine marched in shouting out '*Khitmagar!*' in an imperious voice. The *khitmagar* was the butler or housekeeper. He told him we needed rooms and dinner for five. I am sure that the *dak*-bungalow had never before accommodated anybody so junior as a sergeant! I think we had some kind of chicken curry for dinner; this was the most luxurious accommodation we had stayed in since arriving in India; and what was to come was much more primitive.

The next day we reached the River Bramahputra near Gauhati. It was quite the largest river I had ever seen; it must have been well over half a mile wide. We crossed on a primitive sort of ferry. Again, apart from the crew of the ferry there seemed to be absolutely nobody about. We felt like explorers as we crossed with the thick jungle coming down the banks on each side. We now headed for Dimapur where the mountain road into Manipur and on into Burma began. We were in the region of India known as Nagaland, the Nagas being a primitive tribe of erstwhile head-hunters. We saw a few and had worried whether they would be friendly, but they smiled amiably enough; I think they thought the Japanese would be even worse. Until Dimapur we had not yet met any military personnel; but at Dimapur all changed. This was, as it were, the base camp for all road supplies to the Fourteenth Army in Burma.

The road as far as Imphal in Manipur was a fully made-up road built by the Royal Engineers and climbed steadily up with endless hairpin bends. We made very slow progress because we were stuck behind big artillery guns which barely exceeded two miles an hour. This was where it mattered that we knew nothing about four-wheel drive and only had two-wheel drive engaged, because our stalling speed was around five miles an hour. Somewhere on the trip up we had given a lift to a major; he didn't stay with us long, because the first time we stalled I freewheeled back downhill until we reached a flat spot – nobody had told me how to do a hill start! The major made his excuses very quickly. We found out about four-wheel drive before we ventured onto the mud tracks in Burma. We passed Kohima where there had been a famous battle earlier in the year in which the tennis court had played an important role. Kohima was as far as the Japs

As a Sergeant in jungle green in Burma

got in their invasion of India. The next scene of a battle was some way on at Imphal.

The Fourteenth Army was by this time some miles into Burma, down the Kabaw Valley (Burmese for the Valley of Death) with a tributary river of the Chindwin running through it. By the time we reached the valley it was after dark and we were making very slow progress. The monsoon had only just ended and the track was a sea of black evil smelling mud; the bodies of so many dead Japanese soldiers were rotting in it. Dead Japanese were never buried; there were too many of them and the terrain was impossible. Dead soldiers' identity tags were removed and used to inform the Japanese authorities of the names of the dead. I am afraid that some of the white soldiers also went in for removing such gold teeth as they could find. The other thing that struck me was that every Jap was wearing a cholera belt, a broad flannel band wound round the stomach. I don't believe they were in the slightest bit effective. In India they had not been worn since about 1920.

As I was saying it was after dark when we entered the valley which was thickly forested with teak trees. We constantly became bogged down, which for some reason we found hilariously funny; standing behind the jeep pushing hard and being spattered with that foul mud, we were in fits of hysterical laughter. At one point we met a driver with a six-wheel Dodge who was also stuck. He paid out the winch on the front of the truck, passed

it round a tree, fixed it back to the front of the truck and set the winch in
motion – all that happened was that the tree came down! More hysterical
laughter! We eventually reached the Headquarters of the 11th East African
Division with whom we were to be for about two months. The Division's
badge was the head of a rhino; and we each had one fastened to our sleeves.
I had mine for years, but it has long since disappeared, although I think I
still had it here at Buxlow.

The next day we pushed on down the valley to join the regiment in the
front line. Our daily routine was as follows. Every evening the unit formed
a perimeter with armed *askaris* (East African soldiers) all round. We would
enter the perimeter and dig a trench for the UHF wireless and shallow
trenches for ourselves to sleep in. One of us would then climb the tallest
teak tree we could find and fix the aerial has high as possible. We took it
in turns during the night to man the wireless, twiddling the knobs,
searching for a Jap regimental transmitter. I have to say that in two months
we never found one; the only thing we tuned into was a dance band from
Bangkok, the transmission bounced off the ionosphere! At least we knew
the wireless worked! We tried every day and every night, but to no avail.
These radios and aerials need to be in line of sight, and I suspect that a teak
forest was the worst possible environment for them. I rather wonder
whether the Japs themselves managed to use their radios effectively. If we
had persevered they might have worked when we got through the gap in
the mountains and entered the much more open Chindwin Valley.

But those two months were a great experience. From time to time we
saw Japanese prisoners of war being shipped back to India. We hardly ever
saw the Burmese. I don't think there were any towns or even villages in
the valley but there were occasionally farmsteads and we would see the
Burmese women sitting outside their huts looking at us. I don't remember
any men. The women smoked the most enormous green cigars made of
local tobacco. Almost every night the Japs would come round the
perimeter, setting off firecrackers to simulate machine gun fire. The *askaris*
were terrified and fired round after round at random. Ammunition became
too scarce and the soldiers on the perimeter were given only one round per
rifle. If there had been an attack, ammunition would have had to be passed
up to them rapidly. These trigger happy *askaris* were frightening; if you
wanted to have a pee during the night you didn't dare stand up for fear of
setting them off. A feature of teak trees is that, although they are evergreen,
old leaves fall off from time to time, and as they fall they sound a bit like a
man walking quietly through the jungle.

We were supplied wholly from the air; every day Dakotas (DC 3s) would
fly up from Calcutta and drop supplies into dropping zones behind the line.
Our food, 'compo rations' as they were called, came in large light metal
chests, about a quarter of the size of a tea chest. The food was pretty good,
all supplied from Australia. There were tins of M&V (meat & vegetable
stew), sardines, butter and biscuits. Bread I think came separately and was

often already green with mould, as were the cigarettes. It was here that I became a regular smoker for the next eighteen years; smoking provided a welcome relief to the smells of the latrines!

We had been allocated a West African batman, who brought us early morning tea. We learned a little Swahili; his morning greeting was '*Jambo effendi.*' But he didn't do the cooking, not that that was any more than heating the stews. I did this on a wood fire, using our only cooking utensil, which was a very old kettle; I don't know where it came from. The four of us got on pretty well: two public school boys and two not – Frank Greenland had been at Westminster. Kenderdine kept very aloof; we never really got to know him. Sometimes during the day we swam in the river: probably foolhardy – who knows what noxious creatures there may have been in it! We certainly were plagued with leeches; you used to get rid of them by applying the lighted end of a cigarette to them! I remember once going back one evening to Divisional Headquarters to watch a film – outdoors of course; I cannot now remember what it was, but it was strange to watch the newsreel with pictures of Allied soldiers looking absolutely miserable in the snow at Anzio!

We had almost total air superiority, but on one day Japanese Zeros managed to get through and we watched with horror as they shot down two Dakotas. They then turned their attention on us, diving in low and strafing us with machine gun fire. Because of the trees they couldn't pick out targets, but quite by chance they shot up a truck which caught fire. Without for a moment considering the danger we rushed over to the truck and began shovelling earth onto the fire; the smoke would have given their planes a clear indication that they had hit something. We succeeded in putting out the flames before the enemy made their next run.

My only other experience of coming under fire was when Frank and I were walking down the track on a lovely sunny day in a fairly open clearing and we suddenly heard bullets swishing past us; we were under sniper fire. If you hear the bullet you know you haven't been hit! We both plunged into a nearby ditch and crawled back away from the front quite a long way before standing up again. No harm done – or I wouldn't be writing these memoirs. I don't remember being at all frightened. Just before Christmas when we had reached a place called Yazagio right at the southern end of the valley, it was sensibly decided that our mission had not been a success and we were withdrawn from the East African Division. It was decided that we should try the Arakan instead, the coastal strip in the south.

So we left the Kabaw Valley. We spent Christmas Day at Imphal; it was bitterly cold and for the time being we discarded our tropical kit. There was no snow, but sharp white frost and freezing fog. We bought ourselves some of the local brew, a kind of beer called *zu*; again a foolhardy thing to do; it was a dirty creamy white liquid and could well have contained wood alcohol. But it didn't and was not in fact very nice; but I always believe in trying the local produce!

Our journey to the Arakan took several days. We first had to return to Dimapur and then headed for Sylhet. We drove for most of the night. Now whenever I drive any distance by night I think of that drive. It was warm again, and we passed endless little groups of people round fires, and the smell of the tropics was all around us. But then came another change of climate. Sylhet, now in Bangladesh, is at over 5000 feet and was cold – so winter uniforms again. If you ask the waiters in almost any Indian restaurant in England where they come from, the answer will almost always be Sylhet. Another strange fact about Sylhet is that although it is miles from the sea it provided most of the lascars (sailors on the old P&O liners). Perhaps it had something to do with Indian cooks travelling the world? We also discovered that Sylhetis love slapstick; the only evening we were there we went to the cinema and saw Charlie Chaplin in *The Gold Rush*; we were the only Europeans in the audience and all the Sylhetis around us were in constant fits of laughter.

The next morning we set off again. We were to experience a dramatic change of climate in the space of not much more than half an hour. When we awoke in the morning we had to break the ice on the buckets of water outside our hut. We set off in heavy winter uniforms with added sweaters. Before long we reached the edge of the mountainous plateau and paused to look out over the plains below, stretching to Chittagong and sweltering in the heat. It took us no more than half an hour to descend to the plain, stripping off clothing as we went. At the bottom the heat was overwhelming with the same muggy humidity we had met in Calcutta. By the late afternoon we had reached Cox's Bazaar, the last town in India (now Bangladesh) before entering Burma. We were directed to a military tented camp near the beach. When, having checked in, I returned to my tent there was quite a crowd of people round it. When I asked what the fuss was about they said that they had just killed a krait (pronounced krite) under my charpoy. The krait is one of the most venomous snakes in the world. Just to cheer me up they said that kraits were almost always found in pairs! Worse was to come, Frank Greenland and I decided to cool off by having a swim in the sea and we soon discovered poisonous sea snakes!

Now we entered Burma. Nothing of any note happened until we got to Akyab (which I see from my *Times Atlas* is now called Sittwe), an island which had only been won back from the Japs a few days before. To cross to the island we had to drive our vehicles on to Indian Navy landing craft. There were several craft going at the same time. Our jeep was the only vehicle on our boat. When the petty officer announced that he couldn't get any closer to the shore, I noticed that all the others had managed to get distinctly closer. I urged him to try again. No, sahib, that is as far as I can go, he said. So I took a stick and walking to the end of the ramp, which he had let down, I measured to see if the water was shallow enough to disembark the jeep. I decided that it was. But I think as I walked back down to the jeep the craft must have floated back a bit; I drove off and the jeep sank into the sea! Luckily we had the roof open and Frank and I floated to the surface surrounded with maps and other papers. We manage to push the jeep up on to the beach quite soon, but no amount of towing up and down the beach would get the engine going again. So I wrote off one jeep! Luckily I had never signed for it in Calcutta. We were wet and rather cold as the evening came on. Frank recognised an officer who had been at Westminster with him and he gave us a tent and we sat round a wood fire drying our clothes.

Next day, all now travelling in the Chevrolet, we eventually reached the Arakan front line. We followed much the same procedure, although this time we were with European troops. I regret to say that our mission was once again unsuccessful. After some days we did in fact tune in to Japanese regimental wireless, but what we had not anticipated was that we were quite unable to work out the Japanese pronunciation of Burmese place names. We knew from their broadcast that they had run out of *gasurino* (petrol) but where? So around the end of January our unit was disbanded.

Before I go on there were two events which I still remember. The coast was very lovely with hills going right down to the sea as, for example, on the Costa Brava. The countryside was much more open than in the Kabaw Valley and there were clear views all round. One afternoon I went down to the beach to have a swim and before long found that I was being carried out of the bay; this was worrying. I would certainly have made land somewhere before too long, but most of the islands beyond our bay were still held by the Japs! So I swam as I as I have ever done. I have never been any good at the crawl, so this was a laborious breast stroke. As is, of course, obvious I made it. Looking again at the map I see that this, which was as far as we got, was at a place called Kyaukpyu, which we pronounced Chalk-Pew, near Ramree Island. The map shows a very complicated coastline with hundreds of islands and inlets; I think it is just as well I managed to swim back!

On another occasion we were sitting near the beach opening our *compo* rations and I was just opening a tin of sardines when a Japanese shell exploded near by and I was wounded, not I have to say by shrapnel, but by suffering a severe cut to my thumb on the sardine tin! I had to go to the First Aid station and felt a complete impostor. Everyone else there was suffering from real war wounds. I wasn't even brave enough to have stitches without a local anaesthetic, so they just stuffed the wound with sulphanilamide powder and bound it up. I can still see the scar fifty-eight years later.

One of the great characters of the Intelligence Corps in the Arakan was Captain Barowski, a former White Russian colonel. There was an article about him in the forces' newspaper, SEAC, which mentioned that he had lied about his age when joining up. He must have been in his late 60s; he had learnt his Japanese living in Shanghai after the Japanese occupation. General Slim, Commander in Chief of the XIV Army, came to visit

Barowski's unit. When Barowski was presented to him, Slim said, 'I have heard of you, Barowski,' to which Barowski replied in his heavy Russian accent, 'I have heard of you too, Slim'!

As I was saying, the unit was disbanded. I don't know where the other four went or how they got back to India. I did meet Frank Greenland again, briefly at Oxford in 1946 where he was doing a short course preparing for the entrance exams for the Colonial Service. It was he who told me that my father's book was still required reading. He went to Tanganyika for some years. I saw him again in the early 70s at Sandown racecourse!

My instructions were to take all our equipment back to Calcutta in the Chevrolet truck and to report to a colonel there. It must have been early February when I set off. It was a long journey, some 800 miles or so, and the Chevrolet had been through some rough times, several thousand miles without ever being serviced. It had developed a troublesome fault; the petrol frequently failed to get to the carburettor. So I kept breaking down. As I have said I have no mechanical aptitude and don't know the first thing about internal combustion engines. I found a helpful mechanic who showed me what to do; with an adjustable spanner I uncoupled the petrol lead, sucked the piece that led to the tank and when the petrol came into my mouth, I had to join it up again. My progress was laborious and I relied on units that I passed to give me a bed for a night and provide me with food. I eventually decided that I would never make Calcutta, so I went to the docks at Chittagong and persuaded someone to put my truck on a ship; for some reason I was not allowed on board and had to make my way to Calcutta by train. Eventually my truck and I were reunited and we set off for the military barracks where I was to find my Colonel.

I must have looked very scruffy in my jungle green when I parked the truck. There was a sergeant standing nearby and I asked him where I could find the colonel. His office was in fact quite close by. When I walked in and announced myself the colonel said, 'Where the hell have you been? We've been expecting you for weeks.' I explained about nursing a sick truck back, but clearly he had been expecting me for much longer. He told me that I had been promoted to Lieutenant three or four weeks before and that I was being posted to the Red Fort in Delhi to join a unit called CSDIC(I), meaning Combined Services Detailed Interrogation Centre (India).

'Peter,' he said to his adjutant, 'have you got some pips for this young man?'

Two sets of two pips were found and fastened to my two shoulder straps and I removed my stripes from each sleeve. I was given a travel warrant for the train to Delhi; and that was it. I walked outside and went back to my truck for the last time to pick up my bedding roll; this was a typical Indian piece of luggage – a canvas roll in which you packed all your belongings, rolled it up and fastened it with a leather strap. On my way back to the truck I passed the sergeant I had seen earlier; he did a double take; after all, only ten minutes earlier I had been a sergeant too, now here I was an officer; he paused for a moment and then saluted me, 'Sir'; I saluted back, my very first salute as an officer.

I was to be in Delhi until mid-June. I say Delhi and not New Delhi, because the Red Fort, a Moghul ancient monument, is in the middle of Old Delhi, surrounded by narrow busy streets and bazaars. We did not live in the ancient part of the Fort, but in modern temporary huts with, of course, no air conditioning. Not that it mattered too much in February, but by the summer it became almost unbearable; the temperature often rose to around 110 degrees, and with absolutely no breeze one was strongly tempted to roll up the mosquito net around one's bed; I think as an officer one got something slightly better than a charpoy. I had to kit myself out with proper khaki officer's uniform and a peaked cap; I don't know what I did with my bush hat.

I had a bearer, a personal batman, allotted to me. Mine was Nazir Uddin Khan. His name showed that he was a Muslim, but also that he came from the mountains. We got on very well. It took me a while to get used to having a personal servant. Some time quite recently there was a news item about the Prince of Wales, in which it was revealed that a footman held the specimen bottle when the Prince was giving a urine specimen. I didn't quite go that far with Nazir, but every morning he would dress me, handing me each garment in turn, filling my cigarette case and putting it into the right pocket.

My work consisted of interviewing Japanese prisoners of war. Japanese prisoners behaved very strangely by our standards; they abandoned loyalty to their own country and went out of their way to be helpful; they often helped me when there was a word I wasn't sure of. Their helpfulness sometimes went too far. I spent a week or two interviewing an Air Force man who had been batman to a general at an air base in Java in the Dutch East Indies. He spent a long time giving me details of its defences, where the guns were and drawing primitive maps. Eventually it became clear that he had been making most of it up. He was so keen to give me, his temporary master, a good report!

On one occasion it fell to my lot to be orderly officer for a day; I had to visit every part of the camp, accompanied by the sergeant major, and see that everything was all right. I visited the canteen and the kitchens to make sure that the soldiers were happy with their food and that the kitchens were clean. Of course the wily sergeant major could have pulled the wool over my eyes and perhaps did. One other place we had to visit was Death Row, where rebel Indian soldiers of Subas Chandra Bhose's pro-Japanese Army were awaiting execution. They were not in cells with spy holes, but in cages. It was not a pleasant duty; they seemed to be resigned to their lot.

I had not had any leave since my embarkation leave in May of the year before and I was now due for two weeks'. I did not know where to go until a fellow officer said that his aunt was the matron at St. Paul's School

– an English type public school – in Darjeeling. Since it was the Easter holidays, and most of the boys were away, she was ready to put me up in one of the dormitories. So I set off by train for Calcutta, accompanied by the faithful Nazir Khan. He was absolutely thrilled because he had not been back to the mountains for years. Travelling by train in India with a bearer is quite an experience. The servants had a coach at the rear of the train where, since there were no corridors, they were isolated. At each stop the bearers would run up the platform to find their masters and tend to their needs, making cups of tea or unpacking pyjamas at the right moment. I don't think this was a practice peculiar to the Raj; rich Indians have always had lots of servants who are used to being totally subservient.

From Calcutta we took another train up to Siliguri, where we had been on our journey into Burma the previous year, and from there the mountain railway up to Darjeeling, which is at about 8000 feet. The matron looked after me very well. The school had a superb view across the valley with the snow-capped peaks in the distance, including Kanchenjunga. Nazir and I went out for walks in the hills every day; the going was pretty steep and Nazir insisted on going ahead and pulling me up with a walking stick! I remember once too we found a poisonous snake, which Nazir expertly disposed of. It was a lovely break; it was wonderful to see what pleasure Nazir got from being back in the mountains. I wonder if he ever managed, after his time with me, to get back to his home in the North West Frontier. We soon had to return to the broiling heat of Delhi.

In early May I suffered from another bout of streptococcal fever. In the summer of 1939 it had kept me in bed for over a month, but with M&B tablets (an improved form of sulphanilamide – antibiotics were still not available) I was in bed for no more than a few days. But one of those days was VE Day. I lay in bed with a temperature of about 104 whilst outside noisy celebrations were going on, including the banging of noisy fireworks.

Then in July I was on the move again. I was posted to Bombay to join the 34th Corps who were preparing to invade Malaya. I was about to embark on my first ever flight. I have no idea why I was not instructed to get there by train; it wasn't as if it were urgent, the date for the invasion had already been decided (15 September), not that I had any knowledge of such Top Secret information. My flight from Delhi was in a small plane, not more than half a dozen passengers. We flew at about 10,000 feet, keeping above the monsoon clouds, so we saw nothing. All went well until we reached Bombay; from 10,000 feet we had to descend fairly rapidly through the clouds, and with the rising pressure my ears began to hurt, so acutely that I felt as if they were bleeding. By the time we landed, I was barely conscious and had a very high temperature; an ambulance was called and I was taken to the Colaba Military Hospital.

My condition, it turned out, was nothing to do with the flight; I had malaria, the serious variety known as Blackwater fever, from which you either die or recover completely. The other less fierce form of malaria recurs intermittently for years afterwards. It was all my fault. When we had been in Burma we took regular doses of mepacrine, an anti-malarial drug which turns your skin very sallow. But mepacrine was not a required drug in Delhi; anopheles mosquitos are pretty rare there and anyway we were expected to sleep under mosquito nets. As I have said earlier, I did not obey this injunction because the heat was so stifling. I remember being bitten, only once, but that was enough. I was barely conscious for some days fighting off the fever; the remedy was the traditional one of sweating off the fever. I alternated between being stifled by blankets – in midsummer in Bombay! – and having cooling blanket baths. You know the outcome! I survived.

I then joined my unit – SEATIC (South East Asia Translation and Interrogation Centre). Our commanding officer was a Colonel Heaslitt, a medical doctor and the son of a former British Bishop of Yokohama. He was a dissolute character and was frequently in brothels, where he was said to go always with his black bag to ensure that the girls were healthy! I have few memories of that stay in Bombay, because in the event I was there for only a very short time, apart that is from the three weeks in hospital. I remember swimming from Juhu beach and having a very unpleasant encounter with a Portuguese Man of War which wound its tentacles around my thigh. But they are spectacular and beautiful creatures. I also remember going to a restaurant with a party from the unit, which included Richard Mason, who later wrote the best selling novel *The World of Suzie Wong*. The restaurant had tables in booths, separated by wooden partitions and screened from the main room with curtains. The party became fascinated by the noises coming from the next partition. A knot hole was found and somebody looked through – a British soldier was bonking an Anglo-Indian WACI (Women's Army Corps India) on his lap. Richard Mason was entranced – material for a novel!

Then the atom bombs fell on Hiroshima and Nagasaki and within a very few days we were celebrating VJ Day. It was decided that the 'invasion' of Malaya would still take place on the originally planned date – 15 September – and we were not now to be the first troops into Malaya. The 5th Indian Division, now in Rangoon, were to be the first, going straight to Singapore on 5 September. Since I was keen to find my parents, last known to be in Singapore, I applied for a transfer to the 5th Indian Division. I was taken to see the Commanding Officer of 34th Corps, General Roberts, who agreed and arranged for me to be flown to Rangoon immediately. I should have said that our role with 34th Corps was for one Japanese speaking officer to be attached to each battalion to deal with prisoners of war and local intelligence. It was just as well that the Japanese had surrendered because when 34th Corps made its landing at Moreb Beach it was found that the intelligence had been faulty. Landing craft would have unloaded their tanks and trucks and within a few yards many would have sunk beneath the waves, like my jeep at Akyab; the apparent beach was in fact a sand bar with a trench behind it before the proper beach. Moreover there were five times as many Japanese troops there than had been expected. An armed landing would have been a shambles.

I, however, was now flown to Rangoon in a Dakota. From the airport I was taken straight to the harbour and embarked on a troopship; I think it was the *Maloja* again, on which I had sailed from the Clyde to Bombay. In the early evening light I was standing on deck with a fellow officer, Sandy Brown, looking at the famous Schwedagong Pagoda with its golden top. Sandy commented how attractive it looked with the lights on it. For the first time I realised that my eyesight was not perfect – I couldn't see the lights at all. We sailed that evening, it must, I think, have been 3 September. We were far from sure that General Yamashita, known as the Tiger of Malaya, would in fact surrender without a fight, so we sailed in black-out. The next day we sailed down the Straits of Malacca between Sumatra on our right and the Malay Peninsula on our left. There were enormous columns of black smoke rising on the Malay side; heaven knows what the Japanese were burning. After another night, we anchored to the south of Singapore.

Landing craft were lowered and we climbed down netting into the craft ready to sail into Singapore harbour. There were many claps of thunder; at least that's what we thought, but it might have been gunfire. So we felt apprehensive as we slowly sailed into the harbour. I was in the lead landing craft and the dock area seemed to be totally deserted, except for three little Chinese boys staring at us. How they had got into the dock area I don't know. We finally made fast and our Colonel ordered us ashore and to take up firing positions. I was the first man ashore and lay down by a bollard with my Sten gun aimed at the dock gates, which were about a hundred yards away. We then saw the most extraordinary sight; the dock gates opened and a line of Japanese staff cars drove through towards us. When they stopped, the drivers got out and opened the passenger doors inviting us to climb in. The colonel would have none of it. 'It could well be a trick,' he said and ordered me to accompany him on foot to the dock gates. Apart from the rather bemused Japanese drivers, there was still nobody to be seen. We marched out of the dock gates, just the two of us, and entered the railway station across the road. There was still nobody to be seen. We then rounded a corner into the main concourse and a great crowd of Chinese and Malays suddenly burst into wild cheering. I am not sure that all of them were really all that pleased to see us, but it suited them to show the winners of the war which side they were now on.

It was in fact now clear that there was to be no resistance from the Japanese at all; the whole Japanese Army in Malaya was reacting exactly like my friendly prisoner of war in Delhi; once defeated they went out of their way to help the conquerors. So instead of taking the whole of Singapore City in one fell swoop, which we could have done – just the two of us! – the Colonel stuck to his orders to advance to establish a beach head and it would take three days before the whole City was taken.

I had told my colleagues with other battalions to look out for my parents. On the third day, Peg Bates (known as Peg because those were his initials) came on to me on the field telephone to say that he had found both my parents who were at the Sime Road internment camp. I jumped into a jeep and drove straight there. I parked and from one of the huts a woman came running very awkwardly down, obviously suffering from arthritis, and this was my mother. We had not seen each other for almost exactly six years. She and my father had been reunited the day before after an interval of three and a half years. I have been asked how I knew my mother. The answer is that if we had passed in a street we might well not have known each other; a boy of fourteen looks very different from a young man of twenty in uniform. She on the other hand had been only 42 when we had last met, and was now nearly 50, and because of her deprivation probably looked more like 60. But of course we recognised each other instantly because Peg Bates had told them I was on my way. They were both in reasonably good shape; they had not been well treated, but they were not like the survivors of Belsen or the infamous Burma-Siam railway.

I have described this meeting with my parents in a very matter of fact way. It was not for me a defining moment in my life. At moments of high emotion I always seem to burst into tears. On this day I did not. Pleased though I was to find them safe and well, they were really strangers to me. But for them it must have been an extraordinary experience. Having spent three and a half years apart and unsure whether they would ever be released, they had had the emotional experience of meeting again for the first time the day before. To hear the next day that their son was actually in Singapore, an Army officer, and on his way to meet them, must have been quite unbelievable. My mother had a very good friend in camp, Freddy Bloom, an American married to a South African doctor; now, she had been very badly treated, beaten up by the Kempeitai (the Japanese equivalent of the Gestapo) and suffering from beriberi.

Both parents would have loved to have been allowed to go back to Trengannu, however briefly, to see all the Malay friends they had had to leave in December 1941, but the new Labour Government had a violent prejudice against British colonial civil servants and were determined to get them out of the country as soon as possible. I think I saw them off home on a boat no more than a week later. And to think that if I had had the vote in the General Election of July I would probably have voted Labour; the vast majority of the troops in the Far East did. The *Straits Times* began publishing in Singapore within a couple of days of our landing. They reported that I was the only British soldier there who had found both parents as prisoners; there were one or two who had found one. We managed to have both my parents to dinner in the mess one evening; what they made of it, heaven knows. It must take a lot of getting used to, seeing a man, your son, who had been but a boy when they had last seen him.

But within a very few days they were gone. I remained with the battalion with whom I had landed only for a few days.

I was then posted to CSDIC(I). My first job was a most unusual one. Although the Japanese had surrendered in Singapore and were slowly being taken over throughout the country, the Japanese Headquarters were still in active command of the whole of the Dutch East Indies. I spent a week living with the Japanese signals unit which was still sending cables to all their other units. I was the censor and no cable could be sent until I had vetted it. This was not an arduous task; as I have already said, the Japanese, once captured, bent over backwards to be helpful. I was the only Englishman in the camp and ate their food, everything served with that very glutinous Japanese rice. One thing that really surprised me was their pin-ups; they were all of Rita Hayworth and Betty Grable; there wasn't a single one of a Japanese girl. We chatted quite a bit; I think they thought that I knew Rita Hayworth; they wanted to know what she was really like.

Our CSDIC(I) mess to which I then returned was in a lovely colonial house with a verandah and a nice garden on the Orchard Road. I can still hear the rickshaw men, with their Chinese accents, saying 'Ochaload'. The whole road was lined with these beautiful houses, which I am told have now all gone, replaced with skyscrapers. In the first few days I acquired a lovely 1940 Buick sedan, pinched from the Japs; for the few days we had it, it was called the Passion Wagon as everybody wanted to borrow it for taking out girls. But we didn't keep it for very long. Mountbatten had seen me driving around the town in it and sent one of his officers to confiscate it for his own use. We ate wonderful food, because somehow we had acquired as servants the crew of an Italian submarine and they had a very good cook. Our commanding officer was an American (Combined Services meant not only Army, Navy and Airforce, but also British and American) by the name of Colonel Blunda.

One of our officers was a naval officer, elderly to me, probably close on forty, who had a real drink problem. He often showed symptoms of DTs (Delirium Tremens) with shaking hands. One day he rushed in, greatly alarmed. 'There's a nest of vipers under the house.' We immediately concluded that pink elephants would be next and had him carted off to hospital. Poor chap, for a couple of hours later, one of the Italians came in and said that there really was a nest of snakes under the house! But I think he really did need to go to hospital.

In October I was posted to Kuala Lumpur. I drove there in a jeep; every so often we would pass what looked remarkably like a road block, although the road was in fact open, but there were groups of men in uniform sitting and standing outside roadside huts, rather like toll booths, with big signs up saying 'Malayan People's Anti-Japanese Army'. These were the Chinese Communists who had been carrying out guerilla operations during the Japanese occupation. They had not been disbanded or disarmed; they bristled with guns. They caused no problems whilst I was in Malaya, but were, of course, at the bottom of the war which followed in 1948. On our way the Colonel and I tried out the Japanese pistols we had 'nicked', I suppose I have to say; we were certainly not supposed to have them. Neither of us proved to be particularly good shots with a pistol; we had not yet had the opportunity of being shown how to use them from all the modern American films! Our wavering arms held out before us, one handed, failed even to hit quite substantial trees.

Kuala Lumpur (KL as it was always called) was in those days a modest city, indeed not even that, more of a large country town. KL was not then the capital of Malaya, that was Singapore, but only the capital of the State of Negri Sembilan. KL now has the tallest building in the world and many skyscrapers. Then there were just shops, offices and villas with gardens, or compounds as they were called. But there was one building of distinction, which I hope is still there. The railway station is a unique building looking like a Moghul palace. My job there was to attend daily at the KL jail to interrogate suspected war criminals. There were some nasty characters there. My job was to try and verify the facts in their frightful dossiers. It was not a pleasant job. The jail was very old-fashioned with enormous oak gates, in which was a smaller door for individual admittance.

I have already mentioned how it was there that I rediscovered the durian fruit. I paid a visit to Cameron Highlands, what in India would have been called a hill station. At some height amongst forest trees it has a temperate climate, and here you can have strawberries and cream. This reminds me of all the other delicious Malayan fruit, rambutan and mangostene, and a particularly delicious banana called *pisang emas* (the last word pronounced '*mas*'), which literally means 'golden banana'. It is very small, golden coloured and with a strong taste of honey. I know that durians, mangostenes and rambutan can be obtained in specialist shops in London, but I don't think *pisang emas* have ever got there.

I think it was before the end of the year that I was posted back to CSDIC(I), whose mess was now in Johore Bahru, just to the north of the causeway to Singapore. We had a large spacious house with a big compound and a mixture of British and Indian troops. Our commanding officer was Colonel Heaslitt, whom I had been with in Bombay. Now began a long period of frustration, relieved only by some interesting travel. There really was no work to do, all those who needed to be interrogated had been dealt with and we, all of us, were doing nothing more than marking time until we were demobbed. In my case, having only joined up at the turn of the year 1943/44, demobilisation was not expected before 1947.

But in early 1946, February, I was granted home leave by what was known as air trooping. This was supposed to be a rapid way of giving overseas troops the chance of a week or two in England. I left Singapore in a Dakota. I can't remember whether I have said that military DC3s were not fitted with rows of seats facing forward; we sat in seats with our backs to the windows, facing a central aisle, and the seats were bucket seats, not made for comfort. Seat-belts in those days were called 'lap-straps'; 'seat-belts' must have been an American term. We reached Karachi quite quickly, but we then found ourselves in a log jam. We spent a week or more in a transit camp outside the city in a dusty desert. We managed to get into town, but I don't remember much that was worth seeing. I say 'we', but I was not with anyone I knew.

I was eventually put on another Dakota for the next stage of the journey. This was to Sharjah in the Persian Gulf. Here we spent a night. It seems almost unbelievable, but I don't think there were any buildings other than sheds; everybody lived in tents. Oil had not yet been discovered there. Our next stop was Lydda in Palestine, just outside Tel Aviv. Here I was stuck again for some days. In fact I spent my 21st birthday in Tel Aviv and celebrated as well as I could by having dinner in the Tel Aviv Officers' Club. I have a tangible souvenir of my time in Palestine; it was there at an art exhibition that I bought two very attractive etchings. The artist was a Jew, but his pictures were of Mount Kenya with vignettes of Masai warriors. Both pictures are now at Buxlow. When I next boarded a plane the pilot spoke over the intercom and said that we had a choice of routes and asked us to choose. What the alternative was I don't know, but after some discussion, we chose the route, El Adem in North Africa, Malta and Bordeaux. We did not disembark at either El Adem or Bordeaux, but we spent a night in Malta. We arrived there on a Sunday. The Maltese were very strictly religious, so when we went in to Valetta almost nothing was open. All we could find was 'Auntie's Bar', where a blowsy Romanian woman called Irma sang songs at the piano and we ate typical English café food, fish and chips or sausages, bacon and eggs and chips! The next day we headed for England, landing in the afternoon at Manston in Kent. It was a beautiful day and I particularly remember being able to see at one and the same time the Pyrenees out of the left windows and the Alps on the other side. After disembarking and going through Customs we went into a waiting room for our bus to London. One officer then amazed me by taking off his jacket and shirt and unwinding yards of beautiful silk he had bought in Karachi!

Having left Singapore in February, I had finally arrived in England on about 20 March. So much for rapid air trooping! I made my way to Southborough, just north of Tunbridge Wells where my parents had bought a house called Thurlestone after the sale of my grandfather's house, Lanka. We belatedly celebrated my birthday by going to the theatre in London; we saw *Now Barrabas* by William Douglas Home, somewhere in the Strand and it was snowing.

I never raised with my parents their experiences in prison; I thought it might be too painful for them and that if they wanted to they would raise the subject with me. I found out years later that I had been mistaken. They had talked a lot about their experiences to the rest of the family on their return and probably would have liked to speak to me about them, now six months after their return. This is another of the many missed opportunities in my life that I regret. It was not that I knew nothing of what they had experienced. I knew that my father had devoted himself to religion, reading, and I think writing, but I may be wrong, for paper must have been hard to come by. What he read I don't know; I doubt if Swedenborg's writings were available. In any event he ended the war totally committed to Swedenborg and the New Church. He had of course been brought up in the New Church, but I don't think the church or Swedenborg's writings had been a central feature of his life for the previous thirty years. But after the war it became of prime importance to him. Their decision to retire to Jersey was as much influenced by the fact that there was a New Church there, the Minister being Maurice de Chazal, as by low taxation.

The most important element of prison for my mother was her friendship with Freddy Bloom, a friendship that lasted all her life. Freddy became very well known in the 60s because her daughter was born totally deaf and Freddy, who had been spectacularly successful in teaching her to talk, took a very active part in efforts to devote more resources to teaching such children. When she appeared on 'This Is Your Life' my mother was invited to the studio in London and appeared on the show. The other lasting effect of prison on her was the arthritis which had developed from malnutrition. She became more and more lame and ended up completely crippled. Total hip replacements were just coming in during the 60s but she was advised against it. I am not sure how close my parents had really been before the war – probably not as close as the family liked to think – but after the war I think they drifted apart, although my mother was always a most dutiful wife. But she did not share George's devotion to Swedenborg; she went to church, but she never could make head or tail of his writings. George, she told me late in life, had made her feel very guilty and a living reproach to him for failing to accept his faith.

But to return to England in the early spring of 1946. Loretto had for years had a close relationship with Trinity College, Oxford and it was there that I went in April to sit for their Entrance Examination. Amongst the others taking part was a tall gaunt looking officer, Peter Gem, who was to become my brother in law. He was still in uniform, the Irish Guards as I recall, but was being discharged because he had been suffering from TB. Today the question of the criteria for University entrance is a hot topic of debate. I have to admit that I got in on very dubious academic grounds. I had matriculated, that is had achieved the requisite number of credits in the School Certificate; even then, I had to take the maths paper twice to achieve a credit; but I had never even taken the Higher Certificate, the equivalent of today's A Level. I had been due to take Highers in French and German in the summer of 1942.

In May I set off for the Far East again on an equally long-winded air trooping return. The first leg of the journey was to Cairo, via Tripoli. This flight was I think in a converted Liberator bomber. We stayed for two days in Cairo and were able to visit the pyramids at Giza and to see the Sphinx. Amicia, who has been to Cairo quite recently, was amazed to hear that we were permitted to climb the Pyramid of Cheops to the very top; each step was at least 18 inches high. We also, believe it or not, climbed on to the back of the Sphinx; I used to have a photograph of three of us, I think, sitting and grinning at the camera; it may still be somewhere in the house. We also went to the famous Shephard's Hotel and had drinks. I have never been one for horseplay or high jinks, but one of our party very unkindly slipped a dose of Spanish Fly (the well known aphrodisiac) into the drink of one of our companions. All it did was to make him very ill, shaking as if he had DTs. Such behaviour upsets me. From Cairo we flew on to Karachi and then Bombay. I don't think DC3s could make Cairo to Karachi without an intermediate stop; where it was I don't know, but Viola tells me that she has a bracelet I gave her which is inscribed 'Iraq 1946'; perhaps it was somewhere near Basra.

We were then told we were going to finish our voyage by ship – from Madras! So we set off by train across India with our first stop at Poona. Those who make fun of the Raj usually use Poona as an example of the snobbish high-handed behaviour of the governing class. There is no doubt some truth in it; but I have to say I thoroughly enjoyed having strawberries and cream for tea at the famous Poona Club, sitting outside on the verandah with a splendid view. Our next stop, a brief one, was Madras – where there was now no ship! So we had to return to Bombay by train. I saw virtually nothing of Madras. I remember noticing that the Indians in that area were more dark-skinned than those I had seen elsewhere in India. In particular I remember one little Madrassi boy begging, rubbing his tummy; he said: 'No papa, no mama; poor little bastard; no food.' I, of course, gave him some money. But begging is a profession in India and it is very likely that he took his money to his papa and mama. From Bombay we eventually sailed to Singapore on a P&O liner; the *Maloja* for the third time. What a contrast this time; no hammock down in the hold, but a proper stateroom, room to circulate on deck and the company of a group of nurses!

So I returned to CSDIC(I) again. Colonel Heaslitt and his deputy were now living in a cottage in the compound with their mistresses. I was by now a captain – don't ask me why; promotion just came with the rations. We had absolutely nothing to do. We spent a lot of time trying to keep the troops busy on useless activities in the compound, such as lining the drive with bricks and then painting them white. It kept them from mischief. I became Mess Secretary; I don't know whether I was appointed or elected, but whatever it was it gave me something to do. Each day I had to decide on the menu for the day in discussion with the cook and have it printed. There were some complaints that the quality of the meat was not what it should be. I suspected that the two corporals whose job it was each day to take a truck into Singapore to pick up our provisions were being lazy and

As a Captain in uniform – 1946

getting there too late, by which time the good meat had gone. So one day I ordered them to get into Singapore really early the next morning. In midmorning they were back and, seeking me out, told me that they had got there too early to get the European meat ration and they hoped I would agree that they had done the right thing in getting the Indian troops ration for everybody. Would I like to come and inspect it? At the back of the truck was a live goat! There was nothing I could do about it, as they knew very well. One up for them! I instructed the typist to make out the menu for dinner with 'Roast Lamb'! The officers ate it perfectly happily. They were less pleased when I told them that it had actually been goat. I am not sure how long I remained Mess Secretary! I had plenty of time to indulge in the pleasure of motorcycling. I loved roaring around Singapore Island on my bike; no helmet, not even a cap, just the wind in my hair.

Sometime in midsummer I was so fed up that I wrote to Weaver, President of Trinity, and told him that I was vegetating to no purpose and not doing much for His Majesty either and asked whether there was not anything he could do to get me home earlier. I got no reply and thought no more of it. Then towards the end of September a cable arrived from the War Office, saying, 'Class B release for Captain de Moubray "to resume studies at Trinity College, Oxford".' This clearly wasn't true, so Weaver had obviously pulled some strings. I was not going to quibble. There was not much time to be lost; the Oxford term was to start on 10 October. It only took a couple of days to organise a flight back to England for me. I was to report early in the morning to Changi airport. I arranged for a driver with a jeep to call for me at about six in the morning and went to bed. When I awoke it was already half past six; I hastily got dressed and ran down stairs. The Indian driver was fast asleep behind the wheel of the jeep in the porte cochère. He said I hadn't told him to wake me. Anyway we set off at great speed, but when we reached Changi we could see the other passengers already going on board the converted Liberator bomber. I was told that I was too late and could not board. So I asked what on earth I could do. They gave me a voucher for a flight to England and said, 'You had better go into Singapore and see if British Overseas Airways have anything going.' I think it was already BOAC; Imperial Airways must already have been nationalised. To my great relief they said there was a vacant seat on a flying boat leaving the next morning. So began the most memorable of all my flights over the next fifty years.

Early next morning I reported to the harbour side in Singapore. It was a beautiful day without a breath of wind and the water was like a mirror. We stepped down into a launch and were ferried out to the Sunderland flying boat. The aircraft was not laid out as they are nowadays with rows of seats facing forward. Down each side there were tables with four seats around them; six in all I think, which means a total of twenty-four passengers. At the rear there was an Observation Deck, with a rail you could hang on to whilst looking out of the plate glass windows. There were also some bookshelves – the Library(!) – with Agatha Christie, Dorothy Sayers et al. All the passengers were male and, apart from me, they were all civilians. Here I was in First Class luxury, whilst the other service men were making an uncomfortable journey home in the Liberator. Even before take-off the stewards were offering us glasses of whisky. The take-off from water is much more interesting than from land; you see a bow wave building up and you seem to go for miles before the heavy craft eventually takes to the air.

Our first stop was to be Rangoon. But first we had lunch. This was in fact to be the only meal we had on board in three and a half days. The stewards brought white damask tablecloths to our tables and set the tables with proper cutlery. They then appeared with a large soup tureen from which soup was ladled into proper soup plates. I don't remember what the other courses were. At Rangoon we came down in the harbour from which I had sailed just over a year before in the *Maloja*. A launch took us ashore and we spent the night at a hotel, having dinner there too.

The next morning we took off and flew over the Arakan on our way to India. I spent a long time on the Observation Deck trying to make out familiar places. I think I detected Ramree Island and Akyab. We came down on the Hoogli River at Calcutta; the Hoogli is an arm of the Ganges. Here we had lunch on shore and took off again for our next destination, which was Karachi. Here we once again spent the night in a hotel; much more comfortable than the Transit Camp I had stayed in only a few months before. The next day we headed west over deserts and the Indian Ocean; the view from the Observation Deck was spectacular as we crossed the mountains of Oman – the flying boat did not fly very high and the tops of the mountains below us seemed very close. Our next stop was Bahrein; here we had lunch. At nightfall we came down (landed is hardly the right word!) on the Nile at Cairo; we were taken to a houseboat for dinner, sitting on deck smelling the last of the tropics and looking across the water at the lights of Cairo. We took off after dinner and the stewards announced that the gentlemen's beds were ready in a kind of loft which we reached by a short ladder. There mattresses with bedclothes and pillows were laid out in rows. We all undressed, got into pyjamas and went to sleep. Next morning we came down in the harbour of Catania – an absolutely glorious day, warm and sunny and the sea sparkling around us as we went ashore for breakfast. Our next stop was Caligiari in Sardinia for lunch ashore as usual. We finally reached Poole in Dorset that afternoon and after tea were taken to London by coach; what a way to travel!

I had to go to some depot in West London to be demobbed; I was issued with a suit (a kind of grey Burton's the Fifty-Shilling Tailors' outfit), an overcoat, shoes and I presume some shirts and socks – remember there was still clothes rationing. I then returned to my parent's house in South-borough to get ready for Oxford which was only about a week away. I don't really know what I needed to do, except open a bank account. When I had been at Dulwich I had had an account with Barclays Bank, but I now opened an account with Coutts, where my parents banked, to receive my government grant. All ex-servicemen going to University received grants; mine for Oxford amounted to £270 a year – £90 a term.

CHAPTER 7

Oxford and Trinity College 1946–48

OXFORD IN 1946 WAS VERY DIFFERENT from what it is today, but also very different from what it had been before. The vast majority of the male undergraduates were ex-servicemen and their average age must have been around 22. The women, and proportionately there were many fewer – all in single sex colleges – were much younger, although there were of course ex-servicewomen too. The University authorities tried to behave as if nothing had changed and the disciplinary rules remained the same as before the war. All these ex-officers, some of whom had been Lieutenant-Colonels, were required to be in college by 11 p.m. (or was it midnight?). Many of them ignored the rules, even though there were bowler-hatted proctors trying to enforce them. What most young men did was to climb into college, and this was quite a test, as many of the walls were high and had spikes on top. But it was not too much of a problem for those in Trinity; to the right of the porter's lodge are the 'cottages' with windows right on to the Broad. Whilst all these windows had bars (to keep people out rather than in!) there was one window on the ground floor where they could be moved; the room was occupied by Mike Chavasse, son of the Bishop of Rochester, who kindly allowed many a late night reveller in!

My rooms were on the first floor on a staircase to the right of the main quad with a window overlooking the rose garden with a pool from which in the hot summer of 1947 frequent splashing could be heard as men cooled off in it. I had one of those old-fashioned scouts, Spanner by name, who was as helpful as Nazir had been in India, but less personal – he never tried to dress me. But he brought hot water every morning for washing and shaving and, in the winter, kept me supplied with coal for my fire.

Looking back I see now that I did not make the most of my time at University. I devoted much too much time to the theatre. I should have realised that I would have been a very unsuccessful actor. I wasn't particularly moral, but I have always found it difficult to lie convincingly. And acting is, in a sense, lying. You have to pretend to be what you are not. My academic work was not all that brilliant either. I was reading Politics, Philosophy and Economics (PPE) for no very good reason other than it did not commit you to any particular career. I did not have anything very definite in mind, but was toying with the idea of the Diplomatic Service, influenced by a novel by Henry Seton Merriman whose books, all leather bound, had been at my grandfather's house. Merriman, I later discovered, had himself been a Lorettonian. Diplomacy would have in fact been as unsuitable for me as acting, for the very same reason. I have on occasions been able to get away with being 'economical with the truth' but in the Foreign Office you have to be a great deal more insincere.

But I had interesting tutors. My tutor for economics was Tony Crosland, later to be Secretary of State for Education and Foreign Secretary. In 1946 he was still only 29. Most tutors did not even try to teach; they gave you a weekly essay to write and a book list and expected you to teach yourself. Tony, unusually, actually had a blackboard in his rooms and would use it to teach you the Law of Diminishing Returns. Tony was absolutely charming, but had a terrific chip on his shoulder. He later became known for his blunt statement that he intended to get rid of 'every fucking Grammar School'. When asked in 1946 where he had been to school he would always reply 'Wigan Grammar School'; he could not bring himself to admit that he had actually been to a public school, Highgate. I told this to Tony Benn when I met him last year – he was surprised to hear something about Tony Crosland that he had never heard before. Tony, anticipating Gordon Brown, would never wear a dinner jacket. At the College Commem Ball in the summer of 1947 he received guests in his rooms with a generous supply of drink, but wearing a tweed jacket and grey trousers. We also became friends. I remember once going to the cinema with him to see *Fame is the Spur*, the film of Howard Spring's novel based on the life of Ramsay Macdonald, who had betrayed the socialist cause. As we walked down the street afterwards, Tony was unusually quiet. It suddenly occurred to me – 'Tony, you want to be Prime Minister!' He admitted that it was so.

He had a girl friend called Hilary Sarson. She found him very difficult and asked me once to have coffee with her in the Cadena. She wanted advice on how to handle Tony. I told her bluntly to drop him. He was always going to put himself first and she would have a terrible time if she married him. Not surprisingly, perhaps, she ignored my advice and married him. She was very unhappy and they divorced after a very few years. I saw Tony one or two times after coming down; I remember we once met at Jack Straw's Castle on Hampstead Heath for a drink, but once he was launched on his political career he dropped those who were of no use to him. Tony tried to get me interested in politics, indeed strongly urged me to join the Labour Party. Hayek's *Road to Serfdom* had already made a great impression on me and turned me against socialism. But Tony insisted that the Labour Party was not going to be like that; he foresaw a kind of 'socialism with a human face'; had he been alive today he would surely have been all for 'The Third Way'. He tried to persuade me to go and see his friend Roy Jenkins and talk things over, but I knew it just wasn't me. Looking back it seems a pity that I had not at least gone to see Jenkins. But he had already gone down, and it would have meant a visit to London. And I could not bring myself to join the Conservatives, which I associated with 'Hooray Henrys' – another missed opportunity, I would have met Margaret Thatcher!

It was not until some time in the last ten years that I read Isaiah Berlin's famous essay on Tolstoy in which he identifies a deep division in mankind between foxes and hedgehogs. However it provides a very useful background to the development of my thinking over the next fifty years. Foxes, Berlin says, are sophisticated, pluralist, usually atheist, and distrustful of absolutes. Hedgehogs, on the other hand, are anti-intellectual, single-minded, often religious, and comfortable with certainties, chief among which are 'good' and 'evil'. In 1946 I was already very much a hedgehog, but there was still a good bit of fox in me. You will remember that in the early forties I was a great admirer of Franklin Roosevelt and the Tennessee Valley Authority. The mood of the times was for change. Away with the old ways of doing things and put reason to use for the good of mankind. Tony, and indeed I, was at that time quite convinced that scientific Keynesian economics was much more useful than fiscal or financial prudence. Over the next twenty years my views changed, and by the mid 1960s I was already a 'Thatcherite' and a full grown hedgehog. The other big change just after the war was that most people were convinced that the Tories had been heartless; that Montagu Norman had cared more about the pound than about the people of Britain; that the Empire had exploited the natives and that we were now going to care. The age of compassion had begun. Even then, but increasingly since, I have termed it the age of false compassion. Almost every action taken to help the poor, the unemployed and the colonial people has in the event left them much worse off than they otherwise would have been.

My other tutors had less influence over me. For Politics I had Philip Williams who never inspired me but helped me to a workmanlike understanding of political philosophy. He became known later as the author of a definitive biography of Hugh Gaitskell. For Moral Philosophy I had Austin Farrer, the College Chaplain and later President of Keble. He was not of this world; his theological books are almost incomprehensible. Whilst we were reading our essays, Farrer was in the habit, in the summer months, of throwing a sixpenny piece into the fire grate and listen to it tinkling down to the hearth! I shared my tutes with Harry Travers. Farrer was apt to say as we arrived 'Ah. Mowbray and Maltravers', showing an appreciation of Shakespeare's histories. Harry's essays always seemed to me to be a mixture of quotations from as many sources as possible, I never felt that you knew what he actually believed. My problem with Oxford philosophy was Swedenborg! Wittgenstein once said that philosophy was useless if it did not try to answer questions to which one really wanted an answer, and so far as I was concerned most, if not all, Oxford philosophy failed this test. I already knew the purpose of life. We are on this earth to prepare for the next one; what we do, what we love, determine the outcome.

My own personal problem in moral philosophy was how it could be possible to be truly altruistic if one was in fact motivated by the desire for salvation. Farrer could not help me. One last word about philosophy. In the autumn of 1946 I attended a series of eight lectures by Gilbert Ryle, famous for being the author of the term 'The Ghost in the Machine'. The title of the lectures was 'Freedom of the Will'. After about four lectures he said à propos the title of his lectures, 'You will notice that I have not yet referred to the freedom of the will; that is because, of course, there is no such thing.' That kind of vain posturing, much admired no doubt by Richard Dawkins, put me off Oxford philosophy for good. Not quite true; I have always found R.G. Collingwood very sound.

All this makes me sound much more serious than I actually was. A great deal of my time was devoted to the theatre. It started in the first week of term. A striking figure could be seen striding around Oxford, tall and gaunt and wearing a plum coloured suit. It was Ken Tynan. I have since heard from an article in the *Spectator* by Paul Johnson that the suit was made from curtain material; we were, of course, still subject to clothes rationing. Undergraduates were required to wear gowns whilst walking the streets of Oxford. Scholars wore flowing black gowns and ordinary commoners little short gowns commonly called 'bum freezers'. But Ken's plum suit was never hidden under a gown. Perhaps the proctors did not believe that someone dressed like that could be an undergraduate. I was to meet Ken a couple of days later.

Sandy Wilson was up at Oriel and we soon got together. In his memoirs, published at some time about thirty years ago, he says — I can't remember the exact words — 'Guy came in and said that we must go to the first meeting of the Oxford University Experimental Theatre Club; there are bound to be lots of girls.' How Sandy's friends must have laughed at that. He is well known to be a homosexual. I don't know whether I really said that, but it is not unlikely. The point is, you see, that in 1946 I had no idea that he was homosexual and really wasn't aware that there was such a category of person. I am not sure that even Sandy fully realised it. I remember in the summer of 1947 he tried quite hard to fall in love with my girl friend!

Anyway we went to the meeting. A number of people who became well known in the world of the theatre and films were there; Ken Tynan, Lindsay Anderson, Donald Swann and no doubt many others. More important for me was that Heather Couper was there; we danced together and fell in love. We spent a great deal of time together from then on until the spring of 1948. Heather was young, only just eighteen, attractive, lively and very keen to be an actress. I don't think either of us managed to get a part in anything that term, I know I auditioned for roles in the OUDS, but failed; not surprisingly, I would have been hopeless in a Shakespearian role. If they had been auditioning for *French Without Tears* by Terence Rattigan it might have been different. We both saw a lot of Sandy Wilson.

After Oxford I saw very little of Sandy, but Heather remained a lifelong friend of his. At Sandy's 70th birthday party we were both at the top table, Heather on Sandy's left and then me. To my left was Dulcie Gray and opposite me was a striking dark haired lady, who I realised was the lovely Judy Campbell whom Sandy and I had seen in *Present Indicative* with Noel Coward fifty-two years before!

Cast of Sandy Wilson's Revue at Oxford – 1947

We also saw quite a lot of Ken Tynan. He was a fascinating character; in my view a brilliant actor. I am not at all sure why he turned instead to criticism. I had Norman Scarfe, the historian, to lunch here the other day and found that he had been at Magdalen with Ken and that we both thought his performance in an OUDS play as the bishop in some Scandinavian tragedy (I cannot remember what it was) had been absolutely splendid. A few friends used to meet in Ken's rooms at Magdalen and he would keep us in fits of laughter reading aloud from Robert Benchley's stories with a perfect American accent. But he had a wilder side to him. At parties he used to indulge in the most public snogging with, I am sure this is right, Jill Rowe-Dutton, the daughter of a very senior civil servant in the Treasury. She was eventually to marry good old Peter Parker. I think it troubled Ken very much that he was illegitimate. His full name was Kenneth Peacock Tynan, Peacock being the name of his father, who had acknowledged him and paid for him to go to school, but being a bastard rankled, and it seemed much more important in those days.

Another memorable event of that term was the Trinity 'bump supper'. Trinity was then the top rowing college and had for the second successive year become Head of the River. It has not to my knowledge ever been as good again. It must have been due to the force of character of the President of the college boat club – one A.D. Rowe. Rowe used to have tutes with Philip Williams and I remember one day he poked his head round the door and when asked by Williams why he had not yet submitted an essay, replied, 'Williams, I would have you know that I am up for the sole purpose of reading Rowing.'

The bump supper was one of those rowdy meals in Hall into the spirit of which I find it hard to fit. There was a good deal of bread and mashed potato throwing. The food throwers were not familiar with the words of Robert Raper, a Fellow of Trinity from 1871 to 1915, who when he was Dean posted the following notice outside Hall: 'Gentlemen coming from homes where bread throwing at the dinner table is habitual, and finding difficulty in conforming suddenly to the unfamiliar ways of a higher civilisation, will be permitted to continue their domestic pastime on payment of 5 shillings a throw during their first year. After that the charge will be doubled.' After supper there was the ceremonial burning of an old boat in the front quad. A lot of drunken men cavorted round the bonfire. One of them was a very tall and strong member of the eight who was what I suppose we would today call a born again Christian, and though a complete teetotaller was drunk with the passion of the occasion. He suddenly seized the Dean who, I think, was Nowell Smith and a known atheist and held him over the fire shouting, 'Burn, heretic, burn!' He was restrained with some difficulty.

I spent the Christmas holidays with my parents and two younger sisters at Southborough. I am told that I made my sisters quite miserable by being grossly insensitive to the Christmas spirit, not being a bit interested in the Christmas tree or in singing carols. It was very thoughtless of me. I think I also went to a dance in Tunbridge Wells and had rather too much to drink and drove some girls home rather recklessly in my parents' Lanchester. This was, to the best of my belief, the last time I ever drove under the influence of drink. Indeed only the second time in my life, the previous one in 1945, driving a jeep round the only roundabout in Singapore doing 'wheelies'!

The first term of 1947 started in mid-January. At Oxford station the sun was shining and it was unusually warm; no one was wearing top coats. But a few days later the snows came, heavy snow it was too, at least a foot. The whole of the country was plunged into this severe weather for several weeks. There was a desperate coal shortage; but Spanner somehow managed to provide me with coal. There was no central heating and the only source of heat in my sitting room was the coal fire. The then Minister of Fuel and Power, Manny Shinwell, found it hard to live down; for years he was associated with the failure of socialist planning. But he eventually became Father of the House of Commons and when he died he was over the age of 100. To have a bath or shower at Trinity meant a long trip in a dressing gown across two quads to the bathrooms. For several weeks one walked between walls of snow piled high on either side.

I prided myself earlier in these memoirs on my chronological approach; but not having kept a diary I am sometimes at a loss. I don't know whether it was in early 1947 or in 1948 that I appeared in Ken Tynan's production of Milton's *Samson Agonistes*. It was performed in the University Church of

St. Mary's. Ken's production, not surprisingly, was very avant garde. There was a tall wooden tower, normally used for repairing street lights (in the days before hydraulic lifts); Delilah spent most of her time high up in the tower with Samson desperately trying to climb up to her. The man who took Samson's part looked very like Victor Mature, a Hollywood film star of the 1940s specialising in biblical sagas. Delilah, somewhat ironically for a Philistine, was played by a very voluptuous Jewess! I was the Philistine giant, carried in to the church on a litter surrounded by admiring ladies. To prepare for my battle with Samson I had to run round the church, punching the air with my fists like a boxer preparing for a bout. It was all great fun, but hardly likely to advance my career as an actor.

In the Easter vac, the family went to Jersey to look for a house. We were all charmed by the beauty of Jersey and saw many houses. My own personal favourite was one called La Falaise on the north coast near the Devil's Hole, but I'm sure my parents were right not to buy it; in winter it would have been exposed to bitter north winds. In any event, it turned out that my father had decided to go into a small business of fruit growing, so he needed the right sort of land for an orchard, mainly apples, and for growing raspberries and strawberries; he was also to grow melons. They bought a house called Avalon in the parish of St. Lawrence and renamed it Maison du Douet (the house of the spring). When we – my parents, Viola, Audrey and I – went to Jersey with all our luggage we required two planes! They were only five seaters, so we had three in one and two in the other with all our luggage. We took off from Croydon Airport, which in those days was London's principal airport; Jersey airport in St. Ouens was no more than a field. Had we gone just before the war we would have had to land on the beach at St. Aubyn's at low tide!

My chronology is a bit uncertain here. I am not sure whether Sandy produced one or two revues whilst we were at Oxford. I have since spoken to Sandy who assures me that there were no fewer than three revues and that I was in all three. I was in the chorus line, singing songs like 'Oxford's not what it used to be, in the palmy days of 1938'. Even here my memory has been at fault. Sandy says that it was Michael Godley (of whom more anon) who sang that song. There were sketches in which Heather acted; both Ken Tynan and Lindsay Anderson were in it. Donald Swann also took part, writing his own songs which he played on the piano. It was all great fun.

The summer of 1947 was one of the most glorious summers I can remember; only 1976 was as warm and sunny. The Trinity Commem Ball was a great event. My guests were Heather, of course, and Sandy with, I think, a girl. Tony held court most generously in his rooms. At some point in that summer the Cambridge Footlights Club invited a delegation from the OUETC to visit them and see their show. The delegation was rather an extraordinary one; there were four of us, Ken Tynan, Sandy Wilson, Peter Wildeblood (later notorious for some scandal involving Lord Montagu and guardsmen!) and me. We went by train on a line which I feel sure Beeching did away with in the 50s. We meandered across England, roughly west to east in a single compartment. The people in Cambridge seemed to me to be even more ex-service than we were. They all seemed to be former majors with black moustaches. The Footlights revue was not memorable; this was several years before Alan Bennett, Jonathan Miller et al.

I spent the long vac in Jersey. I had hoped that Heather would join me there, but she decided to take up a post as au pair to a rich Finnish family who owned an island in the Baltic. The weather continued to be glorious and I had a lovely holiday. There were frequent visits to the beach — our favourite was the vast almost deserted beach at St. Ouens — and the bays on the north coast beneath the granite cliffs. I seemed to wear a dinner jacket almost every night. There were parties at people's houses with dancing, ending in the early hours of the morning with breakfast in the kitchen. Viola and I went to most of them together; Audrey at 15 was still a little young. There were not many really rich tax avoiders in Jersey then, so most of the parties were with the old Jersey families — Noemi de Gruchy, Peter Crill, John Coutanche, the son of the Bailiff of Jersey, Peter Falla and others whose names I cannot now remember. There were also one of the new rich families, the 'whisky' Dawsons, whom I remember as being very nice.

In the autumn it was back to Oxford for my last year. Somehow I have failed to say very much about the people in Trinity. The person I saw most of was Peter Gem. He had a room in the Cottages but, luckily for him, not on the ground floor and with no loose window bars! He had a great influence on my taste in classical music. He was devoted to violin concertos and had a great stack of records. I came to love the Bach Double concerto with Yehudi Menuhin, his recording of the Elgar concerto, the concertos of Max Bruch, Tchaikovsky, Sibelius and Brahms. Mozart did not yet mean anything to me and it may be surprising today to know that Mozart was generally not so highly thought of; he did not really become appreciated until the early 60s. Peter had a good friend, Bunt Kimber, whom I saw a lot of, but who was never really my friend. He had been in Bomber Command and was clearly marked by the strain of the experience of being constantly under fire from anti-aircraft guns and from the frequent loss of colleagues. It seemed to give him a macabre sense of humour.

We had rooms in College only for our first year. We then had to move out to 'digs', a phenomenon peculiar to the time. Digs I am sure died out by the early 50s. You had a furnished bed-sitting room and a landlady who provided breakfast and I think dinner, but we still dined most nights in Hall. Peter and I shared digs in a house in North Oxford on the Woodstock Road. Our landlady was very strict about the admission of women, stricter than the authorities at St. Hugh's were about the admission of men. So I saw more of Heather at St. Hugh's than in our digs. During the winter of 1947/48 Heather and I began to drift apart. I was and remained for some years far too self-centred.

An amusing incident occurred at about this time. A friend invited me to have lunch with him at White's in the High; it was *the* restaurant at the time. There was another man with him and he took great pleasure in introducing us: 'Guy de Moubray, I would like you to meet Michael de Mowbray!' Michael was one of the four brothers I have already mentioned and was a medical student at the Radcliffe Infirmary. We got on perfectly well at the lunch, but never in fact ever met again.

Christmas this year was spent in Jersey. I hope I was less insensitive to my younger sisters' views. One of the reasons my father chose to live in Jersey was that it had a New Church, that is to say a Swedenborgian church, whose minister at that time was our cousin Maurice de Chazal. After some years there was some sort of scandal about the death of Maurice and Marcelle's daughter Minou. I do not remember the details, but it meant that he gave up and a new minister came with whom my father frequently clashed on points of doctrine. When he eventually went my father took over the role as a lay preacher right up until his death in 1976. The congregation was tiny, mostly family, and his sermons were heavily doctrinal. My father kept his fruit growing business going for eleven years. It was unlucky that he did it at a time when 'Pick your Own' had not yet been thought of. It meant a lot of labour for my mother and anybody else staying during the strawberry and raspberry seasons. But my father thoroughly enjoyed it. He used to load up his estate car with all the day's produce and drive in to St. Helier early in the morning to sell his fruit in the market. Besides the berries there were apples and melons.

Amongst the guests who stayed with me in Jersey were Sandy Wilson and Peter Gem. Peter and Audrey fell in love; she was only sixteen in 1948, but the parents did not object and they were married in 1949 when she was still only seventeen. During the Easter holidays of 1948 Heather went on a trip to Paris with a group of acting friends from Oxford. On her return she told me that she was now in love with Michael Godley. I was, selfishly, distraught, but of course had to accept it. She and Michael married after she had gone down, presumably in 1949 or 1950.

The summer of 1948 was nowhere near as nice as the year before; the weather was poor and I had lost Heather. I had to endure watching Michael Godley playing the lead part in *Love's Labours Lost* in an outdoor production in the grounds of Worcester College; I just could not see what she found so attractive in this little man! I also took my Finals in June. Daphne always used to say that my academic qualifications were really miserable; not only had I not taken a single Higher Certificate, I also never took a proper degree, because I had only done two years. Ex-servicemen were allowed to take only two-thirds of the final papers. I suppose it would have been possible to stay on for a third year, but the Government grants were limited to two years and it seemed then that at the age of 23 it was high time one got a job. And anyway I found it difficult enough to manage on my grant. My father seemed to think that I should not only live on it, but be able to buy clothes too. Clothes were still rationed, but suits were very expensive so I was always overdrawn.

I had no assets to secure a loan, but somehow Coutts allowed me to stagger on. I used to receive from time to time one of their delightful third person letters: 'Messrs. Coutts & Co. would be obliged if, on his next visit to London, Mr de Moubray would call on them.' If you wanted to see your balance, they would take you behind the counter, lifting a large oak flap, and show you your entries entered in ink in the large leather bound ledger. My entries were always on the left hand side, and rather strangely they never covered up the right hand side which showed the account of the next customer – in my case it was Lord Louis Mountbatten! But I never looked at his entries.

Before my Finals I borrowed a car from somebody in Trinity and went off for a couple of days to stay at the Bay Tree in Burford to do some revision in peace and quiet. On the day of Finals one had to attend the Schools in gown and subfusc; subfusc being a dark suit with white tie. After the end of term I was called back to Oxford for a Viva. Any candidate who seemed to be on the border between one class of degree and another had to attend an oral examination, which lasted about an hour. You sat and faced three or four dons at a table facing you, a little reminiscent of the painting of the Cavalier boy 'When did you last see your father?' I had by then forgotten what I had written in my Finals and was floored when one of the dons said, 'You made an interesting point in your paper. Would you like to expand on it?' Luckily, for another question, *The Times* leader for that day which I had just read was relevant. I know I made one terrible boob; in the forthcoming General Election in Western Germany there were two candidates for Chancellor, Adenauer and Schumacher, and I could not for the life of me remember which was the Christian Democrat and which the Social Democrat, and almost as soon as I said it, I realised that I had got it wrong. That may well have scuppered my chances of a First and I was awarded a Second. The full results, which were revealed later, actually showed that I had alphas in Politics and Philosophy but only a gamma in economics – perhaps I wasn't Keynesian enough.

Before going off on holiday I paid a visit to the Civil Service Commissioners. I was entered to take the Foreign Office House Party entrance test at Stoke D'Abernon, but that was not to take place until the summer of 1949 so I needed to find some other job in the meanwhile. I knew that a bright Oxford girl called Jenny Turner had gone to the Treasury the previous year and it seemed a good idea to try to do the same. The Civil Service Commissioners expressed shock that I should brazenly ask to go to the Treasury; that was a boon which was granted to few. I had of course been brought up to think that the acme of Civil Service life was either the ICS or the Treasury. I knew that the top candidate for the Civil Service in 1906, Otto Niemeyer, had gone to the Treasury; Keynes who came second went to the India Office! So I told them that so far as I was concerned it was the Treasury or nothing – not for me the Board of Trade or the National Insurance Office. In spite of my cheek (or perhaps because of it?) they agreed to send me to the Treasury which I was to join early in October.

For the holidays I stayed with a family in France. Our Mauritian cousin Claire de Pitray (married to Comte Louis de Pitray with a chateau in the claret country) introduced me to the de Calmels family whose son Jean Louis was keen to improve his English. In return he came to stay for a while in Jersey. They lived in the Landes at Dax, north of Biarritz. On my way down there by train I had lunch in the restaurant car and met a French Catholic priest. He was convinced that all Englishmen were heretics. I assured him that there were a lot of English Roman Catholics; '*Mais ils ne sont pas des vrais catholiques*,' he assured me! How the English and the French are ever going to live in harmony in the European Union, I don't know. But more of that at the right time.

Hossegor is now, I believe, a thriving coastal resort, but then I do not remember seeing anything else besides the Calmels' enormous beach house, perched on the dunes. It was a wooden bungalow with no running water. The de Calmels family consisted of father and mother, one son, Jean Louis, who must have been about 20 years old, and two daughters, the eldest of whom, Danielle, was about nineteen. But at meals in the dining room there must have been at least fifteen of us at table. There was a Baron de Noirmont and his young wife; I shocked everyone by calling her *tu*!, but only once; I learned my lesson. Who the others were I am not at all sure. I think they included Madame de Calmels' mother and other cousins with young children. There was also l'Oncle Robert who was a mad anglophile and bought his suits in Saville Row – also his ties. The children found it very funny, particularly that, trying to sound English, '*Il parlait avec les dents sérrés.*'

The ages ranged from about sixty down to three! Everybody had wine at meals. You could tell their age by the colour of the wine; all adults down as far as Danielle drank straight wine, the younger they were the lighter the wine; the youngest drank a very pale pink water. The house was swarming with servants, who would bring us hot water in jugs and we had baths in galvanised iron tubs on the floor. We spent about two weeks there, mostly on the beach. Monsieur de Calmels had one of those old Citroens like Maigret had in the British television films. One evening, father, mother, Jean Louis, Danielle and I went off in the Citroen to a night club in Saint Jean de Luz. Some of the others came too in another car. I danced a lot with Danielle and she flirted madly; we cuddled up together in the back of the Citroen on our return journey.

After two weeks at Hossegor we moved on to the de Calmels' grandfather's chateau in the Gers, with distant views of the Pyrenees. It was a very old castle and I had to be shown around; Danielle who was in charge of my guided tour tried to shock me when she showed me the loo: '*Voici la chiotte*,' she said. I had never heard the word before – and have not ever heard it again – but I could guess the literal translation. So there is a useful addition to your French vocabulary. The top floors of the chateau were infested with bats, quite big ones, not the little pipistrelles. Every night before we went to bed, the men visited the bedrooms with tennis rackets to drive the bats out of doors. It was quite a hard job; the bats would take refuge on top of the canopies of the four-poster beds. But it had to be done; none of the women dared to go to bed until they had the bat 'all clear'.

We spent most of our time out of doors. We did some rough shooting, which I think is much more sporting than shooting with beaters. A party of us would go out with shotguns and search for game to shoot, mostly partridge, but also some hares. I don't remember one day of rain in the whole month. The Gers in the early autumn is beautiful, but I have never been back. I seemed to fit in very well with the whole family and thoroughly enjoyed my stay. And, just as important, my French, which had become a little rusty during the war, was fluent again with, dare I say it, *un accent impeccable*, which was going to be very useful to me in my work over the next twelve years.

There was one last fling of my Oxford life. Late in September Sandy Wilson's Revue was put on for three nights at the Playhouse Theatre in London. The theatre at the bottom of Northumberland Avenue, near the Embankment, has not been a proper theatre for many years now and has been used as a studio by the BBC. I think our performance went down quite well; we had good reviews, but not rave ones. After one of the rehearsals I paid my first visit to the Treasury to see the Establishments Officer, Milner Barry, who was a little shocked, I think, to find me in a sweater and no tie with traces of theatrical make-up on my face! But we agreed on my starting date and I heard what my salary was to be – £400 a year, which seemed pretty good after two years on a Government grant of £270 a year.

CHAPTER 8

His Majesty's Treasury 1948–50

BEFORE STARTING WORK I had to find somewhere to live and I found some tolerable digs in Courtfield Gardens in SW 7. Courtfield Gardens is, or was, a salubrious area, and the digs were friendly; lots of young men starting work in London. Our landlady was strict but produced tolerable food – breakfast and dinner. The rent was £5 a week. But I had a minute room. Our digs at Oxford had consisted of a very spacious bed-sitting room with a desk each but here I had not much more than a cubby hole with room for a single bed and one chair. There was a basin, which during the day was disguised with a wooden cover to look like a small desk! There were communal bathrooms on each floor. All the tenants were, of course, men, and women were not, I think, admitted at all. Not that I would have wanted to show my little room to any visitor.

The only man I knew was Jimmy Leasor whom I had briefly met at Oxford. He had started work as a journalist at the *Daily Express*, the Beaverbrook paper. Every night he would return home with a copy of next morning's first edition and proudly show me all his contributions which had been circled with a blue pencil. I am afraid that I did not usually approve at all of his efforts. 'You can't say that,' I would exclaim, 'you have no evidence for it at all, and it's just not true.' I don't think his career as a journalist continued for very long. He found a much more lucrative career, writing thrillers, which in later years I often saw at bookstalls at airports, but I have never actually read one.

I started at the Treasury at the end of September. I had been appointed to the Overseas Finance Division (OF) in the section concerned with France and the Benelux countries. I was called an Administrative Assistant, the unappointed equivalent of an Assistant Principal. My immediate boss was Armide Oppé. I don't know where the Oppés came from, but she looked Levantine. We shared a room and I got on very well with her. The Assistant Secretary was Ernest Copleston; although Christian names were normally used, he was an exception and was always called Cop. His claim to fame was that he had been expelled from Marlborough for having under his bed a case of Beaune – now there's a touch of class. He ended his Civil Service days as Secretary of the University Grants Committee. The next up in the hierarchy, the Under Secretary, was Eddie Playfair, I think already knighted. He was reputed to have been able openly to discuss Top Secret information on the telephone with Gunston of the Bank of England because they both spoke Cornish. He later became Permanent Secretary of the War Office, a most unlikely appointment for somebody so intellectual and who, under my influence I may say, wore bow ties! Sir Humphrey Mynors, later Deputy Governor of the Bank of England, told me that Eddie had been very worried about the appointment, but that he had told him to wear a bowler hat and carry a rolled umbrella and he would get away with murder. And so it transpired. I once met Sir Eddie in the Mall, looking very dapper and every inch the War Office. More senior still, the Second Secretary was Sir Leslie Rowan. And right at the top was Sir Edward Bridges, the Permanent Secretary, son of the poet Robert Bridges. The Chancellor of the Exchequer was Sir Stafford Cripps, whom I only met once at the Christmas party. Despite his reputation as a puritan he smoked the most enormous cigar and was very civil and friendly to a young man like me.

Two important things happened to me on my first day in the Treasury. I was sharing a room with Armide and she passed me a file and told me to familiarise myself with it. It concerned the negotiations to settle the Anglo-Dutch wartime debt. Negotiations seemed not to have gone very far and there were clearly things which could be done. Armide told me then to get on with it and to settle the debt! The important thing about this was that it gave my self-confidence an enormous boost to have such authority given to me, 23 years old, on my very first day. I very much doubt whether such responsibility would have been given in any other Department of State, or in the City or in industry. After all, the debt was very substantial for those days: somewhere between 8 and 12 million pounds. I have always considered it very important to have the ability to think for oneself and to take decisions. I don't know whether such ability is innate or cultivated; but I do know that this experience strengthened it in me. I was later to see the ability completely atrophied among some young graduates in the Bank of England, where such responsibility would not have been given to anyone under the age of about 45.

The second even more important thing that happened that day was that the door opened and a beautiful girl put her head round the door, took one look at me and realised that the person she was looking for was no longer there. 'Where's Jan?' she asked Armide. So that was the first time I ever saw Daphne Hazell, my future wife. She was also in OF, working on Western Germany, where there was a good deal going on, the forthcoming monetary reform with the introduction of the Deutschemark to replace the Reichsmark and the Berlin Airlift. As I was to discover Daphne had been given every bit as much responsibility as I. On the Airlift she was talking direct to Royal Air Force Air Marshals, authorising emergency expenditure on her own responsibility. It took a bit of time to get to know her. A few days later I remember walking down a corridor behind her, admiring her legs in grey nylon stockings with carefully centred seams under a slim New Look midi-length skirt. All the young ones met for coffee in the canteen every morning, which must have been where I got to know her. We were both members of the Treasury Cinema Club and attended showings together. We once went to a film at the Hampstead Everyman; Daphne was living in a flat in an apartment block called Greenhill, not far from Hampstead Tube Station. But we were not a couple until well into the New Year of 1949.

I wasn't at all sure that she was as keen on me as I was on her. In the Treasury she shared a room with James Collier and I had a vague suspicion that something might be brewing there. Of course, there wasn't. All my doubts were dispelled when she returned from a trip to Paris sometime in January and brought me two presents – a '100 pour cent soie' bow tie and even more significant, a 78 r.p.m. record of Jean Sablon singing 'Si tu m'aimes'. I may have had self-confidence at work, but I desperately lacked it with girls, but the signs were unmistakably favourable.

At work the last three months of 1948 were devoted to settling the Anglo–Dutch wartime debt. I made contact with the Financial Attaché at the Netherlands Embassy, a charming man called Jan Fehmers who was married to an English girl. She had been in the ATS. We became friends, some might say too friendly for a tough negotiation; I spent many an evening drinking Dutch gin with them in their Mayfair flat and returned home late rather the worse for wear. We eventually agreed on the sum of ten million pounds. I am sure that a really tough negotiator could have come nearer to twelve million. But it was I think important to establish a good working relationship with the office of the Dutch Financial Attaché. It certainly helped me later in the Bank of England.

I also managed to find nicer accommodation than the digs in Courtfield Gardens. I ran across Peter Hobson, from the SOAS and Dulwich. He asked me to join him in a flat he had rented at 94 Cornwall Gardens; there was a third person in the flat, a young Malayan student at the SOAS by the name of Zulkifli bin Hashim. The flat was on the first floor and consisted of one very large bed-sitting room, in which we all slept, a kitchen, and a bathroom. I think we had a table for eating meals also in the same room.

Fending for oneself in London at that time was far from easy. Food rationing was still as restricted as at the worst point of the war. There were no self-service shops; one had to stand at the counter to be served, clutching one's ration book to wait to have the coupons cut out. But it was not only meat, butter, sugar, eggs that were rationed. There was also what was known as the points system for tinned foods. Vegetables were sold all covered in mud. There were no avocados, no sweet peppers and still no bananas. The only pasta you could get was Quaker's quick macaroni, no parmesan cheese, no salami, and so it could go on and on. We had no difficulty in keeping slim. But we discovered a grocer in the Cromwell Road who sold tinned haggis, which was not rationed, and haggis is very filling, so we ate a lot of it. There was also whale's meat instead of beef steaks. I found it had a rather unpleasant flavour.

Peter, who was still studying at the SOAS, had lots of Asian friends. One of them was an Indonesian prince called Utomo. He would invite us for

Indonesian meals and we borrowed at least one recipe, *gadu gadu*, which was cauliflower with a curried peanut sauce. The peanuts, of course, came from peanut butter, which perhaps surprisingly was available. Daphne and I after we were married often had *gadu gadu*. Entertaining was very difficult. Peter and Zul concocted excellent curries and Indonesian dishes like *nasi goreng*. But when I invited Daphne and James Collier to dinner one night early in our acquaintance, I gave them, believe it or not, what my mother called a macaroni mess! – Quaker quick macaroni drained and kind of stir-fried (not that I was to hear that term for some years) with a bit of bacon, some pieces of sausage and tinned peas.

Utomo had another influence on our lives, or rather on Peter's, because at some time in 1949 he arranged for an Indonesian gamelan orchestra to come to London and perform in a theatre. When the time came for the performances, they were one player short and, remarkably, Peter Hobson stood in. He was naturally fairly dark with black hair and was not very tall. So, wearing a sarong, Peter from Leeds performed in an authentic gamelan orchestra. The remarkable thing really is that his playing was indistinguishable from the genuine thing. Nobody in the audience knew apart from Daphne and me and Zul. The newspaper critics did not know either; it would have made a good story. Peter's friends were always exotic. He became close friends with the Ballet Nègre (all from the Caribbean) which performed in London for some weeks. Peter certainly could not have stood in for any of the dancers in those performances. Some time in 1949 the Ballet Nègre appeared at a theatre in Jersey and all the cast was invited to Maison du Douet. Daphne and I were there at the time. I remember my grandmother being entranced with them, but she confided afterwards that she had no idea that any negro could be as black. There was one particular dancer whose skin was like polished ebony.

My work at the Treasury continued to be very satisfactory. I was still given remarkable responsibility. Our relationships with our European neighbours were on an entirely bilateral basis; the European Payments Union (EPU) was still a few years away. With each country we had a swing credit. This presented problems only with Belgium, with whom we had a swing credit of £10 million. Since the Belgians had wisely eschewed socialism and adopted a free market economic system, their economy was booming and we kept bumping up against the credit limit and had to reduce the balance back to £10 million by paying them gold. There was some adverse comment at the time about having to pay gold for imports of Belgian azaleas. One day a Principal from the Board of Trade rang me, very deferentially calling me 'sir' because, even though he was senior to me, I was in the Treasury. He said there was an urgent need to import £1 million of steel from Belgium, would I authorise the expenditure. The swing credit was at that time below £10 million and steel was obviously very important, so I authorised the expenditure on the spot without referring to anybody more senior in the Treasury.

There was another incident when some crisis blew up, I forget what about, but a meeting was called in Sir Leslie Rowan's room and OF had to be represented. For some reason Armide Oppé, Cop and Eddie Playfair were all away at the same time so I had to go. I hurriedly read up the file and Daphne suggested that I might seek some advice from Sir Dennis Rickett (OF but for different countries). I told him what I thought I would say, and he told me to make up my own mind, not to worry and go ahead. So I attended the meeting. There were only about five people there including Sir Max Brown from the Board of Trade; after some discussion Leslie Rowan asked for a view from OF. I gave my opinion. Max Brown expressed great satisfaction: 'That's what I have been saying for some time; I am glad the Treasury are now seeing sense.' When my seniors returned they did not reproach me for having gone against their previous line.

I had asked for the Treasury just to fill in time, but now found the world of international finance very appealing. I used to browse back through the files from the 1930s, reading about the tripartite agreement between the Bank of England, the Banque de France and the Federal Reserve Bank of New York to manage their floating currencies after sterling came off gold in 1931. I was due to go to this Foreign Office entrance weekend examination at Stoke D'Abernon and I asked the Civil Service Commissioners whether the exam could also be allowed to count for the Home Civil Service, since I now felt I would rather stay on at the Treasury. The Chief Clerk at the Treasury informed me that my application had been received on the day after applications closed and that the Civil Service Commissioners had therefore rejected my application. I should add that the weekend house party was still some weeks away. All my superiors were incensed and made approaches to the Commissioners; Eddie Playfair and Leslie Rowan were both keen for me to stay but had no better luck than I. So I eventually went to the House Party and was rejected for the Foreign Office; quite rightly I think. I only remember one other person at the House Party and that was Hugh Cortazzi, who had learned Japanese at the SOAS and was later to be UK Ambassador to Japan.

I had one further fling as an actor as a member of the Treasury Amateur Dramatic Club. All I remember about it is that the leading light in the club was Sylvia Stratford-Lawrence who was also a temporary Assistant Principal, who had also been at Oxford and was making tongues wag by having an affair with a Clerical Officer in the Treasury. Members of the First Division Association did not think that sort of thing was really on! The leading lady, playing opposite me, as my wife, was Margaret Reid, an extraordinarily shy girl who was quite out of place as an actress. She later became a very well known financial columnist for the *Financial Times*.

Although I suppose I could have stayed on in the Treasury, hoping one day to become established, I felt I wanted to start in some established career with clearer prospects for the future. I tried for a job with ICI and went for an interview for a job in their tariff office at Millbank. The over jovial man who interviewed me made frequent use of four letter words and quite put me off. Anyway I was not really interested in a statistical job. I also remember trying Shell; but they wanted me as a Japanese speaker and wanted me to go to Japan. I had had enough of the Japanese and knew that Daphne was not ready to give up her work and follow me. It was Daphne who suggested my new career. She said that on her frequent visits to Germany she kept meeting very prosperous looking gentlemen from the Bank of England; why did I not at least think about it. I too had had some experience of the way the Bank lived. I had visited the Bank with Monsieur Cools, the Belgian Financial Attaché, in connection with the validation of Belgian bonds. We visited Mr MacNamee, Principal of the Securities Control Office (part of the Exchange Control) and were given tea served in a silver teapot by a pink coated messenger. At that time banking had absolutely no appeal for me, but of course the Bank was heavily involved in international finance and featured prominently in the files of the 1930s which I had been reading. Moreover in OF I was in almost constant touch with Lindsay Ryan, head of Group II in the Bank's Overseas and Foreign Office, and with his boss, Philip Hogg.

An opportunity to take soundings came with a meeting of the Anglo-Belgian Economic Committee. The Belgian side included Luxembourg and the meeting was held in Luxembourg. The Treasury team consisted of Cop and me, and the Bank of England was represented by Philip Hogg. The meeting took place in the autumn of 1949. We flew from Northolt, then the main London airport, to Brussels, where we were met by a car on the tarmac; we never even showed passports or went through Customs. We then drove to Luxembourg, passing Bastogne, where there had been heavy fighting in the war during the Battle of the Bulge. We entered Luxembourg from the north-west and drove down to the city. I could not help feeling that this was what Ruritania would look like: craggy hills covered in forest with deer and wild boar. I could imagine Black Michael suddenly bursting across the road ahead of us on his horse. We passed near the town of Echternach on the German border. The people of Echternach were very proud of their ancient ruined castle. Our Luxembourg hosts told us that when the Germans had been driven out the Mayor of Echternach had sent a cable to the Grand Duchess in London: '*Echternach en ruine; ruines intactes!*' Apocryphal no doubt. The city when we reached it was no more than a country town with only one hotel; the great steel works were a few miles away. We went looking for the British Ambassador – Luxembourg had only very recently been upgraded to an Embassy from a Legation – but he wasn't at the Embassy, which was just a small town house. He was to be found in the bar of the hotel drinking champagne cocktails. Apparently he spent much of the day there, and we were soon urged to have cocktails too.

The Belgian delegation was headed by Olivier Gerard, Permanent Secretary of their Ministry of Trade, a nasty piece of work, who a few years later went to jail for corruption. The meetings were fairly difficult because the Belgians had the upper hand with their swing credit convertible into gold. We made little progress the first day. We then adjourned for dinner. I remember sitting next to the Dutch observer, who was there because of Benelux. He spent most of the dinner telling me quietly just how unspeakably awful the Belgians were. Gerard then insisted that we should all go to a night club, almost certainly the only night club in Luxembourg. There was a striptease artist. Believe it or not, her few garments were black in honour of the centenary of the death of Chopin! After her performance, Gerard picked her up and dumped her on Philip Hogg's lap – '*Voici la Banque d'Angleterre*,' he said. Philip was the last person this should have happened to. Even in the night club, he was still wearing his mackintosh and clutching his briefcase. He was a very devout Christian Scientist. By this time Cop was very drunk and Gerard took the opportunity to try and get him to agree there and then to make serious concessions to the Belgians. I had to intervene.

'Monsieur Gerard,' I said, 'you can't do this, we will discuss it in committee tomorrow morning.'

At lunch next day I had an opportunity to ask Philip Hogg what he thought about me joining the Bank of England. He seemed to think that it was a good idea and told me to ring him when we were back in London and he would arrange for me to see someone. This I did, and went for an interview with Grafftey-Smith, the Head of the Overseas side of the Bank. He was also very forthcoming, but said that I would have to go through the normal procedures and would have to be seen by a Selection Board. Twenty years later I was to be Chairman of Selection Boards, but on this occasion the Chairman was Humphrey Mynors, then a Director but later to be Deputy Governor. As I fear is often the case I was not particularly humble at the meeting and began to interview them! I said that in the light of my experience at the Treasury the starting salary was really quite inadequate – £360 a year was significantly less than I was earning at the Treasury (£400 a year). Humphrey Mynors put me in my place. 'Young man, you have a lot to unlearn!'

This was a significant remark; although the Bank as a whole was of a significantly lower intellectual calibre than the Treasury, Bank men looked down on the Treasury, who were seen as being too subservient to politicians, not sufficiently committed to sound finance and woefully ignorant of the workings of financial markets.

CHAPTER 9

The Bank of England and Marriage

M Y LAST DAY AT THE TREASURY was Friday 3 February 1950. On Monday 6 February I joined the Bank as a 4th Class Probationary Clerk! The contrast was even greater than I had imagined. In the Treasury one was, as it were, a member of the Officers' mess. In the Bank one was the lowest of the low. Whether a profound sense of my juniority would have held me back, I don't know, but I had the great advantage of having been given great responsibility at a young age in the Treasury. That was a lesson I was not going to 'unlearn'. I started, as all graduate entrants did, in the Accountants Department, Registrars for the National Debt. It was known in the Bank as the 'stock side' to differentiate it from the 'cash side' (Cashiers' Department). We spent our days 'passing transfers', that is to say processing purchases and sales of gilt-edged stocks. We worked in a large open plan office on the first floor of a building in Finsbury Circus. In the corner of the office was a case (a glass panelled office within an office) in which sat the Principal Clerks, keeping an eye on us. In the first few days they did not know what to make of me. We were required to treat them as being near to God and had to call them 'sir'. But in those first days they were constantly having to come to see me to fetch me to the telephone, where the Financial Attachés of Belgium and France wanted to speak to me. It was easier for them to sort little problems out with me than to deal with my successor at the Treasury who knew nothing of what had been going on. I am sure that they thought of the Bank as being nothing more than the 'East End Branch' of the Treasury. But the Principal Clerks found it quite incomprehensible that these senior financiers should want to talk to a 4th Class Probationary Clerk.

Soon after I had joined the Bank, Daphne and I became engaged. Our relationship over the previous year had not always been smooth, but we had no doubt that we wanted to be man and wife. We were married on 1 July 1950 at St. George's, Hanover Square, a lovely church with strong associations with Handel. It was a lovely wedding and Daphne looked absolutely stunning. We had lots of friends (mostly from University and the Treasury; I am not sure whether anybody came from the Bank) and of course family. The best man was my cousin Peter Dalley. Daphne carried a small white leather bound prayer book, which I still treasure. On our way out of the church the organ played Bach's 'Air on a G String'. We have photographs of us and friends and family on the steps outside the church in the days when they were adorned with those two delightful statues of dogs, which have since been stolen. We had our Reception at 94 Piccadilly.

Daphne's engagement photograph by Fayer – March 1950

Daphne said I made a hopeless speech for lack of preparation, but judging from the very poor home movie we have of the wedding, I look to have been fluent enough.

I propose at this point to abandon the chronological approach to my life's history for a short while in order to say something about our marriage as a whole. I see the purpose of these memoirs in some sense to be my own 'judgement' on my life anticipating God's Judgement still to come. Our marriage has been the central pillar of my life and I have to say that my greatest regret is to realise that I failed for over thirty years to give Daphne what she really needed. This has to be explained. I know why I married Daphne. She was spectacularly beautiful, as the engagement photograph by Fayer confirms. What it doesn't show is her heavenly smile, nor does it reveal that she had the softest skin imaginable, like warm silk. She was also intelligent and good company. Since early childhood I had taken it for granted that I would marry and have a family. Ajax, my eldest grandson, seems to feel the same; at the age of four, when asked what he wanted to be when he grew up, he replied, 'I want to be a Daddy and have twelve children.' What I had not considered was what had I to give Daphne. I am not sure why she married me. I wasn't bad looking and I was very kind; she may have thought that was enough, but kindness without imaginative insight (which I conspicuously lacked) is not really enough. She clearly did

Daphne and Guy at St. George's Hanover Square, 1 July 1950

not marry me for my money; I had an overdraft at Coutts of about £70!
Daphne's father was, she later told me, very disappointed in her choice of
husband. During her time at LSE (evacuated to Cambridge until 1946) she
had consorted with a lot of rich men – a Greek, a Parsee from Bombay and

Our parents at the wedding

Micha Battsek, son of German refugees who, if not very rich then, became so later. She had a passionate affair with Micha and I never really discovered why they had broken up. Perhaps his very Jewish parents had objected to him marrying a Gentile; but then I know she was very fond of his parents. He remained obsessed with her for over forty years, so it must have been she who rejected him; I think it may have been that he lacked the one good quality I had – kindness.

Daphne was a very private person and successfully hid her inner nature from all others – perhaps even from herself. She put up a lot of camouflage. In the Treasury she was highly regarded and took a great deal of responsibility without hesitation. When Douglas Allen (now Lord Croham) moved from the Treasury to the Cabinet Office, he took her with him to work in the Central Economic Planning Staff. One of her responsibilities in the years up to 1953 was to prepare the annual pre-budget White Paper on the state of the economy. I am sure that had she remained in the Civil Service she would have become one of the first female Permanent Secretaries, along with Dame Evelyn Sharp.

Outwardly she projected an image of a self-assured strong character. But in fact, inside, she was completely insecure. I think, looking back, that she began to suffer attacks of irrational panic quite soon after we married. Her

Malay and Indonesian friends at wedding

insecurity was the result of a very unhappy childhood and the mutual antipathy between her and her mother. Daphne's father was a kind man, who in the immediate aftermath of the First World War had married a pretty flibbertigibbet, Ione Pestel, a descendant of one of the principal Russian instigators of the Decembrist Revolution of 1825 who had been exiled and whose family came to live in Bedfordshire. Spencer Hazell was an unassuming banker with Barclays Bank and soon realised, I think, that he was out of his depth with this headstrong, flirtatious wife; she should have been married to a rich man.

When Daphne was still very small her mother moved out of the marital home and went to live with her mother in Eastbourne. She had an affair with a man from the Argentine, I don't know whether he was English or Argentinian, and became convinced that he would have married her and taken her away if she had not been encumbered with a little daughter. She resented Daphne for the rest of her life; it took me a long time to recognise this. In the end, I believe, she came to hate Daphne. Daphne admitted to me years later that she had hated her mother and even at one time contemplated killing her. With the economic problems of the Depression weighing on them, Spencer and Ione decided to set up house together again; but it was no more than a *mariage de convenance*. They quarrelled incessantly and Daphne grew up in an atmosphere of bitterness and antipathy. It is not at all surprising that this should have undermined her self-confidence. What is extraordinary, I think, is how well she managed to hide the inner turmoil from others. The slender evidence of this turmoil only served to irritate me. Soon after we were married we had tickets for the theatre in London and I simply could not understand why, at the last minute, she said she could not go and sent me off on my own. She did not look to me unwell and I completely failed to show any imaginative insight. This must have been one of her first bouts of irrational panic. I was not to discover that she had these panic attacks for another thirty years. She seemed happy and serene for much of the next decade, for five years of which we lived in America. Looking back I see now that this was almost certainly because she was three thousand miles from her mother. During the 1960s she was very reluctant to have people to stay or to come to dinner; she claimed that all the people we knew were too rich and that it was embarrassing to be obviously unable to keep up with them. I should again have seen that keeping people at a distance was a mechanism for hiding the inner turmoil. Her argument did not really bear water; we were not rich, but by the age of 34, I was already paying 'supertax'.

Daphne did not keep a regular diary, but I have found some very revealing fragments. I think they are worth quoting from. But with this cautionary note; in January 1980 she wrote:

> Occasionally I regret not having kept a diary, but then recollect that it is precisely when one's life is most interesting that one has no inclination to do so – also there is the everlasting danger (as long as there are relatives about) of causing offence and stupid scenes if it gets read by others; and a cautious 'safe' diary would be a great bore and no fun to write.

So she set great store on keeping all her troubles to herself and would be unhappy to know that these fragments were now being read. But I think they explain much and show her in a very favourable light. In 1965 she wrote:

> I think all my life I have been that 6 year old girl running up the long flight of those steep stairs of my grandmother's house in Eastbourne, up, up, up to the room I shared with my mother at the top away from the newly acquired knowledge that I was to leave my home, that my life was to change, that everything was to be different, that my life as I had lived it was not to go on. I wonder now if the dash from London through the so ugly outer suburbs into the country and then finally up, up onto the Downs above Parham, that used to relieve my anxieties in 1955 wasn't a repeat of that flight up the stairs in 1932.

In 1964 she notes that Aunt Emily had come over for the day. She writes:

> She spoke rather freely to me about the parents; she is completely pro S.T.H. [her father] but nevertheless it is reassuring to me when other people can picture my mother as I have experienced her myself, and that I can know it

isn't my exaggeration that sees her actions in this light. Emily's story about my mother sending Nancie [Arnstein – D's first cousin] a card a week before Peter was born saying she couldn't come over to take her to the clinic 'because she had to see Aline that day' is dead in line with my experience with her when pregnant and a good example of how her kindness is completely limited to her desires and wants. She is a very shallow woman in pursuit of her own pleasure.

In April 1965 she writes:

> To feel ill is to lose touch with all gay and pleasant feelings. It is to go down in a bizarre tunnel and to be rocked mercilessly by one's fears, fantasies, dreads – all those things kept under control when one is whole. When one is whole again it seems a marvel that one was in despair and a surge of joy, almost physical, jumps within one. Oh! God for a painless old age on passing on to keep one's normal self and not to be at the mercy of these subterranean fears and horrors.

There are two other passages that I feel I must quote. In October 1967:

> How a family can suffer and aggravate each other from close and continuous contact. More especially when they are like G. and won't leave me alone when I am obviously unsympathetic. He has to keep proving yet again that I'm in a difficult (for him) mood and make feeble attempts to get me out of it. Separation is to me the obvious necessity at such a time. . . . Sometimes I think I choose country obscurity because here there is no compelling measuring up to other people. . . . I think my present restlessness may at last overcome my fears. I long for this to happen, at times I will it most fervently. If they could be vanquished I veritably believe I could now make a living life for myself – which is hard, nay impossible, when you cannot trust yourself away from your own base.

A final extract must be quoted (this in 1965):

> I feel I want to write down for record the great joy my children are to me. They are wonderful in existing. I who have never felt a part of anyone and they were a part of me. I can never forget the first day of their arrival, the freshness of the new born life that bursts forth. And every day ever since I have gloried in their sweetness, their beauty and their love.

All these extracts fill me with a terrible pain at recognising my inadequacy. If only I could have the time again and really make her feel a part of me.

A turning point in our marriage came quite early in the 1980s. We were all having dinner on the picnic table outside the garden door on a very hot night and the children had been talking about the parents of one of their friends who were going through a messy divorce. I said, 'Thank God we are happily married.' To my amazement Daphne exploded: 'How can you be so complacent?' Only after that did I begin to understand the inner insecurity. When we first came to Suffolk we had been invited to lunches with new neighbours and every time when the morning came she would announce that she was not well enough to go. You can't indefinitely have social relations with neighbours on that sort of basis. So our social life revolved around the children and friends of theirs, but no real strangers. She was at her most secure with me and the children. I discovered that my irritation was quite misplaced. These were panic attacks, and she was said to be suffering from a mild agoraphobia. Even that was pretty well hidden; she had no problem with going shopping or with attending school functions, such as the Fourth of June or Founder's Day. Our local doctor had put her on to a regular dosage of Valium (at that time I had no idea of the dangers of addiction to Valium).

On her own she had got into correspondence with the Phobic Society and was, on their advice, using deep breathing relaxation techniques and had a cassette tape with a man speaking soothing words to help her get to sleep. We began to work together. We would lie on the floor together doing yoga deep breathing exercises, listening to instructions from an Australian woman. In 1984, very bravely, she gave up Valium overnight; she did not seem to suffer from the often reported withdrawal symptoms. Slowly we began to restore our marriage. In her last years we became very close. I will talk about that again in chronological sequence.

There, I have got that off my chest. I so deeply regret my lack of imagination. But I know that she is waiting for me in the next world, and that we shall meet again when God decides that is time for me to go. She, of course, would have hated to have all this revealed. But I feel I should like her family and those who loved her to recognise how brave she was to keep this all to herself and to lead an almost normal life.

I return now to the chronological sequence and to 1 July 1950. After the wedding reception we went to the BEA Kensington Air Station where we checked in to our flight to Paris and went by coach to Northolt Airport, which had by then become London's principal airport, replacing Croydon. We spent the first night in a hotel in Paris. I am usually so bad on names, but I remember it was called Le Louvois. On the Sunday night we set off by night train to the Rousillon in the foothills of the Pyrenees. We spent our honeymoon at Collioure, but since there was no station there, we had to go on to the last station before Spain, Port Vendres. It was extremely hot with the temperature over 100 degrees Fahrenheit. From Port Vendres we took a taxi. A young doctor friend of Daphne's had not only recommended Collioure, but also Madame Torrent who ran a café restaurant facing the inner harbour and who let us a spacious furnished room in a side street; we had all our meals in her restaurant. The weather was perfect and we always ate out of doors – delicious tomato salads, where I first came to know the marmande tomato. There was one feature of Collioure that I did not appreciate and that was the sea urchins; I seemed to be constantly treading on them and getting those awful spikes in my feet. Collioure was known then – and still is – for its anchovy fleet. Collioure is right at the final point at which the Pyrenees reach the sea. There is a very sharp descent to the town and the harbour.

Fifty-three years later, in February 2003, I stopped at Collioure driving back to Perpignan airport from Gerona in Spain and had a delicious lunch there; not in Madame Torrent's restaurant, which had been taken over by a Greek family. Astonishingly Collioure must be, perhaps, the only Mediterranean village still almost unspoilt. It would still be a lovely place to spend a holiday.

We took a coach trip up into Andorra and spent a night there. For the French its main attraction was already duty free goods but the small country was still very unspoilt and rural. When we next visited Andorra in 1978 it was just one vast shopping mall. On our trip the French were, I am afraid, disappointed; the French Customs were very strict and were proposing to confiscate very many bottles. But the angry Frenchmen were not having any of that – they spent some time smashing bottles on the rocks!

When we got back to England we returned to a flat we had rented in Tregunter Road – for about £5 a week, I think. It was a so-called basement flat but the front faced on to the garden and was very light. The house was owned by Josef Josten, a Czech who had been a private secretary to Jan Masaryk and had become a refugee when the Communists took over. He edited a Czech newspaper for émigrés. We were to be at Tregunter Road for just over two years. It is strange to think that those houses now sell for over £1 million.

To return now to the Bank. I was moved at the end of May to the Drawing Office, the main practical banking office, so called because it was where money was 'withdrawn'. The work was desperately dull, but I persevered. All entries in the ledgers were made in ink with scratching pens dipped into inkwells. No deletions were permitted so there had to be no errors, which for someone as untidy as me was impossible. I was soon shown by the old hands how to scratch out the offending ink with a sharp penknife. Some of the pages had such thin patches that if the book was held up to the light you could see the light shining through. The senior people knew perfectly well what we were doing but turned a blind eye; after all they had done it too when they were juniors.

After returning from our honeymoon I was moved to the Chief Cashier's Office (the CCO). This was the office looked on as an essential step in the career of any aspiring clerk. The office did all the 'devilling' for the Chief Cashier himself and for his Deputies, drafting the letters they had to sign (usually following a strict precedent – original ideas were not looked on with favour). There was also some slightly higher level banking to be done. Knowing how important this office was, I deliberately dressed up for my first day in my best suit and wearing Daphne's *cent pour cent soie* bow tie. In the course of the morning I was called in to see the Deputy Chief Clerk, a very pompous creature by the name of John Waddell-Dudley, who worked in a 'case' with the Chief Clerk.

'We have high standards of dress in this office, de Moubray,' he said.

I could not for the life of me think what he was on about; I checked that my fly buttons were done up.

'Bow tie,' he said.

To this I replied, 'It had never occurred to me that what was *de rigueur* in the City in 1910 should no longer be acceptable in the Bank of England in 1950: I wore it to honour the office!'

Another big change from the Treasury; I never again wore a bow tie in the Bank.

A former colleague, David Green, recently sent me this e-mail: 'During one of my training runs in CCO I found myself on the Counter Post. The duties included reporting to the Chief Clerk on late signs, absentees, overtime, etc. and amongst the dusty drawers of my desk I came across a defunct record book in which latecomers were required to explain their lateness. Amongst the usual excuses one entry stood out. It read "becalmed at sea" and initialled G de M. It made me laugh at the time and still amuses me now and I can only guess at the reaction of the Chief Clerk of the day! Were you reprimanded for not paying enough attention to the weather forecast?'

The Chief Cashier of the time was a rather unpleasant and authoritarian man by the name of Percy Beale who could make or break a man's career in the blinking of an eye. This happened whilst I was in his office. Every Friday there was a strange ritual of the Treasury Bill tender. Accepting Houses, or indeed anyone with £5000 cash in hand, could apply for Treasury bills; if one bid £5000 for a £5000 bill one was obviously going to get no interest when the bill was paid off 91 days later. So tenders were invited with the highest bidders receiving their application in full. Tenders had to be received at the Chief Cashier's Office no later than 1 p.m. on a Friday. The Chief Clerk, in his case, would ring the recorded time number on the telephone and when it said, 'At the third pip it will be one o'clock precisely', he would wave his hand to a clerk standing at the door of his case; this clerk in turn would wave to another clerk standing at the office door who would then with a flourish close the door and lock it. On this occasion, however, a messenger from Hambros Bank had still not reached the door when it was locked. So Hambros were denied any bills in that week's tender. But the Chairman of Hambros, Sir Charles Hambro, was the senior non-executive Director of the Bank of England and immediately rang Percy Beale in a fury. Beale not only caved in and allowed their application to be accepted, but sacked the clerk on the door from his office instanter. The poor man had until then had a promising career. Now he was finished. But in a sense, so was Beale. I discovered many years later from a former colleague, Peter Maugham, that the Governor and Deputy Governor, by then Cameron Cobbold and Humphrey Mynors, so disliked Beale that they made sure that he never got onto The Court (the Bank's Board of Directors) like his predecessor Sir Kenneth Peppiatt, and banished him; I seem to remember that he was sent to India to perform some senior function with the Reserve Bank of India.

A number of amusing incidents happened at the Counter to which the public were admitted. On one occasion a man asked to see the Governor and was told that that was not possible. At that moment one of the clerks in the office, Rupert Mahaffy, very tall and distinguished looking, wearing what looked like a morning coat walked across the back of the office. 'If I can't see the Governor, I'll see him,' said the man at the counter! I once went to the counter when an extraordinary looking woman with an ashen face appeared.

'I have come,' she said, 'to collect a million pounds which King Leopold of the Belgians has deposited here for me.'

'Yes madam,' I replied, 'I'll make enquiries, may I have your name.'

'Mata Hari,' she replied!

I went back to my desk, looked at a few papers and returned to the counter to tell her that there was no record of any such deposit and suggested that she should go and see the Belgian Embassy.

In September I moved on to the the Securities Control Office, which I had visited the year before with Monsieur Cools. The work was deadly dull, processing exchange control applications. But the Principal, MacNamee, did a double take when he first saw me! A probationary clerk was the lowest of the low and yet here was one to whom he had served tea in a silver teapot only a few months before. The only other thing I remember about the SCO was a man, presumably a senior clerk, who sat at a desk by himself facing a group of tables with clerks beavering away at exchange control applications. He had a massive bull neck and every day he would go to lunch at midday; when he returned his face would be almost literally purple and he would sit there comatose until 4 o'clock, when he would rise laboriously to his feet, put on his coat and go home; at least, I hope so – I discovered in later years that many commuters went to pubs before catching their trains or went to pubs when they reached their home station, and some also spent the entire train journey drinking in the bar.

In the normal course of events, as a new graduate entrant, I would have spent several more months in a variety of exchange control offices. But as the result of a tragic accident, I was moved to the Overseas & Foreign Office (O&F) in November. A member of Group II of that office and his wife had been killed in an air crash at Le Bourget, so there was a vacancy which I was to fill. It was perhaps surprising that the Bank should have fitted such a round peg to such a round hole. Group II was the group dealing with France, Benelux and Italy and had been my opposite numbers in the Treasury. Somehow I would have expected the Bank to put me on to something quite unfamiliar in the process of getting me to 'unlearn' the experience of the Treasury. Group II sat at a table on the third floor of the Bank overlooking the Garden Court facing east. On the other side of the table was Group IIb who dealt with Scandinavia. My Group Leader was Lindsay Ryan, whom of course I already knew. I checked whether I was now expected to call him 'sir'; but no, I could continue to call him Lindsay. The Deputy Group Leader was P.F. Stephens (I never knew his Christian name). As the junior I sat at the foot of the table. There was one other member, but I am not quite sure who it was; it may have been Kirbyshire, who later became the Bank's Adviser concerned with relations with the Federal Reserve System in the USA or it may have been Peter Harvey, whose father was at that time Ambassador to France. Peter succeeded to his father's title as Lord Harvey. He was clearly thought to be a man of promise. He went to Washington as the Technical Assistant to the British Executive Director of the IMF, but later left the Bank.

The Group's responsibility was to keep the Assistant (of administrative rank), Philip Hogg, abreast of all financial and economic developments in our countries. The junior's task every morning was to go through the relevant foreign press, cutting out pieces of interest and mounting them in the Press Cutting folder. The main papers were, for France, what we called 'Agefi', i.e. the Agence Financière et Economique, printed on pink paper like the *Financial Times*, *Il Sole* from Italy, also on pink paper. I can't at this distance remember the Dutch and Belgian papers – the Belgian one may have been *Le Moniteur Belge*. I was to be on Group II until May 1953.

One piece of work I remember doing was a fairly comprehensive study of the French nationalised industries. Not surprisingly, for a budding 'hedgehog', I concluded that they were hopelessly inefficient and that the only remedy was denationalisation! Some hope; here we are over fifty years on and the French public sector remains much as it was then. I gradually made my way up the Group. The hierarchy in the Bank was stifling; it was easier for me, having already established good relations with Hogg and Ryan. I remember once picking up the phone and hearing a voice say, 'Come in'; I had to guess who it was and it was Maurice Parsons, then I think a Deputy Chief Cashier in charge of the O&F. I knocked at the door and was told to come in. He then kept me standing at the door for at least two minutes whilst he went on reading a letter. When I was finally motioned towards his desk I saw that he had been holding the letter upside down! He had just been putting me in my place. But I may have been wrong; Maurice Parsons when Deputy Governor in the 1960s actually developed Alzheimer's and had to resign; perhaps the upside down paper merely meant that for a moment he did not know where he was or what he was supposed to be doing. On another occasion a voice on the phone said, 'What is the Banque de France's gold reserve?' I said that I was not at liberty to give that figure to just anybody who rang. A furious voice said, 'It's Watson.' Guy Watson was the Assistant Chief with whom I was in later years to work quite closely.

I wasn't at all sure that I wanted to stay in the Bank and I replied to an advertisement for applicants for a post with NATO in Paris (NATO had not yet moved to Brussels). This must have been in the summer of 1951. NATO flew me to Paris for the day. I went from Le Bourget to the NATO offices for an interview in the morning. I feel pretty sure that I would have been offered a job, but it did not appeal to me. I did not like the idea of no career structure; promotions came about by internal advertising of vacancies, and if you thought you were up to it you applied. But I enjoyed my day out. I had lunch at Fouquets in the Champs Elysées, sitting at a table outside in the sun. It seemed strange next day in the Bank that I should have been in Paris the day before; nowadays people fly to New York and back on the same day and think nothing of it.

By the autumn of 1952 I had myself become Group Leader. I remember a charming man under me called Michael Ramsay who, although a graduate, was quite unable to make up his mind for himself; he was trying to do or say what he expected the Bank to want. We were once asked to brief our superiors on points which should be raised at the next meeting of the Anglo-French Economic Committee; Michael just couldn't cope. He did not stay in the Bank very long and in fact went off to NATO as a translator. His mother was French. But before he went he taught me how to cook a real French omelette; his mother's flat cannot have been very far from the Bank because we once went there at lunch time and he made an omelette, *baveuse* as it should be.

Another friend in the Bank was Michael Dealtry. We often used to go up onto the roof of the Bank (almost certainly not permitted) after lunch and sit in the sun. We had to put down newspapers to sit on to avoid being covered in soot. The Clean Air Act was still five or six years off. I took some photographs from the roof of the bank in April 1952, looking in all directions. There was not a building taller than St. Paul's and still lots of blank spaces of bomb damage. Michael went off to the Bank for International Settlements (the BIS at Basle in Switzerland) at some time in the early 50s and spent the rest of his life there. I saw him whenever business took me there, which was not that often, except for a brief period in the mid 60s. I suspect he got the job because he was Otto Niemeyer's nephew and Niemeyer, although no longer a Director of the Bank of England, had an office in the Bank and was Chairman of the BIS.

I did two or three trips abroad for the Bank in the course of my years on Group II. The first was very early on, about February 1951. It had been decided that the Principal of the Issue Office should go to Paris and see how the Banque de France managed to cope with such a large volume of bank notes. But he spoke no French and I was appointed his interpreter. In order to do my part I had to learn something about the note issue. I spent two weeks with the three Principal and Senior Clerks in the Issue Office seeing what was done and learning the terms of art. I had always thought of the word 'garbled' as meaning all jumbled up; but in the Issue Office 'garbling' was the process of sorting notes, discarding those that were not fit to be reissued. I learned that the French word for it was *triage*.

Late one afternoon the Principal and I left Victoria station on the Golden Arrow for Paris and were both seen off by our wives. A sorry couple we were; he had a bad back and I had an upset tummy! We must have spent two or three days at the Banque de France. Whether the Issue Office learnt anything of value from the visit I don't know. In spite of us both suffering we went one evening to a night club in the Place Pigalle! I thought the old man would feel cheated unless he saw some of the naughty Parisian night life; he no doubt felt much the same about me. It was a strip club and we got landed with a couple of women who sat at our table and ordered drinks for us (alcoholic) and soft for them (but charged as if they were alcohol). When it came to time to settle the bill we did not have enough francs, so we were compelled to flog a Bank of England £5 note, which we both knew was unlawful under the Exchange Control Act. I wish I could remember my companion's name. He made a very generous gesture; when I returned to my desk in the O&F, I found an envelope addressed to me in which he had enclosed a crisp white £5 note!

My next trip abroad was as 'bag carrier' on one of the monthly Basle trips. Every month there was a meeting at the BIS of the Governors of the member Central Banks and it was usual for the Governor of the Bank of England to attend with a small delegation and a promising junior would also go to carry their bags, pay tips and generally make himself useful. The Governor used to go by plane I think, but Sir Otto insisted on going by train and would take with him one or two junior members of the delegation and the bag carrier. I had been told by Rupert Mahaffy, who had previously been on one of these trips, that when abroad members of the Bank had to give an impression of affluence and put in a respectably high expense account – this was good for the standing of Sterling! Rupert had somehow managed to feel the need to buy two shirts in Basle and had put these on his expense account! He left the Bank before long and lived a more affluent life with a Merchant Bank.

The journey to Basle was a hallowed ritual. We always crossed the North Sea from Harwich to the Hook of Holland by sea – a night journey with cabins booked for all of us. We went from the Bank to Liverpool Street Station where we were met by the Station Master, wearing his bowler hat, who then escorted us to our seats. On this occasion for some reason the party was very depleted; the Governor did not attend and his place was taken by Sir George Bolton, then one of the two Overseas Executive Directors. From The Hook we went by train through Germany up the valley of the Rhine to Basle. We all had to stay at the same hotel, the Schweitzerhof, where Sir Otto had stayed for innumerable years.

On the first evening there was another ritual; all the Bank members, without any outsiders, dined together at a restaurant called the Schlussel, where it was traditional to have Dover sole. This was intended to give the Governor the opportunity to meet some junior members of his staff on an informal basis. But on this occasion there were only three of us. It was a strange dinner; Bolton and Niemeyer spent the whole time running Cobbold down and telling nasty gossip about him. I suppose they must both at one time have hoped themselves to be Governor. At the end of the meal they turned to me and told me to forget everything they had said. As it happens, I have.

The bag carrier did not attend any formal meetings, but there were cocktail parties where one met staff of the BIS and other central bankers. The most important member of the BIS staff one met was Per Jacobsson, a Swede who was the Bank's Economic Adviser and responsible for producing each year the BIS Annual Report, which was widely seen as the most authoritative independent assessment of the European economies. I met him only briefly. Later he was to play an important part in my life.

This particular Basle weekend was different in one other respect; because he had to be back in London early, Niemeyer consented to fly. We took the train to Zurich and checked in for the BEA flight to Northolt. Zurich airport then, believe it or not, was just a collection of huts on a grass field – no tarmac. The check-in girl had to find our names on a typed manifest – no computers, of course, and she seemed to have great trouble in finding them. Our names were eventually found: Bolton had been shown as 'Bocton', I appeared as 'Dembry' and the third member of the party as 'Sirottoniemeyer'! As we walked across the grass to the plane, Niemeyer turned to me and said, 'What a fuss – perfectly good English names!'

My second Basle trip must have been in 1952. This time the Governor did attend, but the dinner at the Schlussel was cancelled; there was some big dinner that the Governor and Niemeyer had to attend. I had managed to avoid being booked into the Schweitzerhof and had installed myself in the much nicer Euler Hotel. I sat down to dinner by myself that evening at a table which overlooked an area in which a large table had been set, but which was as yet unoccupied. Mindful of Rupert Mahaffy's advice, I ordered a bottle of Pontet-Canet 1923! So I was sitting there quietly enjoying my wine and reading a paperback Simenon to improve my French, when a number of elderly gentlemen filed in to the area below to take their seats. Horrors! – they were the Governors of the European central banks, including my Governor and Otto Niemeyer. I hastily turned the bottle of Pontet-Canet around so that even if they were very sharp eyed they would not see what vintage it was, called for my bill and retreated as soon as possible.

My career seemed to be going reasonably well. By September 1952 I had myself become Group Leader in place of Lindsay Ryan. We had all been told that the shortest time any graduate had taken to become a Senior Clerk was three and a half years; so I was satisfied to be by now a Third Class Clerk. Daphne and I decided (or rather I should have said, Daphne decided, because throughout our married life Daphne took all the important domestic decisions) that it was time to move out of a rented flat and to buy a house. My parents, very generously, gave us £2000 (which was a great deal of money in 1952) and I applied for a Bank of England Housing Loan of £3000 (at a negligible subsidised rate of interest). We had our eyes on a house for £5000. The Senior Clerk on the Housing Loan Section, Denis Erridge, suggested that I was aiming a little high for a man of my standing and made the classic remark, 'de Moubray, the Governors may not think that a 3rd Class Clerk should live in Chelsea!' But he obviously had some information to indicate that I was a rising star and approved the loan, which must have been for about eight times my annual salary.

So in September 1952 we moved in to our very own house, 20 Pond Place, lying between the Fulham Road and the King's Road. It was tiny and the front door opened straight on to the pavement. Downstairs we had a small living room, at one end of which we put a dining table. There was a small kitchen and upstairs two bedrooms, one a double room and the other a single, and a bathroom. When we arrived we only had one small armchair, Daphne's old wooden school trunk, which I sat on and a tea trolley to eat off. Daphne's father had given us as a wedding present a Heal's double bed, which we did not put into the flat at Tregunter Road. So we arranged for Heal's to deliver it. The staircase was so small that they could not get it upstairs so they took it away, cut it into two halves, delivered it back to us and assembled it in the bedroom. We kept that bed for over thirty years. Daphne was very keen on antiques and we slowly furnished ourselves, relying heavily on Miller's Antiques in the King's Road (I wonder if it is still there). The small bow chest which stands outside my bedroom here at Buxlow cost all of £11! But there were other things to buy; we bought a floor polisher on a handle (not electric) and I remember as I walked down the Fulham Road with it over my shoulder some young man said loudly, 'He looks married!'

We entertained a little bit. I remember having two Americans who were renting the house next door in to dinner and how amused he was to be allowed to wear my bowler hat. Anticipating Humphrey Mynors' advice to Eddie Playfair, I had already shown willingness to conform by buying a bowler hat and a rolled umbrella. I also remember having Peter Harvey to dinner and that the best we could do was tinned Danish kidneys in a sauce! Another memory of that house is sitting with Daphne at the gate-legged table helping her with her Cabinet Office work; sometimes on the pre-budget White Paper and once projecting the number of miners there would be at the coal face in five years time. We were of course completely wrong, having relied wholly on extrapolation, taking no account of changing trends. I find fifty years on that sort of abuse of statistics is frequently used by journalists, and of course politicians. Daphne bought a chocolate brown miniature poodle which we called Louis. I cannot quite imagine how she managed it with work; perhaps that was only after she had given up working. I know she used to take Louis to Kensington Gardens on the 49 bus. We chose a poodle because of their beautiful gait. Louis was quite mad; he once jumped out of the first floor window at Daphne's parents' house; they had by then moved from Coulsdon to West Chiltington in Sussex (which was not then divided into East and West).

At this point I suddenly remember that we went on holiday with the Hazells in the summer of 1952. We went in his Austin Cambridge, driving through France down to the Riviera and into Italy as far as La Spezia and then back up through the Simplon Pass to the Swiss Alps. I had not yet realised how bad Daphne's relationship with her mother was, nor indeed quite how strained her parents' relationship was. Nevertheless, we had a nice holiday. The Riviera in those days was quite unspoiled. I remember being particularly attracted by Le Lavendou; when Daphne and I drove through there thirty-five years later it was nothing more than a glorified caravan site. I also remember with pleasure a very nice hotel at Nervi, just to the east of Genoa; again completely spoiled when we next passed there thirty-two years later. I got some hint of the Hazell relationship at Domodossola, just before the Simplon Pass. Daphne's mother stayed in the car when we went for a little walk; when we came back her father sat down in the driving seat and immediately leaped out again; she had spilt a tin of sticky peaches onto the seat; 'The woman's mad!' he said.

Great changes took place in 1953. My first story is again about the Bank. All Bank salaries were reviewed once a year with all promotions and advancements up a scale being announced in February and taking effect from 1 March. The Annual Review was a nightmare for all concerned. All those to be promoted or advanced were bidden to the Establishments Department to see a senior official who would reveal the good news, expecting a grateful acknowledgement. When I walked in to see somebody called Jacques I had no idea what to expect. I thought I would get some significant recognition of the fact that within two years of joining O&F I had become Group Leader. I was astonished to be congratulated on being given an increase in salary of £10 a year. I must have shown my displeasure. Jacques asked me if I was not pleased. I said, 'If you want an honest answer, I think it is bloody mean.' He was outraged; he expected me to realise that the whole process of doing the Annual Review took months and that when I had been considered, I had not yet become Group Leader. I had no doubt that he would devise some means of punishing me for my insubordination – indeed the Bank did; the following year I got nothing at all! But the punishment might have been much worse; at this moment I said to him that in the event it didn't matter very much as I was off to America in the summer. 'How do you know that?' he said, sharply. I said that Sharman Wright, the Assistant on Scandinavia, had told me. I suspect that if I had not already known about it, my posting might well have been cancelled.

CHAPTER 10

Washington DC 1953–54

I WAS BEING POSTED TO WASHINGTON DC, technically as a member of the UKTSD (UK Treasury and Supply Delegation) but also as Technical Assistant to the UK Executive Director of the IMF, Sir Edmund Hall-Patch. This was obviously considered an appointment for a high flyer, although it didn't always work out that way. It certainly worked for the first one appointed, Jasper Hollom in about 1948, because he rose to be Deputy Governor. The second, Peter Rackham, fizzled out; he ended up as a translator, having learned Mandarin; I suppose he was the Bank's expert on China, but that did not seem to count for very much; he remained in a lowly rank. The third appointment went to Peter Harvey, whom I have already mentioned, who left the Bank. Then came my predecessor, Tony Rudd. He was very able but found the Bank stifling and left soon after returning from Washington to work for Richard Fry, the financial columnist on the *Financial Times*. He later set up as a stockbroker in a firm called Rowe Rudd and also became the financial columnist for the *Spectator* for some years. I saw quite a bit of him in the 1960s but lost touch with him when he had to give up as a stockbroker – he was losing his sight.

I cannot for the life of me remember whether Daphne gave up work when we heard of the Washington appointment or whether she had stopped earlier. I was of the generation that took it for granted that when the husband received an overseas appointment the wife went too. It clearly would have been possible for her to stay on in London; the appointment was for only eighteen months. But when you are in love, you don't want to be parted and it wasn't possible to make brief visits to America during the appointment; hardly anybody flew the Atlantic in those days and anyway we could not have afforded it. So Daphne came too. We went to Jersey for Easter and left Louis there; my parents had kindly agreed to look after him for us.

We let 20 Pond Place to some Americans and set sail for New York on the *Queen Elizabeth* in June. In spite of my junior rank we were permitted to travel Cabin Class (the forerunner of Business Class on aeroplanes now). It was very comfortable and we had access to the main dining saloon, where every meal was of five courses, and to the main saloon in the evenings where there was dancing (black tie, of course) and 'horse racing' – large wooden models of horses manipulated across a track by stewards in accordance with the throw of dice with some kind of primitive betting. During the day one would walk around the Promenade Deck or sit there on long wooden chaises longues, with stewards bringing us mugs of beef tea.

120

After five days we arrived in New York. I have a photograph of Daphne on deck in New York harbour ready to go ashore, wearing a splendid beret-like hat which she had bought from Harrods for the phenomenally high price of 6 guineas! We landed on the Queen's Coronation Day. It was a beautiful day in New York and the taxi driver who drove us to our hotel said: 'Gee, I'm glad your Queen has such a lovely day for her coronation.' In London, of course, it was pouring with rain! We went to the Westbury on 5th Avenue, which was then brand new and apparently the place to be. Its coffee shop (an entirely unfamiliar concept to us) was called The Polo Bar! We had been met at the dockside by the Federal Bank of New York's 'welcomer', John Walsh by name. He was an anglophile and tried to speak in a clipped English accent and dropped names in every sentence – Lady Hermione (Cobbold) featured a lot! I don't think he knew much about banking.

The senior Bank of England person in America, Leslie Crick, was Alternate UK Executive Director of the Fund (his Bank rank being an Acting Adviser). Crick was a typical Bank man, who did not think much of these new graduate entrants and who considered 3rd Class clerks very lowly creatures indeed. But he and his wife were perfectly civil when they too met us in New York. We were invited to the house in the suburbs of the Fed's foreign exchange expert – a charming man, Tommy Roche (the predecessor of the better known Charlie Coombs) for the evening for what turned out to be a TV supper; the American networks had managed to arrange for a US military plane to fly tapes of the coronation across the Atlantic in time to show them on evening television. The military planes must have been jets which were not yet used on commercial services, although it would not be long before the British Comet took to the skies. It was 1959 before the American airlines put jets into service with the Boeing 707. We all marvelled at the wonders of modern technology!

Next day we went to Washington, by train from the Pennsylvania Station. The train may well have been the Chattanooga Choochoo, because I am sure that it continued south after Washington, and I think we may well have boarded 'on track 22'. We were very impressed with the train; we travelled in a Club Car with swivel seats that could face the windows or the aisle. The stewards were black, as in all the 1930s movies. We were met at Union Station by Tony and Ethne Rudd and taken to our hotel, the Mayflower, which was then the principal hotel in Washington – Sheratons and Hiltons did not as yet exist. On one of our first mornings we saw a very distinguished guest walk through the Lobby on his way out for a morning walk, former President Harry Truman. Eisenhower had in fact only been inaugurated five months earlier.

Tony Rudd handed over to me and we agreed to take on from the Rudds the apartment they were renting at 4201 Massachusetts Avenue. NW. This was a modern apartment block, but no higher than about six floors in the north-west suburb of Washington D.C. We were in the front of the building looking out over Mass. Ave. to woodland opposite, which adjoined the Irish Embassy. Just down the road from us was the then only mosque in Washington, and near it a magnificent pawlonia tree, which I think started me on my lifelong love of trees. The pawlonia has large leaves like a catalpa and, in the spring, great spikes of purple flowers. I remember an equally lovely pawlonia near Charlottesville in Virginia. The Bank had shown remarkably little interest in the living conditions of the junior. I am told that Hollom and Rackham both rented basement hovels. Peter Harvey had begun to improve things, and the Rudds had done even more; but the flat was very sparsely furnished with quite inadequate furniture and cutlery and it was a bit much to expect us on our salary to furnish a flat. Crick was quite unresponsive; but I found the answer. Soon after we arrived, Guy Watson, the boss from back home, came for a visit and I had the inspiration to invite him to dinner with us in our apartment. He was so taken aback at how little we had that he said: 'Give me a list of what you need and I will authorise the expenditure.' We ended up with a list for expenses of about $300.

Just across the hall from us lived Ray Stevens, an American, a bachelor, whose work was to do with oceanography. He was a wonderful neighbour and helped us settle in. With his help I bought a car (the first car we had ever had). Together we visited used car lots armed with *Which* magazine's 'how to buy a car' supplement which we took care to let the salesmen see! I remember wondering whether to make an offer for a blue Ford, when Ray said to the salesman, 'That's no good; it looks as if a bunch of jigs have been riding around in it'; 'jigs', I learned was a slang term for negroes.

Washington was still very much a Southern town. Segregation on the buses and street cars had only just been abolished – in 1952. Anyway, I ended up buying a lovely 1950 Dodge in metallic bronze, which we called Caramella. 1950 was the first year in which American cars had wraparound windscreens. It also had a strange kind of gear mechanism; although there was a clutch pedal for changing gear, the car did not stall at traffic lights if you did not put your foot on the pedal.

Daphne took a job in the Fund library, which she found absolutely fascinating; all her fellow workers were black and she became very friendly with them. Elizabeth was in charge and twenty-five years later, when I again visited Washington, I called in to see her; she was so pleased to hear again from Daphne.

In my work I was in a strange position; the top man was Hall–Patch and he treated me exactly as the senior people in the Treasury would have done, as a fellow member of the club. But Crick expected me unquestioningly to do his bidding. Back in England I had got used to the Bank practice of juniors doing 'green drafts' – literally on green paper – which you then put up for approval. Crick infuriated me; as soon as I put a green draft before him he had his pencil out and started changing everything before even reading the document through. I did as much as I could to bypass him and go direct to Hall-Patch. Sir Edmund was a charming bachelor with endless gongs, GCMG and I know not what. But neither of my bosses was at all keen on going home at a reasonable hour, Crick because he felt he had to show how hard he was working, and Sir Edmund because he was not yet ready to settle down to his bottle of claret. Crick expected me to stay until he went; but when I thought it was time to go I would go in to Hall-Patch and say, 'If there is nothing more you want this evening, Sir Edmund, I think I will go home.' 'Of course, my dear, off you go,' and there was nothing Crick could do about it. Hall-Patch called everybody 'my dear'.

Those were the days when communications with London were far from easy; you had to book transatlantic telephone calls in advance and the quality of sound was often appalling. There were no telexes yet, just cables. But everything that Hall-Patch wanted to do in the Fund had to be cleared with the Treasury so he put into effect a technique which I am sure he had perfected over the years. We would draft a cable to the Treasury, the last paragraph of which was always: 'If I do not hear to the contrary within 24 hours, this is the line I shall take.' Of course he knew that nobody in the Treasury would be brave enough to take a decision on his own and would have to summon a meeting, and there was no chance whatever of receiving a contrary instruction within 24 hours. I thoroughly enjoyed working with him, and he was absolutely charming to Daphne when we met at cocktail parties, of which there seemed to be a great many.

Crick and his wife began to see that 3rd Class clerks were human and invited us to various things. They once invited us out on a trip down the Blue Ridge Parkway in Virginia, the scenic road which went along the crest of the Appalachian Mountains, with preserved log cabins and little eating places. Crick was a dedicated butterfly collector and always went on these trips with his net. Was it I who was naughty, or was it Daphne? At any rate one of us said, 'Look at that black butterfly!' Crick was out of the car in an instant and spent the next few minutes vainly chasing a non-existent butterfly!

His butterfly collection features in another story. John Stevens of the Bank of England, later to be Deputy Chairman of Morgan Grenfell, had just been appointed Director of the European Department of the IMF. Crick and his wife invited Stevens and Daphne and me to dinner at his house. Stevens, mischievously I fear, expressed interest in Crick's butterflies. They were all beautifully mounted in glass cases. Stevens said of a turquoise butterfly, 'That's a lovely one', and Crick opened the lid to show it more closely. At that point Stevens pursed his lips and blew at the case – disaster – blue wings flew off on to the floor. If Stevens had not been so senior I imagine Crick would have exploded or even struck him. With very poor grace Stevens apologised. It's easy to see that I did not really take to Stevens. It used to sicken me in the evenings at the end of work when he would always manage to appear in the lobby just as Ivar Rooth, Chairman and

Managing Director of the Fund, was leaving and cadge a lift home with him in the Cadillac. Max Stamp who had preceded him was a much more amiable character. I much admired the blue and white seersucker suit he wore in the summer and bought myself an almost identical jacket from Hacketts in the mid 80s.

We had quite a full social life. Ray Stevens had a conviction that the best thing for a hangover was ice cream and drove us miles into Maryland to find what he considered the best ice cream parlour. Those were the days when the Howard-Johnson chain of restaurants made a point of advertising '36 flavours of ice cream'.

There was only one other Technical Assistant to an Executive Director and that was Alesandro Baca-Muñoz who worked for Paranagua, the Brazilian who was Director for Latin America. Alesandro was from Nicaragua, a country about which, at the time, I knew absolutely nothing, but he must in fact have been close to the ruling tyrannical Dictator of his country. Nevertheless we got on pretty well with him and his wife. They were obviously wealthy – she wore a splendid mink coat. We also made friends with the First Secretary at the New Zealand Embassy and his wife. We used to go out together. I remember one particular evening when we went dancing at a night club; the band was Louis Armstrong's. Imagine dancing with Satchmo playing his cornet!

We also had friends amongst the staff of The Federal Reserve Board, in particular Sam Katz and his wife, who lived in a Virginia suburb. He was a respected economist. We often went to their house for meals. Another couple with whom we became friendly were Ed Dale, the economic and financial columnist with the *New York Herald Tribune*, and his English wife, Todd. She was a Hastings from Norfolk. Ed introduced me to baseball; we used to go to the Washington Redskins' stadium to watch games. I became very enthusiastic and soon learned all the rituals, throwing your coins to the hot-dog seller and catching the hot dog when he threw it to you from a couple of rows away! And the 'seventh innings stretch'. Quite often on Saturdays I would settle down in front of the television to watch baseball with a can of cold Budweiser in my hand!

I suppose my closest friend was Brian Rose, a Cambridge graduate who had joined the Fund straight from University. He was in the European Department and about my age. His wife, Imogen, was a very erudite classicist and taught at one of the private schools. Brian spent the whole of his career in the Fund, ultimately becoming very senior. We used often to lunch together, but not in the Fund; we usually got sandwiches from a Greek on 17th Street; here for the first time I discovered that sandwiches could be moist and tasteful, unlike English sandwiches. The Greek stood at a counter taking orders and then with incredible speed sliced bread, spreading it with mayonnaise, some chopped iceberg lettuce and then tuna or bacon and tomato. I don't know why I spell this out in such detail; it is now commonplace and available in any English supermarket; but then it was a revelation. There was also a little restaurant on Pennsylvania Avenue, again with a Greek, where I particularly liked sweetbreads in a white wine sauce. There I go again – food!

I have to say that although my basic instincts were 'hedgehog', all our friends were of the left. All the Americans were Democrats; Republicans were beyond the pale. And yet Eisenhower's government was really very successful. During his term of office there was absolutely no inflation – and I mean 'no', not just two and a half per cent. I think it took me another ten years to grow out of the illusion that everything had to be changed and that there were better ways of doing things. To quote Patrick Hutber, the late journalist of the *Telegraph* – 'better is often worse'.

We returned the hospitality we received with a series of Madeira parties before lunch at weekends. We served Madeira wine and slices of madeira cake; but our American friends missed the subtlety of this; the Americans call Madeira cake 'pound cake' (a pound of flour, a pound of butter and a pound of sugar). I don't know whether I drank more in those days than I do now: possibly not, but it was hardly ever wine and mostly gin (dry martinis) and whisky and I certainly carried it a lot less successfully. Alka-Seltzer featured prominently on the bathroom shelf. I remember going to a very bibulous Oxford and Cambridge dinner in Washington; next morning I felt absolutely wretched with the bed heaving and was quite hurt to find Daphne standing at the foot of the bed laughing at me.

The Fund has never, I believe, been very effective. It was set up for the very same reason that I have mentioned – this belief that things could and should be done better. Fixed exchange rates, with countries requiring the approval of the Fund before devaluing, was supposed to prevent 'competitive devaluation'. I don't myself think that competitive devaluation really had been so much of a problem in the 1930s. And anyway as numerous countries, including the UK, were to discover in the next twenty years, devaluations don't work unless they are accompanied by strict monetary and fiscal policies which few governments favour. Devaluations set off price increases caused by the higher cost of imports and any favourable impact on exports is usually dissipated within eighteen months. The Fund was also set up by people with strong 'left' and 'fox-like' views, Harry Dexter White, the American and John Maynard Keynes, the Englishman. I say all this because in those years the Fund didn't do anything of note; strangely it could be said merely to have provided a forum in which the US Executive Director, Frank Southard jnr., lectured all the socialist countries urging them to adopt essentially conservative policies. I think there were only two European countries doing what he would have approved of: Belgium, and Italy under Einaudi; West Germany would join them before too long. Heaven knows now what I wrote green drafts about – certainly nothing of any importance.

The Fund had every year an Annual General Meeting, jointly with the International Bank for Reconstruction and Development (the IBRD), every other year in Washington and the other years somewhere abroad. In 1953 it was Washington's turn. The AGM was a great jamboree to which Ministers of Finance, Governors of Central Banks, scores of officials, the world's financial press and bankers of all sorts and descriptions came thronging, to make speeches, perhaps listen; but their main aim was to have fun and run up vast expense accounts. Mark you, the cost of the endless cocktail parties and receptions was not borne by those who came.

I had to greet the top Bank of England people at the Union Station; they had, I should say, travelled by sea across the Atlantic; those who attended the Annual meeting had to devote a month or so to the enterprise, often finding excuses to add a holiday or two to the serious proceedings. When I met Sir George and Lady Bolton and loaded their luggage into my car, Bolton wandered around the car questioningly, 'Is this your car?' He clearly hadn't expected a Third Class Clerk to have one! The 1953 Meeting was held in exceptionally hot conditions, the temperature almost every day was over 100°F, but of course the meeting halls were all air-conditioned. From the Bank there was also Maurice Parsons; Crick for some reason kept referring to him as the Pope. Crick was also very wary of Lady Bolton: 'When she has had one gin she is all right, but when she has had a few she is murder.' I didn't find her that bad; indeed she flirted with me. There was a very bibulous cruise on a large yacht down the Potomac; I danced with Lady May and at one point she remarked that she hadn't seen George recently and asked me to go see if he was all right. I'll say he was all right; I found him on the top deck clasping some young woman in a strapless white gown! I managed to indicate that Lady Bolton wanted to see him and he disengaged himself. Daphne and I also kept bumping into Sir Edmund outside receptions; he always seemed reluctant to go in and was much happier chatting outside.

When it was over, Daphne and I went off on a holiday. We took 'Caramella' and drove up as far as Quebec City and back. We stayed at motels, which in those days were available for about $10 a night. We drove right up through New York State, passing Saratoga and Lake Champlain, into Vermont and then into Canada. Daphne and I never liked big cities, so we avoided New York City and Montreal. Perhaps it would be truer to say that I found it almost impossible to find my way in large cities and found, even in those days, parking a nightmare. Daphne actually loved New York.

In Canada we took No. 1 Highway towards Montreal, which was then a dirt road corrugated by the wind – no tarmac. Somebody told us that it would be very uncomfortable if taken slowly; the secret was to drive at at least 50 m.p.h. This turned out to be wise advice. When we visited Quebec City it was still some years ahead of the 'Québec Libre' campaign, but it was immediately made clear to us that French was much more acceptable than English. We went past the Laval University when the students were streaming out; they could see that we were tourists and, hearing us speak, knew that we were probably English and by their glances made us feel like members of an alien occupying force. But we saw all the sights, including the Heights of Abraham overlooking the St. Lawrence River. To make amends, in the shops I made a point of speaking French.

We returned through New England, Vermont, New Hampshire and Massachusetts. The fall colours were at their very best; and the weather matched it in beauty. We visited Plymouth, where I bought a short sleeved shirt made by the 'Puritan Clothing Company' which I wore for years. We visited Newport, Rhode Island. We also ate a lot of lobster. I remember one restaurant where there were two middle aged ladies with napkins tied around their necks tucking in to lobster, eating with their hands. It must have been quite a sight still to be able to picture it fifty years later.

Sometime in 1954 Crick returned to London and was replaced by Jack Portsmore; he came with his wife and small children. John Stevens again made a bad impression; he and his wife Anne invited the Portsmore family to their house one weekend. The Portsmore children played with the Stevens children. Next week Stevens told me how funny it had been hearing the Portsmore children; when they played games racing each other they used to say 'Ready, steady, gow.' Did he really think I would be amused?

Life in Washington was very pleasant. The NW district of Washington was the wealthiest suburb with lots of 'lovely homes' – Americans always said 'homes' where we would have said 'houses'. We did our shopping in the Spring Valley shopping centre – not quite yet a supermarket, but the grocer was, as I remember, a self-service store – with extraordinary delicacies, including chocolate coated ants! For English specialities you had to go to Magruders in downtown Washington which had such things as bath olivers and Dundee marmalade. We take the method of payment very much for granted these days but then there were no credit cards, and you paid either in cash or by cheque. There were no bank cards and no personalised cheque books. In Washington reputable retailers trusted you; on every counter there was a book of blank cheques (or should I say checks?) and when you wanted to pay, you tore out a check, entered the name of your bank and wrote it; there was no question of your account number; if there was one, I certainly didn't know what it was. I don't think shops in England at that time were as trusting.

I used to have my hair cut at the barber's in the Roger Smith Hotel, which was just around the corner from the Fund, and which no longer exists. The barber was English, a former barber on the *Queen Mary*. He was moving from state to state avoiding alimony. When his ex-wife had just about completed the legal procedures to make him pay, he would move to another state and she would have to start all over again. He often used to say, of both of us, 'The trouble with us, sir, is that we have champagne tastes and beer pockets.' He was right about himself, and there was an element of truth in it about me; I have always wanted to live in nice houses which were a little too expensive.

I cannot remember whether we went to church regularly during our stay in Washington. There was a New Church and we went regularly on our next appointment, but I think we did not in 1953/4. But my father gave us an introduction to a New Church American couple in Bryn Athyn, Pennsylvania. Bryn Athyn is a suburb of Philadelphia and is the headquarters of one branch of the New Church. It was, and presumably still is, a wealthy community almost entirely New Church. The patrons of the church were the Pitcairn family, who had made their money from making glass. They had paid for a Gothic cathedral to be built exactly in the mediaeval manner; it was built by stone masons brought in from Italy. We went there for a weekend. We must have driven up on a Saturday morning. Before lunch we were offered, as was the custom in those days, a dry martini. But the drink was preceded by a little New Church ditty which we all sang. That evening we were invited to attend a wedding in the cathedral. It was a lavish affair; all the guests wore evening dress and went on to a dinner and dance afterwards.

We had two holidays in 1954. In April we went off for a week down the Blue Ridge Mountains in azalea and dogwood time. We went as far as North Carolina. For our summer holiday we rented a log cabin on a cliff overlooking the Atlantic Ocean on Cape Cod in Massachusetts. We spent a lot of the time on the beach but we also visited Provincetown on the tip of Cape Cod.

At work there came a change when Sir Edmund Hall-Patch retired. He was succeeded, only very briefly, by Sir Dennis Rickett, who was also Minister at the Embassy. We had an interesting experience together. There was a whole series of meetings of a Committee of the Board discussing whether Czechoslovakia should be expelled from the Fund. The case for expelling them was that they had been unwilling to give the economic and financial information that members were required to give. As Communists they treated all such information as Top Secret. When Czechoslovakia joined the Fund it was, of course, not yet Communist. In 1954 it was the only country in the Soviet Bloc which was a member. All the other countries were already Communist when the Fund was founded. But the Czechs were very keen to remain members of the Fund and had sent a high-powered delegation to argue the case for remaining members. Rickett and I sat side by side, with me briefing him on technical points. Portsmore must have been away, or perhaps the hearings took place in the interregnum between Crick and Portsmore. It was fascinating to hear a dedicated Communist well versed in legal questions arguing their case. The phrase 'on a point of order' was frequently used — a remarkable echo from the Army-McCarthy hearings which had just taken place in Washington where Senator McCarthy finally met his match in the lawyer from New England, Mr Welch. But returning to the Fund, the Czechs were eventually expelled. A Czech member of the Fund Staff, Jan Mladek, who was at that time the Fund's representative in Paris, defected and took American citizenship.

My tour of duty came to an end towards the end of September. I was to be succeeded by Derek Spiers from the Bank of England, whose career never really got going. But he was a perfectly nice fellow. We passed on to him our apartment and our car. It was already a tradition that the retiring Technical Assistant was allowed to make a tour of the States at the Bank's expense. We were no exception and around the end of September we set off on an extended tour, at every city calling on the local Federal Reserve Bank. We were in fact not to return to England until just before Christmas and I was not to be back in the Bank until the beginning of January.

Our first port of call was Cleveland, Ohio, where, whilst I called on banks, Daphne took the Greyhound tour of the city. Wives of members of the Federal Reserve banks were very generous in giving up time to Daphne. After all these years I have only a very hazy recollection of Cleveland. Our next stop was Chicago, where we stayed at the Palmer House Hotel, which was memorable for its breakfast counter – it must have been able to serve 100 people at the same time; and here I learned the ritual breakfast language as the girls behind the counter called the orders to the cooks behind – 'Fried egg – easy over,' meaning fried and then turned over briefly to set the yolk and 'BLT on,' which means bacon, lettuce and tomato on rye bread. I don't know why this so fascinated me, but I could have sat and watched for ages. The main features of Chicago that I remember were the waterfront on the Lake side and the 'Elevated' – that strange feature of a railway that runs above the street at first floor level. If you have ever seen that wonderful film *Twelve Angry Men* with Henry Fonda you will remember that an important piece of evidence related to what a woman with poor eyesight could have seen of the murder through the windows of a passing train on the 'Elevated'. The Federal Reserve Bank also took me on a tour of the United States Steel plant at Gary, Indiana, which was then the largest steel plant in the world.

We then flew to Kansas City, Missouri. There we were taken out to dinner to eat KC (Kansas City) steaks. When we had left England, meat rationing had still been in force and the steaks served to us with pride would have required a full week's ration. We were not yet accustomed to eating such large quantities of meat, and I regret to say that I didn't even think they were very good – tough and overdone! We then flew to Dallas, Texas, calling briefly at Oklahoma City on the way. The view from the plane of the vast expanse of the prairies was quite striking. In Dallas, we stayed at the Howard Baker Hotel and I had the odd experience, a few years ago, of seeing it being demolished on television; quite why they thought that would be interesting to a British audience I don't know. We landed there on Columbus Day, which was a public holiday, but we were met by a couple from the Federal Reserve Bank of Dallas. Wherever we went the Federal Reserve were very hospitable. That evening the couple took us to dinner at an ice show with a table right by the rink; every now and then we were sprayed by ice as the skaters stopped suddenly.

Noble Crawford, Sheriff of Gregg County, Texas appointing me a
Special Deputy Sheriff, October 1954

I spent one whole day doing a tour of the oil fields; it was quite a long drive across the hot plains and this was my first experience of an air-conditioned car; uncomfortable it was too. I sat in the back and there was a cold jet blowing on to my neck. I was accompanied by a man from the Fed but our host was a 'wild cat' oil man. 'Wild cats' bought parcels of land speculatively and were richly rewarded if they struck oil. He was an exuberant man, delighted to show off his wells. On those bare plains one saw endless derricks with the arms of the pumps monotonously going up and down. Our host introduced us to the local Sheriff, the Sheriff of Gregg County, Texas. At a ceremony, with the local press in attendance, I was appointed a Special Deputy Sheriff of Gregg County. I still have my certificate and a press photograph. The journalist, showing off his knowledge, said to me, 'So, you haven't brought the old lady.' I told him that I had, and that she was in Dallas! But he, of course, had been referring to the Old Lady of Threadneedle Street. From Dallas we went to San Antonio and visited the Alamo.

At this point we interrupted our tour of the States and flew off to Mexico for a two week holiday. We stayed first in Mexico City, which at that time had a population of about 1 million; I am told that today it is 18 million. I simply cannot imagine such a vast community. The City must by now have filled up the large plain, which I assume was in fact the crater of an extinct volcano, but at that time was still open countryside. From the balcony of our hotel, the Maria Christina, we had a splendid view of the two extinct volcanoes to the south of the City with their wonderful exotic names: Ixtacihuatl and Popocatapetl! On our first evening we were invited to drinks by some friends of Derek Spiers, but hardly had we set foot in our room than Daphne burst into tears, said she felt awful and went to bed. Could that have been an attack of panic? I don't know; but my host when I arrived alone and explained what had happened said that this was a very common experience; many people found it very difficult to adjust quickly to the height – Mexico City is at 7500 ft. Whilst in Mexico City we visited the Aztec pyramids with their images of their feathered god Quetzelcoatl. The pyramids were then outside the city, but I suppose they must now be in a park within the city. We also admired the strange outdoor murals by Diego Riviera near the University.

One day we went out into the country to visit some more friends of Derek Spiers. Hippies had not yet been invented, but they were the nearest thing to it. They lived in a remote house high in the hills, living off the land and worshipping strange gods. We got there by bus; that was quite an experience as I sat next to a peasant woman with two live chickens on her lap with their legs tied together. In the countryside I remember too, men stripping the fibre from the enormous leaves of agave, which they called 'magay'.

From Mexico we travelled to Cuernavaca, a resort town in the mountains on the road south to Acapulco and spent several days there. We also visited Taxco (pronounced Tasco) the silver town. The main street was lined with silversmiths selling necklaces, cream jugs, paper knives and all manner of trinket boxes in silver, but inlayed with copper, silver and abalone shell. Daphne bought a substantial selection.

We resumed our tour of the States by flying to New Orleans, our hosts again being the local Federal Reserve Bank. New Orleans lived up to its reputation. We visited the docks and saw enormous loads of bananas being carried off the boats by great strong men. The Mississippi is a splendid river and there were then still a few river boats, the large paddle steamers. We also visited the old French quarter, admiring the elaborate iron trellis work of the balconies. But we were also typical tourists; we visited Bourbon Street and listened to jazz and even visited a strip club, which Daphne found amusing; so far as I remember there were as many women in the audience as men. We did not see a street car named Desire, because street cars had already disappeared from the streets of New Orleans, but we did see a bus named Desire. I remember the food as being very special with soft-shelled crab from Lake Ponchartrain and various 'gumbos'.

Our next flight took us to Atlanta, Georgia. As usual I spent a great deal of time talking to bankers. It was already nine years after the end of the war and the bankers wondered why we had not yet made sterling convertible. I could not give the true answer, which was that the new Conservative government was almost as socialist as the Attlee government had been. Daphne meanwhile was being shown the 'fine homes' of Atlanta, mostly built with money derived from Coca-Cola.

From there we flew to New York City; Daphne said she found it exhilarating, but I certainly would not have wished to live there. But I had a very interesting time talking to bankers; I particularly remember spending a morning with all the bright young sparks of J.P. Morgans. They were very impressive and I liked the atmosphere; there were about eight of them, all in the same room, sitting or standing at roll top desks. New York drinking habits were very strange; before lunch you were given two large dry martinis, but lunch itself was dry; I put my foot in it at the Federal Reserve Bank of New York's officers' dining room; when asked what I wanted to drink I asked for a beer — the choice on offer was water, milk or iced tea!

We finished our tour with several days in Canada. We left New York by the night train to Montreal. I have never liked night trains; the constant noise of shunting and stopping at stations meant that I could never sleep. Our stay in Montreal was enlivened by the presence in the city at the same time of Cobbold, the Governor of the Bank of England, who was accompanied by a fairly senior bag carrier in the person of Jasper Hollom, who was at that time I think a Principal. Cobbold invited us to dinner at a night club where he was determined to enjoy himself; I hardly had any opportunity to dance with Daphne as Cobbold monopolised her. The cabaret singer wore a very décolleté dress and Cobbold turned away from us and stared at her eagerly. At one point a woman with a strapless dress appeared at the entrance with a mink stole. 'What do you make of that, Hollom?' asked the Governor. Hollom paused for a moment and replied: 'A little highly coloured, sir!'

We encountered Cobbold and Hollom again in Ottawa. Drinking habits make up most of my memories of Ottawa. Cobbold decided to give a drinks party in his suite at the Chateau Laurier and Daphne and I were invited. Hollom was supposed to have arranged the party, but when we arrived early, before any of the other guests, Jasper suddenly discovered that Room Service were quite happy to send us glasses, tonic, soda water and little nibbles, but they were not allowed to provide alcohol; we would have to buy that ourselves and bring it in. Jasper sent me off to find a liquor store and buy several bottles of gin and whisky. I had the devil of a job finding a liquor store; by law they were not allowed to have any bottles that could be seen from the street so the stores were so inconspicuous as to be almost invisible. From outside they looked like the ration offices in England. I eventually found one, but my troubles were not over yet. In order to be allowed to take away that much alcohol I was required to sign a document confirming that I was an alcoholic! But the party went off smoothly. I don't think that Cobbold even realised what a problem we had had.

The other drinking experience was on a Sunday afternoon, when a couple from the Bank of Canada took us for a drive in their car out to the Laurentian Mountains, which are said to be geologically the oldest mountains in the world. Were they interested? No, all they wanted to do was drink Canada Club whisky from plastic mugs, sitting in the car. They kept telling us how much Jim Keogh had drunk when he had been their guest. Keogh had been Crick's predecessor in Washington. He was highly thought of as a banker, but his career never quite got off the ground; it may have been something to do with his wife's behaviour. At parties in Washington when she was politely asked how she liked living in Washington she was reputed to have replied that she was counting the days until she could go home. I suspect that she didn't accompany her husband on his farewell tour of the States and Canada. I have a vague recollection that Keogh ended up in some senior position in the Singapore Monetary Authority.

We had two more places to visit in Canada – Toronto and Quebec. Toronto in those days was disparagingly referred to as Hog City. It certainly was not then the cultural centre that it has now become. I spent my whole time talking to bankers and industrialists whilst Daphne was taken on a guided tour of Niagara Falls. The only reason Quebec featured on our itinerary was that I had discovered that whilst at my rank we would have to travel Cabin Class on the *Queens*, on any other Cunard liner we would be able to travel First Class, so we were booked to sail for Southampton on the *Samaria*, the last liner to leave Quebec before the St. Lawrence River froze up for the winter. We had of course already seen Quebec the year before, but this time we stayed at the Chateau Frontenac with a room looking out over the river, which already had some ice on it and the shore was sprinkled with snow – we were already into December.

We sailed in the late afternoon with snow falling and lying on the decks. The Gaspé Peninsula looked very bleak. It is no wonder so many Canadian pensioners, even then, arranged to spend the winters in Florida. The next morning we sailed in sight of the last French possessions in the North Atlantic, St. Pierre et Miquelon. Then it was the bleak rough winter North Atlantic. There were not all that many on board, but quite frequently Daphne and I were the only passengers at dinner; the others were all seasick. The dining saloon tables were all fitted with 'fiddles' to prevent the crockery and cutlery falling off when the ship rolled. In the Western Approaches we encountered the fiercest storm of all; we could see smaller ships running for cover; the sky was quite spectacular. We managed to dock at Le Havre, but when trying to leave, being towed out by a tug, with a gale still blowing, the tow rope snapped and wound itself around the propeller. It took several hours to get it free. We eventually arrived at Southampton and returned to our house at 20 Pond Place.

CHAPTER 11

England 1955–56

The Chief Cashier's Office

I THINK WE MUST HAVE SPENT CHRISTMAS in Jersey with my parents and been reunited with Louis the poodle. Early in the New Year I was back in the Bank, this time in CCO, but acting as No. 1 on the posts rather than at the bottom. Jasper Hollom had been Chief Clerk of the CCO but by now I think he was already an Assistant Chief Cashier; he was moving up very rapidly; within a couple of years he had become the Deputy Chief Cashier under Leslie O'Brien. I was never cut out to be a banker, and the atmosphere was quite stifling, with absolutely no opportunity to show initiative and putting in draft letters to Deputy Chief Cashiers who were all non-graduates. There is nothing wrong in being a non-graduate; the only problem was that they found it very difficult to come to terms with young graduates and showed it by constantly making petty objections to drafts. It was not unknown for a rejected draft to be resubmitted unaltered and then accepted!

Some time early in 1955 Sir George Bolton asked to see me. He said that there was a strong possibility that the Bank would be asked to provide an Adviser to the Central Bank of South Vietnam and asked whether I would be prepared to take it on. I said I would have to consult Daphne first. Vietnam – I think it was already called Vietnam and was no longer part of French Indochina; the French Army had been defeated at Dien Ben Phu the year before – was not a particularly dangerous place in 1955. I don't think there were any American forces there yet. I spoke good enough French to do the job and it sounded quite exciting, and a good deal more lively than the CCO. So we agreed to go, if the job came up. In the meanwhile I was taken off the normal CCO work, and whilst still sitting there was told to read up relevant files. V.C. Tong, one of the Deputy Chief Cashiers who could not begin to understand how a young man, only just thirty and with so little experience of the CCO, could possibly advise a Central Bank, said that he supposed I had better have unrestricted access to all the CBP papers (standing for Central Bank Papers) which in fact, merely covered all the work of the CCO – there was nothing of any relevance to the work I might be doing in Vietnam. I think it was then that I bought a book called *Souvenirs d'un Gouverneur de la Banque de France* by Moreau. This covered the 1920s and the period of the Poincaré franc. This was much more relevant. After about a month the project was called off; Vietnam was already coming into the American sphere of influence and Alan Holmes of the Federal Reserve Bank of New York was appointed to the post. I had met Alan in New York the previous November; we neither of us then knew what was pending.

Private Secretary to the Deputy Governor

So I returned to normal CCO duties; but not for very long. Some time in the summer I was made what was called GPS 2 – that is Governor's Private Secretary No. 2, which essentially meant that I was the Deputy Governor's Private Secretary – this was Sir Humphrey Mynors. The role of the Private Secretary in the Bank was much more limited than in the Civil Service. We did not attend meetings in the Governors' rooms and so took no minutes. Our role was to keep their diaries, open all the mail and direct it to the appropriate place and marshal all the papers addressed to them. The GPS was Peter Taylor, a friendly and engaging character who was already of administrative rank, a Principal, I believe. He sat on one side of our vast desk and I sat on the other. In front of each of us was a lectern on which was propped our respective master's diary, consisting of sheets of green paper marked with hours, days, months on to which we entered the Governors' appointments in pencil, being required quite frequently to rub out some engagement and enter another.

Our office had a permanently open door looking into the antechamber of the Governors' Parlours, so that we could see anybody approaching, as pink coated messengers led visitors in to the waiting rooms. We would also see senior officials, the Chief Cashier and the Secretary of the Bank in particular. The Chief Cashier was by then Leslie O'Brien, later to be Governor – the very first Governor to emerge from within the Bank. The Secretary was Arthur Dascombe. We were also frequently visited by messengers bringing or taking away papers, by the Governor's private typist, a charming lady by the name of Jean Pierson. We were also visited by Miss Heather, the Governors' filist, who smoked like a chimney and whose fingers were permanently stained by nicotine.

The advantages of the job were first that one got to know everyone of any consequence in the Bank and, perhaps even more important to one's career, that they got to know you. We also saw every piece of paper that went in to the Governors. The great issues of the day, I remember, were whether and how soon sterling would be made convertible (into US dollars, that is). This issue was always know as 'The Collective Approach'. The problem from the point of view of the monetary authorities, a view shared by the Bank and the Treasury, was a fear of a run on the pound as holders of The Sterling Balances (the war time debts piled up and held in gilt-edged bonds by countries such as Egypt and the Commonwealth) rushed to convert them. The other big issue went by the name of 'Counterblast to Messina'. Both the government and the Bank were at that time totally opposed to the movement towards a European Union which had been launched at a meeting of the six countries, France, West Germany, Italy, Belgium. Luxembourg and the Netherlands, at a meeting in Messina in Sicily, which was to lead to the Treaty of Rome two years later. I am not quite sure why they were so totally opposed, considering that seven years later they were to be enthusiastic about joining the Common Market.

There were four Executive Directors with offices in the Parlours. Next to us was the Finance Director, Sir Kenneth Peppiatt, a former Chief Cashier. Beyond the Deputy Governor was the first of the Overseas Directors, H.A. Siepmann, who was a very remote figure. He always left the door of his office open and could be seen standing at his old-fashioned roll top desk. After lunch he had the habit of lying on his back on the floor! Beyond him was the second Overseas Director, Sir George Bolton. Bolton was a very live wire; I used to say that he had ten 'brilliant' ideas a day, only one of which was actually any good. When he left the Bank he became Chairman of BOLSA (The Bank of London and South America), where he was very innovative; indeed it was thanks to him that the Eurodollar market developed and greatly strengthened the position of the City of London as an international financial centre. The fourth Executive Director was the Staff Director (i.e. personnel) Sir George Abell, formerly with the ICS in India. Also in the Parlours was an Adviser to the Governors, W.M. Allen. I think he is the only person in my whole life whom I have actively disliked. He was an economist, brought in by Cobbold; he had been a don at Cambridge, was with the IMF in its early days and during the war had been in the Intelligence Corps. I discovered that during that brief period that I was at the Wireless Experimental Centre in New Delhi, Maurice Allen had been there too. Although he had a high reputation as an economist, he had, unusually for a don, never published anything. His only claim to fame was in a footnote in a book by D.H. Robertson: 'I am indebted to Mr W.M. Allen for this idea.' He was a distinctly left wing economist and I clashed with him constantly in the mid to late 1960s.

I once made a terrible mistake with the Deputy Governor's diary. One morning I looked up and saw a messenger escorting Lord Bruce to the Deputy's waiting room. Horrors! I had forgotten to cancel his appointment and the Deputy had been called to the Treasury. Lord Bruce was one of the most distinguished characters in the City, a former Australian Prime Minister and member of the War Cabinet. What on earth was I to do? Peter Taylor suggested that I should call on Peppiatt and explain what had happened. Peppiatt was wonderful; no word of reproach passed his lips, he walked with me to the waiting room, greeted Bruce, saying, 'Bruce, there's been a cockup. The Deputy has been suddenly called to the Treasury.' Peppiatt took Bruce by the elbow and escorted him right to the main door into Threadneedle Street. The sight of the two white haired elderly gentlemen strolling gently along the corridor was a most engaging one. If it had been somebody like Beale or even Maurice Parsons, instead of Peppiatt, my career would have been ruined on the spot.

I also made another serious mistake. As I have already said, one of our tasks was to open the Governors' mail, enter it in a register and direct it to the appropriate place. One day I stupidly opened a letter addressed to the Governor which was clearly marked 'Private and Confidential'; imagine my feelings when I saw that the first words were 'Darling Kimmy' and that the letter had been written by the wife of the Chairman of British Petroleum, Sir Maurice Bridgeman! I hastily pasted it shut and wrote on it: 'Sorry; opened in error.' Again, I got away with it. Cobbold never even referred to it. I wonder if he remembered the night club in Montreal! I got on very well with Cobbold, and admired him: a very worthy successor to Montagu Norman. Cobbold was tall and seemed to me to be more at ease with other tall people, unlike his short successor, Lord Cromer.

A number of distinguished visitors came whilst I was there. Harold Macmillan, when Chancellor of the Exchequer, called for lunch. I had to greet him as he entered the Parlours and take him to the lift up to the Governor's Dining Room. I have never encountered such a limp handshake. I used to think that I should have known from that that I was never going to agree with what he did, either as Chancellor or as Prime Minister – he was an archetypal 'wet'. But one should not judge people on such slender evidence; I learned years later that his handshake was the result of a war wound in the First World War. Another distinguished visitor was Princess Alexandra, who came in to the Private Secretaries' office and was perfectly charming.

We move to Sussex

I found commuting to the Bank by tube extremely uncomfortable. I suspect that the tube was last a pleasant means of travel in about 1939! I used to walk from Pond Place to South Kensington tube station and travel to the Mansion House, and almost invariably I had to stand the whole way, hanging on to the overhead strap. And the whole journey often took as much as ¾ of an hour. Daphne found exercising Louis quite a chore; she had to take the 49 bus, dogs allowed only on the top deck, to Kensington Gardens. So we decided to move to the country. House hunting was not easy; we had no car in England as in London we would not have needed one. So *faute de mieux* we relied on Daphne's father to drive us around Sussex (no East or West Sussex in those days). The Hazells had moved to West Chiltington, near Pulborough when he had retired from Barclays Bank as manager of the Vauxhall Road Branch. This was very convenient, but had the unfortunate result of putting us far too close to Daphne's mother – this was a problem which I had not yet taken in.

In November 1955 we bought Codmore Barn, a converted barn at the top of Codmore Hill in Pulborough, with several acres of land. It was a good time to buy; the previous owner, we discovered, had bought it for £6200 in 1952. We bought the house at auction, but since neither of us could get there, it was Daphne's father who bid on our behalf. I think we had instructed him not to go above £5000 which was what we had got for the sale of 20 Pond Place; I seem to remember that the eventual under bidder actually bid £5000 but Daphne's father screwed up his courage and went to £5250 and generously gave us the £250. This was very brave of him, since every time he ever gave Daphne anything, his wife was certain to ask for just as much again for herself! The Deputy Governor said to me one day, 'I hear you are taking one of the iniquitous Bank Housing Loans.' I was a bit surprised. I think all he meant was that they were all dressed up to look commercial, but that the interest rate charged was ludicrously low, and that the Bank would never have risked the public odium of repossessing an employee's house.

We moved in two days before Christmas. Somehow Daphne managed to provide a Christmas lunch for us and her parents. Codmore Barn was not a very good conversion (post war austerity); the wind whistled through holes in the walls, which I spent a long time blocking up with crumpled pieces of *The Times*! It had a small dining room, a small sitting room and a large room which we called the Music Room on the ground floor. Daphne's mother's piano which had belonged to her mother before her was installed there; the piano was the only substantial present Ione ever gave her daughter, everything else she sold – that's not quite right, she also eventually gave her a Welsh dresser which had also belonged to her mother. Upstairs, above the kitchen, dining room and sitting room were three bedrooms and a bathroom. There was no central heating, and we relied on paraffin stoves.

Commuting from Pulborough meant that we had to have a car; the station was too far away to walk. We bought a tiny blue Ford Anglia for about £300 on hire purchase. £300 was probably equal to about 3/5 of my annual salary! The journey from Pulborough to London Bridge Station took about 1 hour and 10 minutes, but starting from Pulborough meant that I could always find a seat; people getting on at Horsham were often not so lucky. We bought another poodle to keep Louis company, by the name of Ginny. Daphne insisted on having her clipped in the true poodle manner, which I must say did not appeal to me very much.

We made a start on the garden; neither of us knew much about gardening, although I had seen my father keenly gardening in Jersey, so we began by buying an advertised collection of Harry Wheatcroft's roses, all of which were hybrid teas or floribundas. We discovered that we were on greensand, which is an acid soil and made it possible to grow rhododendrons. I also planted two trees; the first was a *Metasequoia glyptostroboides* (the dawn redwood), which was in those days still a very rare tree, having been introduced to the UK as late as 1950. Daphne derived a lot of amusement from the fact that I planted it 100 feet from the house – it was supposed to grow to that height at maturity and I didn't want it falling on the house in a gale! I fear that where it was is now a housing estate. The other tree I planted was a tulip tree. But we didn't really make much progress in the garden until we returned from our second appointment in America.

As I said, I got on very well with Humphrey Mynors. He was passionately interested in the art of writing, insisting on immaculate punctuation, but come to think of it that obsession had a lot more relevance when I worked for him again in the 1960s. He encouraged me to take home books from the bookcase in his room to read on the train. I remember in particular vast tomes, bound in leather, of all the minutes of the Macmillan Committee of which John Maynard Keynes had been a member – also Ernie Bevin, later Foreign Secretary in the Attlee government; this gave considerable amusement to my fellow commuters. Next year I finally got the promotion to Senior Clerk which had been denied me in 1953!

In the summer of 1956 Daphne became pregnant; the obstetrician said the baby was due in late January of 1957. I feel sure that his arithmetic failed him – Amicia was not born until 23 February and I am sure that she was a normal full term baby.

Room 1 of the CCO

Late in that summer I was moved on from being GPS and went back to the CCO; this time in Room 1 through which all who aspired to a good career in the Bank had to pass. Its primary responsibility was to produce the weekly Bank Return, which was always posted on a Thursday morning, the same morning that the Court (as the Bank's Board of Directors was called) announced any change in Bank Rate. This meant that we (three of us if I remember rightly) had to stay very late on Wednesday nights, never getting away before about 10 p.m. This made it impossible to return to Pulborough. Martin Mays-Smith, a young high flier about five years my junior, very kindly allowed me to stay in his flat which he shared with the son of Johnny Miller, the Press Relations chief of the IBRD. Young Miller was working for Harveys of Bristol, so whenever we had dinner together we had good wines to taste. So far as I remember, I would drive up to London first thing on a Monday morning in the little Ford Anglia and return home again at lunchtime on a Friday – this was a special concession for those working in Room 1.

Looking back I feel ashamed that I deserted Daphne for four nights of the week; I should have stayed in London for only the Wednesday night. How she managed all alone I don't know. There was only one shop to which she could walk. But even if I had left her the car, she didn't know how to drive. That was another selfish attitude; of course she should have had driving lessons. I think looking back that her very kind father must have helped. This spell in Room 1 must I think have lasted a couple of months and was to end very suddenly and dramatically.

Per Jacobsson

A Friday in late October was to be one of the most remarkable days in my life. I had driven to the Bank and parked my little car in Tokenhouse Yard at the back of the Bank. Anybody who knows the City today would be amazed to hear that it was possible to park there. It is a tiny little lane. Later that morning the Chief Cashier, Leslie O'Brien, asked to see me. I stood in front of his desk and he asked me if I knew Per Jacobsson. I told him that I knew who he was and had met him briefly when a bag carrier to Basle. He seemed not to believe me and asked insistently if I didn't know him a lot better than that. He eventually accepted that this was so, but remained puzzled. 'Well,' he said, 'Jacobsson is in that room the other side of the Garden Court and he wants to see you now.' I had no idea what this was about, but went through the Parlours and entered Jacobsson's room.

He had asked to see me, he said, because he was looking for someone from the Bank to be his Personal Assistant at the IMF in Washington DC to which he had just been appointed as Chairman and Managing Director. As a Swede he felt the need to have an Englishman to help him with his speeches. In Basle, Michael Dealtry had been performing that task for him, but for some reason PJ (as I shall call him) had decided not to take him to America. Jacobsson's appointment had been a total surprise to the international financial community – both previous incumbents had been Governors of their Central Banks, whilst Jacobsson had merely been the Chief Economist at the BIS. His appointment was entirely due to Cobbold who had persuaded the other Governors, Baumgartner of the Banque de France in particular, who had himself declined the appointment, that PJ was ideally qualified for the job. Before joining the BIS in around 1930 he had been very active in the League of Nations' financial committee and had worked very closely with Montagu Norman, who thought very highly of him. So PJ had particularly warm feelings for the Bank of England.

During this week in October the Bank had sent him three or four young men to interview, all of whom he had found quite hopeless. He told the Bank that unless they found somebody more suitable, he would have to find his Personal Assistant elsewhere. During this period he spoke to his daughter Moyra and asked her if she knew of anybody bright in the Bank. She had been at the Ruskin School at Oxford when I had been up and knew that I was in the Bank and had heard, how I don't know, that I would probably be just what he was looking for. So he had asked for me by name; with great reluctance the Bank allowed him to see me. Within a very few minutes we knew that we would hit it off very well; and he was also particularly pleased that I already knew the Fund and all the people in it. So after about half an hour he confirmed that he would like me to go to Washington with him for about two years.

I went back to see O'Brien but he had already gone to lunch. I spoke to his secretary, Mrs Smith, and asked her whether she thought that this being a Friday I could now drive home. We both agreed that nothing could be done about my appointment before the following Monday and that I might as well drive home.

As I was to discover two or three hours later, hardly had I gone than the Governor asked to see me. The Bank gave the police and the AA a description of my car and the number plate and told them to stop me and return me to the Bank as soon as possible. But I drove too fast for them – remember that in those days there was no speed limit outside towns. You only committed an offence if you drove dangerously. In the meantime the Bank (in the person of Peter Maugham, whom I still see today) rang Daphne to say that I would not be home until very late and mysteriously told her that it was about 'crossing the pond' – not particularly informative. So when I finally drove up the drive at Codmore Barn, there was no Daphne, only Elsie our wonderful cleaner. She told me that the Bank of England were on the phone that very moment; I was instructed to return immediately. I pointed out that it would take me at least two hours; was the Governor going to wait for me? 'No,' they said, 'You are to go straight to his flat in Green Street' – that was in Mayfair. So I climbed back into my car; at that very moment a police car came racing up the drive to tell me that I was required to return to London immediately to see the Governor!

I set off up the A29 as fast as I could, but it became clear to me that I was not going to be able to reach Green Street before 7 o'clock, when the Governor was due to leave to go to the opera. So I turned in to Dorking Station, parked my car and took a train to Waterloo. I got there at about 6.45, leaped into a taxi and told the driver to get me to Mayfair in ten minutes and not to worry about red lights! When I arrived, there was Cobbold pacing up and down on the pavement in white tie and tails, with Lady Hermione already in the car and Gale, the chauffeur, standing patiently by the car. Cobbold took me by the arm and walked me up and down, telling me that it was his earnest wish that I should go to Washington with Jacobsson, that I should sail on the *Queen Mary* with Mr and Mrs Jacobsson in two weeks' time and that I was now to go to the Kensington Palace Hotel where Jacobsson was expecting me for dinner. All that in about five minutes! And then they were off in the Rolls.

I made my way to the KPH and had dinner with Jacobsson. We did not agree on everything. I was at that time still sufficiently liberal to be strongly opposed to the Anglo-French invasion of Egypt, whereas PJ was strongly in favour of what today we would call 'regime change'. I now think that the history of the Middle East for the past fifty years might have been very different if we had persevered in spite of American opposition; it was 'wet' Macmillan who caved in. In another two days the whole of the Suez Canal zone would have been in our hands and Nasser might well have been toppled. It was a pity that Eisenhower was President; both Teddy Roosevelt and George W. Bush would have had a quite different view. But PJ and I talked mostly about the Fund and what awaited us in Washington. With the run on the pound, the UK government was going to approach the Fund for a substantial loan to calm the markets.

I had a lot to discuss with Daphne, so I got away as quickly as possible, took a train back to Dorking and drove back to Codmore Barn; it must have been midnight or later when I got home. What a day! We talked on for a long time. Daphne had thoroughly enjoyed her first stay in America and was very pleased to go back; the only problem was that she was thought to be already seven months pregnant and there were dangers in a winter crossing of the North Atlantic. I suggested that perhaps she should stay in England, have the baby and then come to join me, but that prospect filled her with many fears, not least, although she did not express it, was to be at the mercy of her mother without my support. When we told her mother, her first remark was, 'Don't expect me to be pleased; I want to see my first grandchild' – a typically self-centred remark.

Over the next few days we organised all that needed to be done. The Bank organised the booking on the *Queen Mary*; Cunard required us to sign an indemnity, absolving them from any responsibility if the unborn child came to any harm. We arranged for Codmore Barn to be let and we decided to take the dogs with us. Dogs on the *Queens* travel in the care of the butcher with kennels on the top deck. There is a wonderful scene in one of the Fred Astaire/Ginger Rogers films of Fred trying to get off with Ginger by borrowing some hounds to enable him to walk up and down the deck with her.

I spent very little time in the Bank. I never went back to Room 1, but saw all the people I thought I ought to see. Jack Portsmore who was now back in the Bank as Adviser on International Organisations briefed me on the current situation, telling me that with the run on the pound the UK government was going to apply for a loan of $600 million. For those who know about these things, the Fund does not actually make loans; member countries make drawing against their quota of drawing rights. John Stevens had become an Overseas Director (in place of Siepmann) and I called on him; he started calling me 'Guy', a sure sign that he thought I might be useful to him, but rather dismissively suggested that my going was not a particularly good idea: 'The Fund is moribund, you know.' I bumped into Sir George Abell in the Parlours who was equally dismissive; he hoped I knew what I was doing, as it didn't seem to be a particularly good career move. I think this all came about for two reasons; first, they were really very annoyed that Jacobsson had asked for me by name, and secondly, they were among very many people who did not think very much of Jacobsson and didn't think he would make a success of it. This in spite of the fact that the Governor had specifically asked me to go!.

CHAPTER 12

International Monetary Fund – Personal Assistant to the Managing Director

LATE IN NOVEMBER WE MET the Jacobssons at Southampton and embarked on the *Queen Mary*. We had not met Mrs J before; she was older than her husband, but very game for the adventure. Her maiden name had been Nye and she was the sister of General Sir Archibald Nye, who had been Vice Chief of the General Staff during the war. She met her husband when they were both working for the League of Nations just after the war. The League was then in London before moving to Geneva. Before the war she had been a Governess in St. Petersburg, her charge being George Sanders, who became a film star – always the very smooth upper class villain. We also began to get to know PJ himself. I should have said that PJ was 62. I found him quite charming with one rather sweet idiosyncrasy – he was terribly vain and loved dropping names. It seemed particularly appropriate that his daughter, Moyra, had married a celebrity – Roger Bannister.

The journey was uneventful and when we got to New York we hurried on to Washington. Daphne and I stayed at the Mayflower whilst the Jacobssons moved into a suite at the Sheraton Park Hotel (which had just opened) where they were to stay for the next six and a half years until he died. The Fund must have been doing some house hunting on our behalf because we very soon found a nice house on 43rd Street in Wesley Heights, a suburb in north-west Washington, not far from the Glover-Archbold Park, then a wild wooded area, but now I believe with a Freeway through it. I needed a car and spent a couple of days visiting used car lots; I could not make up my mind, but eventually settled on a second-hand 1956 Chevrolet. When I drove up outside the house in 43rd Street Daphne could not believe her eyes; it was scarlet and white – exactly the kind of car which featured in the film *Back to the Future*. The Chevrolet kept us going as the family car until 1967!

Jacobsson and I entered the Fund together on 3 December 1956. The Fund was then in its original building, not purpose built, but converted from an existing apartment block at 1818 H Street, which was shared with the IBRD. PJ's office was large and spacious and overlooked H Street; beyond his office was a small meeting room and on the other side through a connecting door, the office of his secretaries, Mathilde Hamilton and Rachel Dillon. Next came my office, which had a black leather couch on which I was wont to stretch out for half an hour after lunch. Beyond my office, but without a connecting door, was the office of the Deputy Managing Director, Merle Cochrane, an American with a remarkable

To Moyra
with love
Per Jacobsson
Washington
19th Sept 1956.

Per Jacobsson, 1894–1963. Chairman and Managing Director of the IMF
I am grateful to Lady Bannister for lending me this photograph of her father

likeness to the film actor Sidney Greenstreet (always the villain, and notable
in the Bogart film *The Maltese Falcon*).

The Heads of the various Departments were on other floors and were all
the same as they had been during my first appointment in Washington,
except that John Stevens had gone from the European Department and had
been succeeded, I think, by Gabriel Ferras from the Banque de France. The
other people we saw most of were the General Counsel. One of the most
important people in any American organisation is the principal lawyer and
this was James Fawcett, a charming Oxford educated upper class Englishman who was really out of his depth in a wheeling and dealing situation.
He later became Professor of International Law at Oxford. He was to be
succeeded by Joe Gold, also English but quite different, an ingenious and
clever Jew. The Chief Economist was an eminent American, Eddie
Bernstein, with as his Deputy a Dutchman, Jacques Polack, who was to
succeed him. We were also to have frequent dealings with the head of the
Exchange Control Department, Irving Friedman, another American who
in the earlier 50s had come under attack from Senator McCarthy as a

suspect Communist. PJ frequently clashed with him, not about politics, but about exchange rate policies. The head of the Latin American Department was Jorge Del Canto, a Chilean; John Gunter, an American, was head of the Middle East Department and finally the head of the Asian Department was James Raj, an Indian Christian from Madras.

On our first morning we were immediately plunged into hectic activity. There was a meeting in PJ's room with the UK Executive Director, Lord Harcourt, his Alternate, now Roy Heasman from the Bank, Merle Cochrane, the lawyers, Fawcett and Gold and a few others. The UK formally asked for a loan of $600 million. Jacobsson surprised all present, both from the UK and from the Fund, by objecting. In his experience a crisis of confidence on the exchanges, where there was no real underlying economic problem, required a massive show of strength; he therefore proposed a massive loan of $1.2 billion! Joe Gold, I remember, was not at all sure that such a loan was in accordance with the statutes of the IMF. But Jacobsson's view prevailed and we went into a drafting session, setting out a document for submission to the Board. PJ was always dominant in any drafting session and the others had to fight to keep up with him.

A difficulty arose over the wording he had proposed relating to Egypt; I don't remember the details, but Cochrane, who supported the American opposition to the Anglo-French invasion of Egypt, thought that the wording was too critical of Egypt. PJ, of course, thought of Egypt as the 'enemy'. We all dispersed and I produced four or five alternative drafts in succession before I found a form of words acceptable to both PJ and Merle Cochrane. We had no trouble in getting it through the Board – incidentally I attended all Board meetings, sitting at the back behind Jacobsson. The international financial community took a very favourable view of the operation; sterling strengthened, there was in fact no need to draw on the loan and the IMF's reputation soared. The Fund was no longer 'moribund'.

I have recently been reading John Fforde's (of whom more anon) *History of the Bank of England – 1942 to 1958*. To my great surprise he makes absolutely no reference to this drawing, even though it was the first substantial operation undertaken by the Fund since it had been established nine years before. I am at a loss to explain this. It took quite a time for Jacobsson to sort out his relationships with the Heads of Departments. It was also difficult for me. I had known them all previously in a much more junior position and they frequently sought to use me to influence PJ. They also had doubts about me. The first Managing Director had a Personal Assistant, who at a time when there was no Deputy Managing Director had tended to try and wield power on his own, as if he were the Deputy; and they were afraid that I might try and do the same; it would not have been so easy since there now was a bona fide Deputy Managing Director. But I have to confess that once or twice I did tell a Head of Department that the M.D. wanted something or other without first clearing it with PJ. He found me out once and ticked me off severely – quite right too and I didn't do it again.

One of our first problems was with the Economics Department. Jacques Polack and his economists had written the first draft of a paper on gold which was to be published. Jacobsson disagreed with it profoundly; they had, in his view, downplayed the real importance of gold and had not written it with markets in mind. He said it would have to be completely rewritten. Polack and his team declined to do so; they said that they had written what they thought was right and would be unable to put across a different view. So Jacobsson and I rewrote the whole pamphlet. I say 'I' because PJ and I soon established a method of writing his speeches or articles; he would take a pad of unlined paper and start writing in ink very rapidly; I sat beside him and as he completed a page he would pass it to me. I corrected errors of English but would also comment on the contents; 'You can't say that,' I might say, 'you have no evidence for it', or 'Surely that's too extreme.' So it became a very co-operative exercise. The new pamphlet was eventually published; I cannot now remember to whom the contents were attributed in the published version.

Polack's boss, Eddie Bernstein, a real liberal democrat, found Jacobsson extremely irritating. He once said to me, 'Tell the boss that he is not an economist and that we are here to do it for him.' I did not pass the message on, but on one occasion later in the year as I got into the Cadillac with him to drive somewhere or other I said, 'You know, some people tell me that you are not an economist – and I agree with them.'

'Moubray,' he exclaimed with horror, the blood draining from his face.

'No,' I said, 'you are not an economist; you are a political economist.'

The blood returned to his face. But I meant it seriously. I have never had much time for over specialised economists, even less for econometricians. PJ always had political realities in view and always tried to sell sound policies to Finance Ministers as a means of increasing their political standing. But Eddie could not take it. He had resigned from the Fund before the end of the year and, as I have already said, Jacques Polack took over from him.

Relations with Irving Friedman were also strained. Jacobsson was a firm believer in a single fixed exchange rate. Friedman was convinced that many of the South American countries could not, as yet, manage a unitary exchange rate and had to have variable rates – different rates for different categories of imports, a more favourable rate for essential goods and a penalty rate for luxury goods. Irving came to a meeting in PJ's meeting room with a draft paper on Argentina. Jacobsson, quite uncharacteristically, exploded.

'Do you know what I would have done with a paper like this submitted to me at the BIS?'

He proceeded to throw the paper on to the floor behind him; the staples came out and separate sheets of paper had to be retrieved from the floor. I think we were all shocked; but it was a turning point; relations with Friedman improved and PJ came to accept that some countries were just not in a position to adopt the policies that he would have preferred.

Meanwhile at home the pregnancy was going smoothly, although it became clearer and clearer that the baby was not going to be born in January. It was very cold that winter. I used to walk the dogs in the Glover-Archbold Park after getting home in the evenings and I remember one evening looking at the thermometer in the back porch which was registering 32 degrees of frost – Fahrenheit. The running stream in the woods was frozen over. We had a Jamaican cook/maid, Miriam, who lived in; she was a good cook but a very difficult person. Finally, on 22 February in the morning (George Washington Day), Daphne started to have labour pains. I drove her in to the George Washington Memorial Hospital. But her obstetrician said it was too early and sent her home again. In the evening the labour pains began in earnest and I took her back to the hospital and sat with her most of the night.

By 5 o'clock nothing had yet happened and since I had to go to work in the morning, I decided to go home and have an hour or two of sleep. At half past six I was woken by Miriam who said that the hospital had rung and that a baby girl had been born at 6.25. Before going back to the hospital I put in telephone calls to the two lots of parents; it was already nearly noon in England and Jersey. Phone calls in those days were very difficult; reception was poor and you could be troubled with echoes. But at any rate the news was accepted with delight. I went back to the hospital and was shown my daughter. I did not then, and still do not relate at all easily to babies under the age of about 6 months. Had she been born on George Washington Day she would probably have been called Georgina Harriet, but as it was she was called Amicia – after her ancestor (the first woman's name in the family tree – Appendix II).

I drove down town and had a real American breakfast at the counter of the Roger Smith Hotel – pancakes, maple syrup and those little rather sweet sausages. And then into the office. Life at home went smoothly. We had brought with us a beautiful old-fashioned well sprung white English pram and I remember Daphne pushing it up and down the very ornamental suburban streets with dogwood, azaleas, cherry trees, almonds and forsythia, always called forsithia with a short 'i' by Americans, in bloom. I walked the dogs regularly in the Glover-Archbold Park and my interest in trees grew. I bought a pocket book for identifying American trees and came to recognise hickories, various oaks, pin oaks, scarlet and red oaks, etc. One small tree I loved because of its name was the sassafras; it has strangely shaped leaves and its root used to be used in the making of 'root beer'. Easter was particularly warm with temperatures in the 70s. We had a visit from Ray Stevens with his new wife, Alta Mae. I love those American names! He was now settled at the Oceanographic Institute at Wood's Hole in Massachusetts so we didn't see much of them.

We regularly went to the New Church in Washington. The Minister was a sweet old man called William F. Wunsch. I still have a copy of a paperback translation by him of Swedenborg's *The Divine Providence*. Amicia was christened there. We made good friends with one of the members of the choir, Gifford Orwen. Neither he nor his wife Mary were New Church, but he liked the choir. We saw a lot of them over the next few years. Mary was an artist and one of her 'drip' paintings hangs in the kitchen here. She got Daphne very interested in art and, when Amicia was a little older, Daphne went to art classes with her. Mary also knew Patrick Heron and at one of the exhibitions she used to stage we bought the Patrick Heron print which hangs here outside the Winter Drawing Room.

Religion didn't play a very important part of my life until I was about 60, but the New Church upbringing that I had, marked me for life. My attitude to many things was in fact influenced by my Christian childhood. If, like me, you are a committed believer in an after life in which you will lead a human life, with a body (spiritual, but substantial), be married, have a job, listen to music; in other words, lead a perfectly normal life – with the emphasis on 'perfectly'; if you also believe that Jesus was and is God, you cannot help having a significantly different outlook on many things, providence and death in particular. There is a passage in the Anglican Communion service which goes something like this: 'It is our duty and indeed our joy, at all times and in all places, to worship thee, O God.' I have to say that 'at all times and in all places' my mind was not often on God. But I did try throughout my career to do what was right because it was right; self interest crept in however quite frequently – I had far too much concern for my career. But I never, at least consciously, manoeuvred to get myself advanced. It was to be another twenty-five years before religion became really important to me.

Come the summer and we decided (Daphne, of course!) that we had had enough of suburbia. We found a lovely house in McLean, Virginia, by the name of Lower Ranleigh, which we rented at a very favourable rate from the Dorrs, who were with the IBRD and had been posted to Istanbul. The house was about twenty minutes drive from the basement car park in the Fund, the other side of the Potomac across the Chain Bridge, not far from the Great Falls of the Potomac. The house was on an estate with four other houses and quite close to Ranleigh, a mansion built by Randolph Leigh, hence its name. Where the drive turned off from the main road (now I presume the main highway to the Dulles Airport which did not then exist) there was a small house which belonged to Tom Gonder, a bachelor doctor who became our family doctor, although as was the custom in America, a baby was looked after by a paediatrician, in Amicia's case Mabel Grosvenor in Washington; she was the daughter of the Founder of the *National Geographic Magazine*.

About a quarter of a mile down the drive on the right hand side was Lower Ranleigh, a rambling white clapboard house set amongst trees. It was mostly on the ground floor, with at the back a kitchen, the maid's bedroom (Suzetta, another Jamaican; Miriam did not want to go to the country), a spacious dining room in the front and a drawing room, both overlooking a

Lower Ranleigh, McLean, Virginia 1957

terrace with a statue on it, which we called 'Little Basket' (a cherub with a basket on its head); the terrace overlooked a steep wooded incline down to the stream below and the swimming pool which went with the house. The drawing room had the distinction of being panelled in swamp cypress; swamp cypresses stand as their name implies in swamps and suck up a vast amount of water through internal pipes, which in the panelling show up as holes.

Bud Horne, the Secretary of the IMF, could never bring himself to go into the house because there had been a tragedy in the house involving the Leigh family, in which a man had killed his wife and then hanged himself from a beam; the bodies were found by their five year old son. Beyond the drawing room there was another ground floor room which became Amicia's bedroom. Upstairs there were two bedrooms, with their windows right in the tops of the trees and a bathroom. The property must have extended to over eight acres. If you continued down the drive you came to a house by a bridge which crossed the stream in which lived Randolph Leigh, junior, a psychiatrist with his wife and children – and the little boy who had been involved in the tragedy. I cannot remember his name, but Randolph's wife was called Mary, and they had two children of their own, a son and a daughter. Up the hill beyond the bridge lived Randolph's brother Claiborne Leigh with his family. He was a lawyer and involved in local Virginia government; some time after we left America I heard that he had gone to jail for fraud. When the Randolph Leighs first came to call on us, they drove up in Randolph's Ford Thunderbird, a sports car where the

With Amicia and 'Little Basket' on the terrace at Lower Ranleigh, March 1958

driver virtually sat on the floor – I know because I was allowed to try it. What is hard to believe these days is that they both got out of the car, each holding a glass of Bourbon, and this at about 11 o'clock in the morning.

We had a lovely summer. One great advantage of America for Daphne was that she never had even a touch of hay fever. But poor Suzetta suffered badly from an allergy to ragweed that always came in August. I liked Suzetta, but I always looked forward to her day off – it allowed me to get into the kitchen and do some cooking! Suzetta's bedroom was right alongside the kitchen and she usually had the radio going full blast with religious programmes; one would hear her joining in with fervent cries of 'Hallelujah; Praise the Lord.'

We got to know more of American wild life. Amongst the birds the most spectacular was the cardinal, a bright red. And the two most irritating were the cat bird with its endless calls of 'miaow' and the mourning dove with its monotonous wailing call. We entertained quite a lot. We had Mr and Mrs PJ to lunch with the UK Executive Director, Guy Thorold, a charming unassuming man, who came between Lord Harcourt and Lord Cromer. We also had Lucius Thompson-McCausland, an Adviser to the Governor of the Bank, to lunch. If I remember well, it was he who named the statue 'Little

Basket'. He seemed surprised that a senior clerk should be living in a mansion – but that just shows my 'champagne' tastes. I had a lot to do with Lucius in 1962/3. He was Lord Lieutenant of Hertfordshire; he told me that he was glad that the death penalty had been abolished since one of the duties of a Lord Lieutenant was to attend executions in person!

We also had a lot of people from the Washington crowd in; we gave over the next two or three years several dances. I remember buying endless records, by this time LPs or EPs, which I think first appeared in 1956, and carefully marking which tunes were suitable for dancing. One of the most useful records was by Les Brown and his Band of Renown.

In August 1957 PJ arranged to do a three week tour of South America, visiting Brazil, Argentina, Chile and Peru. His whole background had been exclusively European and he felt, quite rightly, that he should see something of Latin America. Our party consisted of Mr and Mrs PJ, Paranagua (the Latin American Director of the IMF, who was a Brazilian), Jorge Del Canto, the Head of the Latin American Department of the Fund, and me.

We were due to leave Washington on a Saturday morning in time to connect with a Pan American Airline 'clipper' from Idlewild (before it became JFK). But the French suddenly caused a serious problem. They had decided to devalue the French franc; one of the main purposes for setting up the Fund had been to prevent 'competitive devaluations' and so no member could change their exchange rate without the approval of the Board of the IMF. I think I have already said that I don't think competitive devaluations were a real problem; in most cases the advantages to exports are quickly dissipated through lack of fiscal rectitude and the rising prices induced by the higher cost of imports. France though might be an exception; fiscal rectitude has never been a French characteristic, but the French economy is probably the least dependent on imports of any other European country; they were, and still are I believe, self sufficient in food and in many raw materials; even their energy needs rely less on oil than most countries with their ample deposits of natural gas. At any rate there had to be an emergency Board Meeting on the Saturday morning. Paranagua did not attend it; he and Jorge and Mrs PJ went to the airport, Washington National Airport which was just on the Virginia side of the Potomac, to wait for PJ and me. The Fund had chartered a small aeroplane to take us straight to Idlewild. PJ and I attended the Board Meeting, which was really a formality; nobody (except the Americans) knew when it might be their turn to devalue, so they were not going to make too much of a fuss about the French.

PJ and I rushed from the Board Meeting down to his Cadillac and were driven at high speed to the airport with a police motorcycle outrider, with his siren blaring. It was quite an experience and it could only have happened in America – no police escort with sirens would ever accompany a Governor of the Bank of England to Heathrow. We were driven on to the tarmac and boarded the plane. We took our seats and the pilot went to the door expecting the co-pilot to climb on board and shut the door. But the co-pilot made it clear he wasn't coming; 'I told you,' he said, 'I promised to take the wife and the kids down to the beach this afternoon.' The pilot then asked me to sit in the co-pilot's seat and help him to navigate! All I had was a map – a road map, I think. With my long legs I was worried that I would accidentally push the 'joy stick' forward and put us into a dive. It was a reasonably clear day with a few clouds and showers. Luckily I am quite good at map reading and I knew the route to New York. I identified Baltimore and then Philadelphia, where the pilot was able to confirm our position with some sort of radio bleep. I got him safely to the Hudson River and the spectacular skyline of New York City (no Twin Towers in those days). From there he made radio voice contact with the Control Tower and we were talked in to Idlewild.

We taxied right up under the wing of the Pan American airliner. All the other passengers had already been aboard for about 15 minutes. So we hastily embarked and set off for Rio de Janeiro only about 20 minutes late. In pre-jet days the flight was a long one; we did not reach Rio de Janeiro until early next morning, but one had the privilege in those days of climbing up into a bunk above one's seat to sleep the night away. However, I do remember the spectacular sight, to me, of the moon reflected on the Amazon delta; the delta is vast, and there were reflections in between the jungle for mile after mile.

It was a lovely day when we arrived and Rio de Janeiro Bay looked splendid, with Copacabana beach below and the unique Sugar Loaf Mountain overlooking the bay. I had done some research into Brazil before leaving Washington. Sir George Bolton was always ready to say that Brazil was the country of the future. My researches suggested that it was true but, unfortunately, that it seemed likely always to be the country of the future. Brazil never managed to make any lasting use of its potential. It had been at one time the world's largest exporter of rubber, diamonds and coffee and yet had managed to lose its supremacy in all three. In 1957 the currency was the cruzeiro; to the best of my knowledge in the last 45 years there have been two new currencies, each worth about a 100th of the previous one. The President of Brazil was Kubitschek (a most unlikely Brazilian name) and he was trying hard to get a balanced budget and sound monetary policies; this was one of the reasons we were there, to give encouragement.

My first impression of Brazil was the extraordinary extent to which the people were of mixed race; here was every colour of skin from negro at one end to pure white at the other; moreover there were also traces of local American Indian origin and many Asians, mainly Japanese. Interestingly, though, there was no sign of multiculturalism; they all shared a passionate attachment to Brazil and to Brazilian music which I happen to find peculiarly attractive, with its melancholia deriving from the Portuguese *fado*, mixed with African rhythms – much more successful I think than anywhere else in Latin America or the Caribbean. If you don't know what popular

Brazilian music is like, you can get a good idea of it if you know the song 'Girl from Ipanema'.

We spent most of our time talking to the Ministry of Finance and the Bank of Brazil; Rio was in those days the capital – it was to be some years before Brasilia was built. But we also enjoyed hospitality. Some of the younger men from the bank took me out to lunch, after a stroll along Copacabana beach. It was the first time I had ever eaten avocado, which then was always called avocado pear. I thought it was delicious and I can even remember the sauce with which it was dressed – *salsa golfo*, a kind of mayonnaise spiced with chilis.

We also attended a most elaborate banquet in honour of Per Jacobsson given by the Brazilian Foreign Office. It was given in a vast hall which one approached along an avenue of extremely tall Brazilian palms. It was a most impressive sight. The banquet was an extraordinary experience. I don't remember how many courses there were, but I know it included a salad of hearts of palm. I am told that every heart of palm harvested kills a mature tree. There were a great many people there, at least fifty I should say, and for every guest there was a waiter. At the end of each course, fifty waiters emerged from the kitchens in military order wearing white gloves, removed our plates, marched out again in unison and returned with the next course.

We also saw something of the seamier side of life; Rio was, and presumably, still is, surrounded by *favellas* (shanty towns) swarming with people, badly drained and very primitive. That is of course a feature of almost all large cities in the Third World. Hernando de Soto, the Peruvian economist, may have the answer to this problem. His book *The Mystery of Capital* produces a most compelling explanation and solution, but this is not the place to go into it.

From Rio we flew to Sao Paulo, which was the largest city in Brazil. It seemed much more European and less tropical; Sao Paulo must I think be at a higher altitude and is marginally south of Rio, which in the winter, which of course it was, would have been a bit cooler. Sao Paulo was where Paranagua lived and we were entertained by his family, who were positively nineteenth century pure Portuguese.

From Sao Paulo we flew to Buenos Aires. The flight was by Air France and they plied us with champagne the whole way. Jorge del Canto and I were almost 'legless' when we arrived. Argentina was of course much cooler; everyone wore light winter clothes. The most striking thing about the city for me was the taxis; the drivers drove like maniacs (the New York taxi drivers were sedate by comparison). There was I think only one crossing with traffic lights in the whole city and there were a few manned by traffic police, but at every other intersection it was 'devil take the hindmost'; the drivers barely paused and risked their, and their passengers', lives at every one. There were wide boulevards, which I suppose made it marginally easier to see other traffic, but it was still terrifying. I remember seeing the Plaza de Mayo with the pink fronted Presidential Palace, where twenty-five years on crowds were to gather to cheer Galtieri on in the battle for the Falklands.

My other memory of Argentina was how pervasive was the English influence; after all the English had built the railways and a lot of the cattle business had been English. We were invited to a barbecue lunch at a ranch in the country; all the young men present could have been old boys of any English public school. They all wore cavalry twill trousers, tweed jackets with four buttons on the cuffs and little flat tweed caps. They were all familiar with horses and were also interested in rugby. I suppose that must have all gone by now – not the horses and the rugger, but the Englishness, particularly after the Malvinas.

From Buenos Aires we flew on to Chile; it was a long flight and the country below rose steadily for mile after mile; we saw Mendoza below and then the Andes ahead. The piston-engine planes could not fly high enough to go over the Andes; we had to fly through a pass just below the peak of Aconcagua, looking up at the giant statue of the Christ of the Andes and the high mountains on both sides of our plane. From the snow covered mountains we descended rapidly into the fertile sunny valley of Santiago. I regrettably did not see much of Chile. On the very first night when we were at a dinner at the Central Bank, I became violently sick and had to return to my hotel with gastro-enteritis; this despite the antispasmodic pills given out by the Fund doctor before we left. I spent a couple of days in bed and recovered enough to join the party on our flight to Lima in Peru.

I had not before realised that the Peruvian coast is virtually a desert. The biggest impression for me were the pelicans in the sea just outside Lima. The Minister of Finance was very much the English gentleman. We spent a day on his estate way out in the country, at least a couple of hours by car; it wasn't desert, but it was pretty arid and bleak. From there we flew back to Washington. We landed briefly in Panama late in the evening; PJ went down the steps and stood on the soil; I stayed at the top of the steps. He made fun of me later.

'Moubray, I have been to Panama, but you haven't; you never set foot on Panamanian soil!'

The next morning we flew over the mountains of Cuba and I remember thinking that somewhere down there in the jungle was the young rebel Fidel Castro trying to overthrow the dictatorship of Batista. I wished him well then.

1957 was the year of Asian flu and Daphne succumbed to it soon after we returned from Latin America. She was very low and had to give up breast feeding. It would shock people to know that she and I were on drugs: specifically, I think, what is known as 'speed'. Tom Gonder prescribed amphetamines generously whenever one felt low; we used to call them 'purple hearts' – the pills were heart shaped and blue rather than purple. We still had some with us in England in 1960. Neither of us had any idea that they were much different from aspirin or a tonic. I was amused in April

2003 to hear on the TV news the shocked discovery by the Channel 4 news team that American pilots in the Second Gulf War had been prescribed amphetamines – they thought this explained the incidents of 'friendly fire'!

Daphne badly needed a holiday, but there was still the Fund and Bank Annual General Meeting to get through. This year it was Washington's turn to host the meeting. I was kept very busy. Every Minister of Finance and Governor of a Central Bank wanted to call on Jacobsson. PJ was not very good at time keeping and I had to keep these distinguished visitors occupied whilst PJ was seeing the previous appointment. I haven't kept a diary, but I think the British Chancellor of the Exchequer was Thorneycroft. He was amongst many people I had to keep entertained with small talk. Another problem with PJ was that he could not keep his pen from paper; I would see him on the dais about to make a speech and realise that he was making changes to his speech. I hurriedly went up on the dais and told him that he could not do that; the text of his speech had already been given to the press and any subsequent changes would be thought to have great significance. He always took it very well and reverted to the speech as initially drafted. He was very good with the press; he gave many interviews to individual financial journalists and performed very well at Press Conferences. He was adept at giving revealing answers obliquely by telling a story. It would be an exaggeration to say that he spoke in parables, but he reminded me of what I had read about Abraham Lincoln; they would have got on well together.

The Fund's Press Relations officer, Jay Reid, found him a congenial boss. As a 'spin doctor' Jay was always pleased when he managed to manoeuvre PJ on to the lead financial story in the *Washington Post* on the very day that Eugene Black, the President of the IBRD, had expected to make the headlines! There was the usual round of parties and dinners. I remember once sitting at a dinner next to the Minister of Finance of Turkey; we did not have much to say to each other and I mention it only because it was a strange feeling a few weeks later to hear that there had been a coup in Turkey and that the Minister of Finance had been hanged!

At last we could go on holiday. We rented a cottage in Bermuda. In those days it was a four hour flight from Washington. Daphne was so weak I had to practically carry her up the steps to the aircraft. Amicia travelled in her blue carrycot. Going through customs at Hamilton Airport people commented on our beautiful Bermudan baby, pink skin and blue eyes. The sandy beaches of Bermuda are pale pink and the sea between the shore and the coral reefs is a deep blue. We had a nice cottage, about five minutes walk from Hungry Bay down a lane lined with papaya trees (I have a feeling that in Bermuda they are called pawpaws). The sea was wonderfully warm and snorkelling was a delight – parrot fish, angel fish and many other brilliantly coloured creatures. The vegetation stays in my mind too, particularly the grape trees with thick fleshy leaves. We went round the island – by taxi, I think; I am not sure that private cars were even allowed. In Hamilton we went round in horse drawn carriages. Daphne bought some paintings by a local artist called Birdsey; they now hang in Buxlow and in Amicia's house in Thorpeness. Birdsey is apparently quite a well known Bermudan artist. When leaving I bought an expensive watch (duty free) for about $50, which Crispin now wears and a gallon (an American gallon which is smaller than an Imperial gallon) package of liqueurs; they lasted over twenty years!

Life in Washington was not quite as it had been the previous time. I did not now eat sandwiches for lunch, but ate in the Executive Dining Room. I don't think PJ often did that; I think he must have gone back to the Sheraton Park to eat with Mrs PJ. I know that it was in their suite that I once joined them for lunch with Roger and Moyra Bannister. One of my favourite luncheon companions was the West German Executive Director, Otmar Emminger, who later became President of the Deutsche Bundesbank. Thinking of Germans reminds me of a story Jacobsson told me. In 1951 the German economy was the sick one of Europe, as it is again fifty years later. The new Deutschemark had not yet really got established and Erhard's free market reforms were still to bear fruit. The OEEC were very worried that the West German balance of payments deficit would overwhelm the new multilateral intra-European settlement system, the EPU, which was to be set up in 1952. They appointed Jacobsson and Alec Cairncross, a Professor of Economics and later the chief economist at the Treasury, on a mission to Bonn to try and sort out the German problem. At one meeting, PJ told me, the Germans said, 'You don't need to worry, Mr Jacobsson, we Germans work very hard and we will get this right.' To this Jacobsson replied, 'Yes, I remember from school that there were some boys who had to work harder than others.' He obviously did not like the Germans! However I remember that he said that he had admired the technical expertise of Helmut Schacht, the President of the Reichsbank under Hitler. I also lunched quite frequently with Jay Reid, keeping him informed of what was going on. I had 'quit' the Bank of England 'with an option to return' and I saw it as my duty to give my loyalty wholeheartedly to Jacobsson; I am sure that a Frenchman in my position would have been plying the Banque de France with inside information; I never did that. I believe I did once write to Maurice Parsons, when it was a question of how long I should stay with PJ.

The next significant event of 1957 was the visit by PJ and me to Paris. Mrs PJ was with us; we also had a young Dutch economist from the Fund's European Department. We stayed at the very luxurious Hotel Meurice on the Rue de Rivoli. We were to spend quite a long time in Paris – about two weeks, I think – trying to help them with a package of financial reforms, which were very badly needed. This was about six months before the return to power of General de Gaulle. We had endless meetings at the Banque de France and at the Ministry of Finance.

One evening PJ said I could have some time off. 'Go and amuse yourself,' he said. I am afraid that I went to the Lido to see the Bluebell Girls! When

I returned to the hotel it must have been after midnight, but the night porter said that Mr Jacobsson had been insistent that I should go up to his room the moment I got in. There he was, pacing up and down in his dressing gown; PJ must have weighed at least 18 stone and I feel sure that the chandeliers in the room below must have been swaying. So we sat down – with a bottle of champagne (his favourite tipple for stimulating the brain) – and rewrote a paper for the Minister of Finance. The Fund had a resident representative in Paris, Jan Mladek, formerly a Czech, whom I have already mentioned. He took no part in these meetings, but he must have provided us with a typist. Jan gave me a short tour of Paris one Sunday morning; I was a little taken aback to discover that he was not married to the girl he was living with – another sign of my innate naivety! They took me to the *marché des puces* where I bought Daphne a sweet little porcelain figure of an eighteenth century court lady dressed as a country girl.

One evening I went out with Harry Travers, whom I had not seen since Oxford. He was working in the OEEC, which later became the OECD, where he spent the rest of his working life. We went to some bars on the Left Bank. The main thing I remember about the evening was the discovery that he had had a passionate affair at Oxford with Moyra Jacobsson and believed she would have married him were it not for her father, who disapproved of him. Moyra says that it was never more than a mild romantic attachment. He married another girl. I met Harry again in Paris forty-three years later; he still wanted to know all that I could tell him about Moyra. Harry was also convinced that on that evening in Paris in 1957 we had had a riotous time and that I had got into some kind of fight. I remember going out with him, but I have absolutely no recollection of being involved in a fight.

Another evening I was invited to drinks with Agnes de Longeville (I think that was her name) who had been Assistant Financial Attaché at the French Embassy in London under René Sergent, whom I had known when in the O&F, and whom I had entertained in London. She was now married to an Inspecteur des Finances and the party was full of young 'Enarques'. I had a difficult time; they were all polite enough, but were clearly incensed that an Englishman should be involved in French financial reforms. They were also very worked up about Algeria and, without even asking seemed to be convinced that I would be violently opposed to '*L'Algérie Française*'; they were unanimously in favour and believed that all foreigners were prejudiced against the French. So I had an interesting evening. I have to say that I did not really have any views on Algeria; I was not well informed on the subject. Our work in Paris finished, I set off back to Washington in time for Christmas. I flew in one of those old fashioned Boeing Stratocruisers, where there was a cocktail lounge in a bubble up a wrought iron circular staircase. The Stratocruisers were on their last legs and being kept going with great difficulty awaiting the arrival of the first Boeing jets – the 707s. We had not go very far from Paris when our plane ran into some kind of difficulty and we were forced to land at Shannon Airport. We were told that the plane would not take long to repair; meanwhile we were encouraged to accept the airline's hospitality – I presume it must have been Pan-American Airways. We sat in a lounge surrounded by lovely young girls dressed in Irish tweeds trying to sell Irish goods duty free and being served Irish coffee, heavily laced with Irish whiskey. After an hour or two they announced that it would still take a little time to get our plane going, and if we wanted, beds were available. But we took them at their word – 'only a little time' – and so went on drinking. It was finally dawn before we were able to take off again; I think that they had to cannibalise a Stratocruiser in Newfoundland to find the spare part needed.

When I got home I discovered that Daphne, Amicia and a girl friend of Daphne's had been snowbound in Lower Ranleigh for two or three days; they had had to put the dogs out of the windows to do their duties. In my later years at work I would have rung Daphne every day to see what was going on, but transatlantic telephones were so difficult and unreliable that I had in fact been cut off from my family for two or three weeks.

We spent a traditional Christmas at Lower Ranleigh with a Christmas tree; Amicia was not old enough to appreciate it, I think, but it was the start of a family tradition that still continues today. A strange thing happened on Christmas Day. Ed Dale of the *New York Herald Tribune* rang and said: 'Guy, I hear you have just returned from France; you can tell me, is the French franc to be devalued?'

'Ed,' I said, 'it's Christmas Day. Merry Christmas, and you don't really expect me to answer that question.' An outright denial might have been misinterpreted, so I said something like this: 'The French are carrying out some useful reforms which I think will be effective.'

So he was denied his scoop; the franc was devalued early in January, for the second time in six months; this was not yet the New Franc which came under de Gaulle. I still think it extraordinary that Ed should have thought that a person in my position, even though a personal friend, would have been prepared to leak market sensitive information like that.

1958 turned out to be a very busy year. But life had a regular pattern. Daphne had at last taken driving lessons and could now drive the Chevrolet – with automatic gear shifts; she could not manage manual gears. I bought a cheap second car, and every morning after breakfast would drive to the Fund across the Chain Bridge; it took twenty minutes in to the private Fund car park in the basement of 1818 H Street. We continued to see many friends. The economist at the Embassy was now Kit McMahon, with his Australian wife Mandy. We were quite close friends, and indeed lent them both our carry cot and the English pram for their first son. I was to see a lot of Kit in the 1960s. I don't think I mentioned at the time that on our previous posting the Embassy economist had been Fred Atkinson with his wife Jane and two small children. Fred had been a don at Jesus in Oxford and occasionally took me for tutes when Tony Crosland was not available.

He was another person I was to work with quite closely in the 1960s. He later became the Chief Economist at the Treasury and is now Sir Fred. I spent a night with Fred and Jane at their house in Kent a couple of years ago and they once visited Buxlow. One of their daughters, presumably now 50, is on the staff of the Fund in Washington.

Another guest from the past was Peter Hobson, who stayed with us briefly at Lower Ranleigh. He was now officially with the Foreign Office, but was actually a spy, specialising in the Far East with his fluent Japanese, Indonesian and Mandarin Chinese. He gave me a jazz record by Thelonious Monk about whom he enthused; but it was just a bit too modern for me. Like Philip Larkin, I incline to the view that not much jazz written after 1945 is worth listening to. This is not quite true; I like Dave Brubeck and Paul Desmond and enjoy very modern players, so long as they play old stuff – like Diana Krall.

In February the Jacobssons and I embarked on another long journey, which was to take us right round the world. The 1958 annual meeting was to take place in New Delhi and it was decided that we should pay a preliminary visit to India. The Jacobssons and I were accompanied by the Head of the Fund's Asian Department, James Raj. We set off from New York one evening, but had not been airborne very long before a passenger became very ill; he was sitting in the aisle seat about two rows ahead of me on the left. We were just being served cocktails when he choked and slumped; the hostesses quickly gave him an oxygen mask and the pilot announced that we were returning to Idlewild to land the passenger. This was a euphemism I am sure – there was no passenger, only a dead body. But they kept up the pretence with the oxygen mask until we landed I am sure that they knew that we all knew and to cheer us up we were plied with complimentary champagne in the VIP lounge.

Eventually we took off again with the conspicuously empty seat. It was a long flight. The first stop was to be at Rome, the old airport, not Ciampino. As usual after dinner we climbed up into our bunks, changed into pyjamas, took a sleeping pill and went to sleep. By dawn we were flying over Ireland and reached Rome in the afternoon. Some passengers disembarked and new ones came on board – but that one seat was still empty. We flew all night, stopping briefly, I think, at Ankara and at dawn landed at Teheran. It was a beautiful sight with the early sun giving a red glow to the snow on the mountains. More passengers disembarked, and new ones came on board; the empty seat was now occupied. I could not help wondering what the man would think if he had known that a man had died there only about 24 hours earlier! Later that day we finally reached New Delhi.

India still seemed to me to be very much as it had been under the Raj. All the senior civil servants we met were very much as one would have expected of the ICS. I also found a great deal of respect for the English. Pandit Nehru is said to have remarked, 'I am the last of the English to rule

India.' One of the high points of our visit was to call on Pandit Nehru, the Prime Minister, in his office. And, of course, he was right – he was in many ways a typical Old Harrovian! He spoke with an English upper class accent, and was quite charming. I made a faux pas. I admired the engraved steel paper knife on his desk; I had assumed that it was Indian craft work, but when I asked him where it came from he said, 'Toledo!' But perhaps I wasn't so foolish; the craft work of Toledo is heavily influenced by the Moorish occupation and thus very like the Moghul art of India. Our stay in India was more like a state visit than a working mission. We stayed at the Ashoka Hotel, which was to be the site of the Annual General Meeting later in the year, so I suppose satisfying ourselves that it would be suitable could have been described as work. We saw all the sights, Lutyens' great buildings and boulevards, the Red Fort, where I had been stationed thirteen years before and the Qitab Minar in black marble.

We were also taken for a day to visit the sights of Agra, which must be over a hundred miles from Delhi. We admired, as how could one not, the Taj Mahal. Until I visited it, I had never appreciated that just behind the usual view of it are the banks of the River Jumna. Even more impressive than the Taj Mahal was Fatehpur Sikhri, a city fortress built of red stone by the Moghul emperors in the sixteenth century, I think, standing remote above the vast Jumna valley. It had been occupied for only a very short time, since it was discovered that the water supply was quite inadequate. The roofscape somehow reminded me of Mervyn Peake's *Gormenghast*. One could imagine horses galloping across it. But standing on one of the ramparts was another mausoleum for an Empress in white marble, just as beautiful as the Taj Mahal and contrasting vividly with the red stone all around.

We continued our visit of India with a few days in Bombay. One evening PJ and I had dinner with all the top politicians of the state of Maharashtra; one of them was Morarji Desai, who was soon to be Minister of Finance of India and later Prime Minister. I sat next to the Maharashtran Minister of the Interior. As is often my wont I was provocative. The state had recently imposed prohibition, and I asked him how he thought he could make it stick without a full scale criminal bootlegging industry. He made it clear that principle was much more important for him than practicality. What actually happened I think was that all those who wanted to drink ignored the law, and that the police turned a blind eye to it, although there must have been a lot of bribery. I spent some time with an old boyfriend of Daphne's from LSE/Cambridge. Noshir Pochkhanawallah was a Parsee from Bombay. He was a wealthy businessman, mainly in the food processing industry. Anyway I spent the day with Noshir and his wife Pinny. When he picked me up in his car, he had already filled the boot with beer. We had dinner at their house.

On the following Sunday Noshir and Pinny took me to the races. Racing in Bombay on a Sunday was a fine sight; everybody was dressed up, all the women wore the most expensive saris embroidered with gold. I have to say that it was in fact the first time in my life that I had ever been horse racing. Bombay racecourse must be the only racecourse that I have been to which neither Crispin nor Jocelyn have ever visited! Our final outing, for the Jacobssons and me, was a visit to the caves at Elephanta. We set out in boats. Once on shore Mrs Jacobsson, sitting in an Indian version of a sedan chair, was carried to the caves by four strong men. The contraption in fact looked rather like the heavy howdahs on elephants. What she made of the caves, I don't know. They are full of elaborate Hindu carving, much of it highly erotic.

From Bombay we flew to Japan, calling briefly at Hong Kong, where we were given a guided tour by car. How things have changed! I don't remember seeing a single skyscraper. The streets were teeming with people, markets everywhere and it all looked spotlessly clean; perhaps we were not shown the dirty areas, if there were any – the population then must have been a great deal smaller than it is today.

In Tokyo we were greeted by the Japanese Executive Director of the Fund, Mr Watanabe. Our time in Japan was again, something of a state visit. We stayed at the old Imperial Hotel designed by Frank Lloyd Wright. I am not at all sure why it has subsequently been pulled down. It was said to have been one of the earliest buildings designed to be able to withstand earthquakes. It had one serious drawback for me – the corridor of gift shops in the basement had a ceiling which was only just over 6 ft; I had to walk with my head bowed. I did not like Tokyo. It was too crowded and already very affected with smog. I found everything large ugly and everything small exquisite; the matchboxes were lovely, every bit of paper had delicate watermarks, but the buildings had no character, except of course the Imperial Palace itself. The parks were lovely; although the Japanese cherries were not yet in flower. At that date many of the women in the street were still wearing kimonos, but it was rare amongst the men.

The Jacobssons were given the great honour of being taken to the Imperial Palace to be received by Emperor Hirohito. This I believe was not so much because he was the Managing Director of the Fund but in recognition of the clandestine work he had done in Basle during the war, using his pre-war Japanese contacts in trying to bring about a peaceful surrender. I am sure that what he did is all public knowledge now, but I remain very ignorant of it.

The Japanese are extremely hospitable and I discovered that you have to be careful not to praise something or it will be given to you. I spent one evening at a dinner with three young officers of the Bank of Japan; we drank a great deal of sake. At one point I said how much I liked the small porcelain sake decanter and thought nothing more of it. But as we left the restaurant the Japanese presented me with a gift wrapped, as their presents always are, in delicate cloth, inside which was the very same decanter. The men from the Bank of Japan must have arranged to buy it from the proprietor of the restaurant. I have it still. On another evening the Jacobssons and I were taken to have dinner at a geisha house. We each had our personal geisha kneeling beside us looking after us. They also performed a number of stylised dances to the music of the samisen. I find the stark whiteness of their makeup quite off-putting. Their kimonos are of course beautiful.

I enjoyed the food. A dinner at a tempura house is a theatrical performance, with the cook behind the counter presenting you ceremonially with a deep fried tiger prawn in a beautiful bowl and with just the right touch of green from seaweed to go with it. One lunchtime I went to have lunch at a sushi bar with an Australian friend of Peter Hobson's, whom I had met in London some years before. He had recently arrived to join the Australian Embassy and did not know his way around any more than I did. We sat at this counter being served endless pieces of raw fish and the accompanying sauces; we wondered when the meal would end. Eventually a Japanese girl sitting next to us spoke up and told us that he would go on serving us until we told him to stop!

When the people from the Bank of Japan heard that I was interested in netsuke they took me to an obscure dealer in a little shack under a railway bridge, who had one of the best collections in the country. I bought several. My favourite in many ways is one which has not been carved at all; it just a small knot of natural wood with two holes drilled into it for the cords. (I may be quite wrong about this memory – it could have happened on my next visit to Tokyo eleven years later!)

We flew back to Washington stopping briefly at Anchorage in Alaska, which was still white with snow. All these flights incidentally were in DC 7Cs, quite a step up from the DC 3 Dakotas I had flown in in 1945/6. Our last stop was in Seattle, where for the first time I was able to ring Daphne; as soon as I heard her voice I broke into tears – tears come very easily from me, but I was moved to hear her voice again. Finally I was back at Lower Ranleigh.

I think it must have been in the summer of 1958 that Jacobsson and I went to have lunch with Dag Hammerskjöld at the UN building in New York. The IMF is a UN Agency, although the UN Secretariat has absolutely no power over it, but a courtesy call seemed appropriate and besides both men were Swedes. But it was a very difficult occasion; both men heartily disliked each other and had done so for years. Jacobsson had publicly blamed Hammerskjöld for debauching the Swedish currency after the war, aided and abetted by Ivar Rooth, PJ's predecessor as Head of the IMF, but then Governor of the Riksbank. Sweden having been neutral during the war came out of it in a very strong economic position. According to Jacobsson, Hammerskjöld, then head of the Swedish Ministry of Finance, and Rooth then embarked on an orgy of tax and spend socialism – anathema to PJ.

At lunch in Hammerskjöld's private dining room there were only six of us – PJ and I, the General Secretary and three of his aides. I remember being

Daphne and Amicia in the drawing room at Lower Ranleigh, 1958

puzzled to find myself seated at Hammerskjöld's left and PJ at his right; according to US etiquette the honoured guest sits at the host's left. Was it intended as a deliberate insult to Jacobsson? Probably not. He was probably just following European practice – and yet at least one of his aides was American and might have been expected to arrange the *placements* in the US fashion. Who knows? In any event, vain though Jacobsson was, I don't think he would have noticed where he was sitting. He wanted to talk about the affairs of the world, where on almost every subject he and Hammerskjöld had totally opposing views; one an archetypal hedgehog and the other a fox.

Come September and it was time for the Fund's Annual General Meeting in New Delhi. It was common practice for those members of the Fund who were required to attend the meetings when they were held abroad to tack on some holiday; after all the fares were paid. My trip to England with Daphne and Amicia, however, was I believe paid for because of a provision which allowed Fund members home leave every other year. We sailed from New York on the SS *United States*, the American answer to the *Queens* – larger and faster. I think it was actually on our sailing that the ship won the Blue Riband of the Atlantic by making the fastest crossing ever. The thing I remembered most about it was that the Promenade Deck, unlike the *Queens'*, was glassed right down to the deck, so that you could see the sea when lying on your wooden chaise longue; not that I did much lying around; I spent a great deal of time following Amicia up and down and round. I left them in England and flew off to India. They stayed first with Daphne's parents and then went to Jersey to stay with my parents.

The Fund meeting involved much the same activities whether it was in Washington or abroad. I helped PJ with his speeches and entertained his visitors as they waited for their interviews. I am sure there must have been some splendid entertaining, but somehow I do not recollect what form it took. The only other incident I remember was having lunch in Jacobsson's suite with William Rees-Mogg, a ginger haired young financial journalist with the *Financial Times*. There is something about flaming red hair which makes the person seem so young and it is great a surprise to see how different they look when their hair goes grey, as Rees-Mogg's did very early.

After the meeting Jacobsson and I and John Gunter, head of the Fund's Middle East Department, paid a fascinating visit to Pakistan. The country was in the middle of a coup; Mirza was still President but the de facto ruler was General Ayub Khan with the Title of Chief Martial Law Administrator. We had a meeting in the President's office with Mirza in the chair; on his left sat Ayub Khan and on his right Jacobsson. Besides John Gunter and me there were two others, I think, one from the Ministry of Finance and the other from the Central Bank. I have never since sat though such a strange meeting; Mirza was still addressed as President, but on every point he gave way to the Martial Law Administrator, who nevertheless maintained all the courtesies to his still nominal boss. It was, of course, not long after we had left that Mirza was ousted and Ayub Khan proclaimed as President.

The remark I quoted earlier attributed to Pandit Nehru could have equally been applied to Ayub Khan. He was, without doubt, the last Englishman to rule Pakistan. He was Sandhurst educated, spoke with an English upper class accent and looked every bit the British General. We had another example of it that evening. We all received invitations to a cocktail party given by the Chief Martial Law Administrator. It was held on the lawns of his Headquarters. It was dusk when John and I arrived. We were greeted by Ayub Khan, who turned to a man and said, 'Hasnie, give these chaps a drink will ya,' in a clipped English voice. Hasnie, by the way was not a servant; he was just about to be appointed Governor of the Central Bank. Muslim or not, cocktails were served and consumed by everybody. It was a warm, balmy night and we sat in large wicker chairs chatting away. The ladies wore the most stunning dark saris, edged with gold and silver. They all gave the impression of being very wealthy. I spent a great part of the evening talking to Beheiry, Governor (or Deputy Governor?) of the Central Bank of the Sudan who happened to be present in Karachi when we were there, on his way back from the Annual Meeting, no doubt. He was another relic of the Empire; although very dark skinned, he had been educated at Cambridge, spoke perfect English and smoked a large pipe. The whole event could easily have been a cocktail party in Oxford or Cambridge.

From Karachi we flew back to London. I called at the Bank of England and saw Jasper Hollom and Maurice Parsons. I have always had an opinion on what was going on around me and was ready to express it. Being with Jacobsson, I mixed with a lot of very senior people and became used to taking it for granted that my views would be listened to with interest. So when I saw Jasper, I commented freely on UK monetary policy. The year before, the Bank of England had made a big break with post-war practice in raising Bank Rate to the unprecedentedly high level of 7 per cent. I seem to remember saying to Hollom, 'And high time too – I don't know why you didn't do it earlier.' I suspect he found this rather outspoken of me; after all in Bank terms I was still only a Senior Clerk, whilst he was the Deputy Chief Cashier. When I had first gone to Washington with Jacobsson it was intended that I should return after two years, so this was really about the time I should have been returning to the Bank; but Jacobsson had made an earnest plea to Cobbold that I should be allowed to stay on with him for another year. And it was decided that I should stay on until after the Fund's Annual General Meeting of 1959.

I then flew to Jersey to join Daphne and Amicia. My parents had sold Maison du Douet earlier that year, when my father gave up fruit farming; he had just turned 70. They had bought Le Marais, an old farmhouse in St. Mary's parish. Why they chose names associated with water, I don't know; *douet* means a spring, and *marais* a swamp or marsh. Jersey is a most attractive island with lovely rocky granite cliffs and sandy beaches. I always enjoyed walking on the beaches and picking up all sorts of attractive water worn pebbles.

Our holiday over we returned to England and sailed for New York on the *Queen Mary*. But we first had a problem; Amicia had travelled to England on Daphne's passport, but when we went to the US Embassy in Grosvenor Square to get visas, they refused to give one to Amicia – visas were for foreigners, and Amicia was a native born American. So we had to get a separate American passport for Amicia, with an endearing photograph of a plump smiling little girl of 18 months!

I find it extraordinary how much it was taken for granted to spend five days sailing across the Atlantic; after all, even though jet planes had not yet come into operation, one could cross the Atlantic in twelve hours. So it was that, of the period of just over a month for which we were away, we had spent ten days on a ship. Mark you, travelling on the transatlantic liners was a holiday – but not without difficulties with a small child; every night the clocks went back one hour and Amicia's internal clock did not adjust that easily and every morning she woke up earlier and earlier!

Life in Washington resumed its normal rhythm. Suzetta was still with us. We now had three dogs, since Ginny had given birth to a puppy whom we called Cindy. Daphne had joined painting classes and was trying oils.

She seemed very happy, but apprehensive, I know, at the prospect of returning to England. Quite a few Bank of England people were in Washington at the same time as us. There was always one member of the Bank's Statistics Office working in the Fund's Balance of Payments section. When we first arrived it was George Blunden, who was very friendly, but began to show signs of – I don't know quite how to describe it; he did not exactly have a chip on his shoulder, but gave the impression that we were adversarial. I did not feel in the slightest bit in competition with him, but he continued this for several years. In the 1980s he became Deputy Governor. His successor in Washington was John Page; we saw John and his wife Gloria socially. He was another who was going to resent me later. He became Chief Cashier, the last I think to hold that job when it was combined with being Chief Executive of the Bank. Whenever the Governor came to Washington, he always held a drinks party to which all the Bank people would come. The Alternate Executive Director for most of my time was Roy Heasman with whom I was to work closely in the 1960s.

There was always, too, a younger man in the post of Technical Assistant, the post I had filled in 1953/4. In 1958/9 it was Martin Mays-Smith, about five years younger than me. He had great charm with a lovely infectious giggle. He distinguished himself in Washington by importing a 1936 Rolls, a very stately car. I have a home movie of him driving the Rolls down the drive from Lower Ranleigh, with his girlfriend doing stately royal waves. Martin was very able and would surely have risen high in the Bank, but he was impatient. He very much resented that a contemporary of his at Cambridge, Raymond Bonham-Carter, had been leapfrogged into the Bank as an Acting Adviser through some influence with Cobbold, whereas Martin had to follow the graduate entry slog of starting as a probationary clerk. It was not long after he returned to London that he left the Bank and joined the merchant bank Kleinworts.

Jacobsson and I did three trips abroad in 1959. The first was to Spain. I think Mrs PJ was with us again. We went to Madrid and had meetings with the Ministry of Finance and the Banco de España. Franco was embarking on a series of economic reforms, strongly influenced by his senior ministers who were all members of Opus Dei. I remember being a little apprehensive on the flight to Madrid by Iberia – up until then I had flown only on American or British airlines. The Spanish crew looked rather untidy and the captain had what would then have been called five o'clock shadow, but was not far off being 'designer stubble'! But the flight went perfectly well! In Madrid Jacobsson again had the privilege of being seen by the Head of State. Franco was to be added to the list of famous people he had met. On the return flight into the prevailing wind we had to make an intermediate stop in the Azores. There was a patch of land right alongside the airstrip on which workers were lifting new potatoes – I mention this only to try and time the trip; new potatoes in the Azores must have been in the very early spring.

Another trip, later in the year, was to Mexico. PJ, although thirty-one years older than me, was indefatigable. When we got back to Washington I was exhausted. Dr Tom Gonder's amphetamines did not cure me. Tom eventually decided to put me into the Doctor's Hospital (where GPs can put their own patients under their care) for observation and tests; I think he suspected Addison's Disease. In the end he decided that it was just a mild case of hypothyroidism – unusual because most people with that condition are fat and I was still pencil thin, as I had been ever since that fearful troopship to Bombay. He said that my natural energy drove me on to burn off the fat, or some such explanation. Anyway he put me on to thyroxine tablets which had an immediately good effect. I also began to put on weight – modestly to start with, but I now have great difficulty in keeping my weight below 17 stone! The doctors in England disputed his diagnosis and would no longer prescribe thyroxine. Finally in about 1998 Dr Seaton in Ipswich came to the same conclusion as Tom Gonder had forty years before! Since I have been back on thyroxine I feel healthier than I have for many years.

One remarkable feature of living in America in the 1950s was the complete absence of inflation. The US retail price index in 1960 was only marginally higher than in 1950, but that was easily accounted for by better quality – cars in 1960 contained much more steel (those great big tail fins) and radios were by then a standard fitting; consumer durables like washing machines and dishwashers were all greatly improved. In the late 1950s there was a much discussed book by an economist by the name of Sumner Schlichter on the subject of 'creeping inflation'; Schlichter advocated it, believing that the economy would only grow with the stimulus of mild inflation. Jacobsson, of course, disagreed profoundly, both because he thought it would inevitably accelerate and also because even mild inflation steadily eroded capital values.

It was actually clear enough from the very experience of the United States in the 1950s that nil inflation was completely compatible with steady economic growth. Even in the UK there was only one year, 1958, in which the retail price index did not rise, and the balance of payments was healthy and the economy grew. That was due to the Minister of Labour, Ian Macleod, who saw off the big unions in that year. I think 1958 is in fact the only year in the last fifty in the UK without any inflation. Jacobsson spoke out against Sumner Schlichter in almost every speech he made in 1958/9; but to no avail I fear. Schlichter won the day and his legacy still dominates official thinking. I find it quite absurd, for example, that today the Government sets a target for the Monetary Policy Committee of the Bank of England of 2.5 per cent inflation – why, for heaven's sake not nil per cent?

Early in 1959 Lord Harcourt was succeeded as UK Executive Director of the Fund and Economic Minister at the Embassy by Lord Cromer. My relationship with him did not get off to a good start. The Fund was pressing the UK to take the final step of making sterling convertible into US dollars and the UK was dragging its heels; the British were very worried about the so called 'sterling balances', the debts that the UK had built up during the war to countries such as Egypt; with sterling convertible they might have all been cashed in, putting intolerable pressure on the pound. Of course, that was a possibility; but the right answer was to run non–inflationary fiscal and monetary policies, making the UK an attractive place for investment. Maggie Thatcher did it in the 1980s, but in 1959 that 'wet' Harold Macmillan was Prime Minister and was heading for a general election (the famous 'you've never had it so good' election). Early in 1959 Cromer made a speech to the Board rejecting convertibility; his arguments were entirely specious. Of course, he had no other option; he had to obey the line laid down by London. But I thought it was awful. As we left the Board meeting I found myself walking alongside Cromer and, looking down at him from my great height, said to him, 'I was ashamed to be British today!' That did not go down well, as can be imagined. I don't know how much, if at all, Cromer held that remark of mine against me. Only a few days later it was announced that Cromer was to succeed Cobbold as Governor of the Bank of England.

I saw a great deal of Cromer over the next few years and I certainly never hit it off with him as I had with Cobbold. It may have been something to do with my height; at 6 ft 5 ins I towered over him. We got on a lot better sitting down! Daphne and I were invited to dinner by the Cromers. It was a very stuffy evening. There must have been a dozen people sitting down to dinner with Lord and Lady Cromer sitting at either end and the guests then placed in strict order of precedence down to G. and D. de M sitting opposite to each other in the middle of the table. Lady Cromer was very pretty, but extremely nervous and tense.

In May we spent another holiday in Bermuda. We again rented a house, this time a little further to the west. Bermuda was still very pleasant then; now being only an hour's flight from New York I suspect it is overcrowded. The only difference I remember from our earlier holiday there was that the sea was distinctly cooler. My memory is not what it was; I suspect now that the purchase of a watch and liqueurs that I mentioned before actually took place in 1959 and not in 1957, but does it matter?

In June I flew to Europe. I was to attend the Annual Meeting of the BIS in Basle with PJ. But I flew on my own – well not strictly on my own since at the airport in New York I ran into Lord and Lady Cromer. Cromer asked me to sit with his wife because she was so desperately nervous on flights. This was to be my first ever flight in a jet, a BOAC Comet, the first commercial jet airliner. Esmee Cromer sat next to me in a terrible state; her knuckles were so clenched that they were white. She was very pretty, rather like the well known actress Margaret Leighton. My presence was I hope soothing. It provided me with a line to shoot: 'I once spent the night with the wife of the Governor of the Bank of England'! Being a jet, the flight was much quicker and there was no question of climbing into bunks; we sat up all night. Lady Cromer was of course not yet the wife of the Governor, so she had no car to meet her at Heathrow (or was it still Northolt?). I was met by a Bank car with a chauffeur and gave her a lift to wherever she was going in Mayfair.

At the Bank I called on Cobbold. He said to me, 'So, you are coming back to us.' I said that I presumed I was, but that I had quit the Bank with an 'option' to return, which seemed to suggest that I had a choice; but did not know what was I choosing between. I asked him what the Bank had in mind for me on my return: '£800 a year may not mean much to you, Mr Governor, but with a wife and family it means the hell of a lot to me.' He was nonplussed. But I had made a point and he did look into it and, as I discovered later, brought me back into the Bank at a salary at least £1000 higher than they had originally intended. When I was in the Parlours I dropped in on Peter Taylor, who was still GPS. I was sitting in my old seat as GPS 2 when the Secretary of the Bank, Dascombe, walked past; he did a double take and also noticed that I had grown a moustache, 'We've matured haven't we?' he said. Perhaps the new 'gravitas' also helped my promotion. For of course at that time I was still in Bank terms a Senior Clerk and not even of administrative rank.

I have spoken rather lightly of my talk with Cobbold, but there was in fact a very serious decision to be made. I had not been told what I would be coming back to. Daphne was very happy in America and was dreading returning to England; on the other hand, I was ambitious and keen to be a top central banker. I eventually decided that we ought to try and remain in Washington. I clearly could not expect to be kept on as Personal Assistant – the Bank had already decided on the man to succeed me. But I talked with Jacobsson at some length, almost begging him to find me some other job in the IMF. PJ was a great admirer of the Bank of England, dating back to the time of Montagu Norman and was very loyal to Cobbold; after all it was Cobbold who had been primarily responsible for his appointment to the Fund. He said, 'I promised Cob that I would not keep you and would return you to the Bank; I cannot let him down.' So I had to return to the Bank. I had decided that if things in London turned out badly I would approach Jacobsson again in a year or two's time and seek a job in the Fund. Cobbold wanted me back; as I have already said, he liked me. But of course his retirement had already been announced, and he would remain Governor for only just over a year after my return. My prospects under Cromer would certainly not be so good. But the die was cast.

So I attended the Annual Meeting of the BIS in Basle in sombre mood. I stayed again at the Euler. PJ always stayed at the Three Kings down by the river. Nothing of any importance occurred. I now knew many more senior people and also made myself known to the BIS economists. The Head of the BIS was now Gabriel Ferras whom I had now known for at least five years. He was very nice and unassuming. Daphne always said that you could judge a person by their eyes, and that she thought that Gabriel's brown eyes revealed a man of great intelligence. He was unfortunately killed in a car crash a few years later.

Back in Washington it was time for the Annual Meeting. But first Daphne and I moved out of Lower Ranleigh; the Dorrs had returned from Turkey. We shipped the dogs back to England by air to go into quarantine, but left Louis in America; the kennel man who looked after the dogs whenever we were away had established a particular rapport with Louis, who would sit on his lap as he sat in his rocking chair on his porch. We now took a house in downtown Washington on S Street. It was a substantial town house on three floors. It was right next door to a girls' school. The girls were all dressed alike in true 1950s style — swirling skirts and bobby socks; just as you can see them now in a film like *Back to the Future*. The only other event I remember from S Street was an occasion when I found that I had locked my keys in the car. The car was parked by the sidewalk with people passing by. I took a hammer and broke the small triangular light in the driver's door. Since it was reinforced glass it took repeated blows before it finally smashed. All this time people were passing by and paying not the slightest attention to this strange sight of a man trying to break into a parked car!

The Annual Meeting went off as all such meetings went, but this time I was not alone, I was working in double harness with my successor, David Somerset. David and his wife, Ruth, and their little daughter Louise arrived in early September. I remember for some reason going with them to a cricket match being played on a pitch with the Washington Monument looming up behind it. Once the decision is taken that you are leaving, you very soon feel quite detached from it.

I was with David when I received the letter from the Bank telling me what I was going back to. From the end of October, I think it was, the Bank was establishing a new Department combining the Overseas and Foreign Office, the Statistics Office and a section known as General Studies to be called the Central Banking Information Department. What a mouthful! In any other central bank it would have been called the Research Department and General Studies would have been called the Economic Section. But Humphrey Mynors had a horror of the two words 'research' and 'economics'. Quite right too, in some ways: 'research' was often a pretentious word for waffle and his views on economics were much what mine were, that is 'political economy' is fine, but pure economics is often far too remote from the real world. Anyway, the Chief of the new Department was to be Guy Watson, the Deputy Chief, Roy Heasman, who had already returned from Washington. James Selwyn was Principal of the Statistics Office; the General Studies Section was headed by John Fforde with the rank of a Deputy Chief and the Assistant Chief on the Overseas side was to be none other than Guy de Moubray! That meant that I had leaped in one bound from Senior Clerk to General Management; a promotion of at least six ranks in one go. That was the result of my talk with Cobbold in the summer. I later discovered that it had been intended that I should return as Assistant Principal in the Discount Office. From the point of view of a career in the Bank that might in fact have been better; to be on the domestic financial side was thought then to be more important; the Overseas side had had its heyday with Montagu Norman. But at one bound my salary had risen to the substantial level of about £3600 and I now became liable to supertax. As a Senior Clerk my salary had not been much more than £500. I could not have lived on that in Washington; the Fund paid me a salary of $10,000 free of tax and the Bank of England underwrote all my medical expenses. On hearing this news I was naive enough to feel excited at the prospect of working co-operatively with the three sections of the department, with the Overseas side contributing to the development of domestic economic and monetary policy based on its knowledge of measures taken in other countries in similar situations. But more of that a bit later.

As was usual with a returning Bank man I planned a tour of the States before returning to London. Basing myself everywhere on the local Federal Reserve Banks, my itinerary took me to St. Louis, Los Angeles, San Francisco, Minneapolis, Chicago and back to Washington. I went alone this time and Daphne and Amicia remained at S Street. There isn't much to say about my trip. St. Louis was very run down; but it was actively being rejuvenated, great swathes of old slum areas on the west bank of the river were being torn down and new buildings going up in their place. My flight to Los Angeles was in a Boeing 707 jet; from now on most flights were to be in jets. The bank in Los Angeles was a branch of the Federal Reserve Bank of San Francisco and I had a very pleasant host who showed me all that I should see – Hollywood, Sunset Boulevard and so on. Los Angeles was plagued by smog; on walking out of my hotel in the morning the fumes caught me in my throat. And when flying in or out, the town was swathed in mist. I enjoyed my stay in San Francisco; it is (or was) a lovely city. I was driven across the Golden Gate Bridge into Marin County to see the giant redwood trees. One evening I spent in a bar with live jazz being played by a wonderful guitarist, Barney Kessel, who used to play with Billy Holiday. In Minneapolis I attended my one and only American football match with the President of the Federal Reserve Bank of Minneapolis, Fred Demming, and his wife. I didn't think they were supporting the local team enthusiastically enough – they were not natives of Minnesota; so I did my best to cheer the home team on! Fred Demming was later to be Secretary of the Treasury (under Nixon, I think).

Back in Washington we packed up to leave S Street. All our belongings were shipped back to England; and they were voluminous – tumble dryer, washing machine, redwood picnic table and benches, a children's swing, the step ladder which I still use forty-five years later! We loaded the Chevrolet and drove to New York; it was by now well into December. We stayed again at the Westbury. I visited banks – my memory is so bad that it occurs to me that my visit to the bright young men at J.P. Morgans may well have been in 1959 rather than in 1954. Daphne and Amicia saw the sights: the Empire State, Central Park (visiting the zoo), they also went shopping and Amicia threw a tantrum in the middle of Bloomingdales! They stocked up for Christmas with decorations for our cabin and a mechanical Santa Claus.

Finally we left America. We sailed on a cruise ship, the SS *Constitution* (the ship on which Grace Kelly had sailed when going to marry Prince Rainier!). It was very sad to see the skyline of New York City disappearing in the mist. We had very much enjoyed our years in the States. But now we were on holiday. Our first stop was Las Palmas in the Canary Islands, which we reached on Christmas Eve. Christmas Day was spent on the island. Daphne went off on a coach tour of Gran Canaria, which included a lunch at a hotel up in the mountains, followed by folk dancing, all of which she took a movie of; including the appearance for a moment of the most famous passenger on our liner, Gracie Fields. Meanwhile Amicia and I toured Las Palmas in a horse drawn carriage. We also bought some lovely embroidered linen including the large tablecloth we use on Christmas Day.

Our next port of call was to have been Casablanca, but the weather was too bad so we diverted to Algeciras, where the weather was not very much better, pouring with rain, but the sea was calm enough for us to get off in little launches. We spent the afternoon in the big hotel, I think it is called the Maria Christina, with very little to do but have tea. Sailing the next day into the Med the weather improved and I think we were able to lunch on deck – an elaborate buffet. We stopped next at Palermo, where I remember the Opera House with palm trees and a trip we made up into the mountains to see a famous monastery (the name has gone!) with elaborate Moorish mosaics. Our last stop but one was Naples. We went up above the city to have a good view of the whole of the Bay of Naples. In the city there was a great covered Arcade with shops; we bought Amicia a doll.

Finally we landed at Genoa; I think it must have been the first day of January of 1960. We watched as our scarlet and white car was lifted from the hold and landed on the dock side. All our baggage was loaded into the van of the Hotel Savoia and Majestica, and we drove behind in our car. Unfortunately I then went down with flu and was confined to bed. Daphne and Amicia had to see the city on their own. Everywhere they went Daphne said they were followed by men chanting '*la bella bionda*' – Amicia had made a great hit!

When I was better we finally set off for the ski resort of Sestriere in the Alps to the west of Turin. We seemed to drive for hours in thick fog, but it was all clear and sunny when we got to Sestriere. We checked in to the 5 star hotel, the Principe di Piemonte. We stayed there for at least a week; I did some skiing, but cracked a rib when skating on rough ice on a pond and had to give it up. We had lunch every day by the pool; snow all around, but steam rising from the heated pool.

The return to England could no longer be put off. We drove our car onto a train through a tunnel into France and went to Dijon, where we stayed a day or two. It was bitterly cold. We visited the museum. Finally we set off for Calais. There were no motorways in those days so we stuck to *routes nationales*. There was virtually no traffic – it was snowing quite hard, and the three of us sitting together on the front seat (American cars had a front bench seat) seemed to be alone in the world. Incidentally, there were of course no seat belts and no child seat. At Calais the car was loaded onto the cross-Channel steamer – roll on roll off ferries had not yet been invented. We landed at Folkestone. Here it was blowing a gale and waves were breaking over the railway station; I was really worried that the car would not be able to be lifted from the hold, but they succeeded and we set off for Codmore Barn. The homecoming was pretty grim. After America the house felt bitterly cold and the very next day I rang a builder and arranged for central heating to be installed. A few days later I reported to the Bank for work – for the first time in just over three years.

CHAPTER 13

The Bank of England – a Critique

I WAS TO BE IN THE BANK for the next sixteen years. But I propose at this point to depart from the chronological approach and devote some time to setting out my views on the Bank as a whole. I think it will make my subsequent career more intelligible. I also feel that my views of the Bank are of some worth per se – I don't think any other of my contemporaries would have seen the Bank from the same perspective, nor can I think of any one of them who would agree with me.

The Bank that I joined in 1950 was still recognisably the Bank of Montagu Norman. Cobbold, Governor until 1961, and Humphrey Mynors, Deputy Governor until 1964, were the last of their kind. They would have shared Norman's view of the role of a central bank. They believed that the Bank's primary task was to preserve the pound and to that end they felt that every effort should be made to restrain the Treasury's, and the Government's (of whatever political party), natural tendency to profligacy. Finally this end also required the stability of the City to be preserved. To be able to defend the pound it was also vitally important to establish and maintain the closest possible relationships with foreign central banks; in this the Bank for International Settlements in Basle had a key role to play. As I have already said many of the European central bank governors attended the monthly meeting of the BIS, as did also representatives from the Federal Reserve in New York. The monthly meetings gave them all the opportunity to get to know each other personally. Norman established very strong personal ties with the Federal Reserve Bank of New York. The Bank also had very close links with the central banks of the Commonwealth and indeed had played a crucial role in setting them up. For many years to come the posts of Governor and Deputy Governor of many of the colonial central banks were filled by Bank of England men on secondment. For this reason the Overseas side of the Bank became in effect its diplomatic service, which gave it a certain cachet. The relationship of the Overseas side of the Bank with the Chief Cashier's Department was analogous to that of the Foreign Office to the Treasury. Those in the Overseas function saw themselves as every bit as important as those in the Cashier's Department whilst those in the CCO and the Discount Office considered themselves the professional elite.

None of these functions could any longer be done in Norman's way. The Bank was nationalised and this gave the Treasury much greater power. The City was changing too. The Bank's relationship was primarily with the Accepting Houses (merchant banks); most of their directors would have

174

been from public schools and Oxbridge; indeed a very great number of those at the top would have been at Eton with Cobbold. They formed an inner circle with as many family relationships as business ones. The Bank had equally close relationships with the Discount Houses, through the Principal of the Discount Office and with stockbrokers through Mullens, the Government brokers for the national debt. The Bank's relationship with the Clearing Banks (in those days, Barclays, Lloyds, National Provincial, Midland, Westminster, Martins and Glyn Mills) was wholly professional — the Accepting Houses were the aristocracy and the Clearing Banks the bourgeoisie.

This was mirrored in the Bank of England itself; the Bank, like first class cricket in those days, was made up of Gentlemen and Players; the Governors and Directors and a small number of Advisers brought in from outside were the Gentlemen, public school and University (mainly Oxbridge), the staff of the Bank the Players, mainly Grammar School and who had not gone to University (a very few had taken degrees in night courses, Philip Hogg and Roy Heasman for example, but for most their qualifications were acquired by taking the exams of the Bankers' Institute). Only two members of the staff had ever been promoted to the Court, Catterns and Kenneth Peppiatt. In the 1960s it became much more common; every Chief Cashier after Peppiatt (with the sole exception of the dreadful Percy Beale) became a Director — O'Brien, Hollom, Fforde and Page. After that the pattern changed when the role of Chief Cashier no longer involved also being the Chief Executive Officer of the Bank. This pattern began to be eroded with the recruitment of University graduates. Cobbold had, I believe, been responsible for pushing this through, probably in the face of some opposition from the Heads of Departments Committee, who represented the old ways.

Similar changes were taking place in the City; more and more outsiders were coming in — in the 60s such names as Jim Slater and, a little later, Robert Maxwell. They were not members of the club and had no natural respect for the office of Governor of the Bank of England. The newly created Eurodollar market in the 60s also attracted a very great number of foreign banks to London; they too had no natural respect for the Governor. For the most part they were accustomed to statutory regulation of their activities. So the ways in which the Bank carried out its functions had to change. The Bank, I believe, took a wrong turning in the 1960s and 70s, which weakened its powers and its reputation. The Bank was not alone in this. The dominant view after the war in all walks of life, academics, politicians, bankers, was that there were better ways of doing things in order to avoid repeating the Great Depression and indeed the war itself. The diagnosis of what had gone wrong was, I believe, flawed. Amongst 'the authorities', the term usually used to refer to the Bank and the Treasury collectively, there was a growing feeling that defending the currency could be too costly and also a feeling, akin to the present widespread objection to 'globalisation', that the benefits of free markets had been seriously overstated. This was the very antithesis of what Norman had believed.

Norman had become something of a hate figure and his influence on Churchill as Chancellor of the Exchequer in putting sterling back on to the Gold Standard in 1925 at the pre-war parity was seen by many as a major cause of the Depression. I think this is a very dubious conclusion. France under Poincaré had also gone on to the Gold Standard in the 1920s, but at a devalued rate; the dollar was also on the Gold Standard and yet both suffered just as much from the Depression. Monetary and fiscal policies in 1931 were clearly at fault; the insistence on high interest rates and balanced budgets was mistaken, but understandable. After all the measures taken then were not at all dissimilar to the recommendations of the IMF in recent years to Latin American and African countries, which in most cases have had the same perverse effects. Norman's advocacy of returning to gold at the pre-war parity had been a very moral stance; if the Bank of England's notes in 1914 had 'promised to pay the bearer on demand the sum of one pound' which was enough to purchase a gold sovereign, to pay the bearer one pound after the war which was now no longer enough to purchase a gold sovereign was tantamount to fraud and, in his view, was harmful to the City's international standing. Was the standing of the City that important? The answer, I have to say, is 'yes'. Without the City's 'invisible' earnings throughout the nineteenth century, and indeed up to the present day, the British economy would have been much weaker and most of Britain's inhabitants a lot poorer.

The downgrading of the importance of maintaining the currency went along with the distrust of free markets and gave rise to the belief that the authorities should control not only financial institutions, but also industry as a whole. During the period of the first post-war Labour government, the Bank could not have stood against the tide; the pound was substantially devalued in 1949, foreign trade was rigidly controlled with import licences and all foreign exchange transactions were subject to Exchange Control; under the 1947 Exchange Control Act the Bank was made responsible for administering exchange control. But as late as 1960 the Bank in its concern for free markets leaned over backwards to make things as easy for business as it was possible. The Head of Exchange Control at that time, Cyril Hamilton, a Deputy Chief Cashier, was of the firm opinion that exchange control was otiose and ought to be eliminated. So far as I remember the number of staff in the exchange control was being steadily cut down and the total number was, I believe, probably less than a hundred.

When the Conservatives were elected in 1951 under the slogan of making a bonfire of regulations, the Bank should have put severe pressure on the Government to abolish exchange control. I have since discovered, reading David Kynaston's The City of London, that Cromer argued very forcibly for the abolition of exchange control in the early 1960s. So perhaps Cobbold too had done so in 1951. But the senior officials of the Exchange

Control in the 1960s and 1970s seemed to have no doubts about its value. Exchange Control had never in my view been effective. Changes in 'leads and lags' could amount to as much as a whole year's balance of payments deficit. Moreover it seriously hampered British industries in their foreign investment. When it was finally abolished, in 1979, nobody missed it, except the now redundant staff who numbered, believe it or not, over 700.

This is perhaps the place to interpolate a personal note. After I had resigned from the Bank in 1976, but before I had actually left, I had lunch in the City with Robin Pringle, the Editor of the *Banker*. In the course of lunch I said that exchange control served no useful purpose and ought to be abolished. He asked me to write an article to that effect for publication. I reminded him that I was still a serving officer of the Bank and could do no such thing. He urged me to write it and said he would publish it anonymously. I agreed and it duly appeared. In the senior officials' mess shortly afterwards I asked Doug Dawkins, then head of the Exchange Control Department, if he had seen it and what did he think of it. 'Absolute nonsense,' he replied. 'Oh, I thought it very pertinent,' I said, but did not of course reveal that I had been the author!

As I have said, the Bank could clearly not try and maintain the stability of the City in the old ways. Many of the new people coming in were impervious to the 'Governor's eyebrows'. But I think the Bank took the wrong turning. The increasing reliance on regulatory powers has, I believe, done more harm than good. The Bank was not alone in giving greater emphasis to regulation. The Labour government's natural instinct was to believe that 'the man in Whitehall knows best'; the phrase is indeed attributed to a Labour Minister, Douglas Jay. I sound perhaps as if I always knew better than everybody else; but in this field I was as mistaken as anybody. I returned from America convinced that central banks needed statutory powers to control the commercial banks as in the United States. During the 60s competition between the banks, clearing banks and merchant banks alike, was suppressed by the instruction that they could not increase their advances (loans) by more than a given percentage. This was not a statutory requirement, although the Act nationalising the Bank gave the Treasury powers to instruct the Bank to take measures over banks. The problem was that the only sanction on banks which overstepped the limit was the disapproval of the Governor. In the mid 60s I remember well seeing figures which showed that Hambros Bank was regularly exceeding its limit and Sir Charles Hambro (already mentioned) did not give a fig for the Governor's disapproval. There were still many in the Bank against statutory controls, but they were eventually overridden. No statutory control can ever eliminate fraud. The Bank needs to keep its ear to the ground to hear what is going on early enough to take action. In a strictly regulatory environment, the regulator becomes increasingly remote from the regulated.

I suspect that the Barings crisis in 1995 would not have gone undetected if Hilton Clarke had still been Principal of the Discount Office and Roy

Bridge, Principal of the Dealing and Accounts Office (who managed the foreign exchanges); they knew the City like the backs of their hands. Ten years after I had left the Bank and had absolutely no locus standi in the matter (I was at the time a self employed management consultant) I became so worried about the regulatory process that I invited the Bank's Head of Banking Supervision, Brian Quinn, to lunch with me in the City and tried to get him interested in the idea of having an informal monthly seminar in the Bank with Directors and Chief Executive Officers of the banks, with wine and sandwiches, at which somebody (a financial journalist or a foreign banker or economist) would present a paper for discussion. The importance was not in the paper, but in sowing the seed of the idea that the stability of the City was not just something of concern to the 'authorities', but of mutual interest to all. I don't think Brian was up to lateral thinking on this scale; that sounds insufferably arrogant, but it was I who had recruited him to the Bank in the late 60s – he had been working for the IMF in West Africa (Ghana I think). It was probably only because of that past relationship that he had agreed to lunch with me. When Barings collapsed much of the fault was attributed to Brian who by then was an Executive Director.

I have been speaking about this to Christopher Bailey, the Bank's current Agent for the South East and East Anglia, who sometimes calls in here for lunch when he is about his business. He tells me that I am quite wrong about this, and that the Bank still had a very close, indeed cosy, relationship with the merchant banks and there was not the more distant, quasi-legal formality that had grown up between the supervisors and the banks in the USA. But, he says, the supervisors 'did not look closely at the Far East treasury operations which seemed to be making a lot of money out of capital and options markets arbitrage – when no other bank was able to do so! What was the magic unique to Barings? The answer, of course, was that there was no magic, only fraud.'

Personally, I am sad that the Bank regulatory function was passed to that monstrosity the Financial Services Authority. I have recently seen an interview with Eddie George in the Bank's staff magazine, *The Old Lady*; the Governor, defending this decision, said: 'There were very powerful arguments for moving the supervisory role from the Bank. Our interest, as a central bank, is in the stability of the system, yet we were responsible for consumer protection – in the sense of depositor protection. There was tension. It shouldn't be seen as a failure of supervision if a bank were to fail, because it is the essence of a competitive market place that institutions can ultimately fail.' Exactly. The problem was that banking supervision should never have been presented to the public as a consumer protection system. All this started a long time ago, probably in the 1970s.

There is no system of banking supervision, however sophisticated, that can eliminate fraud. Perpetrators of fraud should be punished, but those who suffer at their hands very often have only themselves to blame; they have either very imprudently sunk their lifetime savings into a speculative venture or they have allowed greed to blind them to the risks. The Barlow Clowes affair in 1988 is a perfect example. The licensing authority (in this case the Department of Trade and Industry) were clearly negligent. They had apparently for four years ignored warnings from the Bank of England of a 'vague sense of unease' in the City about Barlow Clowes. But the fact that those who lost money were compensated was I think misguided and did a lot to reinforce the disastrously common attitude that 'where there is blame, there is a claim'. Investors should show a degree of self-responsibility. 'Caveat Emptor' is still a very good principle. Politicians have been far too weak. By 1997 the mixture of banking supervision and consumer protection had, as the Governor said, gone too far to sit happily in the Bank.

But I believe that the Bank should again be charged with responsibility for maintaining the stability of the financial system. I hope a future Government then abolishes the Financial Services Authority. It has added immense costs to the the execution of financial transactions and gives a wholly spurious impression that the danger of fraud has been eliminated.

I am grateful to Chris Bailey again for telling me of 'the radically different approach currently adopted in New Zealand where the emphasis is on full disclosure of financial institutions' conditions and then letting the principle of *caveat emptor* prevail. It avoids the risk of "moral hazard" whereby savers can act recklessly in the expectation that the regulators (and courts) will compensate them. It also minimises the number of bureaucrats required.' New Zealand seems to show the way here, as well as in its treatment of agricultural subsidies.

Before leaving this general consideration of the post war Bank I need to say a word about economic policy. I shall come back to this later, but in the 1960s the Bank, as I experienced it, had no monetary policy; its advice to the Treasury was always macro-economic in nature and just a bit firmer than the Treasury. Most of those imported into the Bank — Maurice Allen, John Fforde, Kit McMahon, and many of the rising graduate entrants such as John Page — were all (let's be blunt) left wing. They all succumbed to the 'false compassion' of the age. Throughout the 1960s unemployment in the UK fluctuated between about 1.7 per cent and 2.3 per cent; they and the Treasury and the politicians were all committed to 'full employment', and when the percentage crept up over 2 per cent, they were convinced that reflationary measures were necessary to stop the awful social evil of unemployment. In my view this was totally misguided and had the effect of making the poor poorer than they otherwise would have been. Beveridge, in his famous White Paper of 1944, had defined 'full employment' as a level of 3 per cent unemployed. Nil unemployment is not possible; wherever firms or industries are declining there has to be frictional unemployment, since not all of those being laid off can find new jobs immediately.

The result of this obsession was that from 1945 to 1972 (the first oil crisis) the UK economy was run in a condition of constant excess demand.

Delivery dates could not be met, to the great disadvantage of exporters; there was steady creeping inflation and Trade Unions had excessive bargaining power. I hold all these left wingers very much responsible. It was not until the 1980s that this problem began to be solved. Sometime in the mid 60s I remember giving Harold Wincott, the well known financial journalist, lunch and feeding him information to support this view. It was not secret; I merely drew his attention to an article in the Ministry of Labour *Gazette* (not a widely read publication, I may say) analysing the unemployment figures. At that time those registered as unemployed amounted to no more than about 350,000 out of a workforce of some 21 million. A third of them, no less, were unemployed ex miners from Durham, all over fifty, with no prospect of finding new work as miners and not prepared to move elsewhere and to learn new skills at that age. There was no way in which they could sensibly be considered to be available for work. I said, at that time, it would be better for everyone if these men could be immediately pensioned at a rate of £1000 p.a. By treating them as available for work the Treasury (whatever party was in power) stoked up inflation which added to the misery of 56 million people and did not in fact help the 100,000 men concerned.

I remember running in to Douglas Allen, not yet Permanent Secretary of the Treasury, at a reception at some time in the late 1960s and expressing frustration at seeing the economy being constantly run at too high a level of demand and wondered why nobody seemed to see that the answer was to let unemployment rise. 'Politically impossible, Guy,' he said. But of course, fifteen years later it did become politically possible. One more remark; in the face of this constant inflation which these left wingers thought inescapable, they resorted again to regulation to try and solve the problem and tried endless fruitless measures to control wages and incomes. John Fforde, I think, had a big hand in the first attempt at an incomes policy in 1961 by Selwyn Lloyd, the Chancellor of the time.

Since writing this I have been reading two books. Sarah Millard, the Bank of England's archivist, very kindly let me have a copy of John Fforde's *The Bank of England and Public Policy 1941–1958*. I have also been rereading Per Jacobsson's *Some Monetary Problems – International and National*, published in 1958. John's book would suggest that my criticisms are too strong. There were voices in the Bank in the period covered by his book who recognised that an essential – and missing – ingredient in solving the problems of sterling and frequent exchange crises was a sound budget. Niemeyer and Mynors would have felt this strongly. But Dalton, Cripps and Gaitskell were not willing to deliver. John's theme seems to me to be that the Bank had to recognise that what it thought were the right policies were just not politically possible. This continued with Butler as Chancellor. Cobbold, I see, did once come very near to resigning – perhaps he should have done so; I don't know. I have the strong feeling that the top people in the Bank had somehow come to believe that the Bank of England and

Montagu Norman had actually been in some sense responsible for the Great Depression — which I am sure was not the case — and that they did not therefore have a very strong position from which to criticise.

When there was a sterling crisis the Bank went along with measures such as cutting back import quotas from the dollar area. But cutting import quotas was no more than a tinkering with the symptoms; the root cause was persistent excess demand. To attack that, however, the Bank might be seen as wanting to revert to the bad old days of the 30s and be grinding the faces of the poor in the dust.

Jacobsson's book makes a very clear and persuasive argument to show that a major post war depression was most unlikely. Jacobsson himself had been largely responsible for the very influential BIS Annual Report of 1944. The report analysed in great detail the differences between the the state of the world economy after the First World War and the likely conditions after the Second. It forecast that 'there will be no dearth of openings for the employment of capital for several years after the war; there would therefore be no reason to expect anything but fairly good business.' In other words, excess demand was much more likely than deficient demand. Jacobsson greatly admired the policies adopted in the immediate post war period by the central banks of Belgium and Italy. They both adopted sound money policies and managed to persuade their Socialist Governments to restrain public sector expenditure. Strangely, of course, the President of Italy, Einaudi, had previously been the Governor of the Banca d'Italia. In Italy, Einaudi abolished food subsidies overnight in the face of severe criticism. In both countries, however, the currencies became very strong, the economy grew substantially and unemployment declined dramatically. If only this could have happened in the UK. But here we were hooked on controls. Jacobsson, in an article written in January 1948, said:

> Wise planning consists, on the one hand, in giving the individual citizen an incentive to act voluntarily in the manner desired by the control and, on the other hand, in bringing about a situation in which the control can be gradually lifted. It must not be forgotten that control measures are costly, involving a waste of time and the upkeep of a huge staff of officials; account must be taken of the fact that employees in private industry are kept busy answering letters from official controllers, so that the cost is generally doubled. If all these people could be released for productive work, the national income in real terms would go up, and the standard of living with it.

Nearly sixty years later and we still haven't learned.

CHAPTER 14

Work and Home

L IVING AS WE DID IN SUSSEX, it was quite impossible to marry work and home life. We were to be at Codmore Barn for the next sixteen years. Happy years they were for me and despite her insecurity, there were many happy moments for Daphne too. She had a knack of making a home a warm and welcoming place. But reflecting this dichotomy between work and home, the following sections of these memoirs will alternate between work and home.

Assistant Chief of the CBID

In January I started work as Assistant Chief of the new Department, the CBID. For the first time in the Bank I had a room of my own – but no leather couch for an after lunch nap! My title defined very clearly what my responsibilities were, namely to assist the new Chief, Guy Watson, and keep him informed of all significant monetary and economic developments in any part of the world. There were twelve Groups in the O&F covering every area of the world, with one Group concerned exclusively with international organisations. For every Group there was an Assistant (Administrative rank) and above him usually an Adviser. All of these had to report to Watson, and my job was to co-ordinate all this and produce a weekly summary. The Governors held an almost ceremonial meeting every morning, which went by the name of 'books'. The Chief Cashier attended every day with a report on the Bank's 'books'; on Wednesdays the 'books' was followed by Overseas 'books' at which the Chief of the CBID was present together with the Advisers to the Governor concerned with overseas affairs. So on Wednesdays Watson had his own ceremony of 'books' an hour earlier, attended by Heasman and me. A draft of the weekly summary was put together by the Groups and then submitted to me. This was all fairly routine, although I do remember on one occasion calling in the Group Leader of one of the Groups to object to his statement that, Austria I think it was, had no economic problems with inflation at only 3.5 per cent. I told him that I at any rate considered that a serious problem!

In my new rank I discovered that I was now an alternate member of the Senior Officials' Mess and was allowed to attend for lunch whenever Watson or Heasman were lunching out. The first occasion was taken very seriously and one of the senior officials introduced me to the others – most of whom I hardly knew, since I had been abroad and because of the age difference; most of them were 10 to 25 years older than me. The only other alternate of my age was Alan Whittome, an Assistant Chief Cashier. The procedure then, it became less formal later, was that one helped oneself to a drink (gin & tonic, Bloody Mary or whatever) and then went to sit at one of the three tables. It was strictly laid down by the President of the Mess, Leslie O'Brien, the Chief Cashier, that people should seat themselves in the order in which they had arrived, no doubt to avoid too much chumminess. I soon discovered that it was wise to go to lunch rather later than had been my habit. When I arrived early, I found myself seated at the top of the far table with Douglas Johns, the Agent of the Law Courts' Branch, who had some way to walk to the Bank and always arrived first. He was on the verge of retirement. Very often Leslie O'Brien would also be there and a few other elderly gentlemen; their conversation seemed to be entirely devoted to golf and to pensions! There was always wine to drink and cigars with the coffee; in later years I was to help myself to a cigar every day, but in 1960 you could not have a cigar unless the Chief Cashier offered you one.

I have already said that I was naive enough to think that the three sections of the Department, the Overseas, the Statistics Office and General Studies, would work co-operatively. Nothing could have been further from the truth. Each jealously guarded its own patch. But all letters and memoranda were circulated in a 'letter book', so that the senior officials could all see what was going on in the other sections. I got into the habit, when I had seen something emanating from General Studies and thought I might have a useful idea to contribute, of writing John Fforde a memo. I feel sure now that this was bitterly resented, not so much by John Fforde as by others in his section, particularly John Page, I believe. Early in the year just before the climactic Annual Review I had expressed to Roy Heasman my surprise to discover that John Page had not yet reached administrative rank and he told me that he was to be promoted to the rank of Assistant Principal on 1 March. I think John was already feeling aggrieved that I had overtaken him so spectacularly. In Washington his Bank rank had been higher than mine. These memos of mine had another quite unforeseen effect three years later, which I will come to at the right time.

There was a strange episode that year, in that I was appointed Secretary of a committee on a subject that had absolutely nothing to do with the CBID; the committee's task was to assess whether bank deposit receipts would constitute an acceptable negotiable instrument. It was a a very small and high-powered committee. The chairman was Leslie O'Brien, the Chief Cashier, and the other two members were Hilton-Clarke, Principal of the Discount Office, and Roy Bridge, Principal of the Dealing & Accounts Office, both parts of the Cashier's Department. We did not even meet in an office in the Cashier's Department but in an office adjoining mine. None of them seemed to take it very seriously. Hilton-Clarke in particular spent most of the time teasing O'Brien. They were all contemporaries and had spent their Bank careers together. Hilton-Clarke, I suspect, thought that he was a much more knowledgeable banker than O'Brien, and may even have thought that he was better suited to be Chief Cashier. I have no doubt myself that he was a better banker, but he probably would not have had the diplomatic skills that were needed to be Chief Cashier. At any rate we met spasmodically for a few weeks and, since we seemed to be getting nowhere, I wrote a report and claimed that it was what they had agreed upon; they were happy to accept it! I still wonder what on earth made them appoint me Secretary.

Towards the end of 1960 Guy Watson told me that I was to go on a three months' General Management Course at the Administrative Staff College at Henley from April to June of 1961. I protested that I did not need to learn how to be a General Manager – I already was one – and that I did not want to leave Daphne alone with Amicia and a two month old baby. But he was adamant; all Bank of England 'high flyers' were expected to go; the Bank in fact for some years sent three men a year to such courses.

In April 1961 the time came for me to go to the Staff College at Henley. The college is housed at Greenlands, the former home of the Smith family (of W.H. Smith & Co) in a lovely situation overlooking a lawn running down to the Thames. I was to spend three months there; I don't think I learned anything of any long term value. My considered view of Business Schools and Management Consultants I shall leave until later. But I had a wonderful time. It was a quite extraordinary interlude in my life and quite out of character with what I believe to be the real me. Irrelevant though it was, the strange story deserves recording.

There were six syndicates of twelve students, the syndicates being labelled from A to F. Every syndicate had a member of the Directing Staff to supervise their work; the D/Ss for four of them were provided by permanent staff of the college, and two, including my syndicate 'E', had temporary D/Ss from industry. Our D/S was Robin Prescott, who was, I believe, Company Secretary of a cement company somewhere in Surrey. But his main claim to fame was that in his youth he had played rugby for England; a couple of years later he became Secretary of the Rugby Football Union. On arrival in the early evening we all assembled in our syndicate rooms to meet our fellow students and to meet our D/S. Robin produced a large map of the Henley area on which he had starred several pubs, half a dozen or more. He said he had been reconnoitring and had chosen these as the best, and that we were going to start visiting them that very evening. We were to meet in the car park after dinner! Our first port of call was a pub in Nettlebed; within about an hour we managed to be expelled and told never to come back! One of our number, a delightful rough diamond by the name of Jim Stone, a former miner down the pits and now an Area Manager of the Coal Board, had taken exception to two young men in shorts who had been rowing on the river; he thought they were too stuck-up; so he, and Robin Prescott himself I think, debagged one of them by the bar! So that was that for the time being.

I normally never go to pubs, but during those three months I went virtually every night. We were a very close syndicate and no one was allowed to stay behind, although some of them who found the work hard were keen to stay behind and work. I remember in particular a very meek young man from the Post Office and a South African. After returning from the pub the brightest of us would sit down and write their papers for them. My two inseparable colleagues were the said Jim Stone and Stanley Pollitt, a very bright if unhealthy looking advertising guru, then with J. Walter Thompson and later the moving spirit behind the founding of the Advertising Agency, Boase, Massimi, Pollitt. We had a great time.

The work was not at all demanding; the average standard of the students was not very high; a great number of them came from the so-called Public Services. The Principal, Sir Noel Hall, was an interesting chap and was to retire immediately after the end of our course. He had one idiosyncrasy; he believed in absolute punctuality; if he was to give a lecture at 10 o'clock, you could be sure that he would walk on to the podium just as the clock moved to ten o'clock. But he would never be early, not even by one minute, because that to his mind was also not being punctual! One of our guest speakers, Dr McCarthy, a left wing 'expert' in industrial relations, turned up twenty minutes late for his lecture. The staff member introducing him presented him as 'the late Dr McCarthy'; he had no sense of humour and looked absolutely furious.

There was one evening when every syndicate invited as a guest some distinguished figure; Syndicate E's guest was a very jovial old codger, the former General Secretary of the National Union of Miners. Was his name Deakin? Anyway he was years before Scargill. He was a Geordie and still had a strong accent. I forget how old he was, but he must have been at least in his seventies, but was quite game to accompany us to a pub afterwards. We went to what had become one of our two favourite pubs, the Stag and Huntsman at Hambledon. The other, by the way, was popular because of the landlady; she had two attributes, a splendid cleavage and she made delicious quiches. But back to the Stag and Huntsman; we were still there drinking long after closing time; it must have been after midnight when suddenly the police arrived at the front – we made a mass exodus out of the back, over a lawn and over a small wall and managed to elude them. Our distinguished guest found the whole episode enormous fun. When we got back to Greenlands, Noel Hall appeared in his dressing gown to complain about the noise. Robin Prescott, who was quite a bit shorter than I, pushed me forward so that he should not be seen; so I had to apologise and say that we would go quietly. Near the end of the course Noel Hall asked me to see him. He said that one of the students on the following course was the Deputy Chief Constable of Lancashire and that he had already heard of the disgraceful breaching of the licensing laws, and would I please tell my friends in the pubs around that this must stop. Robin Prescott had managed somehow not to be associated with this behaviour. Years later, at some Henley reunion, I discovered that members of other syndicates thought of me as being the ringleader!

I also discovered that I had a hidden talent; we used to compete against Syndicate F in a strange kind of rowing event; eight members of each syndicate would sit on the floor in the bar, one behind the other; each 'rower' would have a pint of bitter on the floor beside him; nobody could start drinking their pint until the man in front had replaced his empty mug on the floor; the winners were the team which finished first. It was discovered that I could down a pint in ten seconds (I think it was). Jim Stone said he wished he could take me back with him to Yorkshire and visit some miners' pubs; he said he could make a mint of money betting that I would down a pint faster than some miner. They would not have believed for one moment that a toff could beat one of them.

I neglected Daphne woefully. There was great pressure put on us not to go home at the weekends and I suppose I only went home every other weekend. That was very hard on Daphne with Amicia aged four and baby Simon (I think I shall call him Crispin from now on – I never think of him as Simon). But one weekend she found someone to look after Crispin and she and Amicia came to visit me. It was a lovely summer's day and we hired a motor boat in Henley and went up and down the river. At the college, Amicia, an English rose, made a great hit with some visiting potentate (from the Middle East, I think). Near the end of the course there was a ball to which the wives came – a sign of the times that there was not a single woman student.

Roy Heasman came to visit me once and, typically of me, I expressed great concern about the state of the economy and wondered why Bank Rate had not yet been put up. The summer of 1961 was one of many post-war sterling crises. The Chancellor, Selwyn Lloyd, had been as expansive as every other post-war Chancellor, except for two, Thorneycroft and Geoffrey Howe. One other visitor was Clement Attlee; I had tea with him and Lady Attlee in the sitting room; he was very easy to talk to and quite unassuming; I can't for the life of me remember what had brought him to Henley.

Before we left Henley, Jim Stone tried hard to find some means by which he and I and Stanley Pollitt could go into business together but our talents were far too diverse. Anyway, I would never have succeeded in business – unlike Daphne, I may say; I think she would have been very good at running a business.

Adviser: Western Europe and Common Market

When I returned to the Bank, I changed jobs again. I was appointed Adviser, Western Europe. I was still at the same equivalent rank and worked for an Adviser to the Governors, Rupert Raw. He was not a Bank man and had been brought in by Cobbold. We got on perfectly well, but I don't remember doing anything particularly interesting during the year that I held that post.

In the summer of 1962 there was an important change in my working life. The UK applied to join the Common Market and in the Bank I was appointed Adviser, Common Market. Responsibility for negotiations for entry was with the Lord Privy Seal (one Edward Heath); he was backed up by an interdepartmental steering group; I had nothing to do with this; the Bank's member of that group was a more junior Adviser, Ricky Hall. I formed part of an interdepartmental committee known as the Long Term Policies Group under the chairmanship of Brian Tew, Professor of Economics at Nottingham University. There were not very many members: Treasury, Bank, Foreign Office, Board of Trade, Ministry of Agriculture and maybe a couple of others. We met very regularly, each member being charged with drafting a number of papers exploring the long term implications of UK membership of the EEC. I was charged with responsibility for writing all the papers on the financial implications.

I used to have a copy of the final bound document in a green cover, but I cannot now find it. It is probably somewhere in the attic. I have however obtained a copy of one paper which I wrote called 'The Position of Sterling and the Future of the Sterling Area'. Within that document there are references to other papers, most of which I wrote: 'Possible Plans for Pooled Reserves or a Common Currency', 'Harmonisation of Economic Policies', and 'United Kingdom Relations with the IMF'. I worked with a senior mentor in the person of Lucius Thompson-McCausland, whom I have already mentioned. All the first drafts of my papers were discussed within a small committee (I cannot call it a subcommittee, because I was the only member of the committee who was also a member of the Long Term Policies Group). This committee consisted of Douglas Allen, at that time probably a Second Secretary in the Treasury, and later to be Permanent Secretary of the Treasury – and later still, as Lord Croham, a non-executive Director of the Bank of England (if you have been reading this attentively you will remember that Daphne worked for him in the Treasury and that he was a guest at our wedding!). There were two other members besides me, Fred Atkinson, later to be Chief Economist at the Treasury, and Derek Mitchell, who was fairly junior and did not take a very active part in the committee's work (he was later to be Permanent Secretary of the Department of Economic Affairs). I found the work very satisfying and was, at the time, quite proud of what I had written. But my views (and the official views) then were totally at variance with what I now believe to be right.

I have only one of those papers to draw on, but it makes very clear that we expected closer and closer union and even recognised the likelihood in the long run of a common currency. A revealing paragraph is worth quoting in full:

Membership in the EEC provides an opportunity for the strengthening of sterling quite apart from the beneficial effects hoped for in the UK economy. To some extent the UK and the Six are complementary.

The Six have –
(i) large reserves (and the experience of surpluses on external account for most of the period since the Community was established);
(ii) a tradition (admittedly somewhat recent in one or two cases) of stricter monetary policies and an electorate with bitter memories of two great inflations;
(iii) the experience of relatively rapid growth;
(iv) large savings but poor market machinery for mobilising them for international use.

The UK would have –
(i) world-wide banking facilities in concrete form – branches, agencies and correspondents on a greater scale than any other country;
(ii) market skills, both for money markets and commodity markets;
(iii) uncomfortably heavy external (and internal) liabilities;
(iv) an electorate haunted by memories of unemployment rather than of inflation.

I think this shows very clearly what our (and my) main motives were. On the one hand we were disillusioned with our own lax monetary policies throughout the whole post war period. This was not just the Labour Government, for at the time of writing the Conservatives had already been in power for eleven years. We all felt that the Continentals were doing it much better, with Erhard in West Germany and de Gaulle in France (the Belgians and the Italians were pretty sound too). The usual British naivety (or wishful thinking?) is shown in the remark: 'admittedly somewhat recent in one or two cases.' Could it really be counted on? Only in fact in the case of Germany, where the stricter policies were to continue for at least another thirty years. Our underlying assumption was that they would on the whole be stricter because their electorates were predisposed to be anti-inflationary and ours to be inflationary. The other great fear is revealed in the clause 'uncomfortably heavy . . . liabilities'.

Somewhat earlier in the paper our desire for greater discipline is revealed in this passage:

> Should we, therefore, be faced with a sterling crisis at some time after joining the Community, Article 108 would be invoked. . . . In seeking assistance for the support of sterling in any such crisis . . . the UK would need the active support of the Six . . . and we should probably not secure it *without submitting to a thorough and highly critical examination of our economic and financial policies.*

In other words our tax and spend Governments would find themselves constrained by the other members. The other attraction was the possibility that the Continentals' ample reserves would support the UK's external sterling liabilities. This was not explicitly stated. Indeed in the paper I almost dismissed the possibility:

> . . . the Community in accepting the UK as a member, would in a sense become committed to the support of sterling. This does not mean that sterling would be supported at any price or on any terms; nor does it mean that in the near future continental reserves would be married to UK liabilities.

But reading between the lines the hope is clear — note the words 'in the near future'. The only reference I can find to the common currency in this paper is the following:

> . . . if the Community were to adopt a common currency this would be a major step which might indeed be taken if the Community had already reached an advanced stage of pooled sovereignty in other matters (necessarily including national expenditure and taxation) . . . but this could not be looked for in any early stage.

One other quotation from the document reveals, on a purely personal level, why I was attracted to the Community.

> We can expect that our fiscal, monetary and incomes policies and planning, and their effectiveness, will come under even closer scrutiny in Europe than hitherto. At official level the scrutiny will for the most part occur in the Committee relating to Economic Trends and in the Monetary Committee.

If we had become members, Rupert Raw would have been the UK member of the Monetary Committee and I was to be his Alternate. This would have involved frequent visits to Brussels and have enhanced my standing. As an ambitious man that was obviously a pleasing prospect.

For the next few months the Long Term Policies Group occupied most of my working time. But as a fully-fledged Europhile, I got involved with a great number of meetings, conferences, lunches and dinners associated with the European Movement. Sir Edward Beddington-Behrens roped me in to lots of meetings — an official of the Bank of England made an impression. I gave a number of talks on the financial implications of membership. Heaven knows what I said; I am sure I would disown it now. A prominent City man, Henry Tiarks, invited me to lunch with him at his club in St. James's. The only thing I remember from the lunch is that he talked incessantly of his daughter, Henrietta, a leading debutante who was about to marry the Marquess of Tavistock.

I went to Basle for one of the central bank weekends somewhere towards the end of the year. I don't know where the bag carrier was, because I travelled alone with Sir Otto Niemeyer; the rest of the party must have gone by air. Sir Otto and I went the traditional way, by train to Harwich, the sea crossing to the Hook of Holland and then by train to Basle. It was already a bitterly cold winter, but Sir Otto insisted on keeping the heat in the carriage at maximum, and it was stifling. Every time I tried surreptitiously to turn the thermostat down a bit, he saw and objected. For much of the rest of the journey I travelled in the corridor, which was tolerably cool. The Governor must by this time have been Cromer, but I don't remember seeing him in Basle. The main purpose of my visit was to meet future colleagues on the EEC Monetary Committee. I had dinner one evening with my opposite number from the Deutsche Bundesbank, Helmut Schlesinger. We got on very well and looked forward to meeting again at work. But it was not to be. I never met him again, and in fact never heard of him again until the early 1990s when he suddenly appeared in the papers as the President of the Bundesbank; he must have been almost the last President before the establishment of the European Central Bank. In early 1963 General de Gaulle decided to veto the admission of the UK to the EEC. My job disappeared over night.

CHAPTER 15

A Family Home

At home, we were slowly settling in to life in England. Daphne, I have to say, was clearly unhappy, but there was nothing I could do in the short term about trying to get back to the States. Amicia was quite a handful, so Daphne was kept occupied. She had the car and I used to go to the station and back every day by taxi. The owner of the taxi was a charming and very helpful Pole. Daphne had help in the house; Elsie no longer worked for us, but we still saw her since she now worked for the Riggs, who lived at the bottom of our drive in Codmore House; in her place we had Mrs Tullet until she emigrated to Australia.

Daphne's great interest was the garden. We had only just started on it before we had returned to America. There was very little left us by the previous owner, just flower beds along two sides of the house and a very mature wisteria against a wall not far from the front door. Daphne expanded it considerably, building up a very fine collection of rhododendrons and azaleas. By the time we sold the house sixteen years later it had become a very fine display. Indeed the garden was the determining factor in the minds of the new buyers, who had just retired from running a nursery. The garden was not all Daphne's work; I remember once going to the Chelsea Flower Show and returning with six large Exbury hybrid azaleas. With my interest in trees, I added to the metasequoia and the tulip tree which I had planted in 1956 a number of interesting trees, including a liquidamber, a Chinese handkerchief tree (which flowered ten years later) and an *Arbutus andrachnoides* (a hybrid of the Strawberry Tree) with its distinctive cinnamon coloured bark.

Our first gardener was a very old fashioned man by the name of Smith; it would not have surprised me if he had turned up for work wearing a smock. He lived in a tumbledown cottage in a field just outside Pulborough on the road to Stopham; it was pulled down years ago. We had been reading a book by Michael Haworth-Booth about what he called 'close boscage'. With fewer gardeners available it was important to make gardens as labour saving as possible, and to that end Haworth-Booth advocated planting shrubs and perennials so close together that weeds were suppressed – 'close boscage'. Smith would have none of that. He used to say, 'I like to see good clean dirt!

Despite what I have said about Daphne's relationship with her mother, she came with us on our Easter holiday. We set off in the Chevrolet and drove to Cornwall. We stopped briefly at Fowey and then went on to St. Ives where we stayed in a hotel by the beach. I have to say that Ione, however difficult she might have been in other ways, was very good at keeping small children amused. St. Ives is a very attractive little town, which already by then had numerous galleries and resident artists. The harbour is so unusual; at low tide none of the ships is afloat and all lie keeled over on the sand; the harbour can only be used at high tide. I feel sure that Beeching's report on the railways had already been published by April 1960, but a steam train to St. Ives still ran. When we were on the beach we could see it puffing its way round the headland.

We had for some time been trying for another baby, but without success. We had various tests whilst we were still in America and I was found not to be very fertile. Various remedies were tried, to no avail. But now Daphne became pregnant. I have a feeling that it may have been the thyroxine tablets which proved efficacious; I had only started taking them in the late summer of 1959. Anyway I think it must have been in Cornwall that the baby was conceived. This was a great relief.

For our summer holiday we went to Wales. We stayed for a while near Harlech in what was then called Merioneth, a Welsh enough sounding name – why they had to change it I don't know. We had a strange accident. We were sitting in the Chevrolet on the grass verge beside a road, when a County Council tar layer approached. I leaned out of the window, and when I saw that they were going to hit us called out to tell them to stop. They ignored me – perhaps I should have spoken in Welsh – and quite slowly cut off the right hand wing of the car! It was not hard to get it repaired, but it took several weeks to get Merioneth County Council to admit liability and reimburse us. From there we went on to Lake Bala, where we stayed for several days. I had a strange experience there; the owner of the hotel asked me to join two other people to judge a beauty contest. I suspect I looked the right type to do this because on holiday I had grown a trim little beard and looked the artistic type. We chose a young girl who was a cashier with Barclays Bank to be Miss Lake Bala of 1960!

Should one perpetuate with children the myth of Father Christmas? Amicia was so excited that I had to wait until after midnight, before I could slip into her room and fill her stocking – not that Amicia had a 'stocking; she had a very capacious pillow case. Anyway she thoroughly enjoyed Christmas with the tree and its lights. From that Christmas on, with the other children, we kept up the pretence of Santa Claus. But the presents were never piled up beneath the tree; the temptation to open them before the due day was too strong and they were placed out of reach on top of the Welsh dresser.

In the early hours of 31 January, Daphne went into labour, so I had to take her into the Maternity Hospital, the Zachary Merton at Rustington-on-Sea. But before driving in I had to find someone to sit with Amicia. I am not sure why I had first to drive to Findon to pick up Daphne's father; her mother certainly did not want to be up at 5.30 in the morning, but I don't know why he did not drive himself. It was quite a drive; the rain was

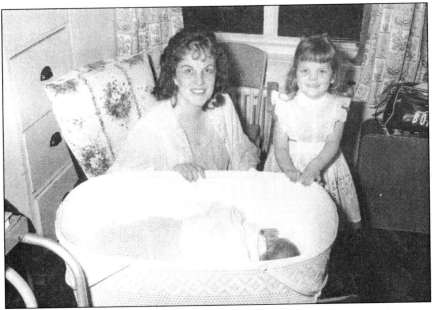

Daphne and Amicia with baby Crispin, Zachary-Merton, January 1961

bucketing down and at one spot somebody ahead flashed his headlights at me and I managed to stop before driving at speed into a severe flood; he was a milkman stuck in his float, but I managed to get through.

I took Daphne into the Zachary Merton and spent the day with her, holding her hand and giving comfort. In those days fathers were not allowed to be present for the birth itself, so I was bundled out, and Crispin was born in the early evening. He was in fact named Simon Crispin and for the first five years of his life was called Simon, but when he went to nursery school we found there were three Simons and two of them had to be called something else. Mrs Barnes's Nursery School did not last very long, but the name Crispin stuck. Amicia was thrilled to go into the maternity home to visit her new brother.

We did not go away for a summer holiday that year – too difficult with a baby. But Codmore Barn was a very pleasant place to be. The garden was still far from fully furnished, but it looked better every year. By this time we had a new gardener, a really helpful and charming man by the name of Pennell. Why is it that gardeners so frequently stand out for their decency and helpfulness? Every one of our gardeners over the last nearly fifty years has been exceptionally nice.

In the autumn we began to build the extension, a Children's Wing opening up from the Music Room with steps leading up to a playroom with three bedrooms off it and a bathroom. We did not use an architect, but planned it all ourselves; it helped greatly that the local builder's mason was imaginative as well as practical. I remember spending hours with Daphne planning the design of the various colours of the vinyl tiles in the playroom on a piece of graph paper. By the time the building started we knew that Daphne was pregnant again; we were going to need the new wing. In the main part of the house there were not really more than two bedrooms; the third, in which we had Simon's crib (with our American background we used that term in preference to 'cot', as we also used diapers instead of nappies) was nothing more than the dressing room for the master bedroom.

By Christmas Crispin was crawling around rapidly and could stand in his playpen. I believe that some modern child experts say that playpens are cruel – imprisoning the child. But the home movies I have show him looking thoroughly happy. We had a fair amount of snow that winter; the home movies again show a very large and splendid snowman with a large carrot for a nose.

An important event for me in 1962 was that I gave up smoking, cigarettes, that is; I still continued smoking cigars for some years. It was in March that the Royal College of Physicians first published a report linking smoking with lung cancer. I felt that with a young wife, two small children and another baby on the way, it was foolish to take unnecessary risks. The Bank of England pension scheme at that time was not very generous for widows. I used to get through a pack of L&M (Ligget & Myers) cigarettes a day; I finished the pack in my pocket before finally giving up. I can still remember the tingling in my fingertips as I inhaled the last of the nicotine! A couple of years later after a meeting in the Governor's room I saw a packet of L&M on his desk and absentmindedly put them in my pocket. Before I got to the door I realised that I had given up smoking and that these were Cromer's! I hastily returned them to him and apologised.

In 1962 Amicia started at some nursery school in Pulborough. I know that because on the afternoon before Daphne went into labour we attended a school display of dancing. The next day, 3 July, Daphne went into labour and went in again to the Zachary Merton under the care of Miss Shipham the obstetrician; she had handled Crispin's birth too. She came from the family that made Shipham's paste – I don't think I have seen any for years. Again I spent most of the day with Daphne, but the birth was taking its time. They sent me home early in the evening, saying that they would call me when anything happened.

Around eleven o'clock I had the most alarming call; the birth was proving very difficult and and they asked me to come in immediately. It must have taken over twenty minutes to get there. When I arrived they would not let me see Daphne; they had decided on an emergency caesarian and I was put in a waiting room as the trolley took Daphne to the operating theatre. I was told that there was a serious risk that I would lose both my wife and the baby. I passed some very anxious moments. I was then told that they had decided that the baby had already got down too low for a caesarian to be practicable. I then went in to see Daphne who seemed in remarkably good heart considering all that was going on. Sometime after one o'clock on the Fourth of July Daphne said that the baby's head was nearly there and I rushed off to tell the doctors. The birth eventually went off successfully; apparently the umbilical cord had wound itself around Jocelyn's throat (for it was he) and could well have strangled him. Jocelyn owes his life to Miss Shipham. He was not in very good shape, yellow with jaundice but within a few days a paediatric specialist (a Dr Washington, would you believe) pronounced him absolutely fit.

The very same day at tea time I brought Amicia and Crispin in to see their new brother. The new Children's Wing was finished just in time. Amicia and Crispin moved in there, and Jocelyn's crib was placed in the dressing room, so as to be handy. We were very lucky to find an excellent 'nanny' to look after the children. I haven't the faintest idea what her real name was, but she was known to us as Twink. She was only sixteen and had just left school. She moved in to the Children's Wing and lived with us until the boys went to prep school. She was not far from home, just a short bicycle ride away, and she had no problem settling in. I haven't heard anything about her for years, but I know she got married and had children of her own. It seems almost inconceivable that she is now not far short of sixty!

Meanwhile at home we were getting used to having three children. Jocelyn was still in the main part of the house, but the other two, with Twink, were in the Children's Wing. They all got on very well together, as they still do forty years on. We had a fully traditional Christmas. Crispin declined roast turkey, saying that he would probably like it when he was grown up! And then on Boxing Day it began to snow. It was a substantial fall, at least a foot. There was to be snow on the ground now until March 1963. Pennell and I did a lot of shovelling to make the drive passable.

In the summer of 1963, we took a summer holiday away from Codmore Barn. We went to a small hotel on the Norfolk coast at Winterton-on-Sea. The drive to Winterton took us past Newmarket racecourse; this was in the days before the Newmarket bypass. Little did we know how well our two boys would come to know the Rowley Mile and the July Course! It must have been at about this time that Ronny Spiers (and his wife Patience) appeared in England. When we had met them in Washington, Ronny had been fairly junior in the State Department. But here he was in London as Minister at the US Embassy; in other words the Chargé d'Affaires whenever the Ambassador was away. I liked them both and Ronny and I lunched together in the City several times.

We invited them and their children down to Pulborough for the day. Their lack of experience of British trains caused a bit of a drama at Pulborough station. We went to meet the train but there was no sign of them and the train was just beginning to pull out when I saw them at a window; they could not fathom the fact that with British trains (in those days, at any rate) it was impossible to open the doors from inside; you had to lower the window, lean out and open the door. But it was too late for

Daphne and the children at Codmore Barn – 1963

that now; I indicated the emergency handle and told them to pull it. The train jolted to a stop. The railway officials were none too pleased; but in those days, without mobile phones, we might have spent all day trying to get in touch. The next stop was Arundel and they might have failed to open the door there. Anyway there was not a diplomatic incident. I would have liked to see more of them. Amicia actually went up to London and stayed with them briefly in their house in Sussex Gardens, but Daphne resisted – she thought they were now too rich for us and too grand. This was nonsense, Ronny and I had been on holiday together in Hunstanton thirty years earlier, but it was of course a symptom of her inner insecurity.

As I write this (June 2003) it is Wimbledon fortnight which reminds me that Daphne adored tennis. We played a lot during our first spell in Washington, but it became rarer the second time; babies have a lot to answer for. We would have played at Codmore Barn had we had a tennis court. I made enquiries but found that with the sloping land it would have required a lot of work and in the early sixties was going to cost £700 or so – a sum which was beyond us. We used to go to Wimbledon in the early fifties; and I went again quite often during the sixties; the Bank had seats on the Centre Court. But the children soon discovered during Wimbledon that Daphne was incommunicado in the television room. This continued to the very end of her life. At Buxlow, of course, we had a tennis court installed in 1979 to celebrate Maggie Thatcher's victory in the election! At Codmore Barn the television pictures – black and white – were of pretty poor quality. We were almost the first people in Pulborough to be able to receive BBC 2 as we were on top of the hill; those down in the town had to wait a few years. Daphne had her heroes (and heroines); one in the early days was the Brazilian Maria Bueno, who played beautiful tennis, but so often just as she seemed to be winning easily, she faltered and gave her fans an agonising time. Björn Borg was a hero and in later years Daphne loved watching André Agassi; I know he was brilliant but I never took to him.

CHAPTER 16

Chief Economist

IN EARLY 1963 THE BITTER COLD was not the only news. General de Gaulle decided to veto the admission of the UK to the EEC and my job disappeared overnight. Whilst I was still waiting to hear what work I might do, I went for the first time on one of the Bank's so-called Industrial Visits. Every one of the Bank's branches was headed by an Agent, whose responsibilities, besides running the branch, included the important responsibility of maintaining close relations with the local business community. And every now and then they would lay on a visit for three or four senior Bank of England officials to look around factories and have lunches and dinners with the local business men. There were then branches at Southampton, Bristol, Birmingham, Newcastle, York, Leeds and Manchester – besides the Law Courts which did not organise industrial visits. During the next few years I think I went on industrial visits to every one of those branches and had some interesting and hilarious experiences. We once had lunch with Kagan of Gannex mackintoshes, the friend of Harold Wilson who was later made a peer and then sent to prison for some skulduggery. I cannot pretend that I saw through him; it is after all the talent of a 'con man' to persuade everybody he meets that he is absolutely to be trusted. On a visit with the Manchester branch we had a dinner with a number of people involved in the ceramic tiles business; we had a lot to drink and had a very merry evening. They commented on how surprising it had been for them to find that Bank of England officials were human. Another highlight was to be driven round the Land Rover test site, up incredibly steep inclines when one felt certain the vehicle would tip over, but of course it didn't.

But the first visit, in late January or early February 1963, was to the Leeds branch. It was a smaller party than usual and for once without an Executive Director. There were only three of us, Lucius Thompson-McCausland, James Selwyn, Principal of the Statistics Office, and I. The industrial visits parties were usually accompanied by the Bank's Industrial Adviser, Ainslie Darby, a Bank man who had made it up from a clerical position in the 1930s. But on this occasion he was sick, and I was asked to write the account of the visit. Our journey north was dominated by the bleak weather. The snow in the south gave way to solid frost. I mention the bleakness because it had also cast a pall of gloom over the economy; business seemed lifeless, and who knew what the spring might bring.

The most important feature of the visit so far as I was concerned was a dinner we had in Lincoln; all the people at my end of the table began saying that they had seen a marked upturn in their order books in the last two weeks. This seemed to me to be very significant; anecdotal evidence, admittedly – no hard statistics to back it up. But I began to feel that the economy was recovering, perhaps strongly, although it would certainly not be evident in the statistics before the spring. I mention this because it was very relevant to the new job I was about to be given. Maurice Allen, not surprisingly, managed to find fault with my report, revealing his talent for nitpicking.

Somewhere towards the end of January or in early February, Guy Watson called me in and said that I should be thinking of a move to another job. I thought he was just thinking aloud about the possibilities, because I said that I could still see a lot I could do in relation to Western Europe. But it transpired that a move had already been decided. I was to take over from John Fforde as head of General Studies. I was absolutely amazed. I did not consider myself a professional economist and here I was being asked to be the Bank's chief economist; I had serious doubts whether I could do it. But that was the Bank's decision and I had to accept it. As I was to discover two years later, the Bank too had doubts; they had in fact already recruited Kit McMahon to fill the post, but his commitments as a don at Oxford meant that he could not take over until 1965, but nobody thought to tell me; nor did they give me any encouragement to help me through the next two years. Maurice Allen indeed went out of his way to belittle me. I have a suspicion that what led the Bank to appoint me as the fill-in were the memoranda on the economy that I had been in the habit of sending to John Fforde. At any rate my appointment was bitterly resented by a number of people in General Studies and in the Statistics Office. John Page, I think, found it particularly difficult. The Bank procedure of putting up green drafts still applied and I remember, on one occasion at least, substantially amending one of John's green drafts; he didn't like it. Personally I think I did a remarkably good job in the next two years, and a number of sceptics, including Tony Carlisle and Gilbert Wood, came to see that I was a great deal better than they had expected.

My new job put me in constant touch with the Governors, Cromer and Mynors, to whom I was responsible for economic assessments. I was also responsible for the Bank of England *Quarterly Bulletin*, which John Fforde had launched in 1961. I had close contacts with the Treasury; I was the Bank's representative on the National Income Forecasts Working Party and on the Long Range Economic Assessment Working Party. Maurice Allen loomed large in my life. He was an Adviser to the Governors on economics; but, luckily, since he was not yet an Executive Director, I was not directly under his command and had the right of direct access to the Governors.

I spent two or three weeks with John Fforde as he handed over to me. It was the only opportunity I had to try and get to know him. He was not of this world; I cannot think of anybody whom I would have thought less fitted to be the Chief Executive of a central bank. But that he was to be; he was immediately going to the Discount Office for a few months to learn domestic banking; he was then to go abroad to visit other central banks to learn something about overseas banking and then, a year later, he was to take Jasper Hollom's place as Chief Cashier.

John seemed to me to be the archetypal absent minded don. He even had some idiosyncrasies which I would associate with a don. The Editor of the *Quarterly Bulletin* at the time was Tony Carlisle, an old Harrovian with a chip on his shoulder. So apart from being much more left wing than me – his views were probably very much in line with John's – he was a perfectly normal human being. But John, rather conspiratorially, warned me very earnestly that Tony was 'mad' – and he meant it, on what evidence I cannot imagine. I was introduced to the economists' jargon – regression equations, endogenous, exogenous (all the words which Gordon Brown now uses to hide any meaning). I also picked up some of the favourite Latin tags – '*a fortiori*' instead of 'all the more', etc.

Just at this time there was a terrible blow – Jacobsson died. Over the past three years whenever he had come to London he had always called at the Bank and made a point of seeing me. We always had a good talk; he revealed his endearing trait of vanity. He once said that he had spent twenty minutes with Nasser in Cairo; considering that in 1956 he had equated Nasser with Hitler, it was surprising that he should think it so great a privilege to have met him face to face. On another occasion he proudly reported that he had spent half an hour with General de Gaulle. He had told de Gaulle that to really establish his reputation on a par with Napoleon he should reintroduce the gold franc! Anyway in April he came to London again for some fairly routine operation. He came to see me at the Bank and we had a long talk. I was still urging him to get me back into the Fund in Washington. He tried to encourage me to stay, believing that this new job I was doing would establish a good career for me. I was not convinced and we agreed to talk again about it after he had recovered from his operation.

The operation was successful, but during the recovery period he had a massive heart attack and died. I was absolutely shattered. Jacobsson had been dearer to me than my own father. I missed him terribly. The funeral took place at the Swedish Church in London. The Lutheran funeral service is utterly depressing; not a word about the after life, just endless variations on ashes to ashes, dust to dust. The three Jacobsson ladies, his wife, Moyra and her elder sister Erin, were dressed in deepest black and wore black veils completely obscuring their faces. I was one of the three ushers, the other two being David Somerset and Peter Cooke (he had succeeded David as Personal Assistant). A very small party of people attended the subsequent interment ceremony at Brookwood Cemetery in Surrey. So ended an important chapter of my life. It also put paid to any opportunity I might have had to return to Washington, so it was a serious blow to Daphne. Later that year when introduced to Jacobsson's successor, Pierre Paul Schweitzer, at a party in Basle, I made one last attempt to get myself recruited to the Fund, but Schweitzer was not interested.

After that sad digression, I must return to my new job at the Bank. The budget was only a few weeks away, so the National Income Forecasts Working Party (NIFWP) was in full swing. We were all Keynesians at that time and believed in 'fine tuning' the economy, so three times a year the Working Party attempted to forecast the growth of demand over the next eighteen months – specifically public sector expenditure, consumer demand, net exports (plus or minus) and stock building (plus or minus). The forecast growth in demand was then measured against what was believed to be the underlying rate of growth of capacity; which, if I remember well, was thought to be about 2.5 per cent. If forecast growth exceeded the growth of underlying capacity, inflation was expected, and tighter fiscal and monetary policies would seem to be called for; and if forecast growth fell short of it, unemployment was forecast to rise and looser fiscal and monetary policies seemed indicated (usually in the form of increased public expenditure – tax cuts were rarely thought of). Changes in interest rates were rarely thought of either, quite mistakenly in my view. The problem was the horizon of the forecasts; changes in interest rates were never thought likely to cut or increase expenditure by more than £100 million or so within the eighteen months time span. I remember arguing this out with Alan Whittome, who was by then the Deputy Chief Cashier; I pointed out that although the change might be quite modest in the forecast period, it was likely to become substantial over two to three years. Alan's line was: 'Don't make a fuss; we are only asked to look eighteen months ahead.'

The time horizon for the Working Party was, I think, partly responsible for the almost constant excess demand between 1945 and 1972. Changes in fiscal policy, including levels of public expenditure, also had substantial 'lags' and would have effects well beyond the forecast period. Changes in public capital expenditure in particular had, throughout that period, an almost constant accelerating upward trend; and changes in projected capital expenditure would in reality have virtually no effect over the eighteen months time span. I should add that the forecasting was purely judgmental; there were no computer models. The Board of Trade seemed to have some kind of simple model for the level of imports and exports, but it seemed to be highly unreliable; the figures produced by the Bank, based on information from Exchange Control, were usually more accurate.

The critical forecast was the pre-budget one, and when I joined the NIFWP it had just started its deliberations. The Chairman was Douglas Allen (who is becoming a familiar figure in these pages). I found my colleagues almost uniformly despondent and gloomy about the outlook. The country was locked into the coldest, bleakest cold winter since 1947 and nothing seemed to be moving, and it seemed very hard to believe that there was anything which would get the economy moving. I remember looking out of the window of my office, looking on to Princes Street and the Head Offices of the Midland and National Provincial Banks and seeing

snow whirling past in a high wind. I would have shared the despondency
had it not been for that dinner in Lincoln a few weeks earlier. I had a very
strong hunch – no more – that the economy was not only going to grow,
but that the rate of growth was going to be well in excess of the underlying
rate of growth of capacity. The Chancellor in the budget should have been
thinking of restraint rather than expansion.

In the NIFWP I had some success in turning my colleagues away from
their despondency, but the final submission to the Chancellor was far too
much on the side of expansion. I spent a great deal of the summer trying
to stiffen the Governors; I was convinced that a boom was on the way and
that it would have dire results for the balance of payments. A substantial
deficit on the balance of payments always meant a sterling crisis, which was
never any good for the Government of the day. I failed. My efforts took
several forms. In my new position I regularly attended Wednesday 'books'
– the overseas day, and Friday 'books' – the domestic day, and there were
opportunities for me to put forward my view. I also wrote memoranda to
the Governors, with copies to Maurice Allen.

For a moment I shall digress from my work as head of General Studies
to remark on another task that senior officials had to perform from time to
time. I mention it now because it was in 1963 that I gave up the chore of
being Official-in-Charge. Every night and every Saturday and Sunday a
senior official was designated 'Official-in-Charge'. He was responsible for
the security of the Bank from 6 p.m. (I think it was) to the following
morning. He had a Deputy and there was another post called Superintend-
ent of the Watch with whom I had no contact so far as I can remember.

The Official-in-Charge had a suite of rooms, sitting room (with
television and radio, telephones and a well stocked drinks cabinet), a
bedroom and a bathroom. Many senior officials who were in the habit of
working fairly late always dropped in for a drink; Roy Bridge I remember
as a particularly frequent visitor. At about this time the Bank Piquet arrived
at the Bank; they were drawn from a Guards regiment and would have
marched from their barracks through the streets, finally marching up Queen
Victoria Street to the Bank. They then mounted guard over the Bank.
Guardsmen with rifles and bayonets were to be found at various strategic
points in the vaults and elsewhere. Both they and the Official had a secret
password, so that I could declare myself when walking round the gold vaults
late at night; I enjoyed looking at the gleaming piles of gold ingots. The
officer commanding the Piquet, usually a Lieutenant, I think, always called
on the Official for a drink. He too had a suite of rooms and had a dinner
with claret and port, and was permitted to invite a guest to dine with him.
Martin Mays Smith, I think, told me that before joining the Bank he had
been the guest of the officer of the Piquet. The Official and the Deputy
also had dinner with claret and port – and cigars! On Saturdays in those
days the Bank was open for work up to midday, so the Official only took
over after lunch. On Sundays one's duty went from 9 a.m. to early evening;

I had to get up very early in Pulborough to make it on time. I may actually be wrong about this; it is conceivable that a Bank chauffeur picked one up and returned one home at the end of the day. For the rest of my time in the Bank I frequently used Bank chauffeurs to take me home from some function in the City (the Lord Mayor's annual banquet at the Mansion House, for example). I don't remember any occurrence of any note on any of the times that I was on duty. I am sure that others had stories to tell, particularly if it was in the middle of a sterling crisis or the Governor was abroad. The Bank Piquet was abolished before the end of the Sixties and I feel sure that the Official-in-Charge has given way to professional security men.

Returning to my job in General Studies, I have already mentioned another interdepartmental committee of which I was a member. This was the Long Range Economic Assessment Working Party (LREA). The Chairman was Fred Atkinson, another familiar figure in these pages. Of course it was good idea to have a body trying to measure prospective demand against prospective capacity over a much longer period than the NIFWP. The LREA looked five years ahead. The trouble with that was that politicians (and indeed senior civil servants) were not the slightest bit interested in such a long horizon; after all within five years there would have to have been another General Election and a new Government. What I believe there should have been, was some marrying of the NIFWP and the LREA, looking first at the relatively short term (eighteen months to two years) with a more speculative assessment of what the trends might be in the next couple of years. I enjoyed working with Fred, but I don't believe we achieved anything worth while. After all anything that we wrote in 1963 went right out of the window when Wilson's Labour Government was elected in October 1964. But more of that when we come to it.

Another important part of my job in General Studies was being responsible for producing the *Quarterly Bulletin*. This consisted of a commentary, several articles commissioned from within the Bank and statistical tables. The Editor, Tony Carlisle at first and later Gilbert Wood, produced a first draft. This was not an easy task. Although the Bank was frequently critical of the Government and of the Treasury the criticism had to be phrased delicately. I believe that it is still true today that to understand what the Bank's view is on anything you have to learn the art of reading between the lines. I would then go through it with Tony making changes that I thought appropriate. The next stage was the most difficult – discussing it with Maurice Allen. His wartime experience in intelligence and cryptography led him to the most obscure thought processes and he would suggest very subtle changes in the text. He would argue that his suggested change would convey just the right impression to the Press. I found this argument unpersuasive; the changes would only be intelligible if the Press knew what the wording had been which was changed – and that, of course, they would never know. Every quarter we successfully struggled through this procedure.

The next step was to get it through the Deputy Governor; Mynors was, as I have said before, a stickler for correct punctuation and Fowler's *English Usage*. But it was all pleasantly done. Articles were often the published results of some research. But I still reserved the right not to publish if it didn't make sense to me. I don't mean by this that I had to agree with it. I remember one article by one of our statistical experts, Peter Burman (on yield curves, I think), which I found quite incomprehensible. So Peter took it away and amended it; it now seemed to be saying the opposite of what his first version had appeared to be saying. So he took it away again and amended it. This again seemed to be an entirely different argument. He agreed, but said that he had come across some new evidence which supported the new version. I refused to publish. As I said to him, how was I to know that three weeks later he would not have decided that a fourth version was more correct.

I commissioned an article from Roy Bridge on the Gold Market. Ever since Jacobsson and I had rewritten the Fund pamphlet on gold this had been a particular interest of mine. Again I found certain passages which did not make sense to me. Roy Bridge was inclined to say: 'Don't ask damn fool questions,' in his typically gravelly voice, but was always amenable and willingly indulged me.

The commentary was then sent to the Treasury for their comments. The Bank never delegated anything that could be kept at the highest level so I was not allowed to send it to the Treasury; I had to produce a draft letter to Douglas Allen for the Deputy to sign. The Treasury always had comments to make, usually about two pages, almost invariably seeking to get us to tone down the criticisms. It was my job to draft a reply for the Deputy; my guiding principle was to keep the major criticisms untouched and to agree to what I considered less important items. Humphrey Mynors shared my view entirely and always approved my draft unchanged. Thirteen years earlier when I had appeared before the Selection Board of which he was Chairman, he had told me, 'Young man, you have a lot to unlearn.' I guess he felt now that I was a true central banker and had cast off my Treasury past!

Leaping ahead a year, the procedure became very different when Leslie O'Brien succeeded Mynors as Deputy Governor. In March 1964 I presented my draft response to the Treasury's comments, which O'Brien completely rejected; he told me to accept all the Treasury's comments. O'Brien from then on seemed to go out of his way to indulge the Treasury, particularly in the person of the then Permanent Secretary, William Armstrong – not to be confused with a later Permanent Secretary, Robert Armstrong. I can't help feeling that he was strongly motivated by the desire to get his GCB!

Talking of Robert Armstrong reminds me that in the mid sixties a Bank-Treasury Dining Club was established, There used to be something like a dozen of us – six from the Bank and six from the Treasury – and we would meet for dinner in some restaurant in the City. From the Treasury

I remember Robert Armstrong, who was then I think a fairly young Assistant Secretary; he had not yet joined the Treasury when I left it in 1950. Another was I think Robin Butler, who later succeeded Robert as Maggie Thatcher's Private Secretary and later still succeeded him as both Permanent Secretary of the Treasury, and also Permanent Secretary of the Cabinet.

On the Bank side I remember a very young Rodney Galpin who was then Assistant Principal of the Discount Office; he later became Chairman of the Standard and Chartered Bank. That was a strange link for me, because at about the time of the dining club my old boss Sir Edmund Hall-Patch was Deputy Chairman of the Standard Bank of South Africa (Standard and Chartered's predecessor) and the Chairman was Sir Frederick Leith Ross, whom my father had known on the Continent before the First World War. They both invited me to lunch with them in their private dining room. Later still Fred Leith Ross invited Daphne and me to lunch with him and Lady Leith Ross at their house in Surrey.

In my work over the next few years I found how badly statistics are interpreted and abused. I have to say, in these days of 'spin', that between 1963 and 1970 the Central Statistics Office (the CSO as it was then called), so far as I could judge, behaved with impeccable objectivity. But statistics were frequently misused. I soon discovered that statistics are practically never just plain facts. Most people probably think that banking statistics at least must be accurate. After all in a balance sheet assets and liabilities have to agree; what many don't realise is that they often do not (errors and omissions); so they have to be made to equal by the use of 'wash accounts'. But not only that; the figures themselves are frequently suspect. When I was in charge of General Studies the Eurodollar market was flourishing and London had hundreds of foreign banks; each one was required to submit statistics of loans and advances to the Bank each month. The banks themselves attached no importance to the statistics and the task of filling them in and sending them to the Bank was often delegated to the most junior graduate recruit. Our Statistics Office frequently found that the latest month's figures were quite incompatible with the previous month's and had to 'massage' them before publication. So I soon realised that all statistics had an element of 'guestimates' in them.

Gross National Product figures were very largely estimated and if one looks back to the published statistics one frequently finds that the figures for any one quarter or any one year have later been substantially revised. The balance of payments figures were equally tentative. The balance of payments deficit for 1964, which may have made an important contribution to the defeat of the Conservative Government in October 1964, was initially published as £800 million. If you look back now at the figures for 1964 you will find that the outcome of the balance of payments for that year is shown as a small surplus! I have to say that that figure seems to me to be suspect; there was every evidence of excess demand in the economy and a balance of payments deficit seems to have been much more likely. But the revision took place under a Labour Government, so it was unlikely to have been motivated by a desire to make things look better for the previous Conservative Government.

Before I leave the subject of statistics, it was at about this time that Jeremy Morse joined the Bank. Before he took over as an Executive Director he spent several weeks making himself familiar with the Bank and spent a couple of days with me. Jeremy had been a high flyer in Glynn Mills Bank, had a first class honours degree, was a distinguished compiler of crosswords – in other words a very intelligent man. But I was surprised to find how naive he was about statistics. He took it for granted that if the figures for any one month were higher (or lower) than they had been a year before this could be interpreted as signifying an improvement (or deterioration) in the situation. I had to explain to him that figures higher than a year before could be indicating a deteriorating situation; the figures might have been rising for a few months after the month in the year before, but have been falling for the last four or five months indicating a worrying trend. I report this not to make fun of Jeremy Morse; I too would have made the same mistake when I started on the job.

In 1964, I think it was, we had an outside economist working for us for a couple of years, a Scot by the name of Andrew Bain; he was later chief economist at the Midland Bank. We got on very well together and jointly wrote a memorandum headed something like 'Should we not be controlling the money supply?' It went to Jasper Hollom, then the Chief Cashier, and spent the next two years in his 'pending' tray! It was to be another fifteen years before anybody in the Bank showed very much interest in the money supply. The Bank, as I think I have already said, did not have a monetary policy; interest rates were seen as having some use in sterling crises, but were otherwise thought much less important than changes in tax or public expenditure. Anyway, we tried!

In the NIFWP I continued to try and get the forecasters to agree that we were already in the early days of a boom, but to no avail. Douglas Allen was no longer chairman, in which post he had been succeeded by Brian Hopkins (later Chief Economist at the Treasury). I forget which post Douglas had moved on to, but whatever it was it took him much closer to the Chancellor, Reggie Maudling. The 1964 budget even managed to ignore the NIFWP's assessment which certainly pointed, if only mildly, to the need for restraint.

Both the Chancellor and the fairly new NEDO were all in favour of what was called the dash for growth. The idea was that inflation would in fact be good for growth. With demand rising strongly, companies would be encouraged to invest more and increase underlying capacity so any balance of payments problems would only be temporary. I believed this to be profoundly wrong. Excess demand, as we had only too painfully seen over the previous years, lengthened companies' delivery dates with adverse effects on both exports and imports, strengthened the bargaining power of trade unions and contributed to rising costs. Companies would not in fact become more profitable, but the very reverse and capital investment would almost certainly decline. This was the intellectual justification for Maudling's budget. But I still saw it as an out and out political budget trying to buy votes for the forthcoming general election. I bumped into Douglas Allen soon afterwards and said that it had been a disgracefully political budget – I seem to be rather prone to making crashing remarks. He earnestly replied, as of course he would, that there was a perfectly good economic argument for the budget.

I never met Maudling as Chancellor, but I had bumped into him at the Fund Annual General Meeting eleven years earlier when he was a young Economic Secretary to the Treasury. He seemed to be completely lost, did not seem to know anyone or even know where to go to get a drink. I took him under my wing, got him a drink and introduced him to some people.

In the summer of 1964 we had a rather more successful holiday. We all went to a holiday camp – not Butlin's, rather more upmarket – on Hayling Island. Twink came too to help look after the smaller children. It was well organised for adults and children. There was also a Punch & Judy show which kept them all in fits of laughter. In their early childhood, the laughter of Crispin and Jocelyn was very endearing. I cannot remember when *Dad's Army* first appeared on television, but I remember being downstairs when they, with Daphne, were watching it upstairs in the television room, all three sitting together on the sofa and peals of laughter came floating down the stairs. At about this time Jocelyn was prone to nightmares, and he would come all the way from the Children's Wing up to our bedroom; I would then carry him back to his bed and sit with him until he went back to sleep. The father/son relationship builds up from small beginnings.

In the world at large the next big event was the general election. As I have already said I think Maudling's budget was a contributory factor to the Labour victory. The 'dash for growth' looked to the electorate more like another impending sterling crisis. But the Labour victory was a very slender one. Harold Wilson had a majority of only a handful of seats in the House of Commons. I was sad to see Alec Douglas-Home go. I honestly believe that he was almost the only disinterested Prime Minister we have had in the last 50 years.

The Labour victory provoked a revolution in the Treasury. Rather like the Labour Party of 1997, but on a smaller scale, they imported a number of Labour minded experts. Even in such a lowly body as the NIFWP, we had evangelical socialists and expansionary socialists from the new Department of Economic Affairs. At a higher level they brought in Tommy Balogh (from Oxford) and Nicky Kaldor (from Cambridge). Cartoons of the period in financial papers showed demonstrators carrying signs calling for 'Freedom from Hungary'! The first post election meeting of the Working Party was extraordinary. Brian Hopkins had great difficulty in controlling it. It was a point of principle with these new experts that 'things are going to be different from now on'; they asserted boldly that with Labour in power the underlying rate of growth of capacity was 4 per cent. When pressed, they could not produce any economic evidence for this assertion. George Brown, the new Secretary of State at the Department of Economic Affairs, had already launched his National Plan which was committed to 4 per cent growth – so there could be no question about it.

Even the Treasury, to whom the 'dash for growth' had been acceptable, were rattled. Ian Bancroft, who was then Private Secretary to the Chancellor, was heard to say about Callaghan: 'Poor old Jim; he doesn't know what is going on; he can't last long.' Of course, Sunny Jim not only stayed on and devalued sterling, but eventually went on to be Prime Minister. But poor old Ian Bancroft had worse things to come; as Head of the Civil Service in the early 80s he fell out badly with Margaret Thatcher.

I continued to be my usual cheeky self. I once went to a meeting in Whitehall chaired by Derek Mitchell at which were present both Kaldor and Balogh. We were considering a paper and I suggested an amendment: 'On page x delete the word "not".' They all turned to the page and found that the passage without the word 'not' would read 'things will be as they were before'!

Kaldor exploded, 'How can you believe that?'

I replied, quietly, that I had no doubt whatever that Governments would continue to spend too much and tax too much; sterling would continue to have periodic crises and things would continue much as they had for the last twenty years! Incredulity all round – and amazement that such a view should be expressed by somebody from the Bank of England. Had Kit McMahon been in my shoes they would have got a very different (and no doubt, more diplomatic) view.

At some time in late 1964 or early 1965 I had another clash with Maurice Allen. He was very close to Cecil King, then editor of the *Daily Mirror*. Cecil King, although a socialist, hated Harold Wilson and began a conspiratorial campaign to bring him down. Looking back I cannot for the life of me think who he wanted to replace him with. Could it have been George Brown (what one might call the John Prescott of his day)? At any rate Maurice Allen joined in this conspiracy and began leaking information to King. It fell to me, on his instructions, to provide the information. I was to give him the data on plain paper so as not to reveal the source. The first piece of paper I took down to him led him to explode; he held the paper up to the light and said, 'You fool, can't you see the Bank of England's water mark?' Not being a natural spy or conspirator, I had not noticed it. And I had to get it retyped on really plain paper. I don't suppose anybody but me knew that Maurice Allen (from now on I propose to refer to him by his initials – WMA) was abusing his position in this way.

CHAPTER 17

Deputy Chief of the EID

A BIG CHANGE TOOK EFFECT in my working life in March 1965. On 1 March the CBID was broken up into two departments. There was an Overseas Department, which there had not been since before the War. Jasper Rootham who had been an Adviser to the Governors was appointed the first Chief of the Overseas Department. The other part of the CBID now became the Economic Intelligence Department (EID). With Humphrey Mynors gone it was now possible to use the word 'economic'. Not that it was really necessary; in every other central bank the department would have been known as the Research Department. The new Chief was Roy Heasman, who was no more a professional economist than I was. Guy Watson I think must then have retired. I was appointed the Deputy Chief of the new department. There were some noses put out of joint. James Selwyn who had been the Principal of the Statistics Office was in fact much better qualified for the job than Roy Heasman, but he was not appointed and was made instead a Deputy Chief of the Department like me. He was shattered and I don't think ever recovered. A few years later he took an early pension and carved out a very successful new career in Hong Kong.

Looking back, nearly forty years on, I am not at all sure that I should not have left the Bank in 1965. I believe that I performed the task placed on me in 1963 with some success. Indeed I feel that the views I expressed would have done the country a lot more good than did those of my successor, Kit McMahon. If I was not really acceptable as an economist, I might have done very well on the Overseas side, but there were now other contenders. The new Deputy Chief of the new Overseas Department was Stanley Payton. But I ask myself, 'Where would I have gone?' I was never really a banker, but I might have done well on the overseas side of a merchant bank.

With my cosmopolitan background the IMF would have done well, but Alan Whittome had very recently been appointed Head of the European Department of the Fund. This is all in the light of hindsight. At the time I did not even contemplate leaving. I was happy to have been promoted to the rank of a Deputy Chief and I suppose I had at the back of my mind the idea that I might one day succeed Roy as Chief of the Department.

The next five years started happily enough. I was not really resentful of Kit McMahon. We had known each other well in Washington. And in 1960 or 1961, when I was still on the overseas side I had been asked by the Bank to help Kit with information for a book he was writing (as an Oxford don) on the Sterling Area. So we saw a bit of each other then. Now, although I began increasingly to distrust his fixation on the desirability of an incomes policy, we worked together very amicably. We also went to the Treasury together and I remember once lunching with him, Douglas Allen and Fred Atkinson. I also introduced him to the Overseas Bankers Club, of which I had been a member since 1960. He came as my guest to a big dinner of the club, where the speaker was the Governor, Cromer. I remember that dinner particularly well because during it Daphne was taken ill, but in the days before mobile phones there was no way she could let me know. When I got home in a Bank car, I found her in bed with a very high fever, nonetheless coping very bravely with the three children. We called the doctor. I cannot now remember what it was; I think it may have been a 'strep' throat; but whatever it was, antibiotics soon cured her.

Many of the new graduate entrants had arts degrees of one sort or another and were not very well versed in economics. I decided that all new entrants to the EID should have a two day course in basic macroeconomics – of the Keynesian kind. Kit helped me to design a course, which I then gave, I think for the next four years or so. I soon modified Kit's outline course because in my view it gave far too much prominence to a modified version of the 'dash for growth' theory, which had to be sustained by a reliance on some form of incomes policy.

Kit and I soon had a clash with Maurice Allen. He was now in a more powerful position: no longer an Adviser to the Governors, but an Executive Director. It was the custom each year after the budget for the Governor to send a letter to the Governors of all the Commonwealth central banks explaining what it meant. This was known as 'the Governor's letter'. For the previous two years I had drafted it and cleared it with the Deputy Governor, no doubt showing it on the way to WMA. This year, because Kit had only just taken over, we drafted the letter together and took it down to WMA's room to clear it with him. Roy Bridge, I remember, was in the room at the time. We showed the letter to WMA. Having read it through he announced loudly, 'Neither of you two fools seem to have any idea of how to write a "Governor's letter"!' Can you believe it? Kit was a recent Oxford don and I had drafted the letter in the two previous years. I don't think Roy Bridge could believe his ears. It is hard to imagine how offensive WMA could be. On several occasions I hung up the phone on him because I was so exasperated. But it was not just me. I was present in Roy Heasman's room when he did the same. And later in the sixties I was present when Roy's successor as Chief of EID, Michael Thornton, did exactly the same thing. If I can manage it I will not mention WMA again!

The Bank of England's management structure would have been almost incomprehensible to an outsider. Everything the Bank did was done in the name of 'The Governors', but neither they nor the four Executive Directors actually ran the Bank. The Governor naturally had a powerful influence on policy; it was he after all who called on the Chancellor once a week, rather on the lines of the Prime Minister's weekly meeting with the Queen. The Deputy Governor and the Staff Director (no longer Sir George Abell but

Jack Davies, who had been a great sportsman – he was famous for having dismissed Don Bradman for a duck) both had a great deal to say on all domestic matters. But the executive authority rested with the Chief Cashier, who worked through the Heads of Departments Committee.

From March 1965, as Deputy Chief of the EID, I attended all meetings of the HOD's Committee. I also became a member of the Departmental Establishments Committee (whose members, one from each department,were known as the DEOs). This was a time consuming task. We were, as it were, the Executive subcommittee of the HODs. It was an entirely new field for me to be involved in. When I first joined the Committee some of the other members were nearly twenty years older than me. C.C. Excell, a Deputy Chief who represented the Cashier's Department, was very close to retirement. The Accountant's Department was represented by Basil Maunder, who was also near retirement. The others were all nearer my age. I was a member of the DEOS for the next nine years and we soon became a fairly intimate group of friends. The others were Peter Taylor (who had been GPS when I had been GPS 2), from the Secretary's Department, Stanley Payton from the Overseas, and Ken Andrews, the Deputy Chief of Establishments, who was ex officio Chairman of the Committee. When Charlie Excell retired his place was taken by Dick Balfour. Dick was – and is – a great character. I had first met him when he was the Bank's Agent at York. He then became a Deputy Chief Cashier concerned with all the domestic matters of the Department. He later became Chief Accountant. He was a great lover of roses and, indeed, an expert. He was for some years President of the National Rose Society. Every day of the year, whatever the weather, he wore a rose in his buttonhole.

Perhaps our biggest and most time consuming task was co-ordinating the Annual Review of staff and making final recommendations for all promotions and accelerations on scales to the HODS. The intention was that all promotions should be fair as between departments; people of equal calibre should progress roughly in line. But this was obviously an impossible job. We were not comparing like with like; the skills required to be a junior economist in the EID were quite different from those required by clerks in the Cashier's Department and the staff of the Accountant's Department. Much as I liked Dick Balfour, he was a pain in the neck, always determined to block promotions of, dare I say it, the more intellectual staff in Overseas and EID, unless he could be allowed to promote clerks in the Cashier's department whom we strongly believed to be of lesser calibre. Before the Annual Review was finalised we used to have interminably long meetings, late into the night, fortified with beer and sandwiches. I remember on one occasion noting in the margin against the name of some clerk in the Cashier's Department whose promotion we had agreed to 'only because it is now 10 p.m.'!

The next five years were probably the least interesting of my Bank career. I had only a marginal involvement in policy, attending 'books' only when the Chief was away. The Bank's involvement in the devaluation of 1966 was handled by Kit McMahon, but I remember going to a high-powered meeting at the Treasury, where I saw the main Treasury architect of the devaluation package in tears. He knew that no devaluation would have any lasting benefit unless it was accompanied by strict fiscal and monetary policies. And that was what he had put together, only to find that the politicians had removed all the disciplinary measures. This was Wynne Godley, the younger brother of John Godley, the Earl of Kilbracken, whom I had known at Oxford. He looked every inch the aristocrat with very finely drawn features. He was a good economist, but also a very sensitive soul.

It fell to me quite often to see foreign visitors. I had to try and be convincing in defence of policies which were, of course, indefensible. One I saw several times was the Director of the Research Department of the Bank of Japan. I'm afraid his name escapes me, but we got on very well and I was more open with him than with many. We had similar views on economics and monetary policy. He was so impressed with the work we were doing in EID that he arranged for a bright young man from the Bank of Japan, Suzuki, to spend several months with us. I could not be as open in the case of other interviews. The Bank's Press officer, John Costello at that time, asked me to give an interview to Sam Brittan of the *Financial Times* to explain the rationale behind the recently introduced import deposit scheme. I don't know how I managed to make that sound plausible, but from what I can remember his subsequent article showed that I had been successful!

During these five years I occupied myself largely with the more domestic affairs of the Department. One of my main interests was to identify and encourage the young graduate entrants with promise – and there were quite a few. They were all placed on the Advanced Training Scheme; in the past nobody was ever told that he was an Advanced Trainee. Some years later I came across a list dating from the early 1950s of twenty-four people who were thought to have high potential – and I was pleased to see that my name was on it. But at the time I was never told. My idea of career planning was of a mutual process between the Bank and the individual. I believed that it was important to tell Advanced Trainees that they were thought of highly and that they should then be encouraged to think ahead about where they might be going and decide what additional skills or expertise they needed.

I found a widespread belief that Keynes, even if he had not quite abolished the trade cycle, had at least given us the tools to ensure that it never got out of hand on the downside. I was at pains to say that since the trade cycle was mainly a reflection of human psychology and that since human nature had not been changed, there was bound to come a day when over-optimism and consequent overinvestment would lead to 'deficient' demand and hence a real recession. I said I didn't know when it would come but felt sure that it would happen in my lifetime. Mark you, the first real post war recession was sparked by the oil crisis of 1973 and not so much by over-optimism. One bright young woman graduate, Maureen Lodge, besides being very bright also made quite a stir by dressing in a real 60s way – miniskirt and a beehive hairdo; she looked a bit like Dusty Springfield. Quite the brightest of the graduates was Andrew Crockett whom I steered on his way to higher things by putting his name forward sometime in the early 70s for the post of Personal Assistant to the Managing Director of the Fund. He was later to be an Executive Director of the Bank and has just retired as General Manager of the BIS in Basle. There are only two or three other things to say about my time as Deputy Chief of the EID. Roy Heasman moved on after a couple of years to become the first Chief of Management Services. He was replaced by Michael Thornton. That left two of us disappointed; I had hoped to succeed Roy and Michael had hoped to become Chief Cashier in succession to John Fforde, but, rather surprisingly (to me at any rate), John Page was made Chief Cashier.

Two other anecdotes may be of interest. We were engaged in negotiations with a number of City bodies in an attempt to improve our financial statistics. One of the bodies we were talking to was the Baltic Exchange. The Chairman invited me to lunch. We ate in an ample dining room, about ten people at table. I sat on the Chairman's right, as guest of honour. After the port had been handed round it was time for the Loyal Toast; I saw the Chairman press a button under the table; this was followed by a whirring sound to my left, directly behind the Chairman; the wall behind was slowly sinking into the ground! When it was right down, topped with carpet to match, we were now seated in a very large hall and hanging on the back wall some distance away was a portrait of the Queen!

In 1968 my passport expired. I had had a British passport of my own since 1935; my first one was signed by Anthony Eden who was the Foreign Secretary. So I applied for a new one. Imagine my surprise when the Home Office informed me that I was no longer a citizen of the United Kingdom and Colonies and that I should apply to the High Commissioner for Mauritius – a country which I had never visited! This was because my father had been born there eighty years previously. My ancestry was a nightmare for the Home Office – born in Malaya, father born in Mauritius, grandfather born in Trieste, great-grandfather born in Jamaica and great-great-grandfather in Scotland in 1773! I suspect that if I had not been in the Bank of England I might still today be classed as a citizen of Mauritius. Perhaps I should have let it happen and applied for the post of Governor of the Bank of Mauritius! At any rate I asked the Governor (now Leslie O'Brien) to intercede for me with the Permanent Secretary of the Home Office. Even then it took some time to get it settled. I have a suspicion that what may have done the trick was that when Amicia was born in America, the British Embassy had granted her UK citizenship on the grounds that she was the daughter of a citizen of the UK and Colonies; if they took away my citizenship, where would that have left her?

Quite early in 1969 I was surprised to receive an invitation to lunch from the Chairman of the National Provincial Bank, Mr Robarts. It seemed odd that a Deputy Chief of a Bank of England Department should be invited to lunch by the Chairman of one of the large Clearing Banks. I rang Dick Balfour and asked him if he thought this was normal practice and did he think I should accept. From what transpired later, I don't think he knew what it was all about but said he did not see how I could refuse. A week or two later I presented myself at the Head Office of the National Provincial Bank to be confronted with an extraordinary sight. The National Provincial and the Westminster Banks were in process of merging and the other guests were all the Executive Directors of both banks — there must have been over forty of them. Robarts walked me round the room introducing me to each one individually. One of them I actually knew — Eddie Playfair from my Treasury days. Not only that, but I was the guest of honour sitting at Robarts' right. What on earth was going on?

Robarts took me aside and said that he was inviting me to be the next Secretary of the Committee of London Clearing Bankers. He made no attempt to interest me in the job — after all it was a dead end job — so he laid out for me all the perks: a salary higher than my present one, a better pension, membership of the City of London Club and lots of free visits all over the world, starting that year with a trip to Brazil. I was really quite shaken by this wholly unexpected offer. It was not my sort of job at all — a position of no influence, and expected to kow-tow to every senior Clearing banker. Showing rather too much vainglory, I suggested that it would be more attractive to me if I was made Director General of Clearing Bank Joint Services! In 1969 that was not an impossible thought; the Clearing banks still operated a tight cartel with the encouragement of the Bank of England. Had I accepted the job I should not have retired for another sixteen years, by which time I am not at all sure that the Committee of London Clearing Bankers still existed; the cartel began to break up in 1971 with the Bank of England's initiative which went by the name of Competition and Credit Control. I left the lunch and walked out with Eddie Playfair, making it fairly clear to him that I was not at all attracted to the post. But I neither accepted nor explicitly rejected the offer that day. The incumbent of the post at that time was 'Porky' Barkshire, whom I had come across in the early 1950s. As an Assistant Chief of the Establishments Department he had interviewed me before I first went to Washington and suggested that I was doing well but that my dress was not quite as it should be. I remember looking down and noticing that I was wearing a pink shirt. When I left Washington in 1954 I remembered that and went out and bought a dozen white Arrow shirts. In my first interview with him after my return he looked at me and said, 'Every inch the central banker, de Moubray'! When he went to the CLCB he had been an Assistant Chief of Department and had, as I discovered, decided that the job had grown in stature during his term of office and had informed the Bank that the new

Secretary should be somebody of at least Deputy Head of Department standing.

At some time in the next few days Barkshire invited me to lunch with him and tried to get me enthused. He too spoke only of the perks, telling me that I would be able to get a large mortgage at a rate even lower than the Bank of England's housing loan scheme. He was very keen that I should take it so as to reinforce his idea that it should be a Deputy Chief of Department. He would feel that the appointment of anybody of a lesser rank would be to downgrade his importance. But I now firmly decided to decline the invitation; mark you I very much doubt whether Robarts was now at all keen on me. If the Bank was looking for a Deputy Chief to appoint, why did they choose me? The answer clearly was that the Bank wanted to get rid of me, or at least to get me away from the economic and monetary policy area. That I can understand; there really was nobody who agreed with my point of view and I would have been a constant thorn in their sides. I said that I would try not to mention WMA again, but I can't help thinking that he may have been the prime mover. There was acute embarrassment at the Bank that nobody had given me any indication of the reason for my lunch invitation. The Governor (Leslie O'Brien) asked me to see him. He apologised for the way in which I had been treated and fully understood why I had decided not to accept. I don't really know what happened next. Did I suggest that a visit overseas would do me some good? Or did he bring up the idea? I don't know, but by the time I left his room we had agreed that I would spend a few weeks visiting New Zealand, Australia and Japan and that I should look into the ways that their central banks organised and co-ordinated research departments, economic studies and overseas research. Was it that the Bank were so embarrassed at the 'cockup' that this was thought appropriate compensation? – for I have to say that nobody showed much interest in my report when I returned! Perhaps there was still a lingering feeling of embarrassment about not having come clean with me about my role as chief economist.

I probably should not have gone on this trip. It was, after all, just a 'swan' and I had to leave Daphne alone with the two boys for quite a long period. But go I did. I took time to plan it thoroughly. I think in the event I cannot have been away for more than about four weeks. The Bank of Japan were particularly keen that I should come and I was invited to give a speech at a meeting of the Tokyo Monetary and Economic Society (I may have that name wrong). I cannot now remember what I said, but I know that Andrew Crockett gave me a lot of help in putting it together. A colleague had advised me to break the journey to New Zealand and have a couple of days in Fiji. I don't usually keep a diary, but I know that I did keep one of this journey, but I am as usual so disorganised that I haven't the faintest idea where it is – probably somewhere in the attic.

But I know that I left Heathrow at about 4 o'clock one afternoon in May. I had done very little flying in the last ten years; probably only a couple of trips to Jersey and the Lydd–Cherbourg crossing. So I had never really done any long distance flying by jet plane. The first leg of the journey seemed quite astonishing to me – non-stop to Los Angeles; there was no question of having to come down at Shannon or having to refuel at Gander in Newfoundland. Even the route seemed extraordinary to me; we flew over Iceland and the frozen wastes of Northern Canada before heading south to California. It even surprised me that it was still light when we reached Los Angeles in the early evening. I had to wait about two hours for my connecting flight, and then took off after dark to Fiji, calling at Hawaii at about midnight. Among the passengers on the plane were the Jacques Loussier trio, well known for playing jazzed-up Bach.

We landed quite early in the morning at Nadi (for some reason pronounced Nandi) in Western Fiji. Fiji has an arid almost desertlike landscape in the west and lush and tropical in the east. I set off for the long drive to my hotel in an ancient taxi with cold blasts of air conditioning to keep off the heat. The hotel recommended to me by Dudley Allen was The Fijian, on the sea. I was by this time, 24 hours after leaving Heathrow, very tired, so I just had some coffee and then retired to bed for a few hours. I then went and swam in the sea; the beaches were absolutely gorgeous with lots of the most exotic shells.

I had been given an introduction by the Head of the Commodity Market in London to a young Australian couple who managed a large sugar plantation. I invited them to dinner that night. I got the impression that they did not often get the chance to eat out in style. The next day he came to pick me up and we toured his estate. This part of Fiji was fertile and well watered, but not yet far enough east to be lushly tropical. The estate looked prosperous and very well run. They invited me to lunch at their house. After lunch I was again very tired and they suggested that I should have a sleep on a chaise longue on the verandah. When I awoke I was surrounded by a swarm of enormous hornets! I don't remember how they rescued me, but rescue me they did.

The next day I was to fly on to New Zealand; the flight from Nadi was so early in the morning that I had to go to Nadi the night before and sleep for a few hours in the airport hotel. We checked in before dawn and were told that we should expect to see a great spectacle; one of the Apollo capsules, returning from orbiting the moon, was due to re-enter the atmosphere just to the west of us and should then be seen blazing across the sky from west to east – it was due to splash down in the Pacific somewhere near Samoa. We went on to the tarmac apron; there were a number of steps on wheels, the kind used for embarking or disembarking from aeroplanes, and we climbed up to look into the night sky to the west. Sure enough we soon saw a spectacular firework display; when the capsule parted from the rocket, both separated and passed across the sky in two bright clouds of sparks.

It was now almost dawn and our plane arrived from Hawaii. We boarded and took off soon enough after the passing of the Apollo that as we climbed we could see smoke trails from the re-entry. I forget which Apollo number it was but it was the last one before the actual moon landing which took place a few weeks later. I had an extraordinary flight; it was a Qantas Boeing 707 and I was the only passenger in the First Class section. I had two stewards and a stewardess to serve me breakfast – Buck's Fizz followed by a proper British breakfast.

I spent about a week in New Zealand as the guest of the Reserve Bank of New Zealand. I was in Wellington for two or three days talking to all their senior people. One economic point I made everywhere on this journey was an idea I had got from a paper by Charles Goodhart, the economist who spent a few years in the Bank in the 60s. This was, first, the fairly obvious point that to assess the impact of interest rates, the actual rate was of little importance; you had to look at the 'real' rate adjusted for inflation. But much more importantly it was necessary to recognise that people and businesses would actually be looking at the 'real expected' rate. A low interest rate might not, for example, encourage investment and consumer spending if prices were expected to fall. This point made a great impact everywhere I went. In Australia I was even asked to run a seminar on the topic by the Permanent Secretary of the Treasury for most of his senior staff. And I feel sure that it must have been one of the topics in my speech in Tokyo. In Wellington the Governor gave a lunch for me; it is amusing to note, thirty-four years on, that he asked very apologetically if I would mind trying one of their new New Zealand wines! I was not in those days as much of a wine drinker as I now am, but I enjoyed the wine – a white wine as I recall. I found Wellington very dated; I felt that I was back in the 1940s. I went one evening to a performance of *Rosencrantz and Guildenstern* in the crypt of a church and I swear all the ladies present were wearing small hats and white gloves!

I spent all my time in North Island and was given a wonderful tour by the Head of Research in the RBNZ. We visited all the main tourist attractions, including the Waitomo caves with the roofs covered with glow worms. We visited the boiling mud and the geysers at Rotorua. We climbed a long way up Mount Ruapehu – what I then understood to be an extinct volcano, but it of course suffered a great eruption a few years later. I learnt something about the New Zealand mania for rugby; we were having a picnic on a hillside when my host produced a radio and tuned in for the next hour and a half to a running commentary on a test match between the All Blacks and Wales!

One of the things that fascinated me on the hillside was that instead of heather the low shrubs around us were all hebes of one sort or another. I think it was that evening that we spent the night in a motel. Before dinner we changed into swimming trunks and ran across the lawn, white with frost, and plunged into the swimming pool, which was in fact a natural hot spring. My host had been in the Air Force during the war and knew all about stars; lying on our backs in the pool he pointed out to me the Southern Cross and particularly Betelgeuse, the giant red star in the constellation of Orion; during the war it had been an important aid to navigation. I was finally delivered to the airport at Auckland for my flight to Sydney.

When one travelled abroad for the Bank of England, the hospitality extended by the central banks was always generous. I spent a few days in Sydney talking to people in the Commonwealth Bank of Australia and to commercial bankers. But I was also taken to see all the sights, including the distinctive shell of the Opera House to be and, of course, Bondi Beach (not particularly crowded since this was midwinter).

The central bank then put at my disposal a car and a chauffeur and we set off for Melbourne, staying for one night in the Snowy Mountains. I stood on a bank of snow under a eucalyptus tree and picked some seeds; eucalyptus are not all that hardy in England and I thought that if I could germinate these seeds they were bound to be hardy. I was never to find out. I had read somewhere that in the wild eucalyptus seeds frequently experience forest fires and that they germinate better in such conditions. When I got home I put the seeds on a baking tray in a warm oven; when I went back half an hour later they had turned to ash! On our way from the Snowies to Melbourne we called in at a winery — I think it must have been the Yarra Valley winery — and had a wine tasting — at about 10.30 in the morning! I don't think I have ever come across an Australian port in England, but I have a firm recollection of tasting a strong fortified red wine that morning.

In Melbourne I did the usual round of talks with bankers and business men. I am sure that I was also taken sightseeing, but I haven't the faintest recollection of the sights of Melbourne. I completed my tour of Australia by flying to Canberra. It must have been there that I talked to the Australian Treasury. When I had joined the Overseas and Foreign Office of the Bank in 1951 I had made a good friend in an Australian called Bob Horan; he did not stay long in the Bank and returned to Australia. Somehow I had discovered that he was the Secretary of the Australian National Library and looked him up in the telephone book, hoping to be able to meet. I found him, and spoke to him, but he was in bed suffering from a bad bout of flu, so we weren't able to meet.

I then flew to Tokyo. I have a feeling that I had first to go to Sydney to catch the flight. My stay in Japan followed the same pattern, talks with people in the Bank of Japan and talks with commercial bankers. My Japanese was very rusty and I only dared try it out with taxi drivers. I don't think I ever told the people in the Bank of Japan that I had been in the Army fighting against them. I wish I could remember the name of the Director of the Bank of Japan with whom I got on so well. He paid me what I am told was the signal honour of inviting me to his home for dinner with his wife and daughter. We sat cross legged at a low table and had course after course; I didn't know how much to take, since I had no idea how many courses there were to be in all. My lecture seemed to go down very well.

I completed my stay in Japan with some quite extensive sightseeing. I found Tokyo singularly unattractive and already suffering from smog; many people in the streets wore face masks. The Bank of Japan gave me an escort for visits outside Tokyo. We took the bullet train to Kyoto which is every bit as fine as one is led to expect. Although this was thirty-four years ago, in the bullet train we never seemed to get into real country; it was built up almost the whole way. I was also taken to see the pearl divers – all women who dive and stay down for a very long time. I think this must have been somewhere south of Nagoya in a bay with many islands. And so back to England; no need on this occasion to refuel in Alaska, the journey across the Pacific and the frozen wastes of Northern Canada was all completed in one go.

The latter part of 1969 was marked by the McKinsey's study of the Bank of England. I have no inside knowledge of why O'Brien invited them in, but I feel pretty sure that it was connected with the fact that, for the first time since it had been nationalised, the Bank was going to be required in 1970 to appear before the House of Commons Select Committee on Nationalised Industries. I suspect that O'Brien fondly hoped that he could appear before the Committee armed with a favourable report from McKinsey's saying that the Bank was in fine shape. This was not to be. McKinsey's were in the Bank for several weeks. I have never thought very much of McKinsey's. They are what I call analytical consultants (as contrasted with process consultants – more of that distinction when I come to describe my time as a management consultant myself in the 1980s and 90s). They talk widely with managers from within the client firm (never so far as I know with people of lower rank) and then report what they consider the client should do. This is worse than useless unless the client firm itself is convinced that its problems are as described and that the solution seems right. Over the years I have on several occasions talked to managers in companies which had experienced McKinsey's, but which had never implemented their recommendation. I am not saying that their recommendations were wrong, but they had not ensured that they carried the client with them in their diagnosis.

The young men from McKinsey's were very bright and I spent several hours talking to them. I never saw their first report, but understood that O'Brien found it too critical and asked them to revise it. Their final report, which I did see, concentrated on two faults – the absence of any strategic planning and the need for a more informed personnel policy, involving the creation of a new appraisal system, proper career planning and the establishment of a manpower plan. What they did not cover was the strange top-management structure on which I have commented earlier; perhaps this was what they had concentrated on in the first report, which O'Brien did not like.

Their two main recommendations were to establish a long term policies committee and to appoint a Management Development Manager to undertake the appraisal and manpower planning recommendations. By this time I was thoroughly disillusioned with the Bank's economic and monetary policies. I went to see Jasper Hollom, the Deputy Governor, and said I wanted a change and wondered whether he would be prepared to appoint me Management Development Manager. He told me that McKinsey's had in fact suggested me for the post and that he would be happy to go along with it. So the Bank had finally got me out of the economic sphere and I was to spend the next four years working in a totally new environment for me. I will just say in passing that a couple of years later I stumbled on an early report on me and found to my amusement that somebody had said that I would be totally unsuited to personnel work!

CHAPTER 18

Life at Codmore Barn

WORKING IN THE CITY and living in Sussex made it quite impossible to blend work and home. There were no colleagues living anywhere near us – the nearest was perhaps in Brighton. It had been very different in Washington. I lived only twenty minutes away from my office and it was possible to have social meetings with any colleagues. Nobody lived more than just over half an hour away. We, for example, lived in McLean, Virginia and some friends lived in Maryland near Bethesda. That was only twenty minutes away, so we had no difficulty in going to dinner with them. I sometimes wish that we could have had a life which combined work and home. But I could never have been a farmer – you have to be practical and I am completely cack-handed. A family business would have been nice, but again, I have no commercial instincts and much as I admire entrepreneurs, I am not one. Daphne could have managed a business. If she had been born even only five years later, I think she would have pursued a full time career. I have already said that she could have become a Permanent Secretary in the Civil Service; but she would have been just as good in an antiques or decorative arts business. But we were stuck with what we had got.

I was ambitious and my work was very important to me, but I never had any doubt that the essential core around which my life revolved was my family. Considering all her inner insecurities, Daphne made a wonderful mother and wife. We were blessed in having three exceptionally nice children. We were from the very start – and still are forty years on – a very close family. Even today hardly a day goes by that I do not speak on the telephone to one or indeed all three of them. They too speak to each other frequently. And we see each other very often. I spend holidays with my sons and often visit Amicia in Kent.

One might have thought that to maintain a close family the children would have to stay at home and not go to boarding schools; but that was not the case with us. Amicia was the first to go in 1968. She was already eleven and we had hesitated for a long time because of her asthma. She was plagued with severe asthma from infancy. The introduction of the small inhalers – what we called her 'blowy thing' – made a vast improvement. But somewhat surprisingly, going to boarding school had a very beneficial effect on her asthma. She went to Windlesham House near Washington. It was run by a go-ahead couple, Mr and Mrs Charles Malden. Mrs Charles, as she was always called, wore mini skirts and bright yellow tights. Windlesham had not been co-educational for very long and Amicia's arrival caused a great stir. Amicia is not a very common name, but I know that there is at least one girl – no doubt in her twenties by now – called Amicia, the daughter of one of the boys who was at Windlesham with our Amicia! Amicia had previously been to nursery school at the Miss Lovelocks in Fittleworth and then to the Convent at Storrington. She was in the charge of a splendid nun called Mother Sabina. The boys went at a very young age to a nursery school run by Mrs Barnes in her own house. They got on well there, but Mrs Barnes suddenly had a stroke and had to give up. This was in the summer and we could not get them in anywhere else until September. In the interim Daphne ran her own school for them in the dining room. It was an absolute delight to see all three of them working together. Daphne seemed to have their full attention and they responded with enthusiasm.

In Washington (DC, I mean) we used to go regularly to the New Church, where Amicia was christened. In England the nearest New Church was in London so it was impossible to go there. Daphne, Amicia and I used to go to the Anglican church in Billingshurst. I am not quite sure why we did not go to Pulborough church, but I think it was because the vicar at Billingshurst was a happy-clappy priest with lots of jolly hymns which appealed to Amicia. The very sort of service which she would now abhor! After Crispin was born we stopped going.

The boys I think have always been puzzled by the fact that they were not christened. I think in fact we got very close to having Crispin christened in Billingshurst, but something intervened. I really don't know what Daphne thought about it. For my part I think that baptism is not all that important. The New Church sees baptism as an introduction to the church – in the widest sense of those in the world who try and follow God's commandments. I have felt that I have introduced them. I know that with my grandchildren I have held them in my arms walking round the garden praying to the Lord and introducing them to heavenly influences. I don't think their parents actually know that!

After Mrs Barnes the boys went to Dorset House, a prep school in Bury, as day boys. Jocelyn was very happy there and had his own gang who had an elaborate 'adventure playground' of their own in a copse. I don't think Crispin enjoyed it as much and he went off in 1969 to board at Highfield, a prep school at Liphook in Hampshire – just over the border from Sussex so within easy reach of Pulborough. During the next year I remember with pleasure walking Jocelyn round Guy Harwood's gallops, which adjoined our paddock, in his blue and grey school uniform early in the morning before he went off to Dorset House. Thursdays were always difficult for Joss; there was always beetroot in a salad for lunch and he could not stand the horrible vinegary taste – and who should blame him? But why did schools make such a fuss and insist that he should eat it all up?

Amicia soon developed an interest in antiques and the decorative arts. At the bottom of Mare Hill there was an antique shop opposite the bus stop where she got off on her return from the convent. She used to go in and

Amicia, Crispin and Jocelyn – 1965

got to be very friendly with the owner. He used to lend her copies of an antiques magazine. She began to acquire the encyclopaedic knowledge of these things that she now has. Crispin's early interest was in tractors, which he called 'tajis'; combine harvesters were known as 'comben harkers'. Jocelyn loved playing on his own. He would spend hours in the sandpit with his toy soldiers. All three learnt to ride; Amicia with Miss Adames just down the lane from us on the way to Pythingdean and the boys with Mrs Rolt. The boys would have been happier galloping than endlessly going round and round the training ring. Neither of them showed any signs yet of their later interest in horses.

The Children's Wing proved a great success. Like most English children they went to bed quite early and were therefore awake very early indeed. In the Children's Wing they could get up and play without disturbing us, but they were close enough to be able to reach us if they had to. As I have already mentioned, when Jocelyn was very young he used to have nightmares and had no difficulty in coming to see me to be comforted. The Children's Wing was amply stocked with toys. The window seats under the plate glass window which gave on to the courtyard contained all sorts of things, building bricks of cardboard, early Lego (so simple compared with the elaborate things which Ajax puts together today), little model cars, electric train sets, Subbuteo, Scalextric and who knows what. Amicia used to organise elaborate games with the boys in which they built a counter from cardboard bricks and played shops.

One serious conflict between work and home concerned the proper time to leave the Bank and go home. As the Deputy Chief of a Department and later, a Chief, one felt under some pressure to give the staff a good example. And yet I considered it absolutely vital that I should on most days be able to see the children before they went to bed. Many staff in offices working fairly late do not in fact achieve anything significant in the extra hour or so. Certainly at more senior levels, decisions are not greatly improved by being pondered on for hours and yet I have seen many who actually made a point of being seen to be working late. I decided quite soon that I would give my family priority and usually aimed to leave the Bank around five o'clock. When the boys were too young for bedtime stories, I spent a lot of the journey down to Pulborough making up stories to tell Amicia. She had a different story every night. When they were a bit older – probably three, four and eight – Daphne would have them lined up in the hall as I approached the front door, all clean and shining after their baths, and as I entered they would bow and say, 'Welcome home, honourable father'! and then burst into laughter. When the boys were old enough – I suppose when Amicia went to boarding school – I read them all the Narnia books and then *The Lord of the Rings*. I also remember *The Borrowers* and *Bedknobs and Broomsticks*. I enjoy reading aloud. Many years later I used to read Dickens to Daphne.

In the summer of 1965 Daphne and I were both unwell. Dr McWhirter, our lady doctor, diagnosed us both as suffering from 'reactive depression'. I am not at all sure that it is properly a disease – surely just a psychological state, in Daphne's case almost certainly reflecting her inner insecurity and great regret that she was not going to be able to return to the United States. Indeed the extracts from her diary fragments dating from 1965 which I have quoted earlier make this quite clear. Mine may have been brought on by reacting to her misery, but I think the sudden unexpected removal from the post of chief economist probably hurt a great deal more than I had initially realised.

My 'sickness' had a most unexpected consequence. The Deputy Governor, Leslie O'Brien, told me to take a couple of months off and go somewhere in the sun with my family and that the Bank would pay half my expenses. This was a very generous offer and I am still not quite sure why it was made. My first reaction was to think that it indicated that the Bank still thought I had a great deal to offer to them. Subsequent developments did not seem to bear this out. Perhaps it was a gesture of compensation for the way they had in fact treated me – using me for two years without telling me that I was only filling in for the interim. Whatever it was, I didn't turn it down.

So one fine afternoon in August, Daphne and I and the children embarked on a cross Channel ship at Newhaven with the Chevrolet. At Dieppe the car was loaded onto a train and we walked down a very long platform to board the train. Amicia was feeling very ill and was extraordinarily brave to walk the whole way. I am sure we could have arranged for a wheelchair to be produced. We had two compartments of couchettes and travelled all night to Narbonne. The boys were fairly boisterous and Dr McWhirter had prescribed for us a bottle of blue liquid which was supposed to be an effective sedative for young boys – it had absolutely no effect on Crispin or Jocelyn! I was very glad to reach Narbonne. From there we set off for the Costa Brava. We were to be away for seven weeks. There was no motorway in those days, so progress was fairly sedate. We had booked accommodation through a firm called Rentavilla.

Our first port of call was at Llanfranch on the coast to the east of Gerona. We were booked in to a self-catering flat on the first floor of a seaside villa. We didn't like it: too near other people and such a bore to have to climb a flight of stairs each time we came in. So I went off to see the Rentavilla representative, who very helpfully moved us to an isolated house on the small cliff at the edge of the little town of Calella de Palafrugel. We stayed there for some weeks. The house had a terrace from which we could see all that was going on out at sea – speedboats, little steamers which plied up and down the coast and the kite man (starting on water-skis behind a speed boat he soon rose into the air on a massive kite). Just below our terrace was a path which was where the Spanish *paseo* took place every evening. Couples, old and young, would stroll past, the girls often stopping to pick wild flowers to put behind their ears. We spent a lot of time on the beach at Calella. You can't really go sightseeing with children as young as three and four, so we never visited Gerona. But we did make several trips up and down the coast on the little steamers; they would run straight onto the beach and let down a ramp from the front for disembarkation and embarkation and then pull away backwards. On one of these trips we discovered the then completely unspoilt seaside port of Estartit.

When we had to leave the house in Calella because other tenants had booked, we took a lovely old country house near Estartit by the name of Mas Basso. There we stayed until nearly the end of September, by which time the beaches were deserted – not that there had ever been very many people on that long beach. We hired a temporary nanny by the name of Enriquetta. She was very good with the children and organised elaborate games for them. She looked after all the children for one day when Daphne and I did eventually go sightseeing. We went north and visited the Greek and Roman remains at Ampurias. The magnificent mosaic floors were not covered and we were allowed to walk on them! Crispin, Caroline and I and their children visited Ampurias (now called Empurias because of the emphasis on using Catalan words, which had not been permitted in the time of Franco) in February 2003. The mosaics were not even visible; during the winter months they are now covered with a layer of sand. In 1965 I also had a go at water-skiing – but only once! Even though I was only forty I found the strain on my thighs too much for me and could not get 'waterborne' before I collapsed into the water. My last memories of Estartit in September were of some spectacular thunderstorms.

So we retraced our steps – train from Narbonne to Dieppe and eventually back to Codmore Barn. Two months did a lot for our health. We both felt fit and I had to return to the Bank of England. As a matter of interest, the bill I put in to the Bank amounted to no less than £1100. Although there was a Labour Government they had not yet made such a mess of the economy that foreign exchange had to be rationed; by the end of the sixties travellers were limited to £50 a head!

Daphne had made Codmore Barn a really lovely family home. She had that knack – and repeated it here at Buxlow Manor in the 1980s. She was the main architect of the garden, where we built up a very fine collection of rhododendrons and azaleas. My job was to plant trees and shrubs. The mowing was done by one of the Pulborough postmen, Mr Hawkins, who always came off duty by midday and came to us in the afternoons. Crispin loved walking beside him as he mowed. Hawkins was later accompanied by his teenage son, who was always known as 'Gladys' (by his father, I think) because he sported the then fashionable long hair.

We saw a lot of Daphne's parents who lived not very far away. The children were fond of them both. Mr Hazell adored his grandchildren and would do anything for them. He would always turn out if there was an emergency. Ione was very good at playing with small children but never helped out; if she had something else on, that took priority. In 1966 Daphne's father was taken ill at Codmore Barn and somehow managed to drive himself home. Later the next day we discovered that he had been taken to hospital and was now in a coma. Ione had been very remiss in not calling for the ambulance for some hours and in not telling us what was happening. Daphne and I rushed in to the hospital. He was unconscious and clearly had a very high fever. The doctors had decided that he had had a stroke; but high fevers do not go with strokes. We hastily called for a private specialist. But it was too late to do anything; he had meningitis and might have been saved if he had been given an injection of antibiotic – during the night, not twelve hours later. He died later that same night. The boys, only 4 and 3, were devastated, but they were, we thought, too young to take to the funeral. We did take Amicia even though Ione did not want any of the children present. I think we were wrong to keep the boys away; at Daphne's funeral both of her young grandsons, then aged three and eighteen months, were present.

During this time I became very interested in orienteering. I have always prided myself on my map reading and used to enjoy treasure hunts across the Downs at Prep School. Roger Bannister invited me to an orienteering afternoon on a misty winter's afternoon at Arundel Castle. I think it must have been in 1965, because the boys, who came with me, were young enough for me to run across the park carrying them, one on my right arm and the other on the left! I was very competitive and determined to win. But, since this was my first time I did not realise the importance of clocking in immediately we had completed the course. So we came second; Lord and Lady Limerick were the winners. But we did beat Chris Brasher; I seem to remember that the son he was carrying was somewhat older and heavier – perhaps a fair handicap for an Olympic gold medallist! Roger Bannister himself could not take part; he had broken an ankle in a car crash. We went on many more orienteering outings with the boys old enough to run with me. One I remember was held at Molecomb House on the Goodwood estate; one of the Blacker twins lived there; he had been at Trinity with me. I even organised an orienteering afternoon myself, setting an elaborate course on Fittleworth Common.

When we had decided that Dorset House was not academically bright enough to get the boys into top rank Public Schools, we had to look at others. We decided to limit our choice to schools in easy reach of Pulborough. One had heard great things of Summerfield, but Oxfordshire was too remote. The only two schools we visited were St. Aubyn's and Highfield. I visited St. Aubyn's alone and found it really too old fashioned – almost Dickensian. The desks had clearly been there since the beginning of the century; they were all stained with ink and still had ink wells for dipping scratchy pens in. The only swimming was in the sea, and to get there you had to cross a very busy road.

We visited Highfield together with the boys. I don't think they took to it at all enthusiastically, but the Headmaster, Peter Mills, seemed all right to me. He played a trick on us. He took us over to the fives courts and then called out 'de Mowbray'; a boy came over. He was the son of Stephen de Mowbray, younger brother of Michael de Mowbray to whom I had been introduced all those years before at Oxford. The son was luckily in his last term. So confusion was avoided, when Crispin started. Crispin went there in September 1969 and we were horrified to receive a couple of days later a short letter from him saying that he was very unhappy and could he please come home. Amicia, who was by then at Windlesham, wrote him an encouraging letter: 'Buck up Bro!' Daphne rang Peter Mills and asked what was going on. Peter Mills replied that he had seen nothing wrong and that at that very moment Crispin was happily playing on the floor in his sitting room. We were reassured, but writing this now it seems very odd that a small new boy should have been playing in the Headmaster's living room; perhaps something had been wrong after all. But Crispin settled down there, although I don't think he ever really enjoyed it.

We had some lovely holidays in the next few years. In January 1966 we flew to Switzerland and spent a couple of weeks in a pension in Grindelwald, beneath the threatening peak of the Eiger. I did some skiing; Amicia and Crispin (aged not quite five) were given lessons on the nursery slopes. Jocelyn, aged three and a half, confined himself to toboggans. It is a tough life being the mother of small children. There was no skiing for

Daphne – not that I think she would have enjoyed it – and keeping small children happy, particularly when it was so bitterly cold was a full time job; and no 'après ski'. But she did it all with great aplomb and never complained. She was a lovely mother.

In the summer of 1966 we all became acquainted for the first time with Normandy, which now plays such an important part in our lives. We actually booked ourselves into a hotel at La Baule near St. Nazaire in Brittany, but moved on quite soon. But how was one to get to France with the Chevrolet? There were no roll-on-roll-off ferries and Brittany Ferries did not yet exist. The year before we had taken the boat from Newhaven to Dieppe and the car had to be loaded into the hold by a crane. I was never very happy seeing our car hanging in the air; might it suddenly fall? So we travelled in quite a different way. We drove to Lydd in Kent and loaded the car on an aeroplane! It seems astonishing to me now to think that it was a viable form of travel; I don't think the plane could take more than about four cars – with the Chevrolet perhaps only three. It must have been fairly expensive. We flew to Cherbourg and set off down the Cherbourg peninsula to La Baule.

We did not enjoy La Baule even though we had rooms looking out to sea. The weather wasn't very good – overcast and fairly wet. We spent a lot of the time on the beach where there was plenty to amuse the children, with slides and a trampoline. I am always amazed at how French children are marshalled when on holiday. Quite near where we were there was a group called *les petits pingouins*; where the children seemed to be constantly being paraded around in circles – '*Allez op, un, deux, trois.*' It was all so organised; I don't think English children would stand for it. In those days many Breton women still wore those enormous elaborate lace headpieces, at least on market days – but perhaps the *syndicats d'initiatives* actually encouraged them to do so to attract the tourists!

After a few days we decided to abandon the hotel and move on. We headed north and adopted the practice which later became our normal way of travelling, even in later years, when there were only two of us – we would do some sight-seeing (even the young boys loved visiting chateaux and climbing on the ramparts), have lunch (usually a picnic), and then, around four o'clock, with the help of the Michelin guide we would look for an *auberge* – we always looked for a remote one – indicated by the little figure of a man in a red rocking chair. We spent some time looking around Vitré. Later we stayed at a lovely inn in the 'Suisse Normande' – Le Moulin at Clécy – almost standing in the river with lots to see and a chance to paddle in the shallow water.

We eventually came across a hotel in the main street of the little town of Barfleur on the north-eastern point of the Cherbourg peninsula. The weather was lovely, the town very attractive, fine beaches and to top it all, Barfleur was *en fête* for this was the 900th Anniversary of William the Conqueror's invasion of England, and William's ship had been captained by

The children at the Lord Mayor's party – 1967

Etienne, a man from Barfleur. The Mayor and his wife took part in a great parade, accompanied by the Mayor and Mayoress of some English town (presumably Barfleur's 'twinned' town); there were typical strident French bands playing military music; lots of people all dressed in what I suppose were meant to be eleventh century costumes – I am sure Norman women did not then wear the lace headgear. By the harbour a plaque was unveiled commemorating Etienne's feat. Celebrations continued all day with barbecues by the harbour and noisy dancing in the evening. We liked Barfleur so much that we stayed there for over a week, I think. Whilst we were there we saw the *Queen Mary* leave Cherbourg on its last voyage.

The regulation restricting one to no more than £50 of foreign exchange per person must have been introduced later that year, because in the winter of 1966/7 it was clear that we would not be able to take a winter holiday abroad. In January 1967 we went instead to Aviemore in the Cairngorms, putting the car on a train and travelling up overnight. There was plenty of snow but the facilities were much restricted compared with Switzerland – and I don't remember much sun! The children, I think, enjoyed it. The hotel was full of children; Amicia made great friends with Joe Coral's daughter. There was also a skating rink and we all went on that (except Daphne – I never saw her on skates as far as I can remember). My cousin Gillian Layard, now Paterson, lived near by at Pitlochry and she and Bill and their two daughters came over to spend a day with us. We visited I remember Loch-an-Eilan – I may have spelt that wrong, but what a lovely name. My mother would have adored it. We were alone in this beautiful landscape; the loch frozen over and deep snow all around and the children throwing snowballs. We returned on the night train again – with the Chevrolet. This was to be our last holiday with the Chevrolet; it had done some travelling in the previous ten years.

In the summer we returned again to Normandy. I think it is usually a mistake to go back again to the same place. We stayed again at Barfleur, but it didn't seem as nice as it had the previous year. But we saw a lot more of Normandy. We travelled this time by sea from Newhaven to Dieppe, now with a rather small Renault 8. Our first stop was at what was to be one of my favourite hotels, La Licorne, at Lyons-la-Forêt. The food was good, the people charming and the little town is most attractive. The children had a lovely time visiting the ruined chateau at Château Gaillard on the chalk cliffs overlooking the Seine.

There was an amusing incident on the 15 August. We had never heard of the *fête de la Sainte Marie*, when absolutely every Frenchman is on holiday. We were following our now regular practice and at around 4 o'clock we began looking for rooms in a hotel; every hotel and *auberge* was full. I remember we even tried the 5 star Hotel La Ferme Saint Simeon at Honfleur. They looked at us as if we were mad. What were we to do? The Renault 8 was pretty small and spending a night in it did not appeal at all. At last in a remote village somewhere between Pont Audemer and Pont l'Evêque we found a little inn called La Cressonière. The young couple who ran it said they had one room free (which could sleep five, two double beds and one single). We were so relieved. They cooked us a good dinner and off we went to bed. But we didn't get much sleep. They were holding a party there for a christening. The baby cried a good deal and the grown ups were having a noisy jolly time. The Godmother must have been very pretty; we frequently heard the cry '*et la belle marraine*' as she was kissed time and time again.

Thirty-six years later on a visit to Normandy I decided to try and find La Cressonière again. It was there, but no longer the same. There was no sign of the stream with watercress, the inn had doubled in size, the terrace on which we had eaten was now incorporated in the hotel as the reception area and the little country lane was now the main road from Pont Audemer to Lisieux. Never go back again! Despite continuing rationing of foreign exchange we had a lovely summer holiday in 1969. We started in Belgium, visiting Bruges and touring the canals; I had to duck to negotiate every bridge! We then went to Holland, taking the ferry to Flushing on the island of Zeeland. Flushing must have been well known to English soldiers in the seventeenth century; it is almost the only town on the Continent whose English name differs quite substantially from its local equivalent – Vlissingen; the only other one I can think of is Munich, which is not in fact all that different from München. We stayed at Veere, a very attractive seaport, not actually on the coast, but on an inland sea, the Veerse Meer. All along the harbour there are houses with a great variety of Dutch gables. I always link Veere with the moon! For it was there one day, that as we were walking past the hotel one afternoon, through the window I could see the black and white television carrying pictures of Neil Armstrong on the moon.

We went on to stay at a hotel in the woods near Zeist, just to the east of Utrecht. Our final stay was at a luxurious hotel, Kastel Wittem, situated in the southern 'panhandle' of Holland which reaches down between Belgium and Germany between Maastricht and Aachen. We drove into Germany to visit the treasures of the cathedral in Aachen – how I prefer the old name, Aix-la-Chapelle! It was extremely hot when we were at Kastel Wittem; I remember seeing in the Dutch newspapers headlines reading 'Body Temperature' (the Dutch equivalent, of course) – English headlines would I am sure have said '100 Degrees'.

CHAPTER 19

Management Development

I STARTED AS MANAGEMENT DEVELOPMENT MANAGER on 1 March 1970. I now moved into the Establishments Department, the Head of which was Ken Andrews. I ranked still as a Deputy Chief, retaining the salary I had had as Deputy Chief of the EID (the Deputy Chief of the Establishments Department had a somewhat lower salary – she was the most senior woman in the bank, Aphra Mansell, with whom I got on very well). I had in the past, like I think most other people in the Overseas Department and the CCO, rather looked down on the Establishments Department, staffed as I thought by people who were not good enough to be in the main policy departments. I was, of course, wrong. There were some very able people there, some of whom will feature in what I have to say. I began with great enthusiasm.

Since I knew nothing about management development I had to educate myself. I went on a number of courses, the most useful of which was at some conference venue near Rugby run by Alastair Mant who was, I think, still nominally with IBM. I was not very happy with the detailed recommendations of McKinsey's on the appraisal system for reasons which I will mention in a minute. There were at that time very few people with the title Management Development Manager – in the City the only other one was with the National Westminster Bank, not surprisingly, since the merger of the two constituent banks had been masterminded by McKinsey's. But I asked McKinsey's whether I could call on their own Management Development Manager. He was a surprise – a good robust retired Brigadier, who I feel sure owned a labrador, if you see what I mean. He had only one piece of advice: whatever appraisal system you created should be changed again after two years! I don't know whether McKinsey's actually did that; it is of course impractical, but there is a serious point to it. No appraisal system can be rigidly specified; it must have some flexibility and the flexibility will need to be managed with some sort of guidelines. The trouble, as I discovered later, is that guidelines very quickly become established as fixed rules, and flexibility is lost. I learned later that by the end of the 70s, guide lines on the promotion of staff with high potential which I had drawn up in the early 70s had already become rigid rules.

It seems obvious that pay and promotion related to performance is better than a system based on seniority. But as soon as you start to try and measure performance you run into difficulties. McKinsey's had for illustrative purposes shown how the performance of the Principal of the Drawing Office (the main banking office) might be assessed; it was based on numbers

– number of accounts, profitability, etc.; but the Principal had no power whatever to affect these figures; the Bank was not concerned with the profitability of accounts, or with their number.

Many of the ills of British public services in the last twenty years or so are, I believe, the result of attempting to define objective criteria for performance related pay. By doing so staff's attention is focused on measurable criteria at the expense of the often far more important subjective criteria. A good headmaster knows full well who are his most effective teachers and should be given the freedom to promote them as he sees fit. To avoid unreasonable personal prejudice he should perhaps be required to consult other senior teachers. And look at the police. Their most important task used to be to prevent crime; but it is virtually impossible to devise objective criteria of an officer's effectiveness in crime prevention. In the past if a constable saw a young hooligan about to throw a brick through a plate glass window, he would have stopped him and probably given him a cuff round the ears. Today he would probably wait until the brick had been thrown; by then arresting the young man his record would now show a measurable contribution to 'crimes solved' and hence enhance his so-called performance.

I was convinced that in the Bank we had to have some more subjective criteria and accordingly rejected McKinsey's recommendations. I should say that, although I was a member of the Establishments Department, Ken Andrews did not try to tell me what to do. I was very much a law unto myself. But of course to get any changes approved I had to secure the agreement of the Heads of Department and the DEOS Committee, of which I remained a member. My main assistant in reforming the appraisal system was Roger Woodley, a bright and very enthusiastic young man. He left the Bank in the 1980s and I tried to persuade him to join the Management Consultancy with which I was then working, but he decided to take some Degree course in the fine arts and now writes and lectures; his speciality is the architecture of London and he has written an excellent guide to London. Roger I am sure would remember the details of the scheme we devised, but after thirty years I cannot now remember what they were. Appraisal in my view had to be closely associated with an assessment of every individual's potential. Managers were required to show on the appraisal form a letter indicating the potential. 'A', for example signified having the potential to reach general management level. People with an 'A' assessment would be expected to be put on the list of Advanced Trainees. They would be told what was expected of them, and encouraged to consider what jobs they hoped to do over the next few years, and prepare themselves for these higher positions by appropriate study. Career planning was intended to be a mutually co-operative process between the individual and the Bank. The DEOs accepted our proposals very readily. I soon realised however that the Heads of Department, with a few rare exceptions, were really not a bit interested in management development.

I tried to get the bulk of the staff enthused with this new approach and gave a series of talks on what I intended in the Oak Room (some 150 people at a time). I had the impression that what I was proposing was very welcome. I remember that after one of the talks a man called Beauchamp came up to me and expressed considerable frustration at his present lot in the Bank. He was at that time in the Cashier's Department and not even of administrative rank, although he must have been close on fifty. And yet during the war in the Navy he had been Principal Private Secretary to three admirals. He was an officer in the RNR, a full Captain no less, and during his summer holidays took command of a naval establishment near Gosport. I suspect he could easily have been a very senior official in the Secretary's Department, perhaps even Secretary of the Bank. When I asked him what had gone wrong, he said that when he returned to the Bank after the war, the Senior Clerks above him had drummed into him a sense of his profound 'juniority'. I discussed his case later with his Department and I am glad to say that by the time he retired he had reached administrative rank.

He was not alone in having been wrongly assessed. I should reword that. Nobody had up to that time been asked as a matter of course to consider what a man's potential was. The very first list of Advanced Trainees, dating from the early 1950s, came about only because Cobbold asked to be given a list of the twenty-four brightest young men in the Bank. I came across that list and it was very interesting; some of those included had gone on to general management positions – including G. de M – but others had fallen by the wayside; was it that their real potential had been wrongly assessed? Or was it that nobody had encouraged them to think what they might do and prepare themselves for it?

I have to tell a story against myself. One of my senior colleagues told me that he had been very amused to attend one of my talks in the Oak Room; I had just come down from the Senior Official's dining room on the fourth floor and was smoking an enormous cigar – behind my head there was a large sign: 'No Smoking'!

Whereas in the past the Bank had taken it upon itself to tell someone that they were to attend the Administrative Staff College at Henley or some other Business School, I instituted a new procedure. Where I thought it appropriate I called the young man or woman to see me and told them that the Bank was willing to send them on a management course at a Business School, talked about the options with them, gave them some brochures from the Business Schools and left them to decide whether they should go at all, and if yes, to choose which School seemed most appropriate to their needs. At that time I ruled out the Harvard Business School on the grounds of expense – and anyway I never really believed in their favourite method of teaching, the case study. But I did include the possibility of INSEAD at Fontainebleau and IMEDE at Lausanne (despite the fact that IMEDE used the case study approach). I was surprised to read in *The Old Lady* an interview with Ian Plenderleith, a recently retired Executive Director of the

Bank, in which he said that he had been allowed to go to Harvard in the early 70s. I thought I had a clear recollection of giving him some brochures and that he had chosen the Manchester Business School – so much for the accuracy of memories thirty years on! Before including INSEAD and IMEDE I went to visit them, accompanied by one of my managers, John Owen. Our journey had one interesting feature. When we were finishing our visit at Fontainebleau there was a sudden rail strike by the SNCF. It looked as if we would have to return to Paris and wait for the trains to run again or take a flight. John, however, suggested that it would in the long run be more economical if we just took a taxi to Dieppe and crossed to Newhaven. And that we did!

The other responsibility put upon me by McKinsey's was to produce a manpower plan. Here again I had no expertise, so I sent myself off on a one week course on manpower planning. I learned something but nowhere near enough to go on my own. Luckily there was a an excellent statistician and expert on manpower planning in my division, John Chilvers. The starting point had to be a strategic plan – but the Bank did not have one, and showed no inclination to make one.

As I have mentioned McKinsey's had recommended the setting up of a long term policy committee and this had been done. I was not a member and only heard what it was up to through Jack Davies, the Staff Director with whom I had a cordial relationship. He told me that the committee was not looking any further ahead than eighteen months! And yet there were some momentous events to take place in the early seventies. The only one on which the Bank seemed to have done some thorough thinking was the break up of the Clearing Bank cartel, the first steps to which were announced in 1971 in a document called 'Competition and Credit Control'. But I am not sure whether the implications of this for banking supervision had been thought through. I do not whether the Bank had looked again at the implications of joining the Common Market – Edward Heath was to take us in in 1973. I don't suppose anybody had foreseen the 1972 Oil Crisis and the abandonment of the fixed exchange rate system in favour of floating rates. Nor do I suppose that anybody would in 1970 have foreseen inflation at over 20 per cent. All of these developments would have consequences for staffing levels but none of them had any effect on the manpower plan which John Chilvers and I put together.

Having been told that there was no Bank strategic plan, I decided that I should have to write one myself. The Cashier's Department did not tell me about 'Competition and Credit Control', no doubt because they thought it was none of my business. In any event I produced the best plan of which I was capable, looking ten years ahead, and sent it to the Governors. I said I would base the manpower plan on these assumptions unless I heard from them within a couple of weeks of any features of the plan with which they did not agree. I was not prescient enough to have covered any of the developments which were to come; and if the Governors were they did not let me know. The only objection they had to my plan concerned the Exchange Control Department. I had said, in my plan, that exchange control served no useful purpose, but that politicians seemed to be set on it and I predicted that in ten years time the Department would either have been abolished or would have virtually doubled in size. The Governors asked me to cut out the reference to the abolition of the Department. In a sense I was right on both counts; by 1979 the Department was at least double the size it had been in 1970, but also in 1979 the new Conservative Administration did in fact abolish exchange control.

In the course of drawing up the plan I made the assumption that it would always be a good idea to recruit some experienced people from outside the Bank to fill senior management posts. If I remember rightly I assumed that something like 5 per cent of top jobs would be held by outsiders. We also made calculations of the percentage of First Class Honours degree people that we should aim to recruit. Again from memory, I think we decided that we did not need more than about two a year, but that we should in fact recruit a few more to take account of early wastage. By the 1970s the idea that graduates would join the Bank for a lifetime career was already waning.

The main feature of the manpower plan was that it showed that there was going to be a need to reduce staff numbers, and that in order to avoid compulsory redundancies a new pension scheme should be devised to encourage staff to take early pensions. The need to cut staff numbers would of course have been even greater had we considered the possibility of the abolition of exchange control. An outside expert who had been recruited from one of the big accountancy firms, John Rumins, designed a new pension scheme with generous terms for early pensions which was instituted forthwith. When I first joined the Establishments Department, the Training Division was not under my command, but it seemed to me logical that it should and with the agreement of Aphra and Ken it was transferred to me. The Division did not do a great deal but it was expanding and building on management training that had been provided from outside by the Industrial Society (which, I believe, still exists, but under a different name). I can't say that the training was particularly useful; what it did primarily was to make staff aware how painfully their own masters fell short of good management standards! One hoped that in the long run, as these younger clerical staff moved into management positions themselves, the standards of management would rise. I am far from sure that it did; by then they may well have been disillusioned and realised that it was quite possible to be rapidly promoted even if one was a bad manager. There were quite a few successful people, like George Blunden, for example, whose theory of management was to 'put the frighteners on' (Nigel Bromage, the Head of my Training Division told me that this was what he had once said).

The great emphasis in management training at that time was on the behavioural sciences; we were all expected to 'really understand' our staff. A caring and concerned management has a lot to be said for it, but this 'touchy-feely' business can be inward looking. Even more important, perhaps, is to know what you and your staff should be trying to achieve. In commercial financial services, with which I had a lot to do in the 80s and 90s, what the customer needed was of supreme importance and far too frequently neglected.

The Training Division had been in the habit of having a monthly meeting of all the members under the chairmanship of a senior manager. This was to exchange views and allow the staff to ask questions of management. I tried out a new format which I have never come across anywhere else. The person who takes the chair at a meeting effectively dictates what is going to be said; if the chairman was the most senior person present it seemed to me unlikely that the staff would have a real opportunity to express their view. I know that some might say that they would get ample opportunity under the heading of 'any other business' but most managers I have encountered are prone to say 'any other business' in a dismissive way, meaning to bring the proceedings to a close. So, although I took the chair for the first meeting, I told them that next month the most junior person present (an eighteen year old girl, as it happened) would take the chair and that from then on the chair would rotate among the sixteen members of the division. The young girl looked appalled. I told her not to worry. All she had to do over the next month was to make a point of asking every member of the division what points they wanted to raise. At the next meeting she would merely have to go round the table and ask each person in turn to speak up. It worked very well; I spoke almost as much as I had as chairman, but the agenda was certainly not dictated by me and many points were raised that I am sure would not have come up if I had been running the meeting. Indeed, I had to get some of my points in under 'any other business'! I believe many could usefully adopt this practice. But there are problems, as I discovered in my next department, where there was great reluctance on the part of managers to take part in a meeting chaired by someone of junior rank!

There was a lot of interest from outside in all the changes we were making in the Bank. Two central banks in particular showed great interest. The first was the Malaysian central bank, the Bank Negara Malaysia. Their Personnel Director, Tungku Aziz, spent some time in London seeking help in running the SEACEN (South East Asian Central Banks) central banking course in Kuala Lumpur in 1972. The Bank of England had for many years run a course every two years for bright central bankers from the Commonwealth. SEACEN had decided to do the same thing in South East Asia. Tungku Aziz spent a lot of time in the Bank and many hours with me. I found him a genial and sympathetic man; our common Malayan roots probably helped. He decided to introduce into his course a special week to be run by the Industrial Society and asked me to collaborate with them and lecture myself for one day of the week. Since the Malaysians were going to pay for my expenses the Bank were quite willing to let me go.

So I went to Kuala Lumpur sometime early in 1972. I decided not to fly directly to K.L. but to start in Singapore, hire a car and drive myself to K.L. retracing the routes I used to follow in a jeep twenty-seven years earlier. Singapore was terribly disappointing; all the lovely old colonial mansions on the Orchard Road had disappeared and the city was nothing but skyscrapers. I think I did just visit the Raffles Hotel to have a drink. I don't think I mentioned earlier in these memoirs that my godmother was a Raffles, a great-niece of the great man himself. From Singapore I crossed the Causeway into Johore, which now involved crossing a national border. In Johore I renewed my acquaintance with Zulkifli bin Hashim, with whom Peter Hobson and I had shared a flat in Cornwall Gardens. I spent a good part of a day at his house, meeting his wife and young children. From Johore I headed for Malacca. One of our neighbours in Codmore Barn was a retired manager from Dunlops and he had arranged for me to be accommodated in the Dunlop bungalow in Malacca. It was a spacious house in a large garden and I was the only guest there that night. It reminded me of the night we four sergeants had spent in a Dak-bungalow in Assam in 1944, but on an infinitely grander scale. Malacca is a very interesting and attractive town, the remains of old Portuguese fortifications are to be seen near the sea and on inland waterways there is a thriving Chinese community. K.L. had of course changed too, but not then as much as Singapore; there were only a few skyscrapers, one of which was the Bank Negara itself, but I doubt whether it was more than about 22 stories high. K.L. now has the tallest building in the world. Who in 1945 would ever have thought that possible! From the top of the Bank one looked down onto the old cricket ground below, which was still being used. K.L. had never had many colonial mansions so nothing was lost by their absence. But happily the railway station, modelled on a Moghul palace, was still there and working as a station.

The people on the course were a mixed bunch. There was one young Chinaman from the Singapore Monetary Authority who seemed to take to me and insisted that I did not wear my tie long enough! The Nepalese representative presented me with a black Nepalese hat on the lines of the hat which Pandit Nehru always wore. I remember being particularly irritated by the questions of the two representatives from Sri Lanka; they were always obscure and destructive. I found the same again to be true of Sri Lankans when in the 1980s I ran a course for the Insurance Institute on service marketing for young insurers from South East Asia, Arabia and Africa. Tungku Aziz was a generous host. We spent one day at his house on the beach with his family.

The other central bank which showed particular interest was the Banca d'Italia. It was the only central bank to have a permanent representative in London. Nominally he represented the Ufficio Italiano dei Cambi (the exchange control), which was of course managed by the Banca d'Italia. Their representative was Nino Zecchi, a charming and engaging native of Rome. He was passionately interested in improving the standards of management in his bank. The system of promotion there was based very largely on seniority; there were exceptions, but I am not sure how they came about. Mario Sarcinelli, their computer chief, could not have been more than 45 years old. Believe it or not, their promotion system continued to operate after retirement; when an older more senior pensioner died the next in line was 'promoted' and drew the appropriate higher pension.

In any event Nino Zecchi arranged for me to be invited to visit the bank in Rome and lecture on management development to all the senior staff. This was, I think, in 1973. I spent a few days in Rome and gave two lectures. I don't think they had any effect whatsoever, primarily because I could not speak Italian and they had to try to understand my English through the medium of simultaneous translation; since the translators did not themselves understand what I was saying, the message must have been garbled indeed.

Nino was particularly proud of Rome and gave me the most wonderful tour of the city. I was enthralled. I loved the piazzas and the Forum and peered with fascination into the little cell in which Saints Peter and Paul were said to have been imprisoned. In the Sistine Chapel I lay on my back on the floor to admire Michelangelo's work. This was before the restoration of the painting. I am not sure that I don't prefer seeing ancient things looking ancient rather than restored. Nino also gave me some wonderful meals: a special roast lamb with herbs in a small restaurant in Rome; a first class meal in the restaurant in Nero's palace; he also took me to Ostia at the mouth of the Tiber where we had fish in a small restaurant where the tables were covered with oil cloth. I don't know when the family's interest in opera started, but by 1973 we were already hooked and with *Tosca* in mind I gazed across the Tiber at the Castel San Angelo. I spent a lot of time on my own and walked and walked and walked. It is just not possible to sit still for long in Rome.

At the end of my stay the Governor and Deputy Governor presented me with a gold medal of Leonardo da Vinci – it was not done within the central bank fraternity to pay me for my lectures. The visit must have been in June, and I must have been flying back on the afternoon of the first Wednesday in June, because I remember asking the stewardess to find out from the pilot which horse had just won the Derby! The answer was Snow Knight.

One of my staff, Nigel Bromage, I think, had met Bernard Taylor, Professor of Strategic Planning at the University of Bradford Business School and brought him into the Bank to see me. We had a chat about what I was doing and he then floated on me the idea that the Bank of England and the University of Bradford should jointly organise a two-day conference in the City on strategic planning for financial institutions. So far as I knew, the Bank had never before been involved in any venture of this kind. But the idea attracted me, even though the Bank could hardly pose as an ardent practitioner of strategic planning, which as I have said, was conspicuously lacking. Another difficulty that I could see was that the

Bradford Business School was not one of the most prestigious; it might well have been more appropriate to do it with the City University or the London Business School. But it was Bernard Taylor who had put forward the idea so I agreed to see what could be done.

I am really not at all sure how I persuaded the Governor to agree, but agree he did. Bernard and I spent a lot of time organising it; we needed a lot of speakers to fill two days and we set about inviting people. The fact that the Bank was sponsoring it eased our task; almost anybody of any distinction in the City was happy to accept. I suggested that the Governor should make an introductory speech, which I drafted. The Bank of England/University of Bradford 2 Day National Conference on Strategic Planning for Financial Institutions was held in the Mercer's Hall in 1972. After the conference we found publishers for a book of all the papers given with an introduction by me. The book therefore has the names of all those who took part. I can only remember a few of them now, but the contacts I made at that time were very helpful later on. One of the speakers I know was Albert Thayre, the Chief Executive of the Halifax Building Society, one of the last of his kind I imagine, a real Yorkshireman with a strong accent and absolutely dedicated to providing the services of a mutual building society; he would have been quite out of place in the same institution today. Another speaker I remember was Dick Lloyd, Chief Executive of Williams and Glynns. I picked on him, not only because he had been successful in managing a merger of two banks, but also because his son was at Highfield with Crispin and I had noticed Dick sitting in a deckchair watching the cricket match with conspicuous on his lap a document marked in large letters 'Corporate Plan'!

My contacts with the Banca d'Italia were to continue. I am not sure in which year it was that Jack Davies, the Bank of England Staff Director, Nigel Bromage and I spent several days at the Banca d'Italia's Training Centre at Perugia. It was certainly high summer and at noon every day we swam in their swimming pool, being served cool aperitifs in the pool(!) and eating lunch al fresco.

The only other thing I did as Management Development Manager was to inaugurate an annual meeting of the top management development people from the central banks of the EEC. I managed to persuade my opposite number at the Banque de France to be the host of the first meeting, which was held in Paris in the summer of 1973. I remember little about the meeting and rather more about a great evening spent by me with Nigel Bromage and the representative from the Central Bank of Ireland. I have forgotten his name, but I remember well his smile, his laughter and his joking. We had a very good meal and drank a great deal in a lot of bars and cafés. It was in fact the only such meeting I attended since in May 1974 I was appointed Chief of the Management Services Department.

It was during these four years that I made my first serious attempt to leave the Bank. In 1972 Sir Noel Hall's successor as Principal of the Administrative Staff College was retiring after eleven years. Applications were invited for a successor. I decided to apply. Although I enjoyed my time as Management Development Manager, the top management of the Bank clearly did not rate it very highly, and I could not see what I was going to be doing in the Bank for the next thirteen years until I qualified for a pension at the age of 60. I felt very confident of my abilities and thought that the College would be a much more interesting challenge. I did not go behind the Bank's back. The Bank had always been closely involved with the work of the College; Sir Humphrey Mynors had been on the Board of Governors from the very beginning and Jeremy Morse was now a Governor. I went to see Jeremy and told him that I wished to apply and that I thought he ought to know, and that I wanted to know whether he and the Bank had any objection. He gave me a clear run.

I must have applied in writing with details of my career and some explanation of why I thought I would be suited to the job. In any event I was short-listed and was called to an interview with a committee of the Governors, which did not include Jeremy Morse. The interview took place on the top floor of the Shell building on the South Bank in the room of the Chairman – CEO of Shell and Chairman of the Board of Governors. He had a terrible cold and left the questioning to others. I told them the story of Pateman at Loretto and his instrument of torture which he had called an 'incita mentis'. I told them that that would be my motto; important though it was to have a thorough knowledge of management techniques, I said that to me the most important attribute of a good manager was the ability to make up his own mind and not seek always just to do what he thought was expected of him by his masters. My aim therefore would be to 'stimulate the mind'.

I have a strong impression that I was the preferred candidate, but my principal rival, Tom Kempner of the Bradford Business School, had the inestimable advantage that he offered them a deal he had done with Brunel University which would allow Henley to award Brunel MBA degrees to Henley students. So Tom Kempner it was. I received a very nice letter from the Chairman saying that I was 'proxime accessit'. Tom Kempner was a difficult chap and not very popular with staff or students, but Henley's mainstay became the MBA degrees. I think it is just as well I was not appointed. Business Schools became obsessed with techniques and managers are still very bad at thinking for themselves. However I think Daphne might well have flourished in that environment. Divine Providence thought otherwise.

I believe that what I did in management development was worthwhile and that I helped to raise morale among middle managers and lower ranks. As with so many things in life, however, what one does tends to be dissipated after a time. I have a feeling that my contribution had sunk into the sands by the end of the 1970s. Certainly by the late nineties morale was reported to be very low again.

CHAPTER 20

Schools and Holidays

B Y THE END OF 1970 all the children were at boarding schools. Amicia had started at Windlesham House in 1968. Crispin went to Highfield either in September 1969 or in January 1970 and Jocelyn joined him at Highfield in September 1970. Amicia went in September 1970 to Cranborne Chase. I think she enjoyed her days at boarding schools even though in those days there were far fewer weekends at home. Her three stepchildren are all at boarding schools, although in fact Leonora has just left King's Canterbury. Her own son Edward will I am sure go to boarding school, presumably at the age of eight. Amicia approves of boarding schools, although she said to me recently that Henry, her younger stepson, seemed to have had his initiative to amuse himself spoilt by the constant organised activities at school; he now spends hours playing computer games. I am not sure that this can really be attributed to school. Computers can be dangerously obsessive.

I am pretty sure that the boys don't approve of boarding schools. They feel, I think, that day schools are much better at forging strong relationships in the family. But it isn't in any event relevant to them as they both live in France and certainly won't be sending the children home to prep schools and public schools. Our children seem to me to have forged pretty strong relationships within the family, incomparably stronger than in my case, where I saw my parents only every three years. But I feel practically certain that Daphne would not have been able to survive another ten years of children at home. In her diary fragments there is a passage, dating from October 1967, which goes: 'I regret that I am becoming disenchanted with child-care, just too soon because I think for years I was a conscientious, loving and delighted mother.' So I have no doubts that in our case it was right. Cranborne Chase was just the kind of school to suit Amicia, short on discipline and long on character.

By 1970 the children were beginning to grow out of the Children's Wing and we decided to build on again, thanks again to the Bank of England. The first wing had been on the east side of the house and this one was now on the west. We added a Sun Room – a broad corridor with a stone back wall and plate glass windows facing south – and a hexagonal bedroom for Amicia. The hexagon was my idea, but we did use an architect to put it into effect. We seemed to have endless 'variation orders' – extra expenses as Daphne kept having new ideas as we went along. Behind the Sun Room was a utility room for washing machine and tumble dryer. It all went well; but there was one variation order which we rejected: the

242

architect had managed to design the shower room and lavatory with a soakaway that ran uphill!

For our summer holiday we rented a top floor flat at Cricket St. Thomas, near Chard in Somerset, for a week and then a small house at Trevadlock in Cornwall. Cricket St. Thomas was a lovely house. This was where we first came across whippets, which have been a feature of our life ever since. The owners of the house had a sweet little whippet bitch called Fawny, who used to creep nervously up the stairs to our flat to see if we had anything to give her. I also remember the boys being allowed for the first time to drive the car very slowly in the grounds. At Trevadlock we got to know Bodmin Moor, which has great character with the ruined wheelhouses of the old tin mines. The children all went pony riding on the moor. We liked Cornwall so much that we returned there again the next year.

Amicia was the first to go back to school in September. We drove to Wardour Castle in Wiltshire and introduced Amicia to the school. From every room in the school could be heard music – all the same, George Harrison singing 'My Sweet Lord'! There was a tea party for new parents. I was taken aback when the wife of Michael Neal, the Headmaster, said that she knew me – she had seen me in Sandy Wilson's revues at Oxford! It turned out that she had been Barbara Carter, a leading light in the OUDS; I remember seeing her take the lead in a performance of *Winterset*. We did not always drive to Cranborne Chase; most terms I would put Amicia on the school train at Waterloo. It was a spectacle. The front of the train was occupied by girls from Sherborne, all wearing brown school uniforms with collar and tie, whilst at the back was the fantastic sight of the Cranborne Chase girls – no official uniforms, but they seemed almost uniformly to be wearing Laura Ashley print dresses down to the ground and many of them wore wide brimmed hats as at Royal Ascot. It was great fun having a teen-aged daughter. She wore all the right clothes – hot pants and snakeskin boots. One day Amicia and I went all along the King's Road and back from Sloane Square to the World's End, popping into every boutique or shop. Art nouveau was all the rage and endless shops were selling Mucha posters.

Then it was the boys' turn. We drove them to Highfield. This was Jocelyn's first time away from home and his parents. He behaved very bravely, but was I think very disturbed. We almost immediately set off for a holiday in France, but were later told that on that very first day Jocelyn had fallen and cut his forehead quite badly. Daphne felt sure that it was a kind of expression of unhappiness. But it didn't last. Neither boy really enjoyed Highfield, but Jocelyn adapted himself rather better than Crispin, I think.

I am convinced that Daphne, in spite of her internal turmoil, thoroughly enjoyed our autumn holiday that year. The weather was glorious and we drove down to the Dordogne. We followed our usual practice of not booking in advance and staying in whatever attractive hotel or *auberge* we were near in late afternoon. I think this was the first time we stayed at the Château de Montreuil not far from Calais and just beyond Le Touquet. It is a wonderful jumping off point for touring Europe. I stayed there again in August 2003; it is still just as nice, but nowadays fantastically expensive. In the future I shall patronise little *auberges*! On our way south we visited Limoges and went to one of the porcelain factories, Pastaud, and bought a dinner service. That's the sort of shopping Daphne indulged in. There were no longer any foreign exchange restrictions, but you had to make sure you had taken enough travellers' cheques. Credit cards were in their infancy; I think we already belonged to Diner's Club. Travelling today is so much simpler, not because of the Euro, which I abominate, but because of credit cards and automated telling machines. We spent a couple of weeks, visiting Perigueux, Bergerac, Sarlat, Souillac and Domme. This is for me above all walnut country; *huile de noix* everywhere and in the autumn the fallen leaves of walnut crackle underfoot and give off a lovely perfume, quite unlike the smell of walnut.

In 1971 our new extension was completed. I don't think Amicia ever really appreciated the hexagonal bedroom which I was so proud of. We spent the Easter holiday in Jersey. I got on perfectly well with my parents, but never felt close. Jersey is a lovely place for a holiday. We particularly enjoyed exploring the rocky north coast, although I have to say Daphne was never very keen on negotiating cliffs. I also started a new hobby — collecting pebbles from the many beaches. I later acquired a stone tumble polisher, and many of the window sills here are covered with polished stones — a great variety of granites and quartzes for the most part.

For the summer holiday we returned to Cornwall. We rented a National Trust property, Old Stan's Cottage on the Tamar. The cottage was on the quayside and we had a large rowing boat tied up there. Every morning before breakfast the children could be found rowing around on the river. They could all by then swim and we none of us wore lifebelts when on board. Just below the cottage was a stretch of water where men set out nets to catch salmon. The cottage was equipped with an enormous fish kettle and we ate a lot of very fresh salmon. Between us and Calstock, just up the river, was the National Trust property Cotehele. Amicia and Daphne enjoyed touring country houses; they both had a very good eye for interior decorations. The boys trailed round politely. I remember at Cotehele Crispin calling us over to look at something — 'a fine twentieth century fire extinguisher,' he proudly said!

1972 turned out to be a momentous year, particularly for the boys. But it started quietly enough. We spent the Easter holiday at Yarmouth in the Isle of Wight, renting a small town house. We did not go far afield, but we visited the Needles and Alum Bay with its multicoloured sands. The boys had a few sailing lessons on a small cruiser. I always remember too the exhibition near the ferry of photographs by that great Victorian, Julia Cameron. Walking down one of the streets of Yarmouth I saw ahead of me a man with a most distinctive gait. I knew at once that it was Peg Bates, the man who had found my parents at the Sime Road camp in Singapore. I went ahead and confirmed that it was really he. He had a family house in Yarmouth and spent many of his holidays there. We were all invited round for a drink.

The next event in 1972 almost deserves a chapter of its own. In late July Daphne said to me one day, 'Why don't we go to Goodwood?' 'Goodwood?' I said. 'Racing?' Apart from that one meeting in Bombay in 1958 I had never been to a racetrack and had a vague feeling that it was a bit raffish. But Daphne said that she hadn't been racing since we were married and that she would like to go again. So I took a day off and we all went to Goodwood.

This was the Glorious Goodwood meeting and children under 15 were not admitted to the members' enclosure, so we had to go in the grandstand. The boys, aged 10 and 11, were enthralled. They backed Lester Piggott on the tote – shilling bets – and he won four races. The boys could tell you today, the names of the horses, their pedigrees, their trainers and their owners. From that day on the boys' primary interest has been thoroughbred racehorses, and they have never had jobs outside that field. We soon had to acquire the form book (*Raceform* or was it *Timeform*?). I don't think we subscribed to the *Sporting Chronicle*, but of course we bought it at every race meeting we went to. From that day on until they were nearly twenty, they each kept what is known as a private handicap, that is to say a list of all the horses currently in training (excluding 2 year olds) and they would give a weight to each horse: the better the horse, the greater the weight. And every evening they would adjust their judgements in the light of the previous day's racing results – all this by hand with no help from calculators or computers. Peter Mills, headmaster of Highfield, said to me one day, 'I don't expect to trip over the form book in the boys' dormitory.' I told him that keeping a private handicap was a much more intellectual exercise than trying to forecast whether Arsenal were going to beat Leeds (which was what interested most of the other boys!).

From 1972 to 1976 I became the boys' chauffeur. We went to race meetings at Ascot, Sandown, Kempton, Newbury, Epsom and Fontwell (a national hunt course very near us in Pulborough). Sometimes it was just the three of us, but Daphne quite frequently joined us, and she always came to Goodwood, where we used to park our car on the grass just the other side of the winning post. We never then ventured as far afield as Newmarket or York. Initially the boys were just as interested in national hunt racing as in the flat; Daphne did not really like national hunt because she hated to see horses fall and sometimes be killed. I began to know the names of all the good horses, trainers and jockeys. Crispin idolised Lester Piggott! As it happened one trainer, Guy Harwood, was established in Pulborough and had his gallops adjoining the top of our paddock so every day we could see horses being exercised. We also used to walk the dogs, whippets by this time, on the gallops. 'Mr de Moubray, can't you control your dogs,' Guy Harwood would shout. The answer was usually 'no'!

Dogs have always played an important part in our lives. Ginny died sometime around 1966 and we were then left with only her daughter Cindy. She developed diabetes incipitis and had to be given an intramuscular injection every day. I think she was the least appealing dog we have had; she had no character. She died in 1970 and we acquired two black and white Dalmatians, Sophie and Chloe. They were great fun as puppies but became quite uncontrollable – by me at least. They were constantly visiting our near neighbours, the Riggs, and scavenging in their dustbins. I finally decided that we would have to get rid of them. In the summer of 1972 we got our first whippet. We rang the owners of Cricket St. Thomas to ask if they had any progeny of Fawny; but the timing was all wrong; there was not a litter in view. So we visited a local breeder and chose a puppy from the litter – a white whippet bitch with black markings. We named her Brie. I strongly suspect that it was Amicia who chose the name; she has always been one for unusual names.

Unfortunately Brie had an accident when still a puppy; she strayed down the drive and on to the main road and was hit by a car. I rushed her to the vet; he said the injury could not be repaired and I only had two options – to have her put down or to amputate the left front leg. On the spur of the moment I chose amputation. The next few days were very hard, but Daphne was superb. Without her I don't think Brie would have survived. She had Brie in a basket near her and constantly urged her to walk. Brie soon recovered and lived another thirteen years. She could run very fast; her only difficulty was cornering. We thought she ought to have company and went and looked at another litter of whippets and chose a dark fawn dog. His breeder was called Trubshaw and for some reason Daphne named the dog Tubshaw, but he very soon became Tubby. Daphne adored Tubby. He had dark eyes, which looked as if they had been made up with kohl like a North African Berber. I think it was the following year that Mr Trubshaw rang to say that he had been diagnosed with a heart problem and had been advised to give up dogs and asked if we could possibly take on Tubby's sister, his one remaining whippet, May. So we agreed and had three whippets for the next six years.

For our summer holiday in 1972 we took a house at Mouguerre near Bayonne in the Basque country. It had been advertised as a farmhouse and I envisaged a house in fields in a real country environment. I have no doubt that it had once been a farmhouse, but disappointingly it now stood in a rough garden of not more than half an acre set in the outer suburbs of Bayonne. But we enjoyed the holiday.

We made frequent trips into the nearby mountains. An oft repeated family story concerns our visit to St. Jean Pied de Port. We were standing on a bridge looking down into the river when my glasses fell off into the water. Crispin, intrepidly, rolled up his trousers and waded in and recovered them. Ajax loves that story and we have it recorded on our home movies. Being in the Basque country there was a lot of pelota being played and there was a very fine court at Mouguerre; the local speciality was pelota *à mains nues* and we watched a number of matches between local teams. We also tried our hand at pelota ourselves. Whilst we were at Mouguerre we listened on the radio to the Benson and Hedges Gold Cup from York; agonisingly the family's favourite horse, the brilliant Brigadier Gerard, was defeated by Roberto. Two other events I remember. All three children developed violent gastro-enteritis at the same time. It was my lot to clear up! And near the end of our stay we visited the home of Edmond Rostand, the author of *Cyrano de Bergerac*; it was a grand Basque villa with extensive gardens. I think it was here that Crispin developed mumps; we had to stay in various hotels on our way back, keeping Crispin out of sight!

In 1973 we took an Easter holiday in the Isle of Wight once more. Our summer holiday was spent in a Landmark Trust property – the Gothick Temple at Stowe. The Landmark Trust does a wonderful job, saving old buildings, doing them up and letting them. I think it was also in 1973 that Crispin, Jocelyn and I spent a week on a sailing course at Dartmouth. We stayed in the Youth Hostel; it had never occurred to me that somebody of nearly 50 would be allowed to stay there. It was tolerable – no more. All the guests had to take a share in the washing up after meals. The sailing was very enjoyable; we were taught in Wayfarers and sailed every day on the Dart, stopping off at pubs for lunch.

It was also the year that Amicia left school. She had taken her O levels and was going to stay on to study History of Art for A levels. But she would have had to study under Mr Brown – and she and Mr Brown did not get on at all well, and we could foresee endless difficulties. So, with Amicia's agreement we took her away from Cranborne Chase.

There was in Pulborough one of the best fine art auction houses outside London. King & Chasemore were the leading estate agents in the area and Mr Weller had built up a thriving auction business. The conditions were still fairly primitive; it still operated out of a large shed. One day I buttonholed Mr Weller in the car park at the back of the shed and urged him to take on Amicia as a trainee helping to write the particulars for the sales. I told him that I was convinced that, although she had no experience and no qualifications, he would never live to regret it. Rather remarkably, he agreed to take her on. She was an immediate success. King & Chasemore later moved into more salubrious premises and was eventually bought by Sotheby's.

1974 was a more significant year. In May I was suddenly, and unexpectedly, promoted to Chief of the Management Services Department – more about that a bit further on. Crispin went to Harrow in the autumn. Peter Mills had said that Crispin should go to a 'civilised' school and recommended Harrow. I went to see some housemasters and we eventually decided on Newlands where the housemaster was Maurice Balme, who had been at Trinity with me. Crispin, I think, never really fitted in to any boarding school; in retrospect he might have been happier at home. But it didn't seem right to discriminate between the children, and anyhow I am convinced that Daphne needed the respite of school terms between the holidays.

For our summer holiday, Daphne and I and the boys (Amicia was already working) took a house on Pont Creek, near Fowey in Cornwall. We had two of the dogs with us, Tubby and May. We spent a lot of time sailing. Having learned from our experience the previous year at Dartmouth we hired a Wayfarer which was tied up at a quay just by the cottage and sailed mainly in the Creek and in Fowey harbour. We had one spectacular accident; for reasons unknown we capsized, luckily in the Creek. We all had to swim ashore, even the two dogs, so it was just as well that three-legged Brie had been left behind. Somehow I managed to get the boat down to our mooring and again, somehow, right her and bail her out. We were very unskilled sailors! We liked Cornwall and visited Bodmin Moor again.

CHAPTER 21

Last Years at the Bank

THE MANAGEMENT SERVICES DEPARTMENT had two sides to it. The major part was to run and manage the Bank's computers, except for those of the Accountant's Department. They had started earlier than the rest of the Bank and used the British supplier, ICL. We relied on IBM. The other part of the Department was concerned with Organisation & Method, essentially concerned with trying to make the clerical work practices more efficient.

I took over the department from George Blunden. My qualifications for the post were no greater than his had been. I knew absolutely nothing about computers and had to learn from scratch the terminology — hardware, software, programs (spelled incorrectly, as I thought). I didn't even know the names of the ranks — programmers (with 2 ms this time!) and systems analysts. I don't know why I was chosen. Perhaps it was just that with George moving on — he was appointed an Executive Director — I was the most senior Deputy Chief with the 'potential' to be a Chief of Department.

I think I must have made it quite clear by now how little I approved of George Blunden's management style. He left me a memo he had written about the work of the department and its structure, which frankly I found incomprehensible. It was involved and convoluted and seemed to bear no relationship to what I actually found. I believe that I managed the department much better than he had done. His great strength however had been his negotiating skills — almost brutal — which he had deployed to recover damages from IBM. That I have to say is not my style at all. However, the department had a number of expert computer people, chief of whom was Ron Gornall, an outsider who had been brought in because of his technical knowledge. But we were heavily reliant on IBM and rather than quarrel with them I sought to improve our relationship.

So what did I achieve with my lack of qualifications? I found that the department was running three projects for three different departments and that all three were desperately behind schedule and that we were unpopular with all our 'customers', most of whom did not really welcome computers at all and felt that if they had to have them the computers should adjust to them and not they to the computers. The department was overstretched and did not seem likely to me to produce good, acceptable schemes for any one of the three departments. The answer I thought was to abandon work on two of them immediately and put them into cold storage and concentrate all our efforts on whichever one of the three seemed most likely to be successful. I suggested that it was likely that the 'customers' involved with the successful project might then do the 'marketing' for us with the other departments.

The proposal was greeted with consternation among all the senior people in the department, and no doubt would have been equally horrifying to the more junior staff if they had known anything about it. My Deputy was a kind and pleasant man who had been deeply immersed in computer matters for some years, Jack Bennet. But he found it desperately difficult to make decisions. He would agonise for days over what seemed to me quite simple issues. I made it clear that my mind was made up, but that since I completely lacked the technical expertise to decide which project was to go on and which were to be suspended, they would have to decide. They made up their minds and one project was decided on. I am not sure at this distance of time which one it was, but I think it was the one for the Cashier's Department. I was in the job for only just over two years, so I do not know whether my strategy was in the end successful.

A serious problem in the department was poor communications. I instituted a regular briefing meeting at which the staff could be informed of what was going on and could ask questions about issues which were worrying them. I tried to import the format I had been using in the Training Department of a meeting with all managers and senior systems analysts (who were not of managerial rank) with the chairmanship rotating monthly from juniors to seniors, but at which I would never be in the Chair. This was adamantly refused by the managers. I had to accept the compromise of having only managers present but still with the chairmanship rotating among all members. I think it improved communications greatly and certainly helped to overcome objections to the concentration on one project.

I was equally unfamiliar with the other side of the department, Organisation & Method. I am, personally, neither organised nor methodical, so I did not have a natural affinity for it. I am not sure that I even really approved of what they were doing. 'Work study' seemed to treat clerical work as if it were a purely mechanical procedure. I have no doubt that it was successful in cutting costs, but at the expense of taking any fun out of the work. Of course work is not intended to be 'fun', but those who enjoy their work and are properly led will tend to find ways by themselves of making the work processes more effective – or so my experience as a management consultant later showed me. However, this side of the department seemed to me to have a much wider potential. I was determined to turn the MSD into the Bank's internal consultants, calling on outside consultants only when necessary. I thought that in time it might also be a good idea to transfer the Training Division from the Establishments Department – they too were dedicated to improving management standards.

To achieve this ambition I started slowly by building up outside contacts. I decided to take advantage of the contacts made in the course of organising the Conference on Strategic Planning for Financial Institutions and try and establish the Bank as a force in the City for encouraging better management.

I instituted a series of seminars on Strategic Planning which met every month in the evening in the Bank and invited a number of City directors to attend regularly. I always invited an outside speaker to deliver a paper which we then discussed. We had an interval for wine and sandwiches. My first speaker was Andreas Whittam Smith, who was then Editor of the *Investors Chronicle* – he was later to be the founder of the *Independent*.

By sheer chance I have kept a copy of the mailing list for these seminars as of June 1976. There were 28 names. Senior managers from insurance companies included General Managers, Managing Directors and Planning Managers from Sun Alliance, Provident Life, Norwich Union and Legal & General. There were senior directors from merchant banks, including Hill Samuel, Warburgs, Morgan Grenfell and Schroder Wagg. From the Clearing Banks we had planning and general managers from Williams & Glyn's, the Midland Bank (Brian Goldthorpe who later became Deputy Chief Executive), two from Barclays Bank including a General Manager and Professor Harold Rose, and the Head of Corporate Planning at the Nat West. We had senior brokers including my former colleague Tony Rudd (senior partner in Rowe Rudd & Co). Bernard Taylor, now Professor of Business Policy at the Administrative Staff College, having moved there from Bradford with Tom Kempner, was also a member. The Building Societies were not very well represented; the CEO of the Halifax, Albert Thayre, was an eager attender initially, but his place was later taken by Callum Macaskill, a General Manager, and the only other Building Society man was a General Manager from the Woolwich.

Besides all of these we also had Robin Pringle, Editor of the *Banker*, Bill Clarke, Director-General of the Committee on Invisible Exports (whom I had first met in 1958 on the plane from New Delhi to Karachi – in the meantime he had been Editor of *The Times*), Eric Glover, Director of Studies at the Institute of Bankers, Charles Read, Director of the Inter-Bank Research Organisation and Brian Emmerson, Finance Director of the Stock Exchange (I have pencilled by his name the comment 'ex Controller of Barclays – extreme Right!'). There was also David Hopkinson, Chairman of M & G Investment Management, who lived near Pulborough and whom I often used to meet on the train.

I have devoted a lot of space to these seminars, firstly to show that they were quite high-powered and then that, in my view, they did a useful job in indicating the Bank's interest in fostering good management in the City. All 28 never attended at the same time, but we usually had an attendance of about a dozen or so. Considering that the seminars did not start until about 6 p.m. this showed that those who attended considered them useful.

I had one other point of contact with the outside world. I was appointed the City representative on a joint committee of the CBI (Confederation of British Industry) and the BIM (the British Institute of Management) concerned with management education. The Chairman when I started on the committee was Sir Fred Catherwood, an ardent europhile, who was later for some years an MEP. The other members were all businessmen, except that there was also a representative of the Treasury. We discussed reports on the state of management education in this country and on occasions made outside visits. The only one I can remember was to Sandhurst where we talked about the applicability of management techniques to the Army. We had a lunch and I sat next to Colonel Blashford-Snell, the well known explorer. He and I had virtually nothing in common, so we neither of us said anything interesting!

For the last two years that I was a member, the chairman was Sir Peter Parker (who was not yet I think Chairman of British Rail), my old bugbear from the School of Oriental and African Studies and Oxford days. We clashed frequently. He was constantly emphasising the importance of manufacturing industry and running down services. I was a fervent believer in the irresistible growth of service industries, besides which I represented the City, without whose invisible exports the British balance of payments would have been in dire straits – indeed even with them, the then Socialist Government were making such a hash of things that in 1976 the IMF had to be called in to recommend an austerity programme. Having known Peter of old I was not cowed by him, though most of the others seemed to be. He was prone to show off. On one occasion he was late for the meeting and a secretary came in to say that Sir Peter had telephoned from his Rolls Royce to apologise – car phones were pretty rare in those days. Also in the last two years the Treasury representative was a Mrs Sluman, who reminded me that when I was in the Treasury she had been Barbara Pilkington-Rogers and then blushed madly; we had had a mild flirtation in 1948!

My only success in providing internal consultation arose when young Eddie George was asked to make some recommendations on the administrative set-up for economic services in the Bank and had been told by somebody that he should think in terms of a matrix organisation. He had never heard the term and referred to me for enlightenment. I was, and still am, highly critical of matrix organisations in which managers report to one superior for administrative purposes and to a specialist for technical matters. It seems to me to undermine the coherence of an organisation; the individual never really knows which of his two superiors he should defer to and this, I think, leads to indecisiveness and inhibits independent thinking. Anyway Eddie did not adopt the idea. He still, however, felt the need for some kind of expert mentor and I arranged with Basil Denning, Managing Director of Harbridge House Europe, a firm of management consultants, to make available to Eddie George one of his bright young men at a relatively modest fee. I think Eddie found it useful. Had I stayed on I would have wanted to do more of this.

My attempts at creating an internal consultancy service did not stop there. I was still dissatisfied with the top structure of the Bank and drew up a number of alternative proposals with charts and took them to Jasper Hollom to see what he thought of them. I am afraid that he was not a bit receptive.

I got the impression that he paid absolutely no attention to my proposals and was really rather annoyed with me for coming forward uninvited. This was not, he clearly thought, the way the Bank did things.

I have been finding this section of my memoirs hard going. I have had to force myself to sit down and write. I am not at all sure why. During the period 1974–76 I felt very confident of my abilities and flung myself into my work with enthusiasm, but I suspect that my reluctance to write about it reveals that beneath the confidence was a growing disillusionment with the Bank and an unhappy feeling that this was leading nowhere. The Bank did not help with what it did in early 1975. At that time inflation was running at well over 20 per cent and the Bank decided to grant an increase of salary to the staff on 1 March of no less than 25 per cent. But the Governor, Gordon Richardson, bowed to pressure from that bully Denis Healey (then Chancellor of the Exchequer) and made a pointless gesture in favour of an incomes policy by announcing that this increase would not apply to the Governors, Executive Directors, Heads and Deputy Heads of Department, who would receive no increase at all! I say 'pointless' because hardly anyone outside the Bank and the Treasury ever knew about it. Needless to say I was shattered and so was Daphne. As Dick Balfour pointed out, to no avail, it hit me harder than all the others, since I was the only one young enough to be having to pay high school fees for my children. The HODS did however protest most strongly to the Governor on behalf of the Deputy Chiefs; Gordon Richardson relented and they were awarded 12.5 per cent. This cut in real salary of course had an adverse effect on the pension I took in 1976. But I will say this for the Bank, towards the end of the 70s the Bank increased my pension to restore it to what it would have been if the cut had not been made.

The MSD was not in the main bank building in Threadneedle Street, but in a property known as Bank Buildings on the corner of Princes Street. The computers however were in the vaults of Head Office in a specially air-conditioned room to keep them at a constant temperature. There were no small computers in those days; they were massive machines with all sorts of whirring tapes.

To be a Chief of Department in the Bank had a certain cachet; it was something more than just being one step up from a Deputy Chief. I had my own personal pink-coated messenger who waited on me hand and foot, served my coffee and my tea and ran errands for me. If he wanted something for me he would say, 'The Chief wants . . .'. In fact I was being constantly known as 'the Chief'. In Bank Buildings I had a very large office; leading off from the anteroom where my secretary sat, the office had three sections – a meeting room for relatively small meetings, then a 'drawing room' as George Blunden called it, with sofas, chairs and coffee tables and then the office proper. On the desk there were a battery of telephones; one circuit for talking only to the Governors, Executive Directors and Heads and Deputy Heads of Department.

As a Chief of Department one was expected to lunch at least once a week in the Governor's Dining Room. It was at lunch there that I met again for the first time since Loretto, Hector Laing, now a non-executive director of the Bank. I perhaps overused my privileges. I remember once that the pressure of work was such that I could not get to Harrow at the end of term to pick up Crispin, so I sent a Bank chauffeur to collect him and bring him back to Bank Buildings. He must have had a very rough night on the last night of term because he was very sleepy. My messenger put him in a room down the corridor which was temporarily vacant. A bit later he beckoned to me to come down the corridor very quietly and look in to the office; there was Crispin fast asleep with his head slumped on the desk!

At home, life was a bit stressful. Inflation made finding school fees very difficult and we did not have a scrap of capital other than the house we lived in. This was made even worse by Gordon Richardson's gesture in 1975. Nevertheless in September Jocelyn went to Eton; he had been down for Eton for some years but it was in the context of a scheme whereby boys had to take an exam and be interviewed. I took him to the interview which was with McIndoe who later became Vice-Provost of Eton. Jocelyn joined Alastair Graham's House. He, and we, got on very well with Alastair. For his last year Jocelyn was made House Captain, but he did not serve under Alastair who left that summer to become Headmaster of Millhill. The new housemaster, Mark Phillips, was not as taken with Jocelyn; they had frequent disagreements.

1975 was, of course, also the year of the Referendum on the EEC. I continued to be a strong supporter; not surprisingly, my lack of trust in either Conservative or Labour governments to manage the nation's finances prudently continued; we had just been through the disastrously inflationary policies of Heath and Barber and were now suffering from the almost worse policies of Wilson and Healey. However, my enthusiasm was waning; when a couple of years later the EEC allowed members of EFTA, which we had left to join the EEC, tariff free access to the EEC markets I remember thinking that we would do much better to leave the EEC and rejoin EFTA. So tariffs had become a more important issue for me than supranational discipline.

1976 was the year in which I finally broke with the Bank. Early that year I was told that the Governor wanted to see me. I walked into his office and sat down. He began to tell me that they had decided to merge the MSD and the Secretary's Department under a new title of the Administration Department and that Peter Taylor, the Bank Secretary, would be the Head of it. I interjected and asked whether he was consulting me about a proposal or was he just telling me; as a Head of Department and part of the top management team, as I thought, I told him that I would have expected to be consulted. Gordon Richardson was quite taken aback; he had expected me to say, 'Yes, Mr Governor, whatever you say.' Clearly he had to spend a little more time with me, but the Government Broker was waiting to see him, so he asked me to go to the waiting room and return when the broker had left. He made no apologies; told me that the decision was a final one and was going to be implemented on 1 March; that I would retain command of the Bank's computers with the title of Head of Bank Computer Services and would no longer be a member of the Heads of Departments Committee, but would retain the salary of a Chief.

I told him straightaway that this was quite unacceptable and that I wanted an immediate pension. He told me that I had better go and talk to the Deputy Governor. I saw Jasper Hollom within a few minutes. He agreed to grant me an immediate pension and, quite generously, said that he was prepared to give me the favourable pension terms which I and John Rumins had drawn up three years before to cut down the impending surplus of middle managers. I hasten to add that when we drew up that pension scheme I had absolutely no idea that I would become a beneficiary. What the Bank did that day in February 1976 amounted I believe to what is now called 'constructive dismissal'. I find it hard to believe that they really thought I would accept such a decision. I was not a computer expert and the new proposal completely eliminated any chance of achieving my ambition to set up an internal consultancy service.

I had made my decision impulsively without even consulting Daphne. But I am sure I made the right decision. The prospect of soldiering on for another nine years until I reached the age of 60 was more than I could face. Jasper agreed to my pension but also agreed that I could put off my formal resignation until I had found myself another job. I met with great sympathy from many of my colleagues, but not I fear from John Page or from George Blunden. In a sense, I think, the Bank gave a great sigh of relief: 'We have got rid of him at last!'

I cannot recollect how Daphne took the news that evening. I suspect that she was worried at the possible financial implications. Had I stayed on my salary would have continued to rise with inflation – Bank pensions are adjusted upwards in line with the Retail Price Index and not in line with earnings so my final pension would have been substantially higher and by then Bank pensioners were also granted free subscriptions to BUPA. But I think she saw that I would have become more and more miserable and that a clean break was preferable.

The question now was what should I do with my life. I was supremely confident in my ability to run almost any organisation, but was never to know whether that confidence was misplaced. I got in touch with a number of head-hunters and had several interviews, but to no avail. I was interviewed for the job of Director of the Tote, but with Woodrow Wyatt in the running I had no chance whatever. Anyway it would have been a most unsuitable job for me; I should have had to rely heavily on the advice of my sons – and that would not have looked good.

I also was interviewed for the job of Head of the University of Aston Business School; I reached the short list and was almost home and dry when

I decided to withdraw my application. Daphne and the children were all horrified at the prospect of living in Birmingham, although I told them that we could live in Worcestershire or Warwickshire and that I would then go in by car. But this was not decisive. Something more attractive had cropped up. Looking back I am puzzled by Daphne's and my reasoning. We had already decided to sell Codmore Barn. Whatever I did, I was determined not to have to commute again daily into London. But even when Birmingham seemed very much on the cards we were already looking for a house in Suffolk!

Why Suffolk? Our main reason was that we wanted a nice house and that meant finding an area of the country where house prices were very good value — and Suffolk qualified. The other consideration was that we wanted still to be within reasonable reach of London, so that the children could easily come home for weekends. In the early summer — perhaps it was before Birmingham was even likely? — I took a day off and went from the Bank to Liverpool Street Station and took a train to Darsham (on the Ipswich–Lowestoft line) in order to have a look at Yoxford Place, a Georgian house in the small town of Yoxford. The daughter of the house picked me up in her car and showed me round the house. Her mother, the widow of a trainer of racehorses, had died of cancer and neither she nor her brother, whose business was the transport of racehorses, wanted to live there. The front of the house was very attractive, and the main reception rooms were very fine. There was also a lovely staircase leading up from the hall. The back of the house, however, was rather dull — a Victorian rectangular wing of relatively small rooms. There was a vast country kitchen. I thought Daphne should certainly have a look at it. A few days later we drove up to Suffolk from Pulborough and stayed at the Crown at Framlingham. We visited Yoxford Place and several other houses; the other possible one was the Old Manor House at Kelsale. We were prepared to buy either one of them. As I remember the Manor House at Kelsale was marginally cheaper and I actually rang the owner, Mrs Edgerley, and made an offer of £42,000. She turned it down on the very moral grounds that she had already accepted an offer of £40,000! Good for her.

We were on the verge of making an offer for Yoxford Place when a new job was offered to me. Jan Mladek, who had been the IMF representative in Paris in 1957, was now head of a service of the Fund in Washington which was concerned with providing technical help and expertise to the central banks of member countries. He was in London and had heard that I was resigning from the Bank. He offered me two possibilities, both in Africa. The first was to be Governor of the Central Bank of the Gambia and the other was to be Adviser to the Governor of the Banque du Maroc in Rabat. I had never visited either country, but the Gambia is a tiny country, sandwiched between two parts of Senegal, and not known to be particularly attractive, although I believe it has some fine beaches. And although I felt very competent to advise on economic and monetary policies, there was not likely to be much call for that in the Gambia and my knowledge of practical banking was negligible, so the executive role of a Governor did not seem to be my sort of thing.

So I – and Daphne – opted for Morocco. Before this could be confirmed it was necessary for me to meet Monsieur Bennani, the Deputy Governor, to see if we got on. I should add that the Governor of the Banque du Maroc was a Prince, an uncle of King Hassan who never once set foot in the bank! If this job was confirmed we might well be living abroad for some years – if not in Morocco in some other client bank of the IMF – so it did not seem sensible to buy a house in Suffolk and we withdrew from Yoxford Place. It is just as well that we did not live there, because the road outside was regraded from a B road to an A road and became for some years the main artery for heavy lorries in the building of the Sizewell B nuclear power station. Not only would it have been noisy, but it would have been murder to have three dogs there.

Bennani came to London and we met and had lunch at his hotel in Portman Square. We got on very well; we clicked immediately rather as Jacobsson and I had twenty years earlier. The language we spoke was French and all the work was to be in French, but I had no troubles on that score. By this time it must have been July and I confidently expected that we would be off to Morocco by September, but for various bureaucratic reasons it was to be November before we actually set off. First, of course, I had formally to resign from the Bank and my resignation became effective in August. Because of our desperate lack of capital and because current expenditure on school fees was proving very difficult after Gordon Richardson's action the year before, I decided to commute half my pension for a capital sum. It was a great relief to have some capital at last. It allowed us first to pay a lump sum to Harrow and Eton covering the boys' fees for the rest of their time at school. I think this amounted to £14,000. We also for the first time in our married life were able to buy a new car – no more hire purchase of a second hand car. It was a Renault 16 (which in Morocco became known as 'le seize'). My pension was substantially more than half my final salary (because of the favourable terms offered by Jasper Hollom), but I don't remember what that was – somewhere around £18,000/ £20,000 I think. That does not sound much today, but it was quite a good salary in 1976. The IMF was to pay me $40,000 a year tax free, which was substantial enough to allow us to fly the boys out to Rabat every school holiday.

It was about now that my father died. I am afraid I felt no sorrow. I had never really felt filial – we had spent far too little time together for that. I was to go to Jersey for the funeral, but fell ill on the day I was supposed to go and arrived after the funeral. Peter Gem seemed to think that this was a deliberate snub, which it certainly was not. It was in fact a migraine, which I suppose is psychological, so underneath there may have lurked some reluctance to go. Who knows?

The pending move to Morocco did not stop us from having a summer holiday. It was to be the last holiday in which all five of us were together, because Amicia joined us. We spent a week or so at the Deer Park, a hotel outside Honiton in Devon. There was a sauna and a swimming pool which took up a lot of Amicia's time. The other four played golf quite often at the Honiton golf course. 1976 was the driest summer for a very long time; indeed it is only in 2003 that it has been matched. The lawns at the Deer Park were absolutely brown. At Codmore Barn many plants were dying. We had already sold Codmore Barn – for £49,000 – to a former nursery man, for whom the garden had been the great attraction. We watered away; it did not seem right to let him arrive and find dozens of dead rhododendrons.

CHAPTER 22

Morocco

UNFORTUNATELY WE COULD NOT GET OFF for Morocco as soon as the boys had gone back to school. There was a preliminary requirement – I had to go to Washington to be briefed and that, for some reason, could not be arranged before October. Completion of the sale was due in early September and there was a lot to be done. We had decided to take a lot of our furniture to Morocco, some was to stay in storage and some was required for the children in England. Pickfords did the moving and storing for us, and there were endless packing cases marked 'Morocco' or 'storage'. It is an exhausting job packing up after twenty-one years. The problem now was where were we going to stay whilst waiting to go. Our first thought was to ask my parents if we could come and stay with them in Jersey. This, regrettably, was not possible. Instead we rented a cottage just north of Pulborough called Staalcot. Daphne then had the brilliant idea that we ought to buy some small property in England for the children to go to at weekends and to maintain some stake in the British property market. We found a small house in the very pretty village of Amberley near the River Arun to the south of Pulborough. Staalcot was a strange enough name, but this cottage was improbably called 'The Stowe'. We were not able to take possession until April of the following year. So far as I can remember the price was around £20,000.

Eventually I was able to go to Washington. This was my first trip to the States since 1959. I took with me my little attaché case which had belonged to Daphne's father; it must by then have already been fifty years old. The inside lining of the top was soft and spongy leather. I had to plead with the customs in New York not to slit it open; they seemed to think I was probably carrying drugs. Washington did not seem to have changed very much, but the Fund was unrecognisable. They had built themselves a grandiose 'palace'; the atrium was immensely tall with quite large trees growing indoors. There were still a few friends from the past. One evening I went to a talk on some economic subject, where Eddie Bernstein put in an appearance and also Jacques Polack. I know I had lunch in the atrium with Jay Reid, the IMF's original 'spin doctor'. I am not really quite sure what the briefing was about, but I spent some time with Jan Mladek. So back to England and off to Morocco.

We had decided to drive there across France and Spain. We set off in November in the Renault 16, packed to the gunwales with luggage. We crossed to Boulogne by hovercraft and then drove off, following our now well established routine; we made no advance bookings and guided ourselves with the red Michelin guide, stopping always at hotels marked with the little red rocking chair – '*situation tranquille*'. In early winter the roads were remarkably empty. I suppose there were then some *autoroutes* but we stuck to *routes nationales*. Our first stop was at Saumur; I always associate the Loire country with hot sunshine, but now it was misty with a hazy sun. We then went on to Pau and stayed at a very grand chateau hotel out in the country. Unfortunately the *confit d'oie* did not agree with Daphne and she had a violent bout of gastro-enteritis.

But we had to press on and climbed into the Pyrenees and stayed a night at Ainhoa in the Basque country. When we arrived there was a violent thunderstorm and all power failed. I got Daphne to bed and later when the power was restored arranged for her to have a simple supper in bed. Ainhoa is the last town in France before Spain, at the westernmost end of the Pyrenees.

By now Daphne had recovered and we crossed into Spain. It is strange now to think that Spain was then still ruled by Franco. We set off south towards Soria. I sometimes have the strange feeling when driving up a valley that I am in fact descending; for in many stretches the road does actually descend, but of course climbing in the long run. In any event I was quite surprised on this bit of the journey to find us running into snow; we even had difficulty in breasting the top of the pass, but we made it. At Soria we had our first experience of the Spanish *paradors*. They are a kind of Spanish equivalent of the British Landmark Trust, but state owned. Sometimes one stays in a converted castle or in a monastery, as at Sigüenza. We found them uniformly good; but the food is disappointing, particularly the puddings which seem to be almost always a dull kind of baked custard.

I always avoid large cities; I find it impossible to find parking places and we both much preferred to stay in quiet hotels. So we bypassed Madrid and went on to Toledo, where the *parador* is spectacularly perched on a cliff top over the river below and with a panoramic view of the city on the opposite bank. It looked better than ever when we there, because the whole city was framed in a double rainbow. We went in to Toledo and saw the sights including the splendid El Greco in the cathedral. We then drove down through La Mancha – Don Quixote country with lines of windmills along the hilltops – to Andalucia. Our next stop was at Cordoba. The old Moorish mosque transformed into a Christian cathedral is to my mind one of the finest cathedrals in the world; the two others that stand out in my mind are St. Peter's in Rome and Lincoln cathedral with its clean white nave.

We next drove on to Granada; for miles before we reached it the white snow-covered Sierra Nevada showed up ahead. The *parador* at Granada, San Francisco, is probably the best known of them all. It is actually situated in the Alhambra and from our room we looked across to the gardens of the Generalife. We then drove south to the Costa del Sol – not as spoiled as it is now – and drove to Marbella. On the way I was particularly struck by the coastal town of Nerja, to the east of Malaga, and have often thought of going there again for a holiday. But Nerja too, I am told, is now spoiled. We spent a night at the hotel at Marbella, which then was part of a chain known as 'The Ten Best Hotels in the World'. I made a great public fuss when checking out the next morning; it hardly seemed in keeping with one of the ten best hotels, I told them, to have mildew in the mini bar!

We crossed the Straits of Gibraltar on a ferry from Algeciras to Ceuta on the North African shore. Ceuta is, of course, still a Spanish enclave in Morocco. It is really strange that the Spaniards cannot see how illogical it is to make such a fuss about Gibraltar when they retain two enclaves in Morocco, Ceuta and Melilla. To my mind Morocco is one of the most beautiful countries in the world, with quite extraordinary diversity. It has both a Mediterranean coastline and an Atlantic coastline. It has several mountain ranges, the Rif, the Middle Atlas, the High Atlas and the Anti Atlas each with quite distinctive characteristics. The first experience was of the Rif Mountains, where under Spanish rule there were endless battles with insurgents. The Rif has nothing as high as the Atlas, but they have a grey, rugged wildness which is quite distinctive. We bypassed Tetouan and spent the night at Chaouen. We were to become very familiar with Moroccan sights, but here for the first time we saw men riding their donkeys, kicking their heels as they went, and Berber women hunched over carrying enormous bundles of dry wood. We also became aware that whenever the donkey traffic became heavy it meant that one was approaching a market. On our final day's travel we reached Rabat. We checked in to the Rabat Hilton, where we were to live for the next few weeks and I reported for work at the Banque du Maroc.

Our stay in Morocco did not turn out as we had expected. My predecessor had been in the job for about five years, I think. Looking back it now seems clear that it was just one of those jobs for the boys, not uncommon, I am sure, with international organisations. It really served no useful purpose, but it made the Department in Washington look good. Moreover at that time, budgetary controls were not yet common. I doubt if the Department actually knew what it was costing. Had we known that we would be staying there for less than two years, we might well not have sold Codmore Barn and we certainly would not have brought out so much furniture. But we made the most of it.

It is perhaps a surprise that my job in Morocco lasted for as long as it did. Bennani, with whom I got on very well, was a very intelligent man and knew just as well as I what needed to be done. He had all the attributes of a sound central banker; but the Government was in no position to run a prudent financial policy. They were fighting a war in the south with the Polisario insurgents from Algeria, so arms expenditure was high and debt was rising. I supported Bennani, but I doubt that that made any impression on the Government. Morocco was not then a democracy, although they had an elected Chamber of Deputies and had a Prime Minister. King Hassan was essentially an autocrat.

Bennani did not lack for other technical advice. Morocco was still very firmly in the French sphere of influence and there were no fewer than five advisers from the Banque de France; most of them very technical (foreign exchange, debt, etc.) but one of them, Gauthier, was quite senior. I think the Banque de France must have been incensed to find themselves with an English adviser imposed by the Fund. Gauthier and I got on very well on a personal level, but we never worked together.

During my time with the Bank I got involved in work not strictly in my sphere; I saw a lot of the senior managers and they put me on some committees dealing with recruitment and other staff matters. There was also a regular economic assessment meeting – from which I remember in particular the phrase '*herbes spontanées*', the fresh new grass which followed rain and was so vital to the peasants in the mountains. As evidence that I had expected to stay much longer I embarked on a course in Arabic and was making good progress with learning to read and write; Morocco became to me '*Al Maghreb*' which literally means 'the West'.

Amicia and the boys joined us for the Christmas holidays. They enjoyed staying in a first class hotel. The food was excellent – mainly French but with a lot of Moroccan touches, particularly with the salads at lunchtime. One day we had a superb *loup de mer en croute*, a whole large sea bass baked in puff pastry. We also had good wines. It is a bit surprising that a Muslim country should produce wine, excellent wine at that, but that of course was the result of the French influence. The best red wine was Ksar and there was a very dark rosé called Boulaouane gris. When Daphne wanted to have a quiet supper in her room with room service, the boys would dine alone in the restaurant. I once went down to see them to find them ordering a bottle of wine and after dinner cigars. They were aged fourteen and a half and nearly sixteen! The hotel also had an excellent swimming pool. The weather in Rabat in December/January is not exactly warm, so nobody else ever seemed to be in the pool, but we all swam quite regularly. Life at the Bank was very leisurely. With two hours off at midday, I always returned to have lunch with the family.

For Christmas week the Banque du Maroc made one of their cottages at Imouzzer available to us. Imouzzer is at the eastern end of the Middle Atlas at about 4,200 ft above sea level, not very far from the mediaeval city of Fez. The Middle Atlas has a temperate climate with Western European style vegetation including hawthorns. The famous Atlas cedars which adorn the gardens of many an old English vicarage and country house originate here. We did not see them in December, but Daphne and I on another occasion walked in the forests of cedar. We tend to think of Atlas cedars growing on their own or in very small clumps, and it is a splendid sight to see hundreds of them all growing together. Another well known plant in British gardens from the Middle Atlas is *Cytisus battandieri*, the Moroccan broom, whose yellow flowers have a delicious scent of pineapples. The main attraction of Imouzzer in the winter was the snow. It was at that time one of only two sites developed – if only primitively – for winter sports. The developed area was in the crater of an old volcano. We did not ski, but the boys did some tobogganing. The only other thing I remember about Imouzzer – food again! – was a first class restaurant, La Chambotte.

In Rabat we joined the golf club, the Royal Dar-es-Salam, owned by the King but available for others, except when he was playing himself. He had already survived one assassination attempt, so security had to be very tight. The club had three courses, two 18 hole ones and a 9 hole course. One of the 18 hole courses – the red one, I think – had a terrifying hole where the the green was on a small island and the tee was only a yard or two from the lake. I don't know how many balls we lost there! Wherever you went on the courses men would suddenly pop out from the adjoining cork oak forests and offer you found balls at a reduced price. The Dar-es-Salam also had a good restaurant and we often lunched there rather than back at the Hilton. Daphne and I tended to concentrate on the nine hole course – much simpler and fewer bunkers!

In January the boys flew back to England and to school. Amicia was between jobs and stayed on with us for a few weeks. We visited Marrakech together for a few days and stayed at the Hotel Mamounia. We must have been some of the last people ever to stay in the old hotel, still as it had been when Winston Churchill stayed there. During the course of 1977 it was completely refurbished and modernised – dread words. For us it was still delightfully old-fashioned. Every evening a man in a gold lamé coat sat at the piano in the lounge playing cocktail hour music – Cole Porter, George Gershwin et al. We had rooms with balconies looking out towards the snow capped peaks of the High Atlas Mountains; the highest peak, Mount Toubkal, is over 13,000 ft. high. The garden was full of bougainvillaeas, oleanders and palm trees, all round an unusually shaped swimming pool.

We were to visit the High Atlas later that year, but in January we confined ourselves to the usual tourist sights in Marrakech. I can still picture in my mind's eye the distinctive outline of the minaret of the Koutoubia mosque, which the guide books describe as 'probably the best known building in North Africa'. The other main attraction is the great square known as the Djmaa-el-Fna (it is always called a 'square' but in my memory it had a most irregular outline and a Spanish word like *plaza* would seem more appropriate). Djmaa-el-Fna, incidentally, means 'Assembly of the Dead', but in fact it was teeming with life, acrobats, storytellers, water sellers (with goatskin bottles), musicians and dancers from the High Atlas, snake-charmers, vendors of love potions and all sorts of food. This is not just an attraction for foreign tourists; many of the spectators are Moroccans and Berbers down from the mountains. I don't know whether it was during this visit or later that we began to collect Moroccan carpets. Buying rugs took a great deal of time; one visited the merchant and over many cups of Moroccan mint tea one would be shown rug after rug. There would follow a lot of bargaining and eventually one would buy one or two.

Moroccan carpets are greatly underestimated. There is a great variety of carpets from different areas of the country. The finest I think are the ones from the High Atlas by the name of Tazenakht. During our time in the country we must have bought well over a dozen. One of my favourites was a very thick piled rug from Khemisset, half way between Rabat and Meknes. It is unfortunately no more – the moths destroyed it this year. There used to be a wonderful anti-moth spray called 'Doom', but the damned European Union outlawed it a couple of years ago on the grounds of safety. The only thing you can use now are moth balls, which are absolutely useless, at least with carpets. We also bought rugs at Imouzzer, made in a disused Christian chapel by very young girls – sweated labour! They looked cheerful enough and at least they earned something for their families.

Back in Rabat we were busy finding somewhere to live. There were no furnished houses to let. We found a large villa in the fashionable suburb of the Souissi. It belonged to a Monsieur Tazi, the Moroccan Ambassador to Paris, I think. The villa and its garden were set behind high walls. Security was an obsession – perhaps rightly. Lahsen, our yardman, gardener and handyman, used to insist that I should lock up every night. His French wasn't very good, but he knew one word and used it frequently – 'voleurs'! In the twenty-six years that we had been married I don't think we had ever locked our house at night. At Codmore Barn we frequently left the house unlocked, even when we went out.

The Villa Tazi, as we called it, was on two floors; on the ground floor there was a very large room, all of 60 ft. in length with plate glass windows and sliding doors giving on to the garden. The room was subdivided into three sections, a dining room and two sitting rooms. Upstairs the bedrooms with balconies also gave on to the garden. The garden itself had shrubs around the edges by the wall, there was lots of grass (which Lahsen cut by hand! not even a push mower) and three or four large orange trees which were in bloom when we moved in with that exquisite perfume of orange blossom and in February still also carrying a large crop of fruit. Oranges taste best when picked by yourself from your own trees!

We took on Fatima as our cook/housekeeper. She was a treasure. She was a very competent cook and did a great deal of the shopping for us. She lived at home but came to us every day; she would appear with a shopping basket full of fish, meat and vegetables and household goods. I used to do most of the other shopping, delicatessen, wine and cheese at a mini self service market called Mam. It was frequented mostly by Frenchwomen and I marvelled at the amount of cheese they bought every day. I don't marvel so much now when I see Crispin and Caroline doing their shopping in France. Before we could move in we had to get our furniture, which Pickfords had shipped in a container and which was now on the dockside at Casablanca waiting for customs clearance. We drove there and signed the necessary documents. We did no sightseeing in Casablanca – there wasn't,

I think, much to see; a vast mosque has, I believe, since been built there. But we had lunch in a seafood restaurant overlooking the harbour – excellent! Our old guide book says of it: 'Le Petit Rocher, in the same area, is also good, but rather costly' – that's what a tax free dollar income does for you!

Later that day, back at Rabat, the container arrived. It was an extraordinary sight: English antique furniture and Daphne's grandmother's nineteenth century burr walnut grand piano being unloaded and carried in to a Moroccan villa. I think it was this that attracted a small crowd of onlookers, amongst whom was Fatima – and that is how we recruited her.

The final step in making the Villa Tazi our home was to collect the dogs from Casablanca airport – all three of them, Brie, Tubby and May. They were almost certainly the only whippets in Morocco. Moroccans do not go in for pet dogs. We did occasionally take Tubby and May walking on leads in the Medina – crowds parted like the Red Sea for the Israelites. Brie never went on a lead; with her three legs it would been impossible. The dogs loved Morocco. They use to lie basking in the sun on the terrace outside the living room. Fatima, even though a Muslim, loved them, managed their feeding and used to have great fun watering them down with a hose when it was very hot. One great disappointment for whippets was that there are no rabbits in Morocco. We used to walk them in the cork oak forest just beyond the golf club and the whippets hunted large lizards instead. The lizards were a sort of turquoise colour; the dogs never killed them; whenever they caught one (it was usually May who did) the lizard in their mouth seemed to induce some kind of allergy and the lizards were very quickly disgorged and ran off again. Before Amicia returned to England we went off on a trip to Meknes. There were endless public holidays in Morocco and I think this must have been on the occasion of the King's Birthday. Meknes was briefly the capital of Morocco – in the seventeenth century. It lies in a plain beneath the Middle Atlas and is surrounded by farmland. As we drove along we would pass great loads of carrots and fennel.

We stayed in a fine hotel, the Transatlantique. I should say that in what I am writing about Morocco I am using names that I cannot in fact remember, but I am helped by still having the guide book that we used – *Fodor's Morocco 1976*. To quote here: 'This is one of the most beautifully situated hotels in Morocco, set in a magnificent garden with superb views over the old town.' The hotel was separated from the old town by the deep gorge of the Oued Boufekrane (the word '*oued*' means river and is the French transliteration of the more familiar term used elsewhere in North Africa – 'wadi'). The old city is surrounded by a massive wall, 15 miles long. I remember, in particular, the sight in the early evening of great flocks of swifts swirling round the minarets and towers of the old city against a violet sky. In the city itself the most memorable sights were the monumental gate, the Bab Mansour, and the ruins of the vast Imperial Palace – at one time the largest palace in the world. Its stables were particularly impressive.

When I look back to the stables of Wentworth Woodhouse where I was billeted in 1944, they pale into insignificance beside those of the Imperial Palace. We also visited another ancient capital of Morocco, the ruined Roman city of Volubilis. It is set in a most spectacular setting in a kind of amphitheatre with the Middle Atlas mountains rising behind.

It was during Amicia's stay with us that she took her driving test and acquired a driving licence, which would later entitle her to an English licence. I am sure she was competent to drive, but she had to take an oral test on the rules of the road, and this had to be in French which Amicia did not speak so I hired an interpreter to accompany her. She passed with flying colours – whatever her answer, he gave the correct reply! She now returned to England to take possession of The Stowe at Amberley. Another lot of furniture had to be moved in by Pickfords. We also bought her a Renault 5 so that she could get around and visit the boys at school. We had told the housemasters that she would be in loco parentis whilst we were abroad. I know that on at least one occasion she went to Eton and had lunch in Jocelyn's house – and made quite a stir.

For the Easter holidays the children all joined us again. We bought the boys a moped which gave them freedom to move around on their own. We discovered that they frequently went to a big beach called La Plage des Nations; it transpired that there were often topless girls bathing there! Together we made an interesting trip into the High Atlas and further south. We started at Marrakech, not staying this time at the Mamounia but in a more modern hotel, the Es Saadi. The boys had not yet seen Marrakech, so we did all the sights again. It was much warmer in April than it had been on our previous visit. We were real tourists – we went round in a horse drawn carriage, rather as one does in Central Park in New York. Crispin distinguished himself by falling out!

From Marrakech we headed for the High Atlas and the Tizi N'Tichka pass, the highest in Morocco, 7,400 ft. at the top. Before taking the other pass which leads south to Taroudant we made a side excursion to the Kasbah of Telouet, the former home of El Glaoui. He, as Pasha of Marrakech, and his family before him, had dominated the High Atlas for at least a hundred years. When Churchill visited Marrakech he was driven to Telouet and royally entertained by the Pasha. By 1977 it was a hollow shell, but still showing what a remarkable palace it had been with spectacular views down to the plains to the west. El Glaoui had disgraced himself in the mid–fifties. In conjunction with the French who still ruled Morocco he was instrumental in having the Sultan Mohammed V exiled to Madagascar and replacing him with an obscure member of the Alaouit dynasty. But the pressure for independence became too strong and Mohammed V returned in triumph. El Glaoui did not live much longer and although the Kasbah is a historically important site, King Hassan had no intention of preserving it; he might well have ordered it to be razed to the ground. I wonder how it looks twenty-six years on.

We then headed south-west up and over the Tizi N'Test Pass towards Taroudant. In 1977 only the beginning and the end were made-up roads, the middle passage (quite long too) was an earthen *piste*, much more suitable for a four wheel drive vehicle than our Renault 16. There were two or three hotels on that stretch of road, all at quite a height – the highest point of the pass is at about 7,000 ft (as high as Mexico City and Darjeeling, the only two other places at that height which I have visited). We bypassed the more expensive looking hotel at Ouirgane – La Roseraie – and settled on an *auberge* a couple of miles further on, Le Sanglier qui Fume, perched on the hillside looking west across the plain to the Atlantic Ocean. It was fairly primitive and all five of us had to sleep in the same room, which we hadn't done since that night in Normandy in 1967 at La Cressonière. We ate outside on long wooden refectory tables. This is the only place in which I have ever eaten frogs' legs – very good. Our host entertained us during lunch with his tame stork, which would clack its long beak on command. We spent a couple of days there, going one morning for an expedition across the mountains on mules; we made quite a sight.

The Tizi N'Test Pass is at the crest of the whole Atlas range with to the north-west a complex quilt of mountains and valleys stretching to the sea. On our left were the snow-capped peaks and Mount Toubkal. Ahead of us were the dry peaks of the Anti Atlas, beyond which lay the Sahara. There were interminable hairpin bends with the road clinging for dear life to the mountain side. Eventually we descended into the valley of the Sous, which flows into the sea at Agadir, and Taroudant. Many people these days stay at the famous Gazelle d'Or outside the town; it was not so well known then, and anyway I much prefer to stay somewhere inside a town. So we chose the Hotel Salaam, set in a secluded garden with a swimming pool. When you walked out of the hotel you were immediately in the noise and bustle of a tropical town. I remember particularly the hordes of swifts screaming up and down the road just missing the people by inches. We hired bicycles for the children and they went exploring. I seem to remember that they did actually visit the Gazelle d'Or.

In the car we went out for a day into the dry desert to the south-east of Taroudant, driving most of the time on dry beaten sand. We saw two great sights. One was a caravan of camels making their way ponderously southwards, presumably heading for the Sahara. The other was a sight which only can be seen in the valley of the Sous – goats climbing into the argana trees, munching the leaves. The tree grows nowhere else in the world. The locals extract cooking oil from its seeds.

From Taroudant we headed into the Anti Atlas, whose main peak is only around 7,000 ft. in height. The Middle Atlas range is green and temperate; the High Atlas also green on the western escarpments with rivers always full of melted snow, but the Anti Atlas are barren and dry. It was pitiful to see crops dying in the sparse fields – mostly sweetcorn. We didn't stay long and visited the town of Tafraoute, where the rocks are tinged with pink.

We then drove down the long valley of the Oued Sous to Agadir, where we didn't linger long. The stupendous earthquake in 1960 destroyed most of the old town, which was not, I gather, even then particularly attractive. Agadir, as I remember it, is made up of lots of modern concrete buildings painted white, but basking in a very warm sun and totally geared towards tourists (which I suppose we were, even though I write as if we were something different). We then headed up the coast road north back towards Casablanca and Rabat. The first few miles, as the coast road clings to the side of the remnants of the Atlas mountains sinking into the sea, is one of the most attractive stretches of shoreline in Morocco. The Atlantic looks particularly inviting and we all thought what a wonderful place it would be to build a house looking down onto the sandy beaches beneath the cliffs.

We stayed next at Essaouira, the ancient Portuguese Mogador, now a harbour for a fishing fleet. The main catch was sardines and we ate them grilled on the quayside. The fortifications beside the harbour are almost identical with the Portuguese fortifications at Malacca, thousand of miles away to the east. No doubt the Portuguese sailors who went to Malacca must have stopped at Mogador on their way and would have taken many weeks to complete the journey. Further up the coast we visited Safi. Safi is distinguished for its ceramic ware, some of which we bought, but we pressed on and stayed at an attractive town called Oualidia, which stands on a lagoon separated from the sea by sand dunes. Our final call before reaching home was a diversion to Boulaouane, which I have already mentioned in connection with its rosé wine, the Boulaouane gris. The kasbah of Boulaouane is a lonely and impressive fortress, dominating the curves of the Oum-er-Rebia, and was built in 1710 by Moulay Ismail, the builder of Meknes. Then home at last to the Villa Tazi. I don't know how long the journey took us but the boys spent a good deal of the Easter holiday in Rabat. They played golf and, as I have said, went out on their moped. Every day I returned from the office to lunch and we usually took the dogs down to the beach at Temara, to the south of Rabat, before returning home for lunch cooked by Fatima.

During the summer – no doubt on the occasion of another public holiday – Daphne and I did a trip across the Middle and High Atlas Mountains to the edge of the Sahara at Rissani. It's a long way, but the roads are so good that the journey there and back can be done in no more than three days. A vast plateau separates the Middle Atlas from the High Atlas and you feel quite alone driving there for mile after mile. Between Middelt and Ksar-es-Souk one passes through the Legionnaires' Tunnel built by hand by the Foreign Legion in 1930.

I always used to think of deserts exclusively in terms of vast flat expanses with large sand dunes. But the moment you arrive on the eastern slopes of the Atlas you are in the desert, but it is a barren mountainous landscape. Not a scrap of vegetation is to be seen for miles, although off to the east, but frequently not visible from the road, is the Oued Ziz in a deep gorge, which makes up an oasis which stretches for miles. Rissani at the end of the made up road is on the edge of the Sahara proper. There is there a famous signpost which reads *Tombouktou – 52 Jours*. We made a little outing to the edge of the first of the rolling sand dunes, tinged with red, like the planet Mars. Here begins danger – one does not venture onto the sand without all the proper equipment – spare fuel, extra water and most important the right kind of vehicle.

Some time that summer the Banque du Maroc held its annual celebration – an elaborate dinner at a hotel near Meknes. Almost all the men wore European dress, but the women were resplendent in the most elaborately decorated kaftans. Following the Muslim practice all the women gathered together on one side of the room and all the men on the other. They seemed to have nothing to do with each other all evening. But Daphne and I and the Gauthiers sat together on benches round a low table. Eating our *mechoui* we were handed pieces of lamb roasted on a spit by one of the hosts. Daphne wore a kind of kaftan and I wore a dinner jacket. We have a photograph of the occasion with me wearing a beard. I grew a beard when I left the Bank of England as a gesture towards a new way of life. But during the summer of 1977 the boys came to visit me at the Banque du Maroc and having enquired for me, the porter said, '*Oh oui, le Monsieur avec la barbe blanche.*' This was clearly now the wrong image – after all I was still only 53; so I shaved it off immediately, just retaining a moustache, which had not yet gone grey.

The children all came again for the summer holidays. We spent a lot of it at the Villa Tazi, but we did make another excursion into the High Atlas; at Ouirgane this time we stayed at La Roseraie and we went on to Taroudant again staying at the Hotel Salaam. This time on our way back from Marrakech we turned away from the main road and embarked on a quite hazardous drive along a *piste* into the foothills of the Middle Atlas. Daphne was always very dubious about going on *pistes*, but the rest of us enjoyed it. There were one or two places where the boys had to bodily lift the front of the car over a rock which was too large for it. Although there was no made up road the route had obviously been used a great deal before the war; every now and again we would come across a signpost marked 'Touring Club de France' or some such wording. We also made a trip in the opposite direction into the Rif Mountains and stayed at the Hotel Asmaa perched vertiginously at the edge of a cliff overlooking Chaouen down below.

Daphne and I also did another trip to the deep south. We went again to the edge of the Sahara, this time to Zagora which lies well to the west of Rissani. It meant another visit to Marrakech and then over the High Atlas to Ouarzazate which is already on the eastern slopes of the mountains and on through a town with the extraordinary name of Agdz. We bought a carpet there which is another one to have succumbed to moths. I think it was on this trip that we admired the small carpet which a Berber was using to cover the saddle of his donkey and managed to persuade him to part with it for a much larger sum than I think he had expected. It still lies in one of the corridors here.

Life was about to change. Bennani came back from attending the IMF Annual General Meeting in Washington to tell me that the Fund had decided to do away with my job. I ought to have seen this coming, but it came as a shock. I had always known that the job was not really essential, but we were enjoying Morocco so much – partly for Daphne, in that she was miles away from her mother – that we had hoped that it would continue for some years. I think it might have lasted rather longer if Jan Mladek had not retired and been succeeded by a Frenchman, who was the last person to see any reason for an Englishman to be an adviser in the French sphere of interest. But even Mladek would have had to deal with his budgetary problems. The Fund wanted the job to cease that autumn, but I managed to persuade them to extend our time to the end of February 1978. When we first went to Morocco I remember Lord Sackville saying to Amicia how brave he thought we were. At the time I was rather puzzled; why was it brave, I thought. Looking back I now see that it was almost foolhardy. We had no assurances about the length of the appointment and I had no fall-back employment, having rejected the University of Aston Business School. So there now began for us a very difficult period, which did not really resolve itself for another eight years. At the time we resolved to make the most of our remaining time in Morocco.

First however we were due for a month's leave. This may sound surprising in view of all the holidays we had had in Morocco, but this was the standard IMF policy of granting home leave. Home leave meant England, but we decided, rather unconventionally, to drive there and back. Since we wanted to spend as much time as possible in England we did not linger over our drive across Spain and France. Rather surprisingly for me I cannot remember much about the trip; I cannot even remember which route we took. In England we stayed for the first time at The Stowe in Amberley. Daphne liked the house very much. We visited both Crispin and Jocelyn at school; I think in fact we may have been there during half term so that they came to stay at The Stowe.

Crispin was going through a bad patch at school. Morrie Balme was quite worried about him. He seemed to be rather antisocial and would spend hours in his darkened room. Racing still meant everything to him. The blotter on his desk was marked LESTER in very large letters and also had the name of a large grey horse he admired, named Scallywag. We were sufficiently worried that we toyed with the idea of taking him away from Harrow. We had two ideas in mind. One was that we might arrange for him to do social work for a year in the slums of Casablanca. The idea had come to me through the knowledge that Dick Lloyd of Williams and Glynns had sent his son to do just that after leaving Eton. The other was that he might get on much better at the rather unconventional American

School in Tangier. But we made no decisions and did not I think discuss this with him at the time. We decided to have him out to Morocco ahead of the other two at Christmas and talk things through then.

So when the Christmas holidays arrived, Crispin came out several days before the others. Jocelyn had a date to go to the Feather's Ball and Amicia was to travel with him. Rather than sit in the Villa Tazi and discuss Crispin's future, we decided to go on a trip together so Daphne, Crispin and I set off to see the Valley of the Kasbahs. The first part of the journey is the same as the route to Rissani, over the Middle Atlas and the plateau in which sits Middelt and then through the High Atlas using the Legionnaires' Tunnel. We turned off into the Valley of the Kasbahs at Ksar-es-Souk. The kasbahs are large imposing fortifications made of dried mud; the first of them at Ksar-es-Souk itself is one of the most imposing. It was a great experience to be with Crispin alone. We soon realised that he was sound enough, even if he did not really fit in to Harrow, and we abandoned thoughts of the slums of Casablanca and the American School at Tangier.

Our first hotel was at Tineghrir, where the Valley of the Kasbahs properly begins. But first we visited the spectacular Gorges of the Todra. The road descends by hairpin bends to the floor of the gorge, a canyon with cliffs rising well over 1,000 ft. on each side. The Gorge is a rift valley, like the Grand Canyon, and divides the High Atlas from the Djebel Sarro (which I suppose could be translated 'the Sahara Mountains') to the south. We did not venture very far up the gorge; if you were brave enough and had a suitable vehicle you could go right round and back again through the almost equally spectacular gorges of the Dades, but we returned to Tineghrir and followed the valley to Ouarzazate, which is in effect an oasis in the bleak desert mountains. We returned through Marrakech, making a side trip again to the Glaoui palace.

On our return Amicia and Jocelyn joined us; they were delayed for a day; somehow they missed their connecting plane in Paris and had to spend the night there – I believe they spent it on the floor in the corridor outside the flat of some friend of Amicia's who was unfortunately away! I suppose telephone communications between Morocco and England are now very simple, but in those days you still had to book a call and the sound was pretty bad; so we were surprised that they were not there when we went to Rabat airport to meet them. I remember Amicia once being hounded by Coutts Bank and having to speak to them in London; 'that terrible Mr Willson – with two ells' reduced her to tears. But it was all sorted out in the end.

So we spent our last Christmas in Morocco at the Villa Tazi. In January we all went and visited Fez, the mediaeval city which lies in the foothills of the Middle Atlas. We stayed in the best hotel, the Palais Jamai, which stands in the very walls of the Medina; from the bedrooms you can look across the ever bustling streets below. No vehicles were allowed into the

Medina and everything had to be carried by donkeys. Fez is frightening if you try to go round it on your own; you feel constantly threatened and are subjected to vociferous begging. The answer, as luckily we soon found out, is to hire a guide. Ours was a venerable white haired old man wearing a jellaba (the French of course spell it *djellaba*) with what we call a red fez on his head (they call it a tarboosh). We saw the famous dyers' souk. My most vivid memory is of the quite enormous pots and pans for sale. Some were quite large enough for boiling a missionary! The children left Morocco for the last time, the boys returning to school and Amicia to her work.

Our time was drawing to an end, but we made one last trip on the occasion of the King's Birthday holiday. We went south again, but to an entirely different area. The fighting with the Polisario was taking place in the far south in what used to be the Spanish colony of Western Sahara. The colony had been annexed by Morocco only a few years previously in a non-violent insurgence, known to all Moroccans as the Green March, and visitors were not allowed to go that far south. But we were making for the town of Goulimine over two hundred miles to the south-west of Marrakech, where the camel caravans arrive from the Sahara. We were at the wrong time of the year to see the great mass of camels coming for the annual camel fair which takes place in July. I am not sure now what route we took. It certainly was not the coast road, because I remember we stopped at a place called Rommani in the hinterland behind Rabat and Casablanca, where we saw a great gathering of Berbers preparing for the feast. In a very large field outside the town there were dozens of the big Berber tents and horsemen were rehearsing for a *fantasia*, a spectacular manoeuvre where a line of horsemen gallop at full tilt straight for the dais where the dignitaries are sitting and at the last minute pull up suddenly and let off a volley into the air from their rifles. We must I think have gone near Marrakech, but we had no time to linger.

Our first real stop was at Tisnit, an oasis in a desert environment about fifty miles due south of Agadir. The town is encircled with ramparts and great gates. There are palm trees and fertile gardens. Here we bought quite a lot of silver jewellery and I bought myself some blue jellabas and *gandouras* (short sleeved gowns) which, twenty-six years on, I still wear in bed in the summer. Goulimine must be another 60 miles on and to reach it you have to cross the last remnants of the Anti Atlas mountains running into the sea; they are still quite high by European standards as the pass is over 3,000 ft. Before you reach Goulimine the last bald hillocks of the Anti Atlas have disappeared and the plain stretches on for ever; it will be flat as a pancake right on through Mauretania and Mali to Timbuktu. Two large palm groves completely surround the town.

The whole purpose of going to Goulimine is to see the Blue Men and there are always some encamped by the oasis. These nomads wear deep blue floating robes over their jellabas and indigo blue twisted turbans. Their skin is often tinted blue as well, where the dye has rubbed off. They have looked

With a 'blue man' at Goulimine in Southern Morocco – February 1978

like this for over four hundred years. An English cloth merchant, Thomas Windham, visited Agadir several times in the sixteenth century and introduced calico, dyed indigo blue. In the town we found a boy, in his early teens, I would say, who offered to take us to visit a nomad. Blue men are reputed to be tall, but this charming man barely came up to my shoulders. We spent most of an afternoon with him; he spoke very little French and the boy interpreted for us. He had just spent several weeks crossing the Sahara with his camels, coming to sell his produce (mainly camels, I suppose) and to buy provisions (particularly salt and sugar). In the corner of his tent he had great leather chests full of material – blue, of course – and ethnic jewellery. He dressed me up in a jellaba and the blue robes and a turban and Daphne photographed us together. We bought some of his things. He was fascinated to meet some English people and wanted to know what England was like. The main difference, we told him, was that England was green and that there were cars instead of camels. He had never seen the sea, even though Goulimine cannot be more than about 25 miles from the Atlantic. All in all a very enjoyable afternoon.

On the coast near Goulimine is Sidi Ifni, once a Spanish enclave in Morocco, 50 miles long and 13 miles wide. It was said to be completely neglected and we decided to go and see it for ourselves. We almost didn't make it; the road too had been neglected and at one point where a bridge had crumbled we gingerly drove down a fairly steep bank and crossed the river bed, which was dry at that time. I quote here from our guide book: 'Sidi Ifni is situated on a cliff above the sea and now presents a sad, melancholy sight with its neat Spanish squares and gardens, promenades lined with white houses and the deserted hotel with its decaying beach club.' The hotel turned out not to be completely deserted, but we were the only guests. There was no hot water, only cold, and the restaurant served only a rather greasy meal, consisting mainly, as I remember, of fried eggs! We didn't linger long and set off on the long journey back to Rabat. Sidi Ifni today is I believe a thriving town, since the Moroccan Government allowed the United States Air Force to set up a base there. The hotel no doubt now serves hamburgers; there may even be a McDonalds. We returned by way of Agadir, Safi and Oualidia.

We now made our final farewells, had all our furniture packed by Bailly Maroc, the shippers, and drove the dogs to Casablanca to put them on an aeroplane back to quarantine in England. For the last few days we stayed at a small hotel, La Feluque, on the beach at Sable d'Or to the South of Rabat.

I still had no clear idea of what I was going to do with the rest of my life; I was still only 53. But I gave serious thought to becoming a dealer in Moroccan carpets. I loved the carpets and it seemed a nice idea to visit Morocco, say twice a year, buy lots of carpets, load the car up and drive back to England. It turned out to be impractical, but I did not discover that for some months yet and we packed the car up with all our carpets. At Chaouen on the way out of Morocco I bought some of the distinctive small Rif rugs, which I eventually sold for £170 to the General Trading Company in Sloane Street! How can I be so precise, you may ask. Well, I was self-employed from 1978 to 1995 and I still have my invoice book, and the first entry in it is for these rugs.

We left Rabat in March and did not immediately set off for England. We had arranged for the boys to come and spend their Easter holidays in Southern Portugal. We drove to Ceuta at the Straits of Gibraltar by way of Fez, Ketama, Chaouen and Tetouan. At Ceuta I made a change in my lifestyle! I bought, in the duty free, an electric shaver and haven't had a wet shave ever since. We crossed to Algeciras and set off for southern Portugal. We were struck by the town of Tarifa on the coast to the west of Algeciras overlooking the Straits of Gibraltar and wondered (for a moment only) whether we should not look at property there and buy a house with such a splendid view! We stayed at the *parador* in Arcos de la Frontera, visited Seville very briefly and took the coast road to Portugal. We had no idea where we were going to stay and we did not have long to go before were due to pick up Jocelyn from Faro Airport; Crispin was on a school trip to Venice and would be joining us later. As we drove west past Faro we stopped at various towns and looked at houses to let; the ones near the innumerable golf courses around Albufeira were very expensive and, with my income now dramatically reduced, we drove on. We spent a night at the Portuguese equivalent of a *parador*, known as a *pousada*. The next day we found a nice villa perched on the cliffs above Luz (pronounced 'louges') Bay near Lagos (pronounced 'lagouche'). Lagos was the port from which Henry the Navigator's ships set off to go round the Cape of Good Hope. The weather was mild; quite warm enough for swimming. The Algarve has a strong English influence. The supermarkets (only mini ones) had English sausages and orange marmalade and the checkout girls could usually speak some English.

We found the atmosphere in the part around Albufeira rather stifling – a bit like Surrey, with endless golf courses. But the western part was much more attractive. Cape St. Vincent, which one knows of from the naval battles, is isolated and windy, facing out into the North Atlantic. From the cliffs the sight of the sea crashing onto the rocks below is mesmerising. Daphne could never understand why I was in the habit of taking movies of waves crashing onto rocks. The beaches running north from Cape St. Vincent were absolutely deserted and went on for mile after mile. The fields just inland were a mass of yellow lupins – so much more attractive a colour than the now ubiquitous yellow rapeseed.

The villa at Luz was part of a small holiday estate with, down near the shore, a sort of community centre with a library – full of English books. During our holiday I think I read every one of Walter Scott's *Waverley* novels! We played quite a bit of golf; there were some courses in this western stretch of coast. We even attended the Portuguese Open at Pennina, the winner that year being Howard Clark, who had an annoying mannerism of pulling at his trouser leg every time before addressing the ball. We played at least one round at Pennina – not my favourite course, because there is too much water; water on a golf course acts like a magnet to any ball I hit! The evenings were quite cool and we lit log fires in the villa. The problem was to find wood, particularly since we had neither axe nor saw; we used to collect what we could find lying on the ground in the Monchique mountains rising behind Lagos. One constant trouble was getting hold of money. With no credit cards and no ATMs we had to write to Coutts in London and have the funds remitted to a bank in Portimao. But I think we all enjoyed that holiday.

After our return, though, life was going to be much more troublesome. But more of that later. The boys flew back to school from Faro Airport. We packed up our car again – and it was very full; the back seats were collapsed and the whole area of the estate car behind the front seats was chock full, luggage, carpets and I know not what. Daphne and I set off fairly leisurely on the long drive back to England in mid to late April. I was to become very fond of Portugal, but it was all new to me then. We spent the first night in a *quinta* (the Portuguese equivalent of a Catalonian *mas* or, I suppose, an English manor house) converted into a hotel in Vila Noguera de Açetao. I am absolutely hopeless at parking in big cities. I don't even really much enjoy driving round them. So we didn't linger in Lisbon, nor even stay there. What was later to be one of my favourite hotels, the Tivoli in the Avenida de la Republica, was far too expensive for us. But we drove around the banks of the Tagus and saw the Tower of Belem. We moved on to Cascais, a fishing port just beyond the resort of Estoril. For some reason we missed out on Sintra, which again I came to know well.

Our next stop was at the mediaeval town of Obidos with its beautiful sparkling white houses and surrounded by ancient walls. I am such a stickler for correct pronunciation that, rather boringly, I am going to say: pronounced 'obidouche'! Obidos used to be a fishing port but is now some 8 miles from the sea as the river has silted up. The Abbey at Batalha was the next great sight. Batalha is to Portugal as Battle Abbey in Sussex is to England. It was built to commemorate the battle which gave Portugal independence from Castille. It presented a remarkable sight the day we were there; it had been raining and the vast terrace in front of the cathedral was glistening wet and the Abbey was fully reflected in the water. The Abbey, started early in the fifteenth century, has a great deal of Manueline architecture added in the sixteenth century. Manueline architecture could be called the Art Nouveau of the sixteenth century and appealed to both Daphne and me.

We briefly visited Nazare on the cliffs overlooking the Atlantic and then headed north to the great city of Coimbra (pronounced – sorry! – 'Queembra'). Coimbra is known for its ceramic ware and here I had to disappoint Daphne, spare cash was running short and we could only afford to buy one of the pair of white ceramic doves she had set her heart on. A few miles north of Coimbra we turned inland, heading for the Spanish border, and spent the night at the hotel at Buçaco. The hotel had been a royal hunting lodge and is by the scene of one of Wellington's battles (in 1810). As the French started their attack in the battle, heavy mist obscured much of the terrain. Rather disappointingly for us, heavy mist obscured our view too. A few years ago I found a very nice print of the battle; I am not sure that it is historically accurate, because there is no sign whatever of mist; the print now hangs on the back stairs here at Buxlow.

Next morning, still in heavy mist, we drove through Viseu to Vila Real in the valley of the river Douro. The lower reaches of the river, down to Oporto, are where the green wine, *vinho verde*, comes from. But at Vila Real we were already in port country. We spent a night somewhere near here and then drove slowly up the Douro Valley to Miranda do Douro on the border with Spain. This being almost the last Portuguese name to be used until I come to the late 1980s I will give one more pronunciation tip: the Douro, the name of the heir to the Duke of Wellington, in Portugal is pronounced 'doh-rou' – the exact opposite of what one would expect. We stayed at a *pousada* there and next morning set off across the dam which spans the river to the Spanish side. But the Spanish customs refused to let us through; this crossing they said was only for tourists and with the amount of baggage we had we were clearly not tourists! So we had to make a long detour back through Portugal and eventually crossed the border without incident a few miles North of Bragança. Charles II's wife we call Catherine of Braganza – the House of Braganza ruled over Portugal from 1640 until the revolution of 1910.

We followed a relatively obscure route across Spain. We rejoined the River Douro, called the Duero in Spain, near Zamora and followed that river, through Valladolid, as far as Aranda de Duero, almost due north of Madrid. We spent some time in Valladolid. The cathedral has some very fine Isabelline architecture (Isabelline being the almost exactly contemporaneous style to the Portuguese Manueline). I also remember a very striking equestrian statue in the square outside the cathedral, which for some reason is not even mentioned in my Michelin green guide to the city. We did not stay in Aranda, but turned away here from the valley of the Duero southwards on to a very minor road to Sigüenza.

The road crossed several mountain ranges, amongst them the Sierra de las Capras (goats) and was virtually deserted. We were almost alone in a vast open landscape; the mountains here are not craggy, and more like the Yorkshire moors, but on a much grander scale. I don't know what we would have done if we had broken down – there were of course no mobile phones yet. There were occasional large flocks of sheep and some goats with lonely shepherds. The most extraordinary sight was to see no fewer than six eagles, all at the same time, circling together high above a flock waiting to pounce on any lamb which strayed too far from the flock.

At Sigüenza we stayed in what we considered one of the most attractive *paradors* in Spain. It is a converted monastery and stands high on a hillside outside the town. From Sigüenza we made fairly rapid progress over a great distance, through Zaragoza and Lerida over the Pyrenees and into Andorra, where we stayed for a night. After twenty-eight years Andorra had been completely spoilt; in 1950 it had been still a very rural town in a lovely valley high in the mountains, with the attraction, for some, of duty free goods. But in 1978 it had become nothing more than a vast shopping mall stuffed full of luxury duty free goods. We bought none. I shudder to think of what it must be like now twenty-five years further on.

We made our escape from Andorra and drove into France and stayed at Carcassonne. The town and the fortifications have been beautifully restored, but I am not too keen on thoroughly restored buildings – they look too new. It is for this reason that I have always resisted having Buxlow's brickwork repointed. The house looks at least three hundred years old, as it should. The hotel we stayed in was outside the town in wooded country and there were nightingales singing all night long. I have never since heard such a splendid performance. By this time it was already May and it was high time we got home so we drove fairly rapidly across France, up the main motorway to Calais and reached home – that is to say the cottage at Amberley.

CHAPTER 23

Suffolk – the Early Years

W E WERE NOW FACED WITH SOME DIFFICULT DECISIONS. The first problem in fact surfaced on the very day we got home. Morrie Balme from Harrow was on the phone. Crispin had been up to some mischief with his close friend, the young Maturin-Baird; something to do with breaking down some door in the garden wall! I can't remember how it was sorted out, but it soon was. The big questions were – what was I going to do with the rest of my life and where were we going to live?

The first question was not to be answered satisfactorily for five or six years. Initially I was still pursuing the idea of being a merchant of Moroccan carpets. I took some very good transparencies of our carpets and began hawking them around buyers in London stores. As I have already said, I sold some Rif carpets to the General Trading Company in Sloane Street. The buyer at Heals in the Tottenham Court Road was showing encouraging signs, but I soon abandoned the idea. It transpired that it was just not going to be possible to take the car to Morocco twice a year, load up with carpets and drive back with them to sell. Enquiries from the Board of Trade showed that a vast amount of bureaucratic paper work was going to be required and that quite heavy duty would have to be paid. If I was not going into this business, there seemed no point in selling them to Heals. I like them so much that I am glad I still have them twenty-five years later. The next question, where were we to live, was not easy to answer either. Whatever I did, I was determined not to commute to London daily; although of course it would have been possible to do so from Amberley, which was not very much further from London than Pulborough. Moreover Daphne was already very attached to The Stowe and would have been quite happy to stay in Amberley. I suppose it was selfish of me to insist on finding a bigger house, but The Stowe only had three bedrooms and two of these were connecting, so that Amicia, when she was there, would not have had any privacy. It would also not have been possible for the children to have friends to stay. And now, twenty-five years on, it would certainly not have been possible to have had seven adults, two children and a baby for Christmas, as we did in 2002. But where should we look? House prices had risen from their low in 1976 but there was still very good value in Suffolk, with which we already had some familiarity. The Stowe itself had appreciated by something like 50 per cent, so we had funds enough to look for a larger house. We went on the lists of all the major estate agents and also looked at *Country Life*.

It was in fact in *Country Life* that we first saw Buxlow Manor. Even today I assert that it is the prettiest house in Suffolk. Built in 1678, seventy-five years after the death of Elizabeth I, it is nevertheless built in the shape of the so-called Elizabethan 'E' in mellow red brick with striking Dutch gables. I fell in love with it at first sight. Amicia and I were, I think, the first to go over and see it. The owner, Frank Hall Hall, had been given the house by his grandfather, Capt. Hawdon, his mother having predeceased her father. Mrs Hawdon moved out in 1972 and went to live in Buxlow Cottage about 400 yards away. Frank, whom I did not take to at all, then ploughed up her beloved garden and put most of it down to grass, emigrated to Canada and put in a couple as caretakers to run it as a B & B. It was the caretakers who showed Amicia and me around. I was enchanted and determined that Daphne would have to come and see it too.

A little later Daphne came with me to look at the house. She was not a bit taken with it. I can see that what was obviously a Bed & Breakfast did not have the atmosphere of a happy family home. But the Hawdons had not, I think, ever been a happy family. You create a happy family atmosphere by living in the house and warming its personality with yours. Daphne also said that there was an unpleasant atmosphere in the area which we now call the library. Win Driver, who cleans for me at the age of 80 and who first worked in this house in 1944 (!), knew the Hawdons well and I get the strong impression from her that Capt. Hawdon was not a very nice man, given to drink and to rages. In spite of Daphne's reservations I persisted.

I said earlier that we had enough funds. This was not strictly true. To meet the purchase price − £70,000 − we would have had to sell a lot of shares to add to the proceeds of The Stowe. My parents had cut me out of their will some years before, on the plausible grounds that I was richer than my sisters and would not need the money. But I was no longer rich. I appealed to my mother and she agreed to sell some of the land in Jersey, reducing her income by not in fact very much, and give me the proceeds. This was a very generous gesture − on a par with what they had done for me in 1952. So she gave me the sum of £40,000. We offered £70,000, which was accepted. But then Hall Hall gazumped us; he claimed he had a higher offer from some people who wanted to make the house a home for delinquent (or was it disabled?) boys. Whichever it was, the house seemed highly unsuited to the purpose; I suspect that the new offer may have been entirely fictitious. But I wanted the house, so we bid £72,000 and this was finally accepted. The sale was to be effective on 5 December.

Meanwhile we saw a lot of the children; we attended both the Fourth of June and Harrow Founder's Day. I think it must have been this summer that I took Crispin to Epsom to see the Oaks on his way back to school after half term. The dogs came out of quarantine kennels at the end of the summer and we used to walk them on the Downs. No lizards now; nor in fact many rabbits; myxamatosis had ravaged the population. In October Hall Hall had a auction of the contents of the house in a marquee in the garden, which we attended. We bought quite a bit; it was so convenient to be able to leave the purchases in the house ready for our arrival. At the end of the sale the auctioneer, rather strangely, said '. . . and I want to thank Mr de Moubray for his contribution!' Around the middle of the auction Daphne fainted and I had to carry her out to the car. I have never really understood what that was about; was it meant to be a signal that she did not want to come to Buxlow? I remain puzzled. Daphne now embarked on another spending spree. We attended many of the sales at King & Chasemore, buying carpets and furniture. Eventually it was time to move.

We started at Buxlow in a tragic fashion. We had spent the previous night at the Crown & Castle at Orford. On the morning of 5 December we packed the car and I took the dogs into the garden to do their duties. Tubby was in a rose bed when he suddenly screamed and lost the use of his hind legs and began to pant heavily. We rushed him into the car and instead of driving to Buxlow we went straight to the vet in Saxmundham. Had I then known about the animal hospital at Cambridge I would have taken him there. The local vet could not make out what the problem was and over the next couple of days his condition worsened and we eventually agreed that he should be put down. Daphne was absolutely shattered by it. Tubby was quite her favourite dog and to lose him just as she was moving into a house which she really did not want was almost unbearable.

And there was a lot to do. The Barkers, Hall Hall's caretakers, had execrable taste. Two of the walls in our bedroom had been painted a lurid orange red. We started immediately to repaint; I still remember that we used magnolia pink. For the next few weeks I became very familiar with paint and rollers. I also papered the summer drawing room, thereby saving £700 which was what Haywards, the builders, would have charged. It was also bitterly cold. We used to huddle over a small coal fire in the library. Daphne was wonderful at making improvements which I would never have seen. We had a wall taken down between the very dark entrance hall and a small sitting room, which then became the summer drawing room. We also put in a new window, replacing one of the windows which had been blocked up at the time of the window tax. They were quite simple things to do but they transformed the ground floor of the north wing and made it a most attractive room. Haywards did a lot of other work for us, making bookshelves for the library and for what became the winter drawing room.

The children all came for Christmas. I don't think we had snow on Christmas Day but we certainly had it by New Year's Day. In January 1979 when the children had all gone, we had a blizzard. In all the next twenty-five years we have never had as much snow as we had then. Behind the back pond there were drifts at least six feet deep and the doors on the north-eastern side of the house were plastered with snow. Another blow came in February with the Iranian revolution, which led to a massive increase in the price of oil. At one time the price of fuel oil for our boiler went as high as 30p per litre. To fill the tank cost about £900 and if we used the boiler regularly we needed to fill the tank at least three times a

Buxlow Manor – winter 1979

year. No wonder then that we huddled over a small coal fire. Thank God things have since changed; a couple of years ago the price of fuel was such that I could fill the tank for under £400.

Daphne was very unhappy. In her diary fragments she says, in 1981: 'I personally did not like 1980', and she surely had not liked 1979 either. It is not until March 1981 that she says: 'I am gradually (too gradually no doubt for Guy) becoming reconciled to this house. Partly inertia, but more that I am slowly moulding it around me.' The 'moulding' consisted of a number of things; in 1981 she arranged for an arch to be knocked through from the kitchen to the morning room making a breakfast room off the kitchen. Until then we had eaten breakfast in the kitchen, which with three outside walls and an outside door facing north-east was freezing cold. The breakfast room was much cosier, heated with a dimplex radiator. In the following winter she decided to stop using the dining room that the Hawdons had used and turned it into the winter drawing room with windows on three sides and turned their drawing room (the old hall) into a dining room.

But to return to January 1979. What was I to do with my life? Basil Denning, whom I have already mentioned, Managing Director of Harbridge House Europe, the management consultants, invited me to become a part time Executive Consultant on a modest retainer and to be paid a consultancy fee whenever I was employed on a project. What he really wanted was somebody with City contacts; he was using me to replace one of the ubiquitous Bruce-Lockhart family who was retiring. I had City contacts and visited them quite frequently but I never got any business for Harbridge House out of them. My problem was that I did not really know what Harbridge House's 'unique selling points' were and was thus not in a position to sell anything.

Basil did use me once on a project for Security Pacific — in a very minor capacity. I also tried to do some management consultancy on my own. I wrote an article on strategic planning in the insurance business, which was published by *Management Today* and gathered a dozen or so strategic planners from the major insurance companies at a meeting at which I presented my conclusions. I don't remember what I had said in my article, but it cannot have been very inspiring. None of them wanted to take it any further. I eventually parted from Harbridge House in May 1981.

Daphne saw an advertisement for teachers for the Borstal at Hollesley Bay and suggested that I should apply. It would never have occurred to me. But I applied and was interviewed by the Head of Training, a bluff Yorkshireman called Ted Gibbins. I nearly talked myself out of the job. I told him that I didn't know what to teach — 'Social studies,' he said. So that was decided. I then said, having heard his strong Yorkshire accent, that I doubted whether the boys would respond to my plummy toff's accent. 'No problem,' he said, 'they'll lap it up.' So I got the job. I was a part time teacher at Hollesley (having bored the reader with the correct pronunciation of Portuguese names it's now time to do it with an English name — Hollesley is pronounced 'Hozeley') from January 1979 to 1985 and then again briefly in 1990.

It was something of a cultural shock; at least Warley barracks had prepared me for the language. The 'f' words were even more frequent here. The boys, ranging in age from sixteen to about nineteen, had completely unfamiliar backgrounds to me. They were almost all urban and the vast majority came from the East End of London. They used criminal language; the police stations were called 'nicks' and their patch of activity was always known as their 'manor'. One of them even claimed to be a member of the Forest Gate mafia! Some of them were already fathers, but none were married. They were almost always polite. They addressed me as 'Sir'. One of them (for some extraordinary reason, I remember his name – Thomson) was very angry with me for something I had said and remarked, 'If we were on the "out" I'd top you – Sir!' Another very unruly boy who lived at Shotley near Ipswich told me that if I ever came to Shotley he would make a point of scratching the paint of my car. I once asked him what his mother did. 'She flogs her muff,' he said. I had to get one of the other boys to explain to me what that meant!

Ted Gibbins gave me a textbook on social studies. Having read it I discarded it; it seemed to concentrate on telling the boys all about their rights and made no mention of their obligations. I had three aims; the first was to keep them interested, the second was to try and inculcate some self-confidence among them – some were on the other hand too cocky and had to be restrained, the third was to try and make them see that they were responsible for being in the Borstal; they could not blame everything on others or on 'society'.

By and large I succeeded in the first aim. I think I did quite well in the second; a number of boys who, when they had first come to me, walked with heads down and drooping shoulders, were walking with head high and shoulders back when they left me. I doubt if I had any success in the third aim. There was one black boy whose father was a solicitor and none of his siblings had ever been in trouble with the police; so it could not have been his background that got him into trouble. I once asked him if he had ever been abroad. 'Oh, yes,' he said; he had been on a school day trip to Boulogne. 'And what did you do?' I asked him. 'We found a shop which sold flick knives and frightened people in the street. It was great!'

I decided after a time that they all had one thing in common: they all acted on impulse and did not seem able to envisage the consequences of what they did. I asked them once whether they looked right, left and right again before crossing the road. With one accord they all answered, 'No.'

'You must hear a lot of squealing brakes,' I said.

'Oh yes,' they replied.

I remember one boy who said: 'Sir. I can't help it. If I was to see an open till, and there was a policeman standing nearby, I wouldn't be able to stop myself from putting my hand into the till.'

My classes usually had about a dozen boys. I had a blackboard and chalk and usually talked about something that was going on at the time – more like current affairs than social studies. Incidentally the boys were allowed to choose which classes they wanted to come to. Many of them chose art or pottery in the certain knowledge that the teachers would normally be women and they just wanted to look at them all evening. I once asked one boy why he had chosen social studies. Despondently, he said, 'I thought it would be taught by a woman.' It took me quite a long time to realise that quite a large minority of the class were illiterate and that they had no idea what I was writing on the board.

In case of any trouble we were supposed to call for the warders (the screws). But if one did so, the boys would certainly be punished, so I settled trouble myself. Two boys in the front row once began fighting. I marched up to them and towering over them pulled them apart and told them to 'f . . . behave'. They were so surprised it stopped them immediately. Today I don't suppose I could do any such thing; I would find myself being sued for assault. I also used to record documentary films and show them to be discussed afterwards. *Horizon* from the BBC was a great source of material. I had also recorded for myself the film *Twelve Angry Men*, starring Henry Fonda. The film takes place entirely in the jury room. At the beginning only one of them believes that the accused is not guilty; by the end they have all become convinced of his innocence. The Borstal boys loved it. I must have shown it a dozen times over the years that I was teaching. The most famous alumnus of Hollesley was Brendan Behan who had been too young to be executed after the IRA bombing in Birmingham in 1939. One of the boys' favourite books was *Borstal Boy* by Behan. I managed to buy a paperback edition of it which they read and passed around amongst themselves.

The only other social studies teacher was an American woman, Virginia Caldwell, married to a former Hong Kong policeman. We got to know each other in the staff room. On one occasion we combined our classes together so that she could show them some of her home movies taken in Africa. We had to combine, because she did not know how to work the projector. I had to explain to her why the boys burst into fits of giggles when she was showing a film of Wankie Colliery — in what is now Zimbabwe. On another occasion Virginia told me that she was going to a concert at the Snape Maltings and didn't know the way. Since I passed it on my way home, I led her there. A few years later she joined the staff of the Aldeburgh Foundation and became a high profile figure as the organiser of the Friends of Aldeburgh.

Besides teaching at the Borstal I was also asked to teach at the Young Persons' Prison just up the road. These were older boys up to their early twenties. Because there was a danger of violence there was a panic button in the class room for calling the warders in an emergency. I never had to use it. Two things I remember in particular from the prison. The first was a very bright half-caste boy. Somebody had told me that he was good at printing. So, trying to encourage, self-employed enterprise I asked him about it. It turned out that his only knowledge of printing was forging credit cards! The boys were allowed to take the morning paper of their choice. This boy took the *Financial Times*. He was very keen on the stock market and kept asking me if I had taken his advice to buy shares in Polly

Peck. Had I done so – and got out before they collapsed – I would have made a great deal of money. One day as we were leaving the class and walking down the corridor to where they had to be searched before returning to their cells he asked me what Euro dollars were. I only had a minute in which to tell him, but he took it in immediately. He was very bright. I wonder what happened to him. He would have done very well as a broker, but could not have been employed with a prison record.

The second was when the warders called away a boy to be interviewed by the police. When he came back the others all wanted to know what had happened. He told them that the Kent police had asked him to confess to a whole lot of burglaries in his area, and that although he had not in fact committed them, he had confessed. The other boys were horrified. But he said to them that it was not going to make any difference to the length of his sentence and that it would be a good mark for him with his local police. At one stroke the Kent police had sharply increased their 'crimes solved' ratio!

This first winter at Buxlow had also been for the country the 'Winter of Discontent' and it was clear that there was going to be a general election. I had never before been a committed Conservative. I would probably have voted Labour in 1945 if I had been old enough to have the vote. I think I must have voted Conservative in the early elections in the 1950s and was abroad for the election of 1959. At some point in the 60s I even voted Liberal; I would not have done so if there had been the remotest chance of their forming a government; I was just registering a protest vote against the the two major parties. The Conservatives seemed to be almost embarrassed to hold free market principles and to advocate lower taxes.

Almost the only Conservative I had admired in the 60s had been Enoch Powell. At a cocktail party in Oxford in the late 60s I went up to Enoch Powell and told him that I was a great admirer of his. He asked me where I came from. When I told him from the Bank of England, he expressed astonishment that he could possibly have an admirer in Threadneedle Street. Not surprising really; I remember once having on my desk a copy of a book of Enoch Powell's collected speeches; when Stanley Payton, Deputy Chief of the Overseas Department, saw it, he was shocked that I should be reading a book by a 'fascist'. This, by the way, was before his notorious 'rivers of blood' speech. My views on Government have been fairly steadily the same since around the mid 1950s. They can actually be rather neatly summed up in the following extract from an article in the *Spectator* by Iain Duncan Smith, at a time when he was still the leader of the Conservative Party:

The Conservative party occupies two intellectual positions of strategic importance – positions that together dominate the landscape. The first is liberty. We represent the whole range of liberal principles – individual endeavour, enterprise, the rule of law, the freedom to choose one's manner and mode of life, and the policies that flow from them: the small state, low taxes, choice in public services, civil liberties. The second strategic position that we occupy is security. We are the party of the family, the neighbourhood and the nation and the traditions that sustain them. Our policies promote stable families, local 'little platoons', national independence and national defence.

To return to 1979; we now had a leader of the opposition who seemed to me to represent exactly my views, Margaret Thatcher, and I was keen to see her party elected. I tried to find out the state of the Knodishall Conservative Association. I discovered that it was virtually moribund and seemed to have only one member, Jan Franklin of Knodishall Place. Jan was still a very active lady even though thirteen years my senior. We reformed the Association with Jan as President and me as Chairman. We co-opted a former member of Lloyd's Bank as Secretary and a few others to the Committee. We did our bit to get the Conservatives elected. John Gummer was our incumbent MP and he called to see me together with the Chairman of the Eye Constituency Association. I no longer agree with Gummer on many things, Europe in particular, but at that time, although not yet in the Government he did write speeches for Mrs Thatcher and I approved of him. Indeed, a year or two later, when the Eye Constituency was abolished and Suffolk Coastal put in its place, I attended with one of the Committee a meeting at Kesgrave school to adopt our new candidate and voted for Gummer..

I did not keep up an active role in the Knodishall Conservatives and had resigned by 1982. This was not in any way due to disillusionment with Maggie Thatcher, but that other interests took precedence. I supported Maggie throughout her years as Prime Minister, with one brief hiccup – in April 1982 I was so shocked at the Government's ineptitude in allowing the Argentines to take the Falkland Islands – and for a brief moment on the Saturday I actually applauded Michael Foot, who made a thoroughly good speech in the House of Commons in the emergency debate. But as soon as Maggie showed real guts in going ahead with the Task Force to retake the Falkland Islands, all was forgiven. Maggie has been quite falsely maligned for having brought about a grossly materialistic society. Even Peregrine Worsthorne, who used to support her, now condemns her. Capitalism, free markets and globalisation are not responsible for the very real materialism which seems to pervade our society these days. Whilst I am on the subject I will here quote a passage from a 'Treatise on the Ten Commandments' which I wrote in 2002.

We see a great deal of covetousness around us in the modern world. Everybody wants to be rich and socialists want to eliminate poverty and yet there is a widespread sanctification of poverty and condemnation of the rich. To quote the late Peter Bauer: '. . . in contemporary debate . . . the poor are often envisaged as a distinct class at the mercy of the environment, with no will of their own, while at the same time they are denied the primary human characteristic of responsibility. The rich are regarded as having a will of their own, but as being villainous. Poverty is seen as a condition caused by external forces, while prosperity is viewed as the result of conduct, although reprehensible conduct. The poor are considered passive but virtuous, the rich as active but wicked' (From *Subsistence to Exchange* by Lord Bauer). This widespread view, shared by both socialists and most of the Christian churches, is based, I believe, on two fallacies, one economic and one theological.

The economic fallacy takes various forms. The first is that the rich have become rich by impoverishing the poor. This is widely thought to be true, not only of people but also of countries. The Western European countries are thought to have exploited their colonial territories. In this context it is worth quoting again from Bauer: 'Nor do income differences normally reflect exploitation, but differences in performance. Income and wealth are usually earned or produced, not extracted from other people by depriving them of what they had, or could have had. Some people and societies have emerged from the surrounding sea of poverty sooner or to a greater extent than others, but the earlier emergence of the former helps rather than obstructs the performance of the latter.'

There is no inherent virtue in poverty and evil in wealth. The capitalist system is very much attacked at the present day. Many people and many countries believe very strongly that free markets and globalisation benefit only big business and not the ordinary people. These are the same people who decry 'profit' and equate it with greed. There is no doubt — from evidence of the experience of the twentieth century — that free markets and capitalism have been capable of producing substantially more goods and services for ordinary people than the centralised command economies. People in this country are incomparably better off than they have ever been before; without free markets and competition we could not possibly sustain a population as great as ours. And profit is the engine that runs it, attracting resources to the most efficient producers and taking it away from the inefficient.

Another good point about the market economy is that it is more likely to encourage people to take responsibility for their own welfare, and those who look after their material needs are more likely to take responsibility for their spiritual needs. Salvation is only achieved in freedom, by the exercise of free will. All the evils which are associated with capitalism are evils of people and not the system. Theodore Roosevelt 120 years ago said: 'But we must keep steadily in mind that no people were ever yet benefited by riches if their prosperity corrupted their virtue.'

A recent leader in the *Sunday Telegraph* put it very well:

> ... in a fiercely competitive world, the more driven the entrepreneur is to make money, the more efficient and successful he is likely to be — up to the point, that is, at which his greed overwhelms his decency and common sense. That is an inevitable risk of a capitalist system which is dynamic, volatile and full of temptation. But the risks are balanced by rewards: entrepreneurship is also one of the great creative forces of human civilisation. It creates freedom of choice; ... it liberates us from drudgery and disease.

But greed is not confined to those in capitalist countries. In non-capitalist countries the greedy seek privileges through the corrupt and violent exercise of control over other people's lives and livelihoods.

After this digression, I return again to 1979. The garden had been neglected for a very long time. There was very little of interest in it apart from some good trees. The best of all is the weeping copper beech, which must be over 150 years old. Copper beeches are not uncommon, but weeping copper beeches are relatively scarce. To stand under one with a copper curtain all around falling to the ground is a special sight. There was also an equally large green beech, which unhappily was killed by honey fungus about six years ago. It was enormous; the woodman who cut it down estimated that it contained at least ten tons of timber. There were also horse chestnuts and around the borders of the property some fairly old oaks. But there was nothing else of any interest.

I have a particular affection for trees and made a point of planting a metasequoia and a swamp cypress; both are now over forty feet high. We also planted a tulip tree, but we had some very severe frosts in the early 80s and it succumbed, as did also a bay tree. I am also very proud of my catalpas. I noticed in Wells & Sons, the ironmongers in Saxmundham, some seeds of what were called 'heritage trees' and bought some catalpa seeds – why they should be 'heritage' I do not know; they originate in the Southern States of the USA. From those seeds I now have three full grown catalpas, one of which, in particular provides a splendid show of flowers and later of beans (the catalpa is also known as the 'Indian Bean Tree'). Indeed the crop of beans is so heavy that on several occasion large boughs have snapped off under the weight.

After the election of Maggie we celebrated by putting in a tennis court. The spoil from the site was piled up as a bank along the edge of the 'canal' and Daphne turned it into a purple and gold shrub border with purple hazels, *Berberis thunbergii atropurpureus*, and some lovely purple shrub roses, William Lobb, Charles de Mills, Tuscany Superb and Zigeuner Knabe. We soon realised that the soil was quite unsuitable for rhododendrons and roses became the speciality. To hide the tennis court we surrounded it with Rugosa roses, Roseraie de l'Haÿ and Blanche Double de Coubert. Over the next few years we put in many more beds of old fashioned shrub roses. We had very little help initially. A rather lazy old rogue by the name of Crisp came for a couple of years, but he had to be picked up from Saxmundham. Later on we had more gardeners, of whom more at the right time.

It is remarkable that almost every gardener we have had has been a really nice person; gardens are obviously good for the character – or perhaps good people take to gardening. It has taken over twenty years to establish a really lovely garden. Daphne would have loved to see the garden as it is now. It owes its present state very much thanks to the efforts of Chris Newman, who only came to work for me after Daphne had died. Chris loves gardens; is not particularly knowledgeable but loves to learn and we learn together

– particularly the secret of pruning old shrub roses (ruthlessness is the answer).

In 1979, though, we neither of us knew very much about gardening and we joined a plant propagation course at Otley Agricultural College. We went once a week for several months. We used to take a picnic lunch and eat it in the car sitting outside Ash Bocking church – an isolated site with only Ash Bocking House nearby. We learned all about heel cuttings and nodal cuttings and I learnt how to make my own compost with the right fertilisers. I acquired an electric propagating frame and the concrete slab, where the Hawdons had an outside dog run, was soon covered with potted cuttings, particularly hydrangeas and hebes. By May 1981, when I gave up my relationship with Harbridge House, I was seriously contemplating going into business – in a small way – as a nursery. I planned to buy a lot of old railway sleepers and make raised beds in the area to the north of the back pond. But I did not pursue it, partly because I started more management consultancy and partly because Buxlow was so remote – two and a half miles from anywhere as I often say – that we were not likely to have many people passing by. So all the potted cuttings eventually stocked the garden.

Crispin left Harrow in 1979 and Jocelyn left school a year later. I don't think 'gap' years were very much in vogue in those days; we certainly never thought of it for Crispin. Jocelyn had his gap year (in fact two) but more by accident than design. So minds were concentrated on which universities they were to go to. In the summer of 1979 I seemed to be constantly on the telephone to UCCA. I cannot remember whether several universities were considered for Crispin, but he won a place at UEA (the University of East Anglia) in Norwich to read English and American Studies. Here again Daphne showed more imagination than I. To start with Crispin stayed in a University hostel near Norwich airport, but Daphne said we ought to buy him a house. We found a very suitable little house at No. 1 Cardiff Road, where Crispin was very happy. He had two or three other undergraduates staying with him – and paying rent. Among them was Caroline Sunderland, who was later to be his wife. In Jocelyn's case I know we tried for Oxford, because I got in touch with Peter Oppenheim, whom I had got to know when he was an economist at the BIS in Basle in 1963–65 and who was now a don at Christ Church. Jocelyn went for an interview but I don't think they hit it off. Again I spent a lot of time on the phone to UCCA and he was given a provisional place at York, but dependent on taking his maths A Level again – he had only been awarded an 'E', I think.

But before this became an immediate issue Daphne saw an advertisement in *The Times* in which Quentin Crewe was seeking a young man to accompany him on an expedition across the Sahara. She urged him to apply. Jocelyn was not particularly keen, but Daphne pressed him. She had known Quentin at Cambridge thirty-five years earlier and had in fact danced with him on several occasions. Nothing remarkable about that you may say, but in fact Quentin had shown astonishing stamina in dancing when already suffering from muscular dystrophy; indeed he was not expected to live beyond his twenties. By 1980 he was confined to a wheelchair and the young man required was to be his constant attendant, pushing the wheelchair. Jocelyn went to London for an interview with Quentin, was offered the job and agreed to go. So from February to June Jocelyn was on the expedition. This was only the first part of the expedition; they were unable to get permission to go through Libya and Chad was inaccessible because of a civil war. They resumed the expedition in the autumn.

This is not the place to describe the expedition; Quentin wrote it all up in his book – *In Search of the Sahara*. But the photographer on the expedition was Tim Beddow with whom Jocelyn is still a good friend. One of the others on the expedition was Anthony Cazalet who has also become a firm friend. They were both at Jocelyn's wedding in 2000. Daphne had very mixed feelings about Jocelyn in the Sahara. The following passage occurs in the diary fragments I have previously mentioned:

> I've decided I am the equivalent of home-sick about Jocelyn – Jocelyn sick – I don't want him not to continue his journeyings; I'd just like to pluck him out of the Sahara and see and talk to him, and then let him go back. I want a Jocelyn refresher.

Daphne later, when she had read Quentin's book was particularly fond of reading Quentin's description of Jocelyn, which she thought very perceptive. It goes:

> Jocelyn de Moubray, whose role was principally pushing my wheelchair, was two people: the shy, blushing, earnest eighteen-year-old schoolboy who started the journey, and the almost easy-going young man who ended it. Both of him lost everything, forgot everything and was wholly unconcerned with everyday practicalities. Among other unsuspected skills he could name and provide the ancestry of every racehorse which has run anywhere in Britain since 1965. He liked to tilt back his chair in the evenings, read T.S. Eliot and smoke a nonchalant cigar. We called him the Pasha. The Arabs thought him wonderfully pretty and the Mozabites pinched his bottom. He had a cynically pessimistic view of human beings, of which his own spontaneous nature was the perfect contradiction. Much of what appears in this book I owe to his observation.

1981 was quite an eventful year. In the summer I paid my first visit to a hospital since Bombay in 1945. I experienced the excruciating pain of kidney stones. Dr Foreman came to see me and gave me some very powerful painkillers. Daphne became very worried because for two or three days I seemed to lie in bed almost motionless like a zombie. The stones did not then dissolve of their own accord and I had to be shipped off to hospital. Jocelyn must have been back from the first part of the Saharan expedition because I remember how amused he was that I called out to him as I was being loaded into the ambulance: 'Don't forget to record the maximum and minimum temperatures!'

This was my first experience of an NHS hospital. I must say I don't like public wards; they always seem to be full of boring people who will find any excuse to describe to you their symptoms. The other problem was that it was virtually impossible to see and talk to the consultant; I could not find anyone to tell me what I was to expect and what would be done for me. Eventually the stones happily dissolved of their own accord and I was able to go home. Looking back I cannot for the life of me think why I didn't get myself transferred to a private ward or a private hospital; after all I was a subscriber to BUPA. Somebody suggested that kidney stones were caused by the very hard water here in East Suffolk. We did not have a water softener installed until at least 1985 and I suffered from kidney stones again the next year and this was almost as easily resolved. But here I am being just a boring as the other patients.

The next big event was my trip to Sierra Leone. Donald Cook of the Bank of England, who was then holding roughly the equivalent post that I had held in 1970–74, rang me up and asked whether I would like to be considered for a consultancy job with the Bank of Sierra Leone, the central bank. They had a number of problems and wanted some expert advice. The Governor, Mr Funna, was in London and an appointment was made for me to see him in the Bank of England. He professed himself happy to have me and we agreed terms. Very helpfully the Bank of England lent me the services of a young Bank of England man by the name of Mike Edwards. Mike would continue to be paid by the Bank of England and all our expenses – flight, hotel, car and chauffeur in Freetown – would be paid by the Bank of Sierra Leone. Daphne wasn't a bit happy to be left on her own. She was still very insecure, and although our marriage was not running that smoothly, it was better to have me than to be alone. But we had an inadequate income and this seemed an opportunity to begin to make a name for myself as a management consultant. As it happened, although I was away for some seven weeks, Daphne was not too unhappy, thanks to darling Crispin. He came down from Norwich as often as he could and spent every weekend with her.

Before setting off for Sierra Leone, Jonathan Coates, the management development man from the Trustee Savings Bank, as I think it was still then called, said he would like me to meet Ken Irons, the Managing Director of KIA (Kenneth Irons Associates), a management consultancy. I had been introduced to Jonathan during the summer. We got on well together and he asked me to give one or two lectures on strategic planning issues to TSB students at their Training College near Coventry. Jonathan had in the recent past worked with Ken in KIA and thought that Ken and I might find ways in which we could be useful to each other. This eventually proved to be the case. Ken and I worked closely together for much of the 1980s – and indeed right up to 1995. We had lunch together at a restaurant in Camden Town, where KIA's offices were. We agreed that I would get in touch with Ken again after I had finished my job in Sierra Leone.

Mike Edwards and I set off from Heathrow towards the end of October. Jocelyn, by the way, was already back in Africa too. There were no direct flights to Freetown so we flew to Schiphol to catch a KLM flight to Sierra Leone. I thoroughly enjoyed my time in Sierra Leone. The country was run by a dictator, Siaka Stevens, but it seemed, at least superficially, a fairly benevolent dictatorship. The people in Freetown always seemed cheerful and smiling. I particularly remember on Sundays walking past churches with their doors open listening to the spirited hymn singing, punctuated with cries of Hallelujah! I never had the courage to walk in myself; more's the pity.

It is desperately sad to see what has since happened in that country. Many of the people we met must have been massacred or mutilated in the fighting. What makes it even worse is that Sierra Leone is one of the loveliest countries on the coast of West Africa — it is the only one I believe which has hills along the coastline — and seemed so fertile and full of promise. Perhaps in the coming decade it will prosper; the trouble is that it may take years before the underlying bitterness between former antagonists abates. The airport is some miles from the city. One has to cross an estuary on a ferry to get to Freetown. But there we were. As I have said before, I love the feel and the smell of arriving in the tropics. We were met at the airport by somebody from the Central Bank and in Freetown were driven right through the city to our hotel which was on a lovely sandy beach at the western tip of the city. Freetown, even then, was not a particularly attractive town. The houses are more like shacks than houses and the main roofing material seemed to be corrugated iron. In Graham Greene's novel set in Sierra Leone (*The Heart of the Matter*, I think) there is a scene in a bar by the waterfront with the monotonous dripping of the rain on the iron roof.

The Mami Yoko Hotel was unexpectedly luxurious. I had a suite overlooking the sea and the cooking was superb. There must have been a French chef; much of the food, at least the meat, was flown in almost daily from Paris, but we also had delicious local fish. Although the weather was superb throughout our time there, the hotel was never really full, but it would I am sure have provided a much better holiday than The Gambia, just up the coast, which had become so popular with tourists. The hotel did lay on tourist attractions, such as folk dancing with African drums on the terrace where lunch was served. I don't think the dancing was particularly authentic. Unlike every other country in Africa, except for Liberia, there are no tribes, since all the settlers were freed slaves. Many of the other people in the hotel were businessmen. I remember in particular seeing quite a lot of two oil men who were engaged in offshore drilling. They were very optimistic about finding oil, but I don't think any has been found. Perhaps it is there, but political conditions may have made it difficult to make the necessary investment. Sierra Leone's main export product is diamonds, which I am sure will also have attracted businessmen, some no doubt unsavoury. Diamonds always seem to be associated with corruption.

We soon fell into a regular routine. Soon after sunrise I would go down to the beach for a swim. After breakfast our chauffeur, Carew (photograph albums can be very useful; without the captions to the pictures I would never have remembered his name), would drive us to the Bank of Sierra Leone, where we spent the day meeting and talking to all the officers. Then at about five o'clock we would drive back to the hotel and I would again go swimming, with the large red sun sinking slowly into the sea to the west. One of the main problems faced by the Bank was what was locally called the 'Vouchergate' scandal. In order to try and staunch the flood of public sector spending the Ministry of Finance had decreed that no vouchers for over 50 leones could be cashed without a confirmatory signature from a senior official. Counter clerks at the central bank then found themselves cashing hundreds of vouchers for 50 leones! I think I soon saw that there was really no way of reorganising the bank in such a way that this practice would not recur. When you live in a dictatorship the wisest course to avoid danger is to follow precisely the regulations laid down; no clerk could be expected to query an official from a Ministry cashing a voucher which, at least nominally, fulfilled all the regulations.

Whilst we were in Sierra Leone, Funna asked me to go and visit the Bank's main branch at Kenema, a town in the interior (what in colonial parlance was still called 'up country'). He asked me to consider whether it served any useful purpose; I recommended that it should be kept going. The visit gave us the opportunity, which would otherwise have been denied to us, to see the interior of the country. It was driving across dirt roads, mostly of packed rich red soil, that gave me the impression of the extraordinary fecundity of the country. I had the feeling that that if you just threw a seed on the ground it would sprout and flourish. But there was in fact very little agriculture. There were some palm oil plantations and a lot of small market garden plots growing food for local consumption, mainly cassava. The trouble with Sierra Leone, and many other African countries, is that in order to keep the urban masses quiet they control food prices in the towns. The low prices have the unintended consequence of making farming unprofitable. Whilst at Kenema the local manager showed us around. We visited an alluvial diamond mine and, according to my photograph album, a little town with the distinctive name of Milestone 91!

Whilst we were in Freetown I wrote regular letters to Daphne and became increasingly alarmed when I never received a reply. My letters became more and more strident. I told Daphne that I felt sure that something terrible had happened to Jocelyn and that she was keeping the news from me until I got home. It turned out that she had written equally regularly, but that her letters were never delivered. Near the end of my stay I did discover (I can't think how) that Jocelyn was in Dakar – not so very far away. With the help of the British Ambassador I got through to the embassy in Dakar on the telephone and tried to arrange to have a conversation with Jocelyn; but was not successful.

Mike and I had quite a pleasant social life. We visited the British Ambassador. It was in his garden that I saw for the one and only time in my life avocados growing on a tree. We also visited Funna in his house and some of the other senior officials. At one of their houses we were given the staple Sierra Leonean dish, groundnut soup. They call it soup but it is really a stew, rather like goulash, but with peanuts rather than paprika. We also once had a jolly dinner at a restaurant near to our hotel with a group of senior officials from the bank.

We spent much of our weekends on the beach, talking to everybody we met; they were all very friendly. We also visited some beaches down the coast which had the rather uninviting names of No. 1 beach and No. 2 beach! But they were almost deserted. Behind them was wild forest. Mike and I ventured into the forest and saw with wonder the enormous termite hills. We were brave enough to poke a stick through the wall and see the animated response of the termites. It was there too that I heard the West African cuckoo. It sounds remarkably like the cuckoo we have here; but I know it is not and the sound was subtly different. I took with me a book of West African birds. Another fascinating bird, which I often saw swooping over the hotel's swimming pool was the black swallow. It is totally black with no trace of white.

One other striking memory of Freetown was the sight of a man claiming to be the 'strongest man in the world' moving down the street outside our office followed by an enormous crowd. They were making such a noise with drums that they disturbed a flock – does one call it? – of giant bats. I presume normally they only emerge at night, but here they were in the middle of the day circling around high above Freetown. They looked rather larger than a European herring gull.

Towards the end of November we felt that we had asked all the questions we needed to ask and I began to write my report. I wrote it rather in the manner that Jacobsson had used. I had a large unlined white pad in front of me and wrote fairly rapidly, passing each sheet as I finished it to Mike for his comments or corrections. But I then decided that I needed more time to reflect on the issues and told Funna that I had decide to return to England and that I would finish the report there. Before returning to London I telephoned Daphne for the first time. It was not very successful; the line was so bad. Daphne at one point said rather crossly, 'Get off the line, I am talking to my husband.' She was in fact only addressing her own echo!

In England, the Bank of England agreed to lend me a typist to finalise my report. Somewhere in the house I have a copy of the report I submitted to Mr Funna, but I don't think my recommendations are now of any interest. Although it was my report and not in any sense the Bank of England's, since they had been so helpful I gave them an advance copy. Loehnis, the Bank's Overseas Executive Director, and Michael Balfour, the Head of the Overseas Department, took great exception to two or three pages I had inserted on the proper role of a central bank. When writing the report I felt sure that Funna would show copies to the government and probably to Siaka Stevens himself.

This seemed to me to be an opportunity to say that the more independence they could give the central bank, the higher would be their repute in foreign markets, and that this would make it easier to finance their foreign debt. Loehnis and Michael Balfour felt, I think, that this was beyond my remit and that I was thereby treading on the toes of Warburgs, I think it was, who were then working for the Sierra Leone government. I think they were also afraid that I might give offence to the Head of State, Siaka Stevens! But I persisted and kept the pages in.

If I had known then what I came to learn in KIA I would have carried out the exercise in a different way. What I had actually done was to follow the McKinsey pattern of analytical consultancy. I decided what I thought they ought to do and then told them. I was almost on to the important point that to be effective any consultation has to win the hearts and minds of those concerned in its implementation. For I proposed to Funna that I should return in the New Year and hold a two or three day seminar with him and all the senior officials to discuss my report and iron out any difficulties. He initially showed some interest in this proposal, but in the end I was not invited back.

As a postscript to my time in Sierra Leone, I should add that some five or six years later, when I was at Gatwick trying to sell KIA's services to BAA, a lift near me opened and out walked Funna. For a moment I did not recognise him; but the penny dropped. He had just arrived from Freetown and was on his way to Washington to take up a post with the IMF. So at least he escaped the massacres and the civil war.

I had not been home very long before we had a nasty shock. The telephone rang one afternoon with somebody from the Bank of England on the line saying that the Foreign Office had rung and asked them to tell me that Jocelyn had been blown up by a mine – but that he was all right. It was alarming and it might have been more tactful of them not to give me such a message and leave it to Jocelyn himself to tell me he was all right. As indeed he did, a few days later, telephoning from Dakar.

What had apparently happened was that they had decided to interrupt their Saharan expedition to spend a few days in Morocco for Christmas and driving through Mauretania had inadvertently entered an unmarked minefield. Luckily the explosion took place under one of the rear wheels, so that even though Quentin was thrown several yards away from the Unimog no one was injured. Jocelyn very bravely risked life and limb rescuing Quentin and they all had to return to Senegal. They were all deaf for several days. So for Christmas that year we were reduced to four and were very grateful that Jocelyn had not been injured.

In March 1982 Daphne and I both had flu and were recovering on an unnaturally warm day for the time of year, sitting outside in the sun in the shelter of the 'E', when quite unexpectedly Jocelyn appeared. He was not looking at all well. I am not quite sure what the matter was, but apparently he had to leave the expedition prematurely at Khartoum. Whatever it was, he was soon over it.

Now we had to concentrate on getting him into a university in the autumn. As I have said, he had already secured a provisional place at York University, but to be accepted he had to get a better result in his maths 'A' level. So we packed him off to a crammers in Oxford, where he not only enjoyed himself but managed to raise his 'A' level result from an 'E' to an 'A' – mission accomplished. So Jocelyn went to York just as Crispin finished at UEA. Crispin embarked on his career in racing that autumn, starting in a very lowly position with a trainer near Newmarket. Daphne for years was in the habit of asking why Crispin could not do a proper job and leave racing as a hobby. Many of Crispin's friends went into the City and still went racing frequently. The difference, I think, was that Crispin was not really interested in gambling, as were so many others. He was completely hooked on thoroughbred horses and wanted to spend his life around them. It took years for Crispin to make a breakthrough and start earning a reasonable income, and Daphne kept trying to persuade me to persuade him to go into insurance. And I suppose I could have done. I had particularly good contacts with the Norwich Union, dating back from my strategic planning seminars. Indeed one summer in the early 80s I was given a lunch by one of the Norwich Union directors in their wonderful marble Head Office in Norwich. I am sure I could have got Crispin taken on as a management trainee. But I was determined to let Crispin make up his own mind. It was not as if we were subsidising him; he was making his own way, fully conscious of what was involved. Looking back now, in 2003, it seems providential that he did not go into insurance. The insurance industry has been going through terrible troubles (mostly of their own making – but more of that when I get on to my time with KIA) and he might well now have been unemployed.

Three years later Jocelyn was to follow him into racing – in a different manner. I have been going through my invoice book and find an invoice made out by Jocelyn to *Harpers & Queens*, to whose editor he had been introduced by Quentin, in connection with his first published article – the October 1983 issue had an item 'Jocelyn de Moubray on the run up to the Arc' (the Prix de l'Arc de Triomphe). Amicia, I should say, having been Secretary of the Victorian Society and for a time with the National Trust, was by this time beginning her journalistic career with the *Architect's Journal*. I called on Ken Irons early in the New Year of 1982 and he asked me to help with the organisation of a symposium on Service Management in Venice later on in the year. My job was to find City people who were prepared to take part, either as speakers or as participants. Unfortunately with the recession of the early Thatcher years, the City was particularly cost conscious and we were not able to get enough people together to make it viable. I may add that a contributing factor was that most financial institutions at that time had precious little interest in service to the customers.

Over the next few years my association with KIA became steadily closer. Ken found me a useful 'elder statesman' – I was by now fast approaching the age of sixty. And I found his ideas very appealing. Ken had for some years been on the marketing side of Beechams, dealing with the non-pharmaceutical products and then with strategic planning. He had a nice story of Beechams' most successful product in India. Horlicks was very popular with men – they had apparently misinterpreted the Horlicks slogan 'For night starvation' to mean that it was an aphrodisiac! In 1972 he was headhunted by Commercial Union, one of the largest British insurance companies at that time, to set up their strategic planning unit. He was with Commercial Union for five years. It took him some time to realise that the methods of strategic planning which had been appropriate in a retail business did not seem to be working in a service organisation. Others may have found that too, but Ken thought deeply about the subject and realised that the essential ingredient in strategic planning for any service industry was to win the hearts and minds of all the staff who interacted with the customer – that is to say not just the salesmen and brokers but the backroom staff dealing with customer correspondence and questions and, an element ignored by many, the secretaries and telephonists, who were often the first point of contact with the customer. Ken felt that these ideas, which had not been enthusiastically received by Commercial Union, would be relevant to all service industries. He decided to leave CU and set up on his own as a consultant on service marketing and strategic planning.

By the time I met Ken, KIA had been going for about five years and was making good progress, but not rapid enough. In the next couple of years KIA worked on putting together a marketing package which they called Total Service Management. I had no part in the creative work, but in 1984 was invited to attend a two day workshop in a hotel in Bayswater to be attended by all the KIA consultants and to give them an opportunity to make last minute adjustments and more importantly to get the whole staff behind the project.

Besides Ken there was Annie Gascoigne, the company's accountant (whom I still see to this day), KIA's director in Belgium, a German by the name of Dieter Hohenstein with his wife Adele who was also a consultant, and the two full time consultants who had been closely involved with Ken in putting the whole thing together, David Low and Frank Hoare. I think Jonathan Coates was also there. David was a Scot and a typical trainer, that is to say articulate, very plausible, good on his feet, but essentially rather superficial. He was good at putting across the message, but was not creative. Frank, on the other hand, was much brighter and had made a considerable contribution to the package.

Both David and Frank had left KIA and set up on their own by the time that I began to work full time for KIA. If they had not left, I probably would not have had the opportunity to work more closely with KIA. Dieter turned out to a bit of a rogue and there was some financial problem between him and Ken and he left the company and the Brussels office was closed down – for the time being; it was in fact revived around 1986 I think. By 1984 Ken was paying me a quarterly retainer and I had begun to do some jobs. My first job was to accompany him on a consultancy with Nationale Nederlanden, the major Dutch insurance company. Being still based at Buxlow I did not fly from London but from Norwich and met Ken at Scheveningen, a seaside resort just to the north of The Hague. Scheveningen is almost impossible for anybody who is not a Dutchman to pronounce. During the war apparently people in the Resistance movement in Holland, as a security measure, used to get possible infiltrators to pronounce it; no German could do so correctly.

We stayed in a vast hotel on the waterfront and there was a jazz band playing on the beach below the promenade. The only other thing that sticks in my mind from that visit was that the part time girl consultant, Jeanette, was the first woman I had ever heard using Anglo-Saxon four letter words. Believe it or not I was really rather shocked. My role in the consultations was minimal; just a senior looking presence, who could be introduced as having formerly been with the Bank of England. It was probably not until about 1986/7 that I began to be confident enough to take the lead in consultancy projects.

One other job I will mention because I think it had a demoralising effect on Frank and David and may well have been an influence on their decision to leave KIA. Early in July 1984 Frank and David were running a workshop for staff of a company called BNRe, the reinsurance subsidiary of Baltica, the main insurance company in Denmark. The workshop was being held in a conference centre on the north shore of the island of Sjelland, some miles from Copenhagen, and because they were running it for fairly junior staff they needed the help of some Danish speakers. So they were in close co-operation with a Danish consultancy with the confusing title of KIO. Ken rang me at Buxlow one Friday evening to say that he was worried that Frank and David were having the wool pulled over their eyes by KIO and that we were in danger of losing the consultancy to KIO. He asked me if I would fly out urgently, talk to the Managing Director of KIO and try and make the project secure.

Twenty years ago it was not a simple proposition to fly to Denmark on a Saturday. I had no cash; I am not sure that I yet had a credit card. I went in to Leiston and called on the owner of a shop selling frozen foods, where I was a regular customer, and asked him if he would be kind enough to cash me a cheque – for £300! Without demur, he produced three hundred pounds from the till; it was lucky that it was at the end of the week and that he had not yet paid in the week's takings. I drove to Norwich, parked my car and took a flight to Schiphol and changed there for a flight to Copenhagen. I then hired a car and drove to this remote estate in a forest by the sea.

David and Frank were not at all pleased to see me, but were polite enough. I found that the Managing Director of KIO was running a course himself at some castle a few miles away, so I had to drive over there to see him. I could not find my way and stopped to ask a man by the road the way to X (I cannot remember the name, but I had it written on a piece of paper). He showed complete incomprehension, so I showed him the piece of paper; whereupon he immediately recognised the name and pronounced it in exactly the same way that I had done! International communication is sometimes difficult! To cut a long story short, I failed in my mission. KIO stole the project from us. And by the end of that same year Frank and David had decided to leave KIA.

Late in 1984 I became even more closely involved with KIA. Ken asked me to spend a couple of days in London interviewing candidates for a consultancy to replace Frank and David. Between us we must have seen a dozen. Such interviews are inevitably subjective. There are no formal criteria. We explained KIA's philosophy and tried to gauge whether it really made sense to the candidate. It turned out that both Ken and I had another criterion; we both rejected an otherwise quite plausible candidate because his face was almost completely obscured by a very large fuzzy black beard!

The next important move was that Ken asked me to work full time on a higher quarterly retainer and with a higher daily rate as a consultant. At first this did not seem possible. It would have been quite exhausting to take the early train every day and return late at night. But at about that time, rather unexpectedly Coutts announced that one of their representatives was going to be calling on customers in this area and we made an appointment for him to call. I had not expected much to come of the meeting, but it turned out that, having seen what sort of a house Buxlow was, he said Coutts were prepared to lend us up to £40,000. Even though my life insurance was to mature in March 1985 and my Bank of England mortgage would be paid off, he did not seem to require the loan to be formally secured on the property; that is, there was no 'mortgage'. So I went flat hunting in London and told Ken that if successful I would join him full time. I looked at several flats in Islington, handy if one was driving in and out from Suffolk, and found a lovely flat – 27 Canonbury Square. Amicia helped me with the search. I took Daphne to London and she approved. So we bought the flat for, I think, about £70,000, putting up £30,000 by the sale of shares and the rest in a loan from Coutts; the rate of interest by today's standards was quite extraordinary – 16.5 per cent! So in March 1985 we moved in to Canonbury Square and I started full time with KIA. I was to be based on Canonbury Square during the week for the next five years, which turned out to be the busiest years of my life, even busier than the Jacobsson years and certainly involving the hardest work.

CHAPTER 24

Further Reflections on our Marriage

I HAVE ALREADY SAID QUITE A BIT about our marriage much earlier on and I do not mean to go over all the ground again, but the years 1984 and 1985 represented a critical watershed. I knew that Daphne was not happy, but I did not recognise how serious a problem this was. In April 1984 we were in the kitchen with an electrician who was trying to put right a problem with the immersion heater when the phone rang. Daphne picked it up and began a long conversation with somebody. Whilst I was going around with the electrician, the conversation continued – for some forty minutes. I did not listen in, but I was puzzled at who it might be on the other end of the line. She then told me that it had been Micha Battsek, her former boy friend, when she had been at LSE evacuated to Cambridge. She told me very little about the conversation. She said he had told her that he could tell by the tone of her voice that she was very unhappy and had suggested that she should go back to him. There seemed to be no imminent intention on her part to take up his offer, so life went on much as before for about eighteen months.

The conversation did have one practical effect; it led Daphne entirely of her own accord, with no prompting from me or her doctor, to give up her tranquillisers. Very bravely she just stopped one day in the early summer. I had hardly been conscious that she was taking Valium regularly. It turned out that it was entirely because of taking Valium that she had kept completely off alcohol. I had been drinking very little in the preceding years – an occasional glass of beer and sometimes a gin and tonic in the evenings. But now we began to drink wine. I knew nothing about wine and Jocelyn was terribly shocked to find that I was buying a wine for £1.99 a bottle! The quality subsequently rose and Daphne began to drink wine regularly. She also developed a passion for cocktails and I was constantly mixing cocktails from a 1930s recipe book in the cocktail shaker that we had bought years ago in America.

Throughout the rest of the year and into 1985 I was not conscious of Daphne being really unhappy; tense, yes, but not unhappy. I remember we went to Glyndebourne to see *L'Incoronazione di Poppea* and Daphne wore a lovely evening dress quite like a kaftan. One of my favourite photographs of her is of her wearing that dress standing at the open front door. Daphne still maintained some contact with Micha, for she told me that she had sent him that photo – and he, miserable man, had said that she looked very unhappy – poppycock! He also had the nerve to send her a boxed set of cassettes of *L'Elizir D'Amore*! It is a lovely opera so I was happy that we should play it. But it was a not very subtle gesture.

Daphne at the front door, leaving for Glyndebourne – 1984

In September we had a lovely holiday in Tuscany. We rented a wing of a house near Siena – Tenuta di Cerbaia. Daphne and I drove there in Jocelyn's Citroen estate car. We left him at Buxlow busy typing his first book, *Horse Racing and Racing Society*. We drove down to the French Riviera and on into Italy. We tried to spend a night at the hotel that we had liked at Nervi in 1952, but it had been quite spoilt. We drove on instead to a delightful little *albergo* on the beach at Parragi, on the road to Portofino. Hanging on a hook in the gun room here is a key with a wooden label '7'; we inadvertently walked off with it! Amicia and her friend Vicki Jaggers came and joined us, flying to Pisa and hiring a car. I have nothing but happy memories of that holiday. At one point Rory Carnegie, Jocelyn's best friend from Eton, turned up with his girl friend, Miranda Cresswell – they were backpacking their way through Italy. Miranda, who later married Rory, painted a fine portrait of Crispin and Jocelyn, which the children gave Daphne for a birthday present in 1989. Daphne and I drove back this time by Lake Maggiore and over the Simplon and through Switzerland.

We were all together for Christmas 1984. Early in 1985 Daphne was still in contact with Micha and actually went to see him in his flat. Believe it or not I drove her there on our way to look at the flat in Canonbury Square. I sat in the car absolutely fuming, pondering the possibility of walking in on them and making a scene. Sensibly, I didn't. When she came out she told me that he had presented her with a ruby pendant – since it was forty years since they had first met! That pendant really annoyed me. I refused to let her ever wear it. She told me that he had asked her not to sell it in order to buy a car but to keep it as a token – what a man! After Daphne died I came across the pendant and decided to get rid of it; the jeweller in Aldeburgh offered me £250 – some car!

As I have said, we moved in to the Canonbury Square flat in March. Daphne was quite extraordinary. We arrived on a Friday and by Saturday afternoon when Amicia turned up to help put things in order everything was already in place. I had fully expected Daphne to spend every week with me in London. Indeed, since we did not believe that May and Brie, both now 13 years old, with Brie going blind and increasingly lame, would be able to stand being put into kennels for four or five days a week, we had them both put down. It was just as well I think; they slept for nearly 23 hours a day and would not have lasted much longer. But after the first week, Daphne decided to spend every week on her own at Buxlow. I am still not quite sure why she decided to do so. It may have just been the obvious answer that there was precious little to do in Islington; Daphne was not one of the world's great shoppers, and she had by this time become very fond of Buxlow, where she had the garden.

In the next five years Daphne rarely came to London. She came, for example, when we had seats for the opera at Covent Garden or the Coliseum and during the week after Christmas, when London was always blissfully empty. It may well have been a good thing for me that she was not constantly in London; Micha would have put great pressure on her to meet him again. Contacts between her and Micha continued nonetheless. At some point Micha's Canadian 'partner' must have picked up an extension in their flat when he and Daphne were on the phone. She became incensed and sent letters to me and to Daphne at Canonbury telling us to lay off and not break up her relationship. But I am sure the relationship was already doomed, whatever Daphne decided.

But life between us continued for the time being, as if there was no question of us not staying together. In May and June we went for a lovely holiday in Provence. We rented a house in Sablet, now one of the Côtes du Rhone Villages, but then I think lying between the Appellations Controllés of Gigondas and Rasteau. On arrival Daphne took a dislike to the house, which was in the centre of the town. We went to see the owners, who ran the *pharmacie*, and luckily they had another property free, a nice house just outside the town in an apricot orchard. From the garden one looked back up the hill to Sablet. A notable feature of the view was the large standard always flying from the flagpole over what was called the Embassy of Patagonia! I have no idea who lived there.

We were joined by Amicia and Crispin. Jocelyn was, I think, busy at Buxlow writing his second book – *The Thoroughbred Business*. We enjoyed our time there, visiting cellars to taste the wines. The view was splendid, looking out to the silhouette of the the small range of mountains called the Dentelles de Montmirail. Micha's presence was still around, but not really threatening. I remember the subject came up between Amicia and me and she was quite incensed with what was going on and hoped fervently that it would soon all die down and go back to normal. In the evenings Daphne and I would stroll down the lane after dark listening to that strange combination of sounds, the croaking of bullfrogs contrasting with the lyrical singing of the nightingales.

Another indication that Daphne was not then contemplating leaving me was a visit we made to a *brocante* in the barn of a farmhouse outside Beaume de Venise. She saw there a a large oak table, some 11 feet long, with eight upholstered chairs. The table top was made of inlaid pieces of oak taken from wine barrels, what are known as *fûts de chêne*. 'Those would be just right for the dining room at Buxlow,' she said. 'Let's buy them.' I was quite taken aback. On previous travels over the years in France when calling on *brocantes* we would buy small things that could be taken back in the car. In Normandy for example we bought many nineteenth century fashion prints. 'How are we going to get them back?' I asked. 'They must have shippers,' she replied. And sure enough, we paid £2,000 for them, and had them shipped back to England by Danzas. Amicia was very upset that we did not haggle more with the owners; she thought we ought to have picked up a chair and thrown it to the ground saying that it was obviously in poor shape. But neither Daphne nor I are good at that kind of thing – although I suppose we did do quite a lot of bargaining in Marrakech. It's not really relevant to our marriage, but when the table and chairs turned up at Buxlow, I was alone in the house. 'Bring them in,' I said. The driver said that he was alone and that he would need my help. Luckily, eighteen years ago I was rather stronger. The table had a very heavy base and the top was separate. We slid both of them in and the only really hard effort was lifting the top on to the base.

It was not until the autumn that Micha posed a real threat. He kept asking Daphne to leave me and go to live with him. She eventually said that she wanted to go and stay with him at his house in Nice. Micha was quite wealthy having built up a travel agency and had, besides the flat, a house in Nice and a house in Gstaad. There was nothing I could do about it. She had, at least, not yet made an irrevocable decision. So I drove her to Heathrow one afternoon in November, I think. I remember the journey well, because I was inwardly in a state of turmoil, which was made worse by being stuck in a traffic jam in the middle of Chelmsford. Ominously, I thought, Daphne was taking a lot of luggage; she must have had five cases! – enough to last her several weeks. By the time I left Heathrow I was distraught, fearing that I might never be with Daphne again. I drove back to London. The sky was black. The rain was pouring down. I was in tears and the music I was playing on the cassette deck was emotionally draining – the last two movements of Saint Saens' Organ Symphony.

I rang Daphne in Nice every day. The children, I gathered, did the same. Micha was apparently very surprised that she should be part of such a close family. I think these constant phone calls must have made him realise that she really belonged elsewhere. One evening sitting miserably alone in Buxlow – probably not much more than a week after she had left – the phone rang. Daphne announced that she was coming home and would I meet her at Heathrow. My spirits soared and, as so often at emotional moments, I burst into tears. Whilst I was waiting outside the customs hall a young boy – probably off her flight – came through and suddenly saw his parents waiting for him; his eyes lit up and he looked ecstatically happy. A few moments later when Daphne appeared with a trolley laden with suitcases, I looked the same as the little boy. I believe it was that that sealed our marriage for ever. She told me later that she had been so touched to see my face suddenly light up. From that day until the day she died we were closer than we had ever been before. She did not entirely subdue the inner turmoil, but she was happy and so was I. I don't think I would have been as distraught as I was, had I seen then the following item from her diary fragments:

April 1984
I suppose I should write about my conversation with Micha, but really I am left, after 5 days, with a feeling of flatness, an interest in the fact that it took place, but little desire to go further. It wasn't really a rounding off, or a nostalgic gambit, rather a weary sounding lack lustre man looking back partly (I guess) because the present is so much a matter of regret. In fact the only animation he showed was in recalling Cambridge and London and the very long ago. I wouldn't have known his voice and yet I would have expected to recognise it at once. It cannot be present satisfaction that makes me detached – perhaps a recognition that so long has elapsed that it is indeed the past, and my present and his present have little of interest to share together. I have my children, he his, he has his regrets (which include me!), I a realisation that it

was indeed an impossibility and now I can listen to it all with interest but no emotion – this surprises me, the lack of emotion – he said, somewhere in the past, that we won all our battles knowing we would lose the last. Well, the last is a historical fact and though he means more to me in the context of that past than the others in it, and though he was closer to me in understanding than nearly anyone in the present, I feel that person is no longer there, in short (and prosaically) he has lived too much and for too long a time away from me to naturally come close to me save in shared memories, and oh! how selective they appear to be, some I remember, some not at all. A kind of memory of closeness, of past possibilities.

I find this almost unbearably moving and very sad. When I started these memoirs many months ago I had no idea that I was going to explore our marriage so deeply. Indeed I could not have done so had I not quite recently found these diary fragments. I am not really sure what I have achieved by doing so. On the one hand I have learnt to my sorrow just how unperceptive I was, for so long – she certainly doesn't mean me when she says, 'closer to me in understanding than nearly anyone in the present'. I wonder whether she was thinking of Jocelyn, for whom she felt a very close affinity. But I have also learnt just what a treasure she was despite her inner turmoil and have a profound sense of gratitude that we did come so much closer together for the last fourteen years of her life. It's strange to realise that I have come to understand and love Daphne more deeply since she died that I did when she was alive. But despite what she wrote in April 1984, I think I may have come close to losing her. By November 1985 I think she may have thought that they might after all have interests to share together and decided to go to Nice to put it to the test. Anyway I still find a sense of profound relief that we got out of the pit and grew together.

I was talking about this with Jocelyn sometime ago. He said he felt that Daphne would have been much happier if she could have had a job after the children were old enough to no longer need full time care. I think he was right. But I don't think she should have done a conventional job, in some office or other. I think she had a talent for writing and should have been writing short stories, or a novel (no, not that, she was so private that in a novel I think she would not have been able to conceal some of her inner thinking that she would not have wanted to reveal). When we were in Sussex, for some time she went to a meeting once a week with a group of women who met in each other's houses to compare what they had written. I should have encouraged that much more. I don't think I even asked to see what she had written, although I think even then she would probably not have wanted me to see it lest it revealed something about her that she did not want me to know. Poetry, I think, could have been her forte.

Amongst the diary fragments there are some poems dating from the 1960s. I have never read much poetry. I find a great deal of it too complex and convoluted. Perhaps I am not as intelligent as I sometimes think I am!

But these poems of Daphne's have moved me very deeply. Her character shines through and they make me love her even more. I am including most of them in an appendix, leaving out only those with which she didn't seem to be entirely happy.

CHAPTER 25

The Canonbury Years

S O THE WHOLE FAMILY WERE TOGETHER for Christmas. I had been dreading
a miserable Christmas with the rest of us all missing Daphne terribly.
Jocelyn had come to live with me in Canonbury after leaving York. The
Haymarket Press had acquired the rights to a horse racing publication –
Update – and had decided to turn it into a glossy weekly magazine and,
thanks to his two books on racing, Jocelyn was appointed the first editor.
Jocelyn was with me for some months, until he found a flat in Notting Hill.
The daily journey to Bayswater and back was rather too much, particularly
because launching a weekly magazine was so demanding.

During these years I had to get used to two changes in my way of life at
home and at work. I had not commuted since 1976 and had never done
weekly commuting. This represented a considerable change, particularly as
I soon discovered that Daphne did not intend to spend the week with me
in London. As I have already said, I am not quite sure why she made this
decision, but in the light of hindsight I am not sure that it did not turn out
to be helpful in rebuilding our marriage. For four days of the week we were
not on top of each other. But Daphne was almost alone. She had always
done all the housework herself and had resisted trying to get Win Driver
to do it for us. Win had worked for the Hawdons and actually started
working at Buxlow as a young woman in 1944. After the death of Mrs
Hawdon in 1982 she would have been available. But Daphne's inner
insecurity put her off; she did not want anyone who might say, 'That's not
how the Hawdons did it.' As I now know, Win is much too nice – and
old-fashioned – ever to have thought of saying such a thing.

But once a week Daphne now had a gardener. When we had returned
from the holiday in Provence the garden was in a terrible state. I had
previously done all the mowing and a good deal of the weeding (though
not with great enthusiasm) and by mid-June the grass in the paddock by the
back pond was nearly waist high. Bill Scarlett was recommended to us by
the publican of the Railway Inn in Saxmundham – not that I was a pubby
type, but I knew him because he also ran a taxi service. Bill was a jewel.
He was always pleasant and worked extremely hard. He was also a
handyman and often did things in the house. The walls in the passage by
the back door and up the back staircase were painted by him. So, when I
was away in London, in any emergency Daphne would always have been
able to call on Bill. Bill worked for us for the next eleven years.

To begin with I used to drive back to Canonbury on Sunday evening
after dinner, but I soon added another night a week at Buxlow and did not

return to London until after breakfast on Monday. I had made it clear to Ken that I proposed to work in London for only four days a week. So I returned to Buxlow on Thursday afternoon. I always used to feel as I drove home that there was a cord pulling me back to Daphne; it seemed almost real to me. Daphne was very touched, I think, when I told her this. When one is working with customers and emphasising the need to put customers first, one has to follow that example oneself; so, if it was necessary in the interest of a client, I would work on a Friday – taking a day off in the next week if possible. At Canonbury I had virtually no social life. By this time I had got used to being on my own in the evenings. The only people – with very rare exceptions – that I saw at Canonbury were the children. I thoroughly enjoyed having Jocelyn with me for a few months. But after that, all three children were working and living in London and used to come and have dinner with me almost every week, I think. Amicia, by this time, had moved on from the *Architect's Journal* to the *World of Interiors* and Crispin was working for *Raceform* – still of course in racing. I have always enjoyed cooking, so I did not subsist on chilled ready cooked meals, but cooked a proper dinner every night. When Crispin and Jocelyn came to have dinner with me, I often cooked a nice warming curry. However there was a very good Chinese restaurant just off Canonbury Square, to which I went occasionally and sometimes collected a takeaway from them.

The other big change in my way of life was at work. At the Bank I had my own private messenger, my own secretary, who could take shorthand, and a substantial office all to myself. Now at KIA, on three small floors above a restaurant – initially a not particularly good Italian one, but later an excellent Chinese Szechwan one – I shared a room with two other consultants, had no secretary; and nobody in KIA could do shorthand, so everything had to be written out by hand. There was no staff canteen, let alone a senior officials' dining room. That first summer, when I seemed to be involved in very few projects, I used to go to a pub and have a cooked lunch every day. When she joined KIA, Tarja Tunkennen (I love that name!), a young Finnish consultant, used to join me. But when work began to flow in, there was no time for lunches in a pub. We had lunch at our desks; sometimes sandwiches, but in my case more often little pots of salads from Marks & Spencers.

For me the next five years were dominated by my work as a management consultant. This may sound desperately dull to some, but I was fascinated by it. I do not propose to mention all the projects I was involved in – there must have been at least fifteen clients over that period. With Ken's background in Commercial Union and mine in the Bank, it is not surprising that almost all of them were financial institutions, insurance companies, banks and building societies. In fact only one was not, I think, BP Portuguesa and also BP Greece. I propose to mention some of them to illustrate what it was that so fascinated me.

I did not discover the term of art which I have mentioned earlier, namely, 'process consultants', until a year or two after starting with KIA. But it is the key to what I enjoyed. I find the most intriguing parallels between religion and consultancy, between process consultants and what I have termed analytical consultants. Consider the following excerpts from the Introduction by Gregory Johnson to a recent American translation of Swedenborg's *Divine Providence*:

> . . . in matters of religion, we should not be compelled by external means to believe and to love. Instead, each of us should *persuade* and at times compel *ourselves* to do so . . . all attempts to compel belief are not only futile but also counterproductive. We value our freedom. When it is taken away, even for our own good, we reassert it by rejecting what is *foisted* upon us.

Swedenborg also adds a very important point:

> that the pleasures of freedom rule over the pleasures of reason, meaning that what we love or value rules over our thoughts, not vice versa. This means that we can be reformed only through a transformation of our *core values*.

I have italicised the three key ideas relevant in a management context.

Any service company which decides to adopt a strategy of putting customers' needs first, has to find a means, not of persuading all those in contact with customers to share their objective, but to find a means whereby the staff can *persuade themselves* that it is right to do so. Any attempt, far too often undertaken, to force compliance with a 'mission statement' will be counterproductive; staff will reject what they see as being *foisted* upon them. The company needs to find a means of getting the staff to share with them their new *core values*. These have to be from the heart; a mission statement which is only on the lips is of no use at all. This internalisation of the strategy is the task that I see as being particularly suited to a process consultant. Analytical consultants adopt an approach which is much more analogous to that of the Roman Catholic Church; they tell the client what he ought to believe and do not set out to devise means to get them to persuade themselves.

Two of the projects I worked on illustrate this very well. The first was with NEM (National Employers Mutual) – a mutual insurance company. They were not doing particularly well. They had been gone over by management consultants (of the analytical variety) to no avail and staff morale was very low. Their Managing Director, Stanley Halliwell, knew Ken and was ready to see if KIA could find a way out of this. The first step in a project like this was for Ken and me to hold a two-day workshop in a hotel with the Managing Director, the Board and senior managers. The NEM workshop got off to a fairly slow start. On the first evening, after dinner, they seemed to be wholly devoted to playing snooker! But by the second day they had come round, of their own accord, to a realisation that something had to be done about the company, and that it made sense to work on a strategy of putting the customer first. This is in fact even more obvious in the case of a mutual company, since the customers are also the owners.

Over the next few weeks I and Mark Langley, a young trainer who had joined KIA, ran a series of workshops with all the rest of the managers. Our aim was not to persuade them that it would pay to give more attention to customer needs, but to try and get them to persuade themselves that it was the right course of action and that they could feel a real commitment to it. In similar situations with other companies I almost invariably found that middle managers became extremely enthusiastic and were really quite impatient to get the project going.

There were always some who were reluctant to change their old ways. In the case of NEM there was one particular manager who was very difficult. He must have been in his forties and as a claims manager had obviously spent most of the previous twenty years firmly believing that his task was to find faults in any claim and if possible disallow it. He reasoned that if the company received premium income and paid out nothing on claims it would be very profitable! He really could not accept that such a course gave the company a bad name. He was convinced that most insurance claims were fraudulent – some of them obviously were, but this was not the way to deal with them. Morale in the company very quickly revived and they soon felt part of a team instituting an exciting new way of doing business. Over the next two years or so the company became increasingly profitable. I felt such a sense of affinity with them that I switched my own household insurance to NEM.

But Stanley Halliwell, the CEO, then dropped a bombshell. I had always had some doubts about his commitment to these new 'core values'. NEM had been having a difficult time with its business in Australia and had a heavy liability to be paid off. As a mutual company, NEM could not raise capital from the market. Stanley then did a deal. He sold all NEM's UK portfolio to AGF, the large French insurance company. I am not at all sure that it was legal. No mutual company can be demutualised without the consent of the existing policy holders. But, very cleverly, he was not actually demutualising, since after this a much attenuated NEM continued to exist as a mutual company. What he had done was to sell off all NEM's British business. But this very act deprived the policy holders of their ownership of the company. So my insurers were no longer NEM, except in name, but AGF – and I had not been consulted. He was allowed to get away with it, but the result was disastrous for all the staff who had become committed to putting customer needs first.

AGF were not in the slightest interested in the customer; they moved the bulk of the business to their offices in the Midlands and there were a lot of compulsory redundancies. Most important was that a large number of decent, intelligent men and women now felt that they could put no trust in senior management and would certainly be very reluctant to get involved with consultants ever again. It was a great experience whilst it lasted, but what a terrible waste in the end. Over the years I have seen many other people in top management who seemed to show more interest in clever 'deals' than in the morale and future well-being of their staff.

Another project is also, I think, worth mentioning. It was a great success, but eventually came to nothing – in a much less traumatic way. This was BP Portuguesa. BP in those days had a devolved constitution, with a self contained subsidiary in every country in which it operated. These companies were run by a Managing Director with a Board of Directors, who were responsible for all the business in their country and who reported to BP in London. The Managing Director of BP Portuguesa was an Englishman, Brian Hughes, but all the staff and managers (with one exception – the IT expert) were Portuguese; the working language at management level was English.

We started as we always did with a two-day workshop for the Board of Directors, run by Ken and me, at a hotel on the coast at Cabo de Roca (the most westerly point of Portugal). The Managing Director had been worried at BP's decline in market share and having met Ken, thought that service might be the key. So the workshop went rather more smoothly than had the one with NEM. We asked them to think about their experience with BP and to try and identify what it was about the company that had been successful in the past and to compare themselves with their competitors. Ken used an intriguing technique, asking them to divide into groups and suggest what animal they would associate with BP and with their competitors. Their competitors were Esso, Mobil and the Portuguese nationalised oil company. Predictably they associated Esso with a tiger; the Portuguese company they associated with ants and, quite unprompted by us, they decided that BP was a Labrador – man's best friend! They recognised that attempts to make the delivery patterns cost effective often went against the customers' needs. They ended the two days committed to trying to launch a campaign to put the customer first.

Ken and I went back to London. For some reason BP Portuguesa then had doubts about going any further. I think it was due to one Director, who had felt very jaundiced by their previous association with consultants. So I flew out to Lisbon again and spent a tricky morning with him and a group of senior managers. Happily, I won them round and it was decided to launch a series of workshops with middle managers. Although the language would be English, we felt that it would be wise to have a Portuguese assistant to help me. Ken had good contacts with the Portuguese insurance companies and through them we found a Portuguese girl, who whilst remaining employed by her insurance company, was released to help me. So far as BP were concerned she was a KIA consultant. Manuela Martins (I have to tell you how to pronounce her name! – mun-wella marteensh!) was very bright and extremely helpful.

I was involved with BP Portuguesa on and off for two or three years. The middle manager workshops were a revelation. They soon built up a strong emotional commitment to change. In all my work as a consultant I have always found a wealth of talent at middle management level. They were soon exclaiming: 'Why haven't we done this years ago?' We carried the exercise right down to quite junior levels. Manuela and I ran a workshop (in Portuguese) for the secretaries and telephonists. They were thrilled to be involved – after all they were the people who most frequently came into contact with customers. By this time I had taught myself enough Portuguese to get by (Hugo's *Teach Yourself Portuguese in Three Months*!); but Manuela had to do most of the talking. I found that I could understand all that they were writing up on flip charts. At one point when Ken and I were asked to speak at a conference in Lisbon organised by the Portuguese Insurance Association. I was bold enough to translate my speech laboriously and deliver it in Portuguese. This was a mistake. It would have been much more sensible to make a few introductory remarks in Portuguese and then give the speech in English. As it was, I lost all spontaneity, since I had to read the speech. I usually speak without notes.

At one stage in the BP project the senior managers agreed that a bright and committed manager should be given specific responsibility for seeing that the project kept moving forward; it is so easy for new initiatives to run into the sand. I suggested, and Brian Hughes agreed, that it should be a young man by the name of Andrew Lancastre – his mother was English but his name showed that his father was descended from John of Gaunt! The contacts between England and Portugal go back a very long way (not that John of Gaunt was all that English – as his name implies, he was born in Ghent!). The project proved very successful. Staff morale improved, as it had done with NEM, and BP's market share began to rise. But once again external forces brought the project to an end. BP's Head Office decided that because of the Single Market and the move towards European Union their activities on the Continent of Europe should be unified and run from Paris. BP Portuguesa ceased to have autonomy, and even worse BP adopted a matrix organisation, whereby the oil operations and the LPG (Liquid Petroleum Gas) operations in Portugal had to report to different heads in Paris. This went against the strong sense of national identity and morale suffered. Andrew Lancastre, whom I by then considered a friend, decided it was time to go. He moved, as I remember, to Renault.

It seems to be the story of my life. When I do something which gives me great satisfaction – chief economist at the Bank, management development manager, seminars on strategic management, NEM and then BP Portuguesa – the effects are quickly dissipated. However the satisfaction in a job well done remains. This was not the only contact that Ken and I had with BP. Before BP became centralised on Paris we spent a few days in Athens running a workshop with the top people in BP Greece. It never went any further; probably because the centralisation was about to take place.

I became very fond of Portugal. In Lisbon I always stayed in the Tivoli Hotel on the Avenida de la Republica. I usually booked the same room, looking out on to the garden at the back and down on the pool; but even more important was the fact that beyond the garden, up the hill, looking over the rustic roofs of outhouses, like Tuscan farmhouses, were the Lisbon Botanical Gardens. So, although one was in the city, the view from the window could have been on the edge of country.

The Portuguese are quite my favourite Europeans. Everybody was pleasant and smiling. There is something very pleasant about the Portuguese word for thank you – *obrigado*. There was a good restaurant on the roof and an excellent coffee shop on the ground floor. I was amused to find that the scales in every bathroom always recorded one's weight several kilos less than the correct weight. I suppose that it was intended to encourage one to eat well in the restaurant!

Lisbon itself had a slightly dishevelled charm; the paint everywhere needed redoing, but I liked it as it was. I haven't been to Lisbon now for at least thirteen years, and I guess that with all the money pouring in from the European Union, the city may well, regrettably, have been smartened up. But apparently not. Andrew Marr in the *Daily Telegraph* in March 2004, speaking of his visit to Portugal with Tony Blair said:

> The previous night we had been in Lisbon, which must be among Europe's loveliest capitals. I was entranced – by the simple fish restaurants, the elegant, slightly battered architecture, the curving hill-streets, with tiny apricot-coloured trams rolling up and down them, the sweet warm Atlantic air – but above all – the friendliness.

When Ken was in Lisbon with me, we used to do a great deal of walking all over the city. We explored the old Moorish quarter, the Alfama, which still has a North African air, with narrow winding streets and lots of little shops and restaurants.

There was an occasion when I was finishing a BP workshop in Estoril on a Friday afternoon, but had to be in their Lisbon offices on the Monday morning. So I decided to stay in Portugal for the weekend and arranged for Daphne to fly out and join me. We booked into a Bed & Breakfast in a *quinta* (a manor house) in Sintra – the Quinta Sao Thiago (the Portuguese equivalent of the Spanish Santiago). Unfortunately Daphne rang to say that she had flu and was not fit to come so I spent the weekend alone. Sintra is a most attractive little town, perched on a hill amongst woods. Looking up from Estoril on the coast it often has a cloud sitting on it, rather as I imagine the 'table cloth' sits on Table Mountain in South Africa. It has a very strange royal palace, with two chimneys almost in the shape of Kentish oasts dominating the roofscape. Sintra also had a very nice antique shop, where I bought things for Daphne on occasions. It was there that I bought the two sixteenth century painted wooden statuettes of St. John and Mary Magdelene, which stand in the dining room. There was also an excellent wine merchant who had quite the best old Madeiras – the Verdelho was especially good.

My hostess at the Quinta was a mad Portuguese woman married to an elderly invalid Englishman. When I rang her from Estoril, she told me to hurry up and come well before dark (it was January). When I arrived she was already standing outside the house wearing heavy walking shoes and a scarf on her head. 'Come on,' she said, 'there's no time to lose.' And we were off, walking through the woods and down the hill in the direction of Estoril. I was not dressed for anything more than a stroll and was quite glad when we got back to the house. She introduced me to her husband, who seemed to be confined to his chair and was, I thought, extremely rude to her. We then arranged to meet for dinner. Her husband did not join us and we were joined by a Hungarian sculptor whose patron she was. I am not sure that he was really Hungarian, since he came from Transylvania, which is for the most part in Romania. Our only common language was French.

The next day I went off up the coast to Mafra and Ericeira, where, according to my hostess, there was an excellent seafood restaurant. She was right; it was very good. I also visited the ornate monastery at Mafra. She had told me to be sure to be back in good time in the afternoon; the sculptor was going to take me for a walk through the woods. In the late afternoon we set off down the hill and through the woods. The adjoining property was the Palacio Montserrate, an extraordinary Moorish folly built for William Beckford. It was not supposed to be open to the public, but since there was a simple gate between the Quinta's grounds and those of Montserrat, we just walked in. Although it was mid-January the azaleas were already in bloom. Montserrat is not as flamboyant as the Brighton Pavilion, but it has something of the same feel. Its architect, as I learned from the notices outside, was James Knowles, who was also responsible for the Grosvenor Hotel in Victoria Station! By a strange coincidence, I have discovered, here in Suffolk, that Caroline Cranbrook of Great Glemham House spent much of her childhood, not just in Sintra, but actually living in the Palace of Montserrat.

On the Sunday I drove off across the Tagus to Evora, an enchanting walled city, roughly half way between Lisbon and Badajoz in Spain. I don't know why Evora is not better known. All the buildings were white and there are some quite well preserved Roman remains, including the columned Temple of Diana. So ended a lovely weekend. What a pity that Daphne could not have been with me. She had been to Sintra the year before at the end of our holiday in Madeira, mentioned below. But she would have enjoyed another visit and I wish she could have experienced the Quinta Sao Thiago.

During those years I spent almost as much time in Spain as in Portugal. Ken and I visited Madrid and felt that there were quite a number of opportunities to be followed up. He had a friend in Madrid, the Managing Director of a company called Data who was prepared to allow us to rent a room in his offices to be our office. He also made available to us a secretary, by the name of Yolanda. She was very bright and eager to extend her knowledge; she spoke very good English. So for about three years I had an office in Madrid and a secretary, and visited Madrid several times a year; sometimes calling in on my way to or from Lisbon.

I taught myself Spanish in the same way as I had learned Portuguese and although I had no problem in reading El Pais every morning, I was never competent enough to carry out sales visits in Spanish. Yolanda accompanied me on all my calls. In spite of frequent visits to Madrid and one trip to Barcelona, we did not succeed in getting any firm business. We came close to some kind of agreement with Banco Hispano Americano – although I am not sure that we were not led on a bit by the fact that the young official in the bank was clearly very taken with Yolanda and was always ready to receive a visit! I came close to some kind of agreement with Banco Nat West, but the manager then got recalled to London. His successor was very friendly – his father had been in the Bank of England and he was Michael Dealtry's brother-in-law – but he was not really interested. The manager who had been recalled to London provided me with an interesting experience. When in London, I called on him in his office in what was then known as the Nat West Tower. When I entered the building at ground floor level it was pouring with rain; when I reached his office on the umpteenth floor, it was snowing! When weather forecasters say 'snow on the hills', they should also add, 'and at the top of high buildings'!

Yolanda and I flew to Barcelona in an attempt to sell KIA's services to the main Catalan bank; again to no avail. Whilst we were there and walking down the Ramblas one afternoon, we passed the Opera House. Yolanda had never been to an opera and I asked her if she would like to go that evening. When she said 'yes' I went and booked two tickets. All we could get were seats in the 'Gods'. Being Spain, the performance did not start until very late. We were desperately uncomfortable sitting so high up, and it was impossible to follow what was happening on the stage. But much more worrying to Yolanda was that we were surrounded by working class Catalans. As a good Castilian she utterly despised Catalans; she huffed and puffed and we eventually left. Not just because of her aversion, but we had an early meeting scheduled for the next morning and at the first interval it was already midnight! However I was very pleased to have seen the Opera House. A few years later it was destroyed by fire, but has I believe been restored.

On one occasion in Madrid I attended a two-day international banking conference. Very little of any interest was said with the exception of an excellent speech by Monsieur Jean Gagné of the Banque Nationale de Paris (BNP). What was strange, however, was that his was the only speech given in French and, since he departed from his prepared speech, the simultaneous translators were unable to cope. Only those in the audience who could understand French (and there were not many) actually heard what he said. I was so impressed that I went up to him afterwards and congratulated him and we agreed to meet in Paris at a later date. I also met a couple of intelligent Englishmen at the conference. I am not quite sure what they were doing there, since they were not bankers, but from BP España. The Spanish BP was a much smaller company than BP Portuguesa and, although we met several times for meals, I was never able to sell them our services.

Ken was very keen to host another international symposium on service management and we prepared to hold one in Seville at the Hotel Alfonso XIII. We prepared a brochure, using a sentence I had taken from Jean Gagné's speech as the theme. KIA's office manager and I flew to Seville to make all the arrangements with the hotel. But once again we were unable to get together enough people to make it worth the expense. I do not like hotels like the Alfonso XIII and in Seville much preferred to stay at a small hotel, the Anna Maria, opposite the Giralda, where the only meal they served was breakfast and where the furniture in every bedroom was antique. So much for Spain. After a couple of years we had to close the office.

In France we had only one commission. I had called on Jean Gagné, but his responsibilities had changed and he passed me on to a colleague. Again we came very close to agreeing on a project – so near, that I even arranged to have the services of a young French lawyer, who had been recommended to me by a friend of Jocelyn's. So the only job I had in France was an interesting one for the Crédit Agricole. This was not a process consultancy; the Crédit Agricole wanted a report on the UK mortgage market with an assessment of whether they should get involved. I made a comprehensive survey, the gist of which was that it had become a highly profitable market, but that as a result new competitors were joining it in droves. I suggested that a useful rule of thumb was that, when everyone is piling into a venture, it is time to think very seriously of getting out of it. Besides, I forecast – this was late in 1986 – that the housing market would soon decline and that there would then be a very large volume of bad debts. So I concluded that they should stay out of it. I had the report translated into French – my written French was not good enough – and Tarja and I went to Paris and presented the report to the top management. They took a keen interest in it, but decided not to accept my advice. They entered the UK mortgage market early in 1987, and had about eighteen months of very profitable business. But the housing market collapsed in the late summer of 1988 leaving many householders with what came to be known as 'negative equity'. I suspect that in the long run Crédit Agricole would have been wiser to take my advice.

It would I think be tedious for most readers to hear about every project I worked on, but I will very briefly mention a few which were of particular interest to me. KIA had a particularly good relationship with Baltica, the largest Danish insurance company. We devoted quite a lot of time to helping them with a strategic study. As 'process' consultants we did not just go away, do our research and tell them what we thought they ought to do. We had many meetings with top management making sure that we were on the same lines. For a time a girl from Baltica was attached to me as an assistant and in our researches across Europe I passed her off as a KIA consultant.

We concentrated on three areas, transport, intruder alarms and health care. I prepared reports on all three. This involved a lot of travelling, some in the UK – I visited an intruder alarm factory in South Wales, interviewed the Professor of Transport at the University of Cardiff and talked to the managers of a number of private hospitals – and some in Europe, where I was accompanied by the Danish girl. I cannot remember her name but she was pleasant enough. Her most marked characteristic was that she was enormously greedy; I am greedy enough, but she out-ate me! With the passage of time I will not now rehearse what was in my reports; except to note that in connection with transport I concluded that electronic means of controlling motor access to cities was going to be inevitable. I also remember that when we were considering the problem of security for lone women drivers, we concluded that something like the nowadays common satellite navigation systems would be highly desirable and noted that Baltica already had a stake in a company developing these systems.

In some ways the most interesting part of the project was health care. The public was already obsessed with anxiety about health, and health insurance was clearly going to be a profitable growth area. Baltica became determined to acquire a reputable company in that field; by reputable I do not just mean financially sound, but a company dedicated to serving the customers and not just to exploiting them. The Danish girl and I were in Paris interviewing a number of people when someone mentioned to me what he considered a very good small health insurance company, La Strasbourgeoise. He thought they might be interested in a good offer. I found out the name of the Managing Director, Monsieur Lehmann, and rang him immediately. He said he could see us that very afternoon. We dashed to the Gare de l'Est and took a train to Strasbourg.

Lehmann and I hit it off very well. For some weeks we pursued the subject and I visited Strasbourg several times, accompanied once by Ken Irons. We finally reached the stage when we revealed that we were acting for Baltica and we had a meeting in Strasbourg with Lehmann and a senior director of Baltica, Lars Dalseger. The whole thing seemed to be cut and dried; but in consultancy, the unexpected often seems to occur. At this very moment Baltica itself was taken over by a German company, Allianz, I think it was, and the deal with La Strasbourgeoise fell through. We got our consultancy fees, but missed out on the large commission we would have received if the deal had gone through. Lehmann was, I am afraid, very upset. He thought, and I suspect he was right, that Lars should already have known of the impending take-over.

Another company with whom we did a lot, a hearts and minds project, was SwissRe UK. Nothing went wrong with this one. At the end, the managing Director gave a small lunch for me and Mark Langley. I was amused to find that the wine he served was Chateau Pitray!

Another slightly unusual project was a hearts and minds one for IPPA Bank in Belgium. We had by this time a Brussels office with two Belgians. One of them, a Hungarian émigré by the name of Stefan Sommsich, worked with me on this one. Belgium has become so obsessed with the cleft between the Walloons and the Flemish that we were required after doing a workshop in French to hold another one in Flemish. Here I had to rely on Stefan. All those taking part in the Flemish one would have been equally at home with French, and I remember that some of them even had Walloon names.

The widespread misunderstanding of the nature of a service industry is illustrated by an exchange I had with IPPA's Managing Director, Bogaerts. He asked me if I could help him with a strategic study. We talked it over and I said at one point that any strategy to be successful had to have the support of the staff. He found this impossible to understand: 'I can't tell the staff; I may want to change the strategy after six months!' That's not what I would have called a strategy. What he clearly wanted was an analytical consultant's report and this, on behalf of KIA, I could not deliver.

I have recently come across my pocket diary for 1990 which has revealed the names of many other clients. They included Zurich Insurance (in Portsmouth, as I remember), Sun Alliance, Cornhill, Victory Re and the City University where I lectured in evening classes to MBA students and also the South Bank Poly, where I also lectured.

Two more things to say about my time as a management consultant. I discovered that I have quite a talent for teaching and for some years I ran (initially with Mark Langley and later on my own) three-day courses for KIA on service management at the Belfry Hotel in Milton Common near Oxford; this continued long after I had given up full time work with KIA. I really enjoyed that.

The other thing is to reflect on why it was that KIA never took off to become one of the leading consultants, as I believe it should. A simple answer would be to say that KIA was too idealistic. So many financial institutions were commanded by very down to earth people who did not really care about the customers, so long as they were making profits. A perfect example of this was our very brief dealing with the TSB Trust Company, the life insurance arm of the TSB Bank. One of their younger marketing people had come across Mark Langley, I think it was, and was impressed with KIA's approach to marketing. He somehow managed to persuade his Board to pay for us to spend a day with them in an effort to produce a new Mission Statement – mission statements were, and I believe still are, all the rage. We ended the day without any hint of agreement.

I should explain what the TSB Trust Company's marketing strategy had been. The Trust Company would have a manager in one of the TSB Bank branches and would arrange for one of the cashiers to pick on some customer and tell him that one of their managers, pretending that it was a TSB Bank manager, would like to have a word with them about their finances. In some trepidation the customer would be led into this room, rather expecting to be ticked off for some financial misdemeanour, to find an amiable manager who would strongly recommend that he should take out some life insurance with the TSB Trust Company. They signed up in droves, only too happy not to have been hauled over the coals.

The Trust Company's 'lapse ratio' in the first two years of a policy was around 30 per cent, that is to say that within two years a third of the policy holders had recognised that it had been a mistake to take out the policy and that they could not really afford it. Even worse, by cancelling a policy within such a short time they got absolutely nothing out of it. For two years they had been throwing their money down the drain. But it was highly profitable. The young marketing man believed that this could not go on without even higher lapse ratios, resulting in the Trust Company getting a very bad reputation – for what today would be called mis-selling. But the Board were perfectly happy for it to continue. And, regrettably, many customers are not articulate enough, or even intelligent enough, to see through this and the Trust Company continued to 'mis-sell' and make hefty profits for many more years.

It is not only insurance companies that have shown a cynical disregard for the real needs of their clients in search of ever higher fees. The Merchant Banks and big accountancy firms have been as guilty as any. I was very impressed, some years ago now, to read the obituary of Daniel Meinertz-hagen, former Executive Chairman of Lazards. Meinertzhagen was said always to have considered the client company's real needs when approached about managing a take-over for them. If he considered that it was not in their best interests, he would say so, even if it risked Lazards losing the contract and the fee of several million pounds. This would not happen today, I fear.

Quite how it came about I cannot remember, but at one stage I spent a day running a course for bright young managers in the accountancy firm which was then called Ernst and Young. I suggested that they needed, when considering their strategic plans, to have a hard look at possible conflicts of interest where their auditing fees were concerned. It seemed to me to be very dangerous to rely heavily on fees for auditing from clients with whom they were also involved as straightforward accountants. The young men found this difficult to accept, partly, of course, because it is very difficult to see how exactly the problem could be solved; a company wholly devoted to auditing would probably not be able to make the sort of profits the large accountancy firms were in the habit of making and would not therefore be able to attract high calibre staff.

Another reason for the lack of interest in customers, I believe, is the result of the McKinsey approach and that of most business schools today. They tend to put heavy emphasis on management techniques and procedures and nowhere near enough on the real substance of the business. This was beautifully illustrated by our experience with the Midland Bank. At one time I had real hopes that we would land a major project with them. Their Deputy Chief Executive was Brian Goldthorpe, who had been a regular attendant at my seminars when I was in the Bank of England. Brian became very enthusiastic about the KIA approach to service management. At a meeting I had with him in the Midland Bank's Head Office he said to his senior loans manager, 'We really must do something on the lines that Guy suggests.' We had a number of meetings with senior managers of the bank and made an elaborate presentation to a group of them. But with the exception of Brian Goldthorpe, they were not very receptive.

Our main obstacle was the marketing Manager, Kevin Gavaghan. He had come to the bank from Marks & Spencers and was quite sure that banking should be sold just like any retailing of consumer products. The rest of the managers found it hard to resist his views and they were mostly inclined to believe that the days of the bank manager were over and that credit risks could be adequately covered by junior staff using credit rating forms.

Any hopes we had of persuading them to use us disappeared when Kit McMahon was appointed the new Chief Executive. Kit swallowed Kevin Gavaghan's view, hook, line and sinker. They introduced a series of brand name accounts with names such as 'Orchard' and, I think, 'Meadow' with separate cheque books with glossy pictures; none of which I think had any real significance for the customers. The differences between us were well illustrated in a couple of articles. Kit wrote one for one of the broadsheets in which he came near to saying that banks were in the business of selling money. This is, of course, nonsense. Customers look to their banks to provide them with means of making payments, to help them manage their finances, to provide effective means of savings and investments and to borrow money for houses or whatever. The money they borrow is not the bank's; it is provided by other customers' deposits. Gordon Brown, the Chancellor, makes the same mistake in thinking that the money he distributes is the Government's.

The other article was by me. It was, I think, the best article I ever wrote; it was published in the *Journal of the Society for Long Range Planning* and was entitled 'Banking is not like selling toothpaste'. Kit's article could well have been entitled 'Banking *is* like selling toothpaste'. I believe the Midland Bank could have continued as a successful commercial bank had it not been for Kit McMahon. Although I sent him a copy of my article, he did not respond.

The failure of KIA to take off may also have been to do with Ken Irons himself. I never had any difficulty working with him, but the other consultants felt that he was reluctant to delegate as much responsibility as they thought they should have. I was already in my sixties and my life and career did not depend on my continuing with KIA. So I took as much responsibility as I felt was needed, even at the risk of annoying Ken. In the event I do not remember ever having any difficulties. Somewhere around 1988 Ken seriously considered appointing a Managing Director, whilst he would continue as Chairman. That might well have worked. But the Managing Director designate, one of our best consultants, Lyn Mailey, did not feel that he was really ready to let go enough for her to feel in charge. Lyn had come to us after having been a client on a small job we did for Granada. She eventually left KIA and set up a consultancy on her own, with a turnover now greater than KIA ever achieved.

CHAPTER 26

Holidays in the 80s

B Y THE END OF THE EIGHTIES I was earning around £60,000 a year from KIA which, on top of my Bank of England pension and income from investments, left me feeling fairly well off so we could afford to have some very nice holidays. But where we went in 1986 I don't know – one of the rare occasions when my chronological mind has not worked. I have no diary for that year and there are no photographs in the albums. We must just have stayed at home. After all, most people would think it a wonderful spot for a holiday; one of the prettiest houses in Suffolk, if not the prettiest, a lovely garden, within ten minutes of the beach and near Framlingham and Orford, not to mention Aldeburgh and concerts at the Maltings.

In 1987 we had no fewer than three holidays. Crispin has for years been in the habit of taking a holiday in January/February, the quietest months of the year for a bloodstock agent. That year he and Caroline, as yet reluctant to marry (to our regret), took a house in a small village called Peygarolles in south-west France and invited us to join them. We flew to Montpellier and hired a car. Peygarolles was in the mountains. For their first few days they had been snowed in. It was still very cold when we got there, but the snow had gone. We spent a lovely week with them. We did a lot of sightseeing and had a memorable lunch in a restaurant which was in a cave up in the mountains. The cave was bitterly cold, but luckily they had a blazing log fire. Daphne and I went off alone for a couple of days, driving along the Riviera. By this time it was February and the mimosa was already in bloom down on the coast. We did a little desultory house hunting at Bandol, between Marseilles and Toulon, where my parents had spent part of their honeymoon in 1921. We saw a couple of very attractive houses on a promontory overlooking the sea, but did not pursue it very far. We drove through Nice and I wondered what thoughts, if any, Daphne had about Micha Battsek. Was she perhaps wondering if she would see him in the street? Who knows.

In the summer we went on an opera tour in Italy. Tours are not really my thing; I find the seating in a coach very uncomfortable – not enough room for my long legs – and I miss the freedom to go wherever one wants at the time of one's choosing. Nevertheless it was a very good holiday. We drove from Bologna to Belluno in the foothills of the Dolomites. Belluno is a most attractive town but really rather far from Verona, to which we went each night to see an opera in the famous Arena. One night one of the party was missing after the performance and we had to hang around for ages till she was found. We did not get back to our hotel in Belluno until after

323

In the dining room at Buxlow – Christmas 1986

midnight. On the first night we saw *Madama Butterfly* – too intimate an opera for the vast Arena – but then we saw *Aida*, for which the Arena was splendid – a vast crowd of the chorus and animals. Were there camels? I think so. We skipped the middle of the three nights – too tiring. Our next opera call was at Macerata, not far from Ancona. But on the way we visited a Palladian mansion in the Veneto and spent a day in Venice. One day is not very long to stay in Venice, but it was enough to give one a real feel for it. At Macerata there is an unusual oval grassy arena, the Sferisterio. Here we saw *Manon* by Massenet. In one of the boxes overlooking the arena sat a former diva, Renata Tebaldi; the knowledgeable Italian audience gave her more of an ovation than the singers that night. She acknowledged their plaudits like a Queen!

Our final opera call was at Torre del Lago Puccini, where there is an open air theatre on the shores of the lake. On our way, though, we visited Assisi. The terrible earthquake had not yet damaged the basilica. It was very fine, but I find the Catholic atmosphere rather stifling (all a bit commercial). We also spent a day in Florence (another desperately short visit, but again time to see the statue of David, visit the Uffizi and have a lunch by ourselves up the hill in Fiesole overlooking the city). For the Puccini leg of our tour we stayed in a hotel in Lucca. At Torre del Lago we saw *Turandot* and *La Bohème*. On our way to the theatre from Lucca we had to cross the lake in a boat. The propeller got jammed with weeds and we had to be towed to the other side! There was far too much coach driving in this tour and we could well have done with only two centres; three was rather overdoing it. But all in all it was a lovely holiday.

In October there was the famous 'hurricane'. One Thursday afternoon I flew back from Munich where I had spent a few days on the Baltica strategic project. I arrived at Heathrow and picked up my car. It was pouring with rain and I set off for Buxlow. It was after dark and I remember listening to the shipping forecast on the radio. I suddenly realised that for every single shipping area, after giving the barometric pressure, they said 'and falling'. I wonder if that happens very often; it seemed to betoken some very serious weather. By the time I got home there was quite a wind blowing, but not yet a gale, let alone a hurricane.

Because I was so tired after a week on the Continent I slept alone in the small Peacock room. I slept soundly throughout the night, but Daphne had been disturbed by the noise of the hurricane. When she came in to see me early in the morning, I looked out of the window and saw the catalpa being blown almost flat. The garden took surprisingly little damage; but more importantly a large branch of one of the horse chestnuts by the drive crashed down, bringing with it the telephone and power lines. The pressure on the electricity companies was so great that we had to wait eight days before power was restored – by a team from Scotland; the hurricane had concentrated its efforts on Kent, Sussex and Suffolk. The damage outside the garden was considerable; great swathes of Tunstall Forest were flattened. The fallen trees were so mangled that they could not be used commercially and for some months the fallen debris was bulldozed into long barrows. They can still be seen sixteen years later among the new plantations. Archaeologists will be very puzzled at the burial practices of twentieth century England!

On the Friday we managed to buy the last small paraffin stove from Wells & Sons in Saxmundham, on which we had to do all our cooking. We warmed ourselves with wood fires and hot water bottles and lit ourselves with candles. We had no idea at the time that we were going to have to wait so long for power to be restored. And rather selfishly, I went back to Canonbury on the Monday. Without a telephone I could not even speak to Daphne – it was to be another ten years before I acquired a mobile phone.

In November Amicia came to have dinner with me and the boys in the flat in Canonbury Square. It turned out to be the night of the terrible tragedy at Moorgate tube station. Amicia had wondered why her train had gone through Moorgate without stopping; it was probably the last train to be allowed through. The dinner was a kind of farewell. Amicia had decided to go and work in New York. She had for some time been a Features Editor of *World of Interiors* and wanted to try something new. Having dual nationality and an American passport she would have no problem in working in the States. She got an introduction to Anna Wintour and was invited to join her at the magazine known as *HG* (previously *House & Garden*). Amicia left in November – I was about to say 'sailed', but of course nobody now went to America by sea! Anna Wintour moved on to be Editor of American *Vogue*, and Amicia stayed on at *HG* for a while, but then went on to *Vogue*. Amicia did very well in New York, but was never really happy. She is quintessentially English and was homesick. She finally returned to England in the summer of 1990.

For our last holiday in 1987 we went to Malta. My previous one day visit to Malta in 1946 had given me no idea of what it was like. I knew of it primarily as a British naval base and knew of its fame during the war having survived under heavy bombing by the Germans. We were lucky, I think, to stay in a very old-fashioned hotel, the Phoenicia, just outside the walls of old Valetta. I am told that it was closed very soon after we stayed there. I am not sure that it has been modernised, more likely pulled down. Happily we avoided the main area of hotels, all of the Holiday Inn type, to the west of Valetta at Sliema. The British, no longer the colonial power, were nevertheless very welcomed. This was after the departure of Dom Mintoff.

Whilst we were there a British warship called for the first time since the naval base had closed. When the frigate, HMS *Brazen*, sailed into Grand Harbour, the battlements were lined with crowds waving their welcome. The loss of the naval base must have meant the loss of many jobs. We loved Malta. Valetta is full of interesting things, and Grand Harbour is a splendid sight. Towns with names like Rabat and Mdina reminding one that Malta is only just off the North African shore; it is indeed located south of Tunis, Algiers and Tangier. We hired a car and drove all round the Island, and even visited the Island of Gozo.

Looking at our photograph albums I am amazed to find that we had no fewer than four holidays in 1988. The first one, in February/March, was a week in Madeira, followed by a few days in Lisbon. Manuela Martins, the Portuguese girl who was helping me on the BP Portuguesa project, did all the booking for me. We wanted to stay at the famous Read's Hotel, but for that you had to book months ahead; so we stayed instead at the Hotel Savoy in Funchal. Our room did not look out to sea, but was just as interesting, looking up into the hills and in the centre of the view a most attractive white and black chapel.

One of the most memorable things about Madeira is the hair-raising experience of flying in. The runway is so short that at least one plane has been known to have gone over the cliffs at the end! It was a surprise to me to discover that there was snow on the ground on the peak of the central mountains; whilst down in Funchal we spent a great deal of time by the swimming pool. I remember telephoning Amicia in New York on her birthday from a pool side phone. The vegetation at sea level in February was tropical. The Botanical Gardens were full of exotic flowers. Somewhat higher up the hill side were the gardens of the Blandy family (one of the Madeira wine families). Here there was an avenue of camellias; the blossom was just fading and the whole avenue, perhaps a hundred yards long, was carpeted in pink petals.

We then flew to Lisbon and stayed at the Tivoli in my preferred room overlooking the garden and the Botanical Gardens. We both enjoyed a few days in Portugal. As was Daphne's wont, whenever visiting a new place we took a tourist bus around Lisbon. Daphne thought I was being very dismissive and eager to finish the bus tour; I was in a hurry, but not in the slightest dismissive – it was just that I did not want to be late for an appointment I had with BP. We also spent a couple of nights in a hotel in Sintra. Unfortunately, we stayed in a rather nondescript hotel. The best hotel, the Sete Ais (meaning Seven Sighs – where Wellington signed a treaty with the French early in the Peninsular War, which nearly cost him his reputation) was fully booked.

Our second holiday in 1988 was a brief stay in a Landmark Trust property, the Water Tower at Sandringham in Norfolk. We had visited Sandringham before on an outing with the Friends of the Historic Houses Association. In our photograph album Daphne has captioned it as 'the Huns' hunting lodge!' I found the garden more interesting than the house. I remember being thrilled to see stinging nettles in one of the flower beds; it made me feel better about my weeding at Buxlow! From the Water Tower we explored the North Norfolk coast, which I had not visited since 1935.

Our third holiday was in Portugal again. This time we took rooms in a small palace, Paço da Gloria, that had belonged to Lord Clark (Kenneth Clark of *Civilisation* fame) and then to his younger son, Colin, who had only just sold it to a Portuguese. Paço da Gloria is in the northern province of Minho (pronounced min-you). It was very grand, on a modest scale, if you see what I mean. There was a pond which was used as a swimming pool. There were lots of fig trees; nobody seemed to want to eat the figs, and as I walked around the garden I would pluck them and eat them as I walked. Senhor Macedo did not provide meals, which Colin Clark had done, so we had to find little country inns for lunch and dinner. We did some sight seeing, visiting Braga and, on the coast, Viana de Castelo.

Not far from Paço da Gloria we found an enchanting abandoned house in the midst of a cork oak forest. There was a drive leading up to the house and attached to it a pretty little chapel. We became so enthused that we made enquiries about the possibility of buying it. Macedo told us that it was quite impossible. The house had been left to members of a family who were carrying on some court case to establish title and this could well take years to settle; in the meantime it was abandoned. It was of course a silly fancy. It was in a remote situation, several hours drive from Oporto and it would have been very difficult for anybody to visit.

Our final holiday of 1988 was a visit to the Lake District in the autumn. Daphne had been to the Lake District as a child and had been longing to go back again. We spent our first night at a luxurious hotel near Chester, the Rookery. It was quite an experience; a half bottle of champagne on the table in your room to greet you, with a large bowl of fresh fruit. In the bathroom there were two voluminous bathrobes to snuggle into. Dinner was almost obscene – six courses, I think, with at least two of them consisting of sorbets to help you recover from what had gone before and to prepare for what was to come.

Starting at Lake Windermere we criss-crossed the Lake District. It was blessedly uncrowded and the weather was fine. We stayed mostly in good B & Bs, but we also indulged ourselves in a stay at the Sharrow Bay Hotel on Ullswater. Like the Rookery this was a tribute to gluttony – every meal enormous. This was the first time I had ever come across sticky toffee pudding. With Daphne's interest in poetry we visited Wordsworth's home at Dove Cottage; memorable to me for a beautiful autumn-coloured maple in the garden. Our final port of call was at Cartmel at the southern tip of the Lake District. It has the smallest race course in England, but it is now equally well known for the Cartmel Village Shop which supplies its own sticky toffee pudding to farm shops around the country!

Late in 1988 the Friends of the Aldeburgh Foundation announced a visit to Hungary in early 1989. We were a bit late in putting in for it and found that all the places had been taken. I got on to Virginia Caldwell and asked whether she could not somehow fit us in. It turned out that there were many more frustrated travellers and the Foundation agreed to double the places available. So in March 1989 we and some fifty others set off for Budapest. In Hungary we travelled in two coaches, one accompanied by Virginia and the other, ours, by the Foundation's accountant. We stayed in the Forum Hotel on the Pest side of the Danube overlooking the Chain bridge. It was an altogether delightful holiday.

Budapest is a splendid city, although almost totally rebuilt after being destroyed in the War. We went to numerous concerts, one of the most memorable of which was the Kodaly Te Deum in the church of St. Matthias on the Buda side of the river; another was a performance of *Parsifal* in the elaborately restored Opera House; we did not have very good seats to begin with, but when the performance had only just begun, a group of German visitors walked out in protest at the opera being sung in Hungarian(!), so we quickly moved to better seats. *Parsifal* is not one of the most favoured of Wagner's operas among Wagnerians, but I myself prefer it to most of the others, besides it has the merit of not being desperately long!

Most of these concerts we attended with the rest of the Aldeburgh group, but Daphne and I went on our own to a performance of *The Magic Flute* (in German!) at the Opera House. We had found a couple of spare tickets from the porter's desk in the hotel. Our seats were in the front row, just behind the conductor. I have the bad habit usually of singing along with operas, particularly the bass parts; in this case Sarastro's arias. The conductor was not a bit put out; indeed he didn't hear me, because he too was humming along!

We went on several trips into the countryside, including quite a long drive across the great Hungarian Plain to Kecskemet, the home of Kodaly. I suppose the Plain must be like the American prairies, but the little huddles of farm buildings, isolated from the road, were most un-American, no red barns but rather shabby groups of farm buildings.

Another striking feature of our time there was the almost palpable feeling that Communism was on its last legs. On one of our coach trips, the Hungarian girl who accompanied us as interpreter and guide was laughing at something the driver had said. When we asked what it was about she said the driver had just told a favourite joke: 'The Russians are very stupid; they have been here for over thirty years and they still can't find their way out!' Before the year was out, of course, the Berlin Wall was down and the communist government of Hungary fell.

In the summer of 1989 Daphne and I did some serious house hunting in Normandy. House values in England had shot up – though they were not as high in 1989 as they had been a year earlier – and, with a strong pound, house prices in Normandy were very attractive. It was possible to buy a nice chateau for around £300,000. We had got Savilles to visit Buxlow and they said we should be able to sell it for at least £800,000; and if we had sold the year before it could well have made £1 million. So a move would have been financially very attractive. We had no particular reason for picking on Normandy other than that communications were very good. There were then flights to England from Caen, Deauville and Le Havre. Besides, I was by this time spending remarkably few nights in Canonbury and my work with KIA seemed to be heavily concentrated on the Continent. Neither of the boys was yet established in France and indeed there was no indication that they might ever be. Although, as I write this, I see on the floor near my desk a copy of the Deauville Bloodstock catalogue for 1987 so Jocelyn at least was obviously visiting Normandy from time to time.

We contacted all the British Estate Agencies who specialised in property in Normandy and started on a tour of chateaux. We confined our search to Lower Normandy, all to the south of a line between Caen and Honfleur; we left out the Cotentin, even though the ancestral home of the Moubrays was at Montbray near St. Lô. Nor did we look in the area near Dieppe. We chateau hunted for a week or two but to no avail. Although some of them were very attractive on the outside, particularly one immediately to the south of Caen and another well to the south, barely in Normandy at all. They were all decorated in abysmal taste; many of them only had a bathroom on the ground floor and it was clear that whatever we bought we would have to spend a lot of time and a lot of money doing it up. So we bought nothing.

I did make one more visit in November. After completing a job for KIA in Paris, I took a train to Caen, spent a night in a hotel and met the estate agent the next morning and we visited a very attractive chateau at a place called St. Georges. This was on 1 November – All Saints Day – and at every cemetery whole families were out visiting the tombs of their relatives. But once again, the amount of work which would need to have been done was impossibly great. I said goodbye to the estate agent and went off by car in the pouring rain to visit Montbray, which was only about an hour's drive away. It is not a particularly nice village – the remains of the old chateau, a church, a *boulangerie* and not much else. It was nevertheless a strange feeling to know that 30 generations back there had been Moubrays there.

So we come to 1990. Although we had not bought anything in Normandy it was already clear that to keep on the flat in Canonbury was an expensive option; we were still paying interest to Coutts at 16.5 per cent and I was frequently spending only one night a week there. So we decided to put it on the market. If I needed to stay in London, it would be more sensible to stay in a hotel near Swiss Cottage. On 15 March I had a streaming cold and was writing some report in a small meeting room at the top of the KIA offices in Park Way when two of the girls appeared with food from Marks & Spencers. I looked puzzled, and they reminded me that it was my 65th birthday and said that all the staff of KIA were on their way up to have lunch with me. Ken and Annie presented me with a wonderful birthday present, a bottle of 1924 vintage port! They told me that their enquiries had revealed that 1925 had been a bad year for port, hence the date of 1924, and, as they said, I had been conceived in that year. We did not, of course, drink it then and there. I and the family consumed it over the Christmas holidays at the end of the year. It was quite delicious.

1990 was a significant year in Daphne's life and mine. I will return to it a bit later. In the meantime, I propose to leave the chronological approach and devote a chapter to what religion has meant and means to me.

CHAPTER 27

Religion

M Y FAMILY AND MY FRIENDS all know that I am Swedenborgian, but I don't think they really know what this means to me and I feel I should try and make it clear. Swedenborg's doctrines are quite unique amongst Christian churches.

I was brought up in the New Church (Swedenborgian) and all my life Swedenborg's doctrines have been at the basis of all my thinking, not just about the Divine, but also about politics, economics, science, ethics and personal relations. As I shall explain a bit later, those who accept Swedenborg's doctrines find themselves in a completely different mind set from all non-Swedenborgians. But I have to say that for most of my life I was not a religious man. Swedenborg's ideas were in my head, but not in my heart. Nevertheless I tried, particularly in my work, always to do what I thought was right and not to be swayed by personal advantage, but in other areas of my life I succumbed to temptation. In the *Short Treatise on the Ten Commandments*, which I wrote in 2002, I said:

> Man's nature is so corrupt that it is virtually impossible not to break some of the commandments some of the time. Few, if any, achieve perfection and become truly regenerate in this life. But that is no reason for not trying, with God's help, to do so. The least that the Lord asks of us is to make some progress in this life in overcoming our hereditary evil. We are not born equal in this respect; some have more hereditary evil than others. What is required of us all is at least to have made some progress in this life in reducing our debit balance. Even those whose debit balance is substantial can be saved, provided they go some way to reducing the debit balance they were born with.

Until recently I have not been religious in the other sense, of attending services in church. In America in the 1950s in Washington DC we went to the New Church every Sunday, but thereafter I went very rarely until we arrived at Buxlow. For the first few years we went fairly regularly to the Knodishall parish church, which, in those days, had a very small congregation. After John Downer, the vicar, left we ceased to go to church and only started again when Christine Brooks, the present vicar, arrived. Under her guidance the church now has a good congregation every Sunday.

I started reading Swedenborg again about twenty years ago and his ideas became steadily more important to me. Although I think Christine is a first class pastor, being myself distinctly more Swedenborgian, I now find some of the Anglican liturgy rather more jarring than I ever did with John

Emanuel Swedenborg 1688–1772

Downer. Since Daphne's death I have begun attending the New Church in Brightlingsea in Essex about once a month – 55 miles there and 55 miles back! Luckily the service does not start until 11 o'clock. When Daphne was ill, I could not have taken her, or been away from home for over three hours. I have said that Swedenborg's doctrines are unique amongst Christian churches so I was rather taken aback at a recent sermon in Brightlingsea when the minister said: 'We do not have a monopoly of the truth; we can learn from the truths of other faiths.' Whilst I am tolerant of all other faiths (except possibly militant Islam) I don't feel I have anything to learn from them. I was delighted to see a few days later an article: 'Unique, we are' in *Lifeline* (The journal of the General Conference of the New Church) – in which the author said:

> . . . one may ask in what respect is the New Church different from the church up the road? Are its members more devout and holy than the members of other churches? Are they necessarily more likely to go to heaven? A chosen people, perhaps? Of course not! But their New Church has one different feature – a feature shared by no other church. And that feature is its Doctrine.

This is a word greeted with distaste in certain quarters, being unfortunately confused with dogma, in its meaning of opinion arrogantly laid down by authority. But Doctrine, in itself, means teaching, means that which is taught. And what is taught by the New Church is so simple, and at the same time so deep and so wonderful, that it is the most precious anyone can have – a pearl of great price. We should renew our confidence in the teaching of the New Church.

The New Church approach is radically different from most other doctrines in that it is what I would call topdown rather than bottom-up. This is well illustrated in a phrase from A.N. Wilson's book *Jesus*, in which he says:

> As Paul said, 'If any man be in Christ, he is a new creature; old things are passed away.' How quickly, though, the believer comes to dislike bobbing about in the sea of faith, and wishes to swim back for his life-belt of plausible historical reassurance. How quickly he believes not out of faith, not from a position of unseeing, but because he imagines himself in that scene with Doubting Thomas, and tries to persuade himself that it is a narrative such as a contemporary observer might have written about the Battle of Jutland.

Andrew Wilson seems to me to describe himself in that passage. I do not find myself 'disliking bobbing about in the sea of faith', nor I believe would any member of the New Church. It doesn't really matter to me whether every story about Jesus in the gospels is historically accurate. I am told, for example, that there is no historical evidence of a census in Judaea at the time of Jesus' birth. To me every word of the Bible is inspired and has an inner spiritual meaning which is much more important than the literal sense. As we read in Jeremiah (1:7–9): 'The Lord said . . . whatsoever I command thee thou shalt speak. . . . Then the Lord put forth his hand, and touched my mouth. And the Lord said unto me, Behold, I have put my words in thy mouth.' Swedenborg incidentally tells us that the only books in the New Testament that do not have an inner meaning are the Epistles and the Acts of the Apostles.

The difference between the New Church approach and the bottom up approach is also illustrated in the following extract from John Howard Spalding's book, *An Introduction to Swedenborg's Metaphysics*:

> The teachings of Swedenborg . . . are a logical, coherent effort to reverse the order which the mind, if left to itself, is disposed to follow in thinking on Divine and spiritual subjects, which is, to bring them to the bar of human reason, and there, and by its canons, to judge them. If these teachings are accepted, they must gradually, almost imperceptibly, perhaps, effect a revolution in men's thoughts about everything Divine and human, and even about physical things regarded from the ontological point of view, as complete as as that wrought by the discovery by Copernicus of the centrality of the sun in the solar system, and of the whole starry universe beyond it. . . . The revolution which he effects is a silent and unperceived one. . . . It is only when we look back and see where we were, and where we are, that we perceive that we have come into a world in which all things are new, even the most familiar.

I quote this at some length because it seems to me to sum up very clearly what I feel and is much better expressed than I could manage. Most Christian theologians (not that I have read that many!) and commentators on the Bible seem to try to bring everything to the bar of human reason. I am reminded of a sentence by Thomas Carlyle in his *Critical and Miscellaneous Essays*: 'Should Understanding attempt to prove the existence of God, it ends, if thoroughgoing and consistent with itself, in Atheism, or a faint possible Theism, which scarcely differs from this. . . .'

So, what is this topdown approach of Swedenborg's? Swedenborg (1688–1772) was an eminent scientist and practical administrator, a member of the Swedish 'Board of Mines' and a member of the House of Nobles. He wrote a number of scientific books, *Principia* and volumes on *Iron, Copper* and the *Brain*. In middle age he taught himself Hebrew and studied the Old Testament in great detail. At about the same time he became aware of meaningful dreams and began to have psychic experiences. He found himself in a state of unusual spiritual awareness, which he claimed was of Divine permission. For over twenty years he claimed that whilst in a waking condition, he was allowed to have almost constant intercourse with spirits, angels and evil spirits. This permitted him to experience in great detail 'life after death'. He also had revealed to him the inner spiritual meaning of the Bible. As a result of these experiences he wrote a number of theological works, the first of which, *Arcana Caelestia*, explained the inner meaning of every verse of the books of Genesis and Exodus. He also described the next world in the book *Heaven and Hell*.

To accept Swedenborg's doctrines you have to believe that Swedenborg was truly an instrument of Divine Revelation. This could be an insurmountable stumbling block for many. I have no difficulty with it, partly perhaps, because I was born into the New Church. But someone like John Howard Spalding, who initially thought that Swedenborg's claims were nonsense, came to believe them. If they were not true, one would have to think that Swedenborg was either mad or schizophrenic. The accounts of his contemporaries show him to have been a perfectly normal man, more intelligent than most, but still normal. Another reason for believing him, so far as I am concerned, is that the doctrines he derives from these experiences make so much sense and are so extraordinarily consistent throughout all his works. Some may say that one should not expect religious doctrine to 'make sense'. All religion, they would say, must be a mystery. It would be quite wrong to try and understand the infinite. One of my sons once said to me that he found it hard to accept Swedenborg 'because he has an answer for everything'. I don't think that is in fact quite true, but I firmly believe that, although there must always be some mystery about the Divine, it is helpful to us in our task of regeneration to have some understanding of the Divine.

This is in marked contrast to someone like Andrew Wilson; in his *Jesus*, for example, he says:

A patient and conscientious reading of the Gospels will always destroy any explanation which we devise. *If it makes sense, it is wrong.* That is the only reliable rule-of-thumb which we can use when testing the innumerable interpretations of Jesus's being and his place in human history.

Swedenborg's doctrines help us to understand a number of issues that trouble many Christians. What can we expect after death? Just who was Jesus? and why did he come into the world? Can we really understand the Trinity? What is the Last Judgement? and when will it be? On all these points the New Church doctrines give plausible explanations that I never hear when I attend an Anglican church (I have been to a Catholic church only about twice in my life and make no claim to understanding their doctrines).

Swedenborg tells us that human beings are spirits clothed in a material body, and that when we die we shed our body as a snake does its skin and awake in the next world with a substantial (but spiritual) body; that is we can see, speak, touch, hear and taste. We are recognisably who we were before we died. Many when they awake in the next world, Swedenborg tells us, don't even realise to begin with that they are no longer in this world. We all eventually become either angels or devils. Angels are not a separate order of creation; they were all at one time in this world. The same is true of devils. To be good we have to be useful. So, in the next world we all have jobs, helping other angels or spirits and also attending on humans in this world. There really are guardian angels. Equally important we are also accompanied throughout our earthly lives with devils. The use they perform is to tempt us; we can only be good by recognising evil and desisting from it. The Lord's Kingdom is a kingdom of uses. This has an important bearing on the questions about who Jesus was and why he came into the world.

Before leaving the subject of the life after death, I have to ask whether it is so different from what other Christians believe. I think the average layman who attends a Christian church believes that his loved ones who have died are already 'somewhere' awaiting him. But this is not true of all the clergy. I have recently been reading a book, *The God of Hope and the End of the World* by the Revd. Sir John Polkinghorne, a leading Anglican theologian/scientist. Polkinghorne as a Christian tries desperately to find some way of contemplating a life after death, even though as a scientist, I think, he finds it hard to deny that when the body dies, we die. His solution is to take the example of the resurrection of Jesus (which he does believe), combine it with the scientists' conviction that this universe will ultimately collapse, and Isaiah's promise of a new creation, and postulate a new creation after the end of the universe in which we shall all once again be re-embodied, but on a different discontinuous level. And we may have to wait billions of years for this to happen. Not having read Swedenborg, he cannot say anything about what it will be like in the next world which to my mind has any credibility. He says; 'Even the man who said that when he went to heaven he would play golf every day, might sicken of the game after a few thousand years. Even less attractive is the caricature notion of sitting on a cloud, eternally strumming a harp.' How right. But what does he put in its place? 'What awaits us is the unending exploration of the inexhaustible riches of God, a pilgrim journey into deepest reality that will always be thrilling and life enhancing.' This seems to me to be an almost meaningless sentence. For my part I confidently expect a heaven with houses, gardens, trees, flowers and rivers, in which I shall for ever be married to Daphne and in which I shall grow in wisdom and the capacity to love in the course of, and this is most important, doing a useful job. Perhaps I shall be a teacher, for which I think I have some aptitude (newcomers from this world who do not know about Jesus or who have muddled views will need teaching). A quite different, Roman Catholic, view was expressed by Cardinal Cormac Murphy-O'Connor in the *Spectator* Christmas Issue 2003:

> In all of our lives we have constantly to choose between right and wrong, good and evil, this road or that road – heaven or hell. As we get older we are bound to realise more and more clearly that we cannot have it both ways. The consequences of not making the clear moral choice are cumulative and deleterious, just as the consequences of making sound moral choices are cumulative and virtuous. Yes, there is heaven and hell, and we all face judgement *at the time of our death* [my italics].

Many people today find it inconceivable that there could be a hell. Surely, they say, it can never be too late to be redeemed. God's offer of mercy and forgiveness is not, they think, withdrawn at death. Interestingly, however, an Anglican theologian like Polkinghorne also seems to believe in hell. He says that 'The Johannine concept of judgement is not that of a divine rejection but of a human self-exposure. In the face of reality ("the light"), we reveal by our actions who we really are.' He also rightly, I believe, says: 'We must ask the question of whether, in the end, the resistance of even the most stubborn and contemptuous of sinners will melt in the fire of God's love, or whether there will be those who resist God for ever. In the latter case, those who make an enduring decision against God have condemned themselves to hell.'

Most Christians believe that God sacrificed his only son to atone for the wickedness of mankind. This postulates an angry God who has to be appeased. I find it extraordinary that so many seem to be able to believe this. We are all appalled at human sacrifice and shrink with horror from the practices of the Aztecs. To me it is unthinkable that a God who is all mercy should ever contemplate such a sacrifice. We know too that Jehovah tested Abraham by telling him to sacrifice his son Isaac, but we also know that he eventually prevented him from doing so.

Swedenborg gives a quite different explanation of why Jesus came into the world. Alone among all God's creatures, man has been endowed with free will, the ability to reflect on his thoughts and feelings and to make choices between good and evil. God ensured that man would always be held in equilibrium between the powers of hell and of heaven – such an equilibrium is in fact a definition of free will. God knew that man's initial innocence would eventually be perverted and that, in consequence, the powers of hell would in time come to threaten that equilibrium. He knew from the very beginning that at that point he would have to come into the world and ensure that that equilibrium was maintained for ever. The only way that the powers of hell could be so restrained was for the Divine to take on human nature and human heredity and overcome every temptation that He experienced.

Jehovah cannot be tempted. God is nothing but good. There is a very significant passage in Paul's Epistle to the Hebrews (last verse of Chapter 2): 'For in that he himself hath suffered being tempted, he is able to succour them that are tempted.' So in order to take on the human, Jehovah impregnated Mary, and Jesus was conceived and born. Swedenborg tells us (*Arcana Caelestia* para 1999):

> The Lord's Internal was Jehovah Himself, since he was conceived from Jehovah, who cannot be divided or become the relative of another like a son who has been conceived from a human father. For unlike the human, the Divine is not capable of being divided but is and remains one and the same. To this Internal the Lord united the Human Essence. Moreover because the Lord's Internal was Jehovah it was not, like man's internal, a recipient of life, but life itself. Through that union His Human Essence as well became life itself. Hence the Lord's frequent declaration that He is Life, as in John: 'For as the father has life in Himself, so he has granted the Son also to have life in Himself' – John 5:26.

So for the New Church, the Trinity is not a trinity of three persons as in the Nicene Creed. The first lines of the New Church creed are: '*I believe there is one God, in whom is the Divine Trinity, and He is the Lord and Saviour, Jesus Christ.*' Jehovah is the soul, the risen Christ is the body (by whom we can know God) and the Divine Proceeding is the Holy Spirit. I have told Christine Brooks, our Anglican vicar, that there is one Sunday in the year when I try and avoid going to her church, and that is Trinity Sunday. I find the Anglican view of the Trinity muddled and rather distressing. It is neatly summed up in the Anglican liturgy, with prayers that are addressed to 'Father Almighty and your only Son, Jesus Christ, who lives and reigns with you in the unity of the Holy Spirit, one God.' This just does not make sense to me. How can three *persons* be one God? It seems to me as if what they are really saying is something like this: 'There are three Gods, but we set great store on being monotheists, so we will say that these three are one God.' Swedenborg was convinced that all facts of every kind may be rationally understood, and that the thing that is not, in some measure, rationally understood is not really believed, however loudly and even sincerely it may be professed.

Another important difference concerns the Last Judgement. Many Christians seem to believe that Christ will come again when the world comes to an end, and that he will appear riding on the clouds in glory. It is at that point, which may be aeons away, that there will be a Last Judgement and that God's Kingdom will be established. Almost none of these Christians believe that the account of creation in Genesis should be taken literally, but, in contrast, they mostly seem to be prepared to take literally Matthew's description of the sun being darkened and the stars falling from the sky.

Swedenborg says that we are all judged at the time of our death, but tells us that there was a Last Judgement, when Jesus rose from the dead. Jesus came into the world at a time when the powers of hell had become so great that devils had taken possession of the lower reaches of heaven. A touch from Swedenborg which I find very appealing is that Christ, presumably on Easter Saturday, actually did 'descend into hell' (as in the Apostles' Creed), freed the good spirits who had been captives 'in the pit' (frequently mentioned in the Old Testament) and sent the devils packing. There was then a Last Judgement.

Jesus coming 'in the clouds' referred to the revelation of the spiritual meaning of the Word in the eighteenth century through the medium of Swedenborg. At this time there was another Last Judgement, as foretold in the Book of Revelations. So 'the Second Coming' has already taken place (some 250 years ago!).

Another feature of New Church doctrine, which is, I think, unique – and to me, very attractive – is that although no one can enter heaven except by way of Jesus (*I am the way and the life*) all people of any religion can be saved. Swedenborg tells us that everyone who sincerely behaves according to the commandments of his religion can be saved. Personally, I go even further; there are now so many people who profess no religion; they too, I think, can be saved, so long as they have tried to do what is right because it is right and not for any personal advantage. At death most people go to the World of Spirits, an intermediary world between heaven and hell – there the good of all religions will be instructed into the truths about Jesus.

Swedenborg's teachings on Divine Providence also play an important part in my religious thinking, and indeed in my life. Divine Providence is concerned with absolutely everything that happens in this universe, from black holes in space to the fall of a sparrow on earth. This does not mean that everything that happens is determined or, indeed, that it is God's will. God permits evil; it is a necessary consequence of granting man free will; no evil comes from God, it all comes from man. Although Providence is concerned with everything that happens in this world, it looks beyond this world and is concerned only with eternity. At every stage, however much evil there is, God always ensures the best possible outcome for the eternal souls of all those involved; God is always restraining the evil and, although it is against Divine order for God, at the end of a wicked person's life, instantly to purify him, He is always restraining the evil and will ensure that the person concerned goes to the least bad hell. When I almost despair at the evil in the world, and wonder why, for example, the New Church, some 250 years after Swedenborg was writing, has not spread more widely, I have to keep reminding myself that Providence is concerned with eternity.

The universe is believed to be somewhere between 12 and 16 billion years old, and God did not make man until very recently – perhaps 50,000 years ago. Whatever the scientists may say, I am convinced that the universe, and probably this planet, will continue for ever. The spiritual universe and the material universe have a kind of symbiotic relationship and neither can continue without the other. Swedenborg says (*Heaven and Hell* para. 304):

> . . . the connection and conjunction of heaven with the human race is such that one continues in existence from the other, and that the human race apart from heaven would be like a chain without a hook; and heaven without the human race would be like a house without a foundation.

So we are at the very beginning of human history; 50,000 years is but the blink of an eye compared to the billions of years still to come. We really have come quite a long way in the last two thousand years. When, in a more mundane way, I worry about what Tony Blair is doing to this country or what horrors the European Union is perpetrating, I have again to remind myself that Providence is watching over it all and will ensure the best possible outcome for our eternal souls in the long run – the very long run.

About five years ago I read in an Anglican church magazine a comment that evolution continued to be a controversial subject amongst Christians. Up to that point I had taken it for granted that scientists had incontrovertible proof that we were all descended from common ancestors; and that the only difference that Christians might have would be over the evolutionists' assertion that it all came about by random chance. But I decided to read Darwin again and a number of other books on evolution. Much to my surprise I found, at least to my satisfaction, that the fossil record is completely inconsistent with the evolution of species. I won't go into my findings in detail – I have expounded them in an article (unpublished) which I have called *A Christian View of Evolution*. Suffice it to say that every species appears in the fossil record fully-formed and departs again millions of years later completely unchanged and un–evolved. And I have come to the conclusion that every species was created, instantly, at the right moment from the point of view of Divine Order.

But it is important in a religious context. I will briefly quote here an extract from my other recent essay, *A Short Treatise on the Ten Commandments*:

> Looking at the world as it is today – where self-seeking is seen as acceptable, where we pride ourselves on man's scientific excellence and where we talk of the sanctity of human life – it is hard not to conclude that for very many,

Man is God. Rather than acknowledge that God made man in his image, we behave as if man made God in his image. A major contributor to this phenomenon is, I believe, the theory of evolution and more specifically the belief that all creatures have a common ancestor. What I think is damaging in this theory is that it implies that man, gradually and almost imperceptibly evolving from anthropoid apes, was initially a brute savage who, if he had a religion at all, was some kind of animist. Monotheism is therefore widely believed to have been invented by the Israelites, from Abraham through to Moses. Religion is seen as something created by man 'to meet his spiritual needs'. I think this is a profoundly mistaken view and incompatible with Christianity, as I understand it.

All humans of whatever age, race or colour have eternal souls and are granted free will, that is the power to choose between good and evil. Man, unlike animals, is born with no innate knowledge of how to survive; a human baby cannot even find its mother's breast; in contrast, a baby kangaroo climbs unaided up its mother's belly and settles into the pouch; ducklings can swim within minutes of hatching from the egg. Man has to be taught everything; how to survive and how to behave. Man cannot exercise that choice between good and evil without instruction. Man's inherited nature is to put himself and the satisfaction of his material needs first. All souls have the power to become regenerate, and to do this they have to be taught what to do to achieve it. The very first men had to have some equivalent of the Ten Commandments, and because of his very nature, man could not have been the source; the only possible source was Divine Revelation. To become regenerate man has to have divine revelation. So it must have been available to the earliest men – in visions, no doubt, since there was not yet the written word. The first men must also have been monotheists, believing in the one God, Jehovah. Animism and pantheism must have been later developments during the decline of the antediluvians.

Reverting again to Divine Providence, I went on to say:

Many scientists claim to see no incompatibility between a belief in evolution and religion. But by denying any supernatural intervention in the process of creation, whether of stars, galaxies, creatures or man, and attributing all creation to random chance, the only room left for religion is some kind of deism – a belief that God set everything in motion, but denies any subsequent Divine intervention. Such a God is really not much more than Mother Nature.

Much of what is accepted as a natural concern with the environment seems to me to be based on two false assumptions. First, that God has nothing to do with what goes on in the universe from day to day and that man therefore must do what God does not do or cannot be trusted to do. Secondly, a quite exaggerated belief in the power of man. We seem seriously to believe that man's technological and administrative powers can, for example, make a significant impact on world climate change. Two verses from Psalm 118 sum up my view:

– 'It is better to trust in the Lord than to put confidence in man.'
– 'It is better to trust in the Lord than to put confidence in princes.'

The world has experienced massive climate changes for millions of years. Even as recently as the twelfth century there was a dramatic warming in Europe, to which man contributed nothing, and which cooled again within a century. Man's emissions of carbon dioxide are dwarfed by natural processes. To quote from a recent article by Philip Stott, Professor of Biogeography at the University of London:

> The idea that climate can be managed in a predictable way by manipulating one factor, carbon dioxide, out of the millions of factors involved is Alice-in-Wonderland science, with the verdict before the trial. This is the ultimate flaw: the sheer hubris of humans maintaining a sustainable climate vividly demonstrates the delusions of the sustainability myth.

The trouble is that, despite what the majority of scientists say, we don't actually know for certain what harms the environment. To give a brief example, most people believe that phasing out DDT was an unmitigated blessing. But was it? Malaria had almost been obliterated in Africa, but without DDT it again became a scourge killing millions of people. We won't ensure salvation by saving the planet. God has looked after the planet for over 4 billion years; man has made it more difficult probably only in the last 50 to 100 years. God can be trusted to go on looking after the planet for many more billions of years, indeed for ever. We need to concentrate on saving our souls by obeying his commandments.

My religious beliefs set me apart from almost everyone I know. I state this not because I am proud to be different, but as a sheer matter of fact. Spalding, as I have said above, says that if Swedenborg's teachings are accepted, they must gradually, almost imperceptibly, perhaps, effect a revolution in men's thoughts about everything Divine and human, and even about physical things regarded from the ontological point of view. As a convinced Swedenborgian I have lived with this revolution; all my thoughts about the Divine, mankind and nature are coloured by his teachings. This gives me a completely different mind set from almost everyone I talk to. This is partly because I see so little of other Swedenborgians.

A couple of years ago, one of my guests at dinner said, 'Guy, doesn't it ever worry you that you are the only person to believe what you do?'! I think this came up in the context of my saying that I did not believe in evolution. Every single individual in the world, past, present and future, is unique. But there are others who believe many of the things that I believe, but perhaps none who believes everything that I believe. But that doesn't bother me. For example, I agree with almost everything Matt Ridley says about the environment, but I don't agree with one word of what he says about evolution. So in my everyday life I am conscious the whole time that Providence is involved in everything that happens and that everything that happens in this material universe has its origin in the spiritual universe. Swedenborg says in *Arcana Caelestia*, '. . . the whole natural order is a theatre representative of the Lord's Kingdom.'

So when I hear people worrying about 'bio-diversity' and campaigning for the preservation of some endangered species, I reflect that all species represent some spiritual reality; if the spiritual reality which some species represents no longer exists, then the species will become extinct. Nothing natural that man can do would stop it. And when I am out of doors, everything I see has, I know, some spiritual connotation: I am far from certain what it is, but I still reflect on it. When I see a large flock of pigeons, several hundred strong, suddenly change direction, as I sometimes do, I wonder about the spiritual significance; I also wonder at the significance of the fact that when the flock turns, there are always a few stragglers who missed the signal! That must mean something. Birds signify spiritual ideas. Trees, gardens and plants also have their significance. Gardens, for example, signify intellect and wisdom. By way of illustration, the following is an extract from the entry for 'gardens' in Swedenborg's *Dictionary of Correspondences*:

> . . . in heaven there appear gardens paradisiacal with fruit trees, according to the wisdom of the inhabitants derived from the good of love from the Lord. But around those who are intelligent and not in the good of love, there do not appear gardens, but grass; and around those who are in faith separate from charity, not even grass, but sand.

I am also constantly aware that I am in the company of spirits, good and evil. I don't mean by this that I am psychic. I am not in any way in touch with spirits; I just know that they are there, either leading me into temptation or strengthening my resistance. I am sure that in dreams the people we meet are spirits. Dreams must have some important use, even when one does not know how to interpret them. I am no Joseph, and am not inclined to ask a psychiatrist to help me interpret them. But my dreams are very vivid.

An interesting aspect of dreams is that I believe they give one an inkling of what the next life is going to be like. Swedenborg tells us that there is no space or time in the next world, but only appearances of both. Dreams which seem to me to last for hours, I am told actually only last for seconds, during periods of what is known as 'REM' (rapid eye movements). And in dreams one moves suddenly from one space to another without being aware of any transition; for example, I seem to be driving along a road in a car, and suddenly I find myself walking along the road; but there has been no transition; I have not had to stop the car, open the door and get out. There are other strange changes in dreams; one can walk into a room and see how it is furnished, and a second later the room has completely changed without any obvious transition. Another fascinating feature of dreams – at least for me – is that I sometimes find myself telling a story. I am not aware of who it is to whom I am telling the story, but I am speaking aloud, and the strange thing is that I don't know where the story is going; it seems to me that the story is being put into my mouth by someone else. I find myself frequently

'Guy contemplating eternity'. The graveyard at Cove Hythe

surprised at the outcome; not that there is always an outcome – sometimes I awake before the end.

Another area where my Swedenborgian views set me apart from most people I meet is death. To me death is a new beginning. I, for example, would never use the phrase, 'he died tragically young'. There is nothing tragic about entering the spiritual world. Providence ensures that the moment of our death is that most suited to our eternal souls. And much as I deplore the suffering and the deaths incurred in the awful famines which still occur in Africa, I am comforted by Swedenborg's assertion that every child goes straight to heaven; they have not yet had time to choose evil over good. I don't fear death. I am looking forward to being reunited with Daphne, and I know that I shall die at the moment which Divine Providence decides is best for my eternal soul. I am ready to go now, but the Lord clearly thinks there is more that I can do in this world to prepare for the next. When I do go, I hope I shall be able to say, with Simeon, 'Lord, now lettest thou thy servant depart in peace.'

CHAPTER 28

Learning to Live with Sickness

AFTER THAT DIGRESSION ON MY RELIGIOUS VIEWS, I now return to the chronological approach. It was in 1990 that Daphne's sad decline began. We had already decided to sell the flat in Canonbury Square. It went on the market in April. A week or two later Daphne went to see a gynaecologist for a minor feminine problem; as a matter of routine he examined her breasts and found a lump, which proved to be malignant. For the next nine years Daphne was in and out of hospital with depressing regularity; in those years she had no fewer than seven major operations. If I had known at the beginning what I knew by the end, I think we could have made things a little easier for her than was actually the case. We all know that on the NHS, articulate middle-class patients have an advantage. It turned out to be just as true with private medicine.

To start with things were not too bad. Daphne went in to the Christchurch Park Hospital in Ipswich and Mr Adair operated to remove the lump. We then had to attend at the old Anglesey Road Hospital twice a week for radiotherapy. Daphne was very brave; we had no idea what the survival rate was, but we hoped for the best and she was not too depressed. Amicia, on the other hand, became very upset and decided that she wanted to be near her mother and decided to leave the States. By midsummer she was back in this country and started work with *Harper's & Queen*. She stayed some of the time at the flat in Canonbury and helped to sell it. We nearly doubled our money and repaid the loan from Coutts.

I felt that Daphne needed a really special holiday, when the radiotherapy was over, and we booked ourselves on a Swan Hellenic cruise for three weeks in late September/early October. Cruises are difficult; you cannot be sure that there will be congenial company and to be really comfortable you need to book one of the most expensive staterooms, which I had not done. We flew to Athens and joined the ship at Piraeus. The Swan Hellenic ship was an old one and not very spacious or comfortable. For the first week we did not have a particularly nice stateroom; the food on board was Greek, and thus never really hot and always too greasy. So Daphne was less than happy to be on the cruise.

But it was a very interesting one. Our trip took us to Rhodes and then up the western shore of Turkey on the Aegean, calling at Patmos, where John wrote the Book of Revelations, and on the Turkish shore, Ephesus and Pergamum. The weather was glorious and the sites more than lived up to their reputation. Our final call in that first week was to the ruins of Troy which, to be frank were not all that impressive. I found it hard to associate this plot of land with all the Homeric heroes. We were not allowed to land on the other side, at the Dardanelles, but could see the monument from the ship. Here I found it easier to associate this with the horrors of the First World War. We then sailed to Thessalonika, passing by all the monasteries on Mount Athos. The monks hate being the object of tourist curiosity, but there is nothing to prevent one sailing past. All the passengers disembarked at Thessalonika except Daphne and me and one other woman. We were then joined by a completely new set of passengers for the next two weeks. We set off for the Sea of Marmora and the Bosporus and sailed past Istanbul in the early morning. For the next two weeks we sailed right round the Black Sea in an anti-clockwise direction. We called at two ports in Turkish Anatolia, Sinope (now shown on maps as Sinop) and Trebizond (Trabzon). Soon after entering the Black Sea and sailing to Sinope a long-eared owl took up its place right on the prow of the ship and stayed there all day, very much a centre of attraction. One of the Swan Hellenic experts on board was a man from the RSPB, who was able to tell us what all the unusual birds were that we saw. We found about five other kindred spirits on board and we met each evening in the bar, carefully avoiding the 6.30 dinner! I forget who they were except for one couple who were Airey Neave's brother and his wife. She was mad keen on racing and we thought we were bound to see each other again at Newmarket one day, but somehow we didn't.

Of course in 1990 the Soviet Union still existed and our three next calls were in the USSR. The first, Sukhumi, was a most attractive town in Georgia in what was called the Autonomous Republic of Abkhazia. I remember particularly the wonderful botanical gardens. It may now be all in ruins, for when the USSR collapsed and Sukhumi passed to the new Republic of Georgia, the Georgians were not prepared to allow the Abkhazians to be 'autonomous' and a civil war raged for some months. Daphne and I stayed on board in the harbour of Sukhumi one morning since we did not want to go on that day's excursion. I got into some kind of conversation with a Soviet soldier on the quayside. He was very homesick and was longing to return home, which in fact was not so far away. His home was on the north shore of the Black Sea at Odessa, which is in the Ukraine.

One of the outings from Sukhumi on which we went was a flight in a helicopter over the Caucasus Mountains. This was my only experience of flying in a helicopter. At one point we were actually able to see a golden eagle soaring below us. The flight also made me less than happy with Aeroflot; the plane was unbelievably dirty! Sochi, now part of Russia, was not very interesting; it seemed to be full of sanataria and health farms for retired Soviet *apparatchiks*.

At Yalta, now part of the Ukraine, most of our fellow passengers opted to visit the hotel where Stalin, Roosevelt and Churchill had met near the end of the war. But Daphne and I went off to visit Chekhov's little house, which is beautifully maintained as a museum. I enjoyed the visit to Odessa, our next stop. We saw the famous Potemkin Steps and toured the city, which has lots of fine buildings. One of our tour guides, a Soviet woman, was infuriatingly anti-Western, attributing the victory in the war exclusively to the Soviet Union. We called at two ports in Bulgaria.

We finished off with a stay in Istanbul. This really is a wonderful city. The Hagia Sophia, a Christian cathedral turned into a mosque (in contrast to the mosque in Cordoba, turned into a Christian cathedral), dominates the sky line and is very beautiful. The Topkapi palace was full of the most splendid works of art – miniature paintings, jewellery, and ceramics. Our final call in Istanbul was to the Grand Bazaar, where we bought three carpets! We left things rather late and only just managed to get back to the ship in time. I wonder if they would really have sailed without us. From Istanbul we returned to Thessalonika, cruising past Mount Athos for the second time. This time a couple of furious monks gave chase to us in a speed boat gesticulating and shouting imprecations. I can understand their feelings. I don't think I shall ever go on a cruise again.

For the next five years I continued to do a certain amount of work for KIA, but living at Buxlow. Some times KIA consultants came to Buxlow to work with me on a strategic report. I also continued to run service management courses for KIA, once a year, at the hotel at Milton Common near Oxford.

In 1991 Daphne and I had our last real holiday together. We went on a tour of Swedish Manor Houses and Castles organised by the Friends of the Historic Houses Association. The photograph album I have of that trip is one of the best I have. They were all beautiful. Sweden was attractive and the company was good. But Daphne was already finding it tiring. Her troubles were just about to begin in earnest.

In January 1992 Daphne was in the car park at the supermarket in Saxmundham and saw a woman with several whippets. She went over and admired them and said that she was seriously thinking of having whippets again. The woman, Sally Aldous, promptly said that one of her whippets did not really fit in with the rest of the pack and she would gladly let us have him! So, the very next day, she came over to Buxlow with a 'blue' whippet – this is the term they use for what I would have called a dark grey whippet. Merlin, for that was his name, was quite enchanting. Initially he missed his previous home; indeed for the first hour or so with us, he howled constantly! But within two or three days he had settled in. Just as Tubby had been Daphne's dog, so Merlin was mine. He was absolutely devoted to me; would lie across my chest on the sofa in the library. When I came home, either from some work I had done for KIA or when I returned on Tuesday evenings from playing bridge with the Aldeburgh Bridge Club, Daphne used to have to let this almost hysterical dog out of the gun room door and he would dash to the garage to greet me.

I am not in favour of having one dog alone; I think they need company. So we looked for another whippet and found one at the RSPCA pound near Manningtree; unfortunately another man had been earlier in the day, and although the whippet was clearly fond of us and was a most unsuitable dog for urban dwelling in Colchester, the RSPCA people said we could not have him. As it happened, two months later the RSPCA rang us and said that the man in Colchester had returned the whippet and asked whether we were still interested. We went immediately to collect him. He was a slightly off-white dog and had been given the unfortunate name of 'Whisky' — the previous owner obviously liked his whisky with a lot of water! With Amicia's help (she loves names) we renamed him Hamo — Hamo d'Albini, you may remember, was Roger de Moubray's brother in the twelfth century! Hamo was also a very sweet dog, not quite as devoted to me as Merlin; so he became very much Daphne's dog. He also adored Jocelyn and would jump three feet in the air to greet him.

I continued to do a fair amount of work for KIA. I have come across a pamphlet which shows that I spoke at the Euroforum Congress at Arnhem in Holland in June 1992 — my speech was, I see, entitled: 'Resources invested in *how* we sell will give incomparably higher returns than in improving *what* we sell' — still very true I think about the insurance industry. I stayed in a hotel overlooking the Rhine and could see the famous bridge. I did not then yet know that Stuart Mawson, one of the Knodishall parishioners, had been the only British doctor at Arnhem in 1944. Nor did I then know that the planes carrying the paratroopers to Arnhem actually flew over Aldeburgh.

It was at about this time that my interest in gardens got me involved in the setting up of the Suffolk Gardens' Trust. I went to the inaugural meeting of interested parties and came away from it finding myself its first Treasurer. The Patron was Lady Marlesford (Gabriella) and the Chairman, Paul Miles. My main work initially was to draft the Articles of Association and negotiate with the Charity Commissioners to obtain charitable status for the Trust. The Committee (later, the Council of Management) used to meet every month in one of the members' houses. One of the very first meetings was held at Buxlow in June 1992. Later, we met regularly in a room at the Otley College of Agriculture. I got into the habit of driving over to Gabriella's at Marlesford Hall and continuing the rest of the way in her car. I have kept up my interest in the Trust ever since; although I had to resign from the Council of Management in 1996 when I became too deaf to take part in committee meetings.

In the autumn of 1992 whilst I was away running a course at Milton Common, Daphne, when walking the dogs at Kenton Hills, collapsed. She said that Merlin was sweet and came and licked her face. Somehow she managed to get to her feet and drive home. She went straight to see the doctor, who said it was almost miraculous that she had been able to get up again — she was very anaemic and her blood count was desperately low. He said we would have to get to the bottom of the anaemia. Medical diagnosis can be very difficult. Dr Seaton in Ipswich soon established that she had a hiatus hernia, but did not think that could be enough to cause such severe anaemia.

We then saw another specialist who was quite unnecessarily alarming; he decided that Daphne had cancer of the oesophagus and said he would have to undertake major surgery. He took a biopsy and we had to go the hospital in Norwich to see him when the results were available. It seemed to me that surgery on the oesophagus was probably more than Daphne could stand and that it would be better to leave things as they were; she was in no pain and the quality of life for however much time she had left would be much better without the operation. I was all primed to confront the surgeon, but when we saw him he apologised profusely and said that there was no malignancy – he had been mistaken. He should not have been so alarming before he had the results of the tests.

But we still had not identified the cause of the anaemia. Finally it was found that she had a small malignant polyp on her colon. This was removed quite simply, but the surgeon said he recommended surgery because there might be still some malignancy in the walls of the colon. So in January 1993 Daphne went into hospital for her second major operation. A piece of the colon was removed and no malignancy was found. So all seemed well. However, I am convinced that Mr Adair removed the wrong portion; he had on that day an entirely new assistant, who I suspect got the measurements wrong. By late 1994 Adair once again suspected cancer of the colon and in February 1995 Daphne had her third major operation, and this time, the portion removed was found to be malignant. Adair still claimed that he had not removed the wrong portion two years earlier – the measurements on this occasion were quite different, he said. So we shall never know. I certainly don't blame Adair.

I have said very little about our home life in these five years. Daphne and I grew much closer. I was always there to comfort her and to cope with the doctors. Daphne would have been inclined to put herself unquestion-ingly in the hands of the surgeons. I, on the other hand, was always ready to question decisions and ask for a full explanation.

Poor Merlin developed a heart problem and died of a heart attack in my arms in the summer of 1994. I found this a quite shattering experience. My religion does not help me much in such a situation, since I do not believe that animals have an afterlife. Once he had gone, that was it. I found it so hard to accept that during the night I went downstairs and out to the workshop to look at Merlin in the cardboard box into which I had put him, in the vain hope that I had been mistaken and that he might still be alive. We buried him next day in the garden. Daphne always felt very strongly that the dead, humans or pets, need a grave.

With Merlin gone, Sally Aldous came to the rescue again. She knew of a whippet bitch who had been very badly treated – locked in a barn for hours on end. One afternoon she turned up with Cassie, who somewhat to our dismay seemed very fat. And indeed she was; she had not had enough exercise. She turned out to be another very sweet and faithful dog. She had one fault; she absolutely adored hunting and at the slightest opportunity would get out of the garden and go up and down the hedgerows looking for rabbits. If one realised soon enough that she had got out, it was not too hard to find her. She had a habit of barking loudly whenever she thought she had a rabbit cornered. All you had to do was walk across the fields listening for the telltale bark. It could on occasions be misleading. I remember once hearing her bark and thinking that she was a long way away, only to discover that she was actually quite close, but half way down a rabbit hole! On one occasion she and Hamo got out at around nine o'clock in the morning and did not return until nine in the evening. At some point on that day somebody had seen them on the dual carriageway of the A12 at Benhall – some four miles from here. They were lucky not to be killed.

By this time – in 1992 – Crispin had taken up residence in France and was the only British bloodstock agent in France, living in Paris with Caroline. In the summer of 1994 Crispin and Caroline decided – at last! – to get married. They gave virtually no notice; Crispin rang one day to say that they were getting married the next day at the Mairie. We certainly didn't have the remotest chance of getting there at such short notice, but neither could Amicia or Jocelyn. I am sure they did not want us to come; they wanted it to be private. Anyhow we were delighted. Crispin and Caroline had been together now for many years and were clearly devoted to each other.

Jocelyn, whilst still living in London, had become thoroughly involved with the Agence Française in Deauville in Normandy – the French equivalent of Tattersalls in Newmarket. It was round about then that both boys began the habit of renting a house in Deauville for the month of August each year. During August there is racing every day and towards the end of the month are the big bloodstock sales so it was more work than holiday. I wish we could have gone and visited them, but after 1992 Daphne was just not strong enough. Amicia continued to be Shopping Editor of *Harpers & Queen*. She had quite a succession of boy friends, but she seemed to value her independence so highly that I suspected she would never get married.

In March 1995 I suddenly found myself suffering from acute breathlessness. I could not even walk up the stairs without having to rest at the top. I was referred to Dr Seaton in Ipswich. He ran an ECG on me and seemed amazed that I had not noticed that my heartbeat was very irregular and rather weak. I was diagnosed as having an enlarged heart. Dr Seaton put me on to a cocktail of drugs, which had an immediate beneficial effect. I had to go into hospital for a couple of days to be tried out on one drug which can have harmful side effects, so that my blood pressure could be taken every twenty minutes. This was my first experience of the private ward at the Ipswich hospital, which I was to come to know all too well. Over the next nine years my cocktail of drugs has kept me much healthier than I had been for several years.

The Moubrays with Caroline Sunderland in the 'E'

This turned out to be providential – for only in good health could I have coped with the ensuing five years. For in early May, came the bombshell. I had spent three days in London running a course on service management for a firm of Lloyd's brokers and returned home on the Thursday. This was the weekend of the Guineas' meeting at Newmarket and both boys were here. We celebrated Caroline's birthday on the Saturday. On Sunday morning Crispin and Caroline left to return to Paris and Jocelyn went off for the day to Newmarket. After lunch Daphne went up to have a rest.

Crispin and Caroline on their wedding day in Paris, 1994

Around four o'clock I was puzzled that she had not yet come down for tea; so I went up to look for her. As I passed the bathroom door I thought I heard a noise and went in – luckily she had not locked the door – and found her lying on the floor, barely conscious; she was obviously just coming round from having been completely blacked out. She was also obviously in pain. She managed to mutter to me asking me just to get her onto her bed and she would be all right.

This clearly wasn't possible and I immediately rang for an ambulance. The ambulance men were very kind and gentle and took her off to the Heath Road hospital in Ipswich. Fearful that the Casualty department might not deal with Daphne sufficiently promptly, I first rang Mr Adair, the surgeon, at his home. His wife answered and said that he was at the hospital; I asked her please to tell him that Daphne was on her way in and that I would very grateful if he would call in and see that all that could be done was being done. I left a message on the kitchen table for Jocelyn and left the house unlocked with the dogs in the library and set off for the hospital. Considering that it was a Sunday and that Casualty was quite crowded, Daphne was attended to quite quickly. It helped no end to have Mr Adair turn up and make his presence felt. The diagnosis was appalling; she had fractured one hip and both shoulders. I won't go into all the details of the following weeks – she was to be in the private ward for some seven weeks. She was so distressed to start with that the nurses put up a truckle bed on the floor near Daphne and I spent every night with her for a week or so. I would return home for breakfast, walk the dogs, do the shopping and then return to the hospital again. I could not get the specialists to be at all interested in what had caused her fall. They had ruled out a heart attack after putting her in the cardiac unit for the first night. They even had the nerve to suggest that Daphne had had a drunken fall – and that the marked disorientation which persisted for the first few days was obviously the result of coming off alcohol!

I did not know in those days that after a broken hip the normal response is to perform a total hip replacement operation. But the Ipswich surgeon said that he did not recommend an operation, and poor Daphne was kept in traction for seven weeks. She returned home at the end of June, with a wheelchair, crutches and a zimmer frame. It was impossible for her to go upstairs, so we set up a bed in the summer drawing room and I washed Daphne at the basin in the gun room. Nobody at the hospital had the sense to recommend to me that I should get a stair lift. After a few days I realised that I had to get one. Having watched endless television advertisements for stair lifts, I rang Stannah and asked them to fit one. They told me that their local agent was away and that I would have to wait three weeks! I found a firm in Ipswich who came immediately and fitted the stair lift the next day. And they were helpful enough to take her bed back up to her bedroom and help me settle her in there.

Daphne, as I think I have said earlier, did all the housework herself; but now we clearly needed help. Our near neighbours, William and Miranda Kendall, suggested that we try Win Driver, whom I have already mentioned. She used to work for the Hawdons and actually started work at Buxlow in 1944. She and her daughter-in-law, Carol, started coming to me before Daphne had returned from the hospital. Carol gave up coming last year, but Win, now aged 80, still comes to me twice a week, as she has done for the last nine years.

CHAPTER 29

Daphne's Last Years

So BEGAN A VERY PAINFUL four and a half years for Daphne. She was always very fastidious and modest and private. And now here she was totally dependent on me. I dressed her, bathed her and even had to wipe her bottom – with two broken shoulders mobility is very restricted. She put up with it all very bravely. She would ask from time to time – 'What would I do without you?' Thank God she did not have to do without me. I am sure she wondered why God had allowed this to happen to her – and so did I. From my point of view I can only say that it at least gave me an opportunity to make up for the years in which I had been selfish, by caring for her as lovingly as possible. I tried never to be away from the house for more than a couple of hours. I also bought a mobile phone and fixed the phone by her bed so that she could ring me by just pressing 'redial'. I left the house only to walk the dogs, to do the shopping, to play bridge one evening a week and to play nine holes of golf once a week.

Getting around was quite painful for Daphne, but she coped very well. At one point I arranged for her to have a powered wheelchair and had a ramp built outside the kitchen door, so that she could go round the garden on her own. For bathing her we had a 'Bathmaster', a contraption which at the press of button could be lowered into the bath. On one awful occasion, it went wrong when in the depressed situation. I had to climb into the bath and bodily lift Daphne out – quite an effort for someone of my age! The children came to stay quite often. We have been very lucky to have both boys involved with bloodstock which requires them several times a year to come to Newmarket – and whenever they do, they have always stayed with us.

Daphne would have been a great deal more mobile if the surgeon had operated to give her a total hip replacement. We settled in to a quiet routine. I would start getting Daphne dressed; she could manage the rest and I would be preparing breakfast when I would hear the familiar noise of the stair lift coming down. Daphne still worried about what she felt was the burden she was placing on me. When she was sitting in the drawing room – in her special reclining chair – she would sometimes say that she felt dreadful just sitting there whilst I was working in the kitchen. I kept telling her that that she must remember that I loved cooking and that I was actually playing not working.

Two other important developments in the family occurred that summer. Amicia had two great friends who lived at Doddington Place in Kent, Richard and Ally Oldfield. She was godmother to their eldest child,

Leonora. Ally developed cancer. At the end of 1994 Amicia took Leo to the *Nutcracker Suite* in London. At Christmas she told us that she had seen Ally and that she was now desperately ill. In early January 1995 Ally died.

I remember saying to Daphne a few weeks later that Amicia seemed to be having lunch with Richard remarkably frequently and that something was, I suspected, in the wind. Sure enough, during Daphne's stay in hospital that summer Amicia confirmed that she and Richard were in love. Regrettably there seemed to be no talk of marriage. Daphne and I continued our quiet routine until November. One day I had taken breakfast up to Daphne and we were sitting in her room chatting, when she suddenly had a violent fit; I immediately rang the surgery and Dr Havard was with us in a very few minutes and was actually able to witness her coming round from it. He immediately diagnosed an epileptic fit and started her on remedial medication. Dr Foreman, our regular doctor, came to see her later in the morning and decided that in the course of the convulsions in the fit she must have broken the other hip – without even falling out of bed. So, once again an ambulance took her to hospital.

This time the private ward was full, so I arranged for her to be moved to Christchurch Park Hospital. The same orthopaedic surgeon treated her. He immediately arranged for her to have a brain scan, which revealed the existence of a tumour. Daphne had been put into traction again, but as soon as she could be moved she went to Addenbrooks Hospital in Cambridge for an operation on her brain. Ipswich is not equipped for brain surgery. The surgeon, a Mr Macgregor, was very skilful and very kind. This, I may say, was by now her fourth major operation. For the fourth time I sat in my car waiting to hear from the surgeon whether all had gone well – I remember I had my mobile phone and was parked on the roof of a multi-storey car park. It was a very long operation and she lost a lot of blood and had to spend that night in intensive care. The tumour was removed and proved to be benign, but had clearly been the cause of both epileptic fits, for even the orthopaedic surgeon now admitted that the first fall had been the result of one. The neurosurgeon inserted a small acrylic plate to fill the hole in her skull.

Addenbrooks is a ghastly hospital; even though Daphne had a private room, it was dirty. The hospital is so vast that I feel that it is in itself a cause of endless infections. So I arranged as soon as possible to have her moved out to the Evelyn Hospital in Trumpington Road. This is a beautifully clean and well run hospital overseen by a strict matron. I spent so much time in Cambridge that month that I rented a nice little cottage in Hinton, a village to the north of the city. Both Amicia and Jocelyn joined me there on occasions. I managed to get Daphne home again by Christmas; but even though all three children and Caroline were there, it was not a very pleasant Christmas. Daphne stayed in bed all the time and I just could not relax when the rest of us were in the dining room. I had to keep popping up to see her from time to time. The brain operation had been a great strain.

Early in 1996 there was another family disaster. Crispin rang me from Paris to say that something awful had happened. He, together with two Frenchmen, had been accused of fraud by the French National Stud. Crispin had been buying stallions at Newmarket, which his principals then sold on to the National Stud. The preferred stallions in England and France are quite different; and Crispin knew that the stallions from lines which would fetch high prices in France could be bought relatively cheaply in England. The two Frenchmen then sold them on with a substantial mark-up, but they were still attractively priced for the Stud. But this was now alleged to be fraudulent. Crispin told me that he was going to have to appear before a *Juge d'Instruction* in a few days' time. He went to court and to his horror was arrested and carted off to prison. The *juge* had decided that there was sufficient prima facie evidence and wanted all three men sent to prison so that they could not communicate with one another and rig the evidence. Caroline, by this time heavily pregnant with her first child, was quite magnificent. It must have been an appalling strain for her, and it was not impossible that Crispin might have to remain in prison for months or even a year. In prison he no longer had any means of earning a living. But Caroline put on a very brave face. She and I were on the phone to each other almost every day, organising private French lawyers to represent Crispin. Crispin turned out to have lots of friends in the French racing world, who all rallied round to provide help and assistance to Caroline. But there were enemies too. Indeed the allegations of fraud were first made by a racing correspondent. The French judicial system moves extremely slowly and it was a real tribute to the lawyers that they were able to have an appeal heard in three weeks; happily all three prisoners were released. It must have been a terrible ordeal for Crispin and for Caroline. But their troubles weren't over yet. It still seemed possible that the case would be brought to trial; and that it might be months away. So the intense pressures remained. Within a year, it became clear that the *Juge d'Instruction* had come round to the belief that the allegations were unfounded. But, believe it or not, it was not until the summer of 2000 (after four and a half years) that all three were finally exonerated.

In the midst of all this, Daphne's troubles began again. She developed a sore spot where the brain operation had been; Dr Foreman didn't seem to be very worried. But I got on to the surgeon in Cambridge. He asked her to come in and immediately decided that some serious infection had got into the wound and that he had to operate again and remove the acrylic plate. It turned out that there was indeed serious infection, which had actually affected the bone of the skull and some of it had to be removed. As I have said, I think Addenbrooks is a major source of infection. For the rest of her life Daphne had a hole in her head only covered with skin. On this occasion I remember waiting for the surgeon's telephone call in my car parked in Grantchester.

One day in April when Daphne was in the drawing room with Dr Foreman and the district nurse, Kathy Hammond, poor old Bill Scarlett came to see me, nearly in tears, saying that he could not go on gardening for us; the pain in his hip was too bad. It was a sad occasion; he had been with us for eleven years. He came in to see Daphne to take his leave. When he had gone I remarked that I would have to find somebody else. Kathy then said that her husband, David, might be willing to come. Sure enough he was willing. We suddenly had, in fact, a much better gardener, since David had a diploma in horticulture from Otley College. The only mistake I ever remember him making was to dig up and throw away my sorrel – but it does look like a weed. David was with us for two years. One day he came and asked me if I would give him good references. This was very disturbing news; but of course I gave him excellent references. He was not leaving for any better employer round here; it was just that David and Kathy had decided to emigrate to New Zealand. They seem to be very happy there and Kathy has become a very important consulting nurse on the treatment of wounds. David continues to be what is known as a 'house husband'. He writes quite frequently and they both came with their children to visit me here at Buxlow in 2002 when they made their first trip back to England. I keep up with Bill Scarlett, who has had two total hip replacement operations and can now get around very well.

The best news of 1996 was the birth of Crispin and Caroline's first child, Ajax. I am not quite sure why they chose that name; neither Ajax the Greater nor Ajax the Lesser seem to me to be particularly attractive Homeric heroes. But I am now completely used to the name. Ajax had lovely red hair and came over to Buxlow with his parents quite early in his life. It was a great pleasure for all of us to see Daphne holding Ajax in her arms.

Daphne was getting along all right, but was still having pain, particularly in the left knee. So she was not very mobile. She spent a lot of time reading. She had always been a voracious reader. Her two favourite authors, I think, were Henry James and Edith Wharton, both very sophisticated Americans. In the autumn we went to see the orthopaedic surgeon in Ipswich to see if there was not something that could be done about the pain. By this time he was surly and unfriendly – we had complained to the Ipswich Hospital Administrator about the allegations that Daphne had had a drunken fall and the failure to give her a brain scan in the summer of 1995 and he felt he had been personally attacked. One of the problems of private medicine is that one is in the hands of a specialist; the surgeon was interested only in bones and the one generalist who had been on her case was a specialist in gerontics and had rejected a brain scan – there was nothing useful it could show, he had said. Anyway, Hudson said there was nothing he could do, and that for the rest of her life she would have to get used to a wheelchair, crutches and a zimmer frame.

I had heard from Gabriella Marlesford of a healer who was said to be very good. We got on to Lilias Sheepshanks. She came to see Daphne several times. Daphne was very impressed with her, Lilias could not heal Daphne

With my first grandchild, Ajax, July 1996

but when she laid her hands on her, Daphne said she felt a wonderful warm glow, and it cheered her up no end. More importantly, Lilias suggested that we should seek a second opinion and recommended a private GP in Melton. He, in turn, referred her to a surgeon in Cambridge who specialised in knees – many of his patients were well known footballers. It was already 1997 when we went to see him at the Evelyn Hospital. He had some X-Rays taken and said that it would be quite unwise to do anything to the knee until someone had done something about the hip above it, and that as it happened, a hip specialist, Mr Scott, was at that very moment at the Evelyn and might be able to see her. Mr Scott was wonderful. He said that a total hip replacement would be very difficult in Daphne's case because the hip had impacted the pelvis, and that it would need a bone graft, but that it was not impossible. He arranged for Daphne to see Mr Mott in Ipswich for some kind of 'nuclear?' test to see the quality of the bones. All this took time – indeed a few months – but eventually Mr Scott agreed to operate. So in September 1997 Daphne had her sixth major operation, this time at the Evelyn. It was a complete success and for the next year she could walk without any pain. She no longer used the electric wheelchair and was able to walk around the garden – usually with a stick in one hand and the other on my arm. She was still completely dependent on me for dressing and bathing, but we became very close.

Since early in 1996 Amicia and Richard had been together a great deal. Amicia still lived in her flat in Notting Hill – which I should have said was bought with a down payment made by us (Daphne's idea again, she was much more imaginative and charitable than I) – but almost every weekend was spent with Richard at Doddington (hereafter always referred to as 'Dod'). Amicia frequently invited us to come and spend a weekend at Dod, but I always refused. I told her that I would not come so long as she was referred to at Dod as Mr Richard's girlfriend. If they were married, of course, we would be happy to come. Early in 1997 Amicia and Richard went to Cuba for a holiday – incidentally nothing would induce me to go to Cuba so long as Fidel Castro was in power – and we all expected a proposal to come out of the holiday. But no such luck. On their return Richard made it clear that he did not want to marry again. I could understand his reluctance having lost his first wife tragically to cancer. But Amicia was very disappointed. Amicia told him that in the circumstances she thought they ought to stop seeing each other. I don't think either of them were very happy about it, but they stayed apart. Suddenly one morning very early, about 7 o'clock, I think, the telephone rang. It was Amicia and she burst into floods of tears. This made me very apprehensive, but at last she managed to say that Richard had just rung her from Boston (Massachusetts) and asked her to marry him. She had accepted, but had said that he must first get her father's permission! She had rung not only with the news, but to warn me that the phone would ring any minute now from Richard. Sure enough it rang and I said that Daphne and I were both delighted.

The question now was where they were going to be married. I felt sure that both Amicia and Richard would have wished for a big wedding with all their many, many friends in attendance. For that they would have to be in London and it would have been quite impossible for Daphne to attend. So we settled on a nice compromise. They were to be married here in Knodishall parish church with only family in attendance and we would have a small lunch for them here at Buxlow. Later on they would hold a large celebratory reception in London. So on 15 March they were married here. Coincidentally, of course, it was also my birthday.

Amicia was dressed by her friends – dress by Serena Blow and shoes by Emma Hope. I thought she looked lovely. She was photographed here at Buxlow by *Country Life* – she was to be the *Country Life* Frontispiece girl that week – one of the nicest they have ever had, I think. The photographer kept taking one shot after another and I found it hard to get her out of the house. When we arrived at the church, Amicia was so moved that she burst

Richard and Amicia on their wedding day with Leonora, Christopher and Henry Oldfield outside Knodishall Church, 15 March 1997

into tears and the vicar, Christine Brooks, was heard to say, 'The bride is here at last!' I was so glad that Daphne was able to attend. She had bought a new dress and hat for the occasion. To make it easier for her, we had to have the wheelchair. Christine has often told me that she thought it was one of the nicest weddings at which she had ever officiated. The three stepchildren, Leonora, Christopher and Henry, came to the altar steps to be blessed as part of the ceremony. On our side there were only Crispin and Caroline with baby Ajax, and Jocelyn. Richard had his children, his sisters, his mother and his stepfather.

We had a lovely lunch in the dining room here – we had to have a second table in the corner. And the excellent food was provided by the Fox & Goose at Fressingfield. As a nice touch for me, after the wedding cake had been cut, another cake was brought in to the sound of 'Happy birthday to you'. It was a lovely day, and Daphne was so happy to be able to be a part of it.

In May, Richard and Amicia held a reception in the Orangery at Holland Park. This was a rather grand occasion with about three hundred people in attendance. There was no way we could get Daphne there, so through a care agency, I found a woman who came in to keep Daphne company for the day and cook lunch for her. I had myself driven to Holland Park by the local taxi of John Miller; he waited for me and drove me home. Richard and Amicia had a steel band in attendance. With my deafness and the noise of the band I found it almost impossible to hear what any one was saying. Amicia led me the length of the Orangery – and it is quite long – introducing me to her friends, saying, 'This is my father. He is very deaf!'

This was now seven years ago now, and I have never been to London again. I am not quite sure why, but I have resolved never to go there again. It is not that the journey would be too tiring; in the past seven years I have frequently been to Dod, which is about two and a half hours away by car. And it is not that it would be too difficult for me to stay in London – Richard and Amicia have a flat in Cheyney Walk. I just feel, I think, that London is a chapter in my life which is now closed.

That summer, Daphne and I paid our first visit to Dod. It was not a very successful one. The trip was quite tiring for Daphne; there is no stair lift and the main guest bedroom is up quite a long flight of stairs on the first floor. I decided that Daphne should have that room to herself; my snoring would otherwise disturb her; so I went up to the second floor. This turned out to be have been a disastrous decision. When I came to see Daphne next morning with a cup of tea, I found her on the floor. When trying to go to the bathroom she had fallen out of bed and was quite unable to get back in. She did not call out; I feel sure that either Richard or Amicia would have heard her; so she spent hours – and I mean hours – lying on the floor. She had managed to pull the duvet off the bed and was not absolutely freezing. But it completely spoilt the visit. It was an awful experience for her and we did not go again.

Life for Daphne and me for the year that followed her hip operation was quiet, but enjoyable. I have pleasant memories of walking round the garden with Daphne on my arm. Daphne was very moved by the death of Princess Diana. I must admit that I did not share her feelings. It seemed to me to avoid several severe problems that would arise from a too close involvement of the royal family with Mohammed Fayed. But we both watched the whole of the funeral on television. It was a quite extraordinary occasion, with a drama matching the funeral of Winston Churchill, nearly thirty years earlier. For me it was marred by Tony Blair muscling in on the occasion and for the appearance of Elton John, whom I find vulgar and very unattractive.

I mention all this because it led, a year later, to Daphne's last trip away from home. She was very keen to visit Althorp and see Princess Diana's tomb so in the summer of 1998 we booked ourselves in to a Bed & Breakfast at Althorp. Daphne was able to negotiate the very short flight of stairs to our bedroom. It was a lovely sunny day and we went round the gardens, and visited the house and the small museum they had established in the stables. Daphne, as I think I have said, had this very strong feeling about the need for the bereaved to have a grave as a focus for their mourning. She had expressed this feeling movingly in one of her poems, which I have included in an Appendix, but which I repeat here:

The body should have a grave
for those who still have bodies,
then they can go and sense the senseless part
of those that have but recently died,
then they can go and stand alone and quiet apart
and let the past come forth before their eyes
While they who grieve are yet alive to feel
the body should be there below the turf
It is most comforting to have so sure a place
where remembered head and hand and face
are yet a part of the earth

Daphne also felt that graves were comforting for our dogs. Merlin already had a grave among the rose beds, surrounded by a frame of black Victorian ribbon edging tiles.

And now, most unfortunately, another was needed. One Sunday morning in April 1998 I had taken Cassie and Hamo for a walk on Blaxhall Common. When we got home I let the dogs out of the car and they suddenly dashed off towards the horse chestnut trees, pursuing a squirrel. I then heard an awful scream, and ran over to find Hamo lying amongst the daffodils screaming with pain. I went to see if I could lift him up to take him to the vet, but he fastened his teeth very firmly on my hand. I had great difficulty prising his mouth open to release myself. By now my hand was bleeding profusely. I staunched the flow with my handkerchief and rushed to the kitchen to phone the vet. Even though it was a Sunday the vet arrived within about ten minutes. Meantime Daphne had struggled out of the house; I found a chair for her to sit on as she watched over poor Hamo. The vet said that Hamo had broken his back, running full tilt into the supporting strut for the overhead power line, and that he could not survive. So he was put down on the spot. It was a quite devastating morning.

The problems were not over yet. The vet was almost more concerned about my hand than about Hamo. With his help I rang the Sunday emergency doctors' number; they said that a home call could not be managed and told me to go to the Aldeburgh Cottage Hospital. I am not at all sure how I managed to drive there with one hand – in the other I was clutching a handkerchief bound round the wounded finger. The doctors stitched me up, but then became worried because the finger had turned completely white. They told me to go straight to the Casualty Department at the Ipswich Hospital. I didn't think I could manage that on my own, so I went to see Carol – she very kindly offered to drive me there. Meantime we had to settle Daphne down with a bite to eat for her lunch. Casualty at Ipswich was crowded, but luckily I did not have to wait long. I think it must have helped that I had been referred there by the doctors at Aldeburgh. They said that there was nothing wrong with the finger, but that the doctors at Aldeburgh should not have put in a stitch! –

so they removed it and taped the wound instead. So poor Hamo's grave joined Merlin's in the rose bed.

To ease the sorrow we rapidly found another dog to keep Cassie company. Rebecca Toller, who was already a good friend, had seven whippets of her own — she races them. Her daughter knew of a male whippet who was in her view being badly treated. There was an extraordinary household in Tunstall (not very far away) — two male homosexuals had eleven dogs (!), four Rottweilers, four Great Danes, two Jack Russells and the poor little whippet, Frankie. I don't think he found it easy to get to the food, and was gaunt; moreover, I think he was also ill treated. Anyway Rebecca's daughter persuaded them that Frankie would be much better off in another home so a few days later he was brought round for inspection — for some extraordinary reason the owner brought this small whippet in a horse box!

Frankie was very neurotic. Daphne was not in favour of taking him, but I felt so sorry for him that I agreed. It took him two or three years to calm down completely, but I have become very fond of him. He looks a bit like Hamo, but differs in that half his face is black. At the beginning he did not even seem to know how to wag his tail. I wondered if the 'wag' gene was missing! But now you should see the tail when he thinks he has a rabbit cornered under some brambles — the wagging is intense. He didn't seem to have much of a bark to begin with either, but now barks wildly whenever anyone comes to the house, but is friendly with everyone — except Jocelyn. Even now, six years later, he steers very clear of Jocelyn. I think Jocelyn must remind him of one of the two Tunstall men who mistreated him.

At around the same time there came the good news that a son had been born to Amicia in Canterbury — Daphne's second grandchild. He was called Edward, but is usually known as Eddo.

Then came another blow for Daphne. At the end of August her right hip packed up. She was quite unable to put her right foot to the ground. Something drastic had to be done. These emergencies always seem to happen at a weekend, when one cannot get hold of the doctors. Happily I had Mr Scott's home telephone number in Cambridge. I rang him and said I wanted to bring Daphne in a soon as possible to have a second hip replacement. Mr Scott told me that he was in the garden and had recently retired. The operation would be a difficult one and since he had done no operations for some months he did not feel that he should attempt it. But he gave me the home number of the surgeon who had taken over from him, Mr Keane.

I promptly rang him and told him that I was proposing to bring Daphne in to the Evelyn as soon as he could arrange a total hip replacement. 'Hang on,' he said, 'I am the surgeon and will have to decide for myself.' I told him that I had no doubt that he would agree with me. We arranged for me to bring her in on the Monday. Mr Keane had no trouble in agreeing that a hip replacement should be attempted, but unfortunately the chest X-ray which they took, as they always do before a major operation, had shown three patches of cancer on a lung and he seemed to want to consult an oncologist before deciding to operate. I was adamant that Daphne needed an urgent hip operation; she was quite unable to walk and it was very difficult for me to look after her. He agreed, but he did not have a free slot for the operation before the Thursday; so I was asked to take Daphne home and bring her back again on the Wednesday.

The operation, which was carried out at the Evelyn Hospital, was completely successful and Daphne was soon able once again to walk without any pain. We then had to decide what to do about the lung cancer. We went to see Mr Mott, the oncologist at Ipswich hospital. Terence Mott was originally a surgeon, but could not continue after a car crash had impaired his sight in one eye. Mr Mott was always very cheerful and felt some affinity towards us, because as a young man he had been assistant doctor on a cruise ship to John de Mowbray – the man who almost married my cousin Françoise Pezzani. Mott decided to put Daphne back on Tamoxifen, which she had taken back in 1990, which had seemed to be very effective with breast cancer. Right up until early in 1999 the X-rays seemed to be very encouraging; the spots were still there but did not seem to be growing, nor did the number increase.

Another blow hit us in April 1999. Cassie, the whippet bitch, had been suffering from heart disease and now took a turn for the worse. A woman vet came to the house. She was a very nice sympathetic girl from New Zealand. Looking back, I think we ought to have had Cassie put down there and then, but the vet seemed to think that there might be a hope if I could get Cassie quickly to the Small Animal Hospital in Cambridge. I set off in the pouring rain and checked Cassie in. About six days later they rang to say that there was nothing they could do for her – except charge us £600 (paid by the insurers!) – and asked me to come and pick her up. Cassie was remarkably brave. Once again I should probably have had her put down, but she lived on for another four or five days. She was able to walk round the garden; and, quite remarkably, two days before she died she suddenly pounced and killed a rabbit. Then one morning when I went down to let the dogs out, there was Cassie, dead on the floor. She had been a very loving dog, but also very demanding; her passion for hunting meant that she was always trying to find a way out of the garden. Sad though it was to have her die – so relatively young – the dogs have since been much easier to manage.

We were never happy to have one dog alone, so we immediately started looking for another. Sally Aldous, who had set us off with whippets again with Merlin, quickly came to the rescue. She knew of a blue whippet bitch at Ixworth, whose owners now were both working all day and had decided that it would not be fair to the dog to leave her alone all day in the house. So I went over to Ixworth with Frankie and we met Milly – the owners had called her Milly Molly Mandy (a name which meant nothing to me). Her owner and I took both dogs for a walk across the fields on leads.

Frankie and Milly seemed to get on perfectly well together, so I agreed to take her. I did however reserve the right to bring her back if she and Frankie did not get on. I asked them when she was due to go into season. They said that she had last been in season just before Christmas, so she would not be due again before June. From Ixworth I drove to Wyken Hall to buy some of Carla Carlisle's delicious white wine, Bacchus. Carla met Milly and said that if she did not get on with Frankie I was not to take her back to Ixworth – she would gladly take Milly. This was on a Saturday.

Daphne was very taken with Milly and that afternoon the two dogs seemed to be getting on exceptionally well together in the garden. Next day, I discovered why. Milly was already in season and I found Frankie and Milly in flagrante delicto! I was horrified – there was no way that I could manage to look after Daphne and at the same time deal with a new litter of puppies. On Monday morning I went straight to the vet and explained my problem. The same New Zealand vet who had treated Cassie saw me and said that she could give Milly an abortive injection, but that she had to warn me that it carried very serious risks; it could have an adverse effect on her bone marrow and be fatal. I had to take the risk. Luckily there were no adverse effects.

But I had a problem. There was no way I could keep Milly and Frankie apart at home for the next ten days of Milly's season. So Frankie had to go to kennels. I can't remember why Rebecca could not take him; but he had to go to some kennels near Wickham Market called Pampered Pets. The same problem loomed later in the summer when it seemed likely that Milly would go into season earlier than normal. I said that she would have to be spayed. Daphne, no doubt after her experience of seven major operations, objected. She had taken to Milly and couldn't bear the thought of her having to undergo serious surgery. The answer suddenly came to me. Frankie would have to be castrated; that was a fairly minor bit of surgery. It seemed to make no difference to him at all. When Milly went into season he was just as frantically interested as he had been before. But, at least we knew that Milly would not have puppies as a result.

Soon after this I took Daphne to see Mott again in Ipswich. He said that the Tamoxifen was not working and recommended that Daphne should be put on chemotherapy. She was to go into Ipswich twice a week for an injection. But after only two injections she decided to abandon it; it made her feel too ill. We had asked Mott what difference chemotherapy, if successful, would make to her life expectancy. He told us that it might prolong her life by 5 per cent. Since it seemed unlikely that she would live more than another two years, this meant in practice adding no more than about six weeks to her life. She was quite prepared to forfeit that for the sake of a more comfortable remaining life.

We had been planning to go together to Dod, where Richard and Amicia were having an outdoor opera performed. But it became clear that Daphne was just not up to it. Around the middle of the summer Daphne paid her last visit to Mott; he confirmed that she was terminally ill and estimated that she might have another 12 to 18 months to live. Daphne was very brave; she must have known this already, and she resigned herself to it. But this was not easy for someone who still then, I think, was inclined not to believe in an afterlife. On 12 August we went into the garden to see the near total eclipse of the sun. I sat Daphne on a chair under the branches of the catalpa. We knew that the eclipse was only going to be 80 per cent or so, but we still thought there would be a noticeable darkening and that birds might behave oddly. Following a tip from a newspaper I had filled a bucket with water and from time to time looked at the reflection of the sun. Sure enough at the maximum, it was possible to see the sun reduced to a crescent, but there was no noticeable diminution in light and the birds behaved perfectly normally. Crispin, Jocelyn, Caroline and Ajax, however were in Normandy and managed to see a total eclipse – very spectacular. They were terribly worried that Ajax might keep looking at the sun after it reappeared and damage his eyes. But all was well.

Daphne's attitude to birthdays had always puzzled me. For the first thirty-six years of our marriage she virtually ignored her birthday and did not want any fuss made. She did not even want birthday cards. Why was this? I don't think for a moment that she did not want to face up to ageing. I suspect it was something more deep rooted. Looking back, I can't help wondering whether it did not mean that she felt that she had no cause to celebrate being alive. That sounds dramatic, but I think it may have been the case. And then, around 1986 she suddenly began to attach enormous importance to her birthday. She was hurt if any of the children forgot to send cards or give her a present. Perhaps now that our marriage had become so secure, she felt there was something to celebrate. Anniversaries have never meant very much to me. I don't remember ever having a birthday party as a child – mainly, I suppose, because my birthday came during term time. Even wedding anniversaries did not mean much in our earlier married years. For our Silver Wedding I bought Daphne an Art Nouveau silver dressing table set of hairbrush, hand mirror and glass dishes for trinkets. I bought the set from a girl in the open air market at Storrington for the remarkably low price of £25. At the time Daphne showed little interest in the anniversary. I thought we then had a happy marriage, but as I have discovered from her diary fragments, she was still desperately insecure.

By the time we reached our Ruby Wedding in 1990 she was much happier to celebrate. Daphne herself bought us for the occasion a set of lovely Dartington glass claret tumblers engraved with our initials intertwined and the date – 1 July 1950. On her last birthday, 24 August, she seemed to be very happy. I remember that she said, 'At least I have managed to get to 73 – that's not bad is it?' The boys had given her a present of caviar from Deauville. A few days later we had our final social encounter. We invited Rebecca around and we drank white wine and ate caviar on little fingers of toast. It was a happy occasion.

A few days later trouble hit us again and there began the worst weeks of Daphne's life – and very stressful ones for me too. One weekend (troubles always seemed to come at weekends) she developed an excruciating pain at the back of her neck. We had to get one of the emergency doctors from Ipswich. He gave her a painkiller which helped a bit. On the Monday I got Dr Foreman round. It seemed clear to me that he suspected that there was now cancer in the bones. From that day on she was bedridden. She could still stand and get herself into the bathroom, but she only went downstairs once again and sat for a while in her electric reclining chair. But she felt more comfortable in bed. Foreman tackled the pain killing with patches which one had to stick onto her chest. They relieved the pain, but had the unfortunate side effect of causing frequent disorientation. This must be bad enough for the sufferer, but it is extremely unsettling for the carer.

One day towards the end of September she collapsed trying to go to the bathroom. I had a terrible job lifting her up bodily and putting her into a wheelchair. Life now became very difficult for both of us. I had to do a lot of lifting. Daphne was not strictly incontinent, but there was no way she could be got to the loo in time and the incontinence pads were not very effective. I seemed to be putting the washing machine on all the time. I think there were days when I put it on at least four times – often in the middle of the night. I had some help from the District Nurses: no longer, unhappily, Kathy Hammond. But I feel they let me down badly. When I asked if they could not arrange for me to have help from the Marie Curie Nurses, they insisted that they could only be called on in terminal cases. Daphne had less than two months to live. If that isn't terminal, I don't know what is.

I was getting some advice from the Macmillan Nurse, but no practical help. For a couple of nights I had some help from a lady from a Nursing Care organisation based at Sibton. She was very good with Daphne but it wasn't enough. I was not up to carrying a second bed into Daphne's room, but I dragged a mattress in and spent several nights on the floor beside her. Early one morning I was in tears and felt I could not go on any longer. I rang Mary Allen, the Macmillan Nurse, and told her that I was at the end of my tether and pleaded for help. She responded very promptly. She got in touch with Mr Mott – who had in fact virtually retired. He arranged for Daphne to be admitted to the Christchurch Park Hospital in Ipswich and Mary sent an ambulance. Daphne looked at me wistfully and said, 'Aren't you getting me out of Buxlow rather quickly?' This made me feel awful, but I knew that I could not have continued on my own. I suppose I could have arranged for full time nursing, but that would have cost the earth.

The move to hospital did wonders for her. Mott completely changed the painkilling regime and fitted her with a pump which was fixed to her tummy and sent a regular flow of some kind of morphine into her bloodstream. She was no longer disorientated and seemed positively cheerful. I began to think that it might be possible at some point to get her home again. BUPA were paying for all this – over the previous nine years they must have paid out over ten thousand pounds. But since she was not being treated for any condition, Daphne could not stay in hospital indefinitely. After a week I was asked to find somewhere else for her. Amicia was with me for a few days then and we looked up Nursing Homes in the Yellow Pages and found one very close to Buxlow at Aldringham. We rang them and they said they had a few vacancies. On the Monday morning we visited the Aldringham Court Nursing Home. We liked the atmosphere. However I was worried that the rooms were a bit poky for Daphne. She had, over the years, become accustomed to living in quite spacious quarters. I asked whether they did not have a larger room. It happened that a double room on the first floor had just become vacant on the death the previous week of an old couple who had been together. I thought it looked just right for Daphne. It cost twice as much as the smaller rooms, but I felt it was worth it.

So Daphne moved in. I took her up and down to the room in her wheelchair in a lift. For the first week or two she made regular trips downstairs and we would have coffee in the dining room. She ate her meals in her room. Both boys and Amicia visited her, Amicia with little Eddo, aged 18 months. He was very sweet. I always carried my mobile phone in my breast pocket and he liked to come and take it and pretend to phone. But here he took it out and very carefully passed it to Daphne through the bars of the hospital bed.

It was then that Crispin told us that Jocelyn seemed to be in love. For some time now he had been working for the Agence Française (Pour la Vente de Chevaux de Pur Sang) and he seemed to have fallen in love with one of the girls who worked there – Muriel Contensouzac. Daphne was absolutely thrilled. It is a great pity that she never had the opportunity to meet Muriel. After two or three weeks, she began to go downhill quite rapidly. One night at about eleven o'clock the phone rang at Buxlow and it was the night nurse from the Nursing Home telling me that Daphne wanted to see me. I went straight over. The male night nurse apologised to me, saying that he had told her that it was selfish to get me out of bed. I rebuked him: 'When you have been married for over 49 years, and your wife says she needs you, you go without hesitation.' We had never removed the second bed from Daphne's room, and the nurse made it up for me.

For the rest of her life I spent almost every night in the room with her. My routine was quite complicated. I would get up and rush home to let the dogs out, have my breakfast and then take the dogs for a walk. I would then go and see Daphne, and usually have lunch with her. Then I had to go home again to give the dogs a run around the garden. On at least two occasions I also played nine holes of golf with Roger Little. I would have an early supper and then return to Aldringham for the rest of the night. Poor Daphne! – she was always so fastidious and modest and private; and now just to go to the loo she had to be lifted from the bed with a hoist and lowered on to the potty; all her intimate bodily functions open to the gaze of carers and me. She never complained, but it must have been terrible for her.

I arranged for Christine Brooks to call on her. Daphne told me that Christine had been very helpful. She had said to Christine that she felt so useless just lying in her bed, but Christine had told her to concentrate on trying to give something to everybody who came in. Disabled though she was, she had the opportunity to give of herself to others. Around this time Daphne once said to me, 'I am worried about how you will get on when I am gone.' I told her not to worry. 'I will have the dogs, I will play golf with Roger and I will probably have people in to meals with me.' At the time, I really thought that the transition from husband to widower would be relatively simple. As I was soon to find, it was not. My routine was becoming very tiring and I arranged to pay a carer privately to spend the night in Daphne's room. She was a very sweet woman called Dagmar with an unpronounceable Polish surname. The last night I spent with Daphne was Tuesday 30 November. I was very touched by one incident that night. Daphne had rung for the night nurse. She was an Irishwoman and as I lay in my bed I heard her say, in her lilting Irish accent, 'Sweetheart, you have a lovely smile.' I believe that the face is a kind of reflection of the soul and I have absolutely no doubt that someone with such a heavenly smile has to be an angel in heaven.

The next day Daphne was not awake very much and I sat with her as much of the day as I could. It was the time of the Newmarket Tattersalls Sales and Crispin arrived and came and sat with Daphne for a while. I think he treasured this last meeting with his mother. Jocelyn was due on the Thursday evening. On the Thursday Daphne was unconscious for most of the day. Dr Foreman came to see her. Crispin and I were there and we asked him if he was happy with the dosage of painkiller; we wondered whether it was not excessive and might be the reason for her unconsciousness. He said that he thought it was right and seemed to think that she would come round and could well live for several weeks. I don't think modern GPs see enough of death at close hand and his judgement was way out. I spent most of the day sitting beside Daphne. I felt sure that the angels were gradually releasing her soul from her body. Mrs Jarvis, the owner of the Nursing Home, looked in and to my surprise said that she would not be seeing me again. I asked her why and she replied that she was going to London the next day and that Daphne would be dead before she returned. In the early evening, just before Dagmar came, Daphne was just conscious for a moment. She had had no nourishment for several hours and I asked the nurse to bring her some ice cream. Daphne took a couple of teaspoonfuls and relapsed again.

On Friday morning at about three-thirty the telephone rang and the nurse told me that Daphne had died. I felt terrible. I had let her down once again. I should have stayed that night with Daphne. But on reflection I realised that Daphne was unconscious all that time and would not have known that I was there. I went and woke both boys. Jocelyn drove us in to the Nursing Home and we paid our last farewells to her. I kissed her on the forehead, which was still warm. We returned to Buxlow and had breakfast. There was no time to grieve; there was so much to do. The undertakers arranged to remove the body to their rooms in Saxmundham. Amicia came up from Kent to be with us and called at the undertakers' with me that afternoon to see her mother's body. I rather wished that I had not gone in too. Undertakers dress up the body in such an artificial manner; she looked cold and white like the effigy on a mediaeval tomb. In the Nursing Home she had still looked human. I arranged with Christine to have the funeral on the following Tuesday. The boys still had work to do at Newmarket, but kept the Tuesday completely free.

I am still remembered by the parishioners of Knodishall for interrupting the preacher in mid sermon that Sunday. Amicia and I went to church and the preacher was Laurie Blanchard, a retired vicar who lives in Knodishall. His views on Christian doctrine are totally at variance with mine, but my interruption was not about doctrine. At some point, using his irritating habit of giving his sermon walking up and down the aisle, as if taking a seminar, he said that forecasting was very difficult, but that he would venture the following forecast: 'In five years time Northern Ireland and the Republic of Ireland will have the same currency – and it will be the Euro.' I exploded, 'You can't say that; that's completely political and nothing to do with the church. And, in any case, the Euro is an abomination.' Consternation in the church! I think Laurie, and perhaps many of the congregation, believed that I only did it because I was suffering from my very recent bereavement; but I am convinced that I would have done the same in any event.

There was nothing in Daphne's will about her funeral, but I found a piece of paper in the drawer of the desk in the winter drawing room addressed to me. I knew that she would not have wanted a cremation, but she also explicitly said that she wanted a completely private funeral. Nobody was to be there apart from me and the three children. I realised that this would upset a number of people who had been closely associated with her in her last years. So I told them all that although the funeral would be private I would give a lunch at Buxlow after the funeral to which they were all invited. In spite of Daphne's wishes I agreed that Richard, Caroline, Ajax and Eddo should be present too. Eddo cannot of course remember it at all but the funeral made a deep impression on Ajax – then three and a half. He still, four years later, seems to remember the occasion. Only last summer he asked me once whether Granny was still in the box in the ground. 'No,' I said, 'the remains of her body are still there but she is now in the next world.'

'Where is the next world?' he asked, 'is it in space?'

What an impossibly difficult question to answer for a seven year old. 'No,' I said, 'it is on a different level of reality.' I am sure we shall come back to discussing it again as he grows older.

I found the lunch a very satisfactory farewell. Beside those of us from the family we had Win and Carol Driver; Mr and Mrs Jarvis, owners of the Nursing Home (the principal nurse was on duty and could not be spared); Dagmar, the carer; Brian Ford (our gardener); Roger Little (my golf and bridge partner – Budge his wife was away); Tina (Daphne's hairdresser, who came to the house to do her hair, and indeed once to the Nursing Home); Bill and Kathy Scarlett (our former gardener and his wife); and Rebecca Toller – roughly twenty people in all. The food was provided and served by the Lighthouse Restaurant in Aldeburgh. I found the lunch deeply satisfying. There were no tears, no speeches, but a lot of friendly conversation and reminiscences of Daphne. Tina, I remember, said that when she had come to Buxlow, Daphne had been the very first person to notice that she was pregnant. Daphne had then insisted that I should thereafter carry Tina's little bag up to Daphne's room for her.

When everybody had gone, the pain of parting began to hit me. I would walk around the garden in tears. Whenever I found myself saying 'my' something or other, rather than 'our', I felt guilty. When I came home after dark, my eyes would go to the window of Daphne's room and I would see no light and realise that she had gone. In spite of my faith and my absolute conviction that Daphne was alive in the next world, I found the parting very painful; much more painful than I had expected. After all I had lived with the prospect for nearly ten years.

Sometime in the middle of December I rang Carla Carlisle at Wyken Hall to see if she had a case of her lovely white wine, Bacchus, that I could pick up. I told her that Daphne had died and she said, 'Come and have lunch and let me give you a hug.' She was very sweet and welcoming. After lunch I went out to my car (or rather, the garage's car – mine was being serviced) and was surprised to find myself staggering. A bottle of Bacchus between us surely should not have had such an effect. But I drove to the garage in Saxmundham to pick up my car – and staggered again. I thought nothing of it and drove home.

Next morning, when I tried to get out of bed my balance had gone; I could not walk across the room without hanging on to pieces of furniture. I rang Roger to say that I was quite incapable of playing golf that day. He asked if I had seen a doctor. It hadn't even occurred to me. But I went to see Foreman. He told me that I had had a mild stroke! – apparently quite a common thing to happen after the end of a long period of strain. I suffered no long term effects, but my left leg seemed less reliable and from then on I walked with a stick.

For the rest of the month I had no time for undue moping. The family were all coming for Christmas and I had to prepare the food and set up the usual 7 ft. Christmas tree. Crispin, Caroline and Ajax were coming, as was Jocelyn, accompanied for the first time by Muriel. Amicia and little Eddo were to join us on Boxing Day. We all missed Daphne, but it was still a happy Christmas.

CHAPTER 30

Widower

THE PAIN REALLY HIT ME in early January, when they had all gone and I was completely alone – except, thank God, for my two dogs. I had a bad attack of flu and was so miserable that I rang the Nursing Home to see if they had a room free and could look after me for a few days. They were fully booked. But I didn't feel I could bear to spend the next night alone. I rang the carers in Sibton and the lady who had come to spend a couple of nights with Daphne in September agreed to come and spend the night at Buxlow. She did not have anything to do, but the mere presence of another live person in the house made all the difference.

January was a bad month, dark, cold and I had this gaping void in my life. It was not just that I loved Daphne; it was that for the previous five years Daphne and I had been locked together. I was never away from her for more than two hours and always available on my mobile phone. Now there was nothing. When I walked the dogs around the garden I would find myself weeping. Whenever I returned home at night (from playing bridge at the Aldeburgh club) my eyes would go to Daphne's room to look for the light. Nothing – and there never would be anything. But there was a lot to do. I answered all the letters of condolence. I also spent a great deal of time in correspondence with Robin Carr, our solicitor, about obtaining probate for Daphne's will and transferring her assets to me.

In the autumn the children had already decided to spend a holiday in Italy in February and had invited me to join them. Daphne had urged me to go, but I told her I would not even contemplate it so long as she was alive. It was remarkably unselfish of her to have suggested that I should go. But now that she was no longer here, I accepted.

The children had taken a Landmark Trust house in the Veneto, the Villa Saraceno, a Palladian villa not far from Vicenza. Amicia and I and little Edward flew from Gatwick to Venice, where we hired a car and drove to the villa. There was quite a large party of us. Besides the three of us there were Crispin, Caroline and Ajax, Jocelyn and Muriel and Jocelyn's great friend from school, Rory Carnegie with his wife Miranda and their three children. The villa could have taken even more of us. When we returned, I showed a postcard of the house to Miranda Kendall, and she asked me in which part of it we had been. 'We took the whole villa!' I said. It was very cheering for me to be with such a loving family and with good friends.

The weather was fine for the time of year. Most days we were able to have lunch out of doors on an enormous refectory table in the porch. With five small children there were no meals out, but we all took turns to do the cooking. There was wonderful shopping in the nearby walled town of Montagnana. Shopping for food on the Continent is always so much more fun than in England; a wonderful butcher, mouth-watering greengrocers and good bread, cheese and pastries. All Landmark Trust houses have a house book; in it, many of the previous tenants had raved about the cooking of an Italian woman who could be hired to cook dinner. Unfortunately she had retired; we tried her successor for one night and had one of the most terrible meals you can imagine to have been cooked by an Italian; the materials were awful and she even served tinned new potatoes. It has only just occurred to me this year that perhaps she was trying to cook us an English meal; if we had specifically asked her to cook us an Italian meal, she might have produced something very much better; surely she could cook pasta!

Although the weather had been fine, it had been rather misty. But on our last two days it became crystal clear and we had splendid views of the snow-capped Dolomites to the north.

When we got back to England I had to start trying to put a new life together. Apart from the five years that we were in America in the 1950s we had had virtually no social life at all. Daphne's irrational fears and panics had made that impossible. But a social life suits me and I soon began to invite people in for drinks or to lunch or dinner. But there was still unfinished business for Daphne. I have absolutely no interest in what happens to my body after I die, but, as I have already said, graves were of very great importance to Daphne. I could have said, rather pompously, that I knew that where she was now she would also have no interest in a grave. But I felt I owed it to her. I knew that she would have wanted a good gravestone, not one of those polished black granite monstrosities.

Daphne had seen an article which referred to the work Harriet Frazer was doing with Memorials by Artists. So early in 2000 I got on to Harriet, who lives not far away at Snape Priory. Amicia and I called on her. I told her that I was thinking of a gravestone which would reproduce the outline of one of Buxlow's Dutch gables. She introduced me to an excellent stonemason, Eric Morland, an American (or was he Canadian?), who lived in Cambridge. He had a lot of work and only took me on, I think, because the idea of reproducing Dutch gables appealed to him. At my request he also designed an old fashioned rose to be carved near the head of the stone – I gave him a photograph of the lovely Charles de Mills rose which had been one of Daphne's favourites. The stone took a long time to make. I visited Cambridge several times to see how he was getting on. One of Amicia's friends from her days on the *Architectural Journal*, Belinda Bamber, lived in Cambridge, and on one of my visits she came to see the work and gave her approval. I then took her out to lunch at the Three Crowns at Maddingley, one of my favourite pubs. The stone was not in fact finished until about February 2001. Not that it mattered; I had been told that one should never erect a stone until about a year after the grave was dug; otherwise it is liable to sink or lean.

When it was finally ready I invited Harriet and Simon Frazer and Eric to lunch at Buxlow. Eric rang that morning to say that he had the most terrible cold and could not come. However the Frazers still came and brought with them a friend of theirs, the poet Herbert Lomas. We had a good lunch. Bertie is very interested in religion and we have since corresponded a bit about religious subjects. He says he thinks that our views are not dissimilar whereas I think we are poles apart. He has this view that the Grace of God can save anyone – however they may have behaved in life. He is prepared to accept a sudden deathbed conversion – a view which I totally reject. If you have spent your life putting your own interests first, it is just not possible to change suddenly.

Daphne's gravestone stands just where I can see it from my pew in Knodishall Church. Although graves are unimportant to me, I always cast a glance at it and think that the plot alongside it is reserved for me!

In the previous summer I had once come into the drawing room to hear Daphne on the phone to Peter Beales, the specialist rose nursery in Norfolk, ordering a dozen shrub roses. I thought to myself at the time that it was very unlikely that she would live to see them bloom. In fact they were delivered only a week before she died. I heeled them in and in early 2000 had to decide what to do with them. Daphne had pretty clear ideas of the gaps that needed to be filled. But I decided on something quite different.

A couple of years earlier, when it was clear that neither of us was ever going to play tennis again, and that the boys were not around enough to play, we decided to dismantle the fencing surrounding the court and to take down the net. A lot of grass had already encroached onto the court and I decided to leave it to grass over on its own. It would have been a big job to dig all the surface up – and there was nowhere obvious to dump the debris. In early 2000 I suddenly decided to get Brian, the gardener, to dig a couple of beds in the middle of the tennis court and to surround them with Victorian black ceramic ribbon edging tiles of the kind we had used for the dogs' graves. He brought in some top soil in his van and we planted the roses all together as a memorial garden for Daphne.

They have flourished and are much admired. There are two Bonica, two Mary Queen of Scots (almost the earliest rose to flower in the spring), two Fru Dagmar Hastrup, a Coupe d'Hèbé, a Fruhlingsmorgen and a Fruhlingsgold in one bed; and then by itself a Comtesse de Lacépède. Two Constance Spry had to go just outside the old tennis court. Caroline still thought they looked a little isolated so I had Brian dig another bed in which I planted four more Bonica and one Daphne! (the rose, not the fragrant shrub). Brian was a pretty hopeless gardener, but very good as a handyman. He did the new rose beds very well and had previously – with no former experience – built a very good brick path in an area which used to be too slippery for Daphne. But one day when I was just off to the Nursing Home, I told Brian that the bed by the old Tudor wall needed a good clean out.

When I got back, I found that he had strimmed the whole bed down to the ground – small shrubs and all!

I consciously tried to build up a social life, inviting people in for drinks, lunch or dinner. I love cooking, so it was no burden for me and I had Win and Carol to clear up for me afterwards. One of the first people I renewed contact with was Jan Franklin, whom I had hardly seen since the early 1980s. In spite of her age – she was already 89 – she was very sprightly. She was totally dependent on carers, who cooked and did the housekeeping for her. Indeed it was always a carer who delivered her to my door by car. We hit it off very well. She liked good food and would always say at the end of the meal, 'Guy, can't you come and cook for me?' One Sunday in church she beckoned to me and said, 'Come and have some sausages with me.' I though she was having some people in for drinks and that there would be cocktail sausages. But when I had been home to let the dogs out and presented myself at Knodishall Place, I found that we were to have lunch *à deux* in her sitting room, served by her carer – sausages and mash. I took her a bottle of champagne on her 90th birthday and that was almost the last time I ever saw her. I had her in to lunch once more with Gabriella Marlesford; Mark Marlesford's parents had been Jan and her husband's best friends. And Gabriella's daughter had just become engaged to one of Jan's grandsons. Jan died early in 2002. I find I miss her company.

I now have quite a large circle of local friends whom I entertain. I have kept my pocket diaries for the last three years and I find that I have given a dinner about once a month, a lunch about the same and rather fewer drinks parties. What a change from the previous forty years! I have also had a few old friends to stay for the weekend, including Fred and Jane Atkinson – they go back a very long way – David and Ruth Somerset (he succeeded me as Personal Assistant to Per Jacobsson), Peter Maugham from the Bank and some friends from KIA.

Quite the most important and delightful event of 2000 was the marriage of Jocelyn and Muriel. The boys had regularly rented a villa near Deauville for the month of August for several years. It was a nice spacious house owned by the architect who had designed it. For the first time I was now free to go and stay with them. August is a very special month for Crispin and Jocelyn; there is racing every day of the month in Deauville and for the last two weeks of the month they (and Muriel) are hard at work with the Bloodstock Sales. So the first half of the month is something of a holiday and that is when guests are welcome. I flew over from London City Airport and two days later Jocelyn and Muriel were married. In the morning there was the civil ceremony at the Mairie, presided over by Philippe Augier, their boss at the Agence, who was also Deputy Mayor – he is now the Mayor. The Mairie is right in the middle of Deauville and there was quite a crowd. Muriel and Jocelyn were smartly dressed in suits. It was the first time I had ever attended a civil ceremony. Philippe's address, taken word for word from the official marriage statute of the Code Napoleon, was quite

Jocelyn and Muriel on their wedding day outside the church at Tourgeville, August 2000

a surprise. It is almost more moral than anything in Cranmer's Book of Common Prayer.

We then returned to the house for lunch and in the afternoon the marriage service was held at the church in Tourgeville. Jocelyn wore a very smart fawn 'Nehru' jacket and Muriel looked lovely in her white wedding dress. The church was packed with friends, racing people, family (on our side, Crispin, Caroline and Ajax, Amicia and Eddo and Ben Worsley, a cousin of Daphne's, and on Muriel's side, her parents and her sister Delphine, and her Aunt Claire with her English husband, Mike), and many other friends. The service was a mixed French and English ceremony. French hymns are, much to my surprise, modern versions of the typical French *chanson*, whereas the English hymns were rousing old fashioned ones, the most rousing of which was 'Praise my soul, the King of Heaven'. Anthony Cazalet sang louder than anybody! There was a lovely reception at the boys' house on the large lawn. I don't know how many people there were, but there must have been a couple of hundred. Muriel's father had found a couple of bottles of 1945 Calvados from a lady in a farmhouse nearby. Many of the French guests were coming up to me and asking me if I would introduce them to him – the two bottles disappeared very quickly!

This was on a Saturday and on the Sunday the Contensouzac parents gave a lunch for some thirty people, again in the boys' house. It was a great occasion. However I did make a bit of a spectacle of myself; I couldn't help breaking into tears at the thought of how much Daphne would have loved the occasion. But I do, I'm afraid, weep very readily.

The summer opera at Dod has become a regular feature. As I have said, Daphne and I had planned to go in 1999, but she was not well enough. I went for the first time in 2000 and I have been in every subsequent year. The four operas I have so far seen at Dod have been, *Don Giovanni*, *The Marriage of Figaro*, *La Traviata* and, last year, *The Barber of Seville*. The audiences – usually two performances on a Friday and a Saturday – seem to love it. The setting for it, in front of vast clipped yews, is superb. The opera group have excellent singers and the production is always good. The producer personally provides English translations of the librettos, which are always elegant and witty. The players and the orchestra are protected from the weather with a covered stage and pit; the audience have to brave it in the open air. But, so far, it has never rained; although on one occasion it was very cold. Most of the audience have picnic dinners in the interval. The Oldfield family and guests eat in the rose garden on a long refectory table. Amicia and Richard are doing a great service in providing this country house opera.

Caroline had a tragic miscarriage in 1998 and both Daphne and I rather hoped that she and Crispin would not try for another baby. But they were determined to. I think Crispin spoke about it to Daphne in the Nursing Home. Anyhow, in the summer of 2000 came the news that Caroline was pregnant again. This meant we had to change our plans for Christmas. The baby was due early in January and Caroline could not possibly come to Buxlow for Christmas so it was decided that I should go and spend Christmas with Jocelyn and Muriel in Normandy. Muriel's father and mother and her sister Delphine also came. Jocelyn and Muriel's flat in Deauville was too small for all of us, so they rented a farmhouse nearby where the three of us stayed. The three Contensouzacs stayed at Muriel's flat.

I travelled to France by Eurostar. I have to confess that I don't much like it. I prefer to feel that I am really going abroad, not just taking the tube under the Channel. But cross-Channel travelling has become relatively easy for me. It is only just over two hours from here to Ashford International station and only about two and a half hours to Dover, when I choose to go by ferry. Christmas in France was an interesting experience. For the French, Christmas Eve is much more important than Christmas Day itself. Muriel's father cooked us dinner on Christmas Eve. The French consume extraordinary amounts of oysters on that day, but we started our meal with smoked salmon. Thibaud's main course was capon and cardoon – apparently a traditional provençal Christmas Eve dish. We followed it with *bûches de Noel*. On Christmas day Jocelyn prepared a traditional English Christmas lunch, including a Christmas pudding bought from Fortnum & Masons.

Whilst I was with them, Jocelyn and Muriel did some house hunting. They both wanted to have children and would clearly not be able to stay in Muriel's small flat. Jocelyn had sold his flat in Notting Hill for a reasonable profit and had funds available. Houses within about fifteen minutes drive of Deauville fetch a considerable premium and they could not find anything suitable. But one day Jocelyn said he would show me a a property they had looked at with a small farm house and a good sized *pressoire* which could be converted, in a most attractive valley with an apple orchard. But he said he thought it was no longer on the market. When we got there, there were builders around and it did seem likely that someone else had bought it. Nevertheless we went in and asked and found that it was in fact still on the market. Muriel was, I think, a little dubious. She had never lived in a house, always a flat, and this valley seemed very remote with no near neighbours. However I suggested that we should drive straight from there to her office in Deauville and time the journey. Quite surprisingly it only took eleven minutes. So it could hardly be considered remote.

Eventually they went ahead and bought the property with the lovely name of La Fontaine Aubray. There were long delays in getting an architect, obtaining planning permission to convert the *pressoire* and there were endless delays in the building. They had hoped to move in by Easter, but did not actually move in until as late as October 2003.

After Christmas, when the lease of our little house was up, I moved into the Hotel Normandie in Deauville for a couple of nights. On New Year's Eve Muriel was giving a dinner in her flat for some of her younger friends, and Jocelyn and I ate together in a restaurant. The whole purpose of staying a few more days in Deauville was to be able to go to Paris and see Caroline and her new baby, which was to be induced (to avoid undue risks) on 2 January. I travelled to Paris by train on the afternoon of the 2nd, still very apprehensive, as there had not yet been any news of the baby. The baby, a little girl, called Alceste, was born whilst I was still on the train. When I got to my hotel near their flat I was greeted by Crispin and Ajax with the wonderful news. How Daphne would have loved to have a granddaughter! I visited the hospital the next day and saw them all. Ajax was absolutely thrilled to have a sister. He was photographed holding his baby sister for the first time. Alceste was one of the very first babies of the new millennium – every country in Europe, except Switzerland, had celebrated the new millennium a year too soon!

In the course of the next three years I have learned to cope with being a widower. I have entertained old friends and made new friends. Amicia, who has a holiday house in Thorpeness and comes to Suffolk quite frequently, always says how lucky I am to live in an area where there are so many nice people. Some, like William and Miranda Kendall, I had seen something of even when Daphne was alive. Both Daphne and I went to their wedding in Kelsale church in 1994. I remember we had to leave the reception early in order to go to a concert at the Snape Maltings. I was driving near Friston when I realised that I had left the tickets at home; we dashed back and made a rather dramatic late entry to the Maltings with me still in morning dress and Daphne with a wedding hat!

But I realise now that Daphne's fears lingered on well into the late 90s. We once invited William and Miranda to dinner with us when Amicia was staying with us. At the last minute Daphne asked to be excused, saying that she did not feel well enough. It must have been irrational fears, but I did not realise it at the time. However I do remember that we ate a turkey and smoked eel stew with apples!

Another friend, whom I first met in 1999, was David Bartleet, a former Bishop of Rochester. He was the guest preacher at a service in Knodishall Church and gave an excellent sermon on the Garden of Eden and the eating of the fruit of the Tree of the Knowledge of Good and Evil. I wrote and congratulated him on it and also sent him a copy of the paper I had written the year before – *A Christian View of Evolution*. I said that I would be interested to hear his views on my paper. We met at Buxlow, for lunch. For some reason I was not there when he arrived and he walked in and introduced himself to Daphne and had a long talk with her. He charmed her.

When we later went to a concert at Snape, he was there with his wife Jean, and Daphne seemed very pleased to see him and commented on how pretty his wife was. I was seriously thinking of asking them both to dinner with us; somewhat apprehensively, in case it proved too much of a strain for Daphne. But she became too ill and it became out of the question. Over the next two years I saw something of the Bartleets at Buxlow and they entertained me at their house in Aldeburgh. David developed cancer in 2002. I paid him a last visit at tea time a few weeks before he died. He was sitting at the kitchen table busy with a tremendously complicated model of a ship. I am sure he knew he was dying, but was still the most perfect and charming host. Although he and I did not agree on Christian doctrines, he seemed to me to be almost saintly.

There have been a lot of other new friends, and I still meet new ones. The garden has played its part in my social life. When I got back from France in January 2001, Brian Ford took me by surprise and announced that he would not be coming again – with absolutely no notice. I am really not sure why he decided to stop working for me, but it actually turned out to be a turning point for the garden. I found a heavy duty gardener – just for mowing, strimming and using a chain saw and hedge cutters – Keith Chapman, who is very reliable and willing and has now been coming to me for three years. But at the same time Carol put me in touch with Chris Newman. She had for many years been 'the Cheese Lady' with a stall in the Saxmundham market. She sold jolly good cheeses too, including cheeses you don't often find in the country like Vacherin and Comté. She had decided to give it up and start gardening, which she loves. She and her husband, Mick, live on a farm in Benhall where, rather surprisingly, he builds yachts – including recently a 70 ft one! She started coming to me immediately on one day a week. Rebecca also decided that she would like to work in the garden and came at the same time as Chris.

They soon transformed the garden. The shrub roses all got properly pruned and Chris had lots of ideas about new perennials. The garden began to look so nice that I thought other people should have a chance of sharing the pleasure with me. That summer for the first time I invited the Aldeburgh Bridge Club to come and spend a Sunday afternoon in the garden. I had not thought about asking them to pay or give to a charity, but one member of the club suggested that I should charge for entry and give to some charity. I didn't like the idea of charging; apart from anything else, that requires somebody at the gate to take the entrance fee. I decided instead to put a Moroccan woven basket on the tea table with a sign saying that donations to the Knodishall Church Organ Fund would be gratefully received. Janet Poll and Betty Gibbs, both members of the club, helped in providing teas. Janet came with an enormous electric tea urn and they both produced sandwiches and cakes. It was a great success. It was one of the hottest days that summer and we raised over a hundred pounds.

The roses, thanks to Chris and Rebecca, looked wonderful. I could not help thinking how much Daphne would have approved of the changes in the garden. I am not sure, however, that she could have coped with the garden full of people. This has now become an annual event and we have even more help and half the donations now go the Friends of St. Andrew's at Aldringham, where Janet worships. I have also taken to providing a wonderful coffee cake, baked by Joan who does the catering for Amicia's garden in Kent.

Some of the members of the Bridge Club who came were also members of the NADFAS painting classes and asked me whether they might come and paint in the garden. I was happy to have them and since that year they have come on two days each summer. They have since been joined – on different days – by the Ufford Art Group and the Kelsale Art Group. The artists mostly try and paint the 'E' from the front and often with it reflected in the main pond. Some are very good, but for many the perspectives are fiendishly difficult. One lady in the summer of 2001 painted something quite different. Enid Lingard painted a delightful picture of the door into the garden from the summer drawing room with all the arum lilies in full bloom. I liked it so much I told her that she must put it in the NADFAS autumn show, She said she had never put a painting in a show. I later invited her and her husband, Tony, to lunch with Tim and Jane Allen; he had been one of my bright young graduates in the EID in the Bank of England in the 1960s – and they all lived at Orford. In November Enid was brave enough to put her painting in the group's annual exhibition. I had had every intention of buying it and was rather disappointed to see the picture marked 'NFS' – Not For Sale. The organiser whispered to me, 'Don't worry. I believe she means to give it to you.' Sure enough, Enid very kindly presented it to me with a lovely inscription. It hangs just inside the door which is the subject of the picture.

Both Enid and Tony told me that they were looking forward to visiting Buxlow again to paint. Unfortunately, Enid became ill very suddenly and died within three months. Tony came the following year and I invited him to lunch with me afterwards to see Enid's painting on the wall. A few months later he invited me to lunch with him in Orford. I was looking forward to it, since he was proud of his cooking. But I never went; a week before the lunch date he fell on icy ground in Leiston and died instantly. He had missed Enid very much, so I was glad that he had lived without her for barely a year.

Through these garden days I have met a lot of new people. Amongst them are Mike and Judith Wilson who live in a large Georgian house in Saxmundham. Judith is an artist and runs the Kelsale Art Group and now, I think, as well the new Saxmundham Art group. In the summer of 2003 the roses in June looked better than ever before. Judith had an artist friend, Dale Pring MacSweeney, who had been commissioned to paint a picture of old-fashioned roses and Judith suggested that she come to Buxlow and see mine and take some to paint. Dale came with another artist friend, Joanna Dunham, and she took some roses away. The final painting was quite lovely; the rose, I think was Grüss an Aachen. This was at about the time of my open Sunday for charity. The evening before I had been to dinner with the Cranbrooks, who have a lovely garden. The guests were shown round the garden and whenever questions were asked about roses, Caroline Cranbrook embarrassed me by saying, 'You must ask Guy, he is the expert.' This is regrettably not true; I know the names of most of my roses but I am hopeless at identifying other people's.

Caroline told them all that they really should see my garden. To my great surprise on the next day – the Open Day – six of the Cranbrooks' guests turned up to see the garden. Later that summer, on a lovely hot day Joanna Dunham invited me to lunch at her house in Sternfield; Dale was also a guest. We ate outside; good food – all my friends seem to be 'foodies'. Over lunch I happened to remark that I was writing my memoirs and had quite recently been writing about acting in *Samson Agonistes* produced and directed by Ken Tynan. Joanna piped up to say that she had once acted in a play produced by Ken Tynan! I went on to say that one of my tutors had been Tony Crosland – 'Oh,' said Joanna, 'I had an affair with him – between his two wives'! I knew that Dale's father had been a very keen jazz fan, and that she had been brought up on jazz records. I also knew that she had until quite recently been living in California. I happened to say that I had written about going to a night club in San Francisco in 1959 to hear a wonderful jazz guitarist, whose name completely escaped me. Dale immediately said, 'Barney Kessel. I had an affair with him!' Suffolk society is not dull!

In 2002 I was host to a most unusual charity function at Buxlow. I had said on one occasion to Pauline Kay, one of the most active members of the Knodishall parish church congregation, that I supposed I should think of holding the annual village fête at Buxlow. She said that she thought we could do something much more interesting. She gave it some thought and came back to me a few days later and said, 'What about a pudding party?' I had never heard of such a thing. There is apparently a pudding club in South-East England which meets about three times a year to have a pudding party. According to Pauline, men love puddings, but their wives try to put them off puddings because they are fattening; so that if you give a pudding party, loads of pudding-deprived men will jump at the chance of having a good tuck in. I remember well from the Bank of England how thrilled Peter Taylor always was when he found that treacle pudding was on the menu. I had rather assumed that a pudding party would be held in the autumn or the winter; but Pauline assured me that it would be fine to have it in May.

The party was held on Friday 31 May 2002; we called it the Jubilee Pudding Party, since it preceded the weekend celebration of the Queen's Golden Jubilee. There was an incredible amount of work involved, all of which fell to Pauline and her friend Marion Wilton to organise. They sold 70 tickets at £10 a head and commissioned puddings – hot and cold – from a large number of willing women in the villages around. The weather had not been very good for most of May, but Friday 31 May turned out to be a lovely warm and sunny day. The guests all assembled at Buxlow at about half past six and were offered white wine and a great variety of canapés – I myself must have made nearly a hundred of my speciality – bruschetta with home made pesto.

We could have sold many more tickets, but had been worried about fitting more than that number in the house if the weather had been bad. As it turned out, there was almost nobody in the house before about 8 o'clock; everybody was drinking wine and eating canapés in the garden. When they came in, Pauline and her helpers had covered the big dining room table with cold puddings – mousses, profiteroles and fruit concoctions. At the end of the room, where I keep the hot plates, there was a great array of hot puddings: treacle puddings, plum puddings, apple charlottes and many many more, being kept warm with several warm trolleys and plates. Everything went with a swing. At one point I heard a man say, 'I'm going back for a seventh helping!' Other helpers were fully occupied pouring out wine – the first glass was covered by the £10 entrance fee, but for the rest there was a basket with a sign suggesting a gift of £1 per glass. And a great deal of wine was sold. But that was not all they got; after the puddings there was cheese and then coffee. In the summer drawing room raffle tickets were being sold. At the end of the party carloads of uneaten puddings were removed. The whole thing was a resounding success and raised over £1200, some for the hospice, some for the church. It would be nice to have another one, but I think Pauline and Marion are not that keen to take on all that work again. Perhaps they will in a year or two; or perhaps we can find some other unusual function.

One feature of social life which took me by surprise was the universal habit of social kissing. When we had lived in America this never happened, and I don't remember it on the few social occasions we had in Suffolk in the early days. I am not sure that I really approve. It is purely ritual. At church I am expected to kiss the three or four women who have been to my house, but I am not expected to kiss any of the other women. Does this make them feel less welcome? It also posed for me a question of etiquette. Does one kiss an Anglican vicar? Christine assured me that it was perfectly proper and showed no disrespect for the cloth! I do not, however, kiss her at the West door on leaving church. It also rather surprises me that a kiss is obviously expected even when one runs into someone in the supermarket or on the High Street.

There are three main occasions in the year when I see a lot of the children and grandchildren. The first is the holiday that Crispin, at any rate, takes almost every February – when the racing world is at its lowest ebb. The second is my annual visit to Deauville and the third is Christmas. In 2001 there was no February holiday – little Alceste was only a month old and Jocelyn and Muriel were busy for some other reason. In the summer the boys decided not to rent again the house where the wedding reception had been held the previous year. The owners had increased the rent substantially over the previous ten years. Instead Jocelyn and Muriel stayed in their flat and Crispin and Caroline and their children took a farmhouse at Clarbec, about fifteen minutes from Deauville and quite close to Pont l'Evêque. I went to stay with them for ten days or so. I decided not to fly but to take my own car with me. Having my own car gave me more freedom to come and go. It also allowed me to go and do the shopping for them in Pont l'Evêque. Nothing would induce me to shop in Deauville – I just could not cope with the parking!

Amicia unfortunately, for me, at least, was not at Dod, so I could not break my journey there. Instead I crossed to Calais on a Seafrance ferry at lunch time on a Sunday – I choose a French ferry for the food! They serve excellent lunches in the brasserie. They served that day *souris d'agneau*. I didn't know what it was going to be until it arrived. It turned out to be lamb shank! – and very good too. I then drove to Le Touquet and stayed at the Hotel Westminster – a mistake. On a blazing hot afternoon it took me over an hour to get from the turn off from the autoroute to the hotel. The drive to Clarbec the next day was very simple – only about three hours on almost empty autoroutes.

Ajax and Alceste were very sweet. Alceste at the age of about 7 months had just reached that stage where I can relate to a baby. She could just sit up and was almost able to crawl. One day, Ajax sitting beside me on a sofa looked up at me with sympathetic eyes and said, 'I'm sorry you have not got Grandma.' I was very touched. The funeral had made a great impression on him.

Christmas 2001 was a very happy occasion. Although Muriel was now pregnant, the baby was not expected until March, so there was no reason why she and Jocelyn could not come to Buxlow for Christmas. Crispin and Caroline were also free to come, but had been prevailed upon to spend Christmas Day with Caroline's mother and stepfather in London. But they came to us on Boxing Day. Muriel's mother and father and her sister, Delphine, also joined us. They had to fly from near Grenoble to Stansted and were due on the Saturday before Christmas. However on the Saturday it began to snow heavily – global warming, you know! – and Stansted airport was closed so they were not able to join us until the Sunday. On that Sunday I had invited a lot of young people from around here with their children to drinks before lunch. My idea had been for the children to meet Ajax and Alceste. That was not now possible, but Amicia came for a couple of days with Edward, so there was at least one child on my side, and it was a very happy party. The garden looked absolutely lovely, covered in snow and bathed in sunshine. The children were left to amuse themselves. The Kendall children had turned up with a sledge and the children pulled each other around the garden on it. The garden is completely flat so there was no real tobogganing. Other children wandered all over the house playing Hide and Seek. When it was finally time to go one of the James's children could not be found . For a moment there was a bit of a panic, but he was found – upstairs, still hiding.

Jocelyn and Muriel went to Stansted that afternoon to pick up the Contensouzacs. Christmas was rather more English than French, but the food was not quite traditional. The first course was some very good French foie gras. I have rather tired of turkey and I find goose very difficult to cook; it is so hard to prevent it drying out so I produced a large English roast of sirloin beef. And of course, we had English Christmas pudding. But, in the absence of both Amicia and Crispin there were no children. Nor was it a typical English Christmas, in that we spoke nothing but French; Muriel's parents and her sister hardly speak a word of English. Jocelyn came with me to church and afterwards, with reference to Christine's sermon, said, 'Well that was all right for you, wasn't it – she actually called Jesus God.' It was one of those rare occasions when she had! On Boxing Day the Contensouzacs left and Crispin and his family came. By this time Alceste was running around. At one point Caroline came and asked where the vacuum cleaner was. When I asked why, she showed me – the breakfast room floor was covered with black peppercorns! Now, whenever a small child is due at Buxlow, all the shelves of condiments and spices are cleared first.

The February holiday in 2002 was again without Jocelyn and Muriel – their baby was due in mid-March. Crispin rented a house on a farm estate overlooking a vineyard in the Penedes region of Catalonia – just to the west of Barcelona. Amicia, Eddo and I flew to Barcelona, hired a car and drove to the farm. Crispin and his family arrived the next day. The weather was unusually warm for the time of year and we had a lovely time. Amicia and Eddo were only able to stay for a couple of days, but I stayed on rather longer. Vila Franca del Penedes was our main town for shopping. This is the region where cava is produced, the Spanish sparkling wine, and we went to several vineyards for tasting. I have rather taken to cava and now always serve it at my drinks parties – livened up with a touch of mûre (the blackberry liqueur). We did some sightseeing, but I did not want to see Barcelona again – I am not at all fond of Gaudi's Sagrada Familia; the others went later, after taking me to Barcelona airport.

The most interesting place we visited was the monastery of Montserrat. The setting is extraordinary; it is set at the top of one of the strangest looking range of hills; from a distance they look like a herd of great humpbacked animals – elephants, perhaps. The main claim to fame of the monastery is the Black Madonna, which was visited by Saint Ignatius de Loyola before he founded the Jesuits. We had to join a vast queue, which shuffled its way up the church to the madonna hanging in an alcove behind the altar; all around me were the 'faithful' crossing themselves as they gazed at it.

I love my grandchildren the more I see of them. Little Alceste, already a year old, is adorable and Ajax is so sweet and sensitive. Edward is very different – boisterous and noisy, but he seems to love me and gets on very well with Ajax. Every night I had to tell them a bedtime story. My stories always revolve around a goblin called Humphrey, who, unlike all other goblins, loves human children and can work the most amazing magic. We kept in close touch with Jocelyn; we thought the the baby might arrive whilst we were still in Spain. But Arthur (pronounced Arture by his mother) was born on 6 March – the first Moubray to be born in Normandy for over 900 years (that's quite a thought isn't it?). He was a very large baby and still is two years later.

That summer for some reason the boys again rented the house that they had been renting for over ten years. Once again I drove to Normandy taking the ferry from Dover. But on this occasion I broke my journey at a B & B in Kent. I had, as always with my family, a very nice holiday. As I have said many a time, I just cannot relate to small babies, so I did not bond with Arthur, but the other two continued to be a delight. Ajax was now six and going to school in Paris, but he could not yet read. He asked me once to read him the *Harry Potter* book that was on the table. Obediently, I began to do so. 'No,' he said, 'in English.' So I had to do simultaneous translation, which is quite demanding. The house had a nice swimming pool, so we divided our time between the pool, the beach and the racecourse.

On my way home, I bought myself some delicious charcuterie in Pont l'Evêque and broke my journey to Calais visiting a lovely garden near

With my three children and five grandchildren at Fontaine Aubray May 2004

Dieppe, le Jardin de Bellevue; it had a particularly fine display of hydrangeas; although I have never ever seen in any other garden except Buxlow, one of my best hydrangeas, *Arboreum sargentiana*. It is, of course, too large a plant for a small garden, but Bellevue was a large estate. I lingered a bit too long and after having a drink at the Aire du Baie de la Somme on the motorway, I suddenly found that I would have to hurry to catch my ferry. I drove the rest of the way at 90 m.p.h. – and was still now and again overtaken! I again broke my journey back to Suffolk at a B & B in Kent.

I think it was in the late summer of that year that I had the most traumatic experience of my life. Viola had come to stay with me and arrived just before lunch so we walked round the garden with the dogs and then came in to eat. After lunch I said to Viola that I was planning to go into the garden with the dogs and have a rest in the pavilion. But there were no sign of the dogs – neither in the house nor in the garden. We had inadvertently left the garden door open and the dogs were gone. When they disappear I know that they usually go down the hedgerows to the east and frequently end up in a small copse down near West Farm and I set off to find them. Normally it doesn't take very long to find them. But this time they had been gone for probably as long as an hour and I could not find them anywhere.

On my way to the copse I carefully negotiated a shallow ditch, but on my way back I misjudged it and fell – into a bed of nettles. Even worse, I was wearing a short-sleeved shirt. And to make things even more difficult, in my fall my mobile phone had fallen out of my breast pocket and had also disappeared in the nettles. I was not feeling particularly strong that summer and I simply could not get to my feet. I kept struggling and then falling back into the nettles. I was in despair. I thought I would never make it. I couldn't ring anybody. Viola did not know in which direction I had gone. I thought it might be hours before I was found. After praying, I finally struggled to my feet; it must have taken twenty minutes. I was shaken and trembling and I knew I could not now negotiate the ditch on my own. I saw Angela Wallis in her garden about a quarter of a mile away and began shouting 'Help!' and waving my stick. She eventually cottoned on and came over the field to me with a man who turned out, quite remarkably, to be Frank Hall Hall, from whom we had bought Buxlow. He had briefly returned from Canada to arrange to sell the land he had kept round Buxlow. Indeed the ditch into which I had fallen was on his land. Angela found my mobile phone and they helped me back to the house.

I was in agony from the nettle stings and eventually decided that I could not stand it and drove to the surgery. I waited impatiently and when the nurse saw me I said, 'Thank God, now you can give me some cream to soothe my pain.' But it turned out that no such cream exists. All they could give me were some antihistamine tablets to chew. It took several days for the pain to disappear. Happily, when I got back to Buxlow, the dogs had

With my five grandchildren on the same day

reappeared. When I told Crispin that it had been the most traumatic experience of my life, he said, 'Surely not; it must have been much worse being fired at by Japanese snipers.' But that had not been anywhere as bad; if you hear the bullet, you know you have not been hit!

Christmas 2002 was for me another lovely family affair. I never understand why I so often read that families hate Christmas reunions. My children do not, I am sure, just come to me because they feel they ought to. This year we had Crispin and Jocelyn and their families for Christmas itself. Crispin and Caroline did not go to Caroline's mother until Boxing Day. On Muriel's side her father was missing – literally; that summer he had walked out on his wife and for some months was not heard of at all. Jacqueline obviously found this very painful, but Muriel was also very upset about it. So from the Contensouzacs we only had Jacqueline and Delphine. We again had a splendid drinks party on the Sunday before Christmas. My suit made a bit of a hit. Rather unusually, Johnny Boden's catalogue had in it that autumn a purple moleskin suit – shades of Ken Tynan in Oxford! One of my guests said how brave it was of me to wear it and he wished that he had the nerve. I never feel brave when people say that I am!

The February holiday in 2003 was again with Crispin and his family. I cannot remember why Jocelyn could not come. Crispin and Caroline again rented a house in Catalonia; this time to the east of Barcelona, near Gerona. Amicia and Eddo could not join us either. So I flew on my own from Stansted to Perpignan, where I hired a car. In England it is not possible to hire a car when you are over seventy, but it is allowable everywhere on the Continent – very sensible. The drive from Perpignan is not much over an hour and a half, and I had hoped to arrive before dark. Unfortunately, Ryanair managed to lose my suitcase, which meant some delay, and I did not quite make it in daylight. It was dark when I left Gerona and headed into the country. Spanish roads are not that good and just before the turning to their house I drove too close to the edge, where the tarmac suddenly falls away. I did not go into the ditch and managed to extricate myself. But I realised I had a flat tyre. Thank goodness for mobile phones. I rang Crispin and within minutes he and Ajax appeared. Regrettably, we discovered that both my near side tyres had been punctured. So we had to leave the car by the side of the road.

My next problem was that I had not carried any hand luggage with me and all my medicines were therefore missing. I take quite a cocktail of pills every morning and a few at night – mainly for my heart – and since we had no idea how soon Ryanair would find my case I thought we ought to try to do something about it. I rang the surgery in Saxmundham and asked them if they would be prepared to fax my prescriptions to a chemist in Gerona. They were happy to do so, but first we had to find a chemist where someone spoke English. Caroline, resourceful as ever, soon found one, and I rang to enquire whether they would supply me with pills on the basis of a fax from my doctor. 'No trouble at all,' said the pharmacist. 'But no need for a fax; just tell me the pills you need.' I had already taken down the full details from the Saxmundham pharmacists, so I was able to give her the information she needed. 'Come along in half an hour, and I will have them ready for you.' I found this quite amazing. I cannot conceive of any chemist in England doing the same thing.

The house they had rented was a modernised thirteenth century farmhouse standing quite alone at the end of a track near some cork oak woods. Whereas in 2002 the Catalonian weather had been unusually warm, in 2003 it was unusually cold, but the house was very well heated. None of us knew that this area to the north-west of Gerona is the site of innumerable extinct volcanoes. We also discovered that not more than a mile or so away was the largest crater in Europe with a diameter of 1.5 kilometres. We explored it one afternoon. We had both cars with us and as I did not feel up to making the full circuit of the crater, Caroline, Alceste and I returned to the house, whilst Crispin and Ajax set out to complete the trip. When we got back to the house, it began to snow. Within minutes there was a blizzard and snow was now lying quite thickly on the ground. We got quite worried about Crispin and Ajax, but we could do nothing but wait. They too were worried. They found it hard to see where they were going, but thankfully they got back safe and sound.

Crispin was too young in 1965 to remember our holiday on the Costa Brava, but it wasn't far away and we went to see some of the old familiar sites. We all visited the Greek and Roman ruins at Ampurias – as I have said earlier, they now keep the beautiful mosaics covered with soil during the winter, but it is still an impressive site. Feeding children in restaurants in Spain is made easy by the existence of tapas; you order a dozen or so separate dishes and everyone can find something they like. One day we drove up the coast to see Estartit, where we had stayed in 1965. What a disappointment – it was hideous; the great long empty beach was now lined with hotels. So we went on to La Escala and had lunch. It was a beautiful day, and very warm in the sun, so we sat at a table outside.

Whilst we were there Crispin's mobile phone rang; it was the airport at Perpignan, saying that my suitcase had turned up. This must have been at least four days after I had arrived. We decided to drive to Perpignan together after lunch and collect my bag. On our way back we suddenly realised that Caroline and the children's passports were in the house in Spain. We hoped desperately that the border guards would not ask to see them. They didn't; they were far too preoccupied with terrorists – we slowed down and there must have been a dozen policemen armed with machine guns looking, I imagine, for Arab looking faces. They even had those spiky chains which can in an instant be thrown across the road to puncture the tyres. We passed muster and drove on. On other trips we explored the extinct volcanoes, which were mostly too steep for me to climb up and then climb down. But it was fun. Crispin, Caroline and their children are always a great pleasure to be with.

Before I set off back to Perpignan, Caroline suggested that I should put my medicines in a separate bag and carry them on the plane. I said that it was inconceivable that Ryanair could lose my bag again. How wrong I was. At Stansted there was no sign of my suitcase. Luckily this time I had medicines at home, so I did not panic. I calculated that Ryanair had my suitcase for no fewer than nine days of the twelve days I was away! On my way to Perpignan I stopped off for lunch at Collioure, where we had spent our honeymoon 53 years earlier. Remarkably, Collioure is still unspoilt. It is a delightful fishing port – anchovies are the great thing on that coast.

In the summer, Jocelyn had hoped that his new house was going to be ready; but even if it had been, we could not all have fitted in. So Jocelyn and Muriel and little Arthur stayed in their flat and Crispin rented a nice little house in Beaumont-en-Auges. This time I decided to break my journey at the hotel that Daphne and I had often used years before when heading off to the south, the Chateau de Montreuil, about an hour's drive from Calais. It was still very good but much too expensive for me. From Montreuil I drove to visit a garden near Dieppe, the Parc du Bois des Moutiers. The house was by Lutyens and the garden was the creation of Gertrude Jekyll. It was quite beautiful. Somewhat like Dod, it has the peculiarity of having acid soil over chalk. Come to think of it, they actually did have a hydrangea *Arboretum sargentiana*. I had a nice lunch in a little *auberge* and then drove to Beaumont.

My main memory of this holiday was the heat. On several days it exceeded 100 degrees Fahrenheit. I also discovered the French word for a heatwave, which I had never known before – *canicule*. The other memory was barbecues; we seemed to have barbecues almost every day; and it was my job to cook – lamb chops, sausages and slices of aubergine and courgette. I was disappointed to find that I did not seem to be able to relate to little Arthur; we had got on so well at Christmas. He did not respond to English or French. On the spur of the moment I tried him with gobbledygook – he loved it! So I can say with conviction that Arthur's first spoken language was Double Dutch. Even today, nine months later, if Jocelyn puts Arthur on the phone we have a great gabble together!

For Christmas 2003 with Muriel pregnant again, we could not have Christmas at Buxlow and we all stayed in Normandy. Amicia and Richard and their family were in Australia. But in mid-December, just before they left for Australia, Amicia came to Buxlow and we gave a party together for all her friends and their children. In Normandy Jocelyn and Muriel were in their new house and Jacqueline and Delphine stayed with them. Crispin had rented a nice house at St. Georges-en-Auge near St. Pierre-sur-Dives, where the rest of us stayed.

This time I travelled to France by Eurostar once again and Jocelyn came to meet me at the Gare du Nord and drove me to their house. I stayed there for a couple of days before Crispin and his family turned up. The house in the country had, rather unusually, a small private golf course of seven holes. Once again we had a lovely holiday, although I have to say I missed Buxlow and my dogs! All went well on my return journey – again by train to Ashford.

However my homecoming was most unpleasant. The house was absolutely freezing cold when I got in; the boiler had been left to go on for two hours a day, but it clearly hadn't been on for days. I pressed the restart button, but it wouldn't go. It was now too late to ring the maintenance engineers. Rebecca agreed to keep the dogs for another night; they would have been frozen. I managed to survive with the help of two electric convection heaters and a hot water bottle. Luckily the engineer came early the next afternoon, but it still took over 24 hours to get the house warm again.

At the beginning of 2004 there was another change in the garden. Chris's husband, Mick, who builds yachts, decided to move to a boatyard in Ipswich and wanted Chris to work for him there. Now I realise what all those computer classes to which she went were for! So she has given up. I have since found an excellent replacement in Richard Pigrome, the husband of Lorraine who handles all my photocopying. I have kept them both very busy in recent months!

Here I am, nearly up to date. I am left only with the February 2004 holiday to describe. Once again Jocelyn and Muriel could not join us, the new baby was due in mid-March. Crispin and Caroline are very clever at finding nice houses on the internet. This time they rented a house in the medina at Essaouira in Morocco. They flew to Marrakech, where Amicia and I and Eddo joined them, having flown from Gatwick. The cousins love seeing each other and there was a great reunion at the airport. Crispin had rented a large 4 × 4, but with the seven of us and our baggage it was a tight squeeze. Essaouira is on the Atlantic coast about 100 miles from Marrakech.

It was dusk when we reached Essaouira. We were outside the Bab Marrakech, one of only three gates into the walled town. I had not been there for 28 years! Superficially Morocco had changed very little; almost everybody was still wearing jellabas and gandouras. The only exception were the school children; female as well as male, wearing European type clothes. Surprising this, I think, when the French government is making such a fuss about Muslim girls wearing head scarfs – I didn't see one in Essaouira. The souks are still much the same, although I noticed that one of the souk stalls was selling nothing but mobile phones and another only CDs! Mobile phones were quite a feature; when we arrived our first task was to ring the housekeeper on her mobile and ask her to come to the Bab to meet us. 'I'll be wearing a red jellaba,' she said. No cars are allowed in and all our luggage was taken to the house by a young boy in a hand cart – on which before too long, there also sat three grandchildren.

I had never thought, when I lived in Morocco, that I should ever be staying in a house right in the medina. It was fascinating; there are no windows in the walls, but there is a central courtyard, many of them open to the sky, but ours covered with a glass canopy; so there was plenty of light. For a view across the medina and over the walls to the harbour and the sea, you had to climb to the very top of the house onto a flat roof. Late as it was, our cook went off into the medina to buy something for our dinner. When we discovered a few shortages of essential household equipment, we just rang the cook on her mobile out shopping and asked her to get them for us! The cook gave us dinner every night, substantial tagines or rich couscous. She also brought us bread and croissants in the morning for breakfast. We always had lunch out. When we had been together in Essaouira in 1977 we had lunch on the quayside; grilled sardines, freshly caught. Now the town has become a major tourist resort and on the quayside there are a dozen stalls with awnings and tables where one can have grilled fish; no longer just sardines, but a vast array of seafood – dorades, prawns, crab, sea bass, little soles and even stranger fish, all beautifully displayed. With it you have tomato salad with red onions and no alcohol. But Morocco is very lax on alcohol; they have excellent wines and Crispin and I used to go the vintner to choose our wines for dinner.

According to a travel book written by a friend of Amicia's, Essaouira is the loveliest of all Morocco's coastal towns, stretching from the Mediterra-nean down to Agadir. It is unusual for an Arab town, because, unlike Fez, where the lanes run in all sorts of strange directions, everything, or almost everything, is in straight lines, for the town of Essaouira was designed by a French engineer in the late eighteenth century. Some of the fortifications are a good deal older. Under the Portuguese, the town had the lovely name of Mogador. The weather was kind to us, but very windy. I became so sunburnt I had to buy a hat (made in Mali). With the 4 × 4 we were able to go on obscure pistes and get right away from it. On one of our trips we had to avoid camels crossing in front of us, and cows, sheep and goats. Crispin and his children had a lovely ride on camels. In one of my bedtime stories for the two boys I introduced a white camel with magical powers! The three children got on very well together. I had a lovely holiday. I do so love my children and my grandchildren – not forgetting my two daughters-in-law.

On our last day we all drove back to Marrakech together. As I have said, Essaouira is some 100 miles from Marrakech and the High Atlas must be another 20 miles further on. When we were at least 80 miles from the mountains I suddenly realised that what I had thought for a moment was a line of white clouds on the horizon was actually the great long sweep of the snow covered Atlas. It is an unforgettable sight. Amicia's and my flight was three and a half hours later than Crispin's. We found that even in Morocco, fear of terrorists makes it impossible to leave luggage in a left luggage store so we took everything with us in a taxi to the Mamounia Hotel. Amicia and I with Daphne had last been there in January 1977. The hotel is still on a remarkable site and the gardens are unchanged, but inside it is now like any other first class hotel anywhere in the world. They were happy to look after our luggage for us, whilst we had a meal, but they were not prepared to allow Amicia and Edward to swim in the pool; that was only possible if you had a room. So Amicia booked a room – for four hours; they charged us half price! The two of them had a long swim in the pool. We then had a small meal; Edward his usual plate of potato chips and Amicia and I a couple of croques-monsieurs.

We still had time on our hands, so we decided to take a taxi to the Djmaa-el-Fna to show Edward the sights. Being a Friday, it was not as crowded as usual. Amicia made the mistake of saying very clearly, 'Oh look, there is a snake charmer.' Within seconds the cobra began to emerge swaying from its basket, but more alarmingly, a snake charmer dashed up to us with a snake in his hands. Edward was absolutely terrified. To reassure him I stood still – and to my horror the man then wound the snake round me and began to make it kiss my mouth! Edward would have none of it. The man then demanded 200 dirhams (about 12 pounds) – the snake's kiss was supposed to have assured me good fortune. I hadn't got a penny on me. 'Je n'ai pas un sou,' I kept saying. I then went off to a chemist to buy something with a bank note from Amicia in order to have some change. When Amicia caught up with me, she said the man had been persistent and she had eventually bought him off with a one pound coin! This seemed a good time to go. To Edward's delight we returned to the Mamounia in a horse drawn carriage. I remembered that in 1977, Crispin had managed to fall out of one of these vehicles.

We arrived back at Gatwick after midnight in freezing cold weather. The next morning – Amicia is a glutton for punishment – they had a Meet at Dod! The sun was out and it was a lovely sight; I do hope that hunting is not abolished. I helped carry out platters of sausage rolls. And then back to Buxlow and my dogs.

On 9 March, around midday, I was at my word processor, finishing off the family tree. I had just got to the very end with Jocelyn marked as having a son, Arthur, and a blank space for the next child. I went down to have lunch and the phone rang. It was Jocelyn to say that their new baby, a girl called Rose, had been born half an hour ago – just at the time that I had put in a blank space for the new baby! So I now have five grandchildren. How Daphne would love to have seen Rose. After lunch I was able to bring the family tree right up to date! This brings me up to the present and I will only add a brief chapter taking stock of my life and the world around me. I will just mention that I have suddenly decided to go to London at least once more. I have been invited to Sandy Wilson's 80th birthday party and will go and stay in Amicia's flat. Sandy and I first met 62 years ago! His voice on the telephone sounds just as it did then.

But before I take stock I shall reflect for a moment on the changes I have seen in Suffolk. Twenty-five years ago Suffolk was much more rural. The girls in the newsagents in the Market Place in Saxmundham wore badges on their lapels which read: 'Don't hurry me. I'm from Suffolk.' Farmers played a much more important part in the community. They were all well

Sandy Wilson's 80th birthday party

off; every single farmer seemed to have a fairly new Mercedes. Now they are reduced to small Suzuki 4 × 4s or battered old Land Rovers. They still had farm workers, not as many as before the advent of tractors, but Stigwood who farmed the land around me had at least three farm workers who all lived in tied cottages. The same cottages have now been sold to weekenders or outsiders. It is they who have the Mercedes, BMWs or swanky 4 × 4s.

The very local nature of the community is illustrated by a story, a true story, that I tell. About twenty-five years ago there was a murder in Saxmundham. An off-duty American airman was stabbed to death by an Englishman in a brawl outside the Bell Hotel. A few days later, I was filling up with petrol at the Windmill Garage (which no longer exists) and I asked the girl who was serving me, whether the murderer had been a local man. 'Oh, no,' she said, 'He was from Kelsale.' Kelsale and Saxmundham are coterminous!

There was much more livestock in the early days; although the farm for Buxlow had not had livestock for many years I think. The old dairy is still here, but has not seen use for over forty years. Flick and Son in Saxmundham had a weekly outdoor market, and the sale of livestock played an important part in it. We bought all sorts of things in the outdoor market – little statues for the garden, the arum lilies which flourish outside the garden door and most of our garden tools. That market must have closed at least fifteen years ago.

And the crops were different. I don't remember seeing the ubiquitous oilseed rape with its vivid yellow flowers until around 1985. There was still the need for casual labour. In the large field on the right driving into

Saxmundham I remember seeing groups of women and small children lifting potatoes. The potatoes were extracted from the ground by a machine, but they had to be lifted by hand. Farmers were still permitted to burn stubble; our local farmer was very inconsiderate – he would set the stubble ablaze upwind from us without prior warning, giving us no time to shut the windows to keep out the soot.

Another important feature around here was the Americans. The American Air Force had a base at nearby Bentwaters. Military aeroplanes were constantly flying noisily around. I had the impression that Buxlow was a landmark for the planes, they seemed to circle the house and then return to Bentwaters. Initially they were very fast jet aircraft, but later they were the A 10 tank busters, which circled around until the end of the Gulf War, in which many of them were used. There were many more coloured people then, because of the American airmen. There were always Americans in Saxmundham, where many of them lived in rented houses. On the lanes one frequently passed American joggers. One still sees people running, but I wouldn't call them joggers; they seem to be more serious, training for the London marathon.

Saxmundham was a miserable town, completely blighted by having the A12 going right through the High Street. The bypass was not to come until the early 90s, I think. There was no supermarket, but three butchers, three grocers and at least two greengrocers. Apart from the heavy traffic, the High Street was probably much as it had been since the war. There was a very old-fashioned emporium, Ashford's, presided over by a dragon of a lady at a desk in the entrance. It was one of those stores where your bill and your money were despatched up to the accountant by a pneumatic tube; your change and the receipt returned the same way. None of my grandchildren will have any idea of what that means.

I suppose there may have been supermarkets in Ipswich, but Daphne and I never did our food shopping there. We soon discovered Baker Bros., the grocers in Leiston who delivered our groceries once a week. When we first went there the owner was still Mr Baker. But he soon sold out to Mr Hurn, who had been with Fortnum & Mason in London. This was the first faint stirring of modernity. Baker Bros. became known as the Fortnum of East Anglia. But I regret to say that it has since declined. It is being driven down-market by the competition from the supermarkets; suppliers are not prepared to supply anything but large quantities of their products. One of the biggest changes in the last twenty-five years has been the quality of the food. The Friday Street Farm Shop opened up very soon after we arrived and from very humble beginnings, with mud coated vegetables, now has expanded to supply a wide range of good local produce, including excellent meat and local cheeses. The one remaining dairy farm in the near neighbourhood, at Friston, just two miles down the road from us, now produces a range of organic cheeses, to all of which they have given the name of Buxlow. Buxlow Paigle, the Suffolk dialect word for cowslip, is a hard cheddar type cheese. A soft cheese, a bit like ricotta, is called Buxlow Wonmill (apparently a Suffolk word for a soft cow's milk cheese); they also have a range of curd cheeses called Buxlow Scransh, flavoured with horseradish, or chives, or fenugreek. The pubs and restaurants have also changed beyond recognition. When we first came here, I guess the best pub was the Crown at Westleton, which served roast beef (rather overdone) and local fish and chips. Now there is a plethora of sophisticated eating places.

The Bell in Saxmundham now does real haute cuisine to a very high standard. And the Old Chequers at Friston has recently been offering crocodile, bison and ostrich! – not that I think they taste very nice. It is not surprising that I saw Suffolk described in a magazine recently as Chelsea-on-Sea!

CHAPTER 31

Taking Stock

AT THE BEGINNING OF THESE MEMOIRS I quoted from a sermon by an American New Church clergyman. It included these words: 'In this huge city of human memories live the wishes, the urges, the demands, the desires, the wants of man. These inhabit the houses and either use them properly or ruin them for habitation.' And I added: 'I hope I have used them properly.' At the time I think I was confident that when I had got to the end, I would indeed feel sure that I had used them properly. But, now that I am at the end, I am not so sure. Crispin has been reading the manuscript of these memoirs as they were up to about two months ago. He has told me that my account of the later years is tinged with melancholy. He added that he thought that was quite unjustified. Unjustified or not, it is I think true.

At the moment the negative aspects of the world and of my life seem to outweigh the positive. Perhaps this is always so for old people. I don't know how old Theodore Dalrymple is – and I don't even know who he is, since that is a pseudonym – but in a recent *Spectator* he said: 'For I have reached the age at which one realises that one has lived, as indeed one must live, in vain.' I am not at all sure that I know what he really means by that. Although the negative tends to outweigh the positive, I certainly don't feel that I have lived in vain. Somebody asked me recently whether I had given my memoirs a title. It had never occurred to me to do so, but when I thought about it, the idea came to me that I should call them *Never Quite*. I think this sums up my dissatisfaction with my own achievements and my anxieties and worries about the the world around me. But that too probably exaggerates my feelings. Sometimes, when I wake in the early hours, I lie in bed and wonder why the Lord is still keeping me alive. Divine Providence must always have a reason. There is still something that the Lord expects me to achieve. But I do not know what it is. Thinking about what I am going to write in this final chapter has given me an idea of a possible answer to that question. I will come back to it at the very end.

My current melancholy relates both to what I have done with my life and to the state of the world around me. And there is not much that I can be expected to do about the world. The world around me has changed to a remarkable degree. Anybody born at any time in the last two hundred years, who had managed to live like me to his 80th year, would be able to say, with some truth, I think, that the pace of technological and social change had never been greater. The BBC was founded a year or two before I was born – and I now have digital television with interactive capacities. I

397

am now on the internet and do e-mails and internet banking. As recently as 1947 in Jersey, to call the telephone exchange you had to crank a handle which rang a bell for the operator. Now I have a mobile and can ring anyone from almost anywhere. I can use it in France, Spain or Morocco, but it actually slightly irritates me that I cannot operate it in the middle of Tunstall Forest, where I walk my dogs. I hope I don't collapse there one day!

Travel abroad has become so much easier. Even fifty years ago most people travelled abroad by ship. Now aeroplanes fly us anywhere with remarkable speed. And when one is abroad one no longer needs travellers' cheques and remittances to banks; a credit or a debit card will make cash available to one almost anywhere. The range of goods available to shoppers in England is now quite extraordinary. There are many who criticise the supermarkets, but I have to say that I think they have played a major role in stimulating competition and in increasing the quality of products on sale. The range of fresh fruit and vegetables and the clean and attractive way they are presented is in marked contrast to what one used to see in a high street greengrocers. Even the farm shops, which started around here about twenty-five years ago, have been forced to improve the way they display their goods. Sure, the supermarkets ought to make a greater effort to display local produce. But even there I have noticed that Tescos at Martlesham Heath display local asparagus from Tuddenham.

In the 1970s the Trades Unions had a dominant role in the economy. The economy was still constrained by the operation of exchange controls. The nation was sick, and everyone knew it. But the free market policies of the 80s have changed all that. One of the most significant developments of the last twenty years has been the growth of competition. Wherever competition can operate, that is to say everywhere except in the public services, standards of service have risen and prices have been kept down. The relative price stability that we have seen since about the end of the 80s owes a great deal more to competition than to monetary and economic policies. I have absolutely no doubt that all these changes have made the people of this country incomparably better off than they have ever been before. Even the poor are much less poor than they were in the 30s. The poor today would find it hard to imagine the conditions in which my uncle and aunt lived in the Manor House at Crowle in the 1930s – with no water, no electricity, no telephone and only an outside loo.

But is the world a better place for it? I say 'the world' because this greater affluence is a world-wide phenomenon – with, I think, the sole exception of most of the African continent. I have been reading *Reformation* by Diarmaid MacCulloch, in which, referring to sixteenth century Europe, he says: 'the Northern Netherlands were one of the first territories in Europe (along with England) to escape the constant danger of mass starvation following harvest failure.' In the twentieth century, until relatively recently the danger of mass starvation has been a potent threat – in Russia, China and India. That threat now seems to be confined to Ethiopia and the African countries lying to the south of the Sahara.

We must be thankful for the improved material conditions, but are we better people? I think that many of those in this country who have grown up since the war, that is the under 60s, sincerely believe that they are more compassionate and less belligerent than my generation and those who preceded us. I am not at all sure that this is so. Much of the 'compassion' is what I consider unrealistic mushiness. Underlying much of the compassion is an economic fallacy. I have absolutely no doubt that the great improvement of material conditions was made possible by capitalism and would not have occurred under a centralised command economy. And yet many people seem to believe that the rich, be they people or countries, are rich only at the expense of the poor. The Christian churches and socialists alike demonise the rich and sanctify the poor. And by doing so, actually make it less likely that the lot of the poor can be improved. As a recent leader in the *Spectator* said:

> This idea relies upon a primitive but pervasive idea of an economy as a zero sum game: that your job is my redundancy, that a pound in your pocket is a pound less in mine, and so forth. It is the governing principle of all socialism and redistributionism, and no matter how many times it is shown to be wrong, both in theory and in practice, it survives because of its superficial plausibility and its appeal to fear rather than to hope.

As I have said, this is as true of countries as it is of people. A large majority of the population consider all humanitarian aid to be 'a good thing'. And, of course aid given to help with the ravages of an earthquake or a famine is in itself a wonderful thing. But permanent aid to poor countries actually holds them back from improving themselves. Excessive aid, be it international, or be it welfare at home, breeds dependency. Salvation comes only to those who take personal responsibility for their spiritual state. And the habit of taking personal responsibility for one's own economic condition makes a good basis for this. If one blames others for all one's economic troubles, it is very easy to make the jump to blaming others for all one's spiritual and moral state as well. Edward Norman, former Dean of Peterhouse College, a distinguished churchman, has said:

> The message promoted by the institutional churches in Britain is scarcely distinctive at all, appearing to be a sanctified endorsement of the Humanist preoccupation with the details of material welfare, which is general in our society. The message of Jesus was clear and simple. It was that men and women needed redemption . . . his primary call was to repentance.
>
> From which pronouncement of Church bodies do we now hear the clear indictment of human sin, and from what pulpit are the follies of each of us regularly condemned? Instead men and women are given a kind of reassurance; the sins of the age are not the consequence of what we are, but of particular material errors; how we have treated the environment, the

economic distribution, the available resources for welfare, the integrity of other people.

This deep distrust of capitalism leads on to the erroneous belief that capitalism is the cause of greed and materialism. Profit is the fuel that drives the capitalist economy, and for many of its critics, profit is synonymous with greed. But, of course, greed and materialism are inherent vices in the corrupt nature of mankind, and are just as evident in centrally controlled economies. Greed in the capitalist economy can do a lot of harm to consumers and employees, but it does not lead to concentration camps and gulags resulting in millions of deaths.

Are we less belligerent? The younger generations do seem to think so. They believe that we have avoided war and should continue to do so by always being prepared to talk and see the other's point of view. Many of them, I think, feel that both World Wars were unjustified. I strongly believe them to be wrong. Without them we would have suffered much worse tyrannies – and almost certainly here in this country too.

The young attribute the avoidance of war in Western Europe to the EEC and now to the European Union. I think this is quite misguided. NATO saved us from war, as did firmness. A vital element in the defeat of Communism came very early on; in 1948, with the airlift to relieve the Soviet blockade of West Berlin. Another important influence on the Soviet Union was, in my opinion, the recapture of the Falklands from the Argentines. It was a close run thing, but it showed guts and determination. Perhaps only a woman Prime Minister would have had the necessary courage! There was an interesting passage in a recent sermon by an American New Church minister in Berkeley, California:

> While mercy is mild, it is not mushy. Mercy can be dispensed too easily, to the point of losing self-respect. People who do not resent moral injuries done to them are not respecting rightfully the need for goodness to prevail. Justice must accompany mercy for it to be wisdom – and therein lies our spiritual growth.

Europe is a real and continuing worry. The original European Movement was motivated by a passionate belief that the existence of the 'nation state' had been responsible for both World Wars. But at the heart of this belief were two fallacies. It doesn't take a nation state to give rise to wars. Even the break up of a single nation state has led to frightful bloodshed – the demise of Yugoslavia, for example. And, if it were true, what are the present drivers of European Union doing if not trying to build a bigger and better 'nation state'? Is this not just as likely at some time to go to war with one of the other big nation states – the USA, Russia, China?

But my main objection to the European Union is that there is not sufficient cultural compatibility to support a new nation state – Europe. The UK's long history of common law is quite at variance with Roman law. What happened to Crispin in France in 1996 could not have happened here

– although one has to suspect that the present Home Secretary would be quite happy with such a regime. Moreover all the continental countries have a view of the role of the state which is at variance with British history. Whether they are Christian Democrats or Social Democrats they all believe in strong central government, which has responsibility for doing what they think is best for the population, whatever the people may think. It is essentially 'fascist'. By this I do not mean to say that they are tyrannical and vicious, but that like Mussolini's emblem of the 'fasces' – all the elements of the state bound together – they think the best government comes from a binding together of government, business and the trade unions. At one time that might have included the church, but no longer. Of course, one has to admit that New Labour seems to share the same beliefs, which is why, in the interests of essential British values, New Labour will have to go as well! The European economies are now driven by a set of sclerotic socialist values. They epitomise the very reverse of what made me in 1962 be in favour of European union. What we need is free trade and close co-operation – and certainly not a common currency or a turgid constitution.

There are many other elements of life today which worry me and contribute to my melancholy. One of them relates to sexual morals. I really don't know whether people's sexual behaviour is more immoral than it was. Perhaps not. But there is one incontrovertible fact and that is that many of the practices that I consider immoral are not seen today in any way as sins. The worst one might say about adultery, for example, is that it might endanger a marriage and therefore be bad for the children. But I get the impression that many consider it quite unreasonable for a wife to make much fuss about her husband's adultery – after all, that is what one must expect from a man! And the worst that might be said about promiscuity is that it would not be 'safe sex'. The safest sex is to be faithful in marriage.

Another worrying aspect of modern life is both the decline of religion and the steady secularisation of the Christian churches. I actually worry more about the state of the Catholic and Protestant churches than I do about the decline in religion overall. As a Swedenborgian, I believe that no one can go to heaven unless they believe that Jesus Christ is God, so I might be expected to be very worried about the growth of the number of people who are not even sure that there is a God, let alone that He is Jesus. So why does it not worry me more? The answer is that I also believe that when we die we all go to the World of Spirits, where we are 'judged' – we in fact judge ourselves and choose whether to be against God or for God. There are many unbelievers who, in my judgement, have behaved well, trying to do what is right because it is right, and not because it gives them any personal advantage. They will soon learn in the next world about Jesus. I suspect that many churchgoers are in fact, in much the same position. I very much doubt whether more than a handful of worshippers, when reciting the Nicene Creed, really reflect deeply on the meaning of the words, 'eternally begotten son'. They recite what amounts to an affirmation of a God in three persons, but I suspect it is not deeply imbedded in their thinking. Neither they nor the unbelievers have 'got a lot to unlearn' – the phrase that Humphrey Mynors used to me 55 years ago. But those who are deeply 'infected' with the mistaken doctrine embodied in the Nicene Creed are much more of a worry. It is unfortunately conceivable that they may never be able to unlearn it.

So, how should I cope with the melancholy which all these worries induce? In the first place I have to admit to being far from sure that people today are in fact worse than when I was young. Daphne once said to me, 'Surely you can't believe that all those people in the supermarket in Sax are going to live for ever.' Of course, I have always been sure of that, but I have to say that I now feel a great sense of satisfaction when I see the people around me in Saxmundham. I should be very surprised if most of them don't go to heaven. At the moment there seem to be a particularly large number of young mothers, clearly doting on their children. I am not sure that that was true twenty-five years ago. In those days there were many very querulous mothers with crying children, being slapped to keep quiet. Today's mothers, by contrast, seem to exude a beautiful innocence. And if you catch someone's eye, you are almost always rewarded with a smile.

And I know so many nice people – all those who have worked in the garden for me and so many friends. We disagree on many things, but most of them seem to me to fall clearly into the category of those who try and do what is right because it is right. Saxmundham may well not be typical of the country as a whole. There are relatively few people round here with spiky hair and rude tattoos; although there are too many women with constantly bare midriffs – even in winter. But I think there is hope. I am also overcoming the melancholia, by concentrating hard on my belief in the overriding power of Divine Providence, and in the knowledge that Divine Providence is not concerned with the here and now, but with eternity. Whether capitalism continues for another thousand years or two, whether there will be a nation state of Europe in 200 or 2000 years' time is profoundly unimportant. But the Lord ensures at all times the best possible outcome for their eternal life of all those in the world today and of all those who will be born in the billions of years still to come. I think many of our worries would seem less alarming if we could hang on to the fact that we are at the very dawn of human history. Fifty thousand years is nothing in relation to eternity. When, at the end of singing one of the psalms, Anglicans say: 'As it was in the beginning, now and ever shall be, world without end. Amen,' I think to myself, exactly so. The Lord's Kingdom is for ever.

The worries of the world can also be lessened by reflecting on the changes for the better which have taken place over a much longer period. In a review of *Mary, Queen of Scots and the Murder of Lord Darnley* by Alison Weir, there appeared the following: 'The real problem is the sheer irredeemable awfulness of 16th century Scotland. . . . And even by the standards of the Stuart royal line the factionalism, greed, venality, savagery, malice, bigotry, treachery and poisonous ambition that blighted the brief reign of Mary stand out.' Five hundred years later, this country at any rate could never be described in such terms. It probably was just as bad in Iraq under Saddam Hussein, and probably still is in Mugabe's Zimbabwe.

However worried I may be about the state of religion today, I only have to reflect on the state of religion in Europe during the Reformation – Catholics burning Protestants, Protestants burning Catholics and Lutherans at daggers drawn with Calvinists. And what is equally bad is that all of them, Catholic, Lutheran or Reformed, had the most awful doctrines. None of them seemed to think that one would be judged by the sort of life one had led; on the Protestant side they were obsessed with predestination and salvation through faith alone; and the Catholics believed that however one had behaved, sufficient masses said for a dead soul could take years off the time he would have to spend in Purgatory.

So the state of the world worries me rather less than when I started these memoirs. But I have learnt a lot about myself. And I am far from happy with what I have learned. The negative feelings are very strong. 'Never quite' almost accurately sums it up. By far my greatest regret is the self-centred lack of imagination I showed in my treatment of Daphne. The undoubted fact that I gave her a great deal in the last few years of her life in no way wipes out the shame at how I behaved earlier on. How could I not have perceived that inwardly she was a mass of fears and irrational panic? I am not surprised that Daphne once wrote me a card addressing me as 'I, I, I!' I don't think even then that I really took in what she was trying to tell me. I have talked about this with both Crispin and Jocelyn, who both say that I should not be ashamed of my behaviour. Daphne was, they say, a difficult person. A lot of it had to do with being an only child, and not only that, but an only child in an acrimonious household.

I also regret that I was so ambitious in a worldly sense in my time with the Bank of England. I wanted to get to the top, and 'never quite' made it. Looking back now, it is of course supremely unimportant. I also have come to think that I am not as wise and intelligent as I used to think I was. So perhaps I have achieved as much as could have been expected.

But there are also many positive elements. At work I always tried to do what was right because it was right and not for any personal advantage. I was never in a position of having a job that was otiose, but I hope that had I been, I would have made every effort to get my job abolished. What would I have done, I wonder, if I had been appointed Chief of the Exchange Control Department, or, more recently, head of the Financial Services Authority? I hope I would have had the courage of my convictions and worked for their abolition.

I am also deeply grateful for my religion, which gives me a solid foundation for all that I do and think. I find it very sad to reflect on those who are afflicted with doubts. And looking at myself and my family there is so much to be thankful for. I have come to love Daphne almost more since her death than before, and I never regret that I married her. Thank God she gave me that 78 r.p.m. record in 1949 – 'Si tu m'aimes'! And my family are a constant source of pleasure. All three of my children seem to me to be very special people. Even in this age, they are all three, people of great integrity – a rare virtue. All three have good marriages. Richard is exactly right for Amicia. He supports her and yet gives her the freedom to be herself and to continue her journalism. They both adore their son, Edward, and Amicia seems to be just right for her stepchildren. Crispin without Caroline is unthinkable. She is a wonderful wife and mother and their two children, Ajax and Alceste, are gems. Jocelyn was the last to marry. A marriage to someone of a different nationality can be difficult, but Muriel has settled in to the family beautifully. I have not yet met the youngest, Rose, but little Arthur is also quite special. So I ask myself, what is the Lord keeping me alive for? It cannot be just to be with my children and grandchildren. Although they all love me and I love them, I serve no essential purpose in their lives. Indeed, if I died they would all be financially better off.

Providence cannot be keeping me going in order to finish these memoirs – can it? If so, with only about a page to go, my days would indeed be numbered! I have finally concluded that my melancholia is a function of my excessive self-centredness. I must learn not to be so constantly looking in. Christine Brook's advice to Daphne in the Nursing Home comes back to me. Daphne, you will remember, told me that Christine had been very helpful. She had said to Christine that she felt so useless just lying in her bed, but Christine had told her to concentrate on trying to give something to everybody who came in. Disabled though she was, she had the opportunity to give of herself to others. That is what I must do; try and give of myself to everybody with whom I come in contact. The words of a popular song of the 1940s (lyrics by Johnny Mercer) come to mind:

> Gather round me, everybody
> Gather round me while I'm preachin'
> Feel a sermon comin' on me
> The topic will be sin and that's what I'm ag'in'
> If you wanna hear my story
> Then settle back and just sit tight
> While I start reviewin'
> The attitude of doin' right.
>
> You've got to accentuate the positive
> Eliminate the negative
> And latch on to the affirmative
> Don't mess with Mister In-Between.

You've got to spread joy up to the maximum
Bring gloom down to the minimum
Have faith or pandemonium's
Liable to walk upon the scene.

To illustrate my last remark
Jonah in the whale, Noah in the ark
What did they do when everything looked so dark?
(Man, they said 'We'd better accentuate the positive')
('Eliminate the negative')
('And latch on to the affirmative')
Don't mess with Mister In-Between (No!)
Don't mess with Mister In-Between.

That's what I have been doing – messing with Mister In-Between. At the
very beginning I quoted from a sermon by an American New Church
minister, Rev. Othmar Tobisch: 'In this huge city of human memories live
the wishes, the urges, the demands, the desires, the wants of man. These
inhabit the houses and either use them properly or ruin them for
habitation.' Perhaps after all, in these past two years of writing I have at last
learned to use them properly. Hence the title I have decided to give to the
whole work – 'CITY OF HUMAN MEMORIES'.

Daphne's Poems

Jocelyn – 1965

Jocelyn wears his trousers every day of the week
Jocelyn's trousers are red, white and blue
striped and buttoned, they once were new
But now they've been worn until they are through
through being worn all the week!

Jocelyn wears his shirt every day of the week
Jocelyn's shirt is orange and flowered
corduroy, buttoned, it once was new
but now it's been worn until his arm's through
through being worn all of the week

Jocelyn sleeps in his blue pyjamas
while his Mummy washes his shirt and trousers
Jocelyn wakes to wear them and then
his Mummy can wash his pyjamas again!
What a good thing he's sometimes asleep

Jocelyn's other clothes look like new
they sit in the cupboard the whole week through
never see the washing machine or feel the soap
But one day, somebody, we respectfully hope
will get him to love some extra things
a yellow shirt, new green pyjamas or bright blue trousers

Meantime we love him however he's dressed
for what's inside doesn't wear out
and it's what's inside that he's all about!

1966 (after the death of her father whose body was cremated)

The body should have a grave
for those who still have bodies,
then they can go and sense the senseless part
of those that have but recently died,
then they can go and stand alone and quiet apart
and let the past come forth before their eyes
While they who grieve are yet alive to feel
the body should be there below the turf
It is most comforting to have so sure a place
where remembered head and hand and face
are yet a part of the earth

In favour of acceptance

You cannot joust, or tilt, or thrust,
you cannot bring me gold,
you cannot conquer, crown or spoil
as could the knights of old

So I will test you
turn you out
send you from my way
To see if testing treatment
Such will prove your worth today

And so I thought, and so I did
bring strife to one young man
and changed a little or a lot
a heart's spontaneous way

I watched and felt the power I had
For dear he was to me
But so contrived a test
must lead to doubt
and though I still had worth,
Love as it was, was out

Dust

Dust on the table top
Dust on the floor
Dust on my glasses
Dust on the ground
Dust it! Dust it!
Let it not be found

And yet we go to dust
And dust is all around
Dust is therefore a friendly thing

A thing of our own kind
We go to dust, and yet we must
Leave only dust behind

'As any woman may'

My hands may bake, may drive, may fill
[My body wills it so]
But yet my mind is free to roam
Full twenty years ago

My legs may dance, may walk, may fall
[My body wills it so]
But yet my mind is free to roam
And let it still be so

And yet I am green and unconcerned
And weakly do I sin
And I am slowly building up the hidden realms within
And am trying, without trying
And I am choosing without choosing
What from the past has gone
And I am starting, going forth
And now am here today
Doing things, and remembering things
'As any woman may'.

Mummy

'Mummy' say the childless
'Mummy' – what a name
'Mummy' say the children
'Oh God!' not again

'Mummy' say the specialists
'Mummy' should be all
'Mummy' say the children
What a bloody bore!

'Mummy' say the preachers
'Mummy' free from sin
'Mummy' say the children
Should be always in

'Mummy' says the father
'Mummy' will decide
'Mummy' say the children
'Take us for a ride'

'Mummy' says the Mummy
has a little right
'Mummy' says the Mummy
'Wants some sleep tonight'

'Mummy' says the Mummy
(and a lot beside)
'Mummy' says the Mummy
'has her own inside'

Riots in Grosvenor Square – March 1968

Why do I pity the horses?
[I who can barely ride]
Why do I feel for them the horror
Of the jeering, angry crowd by their side?
Is it because they are disciplined?
Is it because their stance is upright above the shambles
Of those that around them dance?
Dance in a manner so graceless,
Gesticulate, hit and run back
Waving their protests for Peace,
Then using them for random attack
Marbles are toys for children
Needles for mothers and wives
Ammonia can be used for whitening
Or clearing out someone's insides

Why do I pity the horses?
Dead they are food for my dog,
But then they are cut up, near bloodless
Like the dead in a Vietnamese bog.
Why do I pity the horses?
Because they are no part of the fight?
Because they are brought in to quell it?
Because they are hurt to do right?
Because they are used by their masters?
But wait – what of those in the square?

Who is using their rationalised protest
To keep from the conference chair?

Penguins and Fathers

The penguin gives his love a stone
On returning to the nest
The eggs are laid about with stones
There the stone-like egg must rest

The human gives his love a ring
To show her true to him
The ring is circled oft with jewels
A price for constancy

The penguin gives his body's fat
To keep his young alive
The human gives his body's worth
To warm his young's insides

The penguin father staggers off
To replenish from the sea
His stock of food;
The human father staggers off
To committee, telephone
The young of each demand and grow
And will not take a stone

A telephone call – 22nd October 1968

'How's your cold?' he asked
[For he had a loving conscience and she had flu]
'Foul' she said, for she was honest
And the day was not yet through
'Oh dear' he said. 'I'd better come back'
'Oh! No!' she said, regretting the implied attack
'Are you sure?' he asked – he had plenty of work to do
'Yes, sure' she said, and it certainly was true!

Time – 3rd March 1969

'I simply haven't the time' she said
Wasting time as she spoke
'I simply haven't the time' she repeated

Giving her hair a stroke
But time went on and took her
Took her as she played
Time stopped in its time
The aimless use of her days

'If only she'd had time to enjoy it'
Her fellows chanted aloud
'If only she'd had time – just a little longer'
Went on the busy crowd
But time went on and took them,
Took them as they stayed

Time stopped in its time
Their endless waste of days
Time should only be wasted at leisure
And leisure should be fashioned of use
Time is the gift of the Saviour
But we are the cooks of the goose!

Before the Cock's Crow – Holland July 1969

I am male, crowed the cock, I am male,
And I am fine.
I am male, crowed the cock, I am male
The she's are mine.
I am male, crowed the cock, I am male,
Three times over,
For betrayal, there must be love and then
The last morn's over

Family Tree

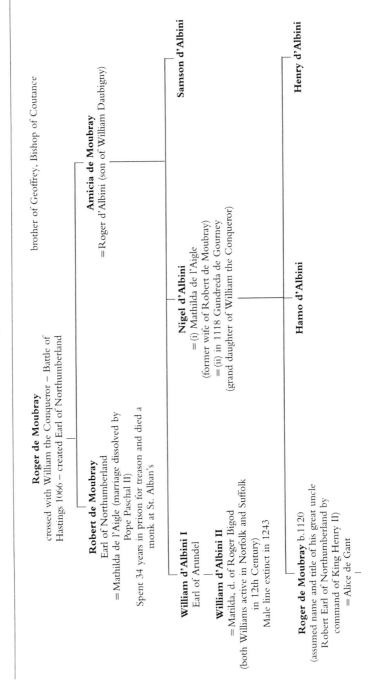

Roger de Moubray
crossed with William the Conqueror – Battle of
Hastings 1066 – created Earl of Northumberland

brother of Geoffrey, Bishop of Coutance

Robert de Moubray
Earl of Northumberland
= Mathilda de l'Aigle (marriage dissolved by
Pope Paschal II)
Spent 34 years in prison for treason and died a
monk at St. Alban's

Nigel d'Albini
= (i) Mathilda de l'Aigle
(former wife of Robert de Moubray)
= (ii) in 1118 Gundreda de Gourney
(grand daughter of William the Conqueror)

Amicia de Moubray
= Roger d'Albini (son of William Daubigny)

Samson d'Albini

William d'Albini I
Earl of Arundel

William d'Albini II
= Matilda, d. of Roger Bigod
(both Williams active in Norfolk and Suffolk
in 12th Century)
Male line extinct in 1243

Hamo d'Albini

Henry d'Albini

Roger de Moubray b.1120
(assumed name and title of his great uncle
Robert Earl of Northumberland by
command of King Henry II)
= Alice de Gant

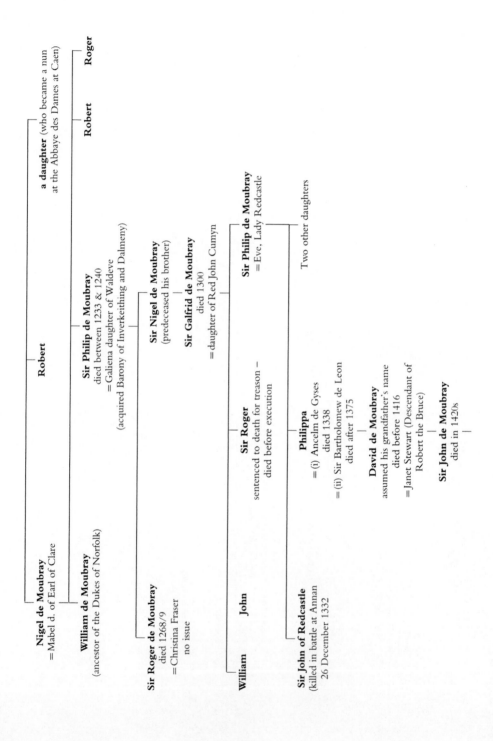

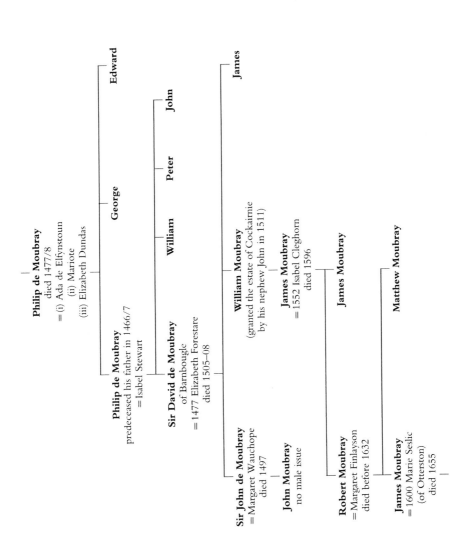

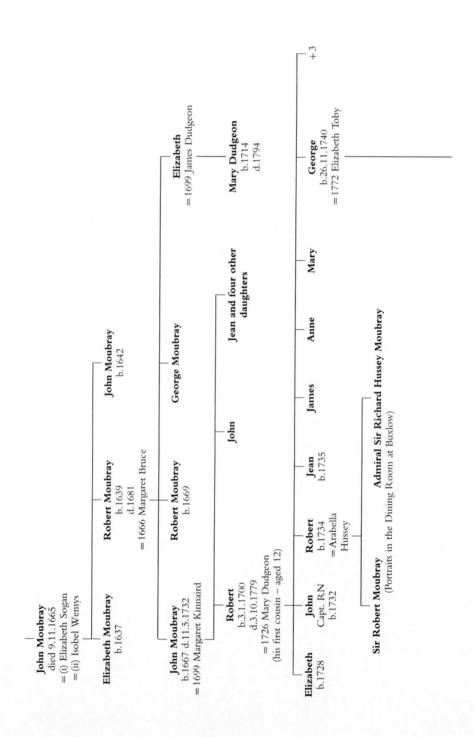

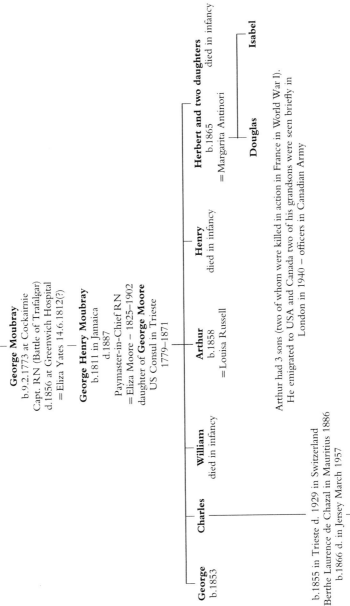

George Moubray
b.9.2.1773 at Cockairnie
Capt. RN (Battle of Trafalgar)
d.1856 at Greenwich Hospital
=Eliza Yates 14.6.1812(?)

George Henry Moubray
b.1811 in Jamaica
d.1887
Paymaster-in-Chief RN
=Eliza Moore – 1825–1902
daughter of George Moore
US Consul in Trieste
1779–1871

George
b.1853

Charles
b.1855 in Trieste d. 1929 in Switzerland
=Berthe Laurence de Chazal in Mauritius 1886
b.1866 d. in Jersey March 1957

William
died in infancy

Arthur
b.1858
=Louisa Russell

Arthur had 3 sons (two of whom were killed in action in France in World War I).
He emigrated to USA and Canada two of his grandsons were seen briefly in
London in 1940 – officers in Canadian Army

Henry
died in infancy

Herbert and two daughters
b.1865
=Margarita Antinori

died in infancy

Douglas

Isabel

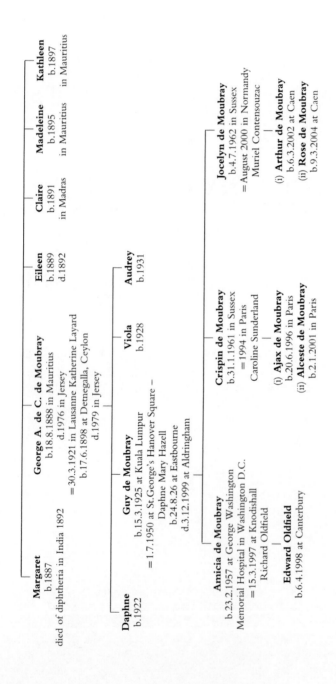

Index